MIRACLES
AND THE
CRITICAL MIND

by
Colin Brown

4609
WILLIAM B. EERDMANS PUBLISHING COMPANY

THE PATERNOSTER PRESS

For Olive

William B. Eerdmans Publishing Company
255 Jefferson Ave., S.E., Grand Rapids, Mich. 49503

and

The Paternoster Press Ltd.
3 Mount Radford Crescent, Exeter, Devon, UK EX2 4JW

Library of Congress Cataloging in Publication Data

Brown, Colin, 1932-
Miracles and the critical mind.

Includes index.
1. Jesus Christ--Miracles. I. Title.
BT 366.B76 1983   232.9'55   83-16600
ISBN 0-8028-3590-2

British Library Cataloguing in Publication Data

Brown, Colin
Miracles and the critical mind.
1. Miracles
2. Title
231.7'3   BT97.2

ISBN 0-85364-385-7

CONTENTS

INTRODUCTION

Several years ago I somewhat foolishly undertook to write a book on a popular level saying why I believe in the miracles of Jesus. This is not that book. However, the present book has grown out of that undertaking. For various reasons the popular book never got written. Among them was a change of job and a change of country. But more important than these was a gut feeling that before I could honestly say what I thought about miracles, I needed to read more and think more.

Some writers, when they begin a book, know what they think and know what they want to say. For them writing is largely a matter of putting their thoughts down on paper. For me the thoughts come as I wrestle with other people's ideas and work out my position as I go along. When I first undertook to write a book on miracles, I knew roughly what I wanted to say. I knew the classical apologetic appeal to miracles as divine accreditation of the Christian gospel. I had read David Hume's classical critique of miracles over and over, and knew its weak spots. As a C. S. Lewis enthusiast, I had found Lewis's best-seller *Miracles* very stimulating. I also had on my bookshelves (unread) the great study *The Miracle Stories of the Gospels* by my first postgraduate mentor, Alan Richardson. There was, furthermore, H. van der Loos's massive study *The Miracles of Jesus,* which I could always turn to in case I got into difficulties.

Armed with these resources, I felt that I could make a reasonable shot at writing a popular paperback that would update the classical apologetic argument. As I saw it in my mind, the book would be in two parts. The first would be largely concerned with philosophical argument. I would do battle with David Hume and his latter-day followers. In the second part I would explain the various miracles reported in the Gospels. However, it did not work out quite like that. I began to see that Hume represented only the tip of the iceberg. In his own day his argument was overshadowed by that of the deistically minded Conyers Middleton. Moreover, it was upon the same Conyers Middleton that the doyen of Reformed theologians, B. B. Warfield, had leaned so heavily in arguing the case that miracles ceased with the last of the apostles. What Warfield apparently chose to ignore was the fact, which John Wesley saw very clearly, that the arguments Middleton deployed against miracles in the early church could equally well be applied to the miracles in the New Testament. It required no great insight to see that what Hume and Middleton were saying was part of a great groundswell of opinion that had been building up for some considerable time.

It became increasingly clear to me that to maintain with integrity a belief in the miracles of Jesus required a fresh examination of the arguments for and against miracles. The result, for better or worse, is the present book. For a long time I cherished the hope that I would still be able to include an exegetical study of the miracle stories themselves. But to do this with anything like the seriousness that such an undertaking demands would take several additional years of research. It would also make the book impossibly long. Some day I would like to write such a book. I even have the title— *Miracles and the Gospel of Christ.* But for the present I have tried to focus attention on the question of miracles and the critical mind. It is not exactly a new problem. It is, in fact, a perennial one. But for both unbelievers and believers over the past two hundred years, the question of miracles has become increasingly acute.

Studies of miracles tend to be either philosophical or exegetical. This is bound up with the relentless pressure to specialize and the fact that expertise in any field requires lifelong dedication. At the risk of being presumptuous, the present book tries to combine both philosophy and biblical interpretation. There are several reasons for this. First of all, the great philosophical debates of the past concerning miracles were not conducted in a vacuum. When philosophers like Spinoza, Hume, Kant, and the English deists discussed the subject of miracles, they were not debating in the abstract the possibility of miracles. They were arguing about the truth-claims of Christianity and the role of biblical miracles in those claims. But quite apart from these classic debates is the fact that the interpretation that anyone gives to the miracle stories raises philosophical questions. Whether we believe or disbelieve the stories, our attitudes are bound up with philosophical positions concerning how we know, what we know, and what we think reality is like. These in turn affect our view of what may count as evidence and what may be inferred from it.

The choice of the title *Miracles and the Critical Mind* is deliberate. It underscores the fact that in talking about miracles we are not simply talking about philosophical questions. But neither are we simply talking about New Testament interpretation as if philosophical considerations did not enter into it. Although we are primarily concerned with identifying and discussing the philosophical issues, we cannot do this in abstraction from what the New Testament is saying. In this book I have tried to look fairly and squarely at what people have said through the ages about the Gospel miracles and their bearing on the truth-claims of Christianity.

As a result of my reading and thinking I have had to change my mind on a number of issues. I do not think that Hume's argument against miracles is any more damning now than I thought it was ten years ago. On the other hand, I think it is more subtle—and more tautological—than I was apt to give it credit for being. At the same time, I do not think that the classical appeal to miracles to establish the divinity of Christ works in quite the same way that the traditional apologists appear to think. To repeat without modification the arguments of Archdeacon Paley, or even of B. B. Warfield, would be like going out to battle wearing Saul's armor. And I have to say that, while I still admire C. S. Lewis, I do not think that all his points are of equal value. Some of them are positively mistaken. If the reader wants to find out what is wrong with the arguments of these distinguished Christian writers, I must refer him or her to the appropriate sections of this book.

But having said all this, I have to confess that I am more than ever convinced that we cannot have Christianity without the miracle-working Jesus of the four Gospels. We cannot have his teaching without his signs any more than we can have his signs without his teaching. The miracles of Jesus provide the key to understanding Jesus and, for that matter, to understanding why the Jewish authorities of his day sought to put him to death. Although this may sound paradoxical to the modern critical mind, the miracle stories themselves are what enable us to make sense of the Gospels as *history*. I would now be prepared to say that without an understanding of the thirteenth chapter of the Book of Deuteronomy and its significance for the Jewish leaders, we cannot begin to understand why they were so opposed to Jesus. I would also be prepared to say that the horizon for the miracle stories is given by John the Baptist's prophecy, "He will baptize you with the Holy Spirit." I would even go so far as to say that the miracles of Jesus are not simply a question of the incarnation of the divine Son of God; they are a question of the Trinity. My conclusions are set out in the last two chapters of the book, but the basis for them must be seen in the light of the argument of the first nine.

ACKNOWLEDGMENTS

I owe a personal debt of gratitude to many people, especially my students, friends, and colleagues at Fuller Theological Seminary. In common with teachers throughout the world I have found that the probing questions of students have forced me to think again and refine my ideas. I have profited from many a conversation with students in the graduate program at Fuller, especially with Dr. Ron Foubister, John McKenna, and Paul Ford. The latter's expertise in C. S. Lewis drew my attention to the vast resources of C. S. Lewis scholarship. Fred Bush and Don Hagner are among the members of the Fuller Faculty who have patiently listened to my ideas and made helpful suggestions at various points. I am indebted to my colleagues Glenn Barker, David Hubbard, Paul Jewett, and Robert Meye who read and commented on various parts of the typescript, and to Richard Muller and Jack Rogers who read the entire work. Without their help my thinking and writing would be much poorer. The faults that remain are mine and not theirs.

I owe a special debt of gratitude to Michael Stribling of the Word Processing facility of Fuller Theological Seminary's School of Theology. Not only did he process and reprocess my typescript; he also spotted many a mistake and helped to turn my English into American. Above all I wish to thank my wife, Olive, who contributed to this work at every step of the way, not least in proof-reading, indexing, and thinking through ideas. It is to her that I dedicate this work.

I

Prologue:
The Prescientific Age

1

MIRACLES AND APOLOGETICS FROM THE EARLY CHURCH TO THE REFORMATION

Apologetics is a subject that no thinking Christian can altogether escape. On the technical level apologetics is the defense and presentation of the truth of Christian faith on intellectual and moral grounds. As such, it is the work of theologians and philosophers. But on the everyday level apologetics is simply the matter of facing up to the questions of what we believe and why. In answering these questions miracles have always played an important part, but it has not always been quite the same part. From time to time miracles have been seen as clear-cut proof of God's hand in history unambiguously underwriting the truth-claims of the faith. At such times apologists have taken the offensive, and have built miracles into the foundation of their apologetic systems. But at other times apologists have been pushed onto the defensive, and have appeared to some to be almost apologizing for their belief in miracles. At such times apologists have argued that miracles are credible against the background of certain beliefs about God and his purposes. When this occurs, miracles have been removed from the foundation of the edifice and have become the copestone of faith.

It is sometimes assumed that the offensive approach to miracles was held uniformly from the early church to the Reformation and by all stout-hearted (or at least tough-minded) believers who follow in their footsteps. But this would be an oversimplification, if not a downright distortion. Moreover, the precise role that miracles play in the truth-claims of Christianity—and indeed in the content of those claims—is not quite so simple as is sometimes imagined. The purpose of this chapter is to probe the minds of some of the leading thinkers who helped to shape the form of Christian orthodoxy, in order to discover the role that miracles played in their faith and thought. We shall focus first on the early church and then on Aquinas, Luther, and Calvin.

THE EARLY CHURCH

From the close of the New Testament period to the third century and beyond, the appeal to miracles was a regular part of the Christian apologist's armor.[1]

Miracles were seen as clear proof of divine intervention in the ordinary affairs of life. Moreover, they served to attest that the one who performed them was doing the work of God. For anyone who had doubts about the Christian message, the apologist could point to miracles as divine confirmation of the truth that was being spoken. Origen (ca. 185–ca.254), who was the greatest of the apologists and the first ecumenical theologian, typifies this outlook with his observation that "without miracles and wonders" the apostles "would not have persuaded those who heard new doctrines and new teachings to leave their traditional religion and to accept the apostles' teaching at the risk of their lives."[2] A similar sentiment was voiced some years earlier by Justin, who was martyred at Rome between 163 and 167. Justin saw himself as a Christian philosopher, having explored various philosophies before becoming a Christian. In a work addressed to Jewish skeptics, Justin observed that Jesus

> was manifested to your race and healed those who were from birth physically maimed and deaf and lame, causing one to leap and another to hear and a third to see at his word. And he raised the dead and gave them life and by his actions challenged the men of his time to recognize him.[3]

Such remarks were addressed to outsiders, but similar arguments were deployed to strengthen the faith of those who were already believers and who were trying to understand the rationale of their faith.

In the fourth century Athanasius (ca. 296–373) wrote the most important work on christology that was to come from the pen of any of the early Fathers. In arguing the thesis that the Logos (Word or Reason) that is manifested in the universe at large is also manifested in a particular way in Jesus Christ, Athanasius urged: "For just as, though invisible, he is known through the works of creation; so, having become man, and being in the body unseen, it may be known from his works that he who can do these things is not man, but the power and Word of God."[4] Later in the same century the champion of orthodoxy, Gregory of Nyssa (ca. 330–395), could roundly state, "His very miracles have convinced us of his deity."[5]

Examples of similar claims could be multiplied,[6] but it should be noted that these early Christian writers were not insensitive to the problems that an appeal to supernatural interventions posed for them and their readers. Today we are apt to assume that our modern world is light-years away from the world of antiquity. But in many ways the two worlds are not all that different. Our technological age is made up of skeptics, the credulous (whether they be devotees of science fiction, wonder drugs, or astrology), and the adherents to numerous shades of opinion in between. In the ancient world the market, which is now supplied by science fiction, astrology, and tales of the supernatural, was met at least in part by pious legends.[7] But alongside this were the philosophers who debated the limits of the possible. The Stoics were prepared to say that God could do anything.[8] Others were less ready to make such concessions. God could not do what was logically absurd and self-contradictory. He could not, for example, make the diagonal of a parallelogram equal in length to one of its sides. Pliny asserted that God could not die, change the past, give mortals immortality, recall the dead, or make twice ten unequal to twenty.[9]

Between the credulous and the skeptical were many who were prepared to accept the paranormal, particularly healings, whether they were performed by Christ, his followers, or by potential rivals to the church. The theologians of the early church met this point not by denying the phenomena as such, but by insisting on the radically different character of Jesus' healings.[10] Just as today Western psychotherapists might recognize the power of witch doctors to heal but question the attendant theology of witchcraft,[11] so the church fathers could acknowledge the healings performed by pagan wonder-workers and at the same time challenge their significance. Such healings were attributed to demonic influence, and their blessings were, to say the least, mixed.[12] But the argument proved to be double-edged. For the same objections were turned against the church by skeptics who, like Celsus, insisted that Jesus was himself a magician who had picked up the tricks of his trade in Egypt.[13] This is a view that has recently been revived by Morton Smith in his book *Jesus the Magician* (1978).

In the meantime it is worth noting Origen's reply. In response to the allegation that parallels could be found in Greek mythology, Origen claimed that the Greek accounts lacked the substantiation of Jesus' miracles:

> We affirm that the whole human world has evidence of the work of Jesus since in it dwell the churches of God which consist of people converted through Jesus from countless evils. Moreover, the name of Jesus still takes away mental distractions from men, and daemons and diseases as well, and implants a wonderful meekness and tranquillity of character, and a love to mankind and a kindness and gentleness, in those who have not feigned to be Christians on account of their need of the necessities of life or some other want, but have genuinely accepted the gospel about God and Christ and the judgment to come.[14]

Replying to the charge that Jesus' works were no different from those that could be witnessed in any Egyptian marketplace, Origen retorted:

> They might have been comparable if he [Celsus] had first given sufficient proof of the similarity to those who employ trickery. But in fact no sorcerer uses his tricks to call spectators to moral reformation; nor does he educate by the fear of God people who were astounded by what they saw, nor does he attempt to persuade the onlookers to live as men who will be judged by God. Sorcerers do none of these things, since they have neither the ability nor even the will to do so.[15]

In other words, the appeal to the miracles of Jesus is not simply an appeal to the stupendous. The miracles of Jesus are to be seen in the context of his life, teaching, and ongoing healing and transforming work.

In the early church, the appeal to miracles hardly ever stood on its own as a single, knockdown argument. What is striking is the way the argument, particularly in Origen's writings, anticipates the classic debates of the eighteenth century and of our own day. It illustrates the perennial dilemma that appears to confront the believer. If the miracles of Jesus are not unique, what then is so special about Jesus? But if they are unique, how can we accept them without incurring the charge of blind credulity? We have just noticed how Origen answered the former question by claiming that Jesus' miracles were inextricably bound up with the unassailable moral character of Jesus' life and his teaching about the righteousness of God. Origen responded to the latter question in a variety of ways. On the one hand, he challenged the implied assumption that there is nothing in ongoing Christian experience that is comparable with the miracles of Jesus. On the other hand, he was prepared to admit that reports of miracles do not have the same compelling power as firsthand experience of miracles. In his *Commentary on John* he conceded that

> Christ's stupendous acts of power were able to bring to faith those of Christ's own time, but . . . they lost their demonstrative force with the lapse of years and began to be regarded as mythical. Greater evidential value than that of the miracles then performed attaches to the comparison which we now make between these miracles and the prophecy of them; this makes it impossible for the student to cast any doubt on the former.[16]

Here Origen admits frankly that the reliability of testimony, especially of that to the miraculous, is always open to question. But if it can be shown that Jesus had fulfilled prophecies that undeniably had been made hundreds of years before, the argument obviously contains fewer ifs and buts. This line of argument was, in fact, the one generally preferred by the early theologians.[17]

In his reply to the deceased but still formidable opponent of the church, the philosopher Celsus, Origen developed this theme more explicitly. Taking his cue from 1 Corinthians 2:4, he observed:

> We have to say this, that the gospel has a proof which is peculiar to itself, and which is more divine than a Greek proof based on dialectical argument. This more divine demonstration the apostle calls a "demonstration of the Spirit and of power"—of spirit because of the prophecies and especially those which refer to Christ, which are capable of convincing anyone who reads them; of power because of the prodigious miracles which may be proved to have happened by this argument among many others, that traces of them still remain among those who live according to the will of the Logos.[18]

As examples of the ongoing power of Christ, Origen went on to speak of healings and exorcisms performed by Christians in his own day who have the same Spirit that empowered Jesus,[19] and of the transforming power of Christ in the lives of believers.[20] With regard to this last point, Maurice Wiles has noted "a shift of emphasis from the increasingly more distant physical miracles of Jesus to the continuing miracles of conversion and continence."[21]

On the face of it the position is substantially weakened; it appears that God no longer acts in abnormal ways. Thus the comment carries with it the implicit question of whether God ever did act in the abnormal ways recorded earlier but no longer directly experienced.

Different theologians have answered the question in different ways. The reader of Wiles's contributions to *The Myth of God Incarnate* might well conjecture that the Regius Professor of Divinity at Oxford would answer this question in the negative, as would R. M. Grant, the leading authority on ideas of science in the early centuries.[22] The contemporary Catholic charismatic teacher, Francis MacNutt, not only answers in the affirmative, but insists that God still heals in such ways today.[23] Between Wiles, Grant, and MacNutt stands B. B. Warfield, the redoubtable champion of old Princeton Calvinism, who believed that miracles ceased with the apostolic age, having served their purpose as "part of the credentials of the Apostles as the authoritative agents of God in founding the church."[24] We shall not attempt to resolve this debate here and now. In their different ways, each of these three theologians has touched on a central issue. We shall be looking at these issues repeatedly in the course of this study.

Before we leave this cursory look at the way the early church interpreted the significance of miracles, we should note the views of Augustine (354–430). Augustine was for many years Bishop of Hippo in the province of Numidia on the coast of North Africa, and was undoubtedly the greatest and most influential theologian of the early church. Augustine defined a miracle as "whatever appears that is difficult or unusual above the hope and power of them who wonder."[25] He went on to divide miracles into two classes: those "which cause only wonder" and those which "procure great favor and good will." To see a man flying would provoke only wonder, but the healings and nature miracles of Jesus produced benefits for those who experienced them. "Thus certain provided for the good of the body by more open benefit, certain again for the good of the soul by more hidden sign, and all for the good of men by their witness to Majesty; thus, at the same time, was the divine authority moving towards Itself the wandering souls of mortal men." It is at this point that Augustine asks and answers the question: "Why, say you, do not those things take place now? because they would not move, unless they were wonderful, and if they were usual, they would not be wonderful." The recurring wonders of nature are no less miraculous than the nonrecurring miracles. But familiarity breeds contempt, and God wants our response to him to be based not simply on the stupendous.

The same point is made even more forcefully in another early work by Augustine:

> We have heard that our predecessors, at a stage in faith on the way from temporal things up to eternal things, followed visible miracles. They could do nothing else. And they did so in such a way that it should not be necessary for those who came after them. When the Catholic Church had been founded and diffused throughout the whole world, on the one

hand miracles were not allowed to continue till our time, lest the mind should always seek visible things, and the human race should grow cold by becoming accustomed to things which when they were novelties kindled its faith. On the other hand we must not doubt that those are to be believed who proclaimed miracles which only a few had actually seen, and yet were able to persuade whole peoples to follow them. At that time the problem was to get people to believe before anyone was fit to reason about divine and invisible things.[26]

The clear implication is that miracles have served their purpose in establishing Christianity. Although they happened, it is now more expedient to base belief on other grounds. He modified this position somewhat (to the discomfort and disbelief of B. B. Warfield) in *The Retractations*, which Augustine composed toward the close of his life in order to correct misunderstanding and set right any errors that he himself had committed. Commenting on this passage, Augustine endorsed its basic thrust, but at the same time made it clear that he believed that miracles still happened:

> Likewise this statement of mine is indeed true: "These miracles were not allowed to last until our times lest the soul ever seek visible things and the human race grow cold because of familiarity with those things whose novelty enkindled it." For not even now, when a hand is laid on the baptized, do they receive the Holy Spirit in such a way that they speak with the tongues of all nations,[27] nor are the sick now healed by the shadow of the preachers of Christ.[28] Even though such things happened at that time, manifestly they ceased later. But what I said is not to be so interpreted that no miracles are believed to be performed in the name of Christ at the present time. For, when I wrote that book, I myself had recently learned that a blind man had been restored to sight in Milan near the bodies of the martyrs in that very city,[29] and I knew about some others, so numerous even in these times, that we cannot know about all of them nor enumerate those we know.[30]

Other writings of Augustine show how he felt the need to provide a further rationale for miracles. Doubtless his philosophical background played a part here.[31] As we have already seen, the biblical miracles had for him a discernible purpose. They were not merely wonders, designed to impress. They always met some human need, and in so doing revealed the graciousness of God. But over and above this, there was the question of whether miracles are arbitrary interventions in the course of nature that are utterly at variance with God's more normal ways of working. For Augustine this was simply not the case:

> There is, however, no impropriety in saying that God does a thing contrary to nature, when it is contrary to what we know of nature. For we give the name nature to the usual common course of nature; and whatever God does contrary to this, we call a prodigy, or a miracle. But against the supreme law of nature, which is beyond the knowledge both of the ungodly and of weak believers, God never acts, any more than He acts

against Himself. As regards spiritual and rational beings, to which class the human soul belongs, the more they partake of this unchangeable law and light, the more clearly they see what is possible, and what impossible; and again, the greater their distance from it, the less their perception of the future, and the more frequent their surprise at strange occurrences.[32]

Elsewhere Augustine entertains the conjecture that God has implanted hidden seeds in his creation that lie dormant until the time is right:

> The being that thus appears has already been wholly created in the texture as it were of the material elements, but only emerges when the opportunity presents itself. For as mothers are pregnant with unborn offspring, so the world itself is pregnant with the causes of unborn beings, which are not created in it except from that highest essence, where nothing is either born or dies, begins to be or ceases to be.[33]

Thus, what we call miracles are in fact part of God's creation. The difference between a miracle and an ordinary event in nature lies ultimately in the rarity of the former. Both, in fact, are wonders and both are ultimately the work of God.

Augustine also considers the suggestion, favored by more recent writers,[34] that miracles might be instances of the accelerated processes of nature. The changing of the water into wine at Cana (John 2:1-11) might be seen as a case of God speeding up the natural process of rain falling to the earth and being transformed into wine through the vine and the fermentation of grape juice.[35] Likewise, the feeding of the five thousand (Matt. 14:17, 21) is no more of a miracle than what God does daily, when out of a few seeds he raises up immense harvests.[36] Close examination of Augustine shows that while he entertains the acceleration theory, he does not press it. His view of the physical world is more akin to that argued by T. F. Torrance, who sees the space-time continuum relatively closed from our side but open to God.[37] For Augustine miracles remain, from our human standpoint, inexplicable. "When such a thing happens, it appears to us as an event contrary to nature. But with God it is not so; for him 'nature' is what he does."[38]

With Augustine we have already moved quite a way from the simple view that the miracles of Jesus provided tangible, compelling proof of his divinity. Certainly, miracles form part of Augustine's apologetic. But they are not a foundation for faith. What Augustine offers is a world view in which miracles can be seen to have a part. But the view itself is an explanation offered from the standpoint of faith. As Augustine expounded Scripture, he saw in the healing miracles of Jesus a deeper meaning that went beyond the act of healing itself. In his *Tractates on the Gospel of John,* which is a collection of sermons he preached on the Fourth Gospel sometime between December 414 and August 416, Augustine pondered some of the acutest questions raised by the healing miracles of Jesus. He asked himself why it was that Jesus did not heal everyone, and why those who were healed fell sick and died in due course. As he reflected on the story of the healing of the lame man at the pool of Bethzatha (John 5:1–18), he observed:

> It ought not to be a matter of wonder that a miracle was wrought by God; the wonder would be if man had wrought it. Rather ought we to rejoice than wonder that our Lord and Saviour Jesus Christ was made man, than that He performed divine works among men. It is of greater importance to our salvation what He was made for men, than what He did among men: it is more important that he healed the faults of souls, than that he healed the weaknesses of mortal bodies. But as the soul knew not Him by whom it was to be healed, and had eyes in the flesh whereby to see corporeal deeds, but had not yet sound eyes in the heart with which to recognise Him as God concealed in the flesh, he wrought what the soul was able to see, in order to heal that by which it was not able to see.
>
> He entered a place where lay a great multitude of sick folk—of blind, lame, withered; and being the physician of both souls and bodies, and having come to heal all the souls of them that should believe, of those sick folk He chose one for healing, thereby to signify unity. If in doing this we regard Him with a commonplace mind, with the mere human understanding and wit, as regards power it was not a great matter that He performed; and also as regards goodness He performed too little. There lay so many there, and yet only one was healed, whilst He could by a word have raised them all up. What, then, must we understand but that the power and the goodness was doing what souls might, by His deeds, understand for their everlasting salvation, than what bodies might gain for temporal health? For that which is the real health of bodies, and which is looked for from the Lord, will be at the end, in the resurrection of the dead. What shall live then shall no more die; what shall be healed shall no more be sick; what shall be satisfied shall no more hunger and thirst; what shall be made new shall not grow old. But at this time, however, the eyes of the blind, that were opened by those acts of our Lord and Saviour Jesus Christ, were again closed in death; and limbs of the paralytics that received strength were loosened again in death; and whatever was for a time made whole in mortal limbs came to nought in the end: but the soul that believed passed into eternal life.[39]

To the skeptic, all this may well look like a piece of spiritualizing of the kind into which preachers regularly fall, in order to avoid the harsher realities of their texts. The historical scholar may well detect in these words traces of a residual Platonism that led Augustine to see a spiritual world behind the physical one. But by whatever route Augustine came to this view of the world, it should not be overlooked that he regarded the present world as a real world. Perhaps it would be more accurate to say that he viewed it as parabolic and sacramental: parabolic in that physical events spoke of transcendent truth; sacramental in that material things were both tokens and means of grace. In this sacramental world miracles were not the sole means of grace. Nor should the sacramental means of grace be confused with the total reality of grace itself. In this sacramental scheme of reality miracles were not seen as isolated acts, having an independent objective evidential value. They had their place as part of a world view that saw God as the fundamental reality and the world only in relation to God. Within this world view miracles had an importance, but it was a relative importance that was determined by their relation to the overall scheme of reality, and was recognized only by seeing them within the frame of reference supplied by that scheme.

As a footnote to this review of the early church, we must observe a point that stands in tension with the general view that miracles are straightforward exhibitions of divine power. It is a comment made by Gregory of Nyssa who, as we have already seen, endorsed the view that miracles demonstrate deity. Gregory suggested that the miracles of Jesus might have been done by Jesus as a man empowered by God.[40] This suggestion fortified Bishop Gore in more recent times in his contention that Jesus'

> miracles in general, and in particular the raising of Lazarus, are attributed by our Lord to the Father, as answering His own prayer, and to the Holy Spirit as "the finger of God," and St. Luke describes His miracles generally as the result of "the power of the Lord" present with him. *This is a point on which—it must be emphatically said—accurate exegesis renders impossible to us the phraseology of the Fathers exactly as it stands.*

Gore went on to cite Bishop Westcott's observation:

> It is unscriptural though the practice is supported by strong patristic authority, to regard the Lord during His historic life, as acting now by His human and now by His divine nature only. The two natures were inseparably combined in the unity of His person. In all things He acts personally; and, as far as it is revealed to us, His greatest works during His earthly life are wrought by the help of the Father through the energy of a humanity enabled to do all things in fellowship with God (comp. John xi.41f.).[41]

AQUINAS, LUTHER, AND CALVIN

Thomas Aquinas (ca. 1225–1274), the greatest of the medieval theologians and the most formative single thinker on subsequent Catholicism, stood firmly in the tradition of Augustine. Augustine's ideas are treated as fixed points. Where Aquinas differs from Augustine, he does so chiefly to express the same ideas in terms of the Aristotelian philosophy that provided the conceptual framework for his thinking. In other words, his discussion of miracles in his magnum opus, the *Summa Theologiae* (I, Q. 105, arts. 6–8),[42] speaks of God as the first cause and creatures as secondary causes. Aquinas defends Augustine's statement that "God does on occasion do something against the usual pattern of nature" by saying:

> Thus if we look to the world's order as it depends on the first cause, God cannot act against it, because then he would be doing something

contrary to his foreknowledge, his will or his goodness. But if we take the order in things as it depends on any of the secondary causes, then God can act apart from it; he is not subject to that order but rather it is subject to him, as issuing from him not out of a necessity of nature, but by decision of his will.[43]

Aquinas also follows Augustine in his definition of a miracle.[44] All works express God's power, "But the word 'miracle' connotes something altogether wondrous, i.e., having its cause hidden absolutely and from everyone. This cause is God. Thus the works God does surpassing any cause known to us are called miracles."[45] For this reason, not all miracles are alike. Some are greater than others. "Therefore the more it exceeds nature's capability, the greater any miracle is said to be."[46]

Aquinas parts company with Augustine, however, through his refusal to conjecture about how God works miracles. Whereas Augustine entertained the idea that God might have implanted certain powers within nature that only come to light when miracles occur, Aquinas insisted that God alone works miracles. Thus, in his major apologetic work, the *Summa contra Gentiles,* Aquinas states his conviction:

> When any finite power produces the proper effect to which it is determined, this is not a miracle, though it may be a matter of wonder for some person who does not understand that power. For example, it may seem astonishing to ignorant people that a magnet attracts iron or that some little fish might hold back a ship. But the potency of every creature is limited to some definite effect or to certain effects. So, whatever is done by the power of any creature cannot be called a miracle properly, even though it may be astonishing to one who does not comprehend the power of this creature. But what is done by divine power, which, being infinite, is incomprehensible in itself, is truly miraculous.[47]

Moreover, "every creature needs for its action some subject on which to act, for it is the prerogative of God alone to make something out of nothing."[48] For Aquinas, miracles are not so much an acceleration of natural processes as a suspension of them. Food can be turned into flesh, "but only when it has been changed into blood."[49] But this is not a miracle in the strict sense of the term. It is a natural process, employing "definite intermediate stages." In true miracles God does not work through the intermediate stages. Nor does he need the natural properties of things.

For Aquinas, it is precisely this which distinguishes divine miracles from those wrought by angels or demons. When either of the latter do astonishing things, "they make use of natural things in order to produce definite effects," using them "as instruments, just as a physician uses certain herbs as instruments of healing."[50] The same is true of magic, which is essentially a power to control or manipulate powers or intelligent natures that belong to the natural order.[51] Such powers are not necessarily evil in themselves; evil arises through the use to which they are put.[52]

When we turn from the Middle Ages to the Reformation, we find the founder of the Reformation in Germany, Martin Luther (1483–1546), both asserting and apparently downplaying the significance of the miracles of Jesus. In the words of the leading authority on Luther's christology, Dr. Ian D. Kingston Siggins:

> They were great miracles and startling deeds, unparalleled, unprecedented. Yet in Luther's thinking they play an incidental role: miracles themselves are the least significant of Christian works, for the devil was defeated by weakness, not magnificent miracles; the earthly effect of Christ's miracles cannot compare with the heavenly effect of faith in Him; and it is one of St. John's superiorities over the Synoptics that he stresses faith where they stress miracles.[53]

In common with earlier theologians, Luther could say that the miracles of Jesus were divine works, wrought by the power of God himself. Commenting on John 14:11 ("Believe me that I am in the Father and the Father in me; or else believe me for the sake of the works themselves"), Luther observes:

> Christ says: "If My preaching does not make you willing to believe that God dwells and is in Me and that I dwell and am in Him, then believe this because of the works you see before your eyes. These works, as no one can deny, are not human; they are divine. They prove and attest powerfully enough that He speaks and works in Me and through Me." These are the works and the miracles which He performed publicly before all the world—giving sight to the blind and hearing to the deaf, healing to all manner of sick, casting out devils, and raising the dead—solely by the Word. These are not only divine works, but they are also witnesses of God the Father. Therefore he who sees and hears these sees God the Father in them; and he is not only persuaded that God is in Christ and that Christ is in God, but from them he can also be comforted with the assurance of God's fatherly love and grace toward us.[54]

There is in this quotation an echo of a note sounded centuries earlier by Gregory of Nyssa: the miracles of Jesus were not purely manifestations of Jesus' divinity.[55] They are rather the works of the Father, or to be still more precise, they are the works of the Word of the Father that became incarnate in Jesus.

For Luther, this thought is grounded in John 14:10 ("Do you not believe that I am in the Father and the Father in me? The words that I say to you I do not speak on my own authority; but the Father who dwells in me does his works"). It is not that Luther wants to drive a wedge between the humanity of Jesus and the divinity of the Father; rather, he wants to express more exactly how we should understand the incarnation of God in Christ. Both John and Paul "join and bind Christ and the Father so firmly together that we learn to think of God as only in Christ."[56] "For, as St. Paul declares (Col. 2:9), in His Person 'dwells the whole fullness of Deity bodily'; and there is no God apart from Him, where I could come to Him or find Him— although He is everywhere else, of course. Now wherever one hears this Man's Word and sees His work, there one surely hears and sees God's Word and work."[57]

Dr. Siggins suggests that Luther was not greatly concerned with miracles. Perhaps it would be more correct to say that for Luther they have their place alongside the other works of God. They are not direct expressions of deity in which we see God as he is in himself. Like the other works of God in the world, miracles may be described as God's masks[58] or garments.

> When we get to heaven, we shall see God differently; then no clouds and no darkness will obscure our view. But here on earth we shall not perceive Him with our senses and our thoughts. No, here we see Him, as St. Paul states (1 Cor. 13:12),"in a mirror dimly," enveloped in an image, namely, in the Word and the sacraments. These are His masks or His garments, as it were, in which He conceals Himself. But He is certainly present in these, Himself working miracles, preaching, administering the sacraments, consoling, strengthening, and helping. We see Him as we see the sun through a cloud. For now we cannot bear to look at his brilliant Majesty. Therefore He must cover and veil Himself, so to speak, behind a heavy cloud. Thus it has been ordained that he who wants to see and apprehend both the Father and the Son glorified and enthroned in majesty, must apprehend Him through the Word and through the works He performs in Christendom by means of the ministry and other offices.[59]

This does not mean that Luther thought that miracles had no evidential value or that they were devoid of spiritual significance. But evidence alone is not enough; there must be also a change of heart.[60] Miracles are like visible, tangible expressions of Christ's teaching. Thus, the feeding of the five thousand teaches us the lesson of Matthew 6:33: "Seek first the kingdom of God and his righteousness, then all such will be well with you."[61] The miracle at Cana (John 2:1-11) also shows how those who believe in him shall not suffer want.[62] In view of this and the fact that Luther could describe both miracles and the sacraments as the masks of God, we might apply to Luther's view of miracles a description that he applies to the sacraments. Luther saw the sacraments as signs accompanying and embodying the promises of God.[63] As such, they were like visible words, and as such they call for the response of faith.

Miracles are set in still sharper focus by Luther's comments on the works that Jesus promised that his disciples would perform.

> We see nothing special that they do beyond what others do, especially since the day of miracles is past. Miracles, of course, are still the least significant works, since they are only physical and are performed for only a few people.[64]

These miracles pale into virtual insignificance compared with the works of conversion and faith that overcome the power of evil and transform lives.

In the last analysis, as the cross itself demonstrates, the ultimate victory is won through the self-surrender of Christ in weakness and not through a display of force. Paradoxically, the way of weakness is the way of strength. Thus, Luther's paraphrase of Jesus' prayer in Gethsemane represents Luther's basic perspective:

> Let it come to pass since the Father wants the devil to be defeated and weakened, not by might and power and magnificent miracles, as has happened heretofore through Me, but by obedience and humility in the utmost weakness by cross and death, by My submission to Him, and by surrendering My right and might. But in this very way I will take and wrest from the devil his right and might over you, since he is attacking and killing Me even though I am guiltless. Then he, judged and condemned by his own guilt, will have to give way, and flee from Me to the ends of the world.[65]

The way of the cross was the way of renunciation and obedience. The glorious vindication of Jesus in his resurrection lies on the far side of the cross. Miracles give glimpses of the glory to come. But the way to glory is the way of the cross.

In contrast to this, the attitude of John Calvin (1509–1564) was forthrightly polemical. In his "Prefatory Address to King Francis," which he composed in 1536 as a preface to the first edition of the *Institutes of the Christian Religion,* Calvin plunged into a discussion of the value and corroborative function of miracles. Replying to the charge that his teaching was novel and lacking in authority, Calvin retorted that it was based on the gospel, which in turn was corroborated by miracles. His opponents had asked whether the Reformers could produce miracles (as the Catholic Church claimed to do) as evidence of divine sanction. Calvin picked up the gauntlet and counterattacked on two fronts. On the one hand, he pointed out that the gospel was attested by miracles. On the other hand, he insisted that where a miracle is associated with false teaching, it should be dismissed as Satanic deceit. Hence, "those 'miracles' which our adversaries point to in their own support are sheer delusions of Satan, for they draw people away from the true worship of their God to vanity [cf. Deut. 13:2ff.]."[66]

In developing both aspects of this counterattack, Calvin cited passages from Scripture to show that this was the position consistently maintained by biblical writers in both the Old and New Testaments. Moreover, both lines of argument exhibit an intrinsic connection between miracles and truth. This comes out in Calvin's use of words like *confirm, attest,* and *seal.*

> In demanding miracles of us, they act dishonestly. For we are not forging some new gospel, but are retaining that very gospel whose truth all the miracles that Jesus Christ and his disciples ever wrought serve to confirm. But, compared with us, they have a strange power: even to this day they can confirm their faith by continual miracles! Instead they allege miracles which can disturb a mind otherwise at rest—they are so foolish and ridiculous, so vain and false! . . .

Perhaps this false hue could have been more dazzling if Scripture had not warned us concerning the legitimate purpose and use of miracles. For Mark teaches that those signs which attended the apostles' preaching were set forth to confirm it [Mark 16:20]. In like manner, Luke relates that our "Lord . . . bore witness to the word of his grace," when these signs and wonders were done by the apostles' hands [Acts 14:3 p.]. Very much like this is that word of the apostle: that the salvation proclaimed by the gospel has been confirmed by the fact that "the Lord has attested it by signs and wonders and various mighty works" [Heb. 2:4 p.; cf. Rom. 15:18–19]. When we hear that these are the seals of the gospel, shall we turn them to the destruction of faith in the gospel? When we hear that they were appointed only to seal the truth, shall we employ them to confirm falsehoods?[67]

Citing John 7:18 and 8:50, Calvin insists that truth in religion is characterized by the desire to seek the glory of God. Conversely, the glorification of anything other than God is a mark of untruth.

Since Christ affirms this test of doctrine, miracles are wrongly valued that are applied to any other purpose than to glorify the name of the one God [Deut. 13:2ff.]. And we may also fitly remember that Satan has his miracles, which, though they are deceitful tricks rather than true powers, are of such sort as to mislead the simple-minded and untutored [cf. II Thess. 2:9–10]. Magicians and enchanters have always been noted for miracles. Idolatry has been nourished by wonderful miracles, yet these are not sufficient to sanction for us the superstition either of magicians or of idolaters.[68]

In short, the stupendous by itself is no attestation of God. True miracles have a signlike quality that exemplifies, reinforces, and attests the teaching of the human agent who performs the miracle. Calvin did not dispute the capacity of many to work wonders. The decisive factor was the claims made by those who performed them. If those claims led away from the gospel, the wonder was to be rejected. This, Calvin pointed out, was the position of Augustine who, rejecting Donatist miracles,[69] appealed to Jesus' warning that false prophets with lying signs would come to deceive, if possible, the elect (Matt. 24:24). It was a warning reinforced by the apostle Paul who predicted the coming of the lawless one "by the activity of Satan . . . with all power and with pretended signs and wonders" (2 Thess. 2:9). Similarly, Paul had warned of Satan's capacity to "disguise himself as an angel of light" (2 Cor. 11:14). The fact that some are deluded by such wonders is of itself evidence that they have rejected the truth of God; it is also a divine punishment for having done so (2 Thess. 2:11).

As Calvin developed this argument in the course of the *Institutes,* he insisted that Moses' doctrine was "sanctioned for all time"[70] by the wonders that he wrought. Events like the deaths of Korah, Dathan, and Abiram (Num. 16:24), the smiting of the rock to produce water (Num. 20:10f.; Exod. 17:6; cf. 1 Cor. 10:4), the giving of the manna (Num. 11:9; Exod. 16:13; cf.

1 Cor. 10:3), and the transformation of his countenance (Exod. 34:29) were all public events, promoting the honor of God and clearly distinguished from the magic that was punishable by death (Lev. 20:6).[71] The same is true of the actions of the apostles whose preaching of the gospel and the kingdom of Christ was "illumined and magnified by unheard-of and extraordinary miracles."[72] However, such works have ceased, having fulfilled their function in establishing the gospel.

There is, however, a basic difference between the miracles performed by Moses and other men of God in Scripture and those performed by Christ:

> How plainly and clearly is his deity shown in miracles! Even though I confess that both the prophets and the apostles performed miracles equal to and similar to his, yet in this respect there is the greatest of differences: they distributed the gifts of God by their ministry, but he showed forth his own power. Indeed, he sometimes used prayer to render glory to the Father [John 11:41]. But for the most part we see his own power shown to us. And why would he not be the real author of miracles, who by his own authority commits the dispensation of them to others?[73]

This last point is illustrated by Jesus' giving authority to raise the dead, cure lepers, and cast out demons (Matt. 10:8; Mark 3:15; 6:7). It is further exemplified by the fact that the apostles healed "in the name of Jesus Christ" (Acts 3:6). Clearly Calvin will not have anything to do with the suggestion that the miracles of Jesus were works of the Father acting through the agency of the man Jesus. For him Jesus is, as it were, the second person of the Trinity incarnated, in whom the "whole fullness of divinity dwells bodily" (Col. 2:9). Whereas Luther could, at least on occasion, see the miracles as the works of the Word of the Father that was incarnate in Jesus, Calvin attributes the miracles to the second person of the Trinity outright.

There is, however, a point that Calvin shares with Luther and that is, I believe, of major importance to an understanding of miracles. It is the observation that Calvin makes, almost in passing, that miracles are sacramental signs.

> The term "sacrament" . . . embraces generally all those signs which God has ever enjoined upon men to render them more certain and confident of the truth of his promises. He sometimes willed to present these in natural things, at other times set them forth in miracles.[74]

The remark is made in the course of Calvin's discussion of the sacraments. The burden of his subsequent arguments is to show that there is nothing inherent in the sacramental material itself that could produce the effect, and that God is not dependent upon any particular means. Thus Jesus could, on occasion, use dust and spittle to restore the sight of a blind man (John 9:6), but sometimes he healed by a touch (Matt. 9:29) and at other times he healed by a word (Luke 18:42). The same was true of the apostles (Acts 3:6; 14:9f.; cf. 5:12, 16), who also used other means (Mark 6:13; Acts 19:12;

cf. James 5:14f.).[75] But whatever the means used, miracles are sacramental signs embodying and exemplifying God's gracious promises. They illustrate and express in the form of an act what God promises in his Word.

SUMMARY

If we try to sum up what we have seen so far, we can point to certain areas of broad agreement and at the same time note a number of issues on which the great thinkers of the Christian church show a variety of opinions. Of the theologians that we have examined up to the time of the Reformation none entertained doubts about the historicity of the biblical miracles. At the same time they do not appear to have been oblivious to the fact that belief in miracles does raise problems. Testimony to the miraculous was no less difficult to believe for the educated person in the second century than for his or her twentieth-century counterpart.

Although these writers believed in miracles, they were well aware of the fact that Christian faith is not based on the stupendous alone. Satan too could perform wonders. For Calvin, following the injunctions of Deuteronomy 13, it was more important to test the teaching of the wonder-worker than to be impressed by his feats. For Origen one of the marks that clearly distinguished the miracles of Jesus from the works of magicians was Christ's concern for righteousness. For Calvin true miracles bring glory to God, whereas pseudomiracles may be recognized by the way that they promote the glory of man. For Aquinas true miracles are distinguished from pseudomiracles by the fact that the former are the work of direct divine intervention, whereas the latter employ means that are ready to hand.

Why was it that Christian thinkers from Justin Martyr to John Calvin were firmly committed to belief in the miracles of the Bible? An immediate and obvious answer is that they believed in them because they believed the Bible to be true, because the Bible was the Word of God. But this was not sheer believism. The writers that we have been thinking about were not content to leave it at that. Three main lines of argument may be discerned.

1. The first is a general one concerning trustworthiness. The reports themselves are to be believed because the stories that they contain were open to public refutation at the time that they happened. Moreover, they come from writers whose judgment is respected and whose honesty is beyond question. Thus, Calvin declared his belief in Moses' miracles, because Moses could have been detected of fraud by anyone present. This was, of course, against the background of Calvin's high view of Scripture as the Word of God. Later generations of thinkers have not been quite so ready as Calvin to take the Bible at its face value, and later on we shall have to examine more closely the pros and cons of this debate.

2. The second line of argument concerns what might be called the intrinsic credibility of the miracle in the light of ongoing experience. The argument could be put like this. We recognize that we have only somewhat remote

testimony for this or that particular miracle. The testimony itself might well be limited to a single source. However, if we have reason to believe that events of the same kind happen today, the intrinsic probability of the reported miracle happening is greatly enhanced. This kind of argument is employed all the time by historians and lawyers in trying to assess whether ordinary alleged events happened. And we may well ask, why should not this argument also be applied to the miraculous? We must note, however, a division of opinion. Such an argument could not be used by Luther and Calvin, because both believed that the age of miracles is past. But it could be used by Origen and Augustine, who believed that God was still working wonders in their own day. Even here a note of caution may be detected. Origen preferred to stress the ongoing miracle of Christ's transforming power in the lives of men and women rather than the abnormal healings and events that broke the normal course of nature. Augustine was inclined to share this view (though with modifications), adding that the recurring wonders of nature are no less miraculous than the unique miracles, but insisting that God does not want our response to him to be based simply on the stupendous. Likewise, Luther believed that we must seek God first through the cross and not in works of power and glory.

3. The third line of argument concerns the conceivability of miracles. Some writers shunned all speculation. For Aquinas, miracles were instances of direct divine intervention in the normal workings of nature, and on that ground alone are conceivable. Augustine was prepared to go further and suggest ways of thinking as to how God might have wrought the events that we call miracles. This would not establish the historicity of any given miracle, but it would enable the believer to see something of its feasibility. Moreover, this feasibility would be further enhanced if it could be seen how the miracle is related to God's other works.

What is clear from all this is the fact that miracles were not thought of as a basic ground for belief in God. God's existence is to be believed in on other grounds. Miracles function as a sign of identification, enabling the one who performs them to be identified as God's agent. But a sign is not the same as a proof. A sign points to something. It may carry with it some indication of its authenticity and veracity. But its function consists in directing us toward that to which it points. Insofar as it does this, it validates itself. The church fathers recognized that signs differed from each other in character and had varying degrees of compelling power. They rarely appealed to miracles on their own. Frequently they linked them with the fulfillment of prophecy. They insisted on seeing them in the context of the gospel generally as expressions of God's loving care, righteousness, creative power, and glory. Luther and Calvin could even suggest that miracles were sacramental acts, embodying and betokening the promise of grace.

The miracles performed by Moses and the apostles were no less miraculous than the miracles of Jesus. What distinguished these men from him was a difference in relationship to God. This is implicit in all the writers we have looked at, but is made most explicit by Calvin. Moses and the apostles saw themselves as agents of God's working. Christ is the incarnation of the divine Creator who in the beginning had created the world and who was now present in Jesus of Nazareth, healing its wounds, bearing its griefs, and redeeming it from all its ills.

II

The Rise of Skepticism

2

THE SEVENTEENTH-CENTURY CRUCIBLE

For Protestant Christians the Reformation in the sixteenth century is the most decisive epoch among all the ages that succeeded the birth, death, and resurrection of Jesus Christ. But from the standpoint of Western culture in general and the scientific and technological changes that affect our daily lives, the turning point was not the Reformation but the age that followed it. The seventeenth century was a crucible into which was poured the philosophy of the Middle Ages, the religion of the Reformation and the Counter-Reformation, and the culture of the Renaissance. For a long period these various elements continued to exist alongside each other. But the chemistry of time brought about the interaction that was ultimately to produce the modern secular outlook. In this interaction several powerful catalysts were to play an important part. The most obvious of these is the rise of modern science, culminating in the physics of Sir Isaac Newton with its seemingly self-contained and self-sufficient mechanistic universe. Science was important not only for the picture that is painted of the universe but also for the questions that it posed about the scope and nature of knowledge. It was with such questions that the two great philosophical movements of the seventeenth and eighteenth centuries—rationalism and empiricism—were concerned. However, rationalism and empiricism were by no means the only philosophical movements of the age. Nor were they exclusively concerned with questions raised by science. The great debates of the sixteenth century had a religious dimension. The quest for certainty in science and philosophy was linked with the question of truth and certainty in religion.

The seventeenth century is a century of paradoxes for the modern mind. We might be tempted to assume that the men of science were the pioneers of skepticism and secularism, and that is was the religious thinkers who were preparing to fight a last-ditch stand before the onslaughts of the Age of Enlightenment in the eighteenth century and of Darwinism in the nineteenth. But skepticism received its strongest encouragement from religious apologists who sought to demolish all claims to knowledge of their opponents in order to make way for their own views. Many of the leading men of science approached nature not as an autonomous closed system, but as God's good creation in which the Creator moved in many and various ways. Among those ways were miracles. At the same time, however, there were those who questioned whether the observed regularities of nature admitted any exceptions and whether the rationality of natural law could tolerate anything so absurd as a miracle.

In this chapter we shall be concerned with the triangular relationship between religion, science, and philosophy. To set the scene we shall look at the new horizons of the critical mind, noting some of the trends and movements that affected seventeenth-century thought. Against this background we shall look at the ideas of some of the most influential figures of the day from Benedict de Spinoza to John Locke.

THE NEW HORIZONS OF THE CRITICAL MIND

Today we are apt to think of rationalism and empiricism as the two major philosophical movements of the seventeenth and eighteenth centuries. But neither movement was as clear-cut or as well defined as we tend to see them from the hindsight of two centuries. Nor were they the sole movements of importance. In our reconstruction of what is important we are inevitably influenced by what we happen to have heard of. The issues and personalities that we pronounce to be significant depend in no small measure upon the traditions in which we stand and the information and viewpoints conveyed by those traditions. A case in point is the image that we have of rationalism, which pictures Descartes as the founder of modern philosophy appearing like a bolt from the blue. Similarly we are apt to think of Locke, Berkeley, and Hume as the trio of British empiricists, with Locke as the originator and Hume as the skeptical genius whose clear-sighted mind readily spotted the elementary mistakes of his predecessors. Rationalism is sometimes presented as a rather absurd continental movement, and empiricism as a superior British alternative. It is questionable whether anyone living at the time would have recognized the compelling simplicity of such pictures. This is not because we have the advantage of broad, historical perspective, enabling us to recognize what is really important; rather, it is because we labor under the disadvantage of not knowing enough about the men and their times.

Prior to the rationalism of Descartes was a movement that had its origins in the sixteenth century. It came to be known as the New Pyrrhonism, or simply as Pyrrhonism, and was so called after Pyrrho, the first great skeptic.[1] In the hands of Catholic apologists Gentian Hervet, Jean Gontery, François Veron (who taught philosophy and theology at the Jesuit Collège de la Flèche during Descartes's student days there), and others, the New Pyrrhonism became a "new engine of war," forged for the destruction of Calvinism. The whole edifice of Calvinism was built on the Bible as the Word of God, in which the internal testimony of the Spirit speaking through Scripture was the ultimate authority for all that was taught and believed. The New Pyrrhonism proceeded to question this foundation of theological knowledge, and sought to undermine all human claims to rational, objective knowledge, including the claims to know Scripture to be the Word of God and to be able to interpret it corrrectly. This was done in order to clear the ground for accepting the authority of the Catholic Church as the guardian of all truth in an act of faith. In short, what skepticism removed with one hand, fideism restored with the other. The method was not unlike Protestant, evangelical, presuppositionalist apologetics in our own day, which seeks to undermine the rational foundation of all other world views in order to make way for a belief system, founded on the Bible, which will also provide a basis for rationality and reality. Indeed, there were Protestant apologists of the period, including the dialecticians La Placette and Bouiller and the Anglican divine and erstwhile Catholic convert William Chillingworth, who redirected the arguments of the Pyrrhonists against their Catholic authors.

Pyrrhonism is important because of the impetus that it gave to the quest for certainty, rationality, and objective knowledge. Both the deism of Lord Herbert of Cherbury and the rationalism of Descartes were in part replies to the growing number of Pyrrhonists, whose interests extended beyond the immediate battle between Catholics and Protestants, so as to encompass the foundation and acquisition of knowledge generally. Both Lord Herbert and Descartes sought a basis for rationality and truth, immune to the arrows of skepticism and built on the solid rock of self-evident ideas, well removed from the quicksands of fideism.

Lord Herbert of Cherbury (1583–1648) was a slightly senior contemporary of Descartes. Between 1618 and 1624 he served as James I's ambassador to France, and it was in Paris that he published the Latin text of *On Truth, as it is Distinguished from Revelation, from the Probable, the Possible and the False* (1624). In it Lord Herbert argued that the mind possesses at birth certain innate truths, or Common Notions, that give meaning to experience and provide the foundation of knowledge. The work received the serious attention of Descartes and the mitigated skeptic Gassendi. It is generally regarded as the first major statement of deism, which will be discussed in the next chapter. In the 1645 edition, Lord Herbert went on to criticize revelation and miracles.

The great French philosopher, René Descartes (1596–1650), was much more circumspect in his pronouncements on religion. In 1634, on hearing of the condemnation of Galileo for teaching the Copernican system, he suppressed his own work *The World,* which shared the same views. By that time he had already developed his method of doubt in response to the skepticism of the Pyrrhonists. The method was modeled on geometry and sought to discover the rationality of reality by resolving whatever he was considering into its constituent elements or ideas. Descartes thought of his method not simply as a way of giving an account of discoveries that had already been made, but as an instrument for new discovery. His first principle was not to accept anything as true that he could not clearly recognize to be true. He next sought to divide the difficulties into their constituent parts. He then tried to arrange the parts in logical order, beginning with the simple and moving to the complex. Finally, he reviewed his analysis to check that nothing had been omitted. At the heart of his method was an emphasis on clear and distinct ideas, the truth of which was self-evident, a conviction about the rationality of reality, every part of which was rationally interrelated, and the further conviction about the rational unity of form and being.

Descartes's celebrated *cogito ergo sum* (I think, therefore I am), which he propounded in 1618 as the first principle of his philosophy, was in part an answer to the skepticism of the Pyrrhonists. It was not, as it is sometimes imagined, intended to be an assertion of radical individualism, but an expression of a rational apprehension of a clear and distinct idea, which thus served as a point of entry in the discovery of the rational structure of reality. Together with Descartes's adaptation of the medieval proofs of the existence of God and an appeal to the attributes of God which precluded the possibility that God would allow the right use of reason to be deceptive, the argument served to guarantee the validity of rational thought and the veridicality of sense perception.[2] But almost immediately Descartes's critics dubbed him as a Pyrrhonist and a dogmatist. Some saw his quest for a rational philosophy based on the method of doubt as an enterprise that only opened wider the Pandora's box of endless doubt. Others saw the *cogito ergo sum* as just another instance of dogmatism. It was not a demonstrative proof of the rational, immaterial self, but the expression of a settled conviction.

All this may seem to have taken us some way from the question of miracles. In fact, however, it bears on the subject in at least two important respects. On the one hand, it raises the question of whether there can be such things as miracles, if reality is a rationally coordinated system. It suggests that, if nature is the expression of rational laws, the phenomena that were previously deemed supernatural exceptions were really natural events that were not understood. Or alternatively, the events just could not have happened as reported. In other words, the world view of seventeenth-century rationalism precludes the very possibility of miracles. This was the view that Spinoza stated openly in Holland and Thomas Hobbes hinted at darkly in England.

On the other hand, Pyrrhonism and rationalism affected the question of miracles in a less direct, but nevertheless very significant, way. For they confirmed the seventeenth-century critical mind in its desire for certainty. They raised the questions of the very foundation of knowledge and the right way to proceed in getting it. Absolute certainty came increasingly to be seen as a mirage that disintegrated just when it appeared to be within grasp—for every point that seems to be established raises in turn further questions. No scheme of interpreting reality is self-contained. The greatest of the skeptics, Pierre Bayle, confessed, "I know too much to be a Pyrrhonist, and I know too little to be a Dogmatist."[3] Others, like Castello, Mersenne, Gassendi, Foucher, Chillingworth, and Glanvill, settled for a "mitigated skepticism."

The issue was still very much alive in the eighteenth century, as David Hume found during his sojourns in France. Hume resolved the question by pronouncing consistent Cartesian doubt to be impossible and by declaring Pyrrhonism to be subverted by everyday life:

> For, as in common life, we reason every moment concerning fact and existence, and cannot possibly subsist, without continually employing this species of argument, any popular objections, derived from thence, must be insufficient to destroy that evidence. The great subverter of *Pyrrhonism* or the excessive principles of scepticism is action, and employment, and the occupations of common life. These principles may flourish and triumph in the schools; where it is, indeed, difficult, if not impossible to refute them. But as soon as they leave the shade, and by the presence of real objects, which actuate our passions and sentiments, are put in opposition to the more powerful principles of our nature, they vanish like smoke, and leave the most determined sceptic in the same condition as other mortals.[4]

In point of fact, Hume's remarks are a form of mitigated skepticism. They constitute an admission of inability to answer Pyrrhonism on an intellectual level and a readiness to settle for a view of life guided by "the real objects, which actuate our passions and sentiments." But this begs the question of what is "real." Hume's view arbitrarily reduces reality to a series of material entities that have objective reality and the passions and sentiments occasioned by them, which are subjective. Together they stand like an island surrounded by a dark sea of mystery that defies all the attempts of reason to traverse.

Descartes's slightly junior contemporary, the great scientist, mathematician, philosopher, and religious thinker Blaise Pascal (1623–1662), put forward an alternative. He, too, was acutely aware of the problems posed by Pyrrhonism and the Cartesian answer. He formulated the issue in this way: "It may be that there are solid proofs, but it is not certain. So the sum of the matter is that it is not certain that everything is uncertain—and Pyrrhonism wins the day."[5] Pascal's answer to the problem was grounded in recognition that neither reason nor material objects are autonomous. Truth is known not only by reason but also by "the heart." It is by the intuitive perceptions of "the heart" that we know God, and it is only by referring reason and the objects of our experience to God that we can obtain a frame of reference adequate to the task of interpreting reality.

The views we have been considering so far were developed largely within the horizons set by French Roman Catholicism. But skepticism, like faith, does not recognize geographical and confessional frontiers. Already in Calvin a need may be detected to defend the miracles of Moses against the doubts of the skeptics. However, these were promptly swept aside in a few sentences ridiculing the possibility of fraud or mistake. For Calvin the public character of Moses' recorded acts was sufficient to preclude such explanations. A century later doubts about the biblical miracles might not amount to a chorus, but the voices expressing them were becoming increasingly audible. By the middle of the eighteenth century the refrain had become familiar.

For most devout Christians in the seventeenth and eighteenth centuries, the fact that the Bible recorded miracles was sufficient to stifle any questions about whether they had really happened. The seventeenth century was the great age of Puritanism and the eighteenth century was the age of the evangelical revival. But a theistic world view was not the exclusive property of either of those Protestant movements. John Donne (1571/2-1631), the Anglican Dean of St. Paul's Cathedral in London, viewed nature not as a separate entity or as a succession of interesting phenomena, but as the work of God's continued providence. Donne saw no radical difference between the miracles that we see every day in nature and those unusual occurrences for which the name "miracle" is normally reserved.

> There is nothing that God hath established in a constant course of nature, and which therefore is done every day, but would seeme a Miracle and exercise our admiration, if it were done but once; Nay, the ordinary things in Nature, would be greater miracles than the extraordinary, which we admire most, if they were done but once . . . and onely the daily doing takes off the admiration.[6]

Such sentiments were an echo of Augustine in particular and of that Christian tradition in general that sought to see nature in the context of belief in God.[7] But such views were not the monopoly of the theologians of the day. The empiricist philosophers and the men of science of the seventeenth century on the whole saw no essential conflict between science and religion. In a general sense empiricism could be traced back to Thomas Aquinas in the Middle Ages and Epicurus in the third and fourth centuries B.C., for both these philosophers stressed the importance of observation. But the forerunner of modern British empiricism was Francis Bacon (1561-1626), who stressed the importance of amassing data followed by judicious interpretation and experimentation, in order to learn the secrets of nature by the planned, organized observation of its regularities. Whereas the continental rationalists emphasized the importance of reason in man's knowledge of reality, the British empiricists stressed the role of experience. Rejecting the innate ideas of the rationalists, the empiricists stressed sense experience as the source of all knowledge. In this respect, British empiricism was not an autonomous movement, completely independent of continental rationalism. It was rather a response to rationalism and an attempt to correct it. Hobbes, Locke, and Hume spent considerable portions of their lives on the continent of Europe, and their writings bear clear marks of continental influence.

Science in the English-speaking world made hitherto unparalleled strides in the seventeenth century. This achievement has frequently been attributed to the ascendancy of Puritanism, but the facts of the matter hardly fit this hypothesis, which could be justified only if the word "Puritan" is stretched to include any Christian who was not a Roman Catholic or a Laudian High Churchman driven into exile or excluded from public life during the

Cromwellian era.[8] The greatest developments took place after the demise of the Puritan commonwealth with the Restoration of the monarchy under King Charles II and of the Church of England. It was Charles II who gave the charter in 1662 to the Royal Society of London for the Improvement of Natural Knowledge, and it was the Anglican Church with its deliberate balance of authority and reason and its encouragement to natural philosophy that gave spiritual blessing to the scientific enterprise. Many of the Royal Society's leading figures were also prominent ecclesiastical figures. John Wilkins, its first secretary, became Bishop of Chester. Thomas Sprat, the Society's official historian, was Bishop of Rochester. Joseph Glanvill was Dean of Bath Abbey. John Tillotson, the son-in-law of Wilkins, was elected to the Society in 1671 and became Archbishop of Canterbury in 1691. Among the lay scientists were Sir Isaac Newton, who joined the Society in 1672 and was its president from 1703 until his death in 1727, and Robert Boyle, "the father of chemistry and son of the Earl of Cork." Boyle wrote numerous treatises defending the harmony of scientific method and Christian faith. In his will he left £50 per annum for a series of eight lectures against unbelievers to be given in some London church—the "Boyle Lectures."

The work of these British seventeenth-century scientists has both a direct and an indirect bearing on the question of miracles. Indirectly, their thought is important in two ways. On the one hand, they saw the laws of science as the laws of God. This was a common theme in an era of natural theology, evidenced by such works as John Ray's *The Wisdom of God Manifested in the Works of Creation* (1691; ninth edition 1727) and John Wilkins's *Of the Principles and Duties of Natural Religion* (1693). Prestige was lent to Ray's work by his reputation as the father of natural history. Robert Boyle anticipated the argument, made famous a century later by William Paley, which compared the universe with a clock, the intricate working of which presupposed a clock-maker. William Derham, who wrote a treatise on clock-making, developed the argument in his Boyle Lectures of 1711-12 on *Physico-Theology, or Demonstration of the Being and Attributes of God from the Works of Creation* (1713). But the analogy of the clock invited criticism. Clocks, when once fully wound, proceed to operate without further assistance. The more the universe resembles a clock, the less it seems to need divine intervention to keep it going. Moreover, a fully mechanistic universe seems to leave no room for miracles.

The writings of the British scientists of this era bear on the subject of miracles in a second indirect way, in that they gave recognition to the importance of probability as distinct from absolute certainty. As spokesman for this outlook we may cite John Wilkins who argued, *"Things of several kinds may admit and require several sorts of Proofs, all of which may be good in their kind."*[9] "Infallible certainty" belongs to God alone, though an "Indubitable certainty" may be achieved on the basis of evidence, testimony, and experience. On many matters man has to settle for less than even this kind of certainty:

> *'Tis sufficient that matters of Faith and Religion be propounded in such a way, as to render them highly credible, so as an honest and teachable man may willingly and safely assent to them, and according to the Rules of Prudence be justified in so doing.* Nor is it *Necessary* or *Convenient,* that they should be established by such cogent Evidence, as to necessitate Assent. Because this would not leave any place for the Vertue of *Believing,* or the freedom of our obedience; nor any ground for Reward and Punishment. It would not be thank-worthy for a man to believe that which of necessity he must believe, and cannot otherwise chuse.[10]

This argument itself is testimony to the inadequacy of the clockwork mechanism as a comprehensive model for understanding the universe, for machines allow no room for autonomous action and independent judgment. Like Pascal before him and Tillotson after him, Wilkins recognized an element of risk and decision that necessitated making a wager with one's life.[11] The choice between the extremes of atheism and Christian faith involved a person's total world view. But the choice was not an irrational one, nor were the alternatives equally balanced. The Christian view of God gave coherence to man's experience of the world, which was impossible on any other view. For this reason the balance of probability favored the Christian explanation. This was the alternative to skepticism and dogmatism of Wilkins and his like-minded colleagues. In arguing for probability rather than absolute certainty, Wilkins anticipated the shape of the argument that was to be used by Bishop Butler on behalf of Christianity and by David Hume against it in the great debates of the eighteenth century.

The views of the seventeenth-century British men of science also had a direct bearing on the question of miracles. Among those who discussed them were Joseph Glanvill and Robert Boyle, whose views will be looked at more closely below. For the time being it must suffice to note that for them miracles were by no means an embarrassment, clung to by a tenacious faith in the face of all their scientific principles. The view that they were to take of miracles was very different from that of Spinoza. The issue, however, was not simply one of particular items of evidence. It was bound up with the way that they understood not only the nature of scientific laws in particular but of reality in general. The most decisive factor in all the debates about miracles was not the specific details of this or that particular case but the world view that determined how particular cases should be evaluated. Nowhere can this be seen more clearly than in Spinoza's critique of miracles in the name of the divine laws of nature.

SPINOZA'S CRITIQUE OF MIRACLES IN THE NAME OF THE DIVINE LAWS OF NATURE

The first major open attack on miracles came from the pen of Benedict de Spinoza (1632–1677). It contributed to his alienation not only from the Calvinists whose thought determined the orthodoxy of his day, but also from the Jewish synagogue from which he had been expelled in 1656. Spinoza's Jewish Portuguese parents had settled in Holland, which in the seventeenth century was not only a bastion of Calvinism but a place of refuge for Jews as well as others whose opinions were not tolerated in their native lands. Thomas Hobbes, in common with numerous others, found it prudent to have his writings published there. For a time John Locke found political asylum in Holland. Earlier in the century Descartes had found Holland a more congenial place to work than his native France, and it was there that he wrote his major works. During his lifetime Spinoza published only two works: the *Principles of the Philosophy of Renati Descartes* (1663) and the *Tractatus Theologico-Politicus* (1670). Whereas Descartes's rationalism had a theistic framework, Spinoza restated Cartesian rationalism in terms of a pantheism in which everything was embraced within a single, rational substance. Inevitably, this brought Spinoza into head-on conflict with both Jewish and Christian orthodoxy and the traditional, theistic view of miracles as divine interventions in the ordinary course of nature.

Spinoza's critique of miracles is contained in his *Tractatus Theologico-Politicus*. He begins with the following observation:

> As men are accustomed to call Divine the knowledge which transcends human understanding, so also do they style Divine, or the work of God, anything of which the cause is not generally known; for the masses think that the power and providence of God are most clearly displayed by events that are extraordinary and contrary to the conception they have formed of nature, especially if such events bring them any profit or convenience: they think that the clearest possible proof of God's existence is afforded when nature, as they suppose, breaks her accustomed order, and consequently they believe that those who explain or endeavour to understand phenomena or miracles through their natural cause are doing away with God and His providence. They suppose, forsooth, that God is inactive so long as nature works in her accustomed order, and vice versa, that the power of nature and natural causes are idle so long as God is acting.[12]

Spinoza saw the big mistake to lie in imagining "the power of God to be like that of some royal potentate, and nature's power to consist in force and energy."[13]

In making this point, Spinoza was criticizing popular belief (both Christian and Jewish) from the standpoint of his philosophy, which identified God with nature,[14] and which was greeted by his contemporaries as a form of atheism. For Spinoza there was a supreme, single ultimate reality that could be called God or nature (*deus sive natura*), depending on which way one looked at it. Spinoza's thought was profoundly influenced by Descartes, to whom he was indebted for his emphasis on clear and distinct ideas and style of reasoning modeled on geometry. But whereas Descartes maintained a theistic view of God existing over and above the world as the necessary ground of all things, Spinoza adopted the pantheistic view of a single supreme reality with many different facets. This pantheism may be traced back to the

Jewish cabala of the Middle Ages.[15] What, however, is more intriguing for our present concern is not only the way in which Spinoza turned to pantheism to undergird his philosophy of science, but also the way in which he used the language of Calvinistic orthodoxy to express his ideas.

The Synod of Dordrecht (1618-19) represents the high watermark of orthodox Calvinism. The Arminians had been routed, and the Canons of Dort had enshrined the doctrine that faith and election (and also reprobation) issue from the eternal decree of God who is perfect and immutable.[16] The Synod had done its work a full decade before Spinoza was born, but doubtless its language formed the very ethos of the Dutch environment in which Spinoza lived. Spinoza proceeded to apply this language to nature and, in so doing, he precluded the miraculous:

> Now, as nothing is necessarily true save only by Divine decree, it is plain that the universal laws of science are decrees of God following from the necessity and perfection of the Divine nature. Hence, any event happening in nature which contravened nature's universal laws, would necessarily also contravene the Divine decree, nature, and understanding; or if anyone asserted that God acts in contravention to the laws of nature, he, *ipso facto,* would be compelled to assert that God acted against His own nature—an evident absurdity.[17]

For the orthodox Calvinist, there was a divine necessity in God's decrees that eliminated chance happenings; for Spinoza, there was a divine necessity in the laws of nature that precluded the possibility of anything happening outside those laws.

Several important consequences followed from this. On the one hand, miracles are rendered impossible by definition, except in the sense that they are something that people wonder at. If there are grounds for believing that they really happened, the cause must have a natural explanation that has not yet been identified. On the other hand, Spinoza went on to conclude that "we cannot gain knowledge of the existence and providence of God by means of miracles, but . . . we can far better infer them from the fixed and immutable order of nature."[18] For miracles are either figments of the uneducated imagination or events that we cannot yet explain. In both cases the miracle tells us nothing about God, for Spinoza refused to recognize "any difference between an event against the laws of nature and an event beyond the laws of science."[19] Any contradiction of a law of nature would be "a mere absurdity."

Writing as a Jew, albeit a highly unorthodox one, in a country where the Calvinistic orthodoxy of the Synod of Dort was the official creed, Spinoza deemed it appropriate, though doubtless provocative, to adduce biblical support for his position.[20] A case in point was the prohibition in Deuteronomy 13 to follow miracle-workers who themselves followed false gods. Spinoza saw his own endeavors as a seventeenth-century counterpart to the Deuteronomic injunction not be to misled by miracles and certainly not to form one's ideas of God on the basis of them without more ado. He viewed the incident of the golden calf (Exod. 32) as a disastrous example of the mistaken ideas formed of God by the Israelites "as the result of all their miracles."[21] On the other hand, Spinoza saw in the Bible numerous instances of miracles that had a plausible natural explanation. The plagues in Egypt were the cumulative product of a series of natural disasters (Exod. 9–10), and the parting of the Red Sea was caused by "a strong east wind all night" (Exod. 14:21). Elisha revived the boy believed dead by some form of resuscitation (2 Kings 4:34f.). "Again, in John's Gospel (chap. ix) certain acts are mentioned as performed by Christ preparatory to healing the blind man, and there are numerous instances showing that something further than the absolute fiat of God is required for working a miracle."[22]

In the light of all this, Spinoza concluded that we can be "absolutely certain that every event which is truly described in Scripture necessarily happened, like everything else, according to natural laws."[23] Anything that contravenes natural law must have been "foisted into the sacred writings by irreligious hands." On this basis, Spinoza proposed what today would be called a new hermeneutic:

> Thus in order to interpret the Scriptural miracles and understand from the narration of them how they really happened, it is necessary to know the opinions of those who first related them, and have recorded them for us in writing, and to distinguish such opinions from the actual impression made upon their senses, otherwise we shall confound opinions and judgments with the actual miracle as it really occurred, nay, further, we shall confound actual events with symbolical and imaginary ones. For many things are narrated in Scripture as real, and were believed to be real, which were in fact only symbolical and imaginary.[24]

Thus, we need a prior understanding of what is possible and a familiarity with "Jewish phrases and metaphors."[25] "The conclusion, then, that is most plainly put before us is, that miracles were natural occurrences, and must therefore be so explained as to appear neither new (in the words of Solomon)[26] nor contrary to nature, but, as far as possible, in complete agreement with ordinary events. This can easily be done by anyone, now that I have set forth the rules drawn from Scripture."[27]

Spinoza's *Tractatus Theologico-Politicus* was published anonymously in 1670 with a fictitious ascription to a nonexistent Hamburg publisher. The general outrage that the work provoked served to confirm its author in his resolve to publish nothing further during his lifetime and to decline the chair of philosophy at Heidelberg, which was offered him in 1673. Spinoza's *Ethics*, which contained a more elaborate discussion of God and the world, first appeared in the *Opera Posthuma* of 1677, which were laconically ascribed to *B.D.S.* Within a century the reservations that Spinoza had voiced concerning the miraculous were still shocking, but they had become more commonplace. In the meantime, a defense of miracles was advanced by other thinkers, both

Catholic and Protestant, which restated the apologetic arguments of the Fathers in terms of philosophies designed to give a much better account of our knowledge of the world than that afforded by rationalism.

THE MUTED SKEPTICISM OF THOMAS HOBBES

Before we examine the appeals to miracles by scientists and philosophers in the seventeenth century, we may note the muted skepticism of the English thinker Thomas Hobbes (1588–1679). Hobbes was born in the Elizabethan Age in the year of the Spanish Armada. In fact, news of the Armada occasioned his premature birth. He grew up in the reign of King James I, and witnessed the rise and fall of King Charles I and Oliver Cromwell's Commonwealth. He lived on for nearly two more decades during the Restoration of the Stuart monarchy and the Anglican Church under Charles II, whom he had tutored for a time in France during the monarch's exile. The age in which Hobbes lived was one of great political upheaval, and it is as a political theorist that Hobbes is best remembered on account of his *Leviathan, or the Matter, Form and Power of a Commonwealth, Ecclesiastical and Civil* (1651). It was published two years after the execution of Charles I, and argued strongly for the absolute sovereignty of the state and the need for conformity in religion. This is a fact that has bearing on his discussion of miracles.

The work derived its title from the Leviathan of the Old Testament (Job 3:8; 41:1; Pss. 74:14; 104:26; Isa. 27:1), which Hobbes proceeded to apply to the state, "which is but an artificial man, though of greater stature and strength than the natural, for whose protection and defense it was intended."[28] In the course of his argument Hobbes set out a rational theory of natural law as the basis of the laws of society, a representative theory of government and the absolute authority of the state that replaced theories of divine right, and an exposition of rational ethics. All this was set in the context of a reappraisal of man, the state, the church, and "the kingdom of darkness." At the climax of the latter comes a discussion of philosophy, reminiscent of rationalism, in which geometry is seen as a model for reasoning, conducive to the discovery of "general, eternal, and immutable truth."[29] Hobbes excludes from philosophy all appeals to *experience*, for the latter has no part in "original knowledge," as it consists in nothing more than prudence. Likewise he excludes from philosophy all knowledge acquired by "supernatural revelation," for such knowledge is not acquired by reasoning.

Hobbes is sometimes depicted as a pioneer of empiricism, but his philosophy was in many ways a transplant of continental thought to British soil. His most productive thinking was done in France during times of travel and exile. But the mitigated skepticism of Mersenne and Gassendi, rather than the dogmatism of Descartes, influenced Hobbes most. Hobbes's early objections to Descartes's *Meditations,* which Mersenne had shown to the great rationalist prior to publication, led to an acrimonious exchange between Descartes and Hobbes. In later years in England Hobbes found himself at variance with the *virtuosi* of the Royal Society on account of his contempt for their inductive methods. In both France and England Hobbes was suspected of atheism; in France because of his criticism of the Catholic Church and in England because his secularism was seen as a cause of the divine wrath that had brought about the Great Plague in 1665 and the Great Fire of London in the following year.[30]

Hobbes's discussion of miracles in chapter 37 of *Leviathan* anticipates both sides of the later debate. Like Hobbes's thinking in general, it gives the appearance of being a halfway house on the road to secularism. At no point does Hobbes question the biblical narratives, which are all taken at face value, whether the subject happens to be the giving of the rainbow after the Flood as divine assurance that such universal destruction will not be repeated, the actions of Moses at Pharaoh's court, or the miracles of Jesus. Hobbes could express wonder at the miracles of creation that occur every day, but these were not to be regarded as miracles in the true sense of the term. For "when we see some possible natural cause of it, how rarely soever the like has been done; or if the like has ever been done, how impossible soever it be to imagine a natural means thereof, we no more wonder, nor esteem it for a miracle."[31] This led Hobbes to define a miracle and its purpose in the following terms:

> A miracle is a work of God (besides His operation by the way of nature, ordained in the Creation) done for the making manifest to His elect the mission of an extraordinary minister for their salvation.

> And from this definition, we may infer: first, that in all miracles the work done is not the effect of any virtue of the prophet, because it is the effect of the immediate hand of God; that is to say, God hath done it, without using the prophet therein as a subordinate cause.

> Secondly, that no devil, angel, or created spirit can do a miracle. For it must either be by virtue of some natural science or by incantation, that is, virtue of words.[32]

It is at this point that Calvinism and rationalism converge. From Calvinism Hobbes derives his theology of the elect and the view that the purpose of miracles is to provide divine attestation. In common with Calvin in particular and orthodoxy in general, Hobbes dismisses as spurious all other alleged miracles. But it is from rationalism that Hobbes derives his method of reasoning. This appears not only in the importance he attaches to definitions that provide clear and distinct ideas and the inferences he draws from them that express rational connections. Hobbes's procedure is the expression of the rationalist conviction about the rational substructure of reality. Whatever is to be found in man's experience of nature and history is but the formal, empirical expression of rational truths. Hence, Hobbes can argue that it is "ignorance and aptitude to error" over "natural causes" that lead people to suppose a supernatural origin for all manner of natural events. Invoking the warnings of Deuteronomy 13 and 18, Hobbes urges that each pretended miracle be tested by every possible means to determine "whether it be such as no man can do the like by his natural power, but that it require the immediate hand of God."[33]

The sting of Hobbes's discussion lay, however, in its tail. The final paragraph contained a reflection of a kind generally associated with David Hume, but which anticipated Hume by almost a century:

> For in these times I do not know one man that ever saw any such won-drous work, done by the charm or at the word or prayer of a man, that a man endued with but a mediocrity of reason would think supernatural: and the question is no more whether what we see done be a miracle; whether the miracle we hear, or read of, were a real work, and not the act of a tongue or pen; but in plain terms, whether the report be true, or a lie.[34]

In arguing along these lines Hobbes was using his present understanding of the world in order to determine the truth or falsehood of reports of events to which he had no direct access. In other words, he was using the principle that came to be known as the principle of analogy. But this was not quite Hobbes's last word. For, in line with his views generally on the totalitarian authority of the state and such institutions that exist to maintain law, order, and the public good, Hobbes proceeded to draw a distinction between private liberty of opinion and public conformity:

> A private man has always the liberty, because thought is free, to believe or not believe in his heart those acts that have been given out for miracles, according as he shall see what benefit can accrue, by men's belief, to those that pretend or countenance them, and thereby conjecture whether they be miracles or lies. But when it comes to confession of that faith, the private reason must submit to the public; that is to say, to God's lieutenant.[35]

Although Hobbes had not denied the biblical miracles outright, he had set a question mark against his own acceptance of them and asserted the right of others to question them privately until such a time when the state itself might sanction public doubt.

PASCAL AND MIRACLES—ANCIENT AND MODERN

Blaise Pascal (1623–1662) is one of those enigmas of history whose scientific genius and austere religion never cease to fascinate. Before he was twenty he had designed a calculating machine to help his father who had been made Commissioner for Taxes in Upper Normandy. His subsequent writings on the calculating machine made a major contribution to the subject, which in turn hastened the advance of the industrial revolution. Pascal also made major contributions to geometry, probability and number theory, and the philosophy of mathematics. In the realm of physics his experiments with barometric pressure demonstrated the existence of the vacuum, and successfully challenged the idea that nature always abhors a vacuum. His work is regarded as a major step in the elimination of the occult from nature and in the establishment of a mechanistic view of the physical world.

But overlapping all this was Pascal's religion. In 1646 Pascal's father had an accident and was cared for by two followers of Cornelis Jansen, the Bishop of Ypres, and the Abbé de Saint-Cyran, spiritual director of the Jansenist Port-Royal movement. This marked the beginning of the Pascal family's involvement with Jansenism, a form of Augustinianism, which was bitterly opposed by the Jesuits and was condemned by the Sorbonne in 1649 and by Pope Innocent X in 1653. Following their father's death, Pascal's sister Jacqueline became a nun at Port-Royal in 1651. Pascal himself was opposed to the move, and for a time led a worldly life. However, on the night of November 23,1654, Pascal had a conversion experience that he described on a piece of parchment that was sewn into his clothing as a perpetual reminder and was discovered after his death. It contained the following reference to his new-found faith:

FIRE

"God of Abraham, God of Isaac, God of Jacob," not of philosophers and scholars.
Certainty, certainty, heartfelt, joy, peace.
God of Jesus Christ.
God of Jesus Christ.
My God and your God.
"Thy God shall be my God."
The world forgotten, and everything except God.
He can only be found by the ways taught in the Gospels. . . .
Let me be not cut off from him for ever! . . .[36]

Pascal was increasingly drawn into the Port-Royal circle. His *Provincial Letters* (1656-57) were a defense of Jansenism, attacking current Jesuit theories of grace and moral theology. In 1656 Pascal began collecting material for what he intended to be an *Apology for the Christian Religion,* putting down his thoughts on scraps of paper. His premature death at the age of thirty-nine prevented the work from becoming anything more than a series of disconnected thoughts. Nevertheless, these thoughts, subsequently published as Pascal's *Pensées,* have an enduring place as a classic of Christian meditation and apologetics.[37]

Pascal's approach to religion in general and to miracles in particular is significant, not least because it reflects the thought of a major figure in the history of science and a pioneer in probability theory. It has as its background the skepticism of the Pyrrhonists and the dogmatism of the rationalists, both of which Pascal rejected as inadequate. Neither the Pyrrhonists nor the rationalists could offer self-sustaining philosophies that did justice to the world that man lives in and to human nature. Nature confounds the Pyrrhonists and reason the dogmatic rationalists. Consistent skepticism is impossible. Reason needs a foundation outside itself. One cannot prove beyond doubt that one is awake, for when one dreams, one dreams that one is awake."There is no certainty, apart from faith, as to whether man was created by a good God, an evil demon, or just by chance, and so it is a matter of doubt, depending on our origin, whether these innate principles are true, false or uncertain."[38] The ultimate mystery of God's existence and the creation of the universe lies beyond the scope of reason. Belief in God as the Creator gives a coherence to the believer's world that is denied to the skeptic and the rationalist. Nevertheless, there is an element of risk that demands of the believer that he should wager his life on the truth of his beliefs. Reason exposes man's plight. Desire for truth and happiness makes man see the futility of science, mathematics, and philosophy as ways of meeting these needs. The basis of the Christian belief-system—like the foundations of mathematics and man's fundamental intuitions about time and space—is known not by reason but by the heart.[39]

Pascal had little use for the God of the philosophers. This is vividly illustrated in a saying not included in the *Pensées* but attributed to Pascal: "I cannot forgive Descartes: in his whole philosophy he would like to do without God; but he could not help allowing him a flick of the fingers to set the world in motion; after that he had no more use for God."[40] Pascal's own view of God was not simply that of a being whose existence is the necessary condition of everything that is. Pascal's God is a God who is known personally through Jesus Christ.

> We know God only through Jesus Christ. Without this mediator all communication with God is broken off. Through Jesus we know God. All those who claim to know God and prove his existence without Jesus Christ have only futile proofs to offer. But to prove Christ we have the prophecies which are solid and palpable proofs. By being fulfilled and proved true by the event, these prophecies show that these truths are certain and thus prove that Jesus is divine.[41]

Pascal's argument at this point recalls that of the early Fathers who maintained that the fulfillment of prophecy offered irrefragable proof of divine activity and authorization. Alongside fulfilled prophecy Pascal also placed miracles. Nevertheless, such demonstrations fell short of carrying absolute conviction. On occasion Pascal could remark that "Miracles do not serve but to condemn."[42] He was aware of false prophets and idolatrous workers of wonders. Moses had given rules to test both: false prophecy does not come to pass (Deut. 18) and false miracles lead to idolatry (Deut. 13). By itself, this leads to the following dilemma: "If doctrine determines miracles, miracles are useless for doctrine."[43] In one sense miracles were redundant: "It is so obvious that we must love one God alone that there is no need of miracles to prove it."[44] But in another sense miracles were important. They did not prove the existence of God, nor establish the framework of theistic belief. They functioned within that framework as revelations of the true God, thus serving to identify Jesus.

Jesus proved he was the Messiah, but never by proving his doctrine from Scripture or the prophecies, but always by miracles.

He proved by a miracle that he could forgive sins.

"Rejoice not in your miracles," said Jesus, "but because your names are written in heaven."

"If they hear not Moses, neither will they be persuaded though one rose from the dead."

Nicodemus recognized by his miracles that his doctrine was from God. *"Rabbi, we know that thou art a teacher come from God, for no man can do these miracles that thou doest except God be with him."* He does not judge miracles by doctrine, but doctrine by miracles . . . .

Therefore all faith rests on miracles.[45]

If prophecy and miracles were not proofs that could be said to be "absolutely convincing," they present evidence that is at least as strong as that of their opponents. "Thus, there is enough evidence to condemn and not enough to convince, so that it should be apparent that those who follow it are prompted to do so by grace and not by reason, and those who evade it are prompted by concupiscence and not by reason."[46]

To the present-day critic it might appear at this point as if Pascal had a split mind. With the scientific side of his mind he was leading seventeenth-century France into the modern age. With the religious side of his mind he seems to read the Bible uncritically, accepting the miracle stories as literally true just because they happen to be in the Bible and be part of the church's faith. Whereas his contemporary Spinoza eagerly sought alternative explanations, Pascal seems to take the miracle stories at their face value. What has to be borne in mind in all this is that Pascal had a double focus that was unified by his theistic Christian belief in God as a God of action and truth. Pascal did not subscribe to the view that the age of miracles is past, and therefore the miracle stories of the Gospels are utterly unlike anything in our ongoing experience. It was because Pascal believed in miracles in his own day that the miracle stories of the Gospels had an added realism.

In point of fact, there was a direct link between a case of healing and the composition of the *Pensées*. Pascal's niece, Marguerite Perrier, had long suffered from a serious, disfiguring lachrymal fistula in the corner of one eye. On March 24, 1656, she was healed through being touched by a Holy Thorn that had recently been presented to the Sisters of Port-Royal. This healing was followed by others, and in time the number of cases reached eighty. The healing of Mlle. Perrier was supported by substantial medical evidence and was authenticated by diocesan authorities. The Jansenists saw it as a sign of divine attestation, as did the Queen Mother who is said to have induced Cardinal Mazarin to withhold persecution of the Jansenists. Mlle. Perrier lived to the age of eighty-seven and identified herself with the cause of the Saint-Médard miracles at the tomb of the deacon, François de

Pâris.[47] The Port-Royal healings did not prevent the suppression of Jansenism, but they did cause Pascal to start collecting material for his *Apology*. He argued that, "When there are parties in dispute within the same Church, miracles are decisive."[48] Since God had never attested the teaching of heretics by miracles, the Jansenist healings were the seal of divine sanction of their cause.

GLANVILL, BOYLE, AND SEVENTEENTH-CENTURY BRITISH SCIENCE

The year 1662 saw both the death in Paris of Pascal and the founding in London of the Royal Society. For some years members of the Society had been meeting informally, but now royal patronage was given to the "improvement of natural knowledge." Among the topics deemed worthy of such improved knowledge by Joseph Glanvill (1636–1680), Dean of Bath Abbey and first secretary of the Royal Society, was witchcraft—a subject that excited the minds of the learned and the unlearned.[49] Its eradication was a goal of both Nonconformist Puritans and Anglicans. Witchcraft trials continued in England until 1712. There were those who, like John Webster, believed that witches were evil-minded persons influenced by the Devil, who wrought their evil deeds by poisons and other natural means. Glanvill, however, contended that disbelief in witchcraft was but a step away from atheism. His major work on the subject, *Sadducismus-Triumphatus* (1681; 2nd ed. 1689),[50] adopted a moderate empiricist approach in line with the scientific outlook shared by his fellow members of the Royal Society.

Glanvill conceded that the possession of supernatural powers seemed improbable, but argued that "many great truths are strange and odd, till custom and acquaintance have reconciled them to our fancies."[51] A scientific skepticism is in order, but it must be applied not only to testimony to the unusual but also to preconceived ideas concerning what is possible and what is impossible. The existence of some cheats and imposters is no guarantee that all are cheats and imposters. "Frequency of deceit and fallacy will warrant a greater care and caution in examining, and scrupulosity and shyness of assent to things wherein fraud hath been practised, or may in the least degree be suspected."[52]

In developing this line of thought Glanvill was charting a course that was followed by the moderate British empiricists of the seventeenth and eighteenth centuries. It differed from the rationalism of Spinoza who was concerned with the discovery of rational laws underlying phenomena and with seeing all phenomena in terms of a rational system. It differed from Pyrrhonic skepticism in its recognition of realities beyond the scope of reason, when empirical evidence warranted it. On this basis Glanvill conceded the reality of malignant, supernatural powers. But this raised the question of how such powers might be distinguished from those of Christ. Indeed, how could one know that the demons exorcised by Jesus were not cast out by Beelzebul (as the Jewish authorities contended in Mark 3)? Glanvill's reply was a seventeenth-century version of the kind of response that Origen, Calvin, and others had made in previous centuries.

> 'Tis not the doing wonderful things that is the only evidence that the holy Jesus was from God, and his doctrine true; but the conjunction of other circumstances, the holiness of his life, the reasonableness of his religion, and the excellency of his designs, added credit to his works, and strengthened the great conclusion, that he could be no other than the Son of God, and Saviour of the World.[53]

In other words, Glanvill was using what R. M. Burns has termed the "principle of context."[54] It involves making a *gestalt judgment* about the pattern of events in terms of one's general perception of reality and of values. In attempting to define criteria for recognizing a divine miracle, Glanvill observed that mere strangeness or unaccountableness did not qualify an event as miraculous, for nature presented many such phenomena. True miracles were distinguished from natural events by transcending "all the powers of mere nature," and from paranormal events wrought by supernatural agents by their character and context:

> They have peculiar circumstances that speak them of a divine original. Their mediate authors declare them to be so, and they are always persons of simplicity, truth and holiness, void of ambition, and all secular designs. They seldom use ceremonies, or natural applications, and yet surmount all the activities of known Nature. They work those wonders, not to raise admiration, or out of the vanity to be talked of ; but to seal and confirm some Divine doctrine, or commission, in which the good and happiness of the world is concerned. I say by circumstances such as these, wonderful actions are known to be from a Divine cause; and that makes, and distinguishes a miracle.[55]

A similar view was advanced by Sir Robert Boyle (1627–1691), who warmly supported Glanvill in his campaign against witchcraft. Boyle, who was a far greater scientist than Glanvill, gave recognition to the importance of both empirical data and doctrine:

> But I think that the use we ought to make of a doctrine in judging of a miracle is not to deny the historical part, if it be substantially attested, but to distinguish whether it be likely to come rather from some evil spirit than from God. . . . Yet I presume not to judge which of these two the miracle is by the articles of any particular instituted religion . . . but for this examination take only the general principles of natural reason and religion, which teaching me antecedently to all particular revelations, that there is a God, that he is, and can be but one; . . . just, wise, good, gracious. . . . If a supernatural effect be wrought to authorize a doctrine yet plainly contradicts these truths, I cannot judge a miracle to be divine. . . . But if the revelation backed by a miracle proposes nothing that contradicts these truths, . . . and much more if it proposes a religion that illustrates and confirms them; I then think myself obliged to admit both the miracle, and the religion it attests.[56]

If there is any substantial difference between Boyle and Glanvill it lies in the fact that Boyle desired to take the widest possible context for judging any alleged miracle. In a sense, this was what Spinoza had done before him and the deists claimed to do after him. But Boyle was an orthodox churchman. Throughout his life he fervently supported the dissemination of Scripture. The above statement was an expression of the empirical approach that Boyle practiced in his chemistry and carried over into religion. For Boyle, as for John Locke, there was no essential conflict between natural and revealed religion.

JOHN LOCKE AND THE APPEAL TO MIRACLES AS PROOF OF DIVINE ATTESTATION

John Locke (1632–1704) was born in the same year as Spinoza. It is not without irony that Locke deemed it prudent in later life to seek political refuge in Holland. For, like Spinoza, Locke was concerned with politics and liberty. But this was some years after Spinoza's death and long after Locke had formulated the foundations of the empirical approach to knowledge. Locke had read philosophy at Oxford, where he developed a distaste for the diet of scholasticism that was currently taught there. When he entered Oxford, Puritanism had already reached its political zenith. But it was not the theological questions of Puritanism that captured his interest, but the problem of knowledge, particularly in the light of the philosophy of Descartes and the methods of modern science with their stress on observation and experiment. In later life Locke obtained a degree in medicine, but he did not pursue a medical career. Locke was a committed Christian who was concerned to integrate religious knowledge with scientific knowledge. It was this combination of interests that led him to write *An Essay Concerning Human Understanding* (1690).

Whereas Descartes and Spinoza had based their philosophies on the ability of reason to discover truth, Locke denied the autonomy of reason. He saw the mind as a blank sheet of paper that receives impressions via the senses.[57] All our knowledge of external reality must come this way. Reason has the job of interpreting the data of our senses. For Spinoza, reason had an autonomous authority; it was also the final court of appeal. For Locke, there were areas of reality that were beyond reason. Therefore, he distinguished between statements that were according to reason, statements that were above reason, and statements that were contrary to reason:

> (1) *According to reason* are such propositions whose truth we can discover by examining and tracing those ideas we have from sensation and reflection, and by natural deduction find to be true or probable. (2) *Above reason* are such propositions whose truth or probability we cannot by reason derive from those principles. (3) *Contrary to reason* are such propositions as are inconsistent with or irreconcilable to our clear and distinct ideas. Thus the existence of God is according to reason; the ex-

istence of more than one God is contrary to reason; the resurrection of the dead above reason.[58]

For Spinoza, this second category of statements *above reason* would have been absurd, but for Locke, it was warranted provided that there were good empirical grounds for making such an assertion. Moreover, it was this way of thinking that furnished Locke with a basis for revealed theology and apologetics:

> *Reason* therefore here, as contradistinguished to faith, I take to be the discovery of the certainty or probability of such propositions or truths, which the mind arrives at by deductions made from such ideas which it has got by the use of its natural faculties, viz., by sensation or reflection.
>
> *Faith*, on the other side, is the assent to any proposition, not thus made out by the deductions of reason, but upon the credit of the proposer, as coming from God in some extraordinary way of communication. This way of discovering truths to men we call *revelation*.[59]

Locke's development of these themes was reserved for two shorter works that he wrote toward the end of his life: *The Reasonableness of Christianity* (1695) and *A Discourse of Miracles* (1702), published posthumously in 1704.[60]

Already in his *Essay Concerning Human Understanding* Locke had formulated his view of the relationship between reason and revelation:

> *Reason* is natural revelation, whereby the eternal Father of light, and Fountain of all knowledge, communicates to mankind that portion of truth which he has laid within the reach of their natural faculties. *Revelation* is natural *reason* enlarged by a new set of discoveries communicated by God immediately, which reason vouches the truth of, by the testimony and proofs it gives that they come from God.[61]

Hence, to do away with reason would be like persuading "a man to put out his eyes, the better to receive the remote light of an invisible star by a telescope." Thus, any claim to revelation must not be contrary to reason.[62] It must be expressed in terms of rational, conceptual thought.[63] Rational understanding of it is a prerequisite of the assent of faith.[64] It must also be accompanied by outward signs that establish its credibility as a supernatural revelation.[65] For Locke, as for the early Fathers, these consisted of the fulfillment of prophecy[66] and miracles.

In his *Discourse of Miracles* Locke defined a miracle as follows:

> A miracle, then, I take to be a sensible operation, which, being above the comprehension of the spectator, and in his opinion contrary to the established course of nature, is taken by him to be divine.[67]

Locke recognized an element of inference in this definition. Clearly, the spectator does not see God act directly as the cause of the miracle. What he observes is one state of affairs before the miracle and another afterward. He observes the effects, and infers a divine cause behind the event that runs counter to the expected course of nature. As in any empirical observation, there is always the possibility of making a mistake, either in what we think we saw or in the interpretation we place upon it. Thus, even if we made no mistake in what we saw, we could mistakenly view an event as a miracle through sheer ignorance of "the force of nature." Locke anticipated this objection not by trying to minimize the possibilities of making such a mistake, but by redefining his concept of a miracle:

> To know that any revelation is from God, it is necessary to know that the messenger that delivers it is sent from God, and that cannot be known but by some credential given him by God himself. Let us see then whether miracles, in my sense, be not such credentials, and will not infallibly direct us right in the search of divine revelation.[68]

The ensuing argument might at first sight seem to evade the issue. For Locke went on to discuss miracle stories in pagan antiquity, pointing out that they were never used to establish the exclusive truth-claims of one particular deity over another. In a polytheistic culture such truth-claims were not a burning issue. Hence, pagan wonders lack the character of a sign or "credential" that the biblical miracles have. Furthermore, no miracles were attributed to Mohammed, and therefore the question of miracles in connection with the truth-claims of Islam does not arise.

However, to appreciate Locke's argument, it must be remembered that he did not use miracles to establish belief in God. His view of miracles is in line with what we have noted about his view of revelation—it does not contradict what is already known and accepted by reason. Rather, it enlarges our understanding and enables us to perceive new truth. Miracles, therefore, function within the wider context of what is already known and believed about God. Their character confirms that the one who performs them does not deviate from the known character of God. The God who is attested by the miracle is the same as the one who is known on other grounds. Thus, miracles function for Locke not simply as impressive wonders that defy explanation but as attestations from God confirming the revelation associated with the miracle. This is the thrust of Nicodemus's remark to Jesus: "Rabbi, we know that you are a teacher come from God; for no one can do these signs that you do, unless God is with him" (John 3:2).[69] Or, as Locke puts it,

> If we will direct our thoughts by what has been, we must conclude that miracles, as the credentials of a messenger delivering a divine religion, have no place but upon a supposition of one only true God. . . .
>
> For example, Jesus of Nazareth professes himself sent from God: He with a word calms a tempest at sea. This one looks on as a miracle, and consequently cannot but receive his doctrine. Another thinks this might be the effect of chance, or skill in the weather and no miracle, and so stands out; but afterwards seeing him walk on the sea, owns that for a miracle and believes; which yet upon another has not that force, who suspects it may possibly be done by the assistance of a spirit. But yet the same person, seeing afterwards Our Saviour cure inveterate palsy

by a word, admits that for a miracle, and becomes a convert. Another, overlooking it in this instance, afterwards finds a miracle in his giving sight to one born blind, or in raising the dead, or his raising himself from the dead, and so receives his doctrine as a revelation coming from God. By all which it is plain, that where the miracle is admitted, the doctrine cannot be rejected; it comes with the assurance of a divine attestation to him that allows the miracle, and he cannot question its truth.[70]

From this it is clear that single instances of miracles do not necessarily have compelling power. On its own, a miracle might be open to an alternative explanation or be sufficiently ambiguous as to warrant suspending judgment. However, the miracles of Jesus have a cumulative force that make it significantly harder to explain them away or to suspend judgment, than if they occurred separately as isolated events associated with different people at different points in history.

For Locke, the argument was an application of the empirical method of observation to the question of miracles. Nor was it irrelevant to observe, as the Fathers had done, that the miracles attributed to the servants of God in Scripture were greater than those of their opponents. "So likewise the number, variety and greatness of the miracles wrought for the confirmation of the doctrine delivered by Jesus Christ, carry with them such strong marks of an extraordinary divine power, that the truth of his mission will stand firm and unquestionable, till any one rising up in opposition to him shall do greater miracles than he and his apostles did."[71] Locke summed up his position by making the following three qualifications:

1. That no mission can be looked on to be divine, that delivers any thing derogating from the honour of the one, only true, invisible God, or inconsistent with natural religion and the rules of morality: because God having discovered to men the unity and majesty of his eternal Godhead, and the truths of natural religion and morality by the light of reason, he cannot be supposed to back the contrary by revelation; for that would be to destroy the evidence and the use of reason, without which men cannot be able to distinguish divine revelation from diabolical imposture.

2. That it cannot be expected that God should send any one into the world on purpose to inform men of things indifferent, and of small moment, or that are knowable by the use of their natural faculties. This would be to lessen the dignity of his majesty in favour of our sloth, and in prejudice to our reason.

3. The only case, then, wherein a mission of any one from heaven can be reconciled to the high and awful thoughts men ought to have of the deity, must be the revelation of some supernatural truths relating to the glory of God, and some great concern of men. Supernatural operations attesting such a revelation may, with reason, be taken to be miracles, as carrying the marks of a superior and over-ruling power, as long as no revelation accompanied with marks of a greater power appears against it.[72]

In several respects Locke's position was similar to that of Calvin. Like Calvin, he believed that miracles ceased with the apostolic age.[73] Like Calvin, he took Scripture at its face value as history. Like Calvin, he saw miracles as signs and insisted on seeing them in the context of the known character of God. But Locke differed from Calvin in two important respects. He gave miracles a more pronounced apologetic role, stressing their place in epistemology in the context of an empirical approach to knowledge. Moreover, he stressed the role of reason, in a way that Calvin did not consciously do, in determining truth in matters of religion. Admittedly, many essential truths of Christianity were *above reason*, but they nevertheless had a foundation that was *according to reason*. A group of thinkers who were unwilling to concede this point and who refused to take the Bible at its face value were the English deists, and it is they who provide the starting point for our next chapter.

3

THE AGE OF DEISM

In his celebrated *Dictionary of the English Language* (1755), Dr. Samuel Johnson defined "deist" as "a man who follows no particular religion, but only acknowledges the existence of God, without any other article of faith." The word seems to have been first used by Calvin's disciple, Pierre Viret, to describe an unidentified group of thinkers who professed belief in God, but rejected Christ and his teaching.[1] In Viret's sense, the deists were opposed to atheism, but by Dr. Johnson's day the word "deist" had been used in both England and France as a euphemism for "atheist." By that time deism in England was already on the decline. It had never been an organized school of thought. Its leaders were freethinking, idiosyncratic individuals who shared a common distaste for institutional religion and a belief in reason and humanity. As they died off, their religion died with them. But their ideas were transplanted in France, Germany, and America, and lived on in the form of critical attacks on the trustworthiness of the Bible and in altruistic moralism, vaguely tinged with religion.

The initial concern of this chapter is with the deists' attack on the New Testament miracles and the replies of their opponents. We shall also consider the thought of Conyers Middleton, Sir Isaac Newton, and Edward Gibbon who, though not deists themselves, lent support to a view of nature and history that pushed divine activity to the periphery of creation. It is not without irony that when the deist controversy was at its height, a number of healing miracles were claimed and attested in Paris. The miracles in the cemetery at Saint-Médard were to figure in various writings, not least those of Conyers Middleton and David Hume. We shall take note of them in the course of the discussion.

THE BRITISH DEISTS

Together with Spinoza on the Continent, the English deists may be regarded as the forerunners of biblical criticism. Today deism is thought of as a kind of absentee landlord theology: God made everything in the beginning, but ever since then he has left the world to its own devices. However, the classical deism of the seventeenth and eighteenth centuries was not the benign, rarified philosophy that such an outlook might suggest. There were two sides to English deism that are not to be separated. One was characterized by its profession of rational religion and commitment to free speech. The other was marked by bitter hostility to the church and the Bible. Deism was born in an age when Puritanism reached its zenith and religious conformity was demanded not only by the dictates of orthodoxy but also by the statutes of the law. Forms of orthodoxy changed as Cromwell's Commonwealth replaced Laudian High Churchmanship, and was itself replaced by the Restoration Settlement. But the demands for conformity continued unabated.

Most historians follow Thomas Halyburton in crediting Lord Edward Herbert of Cherbury (1583–1648) with being "the father of English deism."[2] As we noted in the previous chapter, Lord Herbert's treatise *On Truth* (1624) was in part a reply to French Pyrrhonian skepticism and in part an alternative to both Protestant and Catholic orthodoxy. In its first edition Lord Herbert contented himself with analyzing varieties of truth and the faculties of the mind. Like the rationalists, he believed in innate ideas that give meaning to experience. It was in the second edition of 1645 that Lord Herbert went on to deal with the foundations of religion and to critique the idea of revelation. He further elaborated his views in *De Causis Errorum* (E.T. *Concerning the Causes of Errors,* London, 1645) and *De Religione Gentilium* (Amsterdam, 1663; E.T. *The Ancient Religion of the Gentiles,* London, 1705). Lord Herbert maintained that there are five great religious truths: (1) that there is one supreme God; (2) that he ought to be worshiped; (3) that virtue and piety are the most important parts of worship; (4) that men should regret their sins and repent of them; and (5) that God bestows rewards and punishments in this life and the afterlife. On the basis of these allegedly self-evident truths, Lord Herbert proceeded to chastise the church and its priests. He praised the Ten Commandments but was critical of bibliolatry—a patent allusion to the Puritanism of his day. While acknowledging Christianity to be the best of all revelations because it came closest to the five religious truths, he urged priests to abandon mysteries, prophecies, and miracles, which were used to support unworthy beliefs.

In some respects deism was a counterreaction to Puritanism with its strong emphasis on the Bible, Christ, revelation, and strict religious observance. The age of deism was also the age of the pragmatic rationalism of Hobbes, the idealism of James Harrington, the Christian rationalism of the Cambridge Platonists and Anglican Latitudinarians, the science of Sir Isaac Newton, and the desire for "sweet reasonableness" on the part of men like John Locke. But it was also an age when the blasphemy laws were enforced. Where possible, they were invoked against deists for their attack on Christianity as the official religion of the state. The legal threat to free speech had an indirect effect on deistic writers in causing some of them to write in veiled, ironical, and cryptic ways, sometimes resorting to pseudonymity, anonymity, and dialogue or letter forms. Sometimes authors wrote as if they were attacking the Roman Catholic Church, although England had been continuously a Protestant country since the days of Elizabeth I. Formally they were criticizing Catholicism; implicitly they were attacking Protestantism. All this had the immediate effect of providing some shield for their authors from the severity of the law. It had the long-term effect of making it difficult to ascertain the true opinions of some of the writers.

The most zealous early propagator of deism was the disciple of Lord Herbert and follower of Thomas Hobbes, Charles Blount (1654–1693). Blount's *Anima Mundi* (1679) was a critique of the idea of immortality based on collected sayings from pagan writers. In 1680 Blount published a collection of sayings from Thomas Hobbes criticizing religion. He published two further works in 1680—*Great is Diana of the Ephesians,* an attack on priestcraft, and *The First Two Books of Philostratus Concerning the Life of Apollonius Tyaneus, written originally in Greek with philological notes on each chapter.* The significance of the work lay in the fact that Apollonius, who died about A.D. 98, was a reputed miracle-worker whose activities might seem to diminish the uniqueness of Jesus.[3] Blount drew the implication that the miraculous element in reported history was like a fungus growing around the memory of all religious leaders. The work was followed three years later by a tract ascribed to Blount, *Miracles No Violations of the Laws of Nature,* which was actually a paraphrase of chapter VI of Spinoza's *Tractatus Theologico-Politicus.* Spinoza's work had been published in Latin in 1670, but an English translation did not appear until 1689. Belief in miracles was the result of failing to understand natural phenomena on the one hand or of metaphorical and exaggerated language on the other. Among Blount's other writings was *The Oracles of Reason* (1693), which was published posthumously after the author's suicide.

A major landmark in the history of deism was John Toland's *Christianity not Mysterious: Or, a Treatise Shewing, That there is nothing in the Gospel contrary to Reason, nor above it: And that no Christian Doctrine can be properly call'd a Mystery* (1696). This slim volume was first published anonymously when the author was only twenty-five years old. It drew on the Common Notions of Lord Herbert and the empirical, reasonable approach of John Locke. But in substance it was more akin to continental rationalism. Whereas Locke had argued for Christianity as being both in accordance with reason and yet above reason, Toland relentlessly sought to eliminate everything beyond the scope of reason. The so-called mysteries of Christianity were ascribed to the intrusion of pagan ideas and priestcraft. In the ensuing uproar caused by the book Locke repudiated all claims to his approval that Toland had made. Toland's subsequent writings touched on the canon of Scripture, the Gospel of the Nazarenes, and pantheism.

The most urbane and readable of the deists was the gentleman, magistrate, and friend of Locke, Anthony Collins (1676–1729). In *An Essay Concerning the Use of Reason* (1707) Collins attacked Locke's distinction between things that are above reason and things that are contrary to reason. Together with his *Priestcraft in Perfection* (1709) the essay prepared the way for his *Discourse of Free-Thinking Occasion'd by the Rise and Growth of a Sect Call'd Free-Thinkers* (1713), which argued that free inquiry was the only means of attaining truth and that it was commanded by Scripture. Further writings dealt with free will and liberty. Collins turned to biblical criticism in *A Discourse of the Grounds and Reasons of the Christian Religion* (1724), where he denied that the Old Testament contained prophecies of Christ. By implication this meant a rejection of one of the main arguments used by apologists through the ages to demonstrate objectively the veracity of Christian claims to divine authentication by showing that Jesus had actually fulfilled prophecies about him made centuries before his birth. The argument was further elaborated in *The Scheme of Literal Prophecy Consider'd* (1727), which concluded with the promise of a supplementary work that would deal with miracles, and thus remove the other pillar of traditional apologetics.

It fell, however, to the Cambridge don and disciple of Collins, Thomas Woolston (1670–1731), to fulfill this promise. He did so in a series of six *Discourses on the Miracles of our Saviour* (1727-29). Some years earlier he had advocated the application of Origen's allegorical method of expounding Scripture. His adversaries alleged that he was out of his mind, and in 1720 he was deprived of his fellowship at Sidney Sussex College. The *Discourse on the Miracles of Our Saviour, In View of the Present Contest between Infidels and Apostates* examined some fifteen Gospel miracles and pronounced them fraudulent. The work was cast largely in the form of a dialogue between a rabbi (alias Woolston) and the author (ostensibly a Christian apologist who regularly comes off second best in the argument). The rabbi promises to become a Christian if the resurrection of Jesus be proved to him, but the accounts are soon pronounced to be a Robinson Crusoe romance. The priests and the disciples had made an agreement to open the tomb of Jesus on the day after the crucifixion, but the scheming disciples stole the body the previous night.

Woolston's writings were marked by a coarse, ribald style, and historians of the period have detected signs of mental instability in him. But this did not prevent him from being tried and condemned for blasphemy.

Woolston's slightly senior contemporary and colleague as a fellow of Sidney Sussex College, Cambridge, William Wollaston (1660–1724), taught a form of rationalism that restated Lord Herbert's Common Notions. His *Religion of Nature Delineated* (1722) was an erudite work that, unlike most deistic writings, contained no biblical criticism.

Matthew Tindal (1655–1733) was a fellow of All Soul's College, Oxford. He is reputed to have been the most learned of the British deists and also the most historically significant. In 1730 he published a work that came to be regarded as "the deists' Bible," *Christianity as Old as the Creation: Or, the Gospel, a Republication of the Religion of Nature.* It provoked over 150 replies, including (six years later) Bishop Butler's *Analogy.* Although

Tindal professed to be an admirer of Locke, he deduced the existence and attributes of God by *a priori* rational reflection. Tindal's title was ironically taken from a sermon by Bishop Thomas Sherlock in which the bishop had declared that "The Religion of the Gospel, is the true original Religion of Reason and Nature.—And its Precepts declarative of that original Religion, which was as old as the Creation."[4] Tindal refrained from the kind of all-out attack on miracles that characterized Woolston's writings, though he anticipated Hume's argument that nothing could be proved from miracles. Instead, he contented himself with commenting on the less-than-perfect morals of certain Old Testament heroes, with questioning some of the New Testament parables, and with criticizing clerical practices. He argued that "the Law of Nature either is, or is not, a perfect law; if the first, 'tis not capable of Addition; if the last, does it not argue Want of Wisdom in the Legislator?"[5] Clearly, Tindal's preference was the former alternative.

Both Matthew Tindal and Thomas Chubb (1679–1746) professed to be "Christian deists." But whereas Tindal was an Oxford scholar, Chubb was a self-taught working man. Yet this did not prevent him from mastering the rationalist thought of the day and developing an argument for free will that provoked an extensive reply from no less a figure than Jonathan Edwards in the New World. Chubb's various writings defended reason and natural religion as a proof of Christianity. His *Discourse on Miracles, Considered as Evidence to Prove the Divine Original of a Revelation* (1741) shows signs of influence by Toland and Woolston. Other writings include *The True Gospel of Jesus Christ Asserted* (1732) and *The True Gospel of Jesus Christ Vindicated* (1739).

The Welsh "Christian deist" Thomas Morgan (d. 1743) was a medical doctor. Combining Lord Herbert's Common Notions with the biblical criticism of Toland and Chubb, he sought to exploit ambiguities in Scripture. According to Morgan, history is a matter of probabilities. The idea of infallibility is fostered by priests for selfish purposes. Religion is a purely internal thing. Morgan's writings include a *Letter to Eusebius* (1739) and *The Moral Philosopher, in a Dialogue between Philalethes, a Christian Deist, and Theophanes, a Christian Jew* (2 volumes, 1737–39).

Viscount Bolingbroke (1678–1751) added little that was new to the debate. He left his writings to be published posthumously. Dr. Johnson regarded him as a "blunderbuss" against religion and morality, and David Hume pronounced his works to be unoriginal and feeble.

Peter Annet (1693–1769) was the last of the old-line British deists. His writings included *The Resurrection of Jesus Considered* (1744) and its sequels, which took up the theme of Woolston's trial and Sherlock's reply, *Supernaturals Examined* (1747) and *Examination of the Character of St. Paul* (1742). His assault on miracles, especially those in the Old Testament, in nine numbers of *The Free Enquirer* (1761) brought a charge of blasphemous libel, to which he pleaded guilty. He was imprisoned for a month, pilloried twice, made to do hard labor for a year, fined, and put under bond of security for life. This was deemed a "mitigated" sentence by the court in view of his poverty and old age. There is evidence, however, that Annet was made a scapegoat after a vain attempt to suppress the publication of David Hume's *Four Dissertations* (1757). Annet was the last person to suffer physical punishment for heterodox opinions. He returned to schoolmastering after serving his sentence.

THE DEISTS' CASE AGAINST THE GOSPEL MIRACLES

In 1754 John Leland observed that "there is scarce anything in which the Deistical writers have been more generally agreed than in bending their force against the proof from miracles."[6] R. M. Burns points out in his penetrating analysis of the deists' works on this subject that their major concern was not to deny the possibility of miracles in themselves, but to nullify the evidentialist use of miracles.[7] In this respect, their position was formally much the same as that professed by David Hume who today is revered as the classical opponent of miracles. Moreover, as Burns proceeds to show, Hume's discussion of the appeal to miracles in the second part of his essay "Of Miracles" with its four *a posteriori* arguments "in fact functions as a fairly compendious summary of all but one of the major types of these arguments as presented by the Deists."[8]

Hume's first argument complained of the lack of discerning, competent witnesses to miracles. He spoke in general terms implying in a veiled way that the same could be said of the New Testament writers. Such inhibitions were not shared by Woolston, Chubb, and Annet, whose forthright comments on the biblical text itself anticipated later biblical criticism.[9]

Hume's second argument implied that belief in miracles was in no small part due to the human propensity to exaggerate. His words were almost an echo of Thomas Morgan's observation that "All men are the more than easily imposed on in such matters as the love to gratify the passion of admiration, and take a great deal of pleasure in hearing and telling of wonders."[10] Discussion of this point was very common. In 1727 the orthodox William Warburton had warned against this very danger in *A Critical and Philosophical Enquiry into the Causes of Prodigies and Miracles as Related by Historians*. But whereas Warburton argued that truth should be distinguished from error, the deists were inclined to attribute all supernatural reports to this human frailty.

Hume's third argument that miracles "are observed to abound among ignorant and barbarous nations" is again virtually an echo of a deist. This time it is John Toland who commented that "It is very observable that the more and ignorant and barbarous any People remain, you shall find them most abound with Tales of this nature."[11] In context, it should be noted, Toland was speaking of Satanic wonders and magic. If Hume was drawing on Toland, he would have derived satisfaction from knowing the original application of his phraseology.

Hume's fourth and crowning argument against appeals to miracles was the claim that the miracles of rival religious factions cancel each other out. Although Hume expressed the fear that his argument "may appear over subtile and refined,"[12] it was in fact one that had been well aired in the course of the previous seventy years. Indeed, R. M. Burns contends that "By far the commonest maneuver in the Deistic polemic against the Christian miracles was the making of a suggestive comparison between the miracles of Jesus and those of other religions."[13] This was done in two main ways. On the one hand, Apollonius of Tyana was paraded as a figure who invited comparison with Jesus, suggesting the implication that Jesus was just another none-too-reputable ancient holy man. Blount's translation of the *Life* of Apollonius supplied his successors with a fund of material to draw on. Woolston professed himself not to be "so impious and profane" as to take literally the story of the water turned into wine, and observed that, "If Apollonius Tyannaeus, and not Jesus, had been the author of the miracle, we should have reproached his memory with it."[14] On the other hand, the deists sought to embarrass their orthodox Protestant readers by citing miracle stories from pagan and Roman Catholic sources. The intended effect was to nullify the Protestant appeal to miracles as divine authentication of their beliefs. As Thomas Chubb put it,

> The miracles wrought in, and by the Church of Rome, for ages past, have been looked upon, and in general treated by Protestants, as fraud and imposition; though it has been wholly out of the power of those Protestants to prove some of them to be such; and though some of these facts seem to be better attested than any of the miracles which were wrought or supposed to be wrought in the first century.[15]

In one important respect the deists differed from Hume's later critique. Hume's discussion of 1748 was an oblique attack on the use made of the Gospel miracles by orthodox divines. He scrupulously avoided mentioning the Gospel stories directly. There was an intended irony in all this, for Hume knew full well that his criticism of the evidence for miracles in general would include the Gospel miracles in particular. The irony of the deists was of a different order. Chubb and Woolston especially attacked their subject head on, ironically exploiting what seemed to them to be absurd, trivial, and even immoral. Woolston's *Discourses* were variations on the common theme "That the literal history of many of the miracles of Jesus, as recorded by the Evangelists, does imply absurdities, improbabilities, and incredibilities. Consequently they, either in whole or in part, were never wrought, as they are commonly believed nowadays."[16] They are the kind of acts that one might attribute to "a conjuror, a sorcerer, and a wizard."[17] The stories of the perishing of the Gadarene swine, the cursing of the fig tree, and the turning of water into wine at the marriage feast at Cana present Jesus in a highly unfavorable light. The two former stories picture Jesus as someone who cares little for the property of others, not to mention his peevish and flagrant disregard for nature. The last of these stories makes Jesus out to be a magician of dubious morality.[18] With regard to Jesus' selective concern in healing only one of the many invalids at the pool of Bethesda, Woolston argued that the story destroyed the credibility of Jesus as a miraculous healer. "If he could not cure them, there's an end of his power of miracles; and if he would not, it was want of mercy and compassion in him."[19]

What this line of criticism did was to strike at the heart of the orthodox apologetic that had argued that true miracles could be discerned by the way in which they brought honor to God, had an elevated moral purpose, and were not concerned with trivialities.[20] The deists were not so much concerned with whether miracles were scientifically impossible as with whether they were unreasonable.[21] As John Toland put it, "Whatever is contrary to *Reason* can be no Miracle."[22] The criticism that the Gospel miracles were morally unreasonable was accompanied by the claim that divine interference in the order of nature is unreasonable. Toland argued that "Miracles are produc'd according to the Laws of Nature, tho above its ordinary Operations, which are therefore supernaturally assisted."[23] William Wollaston and Peter Annet thought that any interference with the laws of nature was inconsistent with God's perfection. Any adjustments that God needed to make in order to meet the needs of particular cases would be carried out, Wollaston argued, "without interrupting the order of the universe or putting any of the parts of it out of their channels."[24] Annet stated the point more bluntly: "God has settled the laws of nature by His wisdom and power, and therefore cannot alter them consistently with His Perfections."[25]

There is one further aspect of the deists' argument against miracles that merits attention. Again it is to be found in Wollaston and Annet, and again it anticipates a major argument of David Hume. It concerns the degree of probability that may be assigned to reports of alleged events. Here, too, reasonability is the decisive factor. Wollaston noted three criteria:

> 1. That may be reckoned probable, which, in the estimation of reason, appears to be more agreeable to the constitution of nature. . . .

> 2. When any observation hath hitherto constantly held true, or most commonly proved to be so, it has by this acquired an established credit; the cause may be presumed to retain its former force; and the effect may be taken as probable, if in the case before us there does not appear some thing particular, some ground for exception. . . .

> 3. When neither nature nor other observation point out the probable conjecture to us, we must be determined (if it be necessary to be determined at all) by the reports, and sense of them, whom we apprehend, judging with the best skill we have, to be most knowing and honest.[26]

Further, Wollaston added that "principal regard" should be given to the first of these criteria. The other two were to be used when nature "utterly excludes us from her bosom." When all three agree, the result is "probable in the highest degree."

Wollaston outlined his argument in 1722 in *The Religion of Nature*

Delineated. Peter Annet developed a similar argument in *The Resurrection of Jesus Considered* (1735) and explored it more fully in the fourth discourse of *Supernaturals Examined* (1747). In the latter he compared the report of a man's jumping across the River Thames at Westminster with that of crossing over it by Westminster Bridge. The former is incredible, but the latter is not. Annet drew this conclusion: "That testimony cannot be credible which relates incredible things. . . . The relaters have not an equal right to be believed."[27] In short, reports of miracles are incredible because they tell incredible things. They are "contrary to the course of nature" and must be explained by "the power and possibility of deception."[28]

What is striking in all this is the fact that both Wollaston and Annet clearly anticipate a major argument of David Hume. Admittedly Annet's discussion probably appeared too late to influence Hume directly, and the details of Wollaston's analysis were lacking in philosophical finesse. But Wollaston's work was well known, and R. M. Burns draws attention to strong grounds for concluding that Hume not only knew of the work, but had actually read it.[29] We shall examine the point more fully in the next chapter, as we consider the arguments of David Hume. In the meantime we need to consider the counterattack of the orthodox.

ORTHODOX APOLOGETICS AND MIRACLES

John Locke stood firmly in the evidentialist tradition: miracles provide tangible evidence of divine attestation. But it was a qualified evidentialism. Locke was not prepared to treat every story of the supernatural as compelling evidence of a divine act. The message accompanying the miracle must be rational, moral, honoring to God, and not contradicting other divine revelations. Moreover, Locke was not prepared to argue that any single biblical miracle story on its own was compelling. In other words, Locke's approach to miracles involved what might be called a gestalt judgment. It not only took account of the paranormal particulars of a report, but also considered its moral and spiritual aspects in their immediate and wider contexts. The judgment that any event was a miracle was thus based on the total impression that the event made, when judged within the widest possible frame of reference. Locke's approach was representative of the broad, British evidentialist position.[30] It was in line with that of Calvin and orthodox theologians through the ages who consistently refused to take wonders at their face value, whenever they contradicted the revealed truth of the word of God. Following the prescriptions of Deuteronomy 13, the moral and the theological were held to be the decisive factors in determining whether an event was a miracle wrought by God.

However, alongside this broad, qualified evidentialism emerged a narrower hard-line evidentialism that was sensitive to the charge of circularity in Locke's reasoning. This was seen as trying to prove the truth of doctrine by appealing to miracles, and making doctrinal truth the test of the genuineness of the miracle. But if miracles were discerned by their moral and theological significance, they could not serve to certify moral and theological truth. The moral and theological truths would have to be known independently of the miracle. To William Fleetwood this approach simply begged the question. His *Essay on Miracles in Two Discourses* (1701) argued that God alone can perform miracles, though he allowed a distinction between miracles that attested the teaching of Moses and Jesus and miracles that were "accidental" or "providential." The latter were acts of God performed "by or among the Gentiles" that did not serve to attest divine truth, but were susceptible of misrepresentation and misappropriation by pagan religious teachers.[31]

The argument was further elaborated by Samuel Clarke in his Boyle Lectures, delivered in St. Paul's Cathedral in 1705 and entitled *A Discourse Concerning the Obligations of Natural Religion, and the Truth and Certainty of the Christian Revelation*. Clarke's *Discourse* was a direct response to Hobbes and the deists of his day whose criticisms of miracles were muted, when compared with the later comments of Woolston and Annet. At the outset Clarke declared that "There is no such thing, as a consistent Scheme of Deism."[32] He went on to a full defense of the rationality of Christian beliefs, concluding with an appeal to miracles and fulfilled prophecy. Clarke denied that "we prove in a Circle the *Doctrine* by the *Miracles,* and the *Miracles* by the *Doctrine.*"[33] He conceded that no miracle could ever prove a vicious or contradictory doctrine. The nub of his argument was that

> The *Doctrine* must be in itself *possible* and *capable to be proved,* and then *Miracles* will prove it to be *actually and certainly* true. The *Doctrine* is not first known or supposed to be *true*, and then the *Miracles* proved by it; But the *Doctrine* must be first known to be such as is *possible to be true*, and then *Miracles* will prove that it *actually* is so.[34]

By "impossible" doctrines Clarke meant teaching that was contradictory or patently vicious. As he pointed out, "The moral part of our Saviour's Doctrine would have appeared infallibly true, whether he had ever worked any miracles or no."[35] The crucial case concerned doctrines, the truth of which could not be known apart from revelation, which in turn required rational, objective attestation. By the application of these criteria Clarke could dismiss "the pretended Miracles" of Apollonius of Tyana, "because they are very poorly attested, and are in themselves very mean and trifling." By the same token Clarke pronounced the judgment that

> The Miracles . . . which our Saviour worked, were, *to the Disciples that saw them,* sensible Demonstrations of his divine Commission. And *to those who have lived since that Age,* they are as certain Demonstrations of the same Truth, as the *Testimony* of those first Disciples who were Eyewitnesses of them, is certain and true.[36]

It would be patently unfair to Clarke to charge him with the elimination of the moral test for determining a miracle. On the other hand, he clearly relegates it and presents miracles as having a logically coercive force that goes well beyond Locke's form of evidentialism. This rigorous evidentialism is further exemplified by Brampton Gurdon, Thomas Stackhouse, John Chapman, Abraham Le Moine, and Hugh Farmer.[37] In the words of Farmer:

> The proof from miracles of the divine commission and doctrine of a prophet is, in itself, decisive and absolute . . . full and sufficient without taking into consideration the doctrine they attest. The proof arises out of the nature of the miracles independently of everything else.[38]

When Hugh Farmer wrote this in 1771, the great British eighteenth-century debate on miracles had already begun to die down. Almost everything had been said that could be said. But his words summarize the central issue concerning the miraculous for the deists and for David Hume—the claim that miracles provide coercive proof of the truth of Christianity. As the deistic controversy entered its final, climactic phase in the late 1720's, the focus began to shift from miracles in general to that of the resurrection of Jesus in particular. This was largely due to Thomas Woolston's critique of the resurrection narratives, which denounced the resurrection as "the most . . . barefaced Imposture ever put upon the world."[39] Woolston argued that the body of Jesus was stolen by the disciples who had probably bribed the drunken guards at the tomb. He noted that the resurrection appearances were made only to disciples, who in any case were known deceivers. Eventually the disciples came to believe their own message, but for Woolston *belief* in the resurrection was the true miracle. He himself professed to look to "that Happiness of the state of Nature, Religion and Liberty, which may be looked for upon the coming of the Messiah, the allegorical accomplisher of the Law and the Prophets."[40]

In 1725 an unsuccessful attempt was made to prosecute Woolston. The *Discourses* provided clear evidence of his blasphemy, and in 1729 he was found guilty by the Lord Chief Justice, who sentenced him to a year's imprisonment, a fine of £100, and security for good behavior. Woolston refused to retract or cease to write, and was still technically a prisoner (despite the efforts of Samuel Clarke to procure his release) when he died in his own house.

Among the less savage replies was one from the pen of Bishop Thomas Sherlock (1678–1761), whose numerous appointments included the vice-chancellorship of Cambridge University, and to whom Woolston had dedicated one of his *Discourses*. In *A Tryal of the Witnesses of the Resurrection* (1729) Sherlock reversed the roles and produced a piece of what Dr. Johnson called "Old Bailey theology." As apologetics, it enjoyed the kind of success in the eighteenth century that C. S. Lewis's *Screwtape Letters* enjoy in the twentieth. It was translated into French and German, and was widely used by French Catholic apologists. In the course of the argument, appeal was made to an illustration that figured repeatedly in eighteenth-century debates on miracles: the question whether it would be legitimate for anyone living in a warm climate to believe in ice. The judge in Sherlock's tract put the question in these terms:

appealing to the settled course of nature is referring the matter in dispute, not to rules and maxims of reason and true philosophy, but to the prejudices and mistakes of men, which are various and infinite, and differ sometimes according to the climate men live in, because men form a notion of nature from what they see; and therefore, in cold countries all men judge it to be according to the course of nature to freeze, in warm countries they judge it to be unnatural. Consequently, that it is not enough to prove anything contrary to the laws of nature, to say that it is usually or constantly to our observation otherwise; and therefore, though men in the ordinary course of nature die, and do not rise again, (which is certainly a prejudice against the belief of a resurrection,) yet is it not an argument against the possibility of a resurrection.[41]

When due allowance is made for Sherlock's emotive language, it must be granted that present experience cannot logically preclude the possibility of events occurring that do not conform to our experience or understanding. Moreover, the testimony of others performs an important service in broadening our horizons. But the questions remain whether we have sufficient warrant for believing such events as miracles, what would constitute such warrant, and how we may distinguish history from legend.

In Sherlock's tract the jury duly acquitted the New Testament witnesses of giving false evidence, having listened to arguments concerning their honesty, intelligence, veracity, and motivation. But the debate was far from being laid to rest. It was taken up by Peter Annet in a series of pamphlets, and by Thomas Chubb who wrote a series of works depicting Jesus as a kind of deist before his time. These in turn provoked further replies from the orthodox.[42] In their day these replies were thought of as robust rebuttals of the skeptics. Today they are unread and unremembered, except by historians of the period who are apt to lament their lack of sophistication in the way that they handle history.[43]

BISHOP BUTLER AND PROBABILITY

Alongside the narrower evidentialists who regarded miracles as hard, unambiguous, and irrefragable evidence of divine activity, there was a steady stream of apologists who continued in the tradition of Locke. Among them were Bishop Benjamin Hoadly, John Leng, John Conybeare, James Foster, and Arthur Ashley Sykes.[44] But the one work that emerged as a classic out of this tradition was Bishop Joseph Butler's *The Analogy of Religion, Natural and Revealed, to the Constitution and Course of Nature* (1736), which was written two years before his elevation to the see of Bristol. Philosophically Butler adopted a moderate empiricist approach, following in the footsteps of Locke and Newton. His work was really a response to Toland, who called him "the judicious Mr. Butler."

The modern reader may find Butler's style of writing and way of arguing quaint, precise, and moderate to the point of excess. But in the opinion of

C. D. Broad, Butler's work is "perhaps the ablest and fairest argument for theism that exists."[45] Many of his arguments had already been stated, especially by the various Boyle lecturers. But Butler raised the discussion to a new level: he lifted the debate above personal polemics, and avoided naming his adversaries. He was prepared to admit difficulties, and refused to press points beyond the evidence. Whereas both opponents and defenders of orthodoxy had spoken with serene assurance, claiming total victory for their viewpoints, Butler insisted that in our thinking we must be guided by probability:

> Probable evidence, in its very nature, affords but an imperfect kind of information; and is to be considered as relative only to beings of limited capacities. For nothing which is the possible object of knowledge, whether past, present, or future, can be probable to an infinite Intelligence; since it cannot but be discerned absolutely as it is in itself, certainly true, or certainly false. But to us, probability is the very guide of life.[46]

In other words, if we were God himself, we would presumably know things for certain and have an absolute and immediate knowledge of everything. But since we are not God, we must recognize that we just do not have that kind of knowledge. Our conclusions are at best interpretations, made by beings of limited intelligence on the basis of a limited selection of evidence, which in turn is interpreted in the light of an unknown number of hypotheses, most of which we have never personally examined. Butler was anticipating a point that has virtually become an axiom of modern philosophical discussion—that all facts are theory laden.[47] Moreover, he was insisting that we recognize the element of probability in every aspect of our thinking.

Whereas the deists had urged natural religion as the rational alternative to Christianity, Butler argued that our experience of nature and the Christian faith both point in the same direction. As the title of his work indicates, he saw an analogy between natural and revealed religion. A major part of Butler's case was his contention that the arguments leveled against Christianity may equally well be leveled against natural religion. In some respects, Butler may be seen as a presuppositionalist. Although he alludes to proofs of the existence of God, Butler's case is built upon the presupposition of "an intelligent Author and Governor of nature" as the necessary condition for the rationality of the universe and objective moral values. It would take us too far afield to pursue the ramifications of the argument and anticipate possible objections, but we can at least state Butler's conclusion in his own words:

> For, will any man in his senses say, that it is less difficult to conceive, how the world came to be and to continue as it is, without, than with, an intelligent Author and Governor of it? Or, admitting an intelligent Governor of it, that there is some other rule of government more natural, and of easier conception, than that which we call moral? Indeed, without an intelligent Author and Governor of nature, no account at all can be given, how this universe, or the part of it particularly in which we are concerned, came to be, and the course of it to be carried on, as it is:

nor any, of its general end and design, without a moral Governor of it.
That there is an intelligent Author of nature, and natural Governor of
the world, is a principle gone upon in the foregoing Treatise; as proved,
and generally known and confessed to be proved.[48]

It was against this background that Butler presented the revealed religion
of Christianity. His argument was much the same as that of Bishop Sherlock's
sermon some twenty years earlier, which Matthew Tindal had tried to invert.
Now Bishop Butler sought to rectify it. He presented Christianity

first, as a republication, and external institution, of natural or essential
religion, adapted to the present circumstances of mankind, and intended
to promote natural piety and virtue: and secondly, as containing an account of a dispensation of things not discoverable by reason, in consequence of which, several distinct precepts are enjoined upon us. For
though natural religion is the foundation and principal part of Christianity, it is not in any sense the whole of it.[49]

Although this was not the language of Calvin, there are here discernible echoes
of Calvin's *Institutes,*[50] not to mention Paul's preaching at Athens: "What
therefore you worship as unknown, this I proclaim to you" (Acts 17:23).

Within this general framework "the miracles and prophecies recorded
in scripture, were intended to prove a particular dispensation of Providence,
the redemption of the world by the Messiah."[51] The bishop proceeded to
invite his readers to suppose that a teacher of natural religion had been endowed by God to perform the miracles that Jesus had performed. Would
it not have afforded additional credibility of the strongest kind? But since
Christianity is an authoritative publication of the religion of nature, miracles
should be seen as an instance of God's general providence.[52] Like Origen
and Calvin, Butler argued that "Miraculous powers were given to the first
preachers of Christianity, in order to their introducing it into the world."[53]
He saw the incarnation as an instance of invisible miracles "which, being
secret, cannot be alleged as a proof of such a mission; but require themselves
to be proved by visible miracles."[54]

Like David Hume after him (though with very different conclusions),
Butler appears to have put forward two types of argument concerning
miracles. Both were general, insofar as they did not examine the details of
any particular miracle. And again as with Hume, one might be termed *a priori*
(in that it examined the inherent probability of the miraculous) and the other
might be termed *a posteriori* (in that it considered the type and quality of
evidence advanced on behalf of miracles).

The *a priori* argument answered the rhetorical question: "Is there a
presumption against miracles, such as to make them incredible?" The bishop
answered his question by asking a further question: "If there be the presumption of millions to one, against the most common facts; what can a small
presumption, additional to this, amount to, though it be peculiar?" Indeed,
there must be "a presumption, beyond all comparison, greater, against . . .
particular common facts . . . than against miracles *in general;* before any

evidence of either."[55] But religion supplies a particular reason for miracles, that is, "to afford mankind instruction additional to that of nature, and to attest the truth of it."[56] Finally, miracles should not be compared with "common natural events" or even "uncommon" events, but with

> the extraordinary phenomena of nature. And then the comparison will be between the presumption against miracles, and the presumption against such uncommon appearances, suppose, as comets, and against there being any such powers in nature as magnetism and electricity, so contrary to the properties of other bodies not endued with those powers.[57]

From all this, the bishop concluded that there is no inherent presumption against miracles that would make them incredible. On the contrary, "our being able to discern reasons for them, gives a positive credibility to the history of them, in cases where those reasons hold."[58]

Bishop Butler recognized that a great deal of nature, including the behavior of "living agents," was reducible to general laws. But the science of his day was ignorant of the laws that cause earthquakes, tempests, famines, and pestilence, and also of the laws that affect human genetics. He went on to observe:

> It is only from analogy, that we conclude the whole of it to be capable of being reduced into them: only from our seeing, that part is so. It is from our finding, that the course of nature, in some respects and so far, goes on by general laws, that we conclude this of the rest.

This observation led Butler to entertain the feasibility of the idea that even miracles might be subsumable under the general laws of divine wisdom, which God might use as he judged fit:

> And if it be a just ground for such a conclusion, it is a just ground also, if not to conclude, yet to apprehend, to render it supposable and credible, which is sufficient for answering objections, that God's miraculous interpositions may have been, all along in like manner, by *general* laws of wisdom. . . . These laws are unknown indeed to us. . . . Now, if the revealed dispensations of Providence, and miraculous interpositions, be by general laws, as well as God's ordinary government in the course of nature made known by reason and experience; there is no more reason to expect, that every exigence, as it arises, should be provided for by these general laws of miraculous interpositions, than that every exigence in nature should, by the general laws of nature: yet there might be wise and good reasons, that miraculous interpositions should be by general laws: and that these laws should not be broken in upon, or deviated from, by other miracles.[59]

In making this suggestion, Bishop Butler was anticipating a modern aspect of the debate on miracles by some two hundred years.

With Bishop Butler's *a posteriori* arguments we are brought back to more familiar ground. He began with a reminder that the evidence for Christianity does not depend either on miracles or the fulfillment of prophecy.[60] Miracles and prophecy are to be viewed in the context of the general character of Chris-tianity. A pointer in favor of the historicity of the New Testament miracles is the fact that the narratives that relate them do not seem to have been aimed at impressing and entertaining their readers. The biblical accounts are very different from those of ancient poets and authors who sought to astonish with wonders and prodigies.[61] In reviewing the origin and establishment of Christianity, Butler maintained that it is hard to account for its history except on the supposition that the accounts we have are true.[62] He even went so far as to argue that since, upon the face of it, it is an authentic history, "it cannot be determined to be fictitious without some proof that it is so."[63] Moreover, of all the great religions, Christianity and Judaism alone were attended with public miracles at their foundation.[64] Finally, the fact that people in different ages have been deluded by pretenses to miracles does not invalidate all appeal to the miraculous. The same argument could be applied to ordinary events.[65] The fact that some claims to the historicity of ordinary events are spurious and deceptive does not make all testimony to ordinary events spurious and deceptive.

Bishop Butler's arguments still have a claim to a hearing today, even though we must also listen to the qualifications voiced by the bishop's own admirers and echoed by his adversaries. Mr. Gladstone, the great British Liberal Prime Minister of the Victorian era, who had a keen interest in theology and who edited the bishop's works, was guarded in his approval of Bishop Butler's discussion of miracles. Two questions in particular pro-voked his comments. The first concerns Butler's contention that there must be a much greater presumption against common particular events happen-ing than against the possibility of miracles in general. The chances of any event at all happening must be millions to one against. The chances against a miracle happening were for Butler only marginally greater. The possibility of any event happening (miraculous or otherwise) is decided by the sheer fact of whether or not it has actually happened. Mr. Gladstone argued that the bishop appeared to be confusing two categories of events.[66] The chances of any event happening are indeed millions to one against (e.g., the fact that I might drink this particular cup of coffee with my meal rather than that cup of coffee or a particular cup of tea). But there is a difference between the normal range of experience that determines the range of the probable and of the *kinds* of events that are probable and improbable, on the one hand, and the experience of something that is unique and without parallel in our experience, on the other hand.

However, close reading of Butler's arguments suggests that this is the point he wanted to make. What Butler's argument shows is that we are con-stantly operating within the realm of probabilities, and that there is no com-pelling argument that would require us to dismiss the possibility of a miracle prior to weighing the evidence and considering the presuppositions that we bring to the case. A miracle might appear to be unlikely in view of our normal experience of the way in which things are. Such experience sets for us the parameters for the *kinds* of events that we might expect and the *kinds* of explanation that we may give to them. But we must recognize that the experience and explanations of any given individual are not absolute and normative. Moreover, as Bishop Butler pointed out, it is not simply one's experience that provides the background against which one must make judgments. In questions involving the alleged activity of God, a predisposing factor is what we believe about the character and activity of God and how the alleged event would relate to that belief.

The other question that gave Mr. Gladstone particular concern as he edited Butler's *Analogy* was the apparent difference of emphasis between the bishop's view of miracles and that of the New Testament writers.[67] The bishop, like his predecessors, had appealed to the apologetic importance of miracles. Mr. Gladstone pointed out that the apostles were not themselves converted by miracles. Nor do the miracles appear to have led to extended conversions in the ministry of Jesus, though they seem to have figured more in the preaching of the apostles. An exception was the raising of Lazarus, in that "Many of the Jews therefore, who had come with Mary and had seen what he did, believed in him" (John 11:45). Further, the incarnation could be considered a miracle. But as such, it is not available as a proof; rather, it requires proof. The miracle of Jesus' person and character is too spiritual for the masses, though it affected a few. The resurrection of Jesus is what fulfills the apologetic function in New Testament preaching that Bishop Butler, in common with previous apologists, tended to assign to miracles in general.[68]

FRANÇOIS DE PÂRIS AND THE SAINT-MÉDARD MIRACLES

While in England the deists and their opponents were heatedly debating the possibility of miracles, from France there came reports of actual miracles happening. They were associated with the recently deceased Jansenist deacon François de Pâris (1690-1727).[69] His commitment to Jansenism, which received papal condemnation in *Unigenitus* (1713), and his personal humility precluded advancement in the church. His latter days were spent in austere renunciation and personal devotions in a squalid quarter of Paris where he was known to his poverty-stricken neighbors as M. François. His intense life of benefactions to the poor, public instruction, spiritual devotions, and physical self-mortification hastened his premature death. He was interred in the cemetery of Saint-Médard in the Saint-Marceau quarter, where he lived.

On the day of the interment an elderly illiterate widow knelt in prayer, kissed the deacon's feet, and was reported healed of a paralyzed arm. It was the first of many reported cures. The cemetery became a cultic center of pilgrimage. Within a year of the burial, the deceased deacon's brother erected a monument that consisted of a black marble slab raised upon four supports, leaving just enough space for someone to crawl between the slab and the grave proper. It rapidly became a practice to crawl into this space, seeking the deceased deacon's intercession. Many who came experienced ecstatic convulsions and did not go away disappointed. Already in the spring of 1728 Cardinal Noailles instituted an investigation of the reported cures. The report, which was suppressed by higher authorities, indicated that there were indeed genuine cases of healing.

As time went on there were reported healings of hemorrhages, ulcerous sores, cancerous tumors, fevers, rheumatism, arthritis, paralysis, deafness, and blindness. By the summer of 1731 vast crowds of visitors frequented the tomb, which had become the site of the activities of frenzied convulsionaries, claiming to be inspired by the Holy Spirit through the deceased holy man's intercession. The Jansenists saw the miracles as continued divine vindication of their cause. They were bitterly attacked by their theological opponents and increasingly harried by the civil and ecclesiastical establishment, which was conscious of the political dimensions of the affair. In 1732 the cemetery was closed by royal decree and devotions at the tomb prohibited. The act provoked the anonymous graffiti: "By order of the king, God is forbidden to perform miracles in this place." The attempts to squash the convulsionary movement led to its spread beyond Paris. Revival millenarianism became embroiled in the political unrest that gripped eighteenth-century France, culminating in the French Revolution.

The healings were the subject of detailed investigation at the time, and continue to divide investigators sharply to this day. In the eighteenth century they entered the British debate on miracles, attracting the attention of Arthur Ashley Sykes, Conyers Middleton, and David Hume. Among recent Catholic writers, Ronald Knox[70] and Louis Monden[71] are almost as critical of the Saint-Médard miracles as Middleton and Hume, though for somewhat different reasons. Knox and Monden attribute such cures as there were to psychological factors and stoutly repudiate the suggestion that they might be in any way connected with genuine miracles. Monden, indeed, argues that the Roman Catholic Church has "a *practical* monopoly" of "major miracles,"[72] from which he rigorously excludes even sects within Catholicism. For Middleton and Hume the reports of the Saint-Médard miracles were simply incredible. In all these negative verdicts it is not difficult to see that a preconceived scheme of interpretation and evaluation plays a significant part.

CONYERS MIDDLETON AND CHURCH HISTORY

The work of the controversial Anglican divine Conyers Middleton (1683–1750) has been applauded by different critics for different reasons. The redoubtable orthodox Presbyterian apologist B. B. Warfield noted "the faults arising out of the writer's spirit and the limitations inseparable from the state of scholarship in his day," but pronounced his opinion that the main contention of Middleton's book on miracles "seems to be put beyond dispute."[73]

For Warfield, Middleton had demonstrated beyond doubt that miraculous claims from the postapostolic age onward were unworthy of credence. Middleton's researches provided welcome confirmation of the view that miracles ceased with the close of the New Testament era. Middleton himself professed to hold this view, and it had already been argued by Calvin. But if the arguments leveled against the church fathers were valid, Middleton's work raised the question whether they might be equally valid against the authors of the New Testament. For the youthful Edward Gibbon, Middleton's *Free Inquiry* prompted a temporary conversion to Rome, but subsequently provided the impetus to view the history of the early church critically.[74] For David Hume, the publication of Middleton's work was an occasion of some chagrin, as Hume himself lamented as he reflected on the events of the year 1749: "On my return from Italy, I had the Mortification to find all England in a Ferment, on account of Dr. Middleton's Free Inquiry; while my Performance was entirely overlooked and neglected."[75] The "performance" in question was Hume's *Enquiry into the Human Understanding,* which had been published the previous year. Not only did it fail to procure for Hume the literary fame that he coveted and to provoke the debate on epistemology that would have proved that he had outsmarted his philosophical contemporaries; Middleton's work was a far more comprehensive critique of miracles than the slim essay that Hume had inserted into his *Enquiry.* Moreover, Middleton had robbed him at least in part of his claim to originality.

Middleton entitled his work *A Free Inquiry into the Miraculous Powers which are Supposed to have Subsisted in the Christian Church, from the Earliest Ages through Several Successive Centuries.* Its publication in 1748 crowned a career of polemics. It was preceded by an *Introductory Discourse* (1747) and was followed by a posthumous *Vindication* (1751), directed against the criticisms of Dr. William Dodwell[76] and Dr. Thomas Church.[77] The *Free Inquiry* falls into five main sections, and it is worthwhile to review each briefly in turn.

The first section reviews the principal testimonies to miraculous gifts in the church, citing sources in Greek and Latin from the apostolic fathers in the second century to Cyprian in the third. Middleton observed that the writers of the age immediately after the close of the New Testament period have nothing to say about miraculous gifts. "They speak indeed, in general, of certain *spiritual gifts,* as abounding among the Christians of that age; yet these cannot reasonably be interpreted to mean any thing more, than the *ordinary gifts and graces* of the gospel, *faith, hope, and charity, the love of God and of man.*"[78] This is followed by a brief account of the testimony of various writers, including Irenaeus, Justin, Tertullian, and Origen, from which Middleton draws the conclusion:

> that the silence of all the apostolic writers, on the subject of these gifts, must dispose us to conclude, that in those days they were actually withdrawn. And if this conclusion be thought to have any weight in it, then surely the pretended revival of them, after a cessation of forty or

fifty years, and the confident attestation of them by all the succeeding
fathers, cannot fail of infusing a suspicion of some fiction in the case.[79]

This conclusion is reinforced by the reflection that the passing of the apostles
deprived the church of its "first and ablest champions." One might have
expected that the church would have needed miracles to confirm its faith
and convince doubters. As it was, testimony to the miraculous increased
"in . . . proportion" to its power and credit, as the church gained ground
throughout the Roman empire.[80] Middleton's argument combines acute observation with speculation elevated to the point of dogmatism, which enables
him to dismiss all subsequent accounts of miracles as mistaken or fraudulent.
On the basis of a hypothesis designed to explain the omission of mention
of miracles in the half-dozen authors whose writings survived from the
subapostolic age, Middleton felt free to impute the veracity of subsequent
testimony. Nevertheless, his observations on the New Testament draw attention to the fact that miracles were never performed on demand in the New
Testament era and that their purpose was never simply to impress:

> The apostles wrought their miracles on special occasions, when they felt
> themselves prompted to it by a divine impulse; but at other times were
> destitute of that power; as it is evident from many facts and instances
> recorded in the New Testament. Agreeably to which, though they ap-
> peal sometimes, in confirmation of their mission, to the miraculous works
> which their Master had enabled them to perform, yet we never find them
> calling out upon the magistrates and people, to come and see the mighty
> wonders which they were ready to exhibit before their eyes, on all occa-
> sions, at any warning, and in all places, whenever they thought fit.[81]

Middleton's second section examined the patristic testimony to the
miracle-workers themselves. He observed that, while testimony to miracles
in the early church abounds,

> Yet none of these *venerable saints* have any where affirmed, that either
> they themselves, or the apostolic fathers before them, were endued with
> any power of working miracles, but declare only in general, "that such
> powers were actually subsisting in their days, and openly exerted in the
> church; that they had often seen the same, whenever they pleased:" but
> as to the persons who wrought them, they leave us strangely in the dark;
> for instead of specifying their names, conditions, or characters, their
> general style is, "such and such works are done among us, or by us; by
> our people; by a few; by man; by our exorcists; by ignorant laymen,
> women, boys, and any simple Christian whatsoever:" but in the particular
> case of *casting out devils, Origen* expressly says, *that it was performed
> generally by laymen.*[82]

Again, Middleton draws a contrast between the later church and the New
Testament, maintaining that the apostles and eminent disciples were commissioned to propagate the gospel and were given the exclusive power to work
miracles. In subsequent ages the miracle-workers are largely unnamed. Here

too Middleton overlooks the fact that whereas named church leaders were said to have performed miracles in the New Testament, miracles and exorcisms were also performed by others.[83]

Middleton crowned his second section with the kind of rhetorical flourish that delighted his contemporaries and helped to earn him the reputation of being one of the great masters of eighteenth-century English prose. With regard to the miraculous gifts that the church fathers did not profess to have themselves, Middleton observed:

> But if those venerable saints and martyrs were not endued with them when living, they had amends made to them when dead, if we can believe the reports of their successors, by a profusion of them on their bones and relics: which suggests a farther cause of suspecting the faith and judgment of those early ages. For how can we think it credible, that God should withhold his distinguishing favours from his faithful servants when living, to bestow them on their rotten bones? or employ his extraordinary power to no other use but to perpetuate a manifest imposture in his church? since it is to those ancient tales, so gravely attested, of miracles wrought *by the bones of saints and martyrs,* that the church of *Rome* owes all the trade which she still draws, from the same fund and treasure of her wonder-working relics: and if we can believe such stories, as they are delivered to us by the primitive writers, we cannot condemn a practice which is evidently grounded upon the same.[84]

Without prejudging the issue one way or the other, we should not allow Middleton's wry humor to conceal the several unexpressed premises of his argument. He has not yet shown whether it is the *same* saints whose relics were allegedly instrumental in performing miracles who did not perform such miracles in their lifetimes. Even if it were the same saints, Middleton has already conceded that the apostles themselves performed miracles only as and when they were given the gift. There is no *a priori* reason why God could not choose to work with material means at one point in time and not at another. Mention of such means is made in Acts 19:11f.: "And God did extraordinary miracles by the hands of Paul, so that handkerchiefs or aprons were carried away from his body to the sick, and diseases left them and the evil spirits came out of them."[85] Moreover, Middleton's argument takes no account of a central paradox of Christian faith, that God chooses "what is low and despised in the world, even things that are not, to bring to nothing things that are" (1 Cor. 1:28). This was, in fact, Origen's point as he reflected on the practice of exorcism in his day; it was what Middleton ignored in his comments about unnamed laymen performing exorcism.[86] To note this point is not to prejudge the question of whether miracles continued in the church after the time of apostles. It is simply to draw attention to the oversimplifications in Middleton's rhetoric.

Middleton's third section is devoted to an examination of the competence of the early Fathers with a view to assessing the reliability of their testimony. As B. B. Warfield pointed out, the criticism was "severe and not always perfectly fair."[87] Warfield could also have added that the criticism was largely directed at Justin Martyr and Irenaeus. The premise of Middleton's argument is the observation that

> The authority of a writer, who affirms any questionable fact, must depend on the character of his veracity and of his judgment. As far as we are assured of the one, so far are we assured, that he does not willingly deceive us; and from our good opinion of the other, we persuade ourselves, that he was not deceived himself: but in proportion as there is reason to doubt of either, there must always be reason to doubt of the truth of what he delivers.[88]

In itself the observation is sound, but it could be further qualified by the facts that people are prone to have better judgment in some areas than others, and that lack of veracity in one area does not mean that the person must be lacking in veracity in everything else. Furthermore, the fact that a person might entertain some mistaken beliefs and attitudes does not necessarily mean that all his or her beliefs and attitudes are mistaken. Each of these points requires precise investigation before an accurate judgment is possible.

Middleton pronounced Justin Martyr to be wanting in judgment on account of (among other things) his allegorical understanding of reality and his acceptance of traditional stories concerning the translation of the Septuagint.[89] Irenaeus is impugned (among other things) for accepting the same stories about the Septuagint and for the gross literalism of his millennial views.[90] The section culminates in a brief review of patristic notions of demon possession that Middleton dismisses as "not only a proof of the grossest credulity, but of that peculiar species of it, which of all others, lays a man the most open to the delusive arts of impostors."[91] The same argument, although Middleton forbore to say so, could have been employed against the authors of the New Testament.

In his fourth section Middleton reviewed the different types of miracles alleged to have happened in the early church. He dismissed Irenaeus's story of the raising of the dead on account of lack of clear testimony to any single instance, lack of corroborating testimony, and the difficulty of accounting for withdrawal of such an impressive gift.[92] The healing of the sick by anointing "might be accounted for probably without a miracle, by the natural power and efficacy of the oil itself."[93] In any case, miraculous healing affords "great room" for delusion.[94] Many of the alleged instances of exorcism should be attributed to epilepsy,[95] "the disordered state of the patient, answering wildly and at random to any questions proposed," or to "the arts of imposture and contrivance between the parties concerned in the act."[96] Exorcism was, by the Fathers' own admission, no monopoly of the church. It was, in fact, practiced by Jewish exorcists.[97] Instead of inferring, as the church fathers did, that it was God acting in both cases and that it demonstrated *a fortiori* the truth of Christian claims, Middleton drew the opposite conclusion. Since "these Jewish and gentile exorcists were mere knaves and impostors,"[98] the testimony of the Fathers was equally open to doubt. Claims to visions and ecstatic trances were discussed by Middleton at some length,[99] but in true enlightened fashion they were dismissed as cases of exaggerated enthusiasm. The same applies to the gifts of expounding the Scriptures and speaking in tongues.[100] In short, Middleton contended that appeals to the paranormal and supernatural in the early church were self-defeating:

> Though their assertions be strong, their instances are weak; and when, in proof of what they affirm, they descend to allege any particular facts, they are usually so unlucky in their choice of them, that, instead of strengthening, they weaken the credit of their general affirmation, and, from the absurdity of each miracle related by them, furnish a fresh objection to their power of working any.[101]

In reviewing such later stories as that of Simeon Stylites, the fifth-century saint who lived standing on the top of various pillars and to whom miracles were attributed, Dr. Chapman had urged their probability on the following grounds:

> 1. That they were of a public nature, and performed in such a manner, as left no room for delusion.

> 2. That they were attended with beneficial effects, which could not possibly have gained credit, unless the strongest evidence of sense had proved them to be true.

> 3. That the end of them was not to confirm any idle errors or superstitions, but purely to advance the glory of truth and virtue.

> 4. That the accounts of them are given by men of unquestionable integrity, piety, and learning, who were eye-witnesses of many of the facts, and declare in the most solemn manner, that they knew them to be true.

> 5. That they were far from being vain and unnecessary, so as to render them doubtful to after ages—but were attested by the strongest moral evidence, equal to that by which most of the ancient miracles were supported.

> 6. That they were incapable of giving any countenance to the fabulous pretences of the papists; and that a protestant of common capacity will discern as much difference between them and the popish miracles, as between gold and brass, between light and darkness.[102]

As we shall see, it would seem that David Hume's argument deliberately picks up Chapman's language (though without naming names). In the meantime we may note Middleton's countertheses, which in substance anticipated Hume's retort.

> 1. That they were all of such a nature, and performed in such a manner, as would necessarily inject a suspicion of fraud and delusion.

> 2. That the cures and beneficial effects of them, were either false, or imaginary, or accidental.

3. That they tend to confirm the idlest of all errors and superstitions.

4. That the integrity of the witnesses is either highly questionable, or their credulity at least so gross, as to render them unworthy of any credit.

5. That they were not only vain and unnecessary, but, generally speaking, so trifling also, as to excite nothing but contempt.

And lastly, that the belief and defence of them, are the only means in the world, that can possibly support, or that does in fact give any sort of countenance to the modern impostures of the Romish church.[103]

Middleton's fifth and final section was devoted to a discussion of the objections to his position. He dismissed the suggestion that his low view of the Fathers might reflect adversely on the New Testament itself, since they were instrumental in transmitting the Bible to later ages.[104] The Fathers themselves could hardly have corrupted the New Testament. Although Middleton allowed that his arguments seriously impugned the character of figures venerated in the early church, he sidestepped the question of whether his arguments might be used against the New Testament itself. Middleton made light of the claim that suspicion of fraud is precluded by the public appeals and challenges of Christian apologists to their pagan contemporaries to come forward and examine the cases for themselves.[105] For he doubted whether such appeals ever reached the secular authorities, who would be no more likely to read them than contemporary governments would be to study the writings of cranks. In the early church the difficulty would be intensified by the disposition of authorities to destroy Christian literature and the difficulty of getting it copied and transmitted in the first place. In response to the suggestion that the charge of fraud fits ill with piety and martyrdom, Middleton replied that religious zeal can make a person capable of doing almost anything.[106] To the objection that Middleton's rejection of the unanimous testimony of the Fathers would destroy the credit of all history, Middleton replied that the objection itself was too wholesale.[107] This argument might seem curious and paradoxical in the light of Middleton's general stance, but it is worth examining more closely.

Middleton pointed out that "We find many men in the world, whose fidelity we have just ground to suspect; yet a number of others, whom we can readily trust, sufficient to support that credit and mutual confidence, by which the business of life is carried on."[108] Thus, to impugn the veracity of some is not to impugn the veracity of all. The point is well taken. But the heart of Middleton's objection to the miraculous turns out, in fact, not to depend upon what might be discovered generally about the character and abilities of the witnesses but upon the prior conviction that miracles just do not happen and that testimony to the miraculous merely reveals whether they are naive, fraudulent, or both.

Ordinary facts, related by a credible person, furnish no cause of doubting from the nature of the thing: but if they be strange and extraordinary, doubts naturally arise, and in proportion as they approach towards the marvellous, those doubts still increase and grow stronger: for mere honesty will not warrant them; we require other qualities in the historian; a degree of knowledge, experience, and discernment, sufficient to judge of the whole nature and circumstances of the case: and if any of these be wanting, we necessarily suspend our belief. A weak man, indeed, if honest, may attest common events as credibly as the wisest; yet can hardly make any report, that is credible, of such as are miraculous; because a suspicion will always occur, that his weakness, and imperfect knowledge of the extent of human art, had been imposed upon by the craft of cunning jugglers. On the other hand, should a man of known abilities and judgment, relate to us things miraculous, or undertake to perform them himself, the very notion of his skill, without also of his integrity, would excite only the greater suspicion of him; especially, if he had any interest to promote, or any favorite opinion to recommend, by the authority of such works: because a pretension to miracles, has in all ages and nations, been found the most effectual instrument of impostors, towards deluding the multitude, and gaining their ends upon them.[109]

This somewhat lengthy quotation contains the essence of Middleton's case. It is based upon the conviction that any testimony to the miraculous is more likely to be deceived or deceiving than it is to be true. The point is further illustrated by the claim that there is not a single historian of antiquity, whether Greek or Roman, who has not recorded miracles, sometimes with the gravest assurances. But all are dismissed as erroneous or fraudulent.[110] Coming nearer to his own day, Middleton examined (as David Hume also did) the miracles alleged to have been wrought at the tomb of François de Pâris within the previous twenty years.[111] Despite their public character and abundant testimony, including that of "some of the principal physicians and surgeons in France,"[112] Middleton refused to credit them as miracles. On the basis of a proper demand for careful scrutiny and evaluation of evidence and testimony, Middleton moved to a position that refuses to take any testimony to the miraculous at its face value. Implicit in his position is the view that David Hume was to make explicit in a work published almost simultaneously with Middleton's work: "A miracle is a violation of the laws of nature; and as firm and unalterable experience has established these laws, the proof against a miracle, from the very nature of the fact, is as entire as any argument from experience can possibly be imagined."[113]

Middleton's work was ostensibly written to refute the claims of the Roman Catholic Church that miracles vindicate its truth and authority. His argument involved the rebuttal of any suggestion that miracles had continued in the church down to the age of Constantine in the fourth century and that it was only the growing worldliness of the church that prevented miracles from continuing. Middleton studiously avoided pronouncing on the miracles recorded in Scripture. His argument appears to fit B. B. Warfield's thesis that miracles had the function of providing credentials for the founding of Christianity and therefore ceased with the apostles.[114] But to John Wesley,

Middleton had contrived to "overthrow the whole Christian system,"[115] for the arguments that Middleton had used to criticize the church fathers could well be turned against the New Testament.

NEW DIRECTIONS

John Wesley's view of the potentially damaging effects of Middleton's work was substantially endorsed by that astute critic of the eighteenth century, Sir Leslie Stephen, who saw in Middleton's approach an anticipation of the historical-critical method. He observed that

> Middleton's covert assault upon the orthodox dogmas was incomparably the most effective of the whole deist controversy. It indicates the approach of a genuine historical method. Middleton was the first to see, though he saw dimly, that besides the old hypotheses of supernatural interference and human imposture, a third and more reasonable alternative may be suggested. The conception is beginning to appear, though still obscured by many crude assumptions, of a really scientific investigation of the history of religious developments. Middleton is thus the true precursor of Gibbon.[116]

The contribution of Edward Gibbon (1737–1794), the great historian of the Roman empire, to the debate about miracles was indirect. Gibbon's *History of the Decline and Fall of the Roman Empire* appeared in six volumes between 1776 and 1788. It has been said that Gibbon's combination of Locke's commonsense approach to philosophy and religion, Montesquieu's view of history, and Hume's skepticism led him to seek cultural, social, and political causes in history rather than supernatural ones.[117] With elegant irony he alluded to the supernatural claims of Christianity, while repeatedly offering alternative explanations. Gibbon notes five causes explaining the growth of Christianity:

> I. The inflexible, and, if we may use the expression, the intolerant zeal of the Christians, derived, it is true, from the Jewish religion, but purified from the narrow and unsocial spirit, which, instead of inviting, had deterred the Gentiles from embracing the law of Moses. II. The doctrine of the future life, improved by every additional circumstance which could give weight and efficacy to that important truth. III. The miraculous powers ascribed to the primitive church. IV. The pure and austere morals of the Christians. V. The union and discipline of the Christian republic, which gradually formed an independent and increasing state in the heart of the Roman empire.[118]

It hardly needs to be stressed that for Gibbon the *beliefs* of the early Christians about such matters as the future life and miracles were the important factor. It was the beliefs that affected attitudes quite apart from the question of whether such beliefs were well founded.

In language reminiscent of David Hume[119] and Conyers Middleton, Gibbon observed that:

The supernatural gifts, which even in this life were ascribed to the Christians above the rest of mankind, must have conduced to their own comfort, and very frequently to the conviction of infidels. Besides the occasional prodigies, which might sometimes be effected by the immediate interposition of the Deity when he suspended the laws of nature in the service of religion, the Christian church, from the time of the apostles and their first disciples, has claimed an uninterrupted succession of miraculous powers, the gift of tongues, of vision, and of prophesy, the power of expelling daemons, of healing the sick, and of raising the dead. The knowledge of foreign languages was frequently communicated to the contemporaries of Irenaeus, though himself was left to struggle with the difficulties of a barbarous dialect, whilst he preached the gospel to the natives of Gaul.[120]

Gibbon acknowledged the existence of Middleton's *Free Inquiry*, but his disassociation from Middleton's stance has the air of the disingenuousness of someone who is praising with faint damns. He noted that Middleton's work had met with "the most favourable reception from the public," while exciting a great scandal among divines. Indeed, the University of Oxford had gone to the length of conferring degrees on Middleton's opponents. Nevertheless, Gibbon professed a somewhat different outlook:

Our sentiments on this subject will be much less influenced by any particular arguments, than by our habits of study and reflection; and, above all, by the degree of the evidence which we have accustomed ourselves to require for the proof of a miraculous event. The duty of an historian does not call upon him to interpose his private judgment in this nice and important controversy; but he ought not to dissemble the difficulty of adopting such a theory as may reconcile the interest of religion with that of reason, of making a proper application of that theory, and of defining with precision the limits of that happy period, exempt from error and from deceit, to which we might be disposed to extend the gift of supernatural powers.[121]

Today this remark sounds like a disclaimer on the part of the historian of the responsibility for determining the truth of what happened in history. As it was, Gibbon contented himself with giving ironical descriptions of events as reported, noting the increasing predisposition of Christians to believe in miracles, the evident conflict of miracles with the laws of nature, the widespread disagreement among Christians as to when (if ever) miraculous gifts ceased in the church, the uncritical attitude of some of Gibbon's own contemporaries to the allegedly miraculous in more recent times, and the paradoxical spectacle presented by contemporary believers who remain skeptical about the miraculous in their own time but are willing to accept accounts of it in days gone by. All these points had already been made by Middleton and Hume. Gibbon's conclusion on the subject was in fact an amplified echo of Hume's contention that the *Christian Religion* not only was at first attended with miracles, but even at this day cannot be believed by any reasonable person without one. Mere reason is insufficient to convince us of its veracity: And whoever is moved by *Faith* to assent to it, is conscious of a continued miracle in his own person, which subverts all the principles of his understanding, and gives him a determination to believe what is most contrary to custom and experience.[122]

As Gibbon put it:

The real or imaginary prodigies, of which they so frequently conceived themselves to be the objects, the instruments or the spectators, very happily disposed them to adopt with the same ease, but with far greater justice, the authentic wonders of the evangelic history; and thus miracles that exceeded not the measure of their own experience inspired them with the most lively assurance of mysteries which were acknowledged to surpass the limits of their understanding. It is this deep impression of supernatural truths which has been so much celebrated under the name of faith; a state of mind described as the surest pledge of divine favor and of future felicity, and recommended as the first, or perhaps the only merit of a Christian. According to the more rigid doctors, the moral virtues, which may be equally practised by infidels, are destitute of any value or efficacy in the work of our justification.[123]

Middleton and Gibbon wrote as practicing historians offering accounts of the course of events in the early centuries that relegated the supernatural to the status of improbable beliefs entertained by ignorant enthusiasts. But it was David Hume who offered a philosophical rationale for banishing the miraculous from the realm of history.

As the supernatural was progressively banished from history in the name of scientific history, it was also increasingly banished from the realm of natural science. These two developments were interrelated, for historians operated with a notion at the back of their minds of what was scientifically possible. Whereas the deists had judged miracles by the criterion of rationality, later thinkers operated increasingly with a view of the universe as a mechanism, determined by time and space, in which everything happened in accordance with the fixed laws of time and space. A key figure in this development was Sir Isaac Newton.

Newton (1642–1727) was a slightly junior contemporary and friend of John Locke. He is remembered in the annals of science for his formulation of the law of gravitation, his discovery (apparently simultaneously with Leibniz) of the differential calculus, and for making the first correct analysis of white light. His formulation of the laws of motion helped to establish the mechanical view of the universe that dominated physics from his own day to modern times. Newton was one of the great universal geniuses of all time. His scientific work did not prevent him from taking a keen interest in theology. His various private papers on the subject show him to have been highly critical of the orthodoxy of the later creeds but not of the Bible itself.[124]

Newton believed that time and space had an absolute fixed character.[125] If this is so, it would seem that everything that happens within time and space must be determined by the characteristics of time and space.[126] Newton himself thought of infinite space as the divine sensorium in which God perceives his creatures.[127] He was, however, anxious to point out that we should not think of the world "as the body of God, or the several parts thereof as parts of God."[128] Newton did not engage in any public debate on miracles. But his private *Common Place Book* contains the following observations:

> A man may imagine things that are false, but he can only understand things that are true, for if the things be false the apprehension of them is not understanding.

> For miracles are so called not because they are works of God, but because they happen seldom, and for that reason create wonder. If they should happen constantly according to certain laws impressed upon the nature of things, they would no longer be wonders or miracles, but might be considered in philosophy as a part of the phenomena of nature [notwithstanding their being the effects of the laws impressed upon nature by the powers of God] notwithstanding that the cause of their causes might be unknown to us.[129]

Newton's scientific world view and its bearing on miracles was the subject of a celebrated eighteenth-century debate that was carried on at long range between the eminent German philosopher and scientist, G. W. Leibniz, and Samuel Clarke. Clarke, whose views on miracles we noted earlier, was an enthusiastic Newtonian. In 1717 he published *A Collection of papers which passed between the late Learned Mr. Leibnitz and Dr. Clarke in the years 1715 and 1716 relating to the Principles of Natural Philosophy and Religion, With an Appendix.*[130] Leibniz rejected Newton's view of space as an organ that God uses in order to perceive things, for this suggested to him that things do not altogether depend on God and may not have been produced by him. He went on to complain that

> Sir Isaac Newton, and his followers, have also a very odd opinion concerning the work of God. According to their doctrine, God Almighty wants to wind up his watch from time to time: otherwise it would cease to move. He had not, it seems, sufficient foresight to make it a perpetual motion. Nay, the machine of God's making, is so imperfect, according to these gentlemen; that he is obliged to clean it now and then by an extraordinary concourse, and even to mend it, as a clockmaker mends his work; who must consequently be so much the more unskilful a workman, as he is oftener obliged to mend his work and to set it right. According to my opinion, the same force and vigour remains always in the world, and only passes from one part of matter to another, agreeably to the laws of nature, and the beautiful pre-established order. And I hold, that when God works miracles, he does not do it in order to supply the wants of nature, but those of grace. Whoever thinks otherwise, must needs have a very mean notion of the wisdom and power of God.[131]

Clarke replied that God's continued involvement in the world was not due to some defect in creation:

> Consequently, 'tis not a diminution, but the true glory of his workmanship, that nothing is done without his continual government and inspection. The notion of the world's being a great machine, going on without the interposition of God, as a clock continues to go without the assistance of a clockmaker; is the notion of materialism and fate, and tends, (under pretence of making God a *supramundane intelligence,*) to exclude providence and God's government in reality out of the world.[132]

The discussion of the nature of time and space went on throughout the Leibniz-Clarke correspondence. Its bearing on science, religion, and philosophy grew as time went on. In France, Voltaire popularized Newtonianism in his *Elements of the Philosophy of Newton* (1741). He professed himself to be a theist, though the difference between theism and deism in his thought is barely perceptible. Just as a watch proves a watch-maker, so a universe proves a God. It was the altruistic God of deism that was the object of Voltaire's belief rather than the God of the Bible. Like the English deists, Voltaire consistently refrained from attacking the deity, but remorselessly assailed priestcraft and the church. He was intimately familiar with the corpus of their writings, and was personally responsible for propagating their ideas on the continent of Europe.[133] The deism of Voltaire, like that of Jean-Jacques Rousseau, fed the growing opposition to institutional Christianity in France, but was in turn devoured by the atheism of the *philosophes.*

In Germany the ideas of the British deists found a foothold particularly after the accession in 1740 of Frederick the Great, the first freethinking European monarch. Their writings, together with those of their opponents, enjoyed considerable circulation and pioneered biblical criticism.[134] Their ideas were absorbed and restated by H. S. Reimarus, who in Germany is credited with being the initiator of the quest of the historical Jesus. The philosophy of Immanuel Kant, which in one way or another has affected all later philosophical thought and a good deal of theology as well, was a form of deism.

In America deism exerted a profound influence on the minds of Benjamin Franklin, George Washington, Thomas Jefferson, and numerous other lesser figures who helped to create the United States. Deism found expression in Ethan Allen's *Reason the Only Oracle of Man, Or a Compenduous System of Natural Religion* (1784), which blasted institutional Christianity and ridiculed the Bible.[135] Ten years later Thomas Paine sought to rescue deism from French atheism and at the same time present Christianity as a species of atheism in *The Age of Reason: Being an Investigation of True and Fabulous Theology* (2 volumes, 1794-96). Thomas Jefferson compiled for private use a volume that came to be known as *The Jefferson Bible.* Jefferson himself called it *The Life and Morals of Jesus of Nazareth Extracted textually from the Gospels in Greek, Latin, French & English.*[136] It was literally a scissors and paste production, thought to have been put together around

1819, consisting largely of passages relating the moral teaching of Jesus. Jefferson had no compunction about cutting verses in half in order to eliminate the supernatural. He included the birth narratives, but cut out the reference to the Virgin Birth and the Holy Spirit. He likewise excised all mention of the Spirit in the account of Jesus' baptism. The temptation story was omitted. The work concludes with the burial of Jesus and no hint of the resurrection. Although Jefferson never published his work, he made at one time a similar compilation that he proposed to call *The Philosophy of Jesus of Nazareth,* which he envisaged "for the use of the Indians, unembarrassed with matters of fact or faith beyond the level of their comprehensions."[137] On a popular level an attempt was made by the blind, ex-Baptist preacher Elihu Palmer to spread deism among the lower classes.

In the rise and fall of deism on the Continent and in North America there was a delayed action. By 1750, when deism was getting a foothold in France and Germany, British deism was already a spent force. And it was only in the last quarter of the eighteenth century that deism came to the fore in North America. Its rise coincided with the new golden age of Freemasonry with its altruistic humanitarian ideals combined with esoteric ritual, which provided some compensation for the eighteenth-century enlightened man's loss of the supernatural. Deism was impeded, however, by several factors. Intellectually it was undermined by reasoned orthodoxy, which found its most formidable champion in Bishop Butler, and by the skepticism of David Hume. Perhaps Hume's contribution to the demise of deism has been overestimated. His discussion of miracles was in many ways a refined, urbane restatement of the deists' own case, and the work that most undermined the foundations of deism, the *Dialogues Concerning Natural Religion* (1779), was published three years after Hume's death.[138] By that time deism in Britain was a thing of the past.

In a sense deism was a parasite faith. It had to feed on the very thing that it attacked in order to survive. It could not compete with thoroughgoing skepticism on the one hand or with orthodoxy on the other. Moreover, orthodoxy received a new lease of life through the Great Awakening in North America, the evangelical revival in Britain, and Pietism in Germany. But the ideas of the deists contained the seeds of later liberalism, and their strident criticism of the Bible prepared a way for others to follow in their footsteps.

4

DAVID HUME

If David Hume's essay "Of Miracles" was temporarily obscured in his own day by the clamor provoked by Middleton's *Free Inquiry*, posterity has made more than ample redress. No work on miracles penned in the seventeenth, eighteenth, or nineteenth centuries receives greater attention today than Hume's slim essay. The piece itself consists of scarcely more than twenty pages, tucked into his *Enquiry Concerning Human Understanding* (1748). The apparent irrelevance of the essay to the work at large prompted the Victorian editor of Hume's *Enquiries* to suppose that Hume's motive was thirst for notoriety.[1] The *Enquiry* had been preceded by *A Treatise of Human Nature* (1739). Neither work satisfied Hume's self-professed "ruling Passion," his "Love of literary Fame,"[2] though this was partly met in later years by the success of his *History of Great Britain from the Invasion of Julius Caesar to the Revolution of 1688* (6 volumes, 1754-62). Already in 1745 Hume had been passed over for professorship at Edinburgh, and six years later his candidacy at Glasgow fared no better. After 1751 Hume published nothing new on philosophy. His celebrated *Dialogues Concerning Natural Religion* appeared posthumously in 1777 in accordance with the wishes expressed in his will.

David Hume lived between 1711 and 1776. Today his place in the history of philosophy is secure, though it is still disputed whether he was truly great or only a "very clever man."[3] The same may be said of his essay on miracles. Moreover, in the light of what we have seen so far of seventeenth- and early eighteenth-century discussion of miracles, it is clear that Hume's arguments were far from being original.

We can best assess the significance of Hume's essay if we summarize it first and then discuss various issues that it raises. Hume divided the essay into two parts. Part I is devoted to what may be called *a priori* considerations culminating in the conclusion that a miracle is a scientific impossibility. From what we know of the laws of nature miracles just cannot happen. Part II is devoted to what may be called *a posteriori* considerations, concerning the type of testimony advanced in favor of miracles, concluding that it is always dubious and never strong enough to overthrow the scientific considerations. Miracles can never provide a satisfactory basis for religious belief.

THE IMPOSSIBILITY OF VIOLATIONS OF LAWS OF NATURE

Part I of Hume's discussion begins with a series of general observations and considerations. At first sight they may appear to have only oblique reference to the subject of miracles, but the intention is to provide a basis for questioning testimony to the miraculous. Hume began by seizing on a remark by the late Archbishop of Canterbury, Dr. John Tillotson, noting that the authority of Scripture and tradition depends ultimately on the eyewitness testimony of the apostles. Such observations continue to be commonplace among Christian apologists, on the supposition that they help to establish the historicity and direct personal relevance of Christianity. But for Hume, Tillotson's remark was an admission of weakness that was to be exploited:

> Our evidence, then, for the truth of the *Christian* religion is less than the evidence for the truth of our senses; because, even in the first authors of our religion, it was no greater; and it is evident it must diminish in passing from them to their disciples; nor can anyone rest such confidence in their testimony, as in the immediate object of his senses.[4]

Hume's contention has not gone unchallenged, as we shall see. But for the moment it is important to underscore two points. The first is that the main thrust of Hume's argument was not concerned with the possibility of miracles as such, but with the truth-claims of Christianity as a historical religion based on supernatural events. His essay is thus a comment on the debate that had been going on since the time of Locke and the deists—that is, the debate on the question of whether Christianity could be demonstrated to be true by appealing to history, and in particular the historicity of Jesus' miracles and resurrection. The second point to be underscored is the precise nature of Hume's argument. In it everything turns on the testimony of the senses and how such testimony should be evaluated. The first Christians believed ostensibly because they were persuaded by the testimony of their own senses. Belief on the part of subsequent generations is dependent upon that testimony. On that basis, Hume concludes that the evidence for past alleged events can never be greater than it was for the first eyewitnesses. With the passage of time and the attendant questions and uncertainties as to the veracity of that testimony, there arises a corresponding uncertainty as to the degree of credence that may be placed upon such testimony by a subsequent age, especially (as Hume is about to argue) if that testimony is contradicted by the world view of that later age. This led Hume to make the following claim on behalf of his essay:

> Nothing is so convenient as a decisive argument . . . which must at least *silence* the most arrogant bigotry and superstition, and free us from their impertinent solicitations. I flatter myself, that I have discovered an argu-

ment of a like nature, which, if just, will, with the wise and learned be an everlasting check to all kinds of superstitious delusion, and consequently, will be useful as long as the world endures. For so long, I presume, will the accounts of miracles and prodigies be found in all history, sacred and profane.[5]

The real thrust of this claim has not always been appreciated. Hume is not claiming here to have demonstrated the impossibility of miracles. His logic does not preclude the possibility of some kind of intuitive acceptance of them, "brought home to every one's breast, by the immediate operation of the Holy Spirit."[6] Such claims might have been made by pious followers of the evangelical revival or by eighteenth-century French Catholic enthusiasts whom he knew about through his visits to France, where reports of contemporary miracles were rife.[7] Hume clearly had not much time for such private revelations, and in any case such revelations would have removed the alleged miracles from the arena of public inspection and in so doing would have deprived it of any apologetic value as an objective historical event. Hume's argument is, as Antony Flew has pointed out,[8] essentially *defensive*. It has the triple aim of highlighting (1) the insuperable difficulties of demonstrating from history the historical veracity of miracles; (2) the consequent impossibility of using miracles in apologetics in order to demonstrate the truth of any religion; and (3) the further consequence that, while miracles may be the object of faith, they can never be its basis. In other words, although Hume could not prove conclusively that a miracle could not happen, he was satisfied that no one could prove that any miracle had actually happened.

In line with the empiricist tradition and the growing prestige of natural science, Hume insisted that experience is "our only guide in reasoning concerning matters of fact."[9] Nevertheless, experience is "not altogether infallible." Nature is not always predictable. Moreover, "all effects follow not with like certainty from their supposed causes." In making this point, Hume was not admitting an indeterminism in the processes of nature. Rather, he was insisting upon our ignorance of the full range of natural causes. There is, therefore, an element of uncertainty even in scientific thinking, which Hume expressed in the following account of what he conceived to be scientific method:

A wise man, therefore, proportions his belief to the evidence. In such conclusions as are founded on an infallible experience, he expects the event with the last degree of assurance, and regards his past experience as a full *proof* of the future existence of that event. In other cases, he proceeds with more caution: He weighs the opposite experiments: He considers which side is supported by the greater number of experiments: to that side he inclines, with doubt and hesitation; and when at last he fixes his judgement, the evidence exceeds not what we properly call *probability*. . . . A hundred instances or experiments on one side, and fifty on another, afford a doubtful expectation of any event; though a hundred uniform experiments, with only one that is contradictory, reasonably beget a pretty strong degree of assurance. In all cases, we must balance the opposite experiments, where they are opposite, and deduct the smaller number from the greater, in order to know the exact force of the superior evidence.[10]

At this point Hume recalled the notorious argument about causation that he had propounded in his *Treatise of Human Nature* and had restated earlier in the *Enquiry*. He now claimed that it was "a general maxim, that no objects have any discoverable connexion together, and that all the inferences, which we can draw from one to another, are founded merely on our experience of their constant and regular conjunction."[11] Hume's point is that we do not actually see causes themselves but only the succession of events. As he had already explained in an earlier section of the *Enquiry*,

we may define a cause to be *an object, followed by another, and where all the objects similar to the first are followed by objects similar to the second.* Or in other words *where, if the first object had not been, the second never had existed.* The appearance of a cause always conveys the mind, by a customary transition, to the idea of the effect. We may, therefore, suitably to this experience, form another definition of cause, and call it, *an object followed by another, and whose appearance always conveys the thought to that other.*[12]

Causal connection is something that "we *feel* in the mind"; it is the product of the "imagination."[13]

On this basis, it might be thought that there would be no intrinsic reason for regarding one event as more or less miraculous or wonderful than any other, since the human mind is not in a position to demonstrate its actual causes. The logical implications of such a position would be to call in question the whole structure of scientific explanation and indeed of our everyday behavior. For both scientific explanation and everyday behavior presuppose that some events are causally connected and others are not. At the same time it should be noted that to draw out the logic of Hume's position in this way would not help the Christian apologist, for part of the significance of miracles consists in the fact that miracles are by definition abnormal events, and by that very fact stand out from the regular course of normal events.

In any case, Hume did not pause to allow his readers time to ponder such reflections. Instead, he pressed on to develop an argument that in later times came to be known as the principle of analogy.[14] While Hume was not prepared to speak of causality as inherent in objects themselves, he was (as we have already noted) anxious to stress our *experience* of "constant and regular conjunction." It was on the basis of this regular experience that Hume insisted that all testimony should be evaluated.

And as the evidence, derived from witnesses and human testimony, is founded on past experience, so it varies with experience, and is regarded either as a *proof* or a *probability,* according as the conjunction between any particular kind of report and any kind of object has been found to be constant or variable.[15]

> The reason why we place any credit in witnesses and historians, is not derived from any connexion, which we perceive *a priori,* between testimony and reality, but because we are accustomed to find a conformity between them.[16]

In other words, the crucial test in evaluating any report of an alleged event is to ask how probable that event is in the light of our experience of the world. We clearly do not have direct access to events in the past. We have to employ some criterion that will enable us to ascertain its probability and distinguish, as far as we can, true events from imagined or fabricated events. We should ask, therefore, whether there are any analogies between the alleged event and our experience.

There are at least two kinds of factors involved here: events and evidence. On the one hand, we should ask whether there is any analogy or similarity between the reported event and events in our own experience of the way in which events normally happen. If there is, the alleged event is at least credible. On the other hand, we should also evaluate the evidence in the light of our understanding of evidence. As a matter of fact, Hume confined evidence to spoken or written testimony. Here, too, we have to look for analogies between what we know of human nature and what we can discern in the witnesses:

> Were not the memory tenacious to a certain degree, had not men commonly an inclination to truth and a principle of probity; were they not sensible to shame, when detected in a falsehood: Were not these, I say, discovered by *experience* to be qualities, inherent in human nature, we should never repose the least confidence in human testimony. A man delirious, or noted for falsehood and villainy, has no manner of authority with us.[17]

Hume's readiness to acknowledge on the basis of experience "qualities, inherent in human nature" and reject on the same basis causality inherent in objects raises serious questions about his consistency as a thinker and the limitations of his philosophical approach. At the same time, Hume's weaknesses should not be allowed to obscure the fact that the Christian apologist who wishes to establish the historical credibility of miracles has, in fact, to appeal to the same basic principles that Hume appeals to. On the one hand, he has to contrast the miracle with the events of our normal experience in order to distinguish its unusualness. Miracles thus presuppose a regular uniformity of events, in order for them to stand out as miracles. On the other hand, the character and motivation of the witnesses to an alleged miracle has to be examined against the background of what we know of human character and motivation, if we are to be reassured that they are telling the truth and that their witness is not mistaken.

With this we are brought to the central issue in Hume's argument. His case amounts to a flat rejection of miracles on the grounds of their incompatibility with the laws of nature:

A miracle is a violation of the laws of nature; and as a firm and unalterable experience has established these laws, the proof against a miracle, from the very nature of the fact, is as entire as any argument from experience can possibly be imagined.[18]

The argument immediately raises numerous questions. What is a law of nature? Is Hume entitled to speak of laws of nature in the light of his previous account of causation? Whose "firm and unalterable experience" has established these laws? Has not Hume's flow of rhetoric obscured the distinction between the difficulty in believing in miracles on the grounds of their abnormality and the absolute impossibility of their ever occurring? In doing this, has he not shifted his position from a defensive one to an offensive one? Above all, has not Hume simply handed back the problem of miracles disguised as a negative answer? We shall postpone an examination of such questions until we have completed our review of Hume's essay. In the meantime we should note two further points that arise in Hume's discussion as he completes Part I of his essay.

The first of these points is his discussion of the case of the "Indian prince" who refused to believe in ice, on the grounds that his experience of nature did not include conditions under which water solidified. It was a case discussed by Locke, Sherlock, Butler, and others.[19] Hume contended that the prince "reasoned justly," for the effects of cold "bore so little analogy to those events, of which he had constant and uniform experience. Though they were not contrary to his experience, they were not conformable to it."[20] With a wider experience, the prince would have been able to accept reports of ice. This, of course, raises the question of whether our experience can ever be so sufficiently broad as to enable us to pronounce a definitive negative verdict. But it also raises the question of whether the alleged event could ever be seen as a suspension of the laws of nature (or conceivably the laws of God), or whether it should be seen as an instance of a law of which hitherto we have had no direct experience or knowledge. The case of the solidification of water is clearly an instance of the latter. Hume went on to concede that "the raising of a house or a ship into the air" would be "a visible miracle," whereas the raising of a feather would not.[21] Today airships and spaceships belong to the common facts of experience, thanks to modern technology and a greater understanding of chemistry and physics.

The second of these points is to note Hume's further definition of a miracle, which he gives in a footnote, in which he includes mention of agency. Thus he defines a miracle as *"a transgression of a law of nature by a particular volition of the Deity, or by the interposition of some invisible agent."*[22] This second definition has been called in question, not least for its apparent admission that agents other than God could perform miracles. From Hume's standpoint such an admission would be important, for it would be consistent with his contention that causes cannot be known from their effects. Hence, even if a miracle were to happen, Hume would not be prepared to concede that it could be traced to God as its cause. Moreover, the argument would suit Hume's contention that miracles cannot be used to establish the truth of any given religion. But quite apart from such considerations, Hume's second definition allows for the point generally conceded by theologians, that Satan and demons could also perform wonders. In essence, the definition does not differ from the more orthodox definitions given in the eighteenth century, such as that by Samuel Clarke, a disciple of Sir Isaac Newton. In some respects he was critical of John Locke, but his definition of a miracle followed the lines laid down by Locke, and for that matter by Calvin.

> The true *Definition* of a Miracle, in the *Theological* Sense of the Word, is this; that it is work effected in a manner *unusual,* or different from the common and regular Method of Providence, by the interposition either of God himself, or of some Intelligent Agent superiour to Man, for the Proof or Evidence of some particular Doctrine, or in attestation of the Authority of some particular Person. And if a Miracle so worked, be not opposed by some plainly superior Power; nor be brought to attest a Doctrine either *contradictory* in itself, or *vicious* in its consequences; (a Doctrine of which kind, no Miracles in the World can be sufficient to prove;) then the Doctrine so attested must necessarily be lookt upon as Divine, and the Worker of the Miracle entertained as having infallibly a Commission from God.[23]

Clarke went on to argue that the miracles of Jesus fully met these stipulations and thus afforded a "compleat *Demonstration* of our Saviour's being a Teacher sent from God."

Clarke raises several issues that deserve attention. For the time being, we must confine our observations to noting that "those invisible Agents" that work miracles are, for Clarke, agents of God. His point is to grant the feasibility of God using intermediary agents in the working of miracles, just as he uses intermediary agents in his other works. In the case of a miracle, the work is of such a character that it could not be performed by a human, and therefore it points to God as its ultimate source. It may also be noted that Clarke's definition anticipated some of Hume's argument in Part II of his discussion of miracles. Or conversely, it could be said that Hume's argument in Part II about contradictory miracles was designed to get around the point made here by Clarke. Certainly, Hume knew of Clarke from his student days, and Clarke figures several times in Hume's writings, especially in his *Dialogues*. Indeed, at the close of Hume's life he professed to James Boswell, who was anxiously inquiring about his spiritual state, that "he had never entertained any belief in Religion since he began to read Locke and Clarke."[24]

Hume rounded off Part I of his discussion of miracles by reverting to his earlier defensive position, insisting that one should follow the same principle of weighing evidence that one follows in science and in determining all disputed questions. In this case one should ask which is the greater miracle—the reported miraculous event or the possibility that the report might be mistaken or fraudulent:

I weigh one miracle against the other; and according to the superiority, which I discover, I pronounce my decision, and always reject the greater miracle. If the falsehood of his testimony would be more miraculous, than the event which he relates; then, and not till then, can he pretend to command my belief or opinion.[25]

In other words, Hume is saying that in the light of his view of the constancy and uniformity of nature, it is practically impossible to prove to him from testimony the occurrence of a miracle. The difficulties of proof will, he suspects, always be too great to persuade him that the regularities of nature have been supernaturally interfered with.

THE WEAKNESS OF HISTORICAL TESTIMONY TO MIRACLES

Part II of Hume's argument is devoted to what we have called *a posteriori* considerations. It consists of an examination of the type of testimony adduced by apologists in support of miracles and has four main points.

The first point is Hume's contention that the witnesses to alleged miracles are unworthy of credence on the grounds of incompetence, motivation, or general unverifiability:

There is not to be found, in all history, any miracle attested by a sufficient number of men, of such unquestioned good-sense, education, and learning, as to secure us against all delusion in themselves; of such undoubted integrity, as to place them beyond all suspicion of any design to deceive others; of such credit and reputation in the eyes of mankind, as to have a great deal to lose in case of their being detected in any falsehood; and at the same time, attesting facts performed in such a public manner and in so celebrated a part of the world, as to render detection unavoidable: All which circumstances are requisite to give us a full assurance in the testimony of men.[26]

Having made this round assertion, Hume proceeded forthwith to his second point, which concerns the human propensity to love gossip, to exaggerate, and to enlarge upon the truth:

There is no kind of report which rises so easily, and spreads so quickly, especially in country places and provincial towns, as those concerning marriages; insomuch that two young persons of equal condition never see each other twice, but the whole neighbourhood immediately join them together. The pleasure of telling a piece of news so interesting, of propagating it, and of being the first reporters of it, spreads the intelligence. And this is so well known, that no man of sense gives attention to these reports, till he find them confirmed by some greater evidence. Do not the same passions, and others still stronger, incline the generality of mankind to believe and report, with the greatest vehemence and assurance, all religious miracles?[27]

Without pausing to give an answer to this rhetorical question or even to consider whether any answer but a resounding affirmative one could conceivably be given to it, Hume turned to his third point. This was not so much an argument as an observation creating "a strong presumption against all supernatural and miraculous relations." Here he remarked that such occurrences

> are observed chiefly to abound among ignorant and barbarous nations; or if a civilized people has ever given admission to any of them, that people will be found to have received them from ignorant and barbarous ancestors, who transmitted them with that inviolable sanction and authority, which always attend received opinions.[28]

With tongue in cheek Hume illustrated this by alluding to the history of ancient Greece and Rome. But he clearly had in mind the learned divines of the eighteenth century who had never witnessed a miracle themselves in the centers of Western science and scholarship, but who staunchly defended the biblical miracles wrought among the illiterate Galilean peasantry.

Hume's fourth and final point was set out at considerably more length. In essence it was Hume's contention that the miracles of rival religions cancel each other out.

> Every miracle, therefore, pretended to have been wrought in any of these religions (and all of them abound in miracles), as its direct scope is to establish the particular system to which it is attributed; so has it the same force, though more indirectly, to overthrow every other system. In destroying a rival system, it likewise destroys the credit of those miracles, on which that system was established; so that all the prodigies of different religions are to be regarded as contrary facts, and the evidences of these prodigies, whether weak or strong, as opposite to each other.[29]

This was in fact the copestone of Hume's entire argument. At the same time it was a kind of safety-net. For even if miracles could be proved to be true, nothing conclusive could be proved from them.

Again there is a certain tongue-in-cheek quality about Hume's development of this theme. He clearly has in mind the attempts of Christian apologists to prove the truth of Christian beliefs by appealing to the miracles and resurrection of Jesus. Hume studiously refrained from mentioning New Testament miracles. But his choice of examples appears calculated to offend Protestant susceptibilities, either by the fact that they were drawn from pagan or Catholic sources or by the fact that they exhibit parallels with biblical miracles. The offense is hardly mitigated by the fact that Hume dismisses them as incredible. For by parity of reasoning, the biblical miracles would also have to be dismissed as incredible.

Among the cases that Hume discusses is Tacitus's account of the emperor Vespasian curing a blind man in Alexandria by means of his spittle and healing a lame man by the mere touch of his foot.[30] With added irony Hume insists that this is "one of the best attested miracles in all profane history." Echoing the arguments of Christian writers who are at pains to stress the probity of the evangelists and their subject, Hume stresses the gravity, solidity, and probity of the emperor and the character of Tacitus, "a contemporary writer, noted for candour and veracity, and withal, the greatest and most penetrating genius, perhaps, of all antiquity; and so free from any tendency to credulity that he even lies under the contrary imputation, of atheism and profaneness."[31] Well aware of the implication that this story comes as close as any account in antiquity to meeting the criteria that Hume has laid down, and the further implication that none of the evangelists came close to possessing such impeccable qualifications as objective historians, Hume was not prepared to believe the account.

Turning to more recent history, Hume noted the story of Cardinal de Retz, who was introduced to a man in Saragossa who had recovered a lost leg through rubbing the stump with holy oil. The cardinal rightly dismissed the story as impossible. In such cases, it is unnecessary to be able to disprove the testimony and to identify its falsehood. The very nature of the case makes the story incredible.[32] The same applies to the stories of the curing of the sick and giving hearing to the deaf and sight to the blind connected with the tomb of François de Pâris (whom he calls the Abbé Pâris), despite the fact that

> many of the miracles were immediately proved upon the spot, before judges of unquestioned integrity, attested by witnesses of credit and distinction, in a learned age, and on the most eminent theatre that is now in the world. Nor is this all: a relation of them was published and dispersed everywhere; nor were the *Jesuits,* though a learned body, supported by the civil magistrate, and determined enemies to those opinions, in whose favour the miracles were said to have been wrought, ever able distinctly to refute or detect them. Where shall we find such a number of circumstances, agreeing to the corroboration of one fact? And what have we to oppose to such a cloud of witnesses, but the absolute impossibility or miraculous nature of the events, which they relate? And this surely, in the eyes of all reasonable people, will alone be regarded as a sufficient refutation.[33]

The language here is replete with biblical allusions. The alleged miracles would seem to meet Hume's previously announced criteria. But Hume refuses point-blank to believe any of it on the grounds that it conflicts with his view of scientific possibility. The same applies to his crowning example, which was deliberately hypothetical and for that very reason all the more pointed:

> But suppose, that all the historians who treat of England should agree, that, on the first of January 1600, Queen Elizabeth died; that both before and after her death she was seen by her physicians and the whole court, as is usual with persons of rank; that the successor was acknowledged and proclaimed by parliament; and that, after being interred a month, she again appeared, resumed the throne, and governed England for three years: I must confess that I should be surprised at the occurrence of so many odd circumstances, but should not have the least inclination to believe so miraculous an event. I should not doubt of her pretended death,

and of those other public circumstances that followed it: I should only assert it to have been pretended, and that it neither was, nor possibly could be real.[34]

No one familiar with the Gospel narratives or the orthodox apologetics of Hume's day could have missed the point. Hume's example was deliberately constructed to stress and even exaggerate the arguments used to support the public verifiability of Jesus' death and resurrection. In the last analysis Hume insists that "the knavery and folly of men are such common phenomena, that I should rather believe the most extraordinary events to arise from their occurrence, than admit of so signal a violation of the laws of nature."[35]

Hume concludes by claiming that such reasoning serves "to confound those dangerous friends or disguised enemies of the *Christian Religion*, who have undertaken to defend it by the principles of human reason."[36] Once more with tongue in cheek, he insists that, "Our most holy religion is founded on *Faith*, not on reason; and it is a sure method of exposing it to put it to such a trial as it is, by no means, fitted to endure."[37] As a parting shot, Hume permitted himself to comment on the improbability of the miracles and events reported in the Pentateuch, and to remark that what he has said about miracles applies equally well to prophecy, since prophecies are a form of miracles and are used by apologists as proofs of revelation. In a final ironical gesture Hume concluded that miracles may be deemed to be credible—but only if one is prepared to abandon all the principles of understanding. And with this, Hume tied in his discussion of miracles to the central theme of his book:

> Upon the whole, we may conclude, that the *Christian Religion* not only was at first attended with miracles, but even at this day cannot be believed by any reasonable person without one. Mere reason is insufficient to convince us of its veracity: And whoever is moved by *Faith* to assent to it, is conscious of a continued miracle in his own person, which subverts all the principles of his understanding, and gives him a determination to believe what is most contrary to custom and experience.[38]

HUME'S LEGACY

The controversy engendered by Hume lies buried beneath the dust of centuries. The memory of the principal antagonists, who in their day were noted divines and ecclesiastics, is preserved in the volumes of the *Dictionary of National Biography* and books that chronicle the history of eighteenth-century thought.[39] The first reply was the Reverend Philip Skelton's *Ophiomaches; or Deism Revealed* (1749), which Hume himself commended for publication. Another early work was an *Essay on Mr. Hume's Essay on Miracles by William Adams, M.A., Chaplain to the Bishop of Llandaff* (1752). This was a temperate statement of the argument for the credibility of miracles on the grounds that God's omnipotence is the adequate cause of miracles. As there is no reason for doubting that God could intervene in the course of nature for worthy purposes, miracles may be believed in when there are adequate reasons to do so. Adam's work proved a stepping stone in the advancement of his career that led ultimately to the mastership of Pembroke College, Oxford, and the archdeaconry of Llandaff. Also appearing in 1752 was the *Criterion* by John Douglas, the future Bishop of Salisbury. His work took the form of a letter addressed to an anonymous correspondent, who afterward proved to be Adam Smith. A feature of Douglas's argument was his discussion of contemporary miracles, including Jansenist cures in France and cases of healing by the royal touch, performed by no less a person than Queen Anne. Douglas dismissed some of the instances as due to fraud; others were recorded late and thus the sources were historically unreliable. And other healings were ascribed to what today would be called psychosomatic factors. In short, Douglas was unwilling to give credence to modern miracles, but he readily accepted those recorded in the New Testament on the basis of the undisputed integrity and authenticity of the latter.

A notable Scottish reply came from the pen of George Campbell, whose *Dissertation on Miracles* (1762) was expanded from a sermon preached before the synod of the Presbyterian Church in 1760. Campbell was Principal of Marischal College, Aberdeen, and was a friend of Thomas Reid and other members of the Scottish commonsense school of philosophy. Hume was shown the text of Campbell's work before publication, and the two carried on an amicable correspondence. Hume acknowledged Campbell to be "certainly a very ingenious man, tho a little too zealous for a philosopher."[40] Campbell's tributes to Hume as a thinker offended the more zealous among the orthodox, but John Wesley spoke of Campbell's work as an "excellent Answer to David Hume's insolent Book against Miracles."[41]

John Wesley's verdict was shared by many of his contemporaries, and Campbell's book was long considered to be the ablest reply to Hume. Today we must take a less sanguine view and say that neither Hume nor Campbell resolved the question of how to determine the historicity of unique events in the past. Hume had proposed to judge testimony by asking whether the event testified to corresponded with our experience of the laws of nature. Campbell replied that, on Hume's logic, no one was entitled to believe in the existence of a person with black skin, unless one had actually seen such a person. Likewise, the new phenomenon of electricity would be as incredible as the raising of the dead. He charged Hume with undermining in principle the foundation of inductive reasoning and at the same time applying "numerical computation" to historical questions in an absurd way. For historical issues just could not be settled by appeal to the relative strengths of scientific laws. But if Hume's position was unsatisfactory, Campbell himself failed to give a convincing account of how one should distinguish between fact and fable in reports of the past. On the one hand, he revived Butler's argument that there is a high intrinsic improbability against such natural events as the appearance of a comet at any given time, and that miracles are only marginally more improbable.[42] On the other hand, he suggested that testimony could be confuted "principally in one of two ways; by contradictory evidence, or by evidence discrediting the character of the witnesses."[43] The word "principally" allows room for maneuver. Even so, a consistent story from the mouth of a generally well-intentioned person is of itself no guarantee of truth.

Another noted reply to Hume came from the pen of Hugh Farmer, who in his day was a popular dissenting preacher and teacher. In his *Dissertation on Miracles* (1771), Farmer wrestled with the question that had exercised Samuel Clarke and that Hume had sought to exploit: How could miracles be shown to be works of God and not merely superhuman but still finite works? Farmer (who in a subsequent tract defended himself against the charge of plagiarizing Abraham Le Moine's earlier *Treatise on Miracles*) distinguished between "providential" and "evidential" miracles. The former class included those performed by the heathen, but they were not sufficiently great or impressive as to warrant any evidential inferences. At the same time Farmer proposed what today would be called psychosomatic explanations for cases of demonology. His suggestion that Jesus and the disciples were aware of this true explanation of the phenomenon did little to assuage the opposition to his rationalizing.

When we turn from the eighteenth century to the present day, we find that the debate about Hume and miracles has scarcely abated. Perhaps the most notable admirer of Hume is Professor Antony Flew who has discussed Hume's argument at length in *Hume's Philosophy of Belief* (1961) and who has restated his position more briefly in his article on "Miracles" in *The Encyclopedia of Philosophy* (1967). As we have already noted, Flew argues that Hume's argument is really a *defensive* one.[44] Thus, it would be a mistake to think that Hume had proved (or even thought that he had proved) that miracles are impossible. At most Hume is claiming that no one can prove that any given miracle has happened, and hence one cannot appeal to miracles to prove the truth of any religion. In supporting his point, Flew has no difficulty in citing passages that bear this out. Certainly, there is nothing in Hume's argument to show that miracles could not happen. On the other hand, A.E. Taylor was surely right in his observation that "On the face of it, there would seem to be something amiss with reasoning which proceeds from the principle that 'a wise man proportions his belief to the evidence' to the conclusion that in a vast, if not too well defined, field, the 'wise man' will simply refuse to 'consider the evidence' at all."[45] For as Hume's argument proceeds, it becomes clear that no amount of historical evidence, past or present, is allowed to count, because miracles are judged to be violations of the laws of nature, and as such are by definition impossible.

Despite his conviction that Hume was essentially right, Flew acknowledges that Hume's essay is marked by "a rather wooden dogmatism of disbelief."[46] Hume tended to talk as if he and his enlightened contemporaries could speak "the last incorrigible word" about what was possible and what was impossible in the light of the laws of nature. This position effectively prevented Hume from entertaining as historical events occurrences that today would be attributed to abnormal psychology or psychosomatic factors.[47] In other words, the argument that was to weed out the supernatural from history turned out also to eliminate events that, for want of a better term, might be labeled as "natural." Perhaps Flew's complaint is a little unfair to Hume, for at the outset Hume acknowledged the statistical character of laws and allowed that some laws of nature were more certain than others. However, this qualification was immediately nullified by the contention that the laws of nature have been established by "a firm and unalterable experience." Moreover, Hume's claim that the Indian prince who refused to believe in ice "reasoned justly" contains the implicit acknowledgment that our expectations based on our experience of the world may turn out to be false in view of our limited knowledge. Nevertheless, such considerations would not ultimately destroy Hume's argument. For the recognition of abnormal psychology, psychosomatic factors, and limitation in our world views and understanding of nature do not amount to an admission of the supernatural into our everyday world. They merely enlarge our understanding of the natural, reminding us that we must not be premature in deciding what is naturally possible.

On the other hand, Hume did lapse into speaking of laws that had been established by "firm and unalterable experience" and of "the absolute impossibility or miraculous nature" of alleged contemporary miracles, despite attestation that met the criteria that Hume himself had been at pains to formulate. At bottom Hume rejects all historical testimony wherever it conflicts with his understanding of the laws of nature. His view of what is scientifically possible always wins out, however impressive the historical testimony might be. In adopting this position, Hume epitomized the skepticism that began with Spinoza and characterizes the rejection of the supernatural to the present day. A. E. Taylor has detected a fundamental confusion of thought in Hume's argument. He summarizes it in the following way:

> No testimony to a "miracle" has ever amounted to a probability, much less to a proof, and even if the testimony, in any case, did amount to proof, it would be opposed by another proof from "the very nature of the fact which it would endeavour to establish". Here, as it seems to me, confusion of thought reaches a maximum. To know that it is a fact that no such testimony *has* ever amounted to a probability, we must, of course, have examined the amount and character of the testimony, and thus have made it a duty to do the very things that Hume originally proposed to show superfluous.[48]

In claiming that "a firm and unalterable experience" has established the laws of nature, Hume proceeds to dismiss the testimony of those claiming to have a different experience. This point raises a series of questions that are important for the skeptic and the believer alike.

Hume's rejection of miracles in the name of the laws of nature is, to say the least, paradoxical. Both his *Treatise of Human Nature* and his *Enquiry Concerning Human Understanding* contained extensive critiques of the concept of causation. We saw earlier how Hume drew on this in discussing miracles. On Hume's premises, as Taylor puts it, "Properly speaking, there are no laws of nature to be violated, but there are habits of expectation which any of us, as a fact, finds himself unable to break through."[49] If Hume's understanding of causation is correct, two consequences appear to follow. On the one hand, there is no reason to regard any event as more or, for that matter, less miraculous than any other. For on this basis we must confess that all events, so far as we can see, are random and are not governed by any causally related factors outside themselves. On the other hand, to speak of laws of nature is purely a habit of mind. The deterministic scientist, no less than the believer in the supernatural, is merely testifying to his inveterate habits of speaking.

It is a matter of debate whether Hume deliberately sought to criticize Newtonian science as well as orthodox apologetics.[50] But the claim that causation (however we define it) is no more than something that "we *feel* in the mind," a product of the "imagination," has the effect of undermining not only Newtonian science but contemporary science as well. Admittedly, causes are posited by the mind, reflecting imaginatively on what we perceive with our senses. Nevertheless, all scientific activity is predicated on the premise that scientific explanation provides an objective description, however approximate and subject to future correction, of objective processes that occur quite independently of whether they are observed or not. In point of fact, the net result of Hume's discussion of causation is not so much to call in question the rationality of science and our everyday assumptions as to draw attention to the inadequacy of Hume's position as an account of human knowledge. At the same time we should note that miracles can be regarded as miracles only against a background of the regular uniformities of nature. For unless miracles stand out in some way from the normal and expected course of events, they would remain indistinguishable from the ordinary. It would not therefore be in the interests of the apologist for miracles to abandon a scientific view of natural processes and the concept of laws.

Various writers have drawn attention to the nomological character of the propositions that describe scientific laws. A nomological proposition does not simply express conjunction and contingency; it contains an element of prediction and necessity. It does not say that, as a matter of fact, A happens to be B. Rather, it has the form: Any A must be B. As Flew points out, Hume failed to give an adequate account of the logical character of a law of nature.[51] Indeed, Flew argues that "the lack of an adequate conception of a law of nature would make it impossible for Hume himself to justify a distinction between the marvellous or the unusual and the truly miraculous, and that it prevented him from exploiting to the full his own distinctive conception of the opposition of proofs."[52] In Flew's view, the justification for giving the "scientific" ultimate precedence over the "historical" lies in the nomological character of scientific explanation. "Whatever falls within its scope is physically necessary, and what it precludes is physically impossible."[53]

But to make this point does not, in fact, resolve the issue; it merely restates the problem. In his much-discussed essay "The Miraculous," R. F. Holland complains that the "violation concept" of miracle that Hume propounds is both "unduly restrictive" and at the same time "not restrictive enough."[54] On the one hand, it does not allow for many events that believers call miracles, where it is possible to see natural and other factors. In such cases the miraculous does not lie in any violation or suspension of the natural but in a providential ordering of events in which the believer sees the hand of God. We shall examine Holland's "contingency" or "coincidence" concept of miracle in Chapter Seven. On the other hand, the mere definition of a miracle as a violation of the laws of nature is not in itself a disproof of the possibility of the alleged event occurring. Indeed, it is a definition of what conditions would have to be fulfilled for an event to be regarded as a miracle in this sense of the term. Such a miracle would have to be (1) empirically certain and (2) conceptually impossible.[55] It would have to be empirically certain in order to be regarded as an event at all, and it would have to be conceptually impossible in order to be distinguished from ordinary events or miracles that Holland would classify under the contingency concept.

The crucial question here is whether any given case can really be said to meet the two conditions stipulated by Holland. His own examples of levitation and a horse remaining alive for a considerable period without food would hypothetically meet the conditions. But because they are hypothetical examples, they leave the reader with the nagging feeling that it might prove impossible to provide a clear-cut actual case of a miracle that fulfills the necessary conditions. Hume resolved the dilemma by insisting that one could not have empirical certainty for that which was conceptually impossible. His *a priori* convictions about physical possibility undercut all serious consideration of any given case.

Several philosophers in the Humean tradition have attempted to refine Hume's argument by making it less dogmatic.[56] One way of doing this is to argue that we cannot completely eliminate the possibility that the testimony to any given miracle might be mistaken, fraudulent, or tampered with in some way by those who recorded it or passed it on for posterity. In other words, there are too many factors for human error to permit us to speak of certainty, especially in cases that happened long ago. Certainly we have no way of having some kind of rerun of past events that we could submit to controlled observation and testing. No doubt Hume was wrong in giving the impression that all alleged miracles were one of a kind, and therefore were unique. But even in cases that exhibit similar features or parallels with our experience today the qualifications that inevitably attach to historical reporting do not permit one to speak of absolute certainty on the basis of historical records. Thus, the philosopher in Hume's tradition continues to reserve the right to say that Holland's first condition—that the alleged miracle must be empirically certain—is never completely satisfied beyond all doubt.

Holland's second condition, that of conceptual impossibility, has provoked the rejoinder that this idea is constantly being revised. For Hume it was unthinkable that a ship or a house should be raised in the air. Today airships are part and parcel of everyday life. Admittedly an airship is a very different kind of thing from a house made of bricks and mortar. It remains as true today as it did in Hume's day that houses of bricks and mortar cannot levitate. On the other hand, modern knowledge of aerodynamics enables the construction of heavier-than-air machines capable of transporting hundreds of people at a time from one continent to another in a few hours. Clearly, it is not a case that any given thing that was conceptually impossible in one age can become conceptually possible in another. Rather, it is the case that certain kinds of things and processes may be seen to be conceptually possible in one age, because of actual instances of them, which in previous ages would have seemed absurd. What has changed is not the laws of nature but our understanding of them. What was previously thought to be law L has been revised to become L_1, L_2, L_3 (and so on) in order to embrace the apparent exceptions. Thus an event that at first sight appeared to be an instance of the violation concept of miracle and thus dismissed as an improbable story, contradicted by the laws of nature, might turn out to be an instance of something that comes within the compass of a wider understanding of reality. In so doing it has ceased to become an example of the violation concept and has become an instance of the contingency concept.

This point is not substantially altered if it be argued that modern science is concerned not only with the formulation of laws but also with different levels of explanation. In this case, the word "law" might be said to function as a kind of shorthand to cover scientific explanation generally. The point could be reformulated in terms of explanation E, revised as E_1, E_2, E_3 (and so on) in the light of more comprehensive understanding.

To some this might seem like a radical transformation of the whole idea of the miraculous. But it may be noted that such a view is in line with Augustine's definition of a miracle as "whatever appears that is difficult or unusual above the hope and power of those who wonder"[57] and that of Bishop Butler and John Locke who thought of a miracle as a "sensible operation, which being above the comprehension of the spectator, and in his opinion contrary to the established course of nature, is taken by him to be divine."[58] Both these definitions are open-ended in that they do not preclude future explanation and identification of operative factors. Such considerations have led David Basinger to conclude that since we can never assume total knowledge of all the natural causal patterns that God has used in any given case, "it becomes difficult even for the theist to claim that an event does not in fact have a scientific explanation. This problem can be easily

circumvented in the present context if one does not make scientific inexplicability a requirement for miraculous occurrences.''[59]

Grace M. Jantzen, on the other hand, still wishes to hold the door open
for the more traditional view of miracles. She asks:

> Given that scientific investigation is encouraged, and that the event in
> question cannot be accounted for by means of any natural law nor by
> any plausible reformulation of them which we can now envisage, can
> a sceptical position be maintained indefinitely? Is it always rational to
> hold that if only we knew enough about natural laws we would see that
> this event was not miraculous after all? . . . I submit that, just as there
> could come a point where it would be irrational to deny that the event
> occurred, so there could at least in principle come a point beyond which
> it would be foolish to deny that it was genuinely miraculous. Even if,
> taken by itself, it would not suffice to establish a whole religious system,
> taken in conjunction with other considerations, it could go a long distance
> in making a religious system plausible.[60]

Hume's argument against miracles was intended to be precisely the kind
of rearguard action that would defend him from having to come to the point
where he would have to acknowledge that a miracle had occurred and see
any religious significance in it. As we have seen, this defense was two-pronged.
We have looked at the general *a priori* argument that miracles are scientifically
impossible, since they are by definition violations of the laws of nature and
as such are absurd. We must now look at the *a posteriori* argument concerning the kind of testimony offered on behalf of miracles and the inferences
that may be drawn from it.

Before looking at Hume's actual arguments we may note with Richard
Swinburne that Hume confines his discussion to verbal testimony.[61] This in
turn was evidently based on memory or apparent memory. Hume says nothing
about *traces* left behind by any alleged event. In Hume's defense it may be
pointed out that the credibility of the biblical miracles largely turns on the
credibility of the accounts that report them. However, in the case of the resurrection of Jesus, the historical credibility of the event turns not only on our
evaluation of the resurrection narratives but also on the interpretation that
we place on the existence of the early church after the crucifixion of Jesus.
For the church itself constitutes a trace left by the event that Christians call
the resurrection of Jesus.[62]

A further point to be noted is Hume's initial assumption that the evidential value of the testimony of others (so long as it is considered as the testimony
of others and nothing more) is invariably inferior to that of our own senses
and that it invariably diminishes with the passage of time. The assumption
should not be allowed to pass without challenge or qualification. In many
cases one could put much more confidence in the report of a trained observer
than in one's own senses.[63] Unless one has good, specific reasons for doubting a piece of testimony, the reports of an eyewitness or someone close to
the alleged event is likely to be more reliable as a guide to what actually hap-

pened than our general conjectures made at a distance. Indeed, the conjectures of later historians have all too often swept aside specific testimony in the interests of constructing a picture that fits the historians' preconceived ideas. Hume's *a posteriori* arguments were intended to cast doubt about the veracity and value of testimony to the miraculous. But as we shall see, they take the form of loose generalizations about testimony in general. They never amount to specific, critical evaluation of any piece of biblical testimony in particular.

Hume's four *a posteriori* arguments owe a certain plausibility to the fact that many alleged instances of the miraculous are patently open to his charges. Hume's first argument complained of the lack of discerning, competent witnesses. But the qualifications that he demands of such witnesses are such as would preclude the testimony of anyone without a Western university education, who lived outside a major cultural center in Western Europe prior to the sixteenth century, and who was not a public figure. A hostile critic of Hume might be tempted to think that Hume had formulated his qualifications not so much with the need to define qualities desirable in a witness but with the preconceived aim of deliberately excluding any testimony issuing from the ancient world. As such, Hume's objections were more in the tradition of the Pyrrhonic skepticism that he got to know in France than in the moderate British empiricism of Locke and the British scientists of his time. It is questionable whether Hume would ever have accepted any testimony to the miraculous that met his stringent conditions. For he goes on to admit instances of miracles said to have been wrought in France relatively recently that "were immediately proved upon the spot, before judges of unquestioned integrity, attested by witnesses of credit and distinction, in a learned age, and on the most eminent theatre that is now in the world." Nevertheless, Hume refuses point-blank to credit such testimony on the grounds of "the absolute impossibility or miraculous nature of the events which they relate."

Hume's second argument concerned the human propensity to exaggerate and enlarge upon the truth, not least in the interests of establishing a good cause. It must surely be admitted that Hume was right in his claim that religious people are by no means exempt from such tendencies. But it must also be said that religion can serve as a check on such tendencies. As a general criterion for assessing testimony to the unusual and miraculous, Hume's point just will not stand. It is irresponsible to brand all religious people as naturally prone to disseminate untruth whether wittingly or unwittingly. Although Hume's own circle of friends consisted largely of moderate Edinburgh Presbyterians, he writes as if all believers are either deceivers or the deceived. He fails to take into account the possibility that some people, including religious people, are by nature skeptics. As Richard Swinburne has pointedly remarked, "How many people are in each group, and in which group are the witnesses to any alleged miracle are matters for particular historical investigation."[64]

Hume's third argument is equally imprecise. Clearly the complaint that miracles are said to occur "among ignorant and barbarous nations" and that civilized people believe them on the basis of sanctified traditions stemming from them is designed to cast aspersions on contemporary belief in the Bible. But as a criterion, Hume's point is too wholesale. It is absurd to demand of a witness that he should share the same world view as oneself or have the same level of education and culture. Moreover, Hume's argument does not distinguish between the testimony to any given event and the explanation that a witness to the event may give. We may, or we may not, be competent to give explanations and interpretations in the light of our contemporary understanding. But the validity of the testimony to a claim *that* something happened depends rather upon the honesty, capacity not to be deceived, and proximity of the witnesses to the alleged event.[65]

Even so, the Bible taken as a whole does not see in miracles *per se* an unambiguous vindication of those associated with them.[66] Miracles are not to be severed from the accompanying teaching. False prophets and teachers may perform signs and wonders. It is their teaching and other actions that give them away and disclose their true identity. Judged by their wonders alone, they would deceive. Moreover, the New Testament writers never claim that God shows goodness only to those who share their doctrines.[67] Human nature is such that people habitually persist in false notions of God when they should have known better. Not only is this generally true,[68] it can also happen in the case of healing, illustrated by the story of the lame man at Lystra. The event should have been seen by the populace in the context of the "good news" that they should turn from vain, superstitious practices "to a living God who made the heaven and the earth and the sea and all that is in them."[69] Instead, they jumped to the conclusion that "the gods have come down to us in the likeness of men." Barnabas was hailed as Zeus, the chief god (because he remained silent), and Paul was greeted as Hermes, the messenger of the god (doubtless because he did most of the talking). What they had done was to interpret the event within their existing cultural and religious frame of reference. But the event that had just taken place was a challenge to change their entire frame of reference.

POSTSCRIPT

It is the term *frame of reference* that is the crucial factor in the assessment of miracles as we look back over the rise of skepticism. Antony Flew endorses C. S. Peirce's observation that "The whole of modern 'higher criticism' of ancient history in general, and of Biblical history in particular, is based upon the same logic that is used by Hume."[70] This may well be true, but it cannot stand as an endorsement of Hume's particular arguments. Taken singly, none of Hume's various points offers a decisive argument against miracles. Arguments that at first sight seemed plausible turned out to be confused, self-contradictory, or at best generalizations that may or may not apply to any given case. The significance of Hume's critique lies in the fact that it raises the question of the frame of reference in which any piece of historical data has to be assessed. However, it must be added that Hume's essay was an attempt to foreclose discussion on this very point that had been a feature of earlier British evidentialism.

In point of fact, the historian does not assess each item of testimony on its own in isolation from his world view. He can only determine its credibility for him in the light of a complex of judgments about what is possible, about the kind of document he is dealing with, and the kind of testimony that it contains. What we call *historical facts* are not items of data that can be directly inspected but interpretation placed on data that have commanded acknowledgment. As we noticed in discussing Bishop Butler, all facts are theory laden.[71] In this respect at least the methods of the historian are comparable with those of the scientist. Admittedly the historian cannot perform repeated, controlled experiments and present his interpretations in terms of mathematical equations. But his data, methods, and conclusions are open to public inspection by anyone competent in the discipline. This applies no less to the frames of references that the historian brings to his assessment.

Frames of reference may be determined by all kinds of considerations. They depend partly on the interests of the historian and partly on his world view. He may, for example, be interested in political, economic, ethnic, or cultural questions. If he is interested in politics, he will keep his eyes open for political isssues and examine events and people with these in mind. At the back of his mind he will have his own views of politics and political theories, which will constantly interact with his perceptions. This is not a crass case of bias. It is, rather, an instance of the fact that nothing can be recognized and interpreted without a frame of reference of some kind.

Hume's approach anticipated the doctrine of analogy developed by Ernst Troeltsch in the nineteenth century, which we shall be examining in the next chapter. Troeltsch argued that in order to recognize anything we need to compare it with our experience of life and our understanding of the way in which things work. We look to see if there are any analogies between the past and the present. We can recognize instances of deceit and lying in documents, because we know what deceit and lying are like from our own experience. Thus, our present view of the world establishes the frame of reference for interpreting the past. Hume opted for a frame of reference that excluded the supernatural, because his experience of the world in the present excluded the supernatural. His understanding of science posited only natural explanations for things encountered in the present. Given such a world view, nothing is allowed to count decisively against it. In earlier ages and in those circles where the supernatural is still readily admitted, the same principles and movements of thought are applied (albeit tacitly) in the interests of a religious interpretation of reality. Accounts of the miraculous are deemed credible not simply because they are judged to be backed by sufficient supporting testimony, but because this testimony is seen to be credible in the light of one's overall view of reality.

Does this, therefore, mean that acceptance or rejection of miracles is a matter of making a simple initial choice between a religious view that admits miracles and a secular one that does not? To his credit, it has to be said that Hume sought to establish his world view. But once established, nothing was allowed to change it. It acquired a quasi-religious character beyond further verification and falsification, because no fact could be admitted that could conceivably count against it. It has to be said that world views and frames of reference are not disproved by single facts. Their validity and usefulness lie in their capacity to account for the world that we live in. When they die, they die not from a single blow but from a death of a thousand qualifications. In the field of science, when an existing view is so beset by anomalies and qualifications that a change is needed, there occurs not simply the discovery of a new law but a paradigm shift involving the adoption of a new frame of reference.[72] Hume's essay on miracles gave no final answers to any of the questions surrounding miracles. But it did raise two important questions in a particularly acute form: (1) What is the justification for a religious frame of reference that admits the possibility of miracles? (2) What is the significance of the biblical miracles for us today? More than two hundred years have elapsed since Hume wrote on miracles and claimed to have discovered "an everlasting check" that "the wise and learned" could use to silence appeal to them. Hume did not think that he could stop the report of miracles; he did not even stop the debate. It merely entered a new phase.

III

The Legacy of the
Nineteenth Century

5

CONTINENTAL SKEPTICISM

In terms of the calendar, the nineteenth century began on January 1, 1800. In terms of theology, the transition from the eighteenth to the nineteenth century was less clearly marked. The quest of the historical Jesus was an enterprise that fascinated the nineteenth-century mind. But the quest was already some twenty-five years old when the new century dawned. The nineteenth century was the golden age of theological liberalism, but many of its seminal ideas were engendered in the previous age. For this reason we shall begin our review of continental skepticism concerning miracles with Immanuel Kant. Within a single chapter, however, it is clearly impossible to take into account every important thinker. We shall concentrate on Reimarus and Lessing and the part that they played in launching the quest of the historical Jesus, Schleiermacher as the greatest exponent of liberal Protestantism, Strauss and Feuerbach in view of their criticism of miracles as the product of the myth-making propensities of the religious mind, and the History of Religions school. Finally, we shall take note of Kierkegaard's unorthodox orthodoxy that raised the question of how the transcendent may be known in history.

KANT AND THE AGE OF ENLIGHTENMENT

Long before the eighteenth century had come to its close, it was already being hailed as the Age of Enlightenment. The German philosopher Immanuel Kant described enlightenment as man's coming of age.[1] Enlightenment was man's emergence from his self-inflicted immaturity, perpetuated by servile obedience to the Bible, the church, and the state. The truly enlightened man is one who thinks for himself. His motto is *Sapere aude*—"Dare to be wise." He replaces supernatural explanations by natural ones and bases his outlook on reason rather than faith. In Britain the philosophy of David Hume marked the zenith of the Enlightenment. In Europe it was Kant himself who was the outstanding representative of the movement, with his systematic critical reappraisal of the main areas of philosophy and his insistence that the human mind was not equipped to deal with the traditional questions of metaphysics.

Immanuel Kant (1724–1804) spent most of his life in Königsberg, East Prussia, where from 1770 until his death he was professor of logic and metaphysics. During the previous fifteen years he had been a university instructor, lecturing and writing on metaphysics, logic, ethics, and the natural sciences. In 1781 he published his epoch-making *Critique of Pure Reason* (revised edition 1787). It was followed by a string of works in which Kant elaborated his basic position, and pursued its ramifications in the fields of science, ethics, and religion. Among these works were his *Prolegomena to Any Future Metaphysics which will be able to Come Forth as a Science* (1783), *Critique of Practical Reason* (1787), *Critique of Judgment* (1790), and *Religion within the Limits of Reason Alone* (1793). Kant's thought has both a direct and an indirect bearing on the subject of miracles. The Gospel miracles are treated directly in *Religion within the Limits of Reason Alone,* which we shall examine presently. But Kant's view of the nature and scope of knowledge also has a bearing on the question, albeit an indirect one.

Prior to writing any of these works Kant had come to believe that the metaphysical systems currently taught by the rationalists yielded no real knowledge at all. Kant's alternative was the product of his own analysis of the scope and limitations of reason, which in turn was influenced by his own Newtonian approach to science and his response to Hume's skepticism. Kant agreed with the empiricists in saying that there can be no knowledge of anything apart from sense experience. He rejected rationalist belief in innate ideas, but argued that the human mind operated with certain categories or concepts that were prior to all sense experience. These categories form the mind's conceptual apparatus for understanding the world that is conveyed to us via our senses. Kant listed twelve such categories of understanding, including the notion of causality.[2] He regarded space and time as forms of intuition that make possible a knowledge of the world around us. But what they yield is a knowledge of appearances and not of things in themselves that underlie appearances.[3]

Kant went on to argue that, "If we, as is commonly done, represent to ourselves the appearances of the sensible world as things in themselves, if we assume the principles of their combination as principles universally valid of things in themselves and not merely of experience, as is usually, nay, without our *Critique* unavoidably, done, there arises an unexpected conflict which can never be removed in the common dogmatic way; because the thesis, as well as the antithesis, can be shown by equally clear, evident, and irresistible proofs."[4] Kant called these contradictions or paradoxes "Antinomies." Among those which he noted were these propositions: "The world has, as to time and space, a beginning (limit)" and "The world is, as to time and space, infinite"; and "There are in the world causes through freedom" and "There is no freedom, but all is nature."

All this meant that our knowledge of the physical world is limited. It is conditioned by the mind, and is confined to appearances. Kant rejected as unwarranted and self-contradictory speculation the claims of theology and traditional metaphysics to any knowledge of God and transcendent reality. God's existence could not be proved either by logic or by observation.[5] Nevertheless, he retained the ideas of God, freedom, and immortality as regulative ideas or postulates of pure practical reason.[6] Although science postulates the occurrence of everything in accordance with laws and thus seems to demand determinism, ethics presupposes freedom and responsibility. Ethics also presupposes immortality as the condition requisite for the union of virtue and happiness, and God as the cause of nature and the ground of the highest good. Kant was at pains to stress that such a postulate of pure practical reason was "a theoretical proposition which is not as such demonstrable, but which is an inseparable corollary of an a priori unconditionally valid practical law."[7]

In a sense, Kant's philosophy was a highly sophisticated form of deism that redefined the role of reason and assigned to God the function of a useful, but theoretical, presupposition. Moral behavior should be determined not by custom, society, or religion but by the categorical imperative of "Fundamental Law of Pure Practical Reason." Kant defined this in terms of the following principle: "So act that the maxim of your will could always hold at the same time as a principle establishing a universal law."[8] It was against this background that he interpreted Christianity in *Religion within the Limits of Reason Alone*. Kant began with the observation that, "So far as morality is based upon the conception of man as a free agent who, just because he is free, binds himself through his reason to unconditioned laws, it stands in need neither of the idea of another Being over him, for him to apprehend his duty, nor of an incentive other than the law itself, for him to do his duty."[9] Nevertheless, morality "leads ineluctably to religion, through which it extends itself to the idea of a powerful moral Lawgiver, outside of mankind, for Whose will that is the final end (of creation) which at the same time can and ought to be man's final end."[10]

Like the deists, Kant saw "The Christian Religion as a Natural Religion."[11] He scrupulously avoided mentioning Jesus by name, and insisted that "We need . . . no empirical example to make the idea of a person morally well-pleasing to God our archetype; this idea as an archetype is already present in our reason."[12] Indeed, even if it were a fact "that such a truly godly-minded man at some particular time had descended, as it were, from heaven to earth and had given men in his own person, through his teachings, his conduct, and his sufferings, as perfect an *example* of a man well-pleasing to God as one can expect to find," and even if "immeasurably great moral good" had thereby come about, "we should have no cause for supposing him other than a man naturally begotten."[13] To speak of Kant's christology would be to use too strong a term. To describe this ideal of humanity he used the phrase *Son of God*, and cited various New Testament verses. But the result was "The

Personified Idea of the Good Principle.''[14] It was a secularization and rationalization of biblical ideas. In the twentieth century the process might have been called one of demythologization. Kant saw it as one of divesting theological ideas of their "mystical veil."[15]

Kant's brief discussion of miracles consistently followed his general approach to religion and ethics. His reproof of the desire for miracles to accredit religious truth was in itself a minor essay in secularizing the teaching of Jesus:

> If a moral religion (which must consist not in dogmas and rites but in the heart's disposition to fulfil all human duties as divine commands) is to be established, all *miracles* which history connects with its inauguration must themselves in the end render superfluous the belief in miracles in general; for it bespeaks a culpable degree of moral unbelief not to acknowledge as completely authoritative the commands of duty—commands primordially engraved upon the heart of man through reason—unless they are in addition accredited through miracles: "Except ye see signs and wonders, ye will not believe."[16]

Human expectation might desire the authentication of a new religion by such external means, but the religion of reason that Kant took to be the true nature of Christianity needs no such attestation. Miracles might still be honored among "the trappings which served to bring into public currency a doctrine whose authenticity rests upon a record indelibly registered in every soul." Sensible men may not be disposed to renounce belief in them; "they believe *in theory* that there are such things as miracles but they do not warrant them *in the affairs of life*."[17]

Whereas Hume had put forward a series of arguments designed to undermine the apologetic use of miracles, Kant simply dismissed miracles as irrelevant to natural religion. He felt no need to disprove them. On his premises it was sufficient to attribute them to unknown causes:

> If one asks: What is to be understood by the word *miracle*? it may be explained (since it is really proper for us to know only what miracles are *for us*, *i.e.*, for our practical use of reason) by saying that they are events in the world the *operating laws* of whose causes are, and must remain, absolutely unknown to us. Accordingly, one can conceive of either *theistic* or *demonic* miracles; the second are divided into *angelic* miracles (of good spirits) and *devilish* miracles (of bad spirits). Of these only the last really come into question because the *good angels* (I know not why) give us little or nothing to say about them.[18]

This touch of irony, reminiscent of Hume, is continued in Kant's concluding remarks in which he warns against any appeal to the miraculous in everyday life.

Kant's view of the physical world was one that—conceptually at least—was a closed system of cause and effect. What might lie within it and beyond it could not be determined, for the human mind can only think in terms of causation and the other categories by which it structures reality. Rational, practical humanitarian ethics pointed the only way forward. The obligation to act morally was for Kant a given fact of human life. Reason served to determine particular courses of action. As the nineteenth century progressed, Kantian moralism seemed to offer a solid foothold to liberal theology. Philosophical idealism came and went. The historicity of the Bible and the authenticity of its contents came increasingly under fire. The moral teaching of Jesus seemed to be all that was left. The Jesus of liberal theology at the end of the nineteenth century bore a striking resemblance to Kant's portrait of him at the end of the eighteenth. But in the meantime Kant fell afoul of J. C. Wöllner, the head of the state department of churches and schools, who was an avowed foe of the Enlightenment.[19] In 1788 Wöllner had issued an edict threatening with civil punishment and dismissal anyone under his jurisdiction who deviated from biblical teaching. Kant was personally rebuked by the King of Prussia, who extracted from him a promise to refrain from all public statements on both natural and revealed religion. It was a promise that he kept until 1797, when with the death of the king he felt released from his vow.[20]

REIMARUS AND THE QUEST OF THE HISTORICAL JESUS

Kant was not the first enlightened author to write on religion, nor the first to be censured. The most extensive treatment of Christian origins from an enlightened standpoint came from the pen of Hermann Samuel Reimarus (1694–1768). Reimarus was a teacher in Hamburg who published numerous learned works on a variety of subjects during his lifetime. Outwardly he was a respected member of the community whose many-sided interests marked him as a fine example of the enlightened man. Over the years he nursed doubts about the Bible and the origin of the church, but he reserved them for a private book that he hesitated to publish. It was called *Apology or Defence of the Rational Worshippers of God.* The worshipers in question were none other than the deists. The work has only recently been published in its entirety, but extracts were published by the dramatist and amateur theologian, G. E. Lessing, during his time as librarian to the Duke of Brunswick at Wolfenbüttel. Between 1774 and 1778 Lessing published seven *Fragments of an Unknown Author*, pretending to have discovered them in the depths of the ducal library. To throw would-be witch-hunters off the scent, Lessing suggested that the *Fragments* (now commonly called the *Wolfenbüttel Fragments,* might have been the work of the well-known, deistically inclined deceased heretic J. Lorenz Schmidt. Although intelligent guesses about the author's true identity were made at the time, it was not until the nineteenth century, when the clamor had died down, that Reimarus was confirmed as the author. In the meantime Lessing was censured for publishing the *Fragments* and forbidden to publish anything further on religion. He did, however, smuggle religious questions into his play *Nathan the Wise* (1779).

Reimarus's work ranged widely over the Old Testament, the life of Jesus, and the beginnings of the church. But it was the *Fragments* on the resurrection narratives and *On the Intentions of Jesus and his Disciples*[21] that stirred up the fiercest controversy and brought down on Lessing a prohibition to publish anything further of a theological nature. Albert Schweitzer has gone on record as hailing the work as "perhaps the most splendid achievement in the course of the historical investigation of the life of Jesus, for he was the first to grasp the fact that the world of thought in which Jesus moved was essentially eschatological."[22]

Reimarus depicted Jesus as a Galilean religious reformer who got mixed up in politics and eschatology. Originally Jesus had no intention of founding a new religion. His message of the kingdom of God became a summons to establish a theocratic kingdom, centered on himself. Before he knew it, Jesus had made implacable enemies. At the crucial moment he found himself alone, and he died disillusioned with the cry on his lips, "My God, my God, why have you forsaken me?"[23] At first the disciples were shattered, but after a while they hit upon a daring plan that would restore their former fortunes. Having disposed of the body of Jesus, they put out the story that he had risen from the dead and that he would come again. Thus the whole fabric of Christianity is based on fraud.

Schweitzer went so far as to say that virtually the entire nineteenth-century quest of the historical Jesus appears to be retrograde after Reimarus, who had no predecessors or successors.[24] In point of fact, although eschatology remained largely neglected for the next hundred years, Reimarus's views were not all that far removed from those of D. F. Strauss, who in 1862 published a tribute to Reimarus,[25] and other authors of rationalistic lives of Jesus, like K. F. Bahrdt. In seeing his eschatological preaching of the kingdom of God as the key to understanding Jesus, Reimarus stood alone at this time. But his rationalistic interpretation of what Jesus actually did was in substance no different from these later writers or the earlier English deists. Moreover, the writings of the English deists and their opponents were well known in France and Germany long before the *Fragments* came on the scene.[26] The ground was thus already prepared for Reimarus and the rationalistic interpretation of Christian origins that came to be associated with the nineteenth-century quest of the historical Jesus.

In a manner reminiscent of Hume, Reimarus roundly asserts that "No one can affirm that miracles of themselves establish a single article of faith."[27] In a similar vein he proceeds to argue:

> Other religions, indeed, are quite as full of miracles; the heathen boast of many, so does the Turk. No religion is without them, and this it is which also makes the Christian miracles so doubtful, and provokes us to ask: "Did the events really happen? Were the attendant circumstances such as are stated? Did they come to pass naturally, or by craft, or by chance?"[28]

These were the kind of options offered by Hume. But whereas Hume was content to state them in general terms, Reimarus spelled them out. Sometimes he appears to concede a historical core to the alleged miracle, but in such cases he questions the theological significance: "It does not follow that because Jesus restored sight to a blind man and healed a lame one, ergo God is threefold in person, ergo Jesus is a real God and man. It does not follow that because Jesus awakened Lazarus from death he also must have arisen from death."[29] But almost in the same breath Reimarus could argue that the reports of Jesus' miracles are so full of contradictions that it is impossible to judge whether a *bona fide* miracle really occurred. Hume would have applauded Reimarus's strictures on the gospel testimony, which virtually echo his own arguments about the dubious nature of testimony to the miraculous by suggesting how they might apply:

> Jesus himself could not perform miracles where the people had not faith beforehand, and when sensible men, the learned and rulers of those times, demanded of him a miracle which could be submitted to examination, he, instead of granting the request, began to upbraid them; so that no man of this stamp could believe him. It was not until thirty to sixty years after the death of Jesus, that people began to write an account of the performance of these miracles, in a language which the Jews in Palestine did not understand. All this was at a time when the Jewish nation was in a state of the greatest disquietude and confusion, and when very few of those who had known Jesus were still alive. Nothing was easier for them than to invent as many miracles as they pleased, without fear of their writings being readily understood or refuted. It had been impressed upon all converts from the beginning that it was both advantageous and soul-saving to believe, and to put the mind captive under the obedience of faith.[30]

In a manner reminiscent of the deists, Reimarus claimed that the New Testament writers' use of prophecy was made plausible by "all the tricks of allegorical adaptation."[31] Indeed, the apostles had "learned from their master how to perform miracles, or rather how to give the semblance of them to spectators."[32] It required little or no skill to relate them or even perform them. Moreover, Jesus' prohibition to the healed to proclaim what he had done was an astute publicity stunt. "He forbids them to be mentioned where it was impossible that they should remain secret, on purpose to make the people all the more eager to talk about them."[33] Here Reimarus's argument recalls Hume's argument about the human love of gossip.

In comparing Reimarus with Hume, the point is not to make out a case for conscious literary dependence, though it may be noted that Hume's *Enquiry* had been published in German in 1755 and Reimarus had traveled in Holland and England in 1720-21, when the deistic controversy was nearing its height. The point is rather to draw attention to the parallels and to note the general drift of the argument. There is a further similarity: both writers seem to want to cast the maximum doubt upon miracles, regardless of whether the arguments are consistent or whether the explanation fits any given case. A major feature of Reimarus's argument is his attempted exploitation of inconsistencies in the Gospel narratives. But his own case was itself built on inconsistencies. Reimarus was never able to make up his mind whether any given act of healing was to be explained psychosomatically, whether it was all a trick, or whether it was a piece of pious fiction fabricated long after the alleged participants had passed from the scene. The argument seems predicated upon the unwritten principle that if enough mud is thrown, some of it is bound to stick. Or alternatively, if enough general uncertainty is generated, the true explanation is more likely to be one or other of the reasons proffered than that the event actually happened as described. In essence this was the outlook of Hume and his skeptical forerunners. Reimarus's work was not the bolt from the blue that Schweitzer would have his readers believe.[34] It was more like a bridge between the eighteenth and nineteenth centuries. If it was a prelude to the doubts of the nineteenth-century quest of the historical Jesus, it was also an echo of the skepticism that we have traced from Spinoza through the English deists to Hume.

LESSING AND THE STATUS OF HISTORICAL CLAIMS

The appearance of the *Fragments* precipitated a pamphlet war embroiling both academics and pastors. Today the names of men like J. D. Schumann and J. M. Goeze are remembered as pawns in the game that Lessing was playing, though in their day they were men of weight and stature in the church. The most substantial reply came from the scholar reputed to have founded the modern, critical study of the New Testament and to have coined the term "liberal theology," J. S. Semler (1725–1791). Semler's monumental *Answer to the Fragments* was virtually a line-by-line refutation of the original, recalling Origen's rebuttal of Celsus in the third century. It was far more profound and effective than Schweitzer's summary of it would suggest. But like the other replies, it remains today largely unread and forgotten. The best remembered part in the whole affair was played by Gotthold Ephraim Lessing (1729–1781) himself.

Lessing was never averse to stirring up controversy. His role in the *Fragments* battle oscillated between that of a midwife bringing something new into the world and that of an advocate. Even so, he chose to avoid making it clear whether he was an advocate for the defense or the prosecution. In true enlightened fashion he enjoyed defending ideas to which he was not personally committed. In a series of pamphlets addressed to various participants he disclaimed the position of the Fragmentist, while questioning whether the truth of Christianity could be demonstrated by appealing to history.[35]

In a tract addressed to Schumann, *On the Proof of the Spirit and of Power* (1777), Lessing echoed Paul's claim that his speech and message "were not in plausible words of wisdom, but in demonstration of the Spirit and power" (1 Cor. 2:4). But his argument centered not on the apostle Paul but on Origen's claim that miracles and fulfilled prophecy supplied just such a demonstrative proof of the working of the Spirit of God and hence of the truth of Christianity.[36] Lessing tried to turn the whole argument around by claiming that it would be valid if he had been there to see it for himself. But "reports of miracles are not miracles,"[37] and though he does not doubt that "the reports of these miracles and prophecies are as reliable as historical truths can be,"[38] history is so full of uncertainties that it cannot match the self-evident compelling power of purely rational argument. Nothing in history is capable of demonstrative proof. Lessing's position is enshrined in the following axioms:

> If no historical truth can be demonstrated, then nothing can be demonstrated by means of historical truths.
>
> That is: *accidental truths of history can never become the proof of necessary truths of reason.*[39]

Lessing's position belongs to the quest for certainty based on self-evident truths that stretches back to the rationalism of Spinoza and Descartes. The version of religion Lessing put forward in answer to this demand was a form of eighteenth-century deistic moralism that in some respects anticipated twentieth-century existentialism. Religion is concerned with the divinely decreed, eternal, ethical verities. But these have to be discovered in life and acted upon. The great world religions are but historical, culturally conditioned expressions of these truths, which have to be known and appropriated by each in his own day.[40]

The figure of Nathan in Lessing's *Nathan the Wise* was modeled on Moses Mendelssohn (1729–1786), the leading Jewish thinker of the Age of Enlightenment and grandfather of the composer. An intimate of Lessing and the Reimarus family, Mendelssohn knew of the source of the *Fragments* and their contents before their publication.[41] On Lessing's death he sought to defend his friend of the charge of Spinozism. His views on miracles were a Jewish counterpart to Lessing's. He held that the eternal, necessary truths of reason were grounded in God's intellect and were therefore immutable. To such necessary truths belong the laws of logic and mathematics. But there were also eternal, but contingent truths, which were derived from the will of God but were not immutable. To these belong the laws of nature. Historical truths were, for Mendelssohn, "passages that occur only once, so to speak, in the book of nature." Miracles were not needed to convey God's eternal truths to humanity, but Mendelssohn allowed a place for miracles in instructing people in historical truths:

> It seems to me that only with regard to historical truths does it befit God's supreme wisdom to instruct men in a human way, i.e. by the spoken or written word, and to cause extraordinary things and miracles to happen in nature, whenever this was required to confirm the authority and credibility of the event.[42]

EARLY LIVES OF JESUS AND THE MIRACULOUS

If Reimarus's investigations into Christian origins were designed to undermine the historical foundations of Christianity, Lessing's philosophical reflections were aimed at showing that historical investigation was largely irrelevant. There were, however, numerous authors who deemed it worthwhile to try to explain how the miracles of Jesus really happened in the course of writing a biography of Jesus. The attempts to write a life of Jesus are far too numerous to be mentioned here. Schweitzer's *Quest of the Historical Jesus* provides an extended, descriptive catalogue. Since few of them merit a repetition of Schweitzer's research, all that we need do here is to draw attention to some of the more noteworthy examples.

Some of the earlier instances of this genre were no more than edifying paraphrases of the gospel stories, rewrittten in the pious idiom of the day. But Lessing's contemporary, Karl Friedrich Bahrdt (1741–1792), succeeded in combining pulpit rhetoric with a fictitious plot, worthy of James Bond. At the height of his career, Bahrdt was a popular professor teaching as many as nine hundred students. But his private life and not-so-private opinions resulted in his dismissal, a year's imprisonment, and his resorting to the life of an inn-keeper. Much of his vast literary output took the form of serialized letters, addressed to thoughtful readers.[43] Such readers were assured that "a too frequent contemplation of the miracles in the Bible" robs them of "the profit which they might have from the study of Holy Writ. For the marvellous has the character of drawing a man's attention to itself and away from the moral teaching." Moreover, the more a teacher founds the faith of his hearers on miracles, the more he exposes them to the danger of doubt. As a consequence of this, Bahrdt adopted the rule of seeking natural explanations for all miracles. Thus, the story of Jesus walking on the water is to be explained by Jesus standing on a piece of floating timber, while the inflamed imaginations of the onlookers supplied a supernatural interpretation. In other instances, Jesus was aided and abetted by secret disciples to whom Bahrdt gives the title "Brethren of the Third Degree." It was they who secretly filled the pitchers of water with wine at the wedding at Cana. The same band thoughtfully secreted large quantities of food in order to feed the four thousand at the right moment. Writing at a time when little was known about the Essenes and a century and a half before the Qumran discoveries, Bahrdt could safely identify this group with the Essene community.

This secret order was devoted to diverting the Jewish people from a political messianism that could only result in disaster. They sought a messiah who would lead the people into more peaceful ways, and found him in the figure of Jesus. The link-men in the organization were Nicodemus and Joseph of Arimathea who discovered Jesus as a boy, finding him already versed in Plato and Socrates, and imbued with a desire to emulate the latter's martyrdom. In the marketplace at Nazareth Jesus encountered a mysterious Persian who gave him two remedies—one for eye infections and the other for nervous disorders. Further medical knowledge was gained from Luke, the physician. The crucifixion was rigged by Nicodemus. Luke had already given Jesus pain-killing drugs, and once Jesus was taken down from the cross he was brought to the cave where Luke was already prepared to work on his resuscitation. Jesus duly appeared to people to convince them that he had risen from the dead, but then retired from public life making only the rarest appearances (as to Paul on the Damascus road). Nevertheless, he continued to direct operations until he died from old age.

Bahrdt's work belongs more to the history of religious fiction than the history of serious scholarship. But one point he shared with many scholars after him—his conviction that "The sacred History is subject to the same laws as all other views of the past."[44] Such a view lay at the back of H. E. G. Paulus's *Life of Jesus as the Foundation of a Pure History of Christianity* (2 volumes, 1828). Paulus, who was a professor of theology at Heidelberg, did not go in for the flamboyant conspiracy theories of Bahrdt, and his explanations of the miracles were quite different. Nevertheless, they too were characterized by the desire for purely natural explanation. Thus, Jesus was not walking on the water, but standing on the shore, his features and position being obscured by the mist. The five thousand were fed by the more well-to-do among them, who were shamed into sharing their provisions. Jesus was not actually dead when he was laid in the tomb, and the cool air, the spices, and the earthquake combined to revive him. Mary Magdalene failed to recognize him because he had to borrow the gardener's clothes. The disciples on the Emmaus road failed to identify the once familiar face that was now transfigured by suffering. Jesus lingered on some forty days after the crucifixion before succumbing to his sufferings. Shortly afterward the disciples came to the assurance that Jesus was now in bliss.

A more restrained example of developed rationalism is provided by the textbook *Life of Jesus* by the Jena professor, K. A. von Hase, which in its various editions enjoyed academic popularity for over half a century.[45] Whenever possible, Hase sought natural explanations of miracles. But the key to them lay in understanding the primacy of the divine Spirit:

> Jesus' miraculous gift appears rather as a dominion of Spirit over nature which had indeed been originally given to mankind with dominion over the earth. It was restored in Jesus' holy innocence to its ancient bounds against the abnormal nature of disease and death. Hence, there enters here into the disturbed order of the world not an exception to natural law but rather the original harmony and truth.[46]

Physical miracles may be rendered intelligible by suggesting an acceleration of natural processes in accordance with laws unknown to us. Thus, commenting on the feeding of the five thousand, Hase conjectures: "But if nature annually brings about a similar wonder in the time between sowing and harvest, she could perhaps bring it about by an unknown law in a moment."[47] The point sounds like a nineteenth-century echo of Augustine.[48] Although many have found this view attractive, it leaves unanswered the question of

how the food came to be cooked and prepared. In the case of the resurrection, Hase had some rather more down-to-earth suggestions to hand. There
is no stringent proof that Jesus had actually died. Rather, he might have
returned to consciousness from a coma. It was open to the Christian to believe
either that the Creator gave new life to the body of Jesus or that he aroused
hidden vital power in him who was apparently dead.[49]

In common with Schleiermacher and others in his day, Hase treated the
Fourth Gospel as the most historical and authentic account of Jesus. Indeed,
Schweitzer noted that, on closer inspection, Hase accepted as authentic only
those miracles reported by John.[50] Hase explained the difference between
the teaching of Jesus recorded in the Synoptic Gospels and that related in
John by positing two phases in Jesus' ministry. The first was colored by the
messianic, eschatological ideas of the day; the second is the kind of teaching
preserved by John. When Jesus saw where the former teaching might lead,
he abandoned it in favor of the latter. Matthew, Mark, and Luke failed to
distinguish the two phases, and allowed Jewish eschatological ideas to
dominate their portraits of Jesus. Hase was ready to concede legendary and
mythical elements in the birth, infancy, and resurrection narratives. But in
general he was not particularly interested in the source criticism that was to
characterize biblical studies in the latter part of the nineteenth century.

SCHLEIERMACHER AND JESUS AS THE MAN FILLED WITH THE CONSCIOUSNESS OF GOD

Schweitzer credits Hase with creating "the modern historico-psychological
picture of Jesus."[51] Another theologian who favored this kind of approach
was Friedrich Schleiermacher (1768–1834), who was one of the founding
fathers of the University of Berlin in the Napoleonic era. Schleiermacher's
many-sided genius as a theologian, philosopher, patriotic preacher, and proto-
ecumenical statesman places him in the front rank of nineteenth-century
thinkers. His man-centered approach to theology, set out in *The Christian
Faith* (1821, 2nd ed. 1830-31), was both the acme and prototype of theological
liberalism. For Schleiermacher, theology was not (as it had been in Reformed
orthodoxy) the interpretation of the divine revelation contained in the Word
of God. Rather, it was the analysis of man's religious awareness and, in particular, of man's sense of utter dependence on a higher reality outside himself.
Schleiermacher's approach was the product of various factors. His family
background was one of Moravian pietism, but this had long since been
tempered by Kantian philosophy combined with the Romantic protest against
the Enlightenment's stress on reason. In common with the Romantic poets
and novelists of the turn of the century, Schleiermacher believed that man
could sense a higher realm of reality that was beyond the grasp of reason.
Schleiermacher's view of man was based on a faculty-psychology that viewed
man in terms of his reason, will, and feeling. But these three faculties were
not equally balanced. It was the stream of consciousness that is the realm

of feeling that constitutes the continuum of human existence and thus is the seat of all religion.

For Schleiermacher, true piety consisted in the full development of our sense of utter dependence. God is that reality on which we feel ultimately dependent, and statements about God are statements predicated upon our analysis of our feeling-states of dependence. Sin is the fleshly desire to be independent when we should be truly dependent. Jesus represents the archetype of humanity, as the man in whom the sense of utter dependence upon God was perfected at every moment. This was developed to the point at which it could be said that the potency of his God-consciousness constituted "a veritable existence of God in Him."[52]

Schleiermacher's developed theology was a thoroughgoing restatement of the entire range of Christian theology in the light of this basic position. The two-natures doctrine of the divinity and humanity of Christ was replaced by this view of God-consciousness and divine indwelling. Schleiermacher retained the traditional Calvinistic framework that viewed Christ in terms of the three offices of prophet, priest, and king, but gave them a drastic reinterpretation. The section dealing with the prophetic office of Christ begins with the thesis that "The prophetic office of Christ consists in teaching, prophesying, and working miracles."[53] But the predictive element in prophecy is soon disposed of, and miracles are now pronounced to be "superfluous." The Old Testament miracles were never intended to evoke faith in messianic prophecy; "their purpose was to evoke faith in their conditional predictions in order to induce people to do what had to be done."[54]

> But Christ gave no such conditional predictions about Himself, and faith in His relation to the Messianic idea was meant to proceed solely from the direct impression made by His Person. That is why Christ never availed Himself of His miraculous powers in any definite connexion with the demands He made or His statements about Himself, but (in the same way as everyone avails himself of his natural powers) according as opportunity offered of doing good by them.[55]

Schleiermacher gave reluctant acknowledgment to the historicity of the Gospel miracles in a general, if somewhat theoretical way. But he consistently downplayed their significance:

> In those days the true recognition of Christ might in individual instances be evoked by miracles; elsewhere it found a confirmation in them; but it might never be properly based upon them. Hence for us, so far as our faith is concerned, they cannot but be altogether superfluous. For miracles can only direct the spiritual need to a definite object in virtue of their immediate impressiveness, or, if it has already been directed thither, justify this inner relation in an external way. This impressiveness, however, is lost in proportion as the person who is to believe is at a distance from the miracle itself in space and time. What takes the place of miracles for our time is our historical knowledge of the character, as well as of the scope and duration, of Christ's spiritual achievements.[56]

Schleiermacher went on to say that we have an advantage over the contemporaries of Jesus, insofar as our awareness of his spiritual power increases in proportion as the impressiveness of miracles is lost. The redundancy of miracles is further underscored by the distinction Schleiermacher draws between faith in Christ and faith in Scripture, the latter being by implication of much less significance:

> Our faith in the external miracles wrought by Christ, as deeds which were not wrought by Him in accordance with rules learned elsewhere, and whose success cannot be traced to natural laws recognized by us as valid for all time—this faith belongs not so much to our faith in Christ as to our faith in Scripture.[57]

Furthermore, the Gospel miracles

> have nothing which raises them, in and by themselves, above other similar miracles of which we have stories from many various times and places. But if we consider the total spiritual miracle, then we must declare Him to be the climax, all the more definitely that we recognize that—apart from Him—this total spiritual miracle could not have been achieved by all the powers of spiritual nature as we know it. But equally certainly Christ is also the end of miracle.[58]

Schleiermacher's lectures entitled *The Life of Jesus* [59] (1864) were first published thirty years after his death. Perhaps their most striking feature is Schleiermacher's unique combination of highly critical argument with an almost uncritical attempt to read into the Gospel narratives his own particular christology. In general he readily applies biblical criticism in his evaluation of the narratives. But one is left with the feeling that the picture of Christ that emerges has already been predetermined. Schleiermacher's reflections on miracles in *The Life of Jesus* [60] are an expansion of the position adopted in *The Christian Faith*. There is an underlying sensitivity to the tensions posed by the apparent conflict between miracles and the natural order of things. But Schleiermacher gives the impression of one who does not want to limit the divine power in advance.[61] The decisive criterion is whether any given miracle conforms "to the rules of human morality, as does Christ's entire ministry."[62] In assessing particular miracles, Schleiermacher repeatedly spoke in terms of difficulties in understanding. Those that appear to have self-preservation or display as their motive present the most difficulties and may not represent authentic history. At the end of his rather wordy digression on miracles Schleiermacher presented the following conclusion, which is firm in its general convictions, but vague in its application and tentative as to how given particular accounts might fit in:

> Although we are not able to form a final judgment on all instances of Christ's miracle-working activity, it is nevertheless true that for our task, that of viewing the life of Jesus in its unity and totality, there remain no gaps, to the extent that we have been able to point out adequately the moral motivation involved in all these acts of Christ. Where this has

not been possible we have said: So far as that which cannot be explained by these maxims is concerned, we believe it must have some other context. We have also pointed out that such an existence as we assume was that of Christ makes possible effects in the area of human life such as no other man could have achieved. The only difficulty is that we can not determine the limits of Christ's unique power. So we have obtained a clear picture of the way Christ exercised his miracle-working powers, and that is all that is necessary for our task.[63]

STRAUSS AND MYTH

Following the appearance of Schleiermacher's work, D. F. Strauss, who had attended some of Schleiermacher's lectures in Berlin some thirty years earlier, published *The Christ of Faith and the Jesus of History: A Critique of Schleiermacher's Life of Christ* (1865).[64] His blistering comments were directed at the whole sweep of Schleiermacher's work. Not even the editor emerged unscathed on account of his uncritical use of his sources. Piece by piece, Strauss tore Schleiermacher's argument apart. He highlighted the precariousness of claiming that belief in miracles belonged more to one's belief in Scripture than one's belief in Christ: "For if there were no truth to the miracles of Jesus, then John's Gospel, which most definitely reports them, would no longer be trustworthy; but then the historical basis of Schleiermacher's Christ, which he appears to find in the Johannine portrait, would disappear."[65] Strauss went on to see vagueness, inconsistency, and contradiction in Schleiermacher's rationale for the miracles of Jesus, his indecision as to what was supernatural and what was not, and his lame attempts to justify some miracles as historical events while ignoring others. The gist of Strauss's attack is contained in his conclusion to the book as a whole:

> Schleiermacher, we can say, is a supernaturalist in Christology but in criticism and exegesis a rationalist. His Christ, however many of the miraculous attributes of the old confession may have been removed, still remains essentially a superhuman, supernatural being. In contrast, his exegesis, as far as it pertains to the miraculous in Scripture, is distinguished from that of Paulus only by somewhat more spirit and subtlety—a difference which precisely in the main points, such as the resurrection story, becomes imperceptible. The one appears to contradict the other; rather, however, the one is the basis for the other. Because Schleiermacher wants to remain a supernaturalist in Christology he must be a rationalist in criticism and exegesis. In order not to lose the supernatural Christ as a historical personality he cannot surrender the Gospels as historical sources. But in order to avoid a supernatural Christ in the sense in which the supernatural is unacceptable to him, he must remove exegetically from the Gospels the supernatural which offends him. Indeed, he retreats to one Gospel, the Johannine, and appears to let the other three go. However, they still have too much in common with John, with regard to content and standpoint to be separable in this way. Whoever thinks

that in the miracle stories of the Fourth Gospel he has the facts in the report of an eyewitness will also assume facts in those of the first three, even if in more indirect tradition; and since he no longer believes in actual miracles, apart from the miraculous personality of his Christ, he will have to explain also these in a rationalist way.[66]

Underlying this criticism was Strauss's own rationalism, which had removed the supernatural from history altogether, and which wanted to read the Bible just like any other "human book" and "really put Jesus in the ranks of humanity."[67] It was a consistent rationalism that operated on the assumption of a fundamental analogy between our own experience of life that does not admit divine interventions and the past that could not be in essence any different. It was the principle Hume had tacitly employed, Ernst Troeltsch was soon to articulate, and in fact lies never far beneath the surface of any discussion concerning the credibility of miracles.

In positing a nonmiraculous Jesus, Strauss was no different from the rationalists. But his own explanation of the presence of the supernatural in the Gospels was radically different. Strauss had set this out in a book that had brought him instant fame and at the same time put an end to his prospects as a teacher of theology. Strauss had graduated at Tübingen, but had gone to Berlin to pursue postdoctoral studies with Hegel and Schleiermacher. But the former had died in a cholera epidemic before Strauss could begin his work. Strauss had heard Schleiermacher lecture, though not on the life of Jesus. It was while at Berlin that Strauss conceived the plan for writing *The Life of Jesus Critically Examined* (1835).[68] Strauss declined to follow the paths marked out by previous skeptics. He was unwilling to see with Reimarus the first Christians as "wicked and deceitful men." Nor was he happy with the rationalistic explanations of the supernatural in the Gospels. Like Kant's moral interpretation, the rationalist interpretation of Jesus was "unhistorical" and "unphilosophical."[69] For Strauss the key to understanding early Christianity lay in grasping its essentially mythological character. The role of myth in ancient literature had already been discussed by a number of scholars. Strauss seized on the maxim of C. G. Heyne and applied it to the Gospel narratives: *From myths proceed all the history as well as the philosophy of ancient man.*[70]

Strauss analyzed various kinds of material in the Gospels.[71] *Evangelical myths* were the products of the religious imagery of the community. *Pure myths* have no historical basis whatever. They may be derived from existing popular notions, such as the expectation of the messiah, or they may be conditioned by impressions formed of Jesus that have served to modify the existing popular notions. But in neither case do they have any real basis in history. By contrast, *historical myths* have a foundation in fact that the religious imagination has transformed into a mythological event that did not really happen. Thus, a saying of Jesus about "fishers of men" was transformed, according to Strauss, into a story about a miraculous catch of fishes. Strauss also recognized in the Gospel material *additions* by the author that were not due to myths but to the author's literary designs. The residue of *historical material* consists of what is left when all the above are subtracted from the Gospels.

Basic to Strauss's whole approach is his view that the world is a closed system of cause and effect that admits no interventions:

> In the history of the Israelites we find traces of his [God's] intermediate agency at every step: through Moses, Elias, Jesus, he performs things which never would have happened in the ordinary course of nature.

> Our modern world, on the contrary, after many centuries of tedious research, has attained a conviction, that all things are linked together by a chain of cause and effects, which suffers no interruption. It is true that single facts and groups of facts, with their conditions and processes of change, are not so circumscribed as to be unsusceptible of external influence; for the action of one existence or kingdom in nature intrenches on that of another: human freedom controls natural development, and material laws react on human freedom. Nevertheless the totality of finite things forms a vast circle, which, except that it owes its existence and laws to a superior power, suffers no intrusion from without.[72]

In other words, "God acts upon the world as a Whole immediately, but on each part only by means of his action on every other part, that is to say, by the laws of nature."[73] Such views, Strauss maintains, were shared by other Christian thinkers, including Schleiermacher.[74]

Although Strauss allowed a minimal historical framework for the life of Jesus, by far the majority of material preserved in the Gospels is the product of myth making, inspired above all by the tendency to read Old Testament messianic expectations into the story of Jesus. The miracle stories provide a case in point. Strauss began his extensive discussion of the miracles of Jesus with this observation:

> That the Jewish people in the time of Jesus expected miracles from the Messiah is in itself natural, since the Messiah was a second Moses and the greatest of the prophets, and to Moses and the prophets the national legend attributed miracles of all kinds: by later Jewish writings it is rendered probable; by our gospels, certain. When Jesus on one occasion had (without natural means) cured a blind and dumb demoniac, the people were hereby led to ask: *Is not this the son of David?* (Matt. xii. 23), a proof that a miraculous power of healing was regarded as an attribute of the Messiah. John the Baptist, on hearing the *works* of Jesus (*erga*), sent to him with the inquiry, *Art thou he that should come* (*erchomenos*)? Jesus, in proof of the affirmative, merely appealed again to his miracles (Matt. xi. 2ff. parall.). At the Feast of Tabernacles, which was celebrated by Jesus in Jerusalem, many of the people believed on him, saying, in justification of their faith, *When Christ cometh, will he do more miracles than these which this man hath done?* (John vii. 31).[75]

Not only was the messiah popularly expected to perform miracles in general; certain types of miracles were already anticipated in the Old Testament or at any rate prophesied there of the messiah. Moses had dispensed meat and drink in a supernatural manner (Exod. 16:17). At the prayer of Elisha, eyes that had been closed were supernaturally opened (2 Kgs. 6:17, 20). Elijah and Elisha had raised the dead (1 Kgs. 17; 2 Kgs. 4). Messianic expectation was already focused on the coming miraculous healings by prophecies like Isaiah 35:5f.: "Then the eyes of the blind shall be opened, and the ears of the deaf unstopped; then shall the lame man leap like a hart, and the tongue of the dumb sing for joy" (cf. also Isa. 42:7). Whereas the church from New Testament times onward had seen in these words a prophetic prediction of Jesus, endorsed by Jesus himself (Matt. 11:5; Luke 7:22), Strauss saw in them only the material out of which myths were made.

In principle, Strauss distinguished two types of miracle: miracles in the strict sense of the term (*Mirakel*), which require divine intervention in the normal sequence of cause and effect; and wonders *(Wunder),* which defy the understanding of those who give credence to them but are susceptible to scientific explanation. Strauss dismissed miracles in the former sense as sheer products of the myth-making mind. But some of the exorcisms were at least plausible in the light of the new science of psychological medicine.[76] Strauss's examination of the accounts of Jesus' healing cases of leprosy led him to conclude that on occasion Jesus may have expressed his opinion that particular patients were no longer in a contagious state. But claims to instantaneous and total healing are beyond belief and are more likely to be legends or parables transformed into history.[77] Alleged cases of the restoration of sight to the blind are even less credible, not least because of the general lack of psychological explanations for such healings.[78]

The healings of paralytics present further difficulties, not least because of the connection made between sin and sickness in the story related in Matthew 9:1–8, Mark 2:1–12, and Luke 5:17–26. Strauss detected a tension between this connection and Jesus' refusal to attribute blindness to sin in the case of the man born blind reported by John (9:2ff.), and Jesus' attitude toward calamity recorded by Luke (13:1–5).[79] In this instance Strauss preferred to see John's account of Jesus' attitude toward sin and sickness as more authentic and representative of Jesus' outlook. He dismissed the Synoptic story as a piece of "accommodation" to the assumptions of the day and treated it as yet another example of the potential of messianic expectation to create myths and legends. For Strauss the decisive question turned on analogy, but the analogy that counted with him was that between the Gospel accounts of the healing of the lame and Isaiah 35:6. He acknowledged modern instances of rapid healing and psychosomatic factors in nervous disorder, but rejected attempts to see parallels between them and the Gospel narratives as "purely arbitrary" expedients. "If in the alleged analogies there may be some truth, yet it is always more probable that histories of cures of the lame and paralytic in accordance with messianic expectation, should be formed by the legend, than that they should really have happened."[80] In saying this, Strauss was sounding a variation on a theme already stated by Hume and others before him. The novelty with Strauss consisted in the rigor and precision with which he worked it out.

If anything, Strauss was more scathing in his criticism of the rationalists with their conjectures as to how the healing miracles might have taken place than he was of the orthodox who simply accepted them at their face value. Both missed what Strauss regarded as the decisive factor in the origin of the stories, the desire of the religious mind to create history out of myth and legend. Comparison of the story of Jairus's daughter and the woman who touched Jesus (Matt. 9:20ff.; Mark 5:25ff.; Luke 8:43ff.) "with kindred anecdotes" left Strauss in "no doubt as to its proper character."[81] In dealing with the numerous stories of Jesus' healings on the sabbath, Strauss anticipated twentieth-century form criticism by suggesting that the original historical core may have been a pronouncement by Jesus on the subject of the sabbath that had nothing at all to do with a miracle of healing.[82] The accounts of Jesus' acts of raising from the dead Jairus's daughter, the widow of Nain's son (Luke 7:11-17), and Lazarus (John 11) were seen by Strauss to be modeled on the stories of Elijah and Elisha (1 Kgs. 17:17ff.; 2 Kgs. 4:18ff.). Whereas a rationalist like H. E. G. Paulus sought natural explanations for the Old Testament stories, Strauss noted that "theologians of more enlarged views have long ago remarked, that the resurrections in the New Testament are nothing more than mythi, which had their origin in the tendency of the early Christian church, to make her Messiah agree with the type of the prophets, and with the messianic ideal."[83] Strauss himself clearly sided with the "theologians of more enlarged views."

The nature miracles present the same spectacle, differing only by their greater intensity. Elisha walked dry-shod through the Jordan and caused a piece of iron to float (2 Kgs. 2:14; 6:6). Job addressed God as one who "trampled the waves of the sea" (Job 9:8). Jesus is elevated to divine status in performing an act greater than that of Elisha that properly belongs to God himself (Matt. 14:25; Mark 6:48; John 6:18). The existence of stories in classical authors of miraculous abilities to traverse rivers, seas, and abysses serves only to confirm Strauss in his convictions about the legendary nature of the "anecdotes" about Jesus "relating to the sea."[84] The accounts of Jesus' feeding the multitudes (Matt. 14:13-21; Mark 6:30-44; Luke 9:10-17; John 6:1-15; cf. Matt. 15:32-39; Mark 8:1-10) are modeled on the stories of Moses feeding the hungry in the desert with manna and flesh (Exod. 12 and 16; Num. 11) and the miraculous provision made for Elijah (1 Kgs. 17:8-16).[85] Anything that Moses or Elijah could do, Jesus could do better according to the pious belief of the first Christians. Whereas Moses produced water from the flinty rock (Exod. 17:1ff.; Num. 20:1ff.), turned the Nile into blood (Exod. 7:17ff.), and on occasion, like Elisha, made bad water good (Exod. 14:23ff.; 2 Kgs. 2:19ff.), Jesus turned water into wine (John 2:1-11).[86]

In 1838-39 Strauss produced a third edition of his *Life of Jesus*. It was written at a time when he still entertained hopes of obtaining a theological teaching post. Partly on account of these hopes, and partly on account of the doubts about the severity of his conclusions,[87] Strauss moderated his position. He now admitted the possibility of another type of explanation that, though it bore some resemblance to some of the views entertained by the rationalists whom he so disdained, he now considered feasible. Strauss now admitted the possibility of cures based on unusual powers of nature, similar to "animal magnetism" or hypnotism.[88] Although this now made it possible for him to enlarge the number of healings capable of being regarded as historical events and in so doing partially undermine his myth thesis, the reasons that he permitted belonged firmly to the natural order. The concessions brought him no nearer orthodoxy, and Strauss's attempts at conciliation were abandoned in the fourth edition (1840) on which George Eliot's English translation of the book was based.

Strauss concluded his *Life of Jesus Critically Examined* with a series of reflections designed to reassess the significance of Christianity for his readers. Regretfully, Jesus must be seen as "nothing more than a person, highly distinguished indeed, but subject to the limitations of all that is mortal."[89] But what was taken away by historical criticism was more than made up for by the dynamic pantheism of Idealist philosophy. Following Hegel, Strauss professed his belief that since God and man are both Spirits, "the two are not essentially distinct."[90]

> As man, considered as a finite spirit, limited to his finite nature, has not truth; so God, considered exclusively as an infinite spirit, shut up in his infinitude, has not reality. The infinite spirit is real only when it discloses itself in finite spirits; as the finite spirit is true only when it merges itself in the infinite. The true and real existence of spirit, therefore, is neither in God by himself, nor in man by himself, but in the God-man; neither in the infinite alone, nor in the finite alone, but in the interchange of impartation and withdrawal, between the two, which on the part of God is revelation, on the part of man religion.[91]

The idea of a man of divine essence subduing nature and performing miracles is replaced by that of God manifested in humankind and nature generally, subject to the laws of nature. Noting that Luther subordinated the physical miracles to the spiritual, Strauss went on to ask:

> Shall we interest ourselves more in the cure of some sick people in Galilee, than in the miracles of intellectual and moral life belonging to the history of the world—in the increasing, the almost incredible dominion of man over nature—in the irresistible force of ideas, to which no unintelligent matter, whatever its magnitude, can oppose any enduring resistance? Shall isolated incidents, in themselves trivial, be more to us than the universal order of events, simply because in the latter we presuppose, if we do not perceive, a natural cause, in the former the contrary?[92]

The answer to these questions was clearly intended to be in the negative. It was a response that had long been anticipated by Spinoza in the seventeenth century, but it is one that has continued to be echoed to the present day. In some respects Strauss was the most radical of all the nineteenth-century critics; he was certainly one of the most meticulous. The account given above of his treatment of miracles merely outlines his general approach. It gives no indication of the detail of the discussion of the individual miracle stories or of his handling of the writings of his contemporaries. For this reason Strauss must rank as the most formidable nineteenth-century critic of the New Testament miracle stories.

Strauss was both a child of his time and a forerunner of modern thought. None of the weapons he wielded against orthodox Christianity were forged by Strauss himself. The possible presence of myth had already been discussed by others, as he noted in his own introduction.[93] Philosophical Idealism had already reached full flower when Strauss went to Berlin as a postgraduate student in the hope of studying under Hegel. The underlying reasons beneath Strauss's rejection of the miraculous lay in his naturalistic view of the world and the workings of nature. What was new was the combination of these various elements, Strauss's willingness to face the logic of his position, and the unrelenting vigor with which he pursued his conclusions, once he had made up his mind.

The various elements in this synthesis have reappeared from time to time in different guises. In the mid-twentieth century the need to demythologize the gospel in the interests of truth was vociferously urged by Rudolf Bultmann and his followers. But Bultmann studiously refrained from acknowledging any debt to Strauss.[94] Bultmann ascribed the mythological world view of the New Testament to Jewish apocalyptic and Gnosticism rather than the desire of the first Christians to make Jesus fulfill Old Testament prophecy at all costs. Moreover, Bultmann's restatement of the gospel was a unique blend of Marburg Neo-Kantianism and Heidegger's existentialism, which permitted him to say that the message of the cross and the resurrection of Jesus confronted the hearer with the transcendent and at the same time with the possibility of understanding existence. Although both Bultmann and Strauss spoke a good deal about myth, Bultmann approached the question from a quite different angle. Strauss's views find more of an echo in *The Myth of God Incarnate* (edited by John Hick, 1977), whose contributors generally disclaim belief in a particular incarnation, preferring to see a general incarnation of the divine more or less in all, and ascribing traditional Christian beliefs to the myth-making factors at work in religion.[95]

FEUERBACH AND MIRACLES AS THE PROJECTION OF HUMAN WISHES

In his own day Strauss's views found an echo in those of Ludwig Andreas Feuerbach (1804–1872). Like Strauss, Feuerbach was to make a pilgrimage from the study of theology, through Hegelianism, to a position on the "Hegelian left,"[96] and eventually to post-Hegelianism. Feuerbach had studied theology under Paulus and philosophy under Hegel. His *Essence of Christianity* (1841) belongs to the same era as Strauss's *magnum opus*. It was also translated into English by George Eliot, whose translation appeared in 1854, some eight years after her rendering of Strauss's book. It took Strauss a number of years to slough his Hegelianism in favor of a form of Kantianism. But Feuerbach had already jettisoned the Absolute Spirit by the time that he wrote *The Essence of Christianity*. By then he was as fiercely critical of the Idealists as he was of the orthodox theologians. In the preface to the second edition, dated February 14, 1843, Feuerbach outlined the basis of his new philosophy:

> This philosophy has for its principle, not the Substance of Spinoza, not the *ego* of Kant and Fichte, not the Absolute Identity of Schelling, not the Absolute Mind of Hegel, in short, no abstract, merely conceptual being, but a *real* being, the true *Ens realissimum*—man; its principle, therefore, is in the highest degree positive and real.[97]

For Feuerbach, religion was a projection of man's deepest hopes and strivings. The religious mind has imagined that "all its involuntary, spontaneous affections are impressions from without, manifestations of another being."[98] But this is illusory:

> The contents of the divine revelation are of human origin, for they have proceeded not from God as God, but from God as determined by human reason, human wants, that is, directly from human reason and human wants. And so in revelation man goes out of himself, in order, by a circuitous path, to return to himself! Here we have a striking confirmation of the position that the secret to theology is nothing else than anthropology—the knowledge of God nothing else than a knowledge of man![99]

In dealing with miracles, Feuerbach conceded that "Miracle is an essential object of Christianity, an essential article of faith. But what is miracle? A supranaturalistic wish realised—nothing more."[100] In point of fact, Feuerbach went on to say a little more about the precise nature of a miracle from his standpoint. Not only is a miracle a supranaturalistic wish realized; it is realized "in the most desirable way" by being fulfilled without delay:

> Miraculous power realises human wishes in a moment, at one stroke, without any hindrance. That the sick should become well is no miracle; but that they should become so immediately, at a mere word of command,—that is the mystery of miracle.[101]

Feuerbach's argument ostensibly provided a psychological rationale for the process that Strauss professed to detect in the origin and formation of the miracle stories. In one sense the argument was a variation on Hume's attempt to trace miracles back to human inclinations. But whereas Hume looked no further than the human love of gossip and exaggeration, Feuerbach detected a deep-felt religious need for supernatural intervention. On the other hand, Feuerbach's reason for rejecting miracles is rooted in their downright impossibility:

> Miraculous agency is distinguished from the ordinary realisation of an object in that it realises the end without means, that it effects an immediate identity of the wish and its fulfilment; that consequently it describes a circle, not in a curved, but in a straight line, that is, the shortest line. A circle in a straight line is the mathematical symbol of miracle. The attempt to construct a circle with a straight line would not be more ridiculous than the attempt to deduce miracle philosophically. To reason, miracle is absurd, inconceivable; as inconceivable as wooden iron or a circle without a periphery. Before it is discussed whether a miracle can happen, let it be shown that miracle, *i.e.*, the inconceivable, is conceivable.[102]

Philosophically Feuerbach's argument is a curious one, and is marked by greater zeal than sophistication. It conflates logical impossibility (a circle in a straight line) with physical impossibility (wooden iron). It then proceeds on the basis of these examples to the general conclusion that the inconceivable is impossible. Feuerbach's demand of conceivability as a precondition to acceptance of factuality would, if applied generally, overthrow the whole fabric of modern science and technology. For in science, as in other disciplines, conceptual understanding follows experience and observation, rather than the other way around. Man's understanding of what is possible at one stage in his history has repeatedly been overturned by later generations.

Feuerbach's argument took the form of a generalization about possibility on the basis of selected instances of nonsense concepts that no one has ever claimed to be examples of the miraculous. To this Feuerbach added the assertion that "Where miracles happen, all definite forms melt in the golden haze of imagination and feeling; there the world, reality, is no truth; there the miracle-working, emotional, *i.e.* subjective being, is held to be alone the objective, real being."[103] Feuerbach's discussion contains a hint that he himself felt somewhat uncomfortable with this wholesale kind of argument. Anticipating the charge of superficiality, he sought to turn the tables by raising the level of rhetoric and by accusing his critics of even greater superficiality:

> The explanation of miracles by feeling and imagination is regarded by many in the present day as superficial. But let any one transport himself to the time when living, present miracles were believed in . . . and he must himself be very superficial to pronounce the psychological genesis of miracles superficial. . . . If the explanation of miracles by feeling and imagination is superficial, the charge of superficiality falls not on the explainer, but on that which he explains, namely, on miracle; for, seen in clear daylight, miracle presents absolutely nothing else than the sorcery of the imagination, which satisfies without contradiction all the wishes of the heart.[104]

This approach foreshadowed the classic Marxist approach to religion and miracles.[105] In itself this is not surprising, since Marx and Feuerbach came from the same milieu. Despite later differences, Marx and Feuerbach were both ex-Hegelians who adopted thoroughly secular world views. Feuerbach's discussion of miracles anticipated the more elaborate and more sophisticated treatment by the twentieth-century Marxist, Ernst Bloch.[106] The argument bears a family resemblance to Hume's claim that because some people love to gossip and enlarge upon the truth, it is safe to assume that all reports of miracles are the product of the imagination. But whereas Hume was concerned only with the human propensity to gossip and exaggerate, Feuerbach professed to detect a psychological explanation for all religious truth-claims that relieved him of the necessity to examine their factual content. Underlying this was the conviction common to Strauss, Feuerbach, Hume, Spinoza, and many others, that miracles are scientifically impossible because they violate the laws of nature.

In the course of time D. F. Strauss came to question the role of the unconscious as a common factor in the formation of the miracle stories. In the introduction to *A New Life of Jesus* (1864) Strauss reported that, mainly as a consequence of the research of his former teacher, F. C. Baur, he now "allowed more room than before to the hypothesis of conscious and intentional fiction."[107] He defended the propriety of retaining the term *myth* for such stories on the grounds that they had become a form of myth once they had gained belief in a religious community. By this time Strauss had also abandoned his former Hegelianism and had reverted to a form of Kantianism. The resultant picture of Jesus was that of an impressive moral teacher who, despite his tendencies to megalomania, should be allowed to take his place among the great ethical teachers of humankind.[108]

THE JESUS OF END-OF-THE-CENTURY LIBERAL PROTESTANTISM

It would require a separate study of massive proportions to trace the course of the debate about miracles through the countless lives of Jesus that were written in the nineteenth century.[109] The majority did not add anything new to what we have seen so far, although techniques and methods changed with the years. Schleiermacher's predilection for the Gospel of John as the original, authentic historical Gospel was soon outmoded. In the earlier part of the century scholars generally followed Augustine's view that Matthew was the first of the evangelists, and that Mark's Gospel was an abbreviation.[110] By the end of the century this order had been reversed, and Mark was widely regarded as the first Gospel. A factor in this reversal was the literary arguments which claimed that better sense could be made of the common features of Matthew, Mark, and Luke if Mark was seen as the primary account of the life of Jesus. As originally proposed by Karl Lachmann in the 1830s, this argument dealt with the order of events in the Gospels.[111] But an added attraction for the antisupernaturalist in arguing for the priority of Mark lay in the fact that Mark's Gospel was perceived to be the least supernatural of the four Gospels.

The antisupernatural interpretation of Jesus took different forms and was reached by different routes, but the result was often a combination of ideas already found in Kant, Schleiermacher, or Strauss. To F. C. Baur, the founder and most important member of the Tübingen School of Theology, the Jesus of history had to be discovered beneath the layers of church tradition and ecclesiastical in-fighting that are preserved in the writings of the New Testament. Baur posited a fundamental conflict in the early church between the Jewish faction, headed by Peter and the Jerusalem apostles, and the more liberal Hellenistic party, headed by Paul. An essential tool of his theological method was tendency criticism, which he used in an attempt to discern the tendencies of each writing in order to determine its place in history. Baur assigned to a late date many of the New Testament writings on the grounds that their tendencies better fitted his reconstruction of the church at the end of the first century and later. But he was not altogether skeptical of the historical Jesus. However, the portrait of Jesus that he painted bore a striking resemblance to the moral teacher of Kant and the Christ of Schleiermacher, whose message consisted of "the immediate utterances of the religious self-consciousness."[112]

The moral aspect of Christianity was particularly pronounced in the liberalism of later German theology. A. B. Ritschl interpreted the kingdom of God in terms of Jesus' vocation to be "the Bearer of God's ethical lordship over men."[113] At the turn of the century the great church historian Adolf Harnack delivered a series of popular lectures at Berlin in answer to the question *What is Christianity?* His reply stressed the spiritual and moral content and pushed the supernatural into the background. He insisted that "Jesus himself did not assign that critical importance to his miraculous deeds which even the evangelist Mark and the others all attributed to them."[114] Harnack saw the essence of Jesus' teaching grouped under three headings: "Firstly, the kingdom of God and its coming. Secondly, God the Father and the infinite value of the human soul. Thirdly, the higher righteousness and the commandment of love."[115] Jesus took over two views of the kingdom of God that were related to each other as a husk is to the kernel. From Judaism he inherited the husk: the kingdom as a future event—the external rule of God. But he also saw the kingdom as an inward reality that elevates people spiritually and transforms them morally. This was the central reality of Jesus' message. The stories of exorcisms belong to the outer husk of contemporary beliefs that the evangelists shared. Harnack treated them as primitive ways of describing mental disorders that are "of rare occurrence nowadays." "Where they occur the best means of encountering them is to-day, as it was formerly, the influence of a strong personality."[116] Jesus was concerned not with himself but the Father.[117] He who had nowhere to lay his head "does not speak like one who has broken with everything, or like a heroic penitent, or like an ecstatic prophet, but like a man who has rest and peace for his soul, and is able to give life and strength to others."[118]

The most memorable comment on Harnack's best-selling portrait of

Jesus came from the pen of the Catholic Modernist, Father George Tyrell. "The Christ that Harnack sees, looking back through nineteen centuries of Catholic darkness, is only the reflection of a Liberal Protestant face, seen at the bottom of a deep well."[119] At the time that Tyrell was objecting to the liberal Protestant theologian's tendency to remake Jesus in his own image, Albert Schweitzer detected a major flaw in the Protestant quest of the historical Jesus. The whole undertaking was vitiated by the neglect of eschatology. Liberal theologians had modernized Jesus by emphasizing his moral teaching and by ignoring his eschatology. They had taken his teaching about the kingdom of God in a purely moral sense and had failed to see the eschatological thought-world of Jesus, which provided the key to everything that he said and did. Although Schweitzer is frequently credited with restoring the eschatological dimension of Jesus' teaching, it must be pointed out that Schweitzer himself did not believe it any more than did the liberals whose shortcomings he devastatingly displayed. Nor could Schweitzer find any room or sense for the miracle stories. He concluded that "It is not Jesus as historically known, but Jesus as spiritually arisen within men, who is significant for our time and can help it."[120]

TROELTSCH, BOUSSET, AND THE HISTORY-OF-RELIGIONS SCHOOL

Despite their differences over the role of eschatology in Jesus' teaching, Harnack and Schweitzer shared a common assumption that the uniformities of nature, as perceived by modern Western man, must determine the limits of what is possible at all times. Although Schweitzer allowed that Jesus entertained ideas of the kingdom that involved the radical inbreaking of God's theocratic reign, and went so far as to insist that Jesus could not be properly understood apart from these ideas, Schweitzer did not believe that such ideas should be taken seriously today. The scholar who did most to articulate the theoretical basis of such a critical approach to history was Ernst Troeltsch (1865–1923), who taught theology at Göttingen, Bonn, and Heidelberg. In 1915 he moved to Berlin, where he taught the history of philosophy and civilization.

Underlying Troeltsch's approach were the three principles of criticism, analogy, and correlation. Criticism demands the critical weighing of all evidence and the recognition that all judgments are open to revision in the light of new knowledge. Correlation is the idea that every event in history is in principle connected with all others, and thus history is a network of interrelated events. Analogy is the key to criticism and correlation. In 1898 Troeltsch wrote a paper "On Historical and Dogmatic Method in Theology" in which he stated the principle of analogy as the criterion by which events are identified and their historicity assessed:

> For the means by which criticism first becomes possible at all is the application of analogy. Analogy with what happens before our eyes and

comes to pass in us is the key to criticism. Deception, dubious dealings, fabrication of myth, fraud and party spirit which we see before our eyes are the means by which we recognize the same kind of thing in the material which comes to us. Agreement with normal, ordinary, repeatedly attested modes of occurrence and conditions, as we know them, is the mark of probability for the occurrences which criticism can acknowledge as having really happened or leave aside. The observation of analogies between homogeneous occurrences of the past makes it possible to ascribe probability to them and to interpret what is unknown in the one by the known in the other. This universal power of analogy includes the essential homogeneity [German: *Gleichartigkeit*] of all historical events. Admittedly this is not an identity [German: *Gleichheit*]; it leaves all possible room for differences. However, on each occasion it presupposes a nucleus of common homogeneity, from which the differences can be understood and felt.[121]

In saying this, Troeltsch was not only stating a basic principle of historical study, he was also summing up the basic difficulty underlying all the objections to miracles from the ancient world onward. The argument is basically simple: we must use our present experience and knowledge to understand the past. Since we do not experience anything that violates the regularities of nature, we must be skeptical of all claims to the contrary. Our experience of all events as similar or homogeneous (German: *gleichartig*) suggests that the universe is a closed system that cannot admit interventions. This clearly rules out miracles, as popularly understood. From Celsus to Feuerbach and beyond to the present day, the objections to miracles are essentially variations on this theme. On the face of it, Troeltsch seems to be correct in saying that analogy is the key to historical study. We could go even further and say that analogy is the key to identifying and assessing people, things, events, and situations in everyday life. But how far should analogy be pressed? If I judge everything by my limited experience of life and partial knowledge of the world, I may turn out to be like the King of Siam in the seventeenth- and eighteenth-century debates who resolutely refused to believe in ice, because he had never seen frozen water. Use of analogy must be sufficiently flexible for our present understanding and experience to be enlarged and modified by new experience and insights.

The question of analogy lies at the heart of all discussion concerning miracles and God's action in history. It was the tacit appeal to uniform experience that led early skeptics to mock Paul's preaching of the resurrection (Acts 17:32). But it was also Paul's appeal to the analogy between Christ's resurrection and the believer's that provided his grounds for proclaiming the future Christian hope (1 Cor. 15:20–58).

We shall return to the question of analogy as we examine contemporary New Testament criticism in Chapter Nine. In the meantime we may note the general direction of Troeltsch's thinking. Troeltsch was critical of Harnack's attempt to define the essence of Christianity by lifting it out of its historical context and making its central ideas the essence of religion itself.[122] Troeltsch himself not only rejected the dogma of the normative character of Christianity based on divine authority and miracles; he urged that Christianity should be seen in the context of the historical development of religion in general. In the end he favored Christianity as "the pinnacle of religious development thus far and the basis and presupposition for every distinct and meaningful development in man's religious life in the future."[123] This judgment was based not on any assessment of particular historical events but upon fundamental convictions concerning personal and ethical values. Troeltsch believed that

> It is necessary to make a choice between redemption through meditation on Transcendent Being or non-Being and redemption through faithful, trusting participation in the person-like character of God, the ground of all life and of all genuine value. This is a choice that depends on religious conviction, not scientific demonstration. The higher goal and the greater profundity of life are found on the side of personalistic religion.[124]

Despite his protests against Harnack and the Ritschlian school, and for all his professed interest in the world's religions, Troeltsch's views bore a marked family resemblance to the German liberal Protestantism of previous generations.

Troeltsch was connected with the *Religionsgeschichtliche Schule* (History of Religions school) that flourished between 1880 and 1920. It largely consisted of biblical scholars who urged the importance of seeing the Bible against the background of Egyptian, Babylonian, and Hellenistic religion. Its leading members included Hermann Gunkel, Hugo Gressmann, Wilhelm Bousset, Johannes Weiss, Richard Reitzenstein, Wilhelm Heitmüller, Hans Windisch, and William Wrede. Troeltsch's friend from student days, Wilhelm Bousset (1865-1920), argued that the eschatological ideas underlying the terms "Messiah" and "Kingdom of God" came largely from other religions. His *Kyrios Christos* (1913) traced the title of "Lord" to Hellenistic religion, and saw the ascription of divinity to Jesus as the result of alien influences on the church. Part of this process was the growing tendency to attribute miracles to Jesus. Bousset's writing was characterized by his manner of stating his hypotheses as if they were obvious facts. Thus, he could claim that

> We are still able to see clearly how the earliest tradition of Jesus' life was still relatively free from the miraculous. It is characteristic that the older part of the evangelical tradition, as over against the narrative portion, was probably a collection of the words of the Lord (or a gospel consisting essentially of the Lord's words), in which miracle naturally played no role. At the most, here and there a catena of Logia was joined to a briefly told miracle story (e.g., the Beelzebul saying). Certainly when the Logia were collected there were many miracle legends of the life of Jesus already in circulation. But people did not consider these things to be the truly and important decisive matters.[125]

This conclusion is at best a conjecture, bound up with an evolutionary theory of christology and predicated on the premise that the original Gospel material was free from all miracles. Moreover, the presence of miraculous and supernatural traits in a story is used as evidence of its lateness. Thus, Bousset confidently asserted that the passion narratives were among the earliest parts of the history of Jesus and were miracle-free. But to sustain the theory, Bousset had to treat "the bizarre miracle of the blighted fig tree" as "probably a literary addition of the evangelist Mark,"[126] and ascribe to late legends the accounts of the empty tomb and the bodily resurrection of Jesus.[127]

Bousset confidently separated the teaching and controversy accounts in Mark from the healing and miracle stories. Where Jesus' pronouncements were attached to miracle stories, Bousset had no doubt that the miraculous element was a later embellishment. On the whole, Bousset was reluctant to follow Strauss in attributing the supernatural elements in the Gospels to the myth-making desire of the early church to make Jesus fulfill the Old Testament. In a manner recalling David Hume, Bousset suggested that "the fabrication of miracles in the life of Jesus probably took place as such procedures usually take place." But whereas Hume was content to attribute this phenomenon to a common human tendency to enlarge upon the truth, Bousset claimed that "People transferred to Jesus all sorts of stories which were current about this or that wonderworker and decorated gospel narratives that were already at hand with current miraculous motifs."[128] Bousset's method of procedure at this point consisted in drawing attention to a small number of ostensible parallels in pagan writings, implying that the Gospel writers had drawn on them. It scarcely needed saying that such stories could be readily dismissed as incredible. Evidently Bousset did not feel under obligation to point out that the sources of the stories he cited were chiefly post-Christian. Nor did he feel it necessary to offer any account of how these particular stories might have influenced the Gospel narratives. He was content to refer to secondary sources[129] and take it as a self-evident fact that the ostensible parallels noted there were clear evidence of unashamed plagiarism by the evangelists, who freely drew on them to enhance their portraits of Jesus.

Moreover, Bousset failed to point out the dissimilarities between the stories he alluded to and the Gospel stories. In mentioning the story of the vinedresser, Midas, told by Lucian of Samosata (ca. 120–ca. 180) in his dialogue about Greek credulity, *The Lover of Lies, or the Doubter,* he took the statement that "Midas himself picked up the litter on which he had been carried and went off to the farm"[130] as clear "proof" of borrowing. In Lucian's story Midas had been bitten by a poisonous viper and was dying. He was healed by "a Babylonian, one of the so-called Chaldeans," who cast a spell and bound his foot with "a fragment which he broke from the tombstone of a dead maiden." The Babylonian went on to charm all the snakes of the farm through ritual incantation and destroy them by breathing on them. Quite apart from its lateness, the story bears little resemblance to Jesus' healing of the paralytic, which focuses on Jesus' forgiving the man's sins and the skeptical attitude of the onlookers who question whether Jesus has committed blasphemy, since only God can forgive sins (Matt. 9:1-8; Mark 2:1-12; Luke 5:17-26).

Whereas Lucian was patently skeptical of the stories he related, the Elder Pliny (ca. A.D. 23-79) uncritically assembled a vast and variegated volume of lore in his *Natural History*. In the course of it he told of the achievements of Asclepiades of Prusa, the physician who discovered a method of preparing "medicated wine for the sick" and "brought back a man from burial and saved his life."[131] Bousset does not make it altogether clear whether he sees here a parallel to the raising of Jairus's daughter (Matt. 9:18-26; Mark 5:21-43; Luke 8:40-56), the widow of Nain's son (Luke 7:11-17), or the centurion's servant (Matt. 8:5-13; Luke 7:1-10; John 4:46-54). He appears in fact to conflate the stories and see general parallels between the coming of the physician, his appearance at the head of the bed, his meeting the corpse on the bier, the disparagement of the futile efforts of the physicians, and the sudden accomplishment of the miracle. But in Pliny's account the intention is not to relate a miracle but to stress the skill of the physician, when others had given the victim up for dead. This same point is emphasized in the account of the same event given by Celsus (A.D. 14-37) in his *De Medicina* who records that "Asclepiades, when he met a funeral procession, recognized that a man who was being carried out to burial was alive; and it is not primarily a fault of the art if there is a fault on the part of its professor."[132] Whereas Pliny stressed the medical skill and diagnostic powers of Asclepiades, the Gospel stories point out that Jesus was not a physician at all. He healed by speaking the Word of God.

Bousset's attempt to find parallels to the nature miracles of Jesus in extraneous sources was equally strained. He cited the stories of Rabbi Gamaliel II and an unnamed Jewish boy who prayed for deliverance in storms at sea as parallels to Jesus' stilling of the storm, but whereas Jesus stilled the storm with his word, in the Talmudic stories it was a case of God answering the prayers of the devout.[133] Bousset failed to point out that Lucian's story of the Hyperborean walking on water wearing peasant brogues also mentions him walking through fire and soaring through the air in broad daylight.[134] In the case of the Gadarene or Gerasene swine and other stories, Bousset admitted that proof was lacking and that one was left to conjecture. Nevertheless, he did not hesitate to say that the original form concerned "an amusing story of poor deluded devils who against their wills do what they most earnestly wish to avoid doing."[135] This little story about an unknown exorcist was transferred to Jesus who, according to Bousset, never traveled either to Gadara or to Gerasa. With regard to the miracle at Cana, Bousset believed that there was "a demonstrable parallel" from the cult of Dionysos that could be traced to the New Testament period. A temple fountain of

Dionysos on the island of Andros was said to flow all year long with wine. A similar story was told of a sacred place in Teos. In Elis on the eve of a festival three jugs were put in a sacred place and were filled overnight with wine behind locked doors. Bousset concluded, "Here, we may surmise, is the genesis of the wine miracle at Cana! People set the epiphany of the new God over against the epiphany of the god Dionysos and its miracle: And he revealed his glory and his disciples believed on him!"[136]

Although other scholars like Richard Reitzenstein examined the mystery religions and Hellenistic miracles stories in more detail,[137] it was Bousset's *Kyrios Christos* that (in the words of Rudolf Bultmann) brought the demands of the History of Religions school "to fulfillment in a coherent and comprehensive presentation."[138] Bultmann himself proved to be Bousset's heir in a double sense. On Bousset's death in 1920 Bultmann succeeded him in the chair of New Testament at the University of Giessen. But in a more general sense Bultmann's own treatment of Jesus and the miracle stories followed the path marked out by Bousset, as we shall see in a later chapter. Both men approached the stories from a standpoint of frank disbelief. In order to explain how such stories found a place in the New Testament and how Jesus came to be divinized, they invoked the hypothesis of the free application of stories and beliefs drawn from the religious world of the early centuries of the Christian era.

KIERKEGAARD AND THE DIVINE INCOGNITO

Before we leave this review of continental skepticism, mention must be made of the Danish philosopher Søren Kierkegaard (1813–1855), if only to correct some misconceptions. Kierkegaard is sometimes seen as a pioneer existentialist whose doctrine of the leap of faith was designed to enable the believer to get by with only a minimal historical faith. Hence, it does not matter how little Bultmann and other radical critics permit us to believe; Kierkegaard's existentialist faith enables us to face life with an open attitude. Some support for this view might seem to be given by this statement in his *Philosophical Fragments:*

> If the contemporary generation had left nothing behind them but these words: "We have believed that in such and such a year the God appeared among us in the humble figure of a servant, that he lived and taught in our community, and finally died," it would be more than enough. The contemporary generation would have done all that was necessary; for this little advertisement, this *nota bene* on a page of universal history, would be sufficient to afford an occasion for a successor, and the most voluminous account can in all eternity do nothing more.[139]

However, this statement must not be taken out of context. It needs to be seen in relation to Kierkegaard's views on the New Testament and in relation to the argument of the *Philosophical Fragments.* A study of Kierkegaard's writings shows that he was anything but skeptical about the contents of the Bible. Although he was aware of the debates surrounding Lessing and Strauss, he himself took Scripture at its face value. His concern was not with the historicity of the biblical narratives but with the relationship of history in time and space and God who is transcendent. By definition God is not an object in time and space. There is an infinite qualitative difference between man and God, for God exists on a different plane and in a different way from creatures who exist in time and space. Man's reason is capable of grasping only objects in time and space and its own deductions. Man cannot, therefore, know God by his own efforts. On the other hand, God might conceivably seek to make himself known to man. But if he were to do so, he would have to accommodate himself to the human mind. He could do this only by taking human form as in the incarnation. But in this case God would remain *incognito*. For in seeing the human form of Jesus, people would see not God directly but a human being.

Basic to Kierkegaard's thought is the fact that the divine cannot be seen directly by humans. In *Training in Christianity* Kierkegaard complained that people (particularly Hegelian thinkers)

> confuse the Christian conceptions in every way. They make Christ a speculative unity of God and man; or they throw Christ away altogether and take His teaching; or for sheer seriousness they make Christ a false god. Spirit is the negation of direct immediacy. If Christ is very God, He must also be unrecognizable, He must assume unrecognizableness, which is the negation of all directness. Direct recognizableness is precisely the characteristic of a pagan God.[140]

In other words, divinity is something that is hidden and is incapable of being seen directly with the senses or reduced to the logical conclusion of a piece of reasoning. When people saw Jesus, they saw a man. When they heard him, they heard human words. Even when they saw his miracles, they did not see the divine directly. What they saw was a condition beforehand and a condition afterward. It was not that Kierkegaard was historically skeptical in the same sense that Strauss and Bousset were skeptical. He did not doubt the veracity of the reports as items of historical testimony. What he questioned was whether one could prove by sheer historical argument the divinity of Christ and know him to be God apart from faith. For Kierkegaard there was an intuitive perception in faith that could not be replaced by rational argument or historical evidence. Both reason and history belong to the sphere of the finite and human. But God is transcendent even in the incarnation, for in Christ God does not cease to be God. Hence, the Christian belief of the incarnation of God in Christ is a paradox that is offensive to reason. Thus in answer to the question "Can one prove from history that Christ was God?" Kierkegaard replied:

> Let me first put another question: Is it possible to conceive a more foolish contradiction than that of wanting to *prove* (no matter for the present purpose whether it be from history or from anything else in the wide

world one wants to *prove* it) that a definite individual man is God? That an individual man is God, declares himself to be God, is indeed the "offence" *kat' exochen [par excellence]*. But what is the offence, the offensive thing? What is at variance with human reason? And such a thing as that one would attempt to prove! But to "prove" is to demonstrate something to be the rational reality that it is. Can one demonstrate that to be a rational reality which is at variance with reason? Surely not, unless one would contradict oneself. One can "prove" only that it is at variance with reason. The proofs which Scripture presents for Christ's divinity— His miracles, His Resurrection from the dead, His Ascension into heaven—are therefore only for faith, that is they are not "proofs", they have no intention of proving that all this agrees with reason; on the contrary they would prove that it conflicts with reason and therefore is an object of faith.[141]

In coming into the world in the form of a servant, God was not directly recognizable. He appeared *incognito,* which Kierkegaard explained as meaning "not to appear in one's proper role, as, for example, when a policeman appears in plain clothes."[142] For the Creator and Sustainer of the world to become an individual man is "absolute unrecognizableness." "To be the individual man, or an individual man (whether it be a distinguished or a lowly man is here irrelevant), is the greatest possible, the infinitely qualitative, remove from being God, and therefore the profoundest incognito."[143] But the modern age has "done away with Christ" either by rejecting his person, while appropriating his teaching, or by trying to make the incarnation something that is demonstrable or directly recognizable.

Kierkegaard went on to argue that to be a contemporary, in the sense of merely living at the same time as Jesus, would be of no particular advantage, so far as knowing Jesus as the God-man is concerned. For mere contemporaneity means to live on the level of the finite. The recognition of Jesus for who he is requires faith. Thus, the incarnation—like a miracle—is a *sign.* A sign is not the same as a proof. It is a pointer, an indication that has to be understood as a sign:

A nautical mark is a sign. Immediately it is a post, a light, or some such thing, but a sign it is not immediately, that it is a sign is something different from what it immediately is.—This [viz. the failure to observe this distinction] lies at the bottom of all the mystifications by the help of "signs"; for a sign is a sign only for one who knows that it is a sign, and in the strictest sense only for one who knows what it signifies; for everyone else the sign is only what it immediately is. . . .

And in the Scripture the God-man is called a sign of contradiction—but what contradiction might there be in the speculative unity of God and man in general? No, in that there is no contradiction; but the contradiction, the greatest possible, the qualitative contradiction, is that between being God and being an individual man. To be a sign is to be, beside what one immediately is, also another thing; to be a sign of contradiction is to be another thing which stands in opposition to what one immediately is. Immediately He is an individual man, just like other men, a lowly, insignificant man; but the contradiction is that *He is God.*

Yet in order that this may not result in a contradiction which exists for no one and which does not exist for everyone (as when a mystification succeeds so well that its effect is null), some factor must be present to draw attention to it. The miracle serves essentially this purpose, and so does a single direct assertion about being God. Yet neither the miracle, nor the single direct assertion is to be regarded as absolutely direct communication; for in this wise the contradiction would *eo ipso* be removed.[144]

This argument appears in *Training in Christianity,* which was published in Copenhagen in 1850. For the next half-century Kierkegaard's thought made little impact outside Denmark, not least because Kierkegaard's numerous books remained untranslated. Within Denmark Kierkegaard was thought of as a brilliant, eccentric private scholar who was overshadowed in the academic world of theology by Hegelians like H. L. Martensen. Martensen's works, not Kierkegaard's, were translated into English and influenced British and American scholarship in the second half of the nineteenth century. It was only in the early years of the twentieth century that Kierkegaard's writings were translated into German and began to influence German thought to any marked degree, and it was only in the 1930s through the American translation of Kierkegaard that the English-speaking world obtained a first-hand acquaintance with his thought. Even so, Kierkegaard was apt to be dismissed as a forerunner of skeptical existentialism instead of being seen as a thinker who saw more clearly than anyone else the questions that arise when we begin to take seriously divine transcendence.

6

ORTHODOXY EMBATTLED

There was no shortage of defenses of miracles by orthodox theologians, whose righteous indignation and belief in the truth of traditional Christianity were displayed in numerous works published on both sides of the Atlantic. It would, however, be a mistake to think that these writers were all responding to continental skepticism, or indeed that orthodoxy was confined to the English-speaking world. There was frequently a time lag between the writing of the continental skeptics and the appearance of their works in English garb. Moreover, there was enough home-grown skepticism to occupy the orthodox apologists of the Anglo-Saxon world. For the sake of convenience we shall focus attention in this chapter on three areas: Roman Catholicism, British Protestantism, and the American Scene. We shall concentrate on the discussions of the othodox, but from time to time we shall have occasion to note the comments of the unorthodox as the debate proceeded.

ROMAN CATHOLICISM

Nearly half a century before Troeltsch's paper "On Historical and Dogmatic Method in Theology," John Henry Newman had given his own answer to the problem posed by Troeltsch. Troeltsch had ruled out belief in miracle stories of the past because they bear no analogy to present experience. It was precisely this point that Newman was concerned to challenge:

> Miracles are not only not unlikely, they are positively likely; and for this simple reason, because, for the most part, when God begins He goes on. We conceive that when He first did a miracle, He began a series; what He commenced, He continued: what has been, will be. Surely this is good and clear reasoning. To my own mind, certainly, it is incomparably more difficult to believe that the Divine Being should do one miracle and no more, than that He should do a thousand; that He should do one great miracle only, than that He should do a multitude of less besides. This beautiful world of nature, His own work, He broke its harmony; He broke through His own laws which He had imposed on it; He worked

out His purposes, not simply through it but in violation of it. If He did this only in the lifetime of the Apostles, if He did it but once, eighteen hundred years ago and more, that isolated infringement looks as the mere infringement of a rule: if Divine Wisdom would not leave an infringement, an anomaly, a solecism on His work, He might be expected to introduce a series of miracles, and turn the apparent exception into an additional law of His providence.[1]

These remarks appeared in the context of a series of *Lectures on the Present Position of Catholics in England* (1851). They were addressed not so much to the skeptic, whose secular world did not admit divine intervention, as the Protestant, who readily believed the miracles in Scripture, but who followed Luther, Calvin, and others in saying that miracles ceased with the apostolic age. At this point in his life Newman was writing as a Roman Catholic, but the position that he adopted summed up his earlier *Two Essays on Biblical and Ecclesiastical Miracles,* which he had written as an Anglican.[2]

Newman defined miracles in terms of events that were *inconsistent* with the laws of nature, as we know them:

A Miracle may be considered as an event inconsistent with the constitution of nature, that is, with the established course of things in which it is found. Or, again, an event in a given system which cannot be referred to any law, or accounted for by the operation of any principle, in that system. It does not necessarily imply a violation of nature, as some have supposed,—merely the interposition of an external cause, which, we shall hereafter show, can be no other than the agency of the Deity. And the effect produced is that of unusual or increased action in the parts of the system.[3]

Newman clearly had in view the argument of Hume and the replies of Campbell, Farmer, Butler, Paley, and others. He recognized that it was often difficult to draw a line between unexplained events and miracles proper, and that "A miracle is no argument to one who is deliberately, and on principle, an atheist."[4] In dealing with the question of the probability of miracles, Newman urged that they should be viewed in the context, not only of the physical, but also of the moral order. Few people have difficulty in seeing that physical acts have a moral dimension in everyday life. Newman urged that, "If . . . the economy of nature has so constant a reference to an ulterior plan, a Miracle is a deviation from the subordinate for the sake of the superior system, and is very far indeed from improbable, when a great moral end cannot be effected except at the expense of physical irregularity."[5]

This last remark forms part of a general argument for "the antecedent credibility of a miracle, considered as a divine interposition."[6] In it Newman sought to turn against Hume the latter's argument that, "As the Deity . . . discovers Himself to us by His works, we have no rational grounds for ascribing to Him attributes or actions dissimilar from those which His works convey."[7] Newman argued that miracles are antecedently credible on the ground that they are consonant with what the Christian believer knows of

God on other grounds. Conversely, cases of alleged miracles that are obviously inconsistent with God's character are deemed to be "antecedently improbable."[8]

Newman's first essay was written at the high watermark of his Protestantism. He clearly distinguished between the biblical miracles and those of the early church. He could even cite Conyers Middleton with approval on this point.[9] Although he did not deny to the miracle stories of the early church "the privilege of being heard,"[10] he maintained that "on the ground of this utter dissimilarity between the Miracles of Scripture and those reported elsewhere, we are enabled to account for the incredulity with which believers in Revelation listen to any extraordinary account at the present day; and which sometimes is urged against them as inconsistent with their assent to the former."[11] In the second essay, however, which was written during Newman's final years as an Anglican, during which he was persuading himself of the propriety of becoming a Roman Catholic, Newman changed his tune. The ecclesiastical miracles of later ages are now seen to be antecedently probable. What God has done once, he may well continue to do. Admittedly, some of the alleged miracles of church history "often partake of what may not unfitly be called a romantic character,"[12] and the true must be discerned from among the spurious. But when this is done, some point at least can be seen in some of the miracles, as in the case of Gregory Thaumaturgus whose miracles were instrumental in mass conversions.[13]

Newman's argument about "antecedent probability" runs remarkably parallel to the position that he adopted in *The Development of Christian Doctrine* (1845).[14] This latter work also dated from the time when Newman was agonizing over whether to join the Roman Catholic Church. He felt acutely the need to explain why so many Roman Catholic beliefs either lacked biblical attestation or seemed at such variance with the early church. Newman found a rationale in the idea of development that supplied both continuity and diversity, as the divine purposes were continually unfolded and adapted to the needs and situation of the church. In both books the idea of "antecedent probability" provided the ground for accepting events and doctrines that in themselves were improbable and ill attested. The notion is, in fact, an important one. Similar ideas have been put forward in more recent times by C. S. Lewis and Richard Swinburne. We shall keep coming across them in the next three chapters, where we shall see that the crucial question lies not with the notion of "antecedent probability" in itself, but with what actually constitutes "antecedent probability." In the meantime, Newman's handling of ecclesiastical miracles met with a good deal of hostile criticism, not least from the pen of A. E. Abbott.[15]

In 1858 fresh impetus was given to the Catholic belief in continued miracles in the church by the visions of a fourteen-year-old peasant girl, Bernadette Soubirous, at Lourdes in the South of France. The visions of the Virgin Mary, who told Bernadette that she was the Immaculate Conception,[16] were followed by accounts of miraculous healings that have continued to the present, making Lourdes a center of pilgrimage. But Lourdes was by no means an isolated instance. As in all cases of canonization of the saints, evidence is required of miracles attributed to the candidate for sainthood.[17] This is examined by the Consulta Medica and published in a *Positio super Miraculis* on completion of the canonization procedure. Even so, the documentation and investigation have not always been as thorough as they might have been. In the opinion of the contemporary Catholic scholar, Leopold Sabourin:

> A close analysis of the evidence presented for the Lourdes miracles and for the miracles of the saints reveals the potential fallibility of human assessments of miracles and the difficulty to ascertain God's direct intervention in extraordinary cures. This does not put into question the opportunity of beatification or canonizations, since the Pope's pronouncements are not invalidated by mistakes in the verification of the miracles. It does, however, pose the question of the opportunity of requesting miracles almost as *sine qua non* conditions for these solemn acts. It would certainly be better for the church to recognise fewer miracles than to have her judgment tied to dubious ones. But this writer acknowledges that even a modest suggestion in that sense may not be adequately founded on an investigation of some limited proportions.[18]

From time to time the Roman Catholic Church has officially reaffirmed its position on the credibility and evidential character of miracles. The First Vatican Council (1869-70) pronounced that since miracles and prophecies "so excellently display God's omnipotence and limitless knowledge, they constitute the surest signs of divine revelation, signs that are suitable to everyone's understanding."[19] The *Oath Against Modernism* (1910), which was required of all clergy to be advanced to major order, pastors, professors, preachers, religious superiors, and seminary professors, reaffirmed this view. Among the explicit affirmations made by the oath-taker was the declaration that "I accept and acknowledge the external proofs of revelation, that is, divine acts and especially miracles and prophecies as the surest signs of the divine origin of the Christian religion and I hold that these same proofs are well adapted to the understanding of all eras and all men, even at this time."[20] The presence of this clause clearly indicates that the Roman Catholic Church was having its own domestic difficulties on this score.

Even before the Vatican Council, J. E. Renan (1823-1882) had published his *Life of Jesus* (1863), the ripple effects of which continued to be felt in France well into the twentieth century. In some ways it was comparable with Strauss's *Life of Jesus* a generation earlier. Both works cost their authors their teaching positions. But whereas Strauss's work was a detailed critical study by a German Protestant making extensive use of the concept of myth, Renan's work was the first nonsupernaturalist biography of Jesus to be penned by a French Roman Catholic. From an early age Renan had been destined for the priesthood, but his growing doubts had already precluded him from that vocation. By the end of 1863 Renan's biography had gone through ten editions of 5,000 copies each, and by the end of the following year it had been translated into most major European languages. The British Museum catalog lists no less than 180 replies to Renan.

The thirteenth edition of Renan's work contained a Preface defending his standpoint and an Introduction discussing sources. Renan expressed two "negations" that were prior to all historical interpretation. He insisted that they were not the result of a particular philosophy, but simply "the outcome of an experience which has not been denied." They concerned miracles and inspiration:

> Miracles are things which never happen; only credulous people believe they have seen them; you cannot cite a single one which has taken place in presence of witnesses capable of testing it; no special intervention of the Divinity, whether in the composition of a book, or in any event whatever, has been proved. For this reason alone, when a person admits the supernatural, such a one is without the province of science; he accepts an explanation which is set aside by the astronomer, the physician, the chemist, the geologist, the physiologist, one which ought also to be passed over by the historian. We reject the supernatural for the same reason that we reject the existence of centaurs and hippogriffes; and this reason is, that nobody has ever seen them. It is not because it has been previously demonstrated to me that the evangelists do not merit absolute credence that I reject the miracles which they recount. It is because they do recount miracles that I say, "The Gospels are legends; they may contain history, but, certainly, all that they set forth is not historical."[21]

The argument sounds like an echo of David Hume. In a manner also reminiscent of Hume, Renan went on to declare, "We do not say, 'The miracle is impossible.' We say, 'So far, a miracle has never been proved.' "[22] But this amounted to a moral certainty that miracles could not happen in the presence of accredited experts under controlled conditions. Underlying the argument was the principle of analogy. However, Renan started where Hume left off. Hume was content to formulate the objections to miracles in principle. Having declared that "If the miracle and the inspiration of certain books are actual facts, our method is detestable,"[23] Renan proceeded to write a biography of Jesus on precisely these principles and simply eliminated the divine and the supernatural from his account.[24]

In the course of the half-century following the publication of Renan's *Life of Jesus* the Roman Catholic Church went through a series of crises occasioned by the spread of Modernism.[25] Even the official condemnation of Modernism by the decree *Lamentabili*, the encyclical *Pascendi* (1907), and the *Oath against Modernism* (1910) did not altogether root it out. In general the Modernists urged the critical study of the Bible in the Catholic Church. They believed that the essence of Christianity was to be sought in life rather than in traditional intellectual dogmatic schemes. Some were prepared to say that the truth of Catholic Christianity was quite independent of its historical origins. The question of miracles came into sharp focus when Maurice Blondel

(1861–1949) published *A Letter on the Requirements of Contemporary Thought and on Philosophical Method in the Study of the Religious Problem* (1896).[26] In the course of his argument Blondel propounded the thesis that

> The proofs are valid only for those who are thoroughly prepared to accept and to understand them; that is why miracles which enlighten some also blind others. Let us use the strictest language about this: since for philosophy no contingent fact is impossible, since the idea of fixed general laws of nature and that of nature itself is only an idol, since every phenomenon is a special case and a unique solution, there is nothing more in a miracle, if one thinks it out fully, than in the most ordinary events. But equally there is nothing less in the most ordinary events than in a miracle.[27]

Blondel went on to define the purpose of miracles and to insist upon the importance of the framework of ideas and predispositions with which we approach miracles:

> The purpose of these interventions, which provoke reflection into making conclusions of a more general character by breaking through the deadening effects of routine, is to show that the divine is to be found not only in what seems to surpass the familiar powers of men and of nature but everywhere, even where we are tempted to think that man and nature are sufficient. So miracles are truly miraculous only for those who are already prepared to recognize the divine action in the most usual events. And it follows that philosophy, which would offend against its own nature by denying them, is no less incompetent to affirm them, and that they are a witness written in a language other than that of which it is the judge.[28]

In the ensuing debate Blondel was denounced for departing from the traditional Catholic stance and for overturning the teaching of the Vatican Council. However, he and his friends protested that he had never denied miracles as such or their importance as signs. He was concerned to protest against Extrinsicism. In other words, he was attacking as naive, simplistic, and ultimately derogatory to miracles themselves the view that values miracles only for their external apologetic value as events providing divine attestation. Such an attitude is not concerned with the particular character of any given miracle. The extrinsic character is all that matters. To appeal to miracles in this way is to use them as a sign or label.

> detached from the facts and placarded at the entry to the dogmatic fortress. But it is noteworthy that this label remains external both to the events, which only support it arbitrarily, and to the ideas themselves, which accept it from outside, as an adventitious and empirical fact. From which it follows that the historical facts are merely a vehicle, the interest of which is limited to the apologetic use which can be made of them; for, whether *this* or *that* miracle is involved, provided it is *a* miracle, the argument remains the same.[29]

Although the target of these remarks was traditional Catholic apologetics, they could have been directed with equal justice against a good deal of Protestant apologetics.

Blondel was no less concerned over the shortcomings of historicism, which had been exemplified by Alfred Loisy's *The Gospel and the Church* (1902).[30] Loisy's work was intended as a modern Catholic reply to Harnack's *What is Christianity?* It contains the memorable dictum: "Jesus foretold the kingdom, and it was the Church that came."[31] The saying is remembered as a cynical comment on the difference between Jesus' lofty teaching and the realities of the institutional church. But in context it was actually a defense of the church, as may be seen when the sentence is quoted in full:

> Jesus foretold the kingdom, and it was the Church that came; she came, enlarging the form of the gospel, which it was impossible to preserve as it was, as soon as the Passion closed the ministry of Jesus. There is no institution on earth or in history whose status and value may not be questioned if the principle is established that nothing may exist except in its original form.[32]

The kind of sociological, nonsupernatural justification of the church that Loisy developed was hardly congenial to the authorities of the Catholic Church. The Archbishop of Paris condemned *The Gospel and the Church*. All of Loisy's writings were placed on the Index of Prohibited Books in 1903. He abandoned his priestly functions in 1906 and was excommunicated two years later. From 1909 to 1930 Loisy was professor of the history of religions at the Collège de France. His views became increasingly skeptical. His study *The Birth of the Christian Religion* (1933) treated the Gospels as catechetical and cultural literature with only slight historical basis. The miracles of Jesus were treated as symbolic stories, invented to enhance the church's catechesis.[33]

In the meantime, Blondel—who remained within the Catholic Church—criticized historicism for failing to perceive the reality behind historical phenomena and for mistaking external acts for the object itself.[34] Historicism was preoccupied with a surface view of history, being preoccupied with the chain of events, understood in a shallow secular way. Blondel argued that history could not be approached from a neutral, objective standpoint. Such a standpoint did not exist. The meaning of gospel history could be understood only from the standpoint of Christian life and faith, as lived out in the church. Hence, he claimed,

> In that profound sense, when it is a question of finding the supernatural in Sacred History and in dogma, the Gospel is nothing without the Church, the teaching of Scripture is nothing without the Christian life, exegesis is nothing without Tradition—the Catholic Tradition which is now seen not to be a limitative and retrograde force, but a power of development and expansion.[35]

The French Modernist debate about miracles reached a new level of intensity in the confrontation between Blondel and Edouard Le Roy, the Idealist who defined a miracle as "an act of an individual spirit (or group of individual spirits), acting as a spirit in a degree higher than normal, finding in fact and as in a flash of lightning its power as law."[36] Blondel found inadequate this view of action, the supernatural, and matter. The debate reached its climax in the discussions of the *Société Française de Philosophie* in 1911, where both Blondel and Le Roy further clarified their position, though not to the satisfaction of all. Le Roy protested that he had been misunderstood over the role of faith, but this did not prevent Léon Brunschvicg from complaining that, whereas miracles were traditionally understood as being given for faith, with man as the astonished witness, Le Roy was making miracles the creation of faith with man as their agent. Blondel saw miracles as spokesmen of the divine philanthropy that cause God's unusual goodness to appear in unusual signs. Lucien Laberthonnière argued that a miracle was a divine intervention aimed at "working in us disenchantment with things and causing us to look higher than the order of things which pass by means of this same order."[37]

In the years that followed the Modernist crisis the Roman Catholic Church has tended to combine the strict evidentialist view of miracles with an appreciation of their significance. In 1964 the Second Vatican Council maintained that "The miracles of Jesus also demonstrate that the kingdom of God has already come on earth: 'If I cast out devils by the finger of God, then the kingdom of God has come upon you' (Lk. 11:20; cf. Matt. 12:28)."[38] But the Council went on to insist that, "principally the kingdom is revealed in the person of Christ himself, Son of God and Son of Man, who came 'to serve and to give his life as a ransom for many' (Mk. 10:45)." This more balanced statement moderates the one-sided impression given by the First Vatican Council that miracles on their own provide self-evident proof to all and sundry. Alongside this may be placed the view of the contemporary Catholic theologian Richard P. McBrien, who concludes that "Miracles are manifestations of the power of God and as such are consistent with divine Providence. They were central to Jesus' ministry. They enter into the formation of our own faith. Beyond that, many questions remain open."[39] Taken together, Vatican II and McBrien seem to represent a return to something like Newman's position that miracles are not free-standing, isolated events, any one of which provides a knock-down proof of divine intervention. Rather, they should be seen in the wider context of God's actions and purposes.

PROTESTANT ORTHODOXY

The shifts of emphasis that may be seen in Roman Catholicism were paralleled in Protestant orthodoxy. The basic evidentialist position was advocated by William Paley (1743–1805), whose writings were long regarded as standard textbooks in the field of apologetics. Paley's *View of the Evidences of Christianity* (1794)[40] and *Natural Theology* (1802) form companion pieces that address the basic questions that Bishop Butler asked over half a century earlier, giving substantially the same reply. There was, however, a major difference. Whereas Bishop Butler had written in reply to the deists, Paley was responding to Hume. This is evident right from the first page of the "Preparatory Considerations" that preface Paley's *View of the Evidences of Christianity*, which seek "to shew that there is not such an antecedent improbability in the Christian miracles as no human testimony can surmount, in opposition to Hume's objection, 'that it is contrary to experience that miracles should be true, but not contrary to experience that testimony should be false.' "[41] The term "antecedent improbability" was one which John Henry Newman was to take up a generation later, as we have seen, and respond to it by offering a catholicized version of Paley's argument. Paley himself urged that miracles were not improbable, if it be granted "first, that a future state of existence should be destined by God for his human creation; and secondly, being so destined, he should acquaint them with it."[42]

These presuppositions that Paley brought to the interpretation of the evidence for miracles were bound up with further presuppositions. The latter included the existence of God as the Creator of the universe, his ability to interrupt "the course of nature," the propriety of such interruptions as and when justified by divine purposes, Paley's own inability to conceive of divine revelation without miraculous attestation, and the consequent lack of need for further miracles, once the revelation had been attested.[43] In seeing miracles primarily as attestations of divine revelation, Paley was following the path of the Calvinistic tradition that Locke had marked out so clearly for English Protestant theology. Such considerations led Paley to conclude that, if twelve men whose "probity and good sense" he had long known were to be arrested and tortured for relating "an account of a miracle wrought before there would not exist any skeptic in the world, who would not believe them, or who would defend such incredulity."[44]

As the argument of the book unfolded, Paley elaborated these arguments in more detail. What is striking is that Paley's position is not strictly an evidentialist position, which regards evidential data in and of itself as sufficient proof of the conclusions to be drawn. At the outset Paley granted that miracles do not prove the existence of God; they are apprehended and understood in the light of beliefs about God that are established on other grounds.[45] Paley went on to give tacit recognition that we do not have direct access to the miracles in question, but have to form our beliefs about their probability in the light of various general considerations that he brings to the interpretation of the evidence. In other words, all facts are "theory-laden," and Paley's view of the evidence for miracles is clearly no exception to this rule. This is not necessarily to say that Paley's position was wrong. It is rather to recognize that Paley's acceptance of miracles was part of a belief-system that was not validated or invalidated by appeal to single facts. Rather, it was a way of interpreting clusters of data in the light of a cluster of beliefs.

Before we leave Paley, one point in particular calls for comment: his appeal to the testimony of twelve honest men under extreme duress as a refutation of skepticism to the miraculous. It has to be said that Paley's reputation as a clear, logical thinker wears thin at this point. The most that it would prove is their willingness to suffer for their beliefs, whatever their cause. The argument could be inverted and applied to the deists, Thomas Woolston and Peter Annet, who were also prepared to suffer for the integrity of their disbelief in miracles. Moreover, if Paley was referring to the twelve apostles, it must be pointed out that he did not know them personally, that we do not have the testimony of all twelve to the miracles of Jesus in general but only to the miracle of the resurrection in particular. Even so, we do not have the testimony of all twelve: Judas must be discounted, and we have only the reports in the Gospels and Acts from which the testimony of the others must be inferred. So far as we know, the apostles were not put to the test that Paley describes for their witness to miracles in general. The report that comes nearest to what Paley describes concerns not an apostle at all, but the man born blind whose healing poses questions that demand an existential response (John 9). Even so, the man was not tortured for his testimony to Jesus' healing.

Paley's *View of the Evidence of Christianity* focused on miracles, but it also appealed to such "auxiliary evidences of Christianity" as prophecy, the morality of the gospel, and the identity and originality of Christ's character. As part of the argument, consideration was given to the authenticity of Scripture. For Paley, miracles cannot be separated from the Christ of the Gospels. The choice before the modern reader is whether to dismiss them as an "idle report or frivolous account"[46] or see them as the divine attestation of Jesus as the Messiah.[47] Paley's argument did not anticipate the objections of Strauss. Moreover, it made certain assumptions about the existence and activity of God. What Paley succeeded in doing was not to prove beyond all reasonable doubt that the miracles reported in the Gospels had actually happened, but that they were feasible, if certain conditions were stipulated. It was not accidental that the *View of the Evidences of Christianity* was followed by Paley's *Natural Theology,* which sought to demonstrate the feasibility of a theistic view of God by examining the evidence of design and purpose in nature. Taken together, Paley's two books form an argument comparable to Bishop Butler's for an analogy of natural and revealed theology, both of which point in the same direction. But whereas Butler treated the natural order first, Paley inverted the order. Paley's arguments lacked the sophistication of Butler's. Perhaps it was for that very reason that Paley, with his robust appeal to the honesty and veracity of the biblical witnesses, became the standard bearer of English apologetics in the nineteenth century.

In a similar vein were the arguments of Richard Whately (1787–1863), who was a prominent Oxford figure in the 1820s. A profuse writer, Whately became Archbishop of Dublin in 1831. For a time he exerted considerable influence on John Henry Newman, but later became a vigorous opponent of the Catholic movement within the Church of England. He was scarcely less opposed to evangelicalism. His writings exhibited a concern to show the reasonableness of broad-church orthodoxy. Whately's *Christian Evidences, Intended Chiefly for the Young* (1864) was a clear and concise restatement of familiar arguments. The appeal to fulfilled prophecy and miracles constituted the major part of the discussion of external evidence. Somewhat earlier Whately achieved fame with his tract *Historic Doubts Relative to Napoleon Buonaparte* (1819), which was an attempted *reductio ad absurdum* of Hume's doubts about the force of historical testimony. The work enjoyed considerable popularity on both sides of the Atlantic, and continued to be reprinted after its author's death. However, it belongs more to the history of rhetoric and light entertainment than to serious scholarship. It confuses two kinds of uniqueness. On the one hand, there are reports of events that are without strict parallels, but that nevertheless fall within the range of the normal, since they do not violate patterns of recurrent types of behavior. On the other hand, reports of certain miracles testify to events without any parallel within recurrent experience. Although Whately's essay continued to be admired by certain types of apologists, its confusion of categories offered little real help to the troubled doubter. As a reply to Hume, coming some seventy years late, it was a testimony to the continuing impact of Hume's skepticism. It possessed a certain degree of novelty, as Napoleon's exploits were still vivid in the memory at the time of writing. However, Whately's implied assumption that the witness of the four evangelists to the supernatural works of Jesus was just as strong as contemporary testimony to the nonsupernatural actions of Napoleon was one that could not survive unquestioned forever.

As the century wore on, the groundswell of skepticism about miracles and their evidential value became more pronounced. Already in 1825 the poet and amateur philosopher and theologian, Samuel Taylor Coleridge (1772–1834), expressed his misgivings concerning

> the prevailing taste for Books of Natural Theology, Physico-Theology, Demonstrations of God from Nature, Evidences of Christianity, &c., &c. *Evidences* of Christianity! I am weary of the Word. Make a man feel the *want* of it; rouse him, if you can, to the self-knowledge of his *need* of it; and you may safely trust it to its own Evidence—remembering only the express declaration of Christ himself: No man cometh to me, unless the Father leadeth him! Whatever more is desirable—I speak now with reference to Christians generally, and not to professed Students of Theology—may in my judgment, be far more safely and profitably taught, without controversy or the supposition of infidel antagonists, in the form of Ecclesiastical History.[48]

By the time that Coleridge wrote these words his creative period as a poet was already well behind him. He had made an involved spiritual pilgrimage from Unitarianism, through the pantheism of Boehme and Spinoza, to a form of Christianity that was much more indebted to German Idealism than these words might suggest.[49] In the course of time Coleridge came to be regarded as the Father of the Broad Church Movement in the Anglican Church.

With regard to miracles, Coleridge did not believe that the important thing about them was that they contradicted the laws of nature and thus offered clear evidence of supernatural intervention. He was willing to entertain the view that with the increase of scientific knowledge miracles might be "resolvable into the universal laws." Yet he went on to add:

> But should that time arrive, the sole difference that could result from such an enlargement of our view, would be this;—that what we now consider as miracles in opposition to ordinary experience, we should then reverence with a yet higher devotion as harmonious parts of one great complex miracle, when the antithesis between experience and belief would itself be taken up into unity of intuitive reason.[50]

For Coleridge the significance of miracles lay in their value as signs. As such, faith played a major part in their discernment. "The Miracles are *parts* of our Religion and Objects of our Belief, not the Grounds of it."[51] By abandoning the evidentialist approach to miracles, Coleridge was able to see their doctrinal significance. Hence, he could ask:

> Is it not that implication of doctrine in the miracle and of miracle in the doctrine, which is the bridge of communication between the senses and the soul;—that predisposing warmth which renders the understanding susceptible of the specific impression from the historic, and from all other outward seals of testimony? Is not this the one infallible criterion of miracles, by which a man can know whether they be of God?[52]

Alongside this quotation taken from *The Friend* may be placed an extract from one of Coleridge's notebooks:

> As a general *rule*, we may say—that without faith in the Patient the Miracle would not have been *symbolic*—or the outward sign of the yet more aweful Miracle worked by the indwelling Christ in the Soul. Faith was, as it were, the Bond or common term between the operation of Christ ab extra, and that of the indwelling Saviour.[53]

Coleridge was not saying here that miracles were the product of faith. Nor was he addressing the issue of whether we can be reasonably certain that any given miracle had actually occurred. His point has to do with the understanding of the significance of a miracle as a miracle, as a distinct occurrence that may or may not have an explanation. Coleridge's thoughts were moving in the same direction as those of Søren Kierkegaard, his contemporary, who in the next twenty years was to develop his own understanding of the role of faith in apprehending and discerning Christ. Curiously enough, both Coleridge and Kierkegaard developed their views in the wake of Kant and German Idealism.

In an appraisal of Coleridge, John Stuart Mill ranked him together with the utilitarian and philosophical radical, Jeremy Bentham, as possessing "the two great seminal minds of England of their age." Bentham, he went on to say, taught men to ask, "Is it true?" Coleridge, on the other hand, taught them to ask, "What is the meaning of it?"[54] Despite his respect for Coleridge, Mill's own mind was of a somewhat different cast, especially in matters concerning religion. His *System of Logic* (1843) contained a chapter reiterating and developing Hume's position. In it Mill argued that:

> If we do not already believe in supernatural agencies, no miracle can prove to us their existence. The miracle itself, considered merely as an extraordinary fact, may be satisfactorily certified by our senses or by testimony; but nothing can ever prove that it is a miracle: there is still another possible hypothesis, that of its being the result of some unknown natural cause; and this possibility cannot be so completely shut out as to leave no alternative but that of admitting the existence and intervention of a Being superior to nature.[55]

Mill elaborated this position in his *Three Essays on Religion* (1874), in the course of which he stipulated the following conditions for an event to qualify as a miracle:

> To make it a miracle it must be produced by a direct volition, without the use of means; or at least of any means which if simply repeated would produce it. To constitute a miracle a phenomenon must take place without having been preceded by any antecedent phenomenal conditions sufficient again to produce it; or a phenomenon for the production of which the antecedent conditions existed, must be arrested or prevented without the intervention of any phenomenal antecedents which would arrest or prevent it in a future case.[56]

Mill acknowledged the possibility of the deity using secondary means to bring about an event in a way analogous to that of human agents directing the course of events by an act of the will. But he insisted that "divine interference with nature could be proved if we had the same sort of evidence for it which we have for human interferences."[57] On this score Mill remained skeptical, insisting that there might always be reasons of which we have not thought that might explain the event in a nonsupernatural way.

The mid-nineteenth century witnessed a growing profusion of testimonies to skepticism. George Eliot's translations of Strauss and Feuerbach contributed to the chorus of doubt, but by no stretch of the imagination could they be held solely responsible for the atheism and agnosticism of the times. More muted and at the same time more poignant than Mill's rigorous logic was the work of Francis William Newman (1805–1897), the younger brother of John Henry Newman. For many years he was professor of Latin at University College, London. In his earlier days he had been strongly influenced by J. N. Darby, the founder of the Plymouth Brethren. By 1850 Newman was a thoroughgoing liberal and had described his odyssey in *Phases of Faith*. Although the apostles might err on scientific matters, their moral and spiritual wisdom could still be accepted. Miracles must not be made to be the prop of faith. Otherwise, they could well prove to be its destruction.

Charles Darwin's *Origin of Species* (1859) was felt by many to be an assault on Christianity, since it proposed the theory of natural selection as an alternative to direct creation and as an explanation of the design and order in the world that Paley had appealed to as the basis of his natural theology. In 1860, a group of scholars largely connected with the University of Oxford published *Essays and Reviews*—a professedly Christian book. At the same time, the contributors insisted that Christian beliefs should be brought into line with modern knowledge. Compared with later views, the opinions of the authors were relatively mild. Nevertheless, the book provoked a scandal, involving a protracted court case.[58] Darwin's work was endorsed by Baden Powell, Savilian Professor of Geometry at the University of Oxford, in his essay "On the Study of the Evidences of Christianity." The title was consciously reminiscent of Paley's work, but the stance adopted by Powell was vastly different from Paley's. Powell argued that the orderly system of nature is incompatible with belief in the miraculous. For a miracle is an "arbitrary interposition" in nature.[59] In a way similar to Mill's, Powell argued that sooner or later science will be able to explain phenomena that are at present inexplicable. Like Francis William Newman, he argued that revelation is not established by "alleged external attestations."[60] God's moral government does not need such proofs. Powell claimed that, "in the popular acceptation, it is clear the Gospel miracles are always *objects*, not *evidences;* and when they are connected specially with doctrines, as in several of the higher mysteries of the Christian faith, the sanctity which invests the point of faith itself is extended to the external narrative in which it is embodied."[61] He concluded that "the *reason* of the hope that is in us is not restricted to *external* signs, nor to any one kind of evidence, but consists of such assurance as may be most satisfactory to each earnest individual inquirer's own mind."[62]

Powell's conclusion appears to give back with one hand what his other hand had already taken away. Matthew Arnold (1822–1888) made no such concessions. To insist on "the miracle of the incarnation," he wrote in *Literature and Dogma* (1873), is to insist

> on just that side of Christianity which is perishing. Christianity is immortal; it has eternal truth, inexhaustible value, a boundless future. But our popular religion at present conceives the birth, ministry, and death of Christ, as altogether steeped in prodigy, brimful of miracle;—*and miracles do not happen.*"[63]

To Arnold it did not matter whether miracles were attacked or defended. The spirit of the age was turning against them for the simple reason that *"it sees, as its experience widens, how they arise."*[64] Arnold himself, who was fond of sprinkling his essays with German words (though he did not always translate them correctly) and was evidently well-read in recent German thought, did not hesitate to attribute belief in miracles to *Aberglaube,* superstition.

Arnold elaborated his themes in *God and the Bible: A Review of Ob-*

jections to "Literature and Dogma" (1875), in which he disarmingly claimed that his earlier work had been written to restore the use of the Bible to those who were disposed to throw it aside. He insisted that the Bible requires for its basis nothing that cannot be verified, and that the language of the Bible is not scientific but literary. Arnold now responded to critics to the right who claimed that he might have taken a more favorable view of miracles if he had paused to study J. B. Mozley's recent Bampton Lectures on miracles, and he responded as well to critics to the left who felt that he could have gone still further and given a thorough refutation of miracles. In response to both sets of critics Arnold cheerfully stood his ground. He acknowledged Mozley's ability, but declined to refute his arguments on the grounds that such a reply would be to engage in what Strauss called "going out of one's way to assail the paper fortifications which theologians choose to set up."[65] On the other hand, he felt that Strauss himself had gone too far in explaining the miracles of the New Testament in terms of the Old Testament. The explanation might fit the transfiguration of Jesus as a repetition of the transfiguration of Moses,[66] but it hardly fitted the walking on the water, the coin in the fish's mouth, the cursing of the fig tree, and sundry other episodes. Although Strauss's idea was "acute and ingenious," Arnold felt that "every miracle had its own mode of growth and its own history, and the key to one is not the key to others."

Arnold also paused to comment on W. R. Cassels's *Supernatural Religion,* which had been published anonymously in 1874.[67] The latter had taken up Hume's and Mill's appeal to induction as the means to establish scientific possibility. Mill had observed that "Hume's celebrated doctrine, that nothing is credible which is contradictory to experience or at variance with the laws of nature, is merely the very plain and harmless proposition, that whatever is contrary to a complete induction is incredible."[68] Cassels endorsed this view and with it Mill's further claim that

> If these observations or experiments have been repeated so often, and by so many persons, as to exclude all supposition of error in the observer, a law of nature is established. . . . We cannot admit a proposition as a law of nature, and yet believe a fact in real contradiction to it. We must disbelieve the alleged fact, or believe that we were mistaken in admitting the supposed law.[69]

Cassels proceeded to apply this to Paley's notorious appeal to the testimony of the twelve honest men that we have already noted, pointing out that "martyrdom cannot transform imaginations into facts," and expressing his astonishment that "arguments like these should for so many years have been tolerated in the text-book of a University."[70]

While sympathizing with the disbelief of Cassels, Matthew Arnold could not refrain from observing that the argument had been overstated: "No such law of nature as Mr. Mill describes has been or can be established against the Christian miracles; a complete induction against them, therefore, there is not.''[71] On the other hand, the reporters of the miracles were not the sort of "picked jury" that Paley's argument required, and no one can be certain that they had fallen into "error and legend." Arnold felt safe in consigning the miracles to "the unreal world of fairy-tale. Having no reality of their own, they cannot lend it as foundation for the reality of anything else.''[72]

The nearest counterpart to the lives of Jesus by Strauss and Renan was the anonymous *Ecce Homo* (1865), whose author, John Seeley (1834–1895), was professor of Latin at University College, London. Seeley went on to become professor of modern history at Cambridge, and was knighted shortly before his death. The title of the book was taken from the words of Pontius Pilate in John 19:5: "Behold the man!" It was indicative of the contents of the book, which consistently toned down the supernatural and miraculous in the Gospel stories of Jesus. Seeley stopped well short of Strauss and Renan in his criticisms of miracles, however. His style was more muted and his comments more vague. He did not deny miracles outright, but insisted that "Miracles are, in themselves, extremely improbable things, and cannot be admitted unless supported by a great concurrence of evidence."[73] Seeley went on to say that there was such a concurrence of evidence for the resurrection and "the general fact that Christ was a miraculous healer of disease. The evidence by which these facts are supported cannot be tolerably accounted for by any other hypothesis except that of their being true. And if they are once admitted, the antecedent improbability of many miracles less strongly attested is much diminished." The language here is reminiscent of Newman, but Newman would certainly have not gone on to say that "Nevertheless nothing is more natural than that exaggerations and even inventions should be mixed in our biographies with genuine facts.''[74]

Where possible, Seeley offered natural explanations for miracles. In commenting on Jesus' baptism, he wrote, "There is nothing necessarily miraculous in the appearance of a dove, and a peal of thunder might be shaped into intelligible words by the excited imagination of men accustomed to consider thunder as the voice of God." Elsewhere he quietly passed over the question of miracles, and dwelt on "the combination of greatness and self-sacrifice" which won people's hearts.

> This temperance in the use of supernatural power is the masterpiece of Christ. It is a moral miracle superinduced upon a physical one. This repose in greatness makes him surely the most sublime image ever offered to the human imagination. . . . It was neither for his miracles nor for the beauty of his doctrine that Christ was worshipped. Nor was it for his winning personal character, nor for the persecutions he endured, nor for his martyrdom. It was for the inimitable unity which all these things made when taken together.[75]

If Seeley started out to write a life of Jesus, giving a milder British version of the antisupernaturalism of his continental counterparts, the result anticipated the moralistic conclusions of Ritschl and Harnack. His book reads like an extended Victorian obituary, assessing Jesus' place in history as one who responded to the divine call to renew the ancient Jewish theocracy. His goal was to establish the kingdom of God, the object of which was that God's will may be done on earth as it is in heaven. In the language of our own day, its object was "the improvement of morality."[76]

A somewhat more temperate approach to the same subject had been put forward earlier by Frederick Denison Maurice (1805-1872) in *The Kingdom of Christ, Or Hints to a Quaker Respecting the Principles, Constitution and Ordinances of the Church* (1838, revised edition 1842).[77] Maurice's father was a Unitarian minister, and Maurice himself had been brought up among Unitarians and Quakers. His Unitarian background gave him a certain affinity to Coleridge, to whose thought Maurice felt himself indebted, especially in his earlier years. Maurice became an Anglican in 1831. Maurice's career was controversial. He was professor of theology at King's College, London. He started a Working Men's College. He was a prolific author. Toward the end of his life he became professor of moral philosophy at Cambridge. In his theology Maurice tried to steer a middle course between the extremes of Catholicism and evangelicalism, avoiding dogmas and dogmatism. What he succeeded in producing was a christocentric theology that anticipated the theology of the later Karl Barth, although Barth seems to have been unaware of Maurice's existence. He believed that "Mankind stands not in Adam but in Christ."[78] Thus all people are elect in Christ. Sin is a falling from the grace in which people already stand. "The world is the Church without God; the Church is the world restored to its relation with God, taken back by Him into the state for which He created it."[79]

On the question of miracles Maurice followed in the footsteps of Coleridge in rejecting the idea of miracles as the chief evidence for the truth of Christianity:

> Now if it is meant by this that a miracle or prodigy, as such, proves the divine commission of the person who enacts it, we have the strongest reason for rejecting such a notion, for the Bible commands us to reject it. We dare not believe anything merely because something which strikes us as a departure from ordinary experiences or laws is done to confirm it: we are warned in Scripture that we shall see such wonders, and that we are to beware of being deceived by them. Again, the Bible is remarkably a book of laws, a book explaining the divine order of the universe; if it be not this it is nothing. Can we suppose that violations of laws, infringements of order, would be the great signs and witnesses in confirmation of it?[80]

The point that Maurice is making here was not an attempt to prepare the ground for jettisoning miracles from the Christian faith. In his own way he was anticipating Blondel's protest against extrinsicism with its appeal to supernatural events as a sanction for dogma. To Maurice miracles were not proofs but signs arousing people from materialism, demonstrating that "spiritual power is superior to mechanical; that the world is subject to God, and not to chance or nature."[81] Every miracle recorded in the Old Testament is recorded expressly as a witness that the Jehovah, the I AM, the Lord of the spirits of all flesh, is the King of the world, and that gods of sense are not its kings. Every miracle recorded in the New Testament is recorded expressly and professedly for the purpose of showing that the Son of man is the ruler of the winds and the waves; the sustainer and restorer of animal life; the healer and tamer of the human spirit; and that those who are adopted children of God in him, while they are doing his work, are not the servants of visible things, but their rulers.[82]

To the evangelical leader Lord Shaftesbury, Maurice was "neither sound Protestant nor true Papist."[83] But this verdict was mild compared with his judgment delivered at a meeting of the Church Pastoral-Aid Society on *Ecce Homo,* which he denounced as one of the "most pestilential books ever vomitted from the jaws of hell."[84] More muted, but nonetheless negative, were the comments of Brooke Foss Westcott, who in a letter to F. J. A. Hort described his sentiments on noticing the book in J. B. Lightfoot's study:

> You will imagine that I felt its defects far more than its merits. I cannot think that any estimate of our Lord's work and person which starts from its ethical aspect can be other than fatally deceptive. This was not that which the Apostles preached, and not this could have conquered the world. I feel more strongly than I dare express that it is this so-called Christian morality as "the sum of the Gospel," which makes Christianity so powerless now.[85]

When he wrote this in 1866 Westcott was an assistant master at Harrow School. He went on to become Regius Professor of Divinity at Cambridge (1870). Together with Hort he prepared the celebrated critical edition of the Greek New Testament (1881). The "Cambridge trio" of Lightfoot, Westcott, and Hort planned a series of scholarly commentaries on the New Testament. Although they did not succeed in covering the entire New Testament, they raised British New Testament scholarship to a new level. Their solid, devout approach did much to preserve faith in the integrity of the New Testament at a time when it was widely assailed.[86]

In 1859 F. D. Maurice launched a bitter attack on H. L. Mansel's Bampton Lectures, *The Limits of Religious Thought* (1858). Maurice entitled his reply *What is Revelation? A Series of Sermons on the Epiphany.* In the course of his argument he further developed his view that the miracles of Jesus were not performed to provide empirical evidence of his authority. Rather, they were themselves epiphanies or works wrought "for the *manifestation* of Christ's glory."[87] Maurice noted that this was the expression used in John 2:11 to describe the miracle at Cana, and that in the lectionary of the ecclesiastical year the church chose this and other miracle stories for the Gospel readings on the Sundays after Epiphany. These stories were not "arguments to convince the understanding that it ought to suspend its own proper exercises; they are unveilings or manifestations to the whole man, of the nature, character, mind, of the Son of Man; and therefore, as He shows us in the passage of which my text forms a part, of the nature, character, mind, of the Father who sent Him." The text in question was John 10:37-38: "If I do not the works of my Father, believe me not. But if I do, though ye believe not me, believe the works: that ye may know, and believe, that the Father is in me, and I in Him." Jesus' acts of healing likewise "bear witness of a Father who is full of grace and truth, of a Father who is not the destroyer but the restorer of men, who is pursuing them into all the secret places of their sorrow and misery to make them right."[88] If they were not such works, Jesus should not be believed. In the same way, Jesus' exorcisms are manifestations of the love and power of God over the forces of evil. "Was not He showing that there are no usurpers over the human spirit so mighty that He cannot overcome them?"[89]

In the same year (1859) Brooke Foss Westcott also published three sermons during the Epiphany season, which he entitled *Characteristics of the Gospel Miracles: Sermons Preached before the University of Cambridge*. In several ways, not least in his Christian Socialism, Westcott was a disciple of Maurice. His sermons on miracles show a marked similarity of approach. Westcott was acutely aware of the difficulties that miracles posed for the modern mind. At one time they had been singled out as the master-proof of the Christian faith; now they were kept back as difficulties in the way of its reception. Westcott wisely refrained from trying to justify miracles as but particular instances of the general processes of nature. He recognized that whereas we can trace each step of the process by which rainwater becomes wine through the growth of the grape and the fermentation of its juice, no such steps can be traced in the miracles.[90] He preferred to compare miracles with God's acts in creation and providence: "They are unimaginable; and yet they *are*."[91]

Westcott saw the Gospel miracles as "a Revelation, an Epiphany of Christ."[92] In so doing, he detected a difference between the miracles of the Old Testament and those of the New:

> Under the Law the miracles were given specially to attest the messenger, that men might know that the Lord had sent him: in the Gospel they are peculiarly part of the work, part of the message; or, if Christ *once* confirmed His word by an outward sign, it was to convey the most comforting of spiritual promises, to give a sacrament of pardon in restored strength, that we might know that *the Son of Man hath power on earth* not to declare the word of the Lord only, but *to forgive sins*.

> The connexion between a sign and an inward truth which is revealed in these words, underlies all the other miracles of the Gospel.[93]

In each of his three Epiphany sermons on miracles Westcott considered one of the three types of miracle performed by Jesus: miracles performed on nature, those performed on man, and those performed on the spirit-world.

Westcott discerned two types of nature miracles, miracles of power and miracles of providence. The miracles of power included the changing of water into wine, the multiplication of the loaves, and the walking on the water.

They were signs of Christ as the source of joy, subsistence, and strength.[94] Whereas the miracles of power were unimaginable, the miracles of providence had a natural aspect. It was not beyond nature to produce a great draught of fishes, to still a storm, or for a coin to be found in a fish, or a fig tree to wither. "The miracle lies in the circumstances and not in the mere fact."[95] To Westcott all these miracles were sacramental signs of God's graciousness in Christ.

Whereas the nature-miracles were "an Epiphany of sovereignty," the miracles on man were "an Epiphany of mercy."[96] The redemption of man was more glorious than the redemption of nature, and it was not without significance that the miracles of healing occupy so large a place in the Gospels. Some were performed in response to personal faith. Others came about through intercession, whereas others were the work of sheer love.[97] In this sermon Westcott introduced a thought that has figured only rarely in Christian discussions of miracles, which has tended to see Jesus' miracles only in connection with his divinity. Westcott argued that the miracles were "not deeds of His Divine Nature only. . . . In the miracles, as elsewhere, a perfect manhood acts in absolute harmony with a perfect Divinity."[98] As we noted in Chapter One, Westcott developed this view in later life, to the point where he was ready to attribute Jesus' works to "the help of the Father through the energy of a humanity enabled to do all things in fellowship with God" (cf. John 11:41f.). This prompted Charles Gore to see the miracles as the work of the Father acting through the Son by the Holy Spirit.[99]

The healing miracles culminated in the raising stories. Westcott saw "the whole Gospel" contained in the words of John 11:25: "I am the Resurrection and the Life: he that believeth on me, though he were dead, yet shall he live."[100] The exorcisms, or miracles of the spirit-world, were likewise sacramental revelations of God's "absolute antagonism with evil" coordinated with "a boundless compassion for the sufferer."[101] The miracles were thus all "sacraments of heavenly realities" carrying lessons of creation, providence, mercy, and judgment for the church until it shares in "the unspeakable triumph of His future Epiphany of glory."[102]

In assessing Westcott's thought at a whole, Henry Chadwick speaks of his "fastidious scholarship" and also of his Platonism:

> To many who already believed in God Westcott spoke words of gold. . . . But to materialists, pantheists, and atheists, and to anyone who did not intuitively understand his passionate sense of the mystery of life and of the inconclusiveness of our space-time existence, Westcott's words could never be effective or impressive in the same way.[103]

Westcott's Victorian homiletical style is no longer to the modern taste. Nevertheless, there is much that is suggestive in his sermons on miracles, not least the thought of the miracles as sacramental signs, his refusal to attribute miracles unequivocally to Christ's divinity, and his desire to understand them in relation to his humanity. Alec Vidler speaks of Westcott's "sense of all life's being lit up by the eternal."[104] Although they had probably never heard of each other's names, Westcott's position was not unlike that of his recently deceased Danish contemporary, Kierkegaard. Both saw the miracles of Jesus as signs, and both approached them from the standpoint of faith. Moreover, both discussed them within the context of homilies. But whereas Kierkegaard reflected on the indirect character of revelation and the consequent demands on faith, Westcott found comfort, hope, and strength in the miracles of Jesus as tokens of God's graciousness in Christ.

Westcott's rejection of the evidentialist approach to the Gospel miracles was anticipated by *Notes on the Miracles of Our Lord* (1846) by Richard Chenevix Trench (1807–1886), which Trench published as a sequel to his *Notes on the Parables of Our Lord* (1841). Educated at Harrow and Cambridge, Trench was a professor, first of divinity and later of New Testament, at King's College, London (1846–1858), where he was a colleague of F. D. Maurice. In later life he was Archbishop of Dublin. Trench repeatedly revised his writings in order to keep them abreast of current thought, and his book on miracles has been kept in print as a valued expository tool for preachers down to the present day. The bulk of the book was devoted to devotional exposition of the Gospel miracles, illuminated by references to the church fathers. Before proceeding to the "more pleasant and more profitable" task of examining the biblical narratives,[105] Trench set out his thoughts on the purpose and apologetic value of miracles in the light of criticism from Spinoza onward. When compared with Paley and earlier apologists, a distinct shift of emphasis becomes apparent.

Trench complained that the traditional apologetic use of miracles as unassailable events that establish the truth of Christian beliefs reduces Christianity to "a sort of revealed Deism."[106] Although Trench himself did not doubt any of the Gospel miracles, he admitted that miracles raised many questions that could not be answered with complete certainty:

> Were the witnesses of these miracles competent? Did they not too lightly admit a supernatural cause, when there were adequate natural ones which they failed to note? These works may have been good for the eyewitnesses, but what are they for me? Does a miracle, admitting it to be a real one, authenticate the teaching of Him who has wrought it?[107]

Both Scripture and the church fathers recognize miracles wrought by false teachers. But the miracle in and of itself is not sufficient ground for following the teachers. The latter must be judged by what they teach:

> But the purpose of the miracle being . . . to confirm that which is good, so, upon the other hand, where the mind and conscience witness against the doctrine, not all the miracles in the world have a right to demand submission to the word which they seal. On the contrary, the supreme act of faith is to believe, against, and in despite of, them all, in what God has revealed, and implanted in the soul, of the holy and true; not to believe another Gospel, though an Angel from heaven, or one transformed into such should bring it (Deut. xiii. 3; Gal. i. 8).[108]

To Trench, the decisive factor is "the testimony of the Spirit, which is above and better than all."[109] Hume's mistake was to see miracles as "solely an intellectual question; but it is in fact the moral condition of men which will ultimately determine whether they will believe the Scripture miracles or not; this, and not the exact balance or argument on the one side or the other, will cause this scale or that to kick the beam."[110] What tipped the scale for Trench was his belief in the kingdom of God and the "*final* causes" that carry humanity forward under a leading mightier than its own.[111] Such views create a predisposition to grant the intelligibility of the two great miracles of the incarnation and resurrection, which in turn provide the context for belief in the satellite miracles attending the incarnation:

> He who counts it likely that God will interfere for the higher welfare of men, who believes that there is a nobler world-order than that in which we live and move, and that it would be the blessing of blessings for that nobler order to intrude into and to make itself felt in the region of this lower, who has found that here in this world we are bound by heavy laws of nature, of sin, of death, which no powers that we now possess can break, yet which must be broken if we are truly to live,—he will not find it hard to believe the two crowning miracles, the coming of the Son of God with power by the resurrection from the dead; because all the deepest desires and longings of his heart have yearned after such a deliverer, however little he may have been able to dream of so glorious a fulfillment of those longings. And as he believes the mightiest miracles of all, so will he believe all other miracles, which, as satellites of a lesser brightness, naturally wait upon these, clustering round and drawing their lustre from the central brightness of those greatest.[112]

Trench drew a distinction between "providential" and "absolute" miracles. In the case of providential miracles, natural causes could be seen as the means that God used to strengthen faith, punish disobedience, or awaken repentance. To this category belong the signs and wonders in Egypt (Deut. 4:34; Ps. 78:43; Acts 7:36), the coin in the fish's mouth (Matt. 17:27), and the thunderstorm summoned by Samuel (1 Sam. 12:16–19). But not even absolute miracles are *against* nature. They are "*beyond* and *above* the nature which we know," but they are not contrary to it:

> The healing of the sick can in no way be termed against nature, seeing that the sickness which was healed was against the true nature of man, that it is sickness which is abnormal, and not health. The healing is the restoration of the primitive order. We should see in the miracle not the infraction of a law, but the neutralizing of a lower law, the suspension of it for a time by a higher.[113]

The Gospel miracles are thus to be seen as instances of the breaking in of a higher order into our present order and pointing us beyond it. In the past apologists have been inclined to treat the miracles as independent wonders that by their sheer supernatural character provide a basis for belief. Instead of this, Trench urged his readers to see the "mutual interdependence" of miracles and the doctrine that they attested. He perceived a unity between the miracles of Jesus, his teaching, and his person which led him to say,

> We believe the miracles for Christ's sake, than Christ for the miracles' sake. Neither when we thus affirm that the miracles prove the doctrine, and the doctrine the miracles, are we arguing in a circle: rather we are receiving the sum total of the impression which this divine revelation is intended to make on us, instead of taking an impression only partial and one-sided.[114]

In saying this, Trench was laying a foundation on which, consciously or unconsciously, a number of twentieth-century apologists were to build. He had abandoned the strict evidentialist position, but so had Paley. For Paley had acknowledged presuppositions about God's purpose which, when granted, lent to miracles an antecedent probability. Although his thoughts were couched in the devotional language of his day, Trench saw more clearly than Paley the logic of his position. In one sense Trench's approach tacitly acknowledged that Hume was correct in saying that miracles cannot be assented to without faith. But this was not the blind credulity that Hume had in mind. Rather, it was a question of the kind of world view that one brought to the examination of any particular item of evidence. Trench's re-appraisal of the apologetic value of miracles was closely linked with his perception of the theological significance of the miracles. What Strauss saw as the product of myth-making tendencies in the early church Trench saw as the divine significance implied in Jesus' acts. This was the central issue of the second part of his book; it will also be the central issue of the final part of the present work.

One of the most learned defenses of the miraculous came from the pen of James Bowling Mozley (1813–1878), whose career spanned a fellowship at Magdalen College, parish ministry in Sussex, and the Regius Professor-ship of Divinity at Oxford. In 1865 he delivered the Bampton Lectures at Oxford, which were subsequently published as *Eight Lectures on Miracles, Preached before the University of Oxford in the Year MDCCCLXV*. Each lecture was prefaced by a text from Scripture that focused attention on the philosophical argument that followed.

Mozley began by adopting a strong evidentialist position, citing John 15:24: "If I had not done among them the works that none other man did, they had not had sin." He conceded that the founder of Islam might have contrived false miracles in support of his teaching, but in fact he did not. Mozley went so far as to say that Jesus admitted "the inadequacy of His own mere word, and the necessity of a rational guarantee to His revelation of His own nature and commission."[115] Miracles bear the stamp of divine power. "Whatever value, then, the testimony to the Christian miracles had when that testimony first took its place in public records, that it has now, and that it will continue to have so long as the world lasts."[116]

Mozley then turned to the order of nature to address Hume's objec-tions to miracles. He pointed out that the uniformity of nature is not self-evident or demonstrable. To know it as a rational principle, one would have to be conversant with the ultimate structure of the world. The scientist observes facts and makes generalizations on the basis of his observations. But these generalizations are really presumptions. They have a practical value, but they do not entitle anyone to "lay down speculative positions, and to say what can or cannot take place in the world."[117] Expectation of absolute uniformity goes beyond reason and experience. It is the product of the imagination, based on a limited experience of repetition. "The order of nature thus stamps upon some minds the idea of its immutability simply by its repetition."[118] What is disturbed by the idea of a miracle is the mechanical expectation of recurrence, which gives rise to the expectation of the immutability of nature.

The marvels of nature excite wonder, but they do not perform the same function as a miracle. For the latter speaks directly of eternity:

> A miracle shows design and intention, *i.e.* is the act of a Personal Being. Some one, therefore, there is who is moving behind it, with whom it brings us in relation, a spiritual agent of whose presence it speaks. A miracle is thus, if true, an indication of another world, of an unseen state of being, containing personality and will; of another world of moral being besides this visible one.[119]

However, miracles do not establish belief in the existence of God. Taking as his text Hebrews 11:3 ("Through faith we understand that the worlds were framed by the word of God"), Mozley summed up the central argument of his book with the acknowledgment that

> The peculiarity of the argument of miracles is that it begins and ends with an assumption; I mean an assumption relatively to that argument. We assume the existence of a Personal Deity prior to the proof of miracles in the religious sense; but with this assumption the question of miracles is at an end; because such a Being has necessarily the power to suspend those laws of nature which He has Himself enacted.[120]

Mozley conceded that such belief went beyond philosophical notions of God as a universal first cause and the beliefs of non-Christian religions. The Bible itself presupposed the existence of this God. But such belief is not blind credulity, for it is congruent with our experience and our rational understanding of the world. Mozley refused to draw a sharp line between faith and reason. To him, "faith *is* reason, only reason acting under particular circumstances."[121] Both faith and reason operate on the basis of accepted premises. The difference lies in the nature of the conclusions. In everyday life reasoning involves faith in the premises and trust in the conclusions. The difference between religious faith and reason in the ordinary sense again lies in the nature of the conclusions. The scientist is able to verify the conclusions in which he has come to believe by devising controlled experiments. At this point Mozley anticipated John Hick's idea of "eschatological verification" by nearly a century, contending that the religious believer sees in the moral and physical constitution of the world

> the strongest arguments for certain religious conclusions—such as the existence of a God, and a future life; and yet waits for that final certification of these great truths, which will be given in another world. . . . Faith, then, is *unverified* reason; reason which has not yet received the verification of the final test, but is still expectant.[122]

Thus, for Mozley miracles were to be seen within the context of a belief system that was rational, but that, by the very nature of the case, lacked conclusive verification. In this respect, it was not unlike Paley's scheme, which also presupposed a theistic, personal view of God, and which found confirmation of this in natural theology. This belief system in turn provided the context for the evaluation of testimony to miracles. Such testimony does not establish the belief system in the first place. Nor is it sufficient to convince everyone of the truth of Christian beliefs. However, it is sufficient to modify and establish further beliefs within the system itself. Following Pascal, Mozley contended that the evidence "was not designed for producing belief as such, but for producing belief in connection with, and as the token of, a certain moral disposition; that that moral temper imparted a real insight into the reasons for the marks of truth in the Christian scheme, and brought out proof which was hidden without it."[123]

Mozley concluded his discussion of miracles by examining the question of unknown laws, the practical results of miracles, and false miracles. He rejected the suggestion that miracles were the product of unknown physical laws. Just as human agents are able to control laws of nature, so divine agency is able to act on physical matter in ways beyond our conception.[124] Mozley went on to reiterate the traditional reformed view that miracles no longer occur, because the need for them in establishing revelation is now past.[125] He rejected nonbiblical miracles, insisting that, while each case demanded individual review, the general considerations that led him to accept the Gospel miracles would lead him to question miracles of a different character.[126]

Mozley's discussion of miracles was one of the most notable of the many nineteenth-century treatments of the subject. Dean Church prophesied that Mozley's approach "will remain a characteristic feature of the religious and philosophical tendencies of thought amongst us."[127] But not everybody shared the dean's enthusiasm. In his Bampton Lectures of 1877, C. A. Row claimed that "The conception of a miracle involves neither a suspension of the forces nor the violation of the laws of nature."[128] Further, he stated:

> What man can do on a limited scale, the Creator of the universe must be able to effect on a much larger one. If man, without actually suspending any of the existing forces of the universe, can change their direction, combine them, or neutralize one by the superior energy of another in such a way as to effectuate the results of purpose, much more must God be able to do the same for the effectuation of His purposes; since His ability to do so must be so much the greater as He is mightier and wiser.[129]

Such views found echoes elsewhere among British scholars who were moving away from supernaturalism and evidentialism. Indeed, Mozley has been hailed as "the last great exponent of the evidential idea of miracles."[130] In his Ely Foundation Lectures at Union Theological Seminary, New York, on *The Miraculous Element in the Gospels* (1886), A. B. Bruce observed that "The apologist of the present time has an interest in minimizing the miraculousness of miracles, and making them appear as natural as possible."[131] Bruce, who was professor of apologetics and New Testament exegesis at the Free Church College, Glasgow, went on to complain that Mozley's bold and ingenious argument "belongs to that class of arguments which silence rather than convince."[132] He felt that Mozley was saying much the same thing as David Hume. By unsettling the fixity of nature's order Mozley was opening the door to belief in centaurs or the return of the dead to life. By questioning the order of nature Mozley seemed to be precluding the possibility of attributing anything to supernatural intervention. Bruce himself viewed the Gospel miracles as "the forthflowing of that love which, according to prophetic oracles, was the chief Messianic charism."[133] He went on to suggest that the miracles of Jesus might be viewed as *parables*. By this he did not mean to imply that they did not happen or that an original parable had been transformed into event through the wishful thinking of the early church. Rather, the healings and exorcisms performed by Jesus were intimations of redemption:

> He healed their diseases that they might think of their sins and seek deliverance from them. In this point of view the whole healing ministry was one grand parable of Redemption. Jesus dealt with the physical effect, the evil of which all could appreciate, to advertise Himself as one prepared to deal with the spiritual cause, to the evil of which many were insensible. He healed disease with an unsparing hand that the presence of the Spiritual Physician might be the better known, and to proclaim a plenteous redemption.[134]

In making this point, Professor Bruce was drawing attention to an aspect of miracles that has frequently been overlooked. But the point was even more significant than perhaps he himself realized. Bruce focused attention on the healings and exorcisms of Jesus. More recent scholarship has shown the essentially parabolic character of the Gospel miracle stories in general and their bearing on creation, redemption, and the person of Christ.

THE AMERICAN SCENE

American Protestant theology in the nineteenth century was affected in no small measure by its reaction to deism and its response to European thought. In 1812 the Presbyterian Church founded at Princeton its first seminary for ministers. The Princeton theologians were called upon to show from reason itself the fallacy of the deists' principles. The "Plan" of the seminary provided that "every student . . . must have read and digested the principal arguments and writings relative to what has been called the deistical controversy—Thus he will be qualified to become a defender of the Christian faith.''[135] This outlook was amply evidenced in the teaching of Archibald Alexander (1772–1851) who chaired the committee that drew up the "Plan," became the seminary's first professor, and exerted considerable influence on American theology. Alexander's *Evidences of the Authenticity, Inspiration, and Canonical Authority of the Holy Scriptures* (1825, revised 1836) was in some ways an American counterpart to Paley's *Evidences.* It was clearly focused on the deistic question, beginning with an affirmation of the authority of reason and proceeding to a vindication of the authority of Scripture. In this argument the classical appeal to miracles and fulfilled prophecy played a key part in providing objective evidence for the divine authority of the Bible. In his discussion of miracles, Alexander kept a constant eye on the arguments of "Mr. Hume." In Chapter 6 he argued that "Miracles are capable of proof from testimony," and in Chapter 7 he claimed that "The miracles of the Gospel are credible."

Alexander summed up his position by saying:

> Since it has been shown that there is no antecedent presumption against miracles, from the nature of God, or from the laws by which he governs the universe; since a miraculous fact is not more difficult to be accomplished by omnipotence than any other; since miracles are not further improbable than as they are unusual; since they are the most suitable and decisive evidences which can be given of a revelation; since even by the concession of Mr. Hume himself, there may be sufficient testimony fully to establish them; and since many false pretences to miracles, and the general disposition to credit them, are rather proofs that they have existed than the contrary; we may safely conclude, that Mr. Hume's argument on this subject is sophistical and delusive; and that so far from being incredible, whatever may be their evidence, when brought to support religion, this is, of all other, the very case in which they are most reasonable and credible.[136]

In saying this, Alexander was following in the footsteps of Calvin's evidentialism, adapted to the post-Humean situation. Archibald Alexander was not an innovator but a synthesizer. None of the arguments here laid any claim to originality. Indeed, it was Alexander's view that his case was self-evidently rational and empirical. "The conclusion which is rational on this subject, is, that all things are possible to God, and whatever is possible may be believed on sufficient testimony; which testimony, however, must be strong, in proportion to the improbability of the event to be confirmed."[137] He then proceeded to expand on the general trustworthiness of the historical testimony to Jesus, comparing it (as Whately had done a few years earlier) with the historical evidence for Napoleon Buonaparte.[138]

Archibald Alexander thus reiterated the evidentialist approach to miracles as historical events, accrediting the truth of the gospel and unassailable by anyone following the canons of reason, common sense, and impartial criticism. In doing this, Alexander was marking out the path that Reformed American evangelicalism was to follow. Nevertheless, it was a *qualified evidentialism* that Alexander advocated, insofar as (like Paley) Alexander tacitly conceded that certain presuppositions were required in order to appreciate the evidence for miracles. These included "the simple truth" that

> the laws of nature are nothing else than the common operations of divine power in the government of the world, which depend entirely for their existence and continuation on the divine will; and a miracle is nothing else than the exertion of the same power in a way that is different from that which is common; or it may be a mere suspension of that power which is commonly observed to operate in the world.[139]

In making such faith-claims, Alexander was apparently unaware that he was making an important concession to Hume by tacitly agreeing that an element of faith is necessary for acceptance of miracles.

A faith-approach to miracles was adopted by the pioneer of liberal theology in New England, Horace Bushnell (1802–1876). In contrast to European liberals who rejected miracles altogether, Bushnell explained them as part of the divine law of nature. In *Nature and the Supernatural as Together Constituting the One System of God* (1858) he argued for a spiritual hierarchy in the universe. Upon nature with its laws "God has, in fact, erected another and higher system, that of spiritual being and government, for which nature exists; a system not under the law of cause and effect, but ruled and marshaled under other kinds of laws and able continually to act upon or vary the processes of nature."[140] God, who is personal, perpetually repairs the disorder of nature, whose laws would penalize, if left to themselves. Bushnell believed that miracles do not prove the truth of the gospel for us at this point in time. Nevertheless, they can become for us

> arguments of trust, a storehouse of powerful images that invigorate courage and stimulate hope. Broken as we are by our sorrow, cast down as we are by our guiltiness, ashamed, and weak and ready to despair, we can yet venture a hope that our great soul-miracle may be done; that, if we can but touch the hem of Christ's garment, a virtue will go out of him to heal us.[141]

The miracles do not stand alone as "raw wonders only of might," for the character of Jesus shines through them, covering them with glory "as tokens of a heavenly love."[142] For Bushnell, the truth of Christianity did not rest upon objective arguments that in turn guaranteed those items of faith that could not be directly demonstrated. Instead, he took the traditional Calvinistic argument concerning the inner testimony of the Spirit to the authority of Scripture and applied it to Jesus:

> It is no ingenious fetches of argument that we want; no external testimony, gathered here and there from the records of past ages, suffices to end our doubts; but it is the new sense opened in us by Jesus himself—a sense deeper than words and more immediate than inference—of the miraculous

grandeur of his life; a glorious agreement felt between his works and his person, such that his miracles themselves are proved to us in our feeling, believed in by that inward testimony. On this inward testimony we are willing to stake everything, even the life that now is, and that which is to come.[143]

With W. G. T. Shedd and Charles Hodge we are brought back to a more traditional evidentialist approach to the miracles of Jesus. Even so, it was an evidentialism that was qualified in various respects. Moreover, Hodge and Shedd did not see eye to eye on every issue. Charles Hodge (1797–1878) studied under Archibald Alexander at Princeton, and as a young tutor lived in Alexander's home. He served on the faculty at Princeton for fifty-eight years, and was credited by Shedd with having done more for Calvinism than any other man in America. When celebrating his jubilee in 1872, Hodge declared, "I am not afraid to say that a new idea never originated in this seminary."[144] Hodge's gift was one for systematization and dogged defense of traditional Calvinism. William Greenough Thayer Shedd (1820–1894) was scarcely less a Calvinist in his basic position, but possessed a more flexible mind. As a student at the University of Vermont, he became an enthusiastic reader of Plato, Kant, and Coleridge. He went on to become professor of English literature at the university. His seven-volume edition of *The Complete Works of Samuel Taylor Coleridge* (1853 and 1884) has long remained the standard version of Coleridge. Coleridge's influence may well be discerned in Shedd's approach to miracles. After teaching at Auburn and Andover seminaries, Shedd enjoyed a distinguished career at Union Theological Seminary, New York City, teaching first sacred rhetoric and then systematic theology.

The subject of miracles occupies an important place in the systematic theologies of Hodge[145] and Shedd.[146] Both writers were fully familiar with the arguments put forward on the other side of the Atlantic by J. S. Mill, Baden Powell, and J. B. Mozley, as well as with the earlier debates. Both writers staunchly maintained that the miracles of Jesus were actual, historical events and that they indicated truths about Jesus. But in general their arguments were defensive. Much of their energy was devoted to arguing the feasibility of miracles in view of their prior commitment to a theistic view of God. Both Hodge and Shedd appealed to the Westminster Confession's article on providence in which it is declared that "God, in his ordinary providence, maketh use of means, yet is free to work without, above, and against them, at his pleasure."[147] Hodge and Shedd both sided with Mozley in rejecting the idea that miracles were instances of natural laws not yet known to man. They also endorsed the argument that just as the laws of nature can continually be modified by the interference of the human will, *a fortiori* they could be modified by the divine will.

All this presupposed a view of reality in which God is omnipotent and personal. The situation is summed up by Shedd's observation:

> Miracles are natural to a personal deity, but unnatural and impossible to an impersonal. All the arguments against them by Spinoza, Baur, and Strauss proceed upon the pantheistic assumption that the Infinite is impersonal, and that everything occurs through the operation of an impersonal system of natural law. But if the existence of a personal Infinite is conceded, it would be strange and unnatural, if there were never any extraordinary exertion of his omnipotence. Miracles are tokens of a Person who can modify his plans, and make new arrangements in space and time.[148]

Shedd's use of the word *token* in this passage is significant. For a token is not the same as demonstrable proof. The thrust of Shedd's argument, in common with that of Mozley and Hodge, is defensive. Miracles are credible when seen in the larger context of a theistic view of God and the world. They indicate truths, but the miracles themselves and the truths that they point to are not separable from the belief-system of Christianity. This is not to say that there are no rational grounds that confirm this system, but it is to concede that miracles are not isolated events that for us today compel belief in and of themselves.

Shedd went so far as to conclude:

> He who believes that God incarnate has appeared on earth to save man from sin, will have no difficulty with the miracle. He who disbelieves this, cannot accept it. It is the first step that costs. If the human mind does not stumble over that Divine-human Person who is "set for the fall and rising again of many," it will not stumble over the supernaturalism that is naturally associated with him.[149]

To go so far is to invert the logic of traditional Reformed apologetics that saw miracles as evidence from which the divinity of Christ might be inferred. Hodge was more guarded in his view of the apologetic value of miracles. Nevertheless, he too conceded that "However uncertain or unreliable [human] testimony may be, such events as miracles may happen, if consistent with the nature of God, and may be rationally believed."[150] Hodge proceeded to enumerate the various stipulations that he would make in evaluating human testimony. These included the intrinsic possibility of the event, the admission of "easy verification," the possession of "satisfactory knowledge or evidence" by the witnesses, the sobriety and intelligence of the witnesses, together with evidence of their good character.

Hodge himself did not venture to enlarge on how these stipulations applied to the Gospel miracles, except in the case of the resurrection of Jesus whose appearances were public events witnessed over a period of time by numerous witnesses in whom there was good reason to place trust. Instead, Hodge went on to expose Hume's various fallacies, culminating in his failure to appreciate that belief in miracles does not rest exclusively on human testimony:

> The miracles recorded in Scripture are a competent part of the great system of truth therein revealed. The whole stands or falls together. Our faith in miracles, therefore, is sustained by all the evidence which authenticates the gospel of Christ. And that evidence is not to be even touched by a balance of probabilities.[151]

Hodge concluded that the evidence of miracles was "important and decisive," but "nevertheless, subordinate and inferior to that of the truth itself."[152]

In arguing his case, Hodge was less clear-sighted than Shedd. He evidently failed to recognize that it was precisely the acceptance of a biblically based theistic view of God's character and purposes that affected the intrinsic possibility of the events in question and so radically tipped the balance of probability. At those points at which Hodge comes closest to Paley, his argument is open to the same objections. His argument glosses over the fact that the individual miracle stories are not open to "easy verification." Nor do they have the same degree of historical attestation as the resurrection of Jesus. Hodge wanted to appeal to miracles as proof of the divine mission of him who performed them. At the same time he invoked a moral argument to the effect that "the highest evidence of goodness is goodness itself," without however explaining the precise logical force of the point or its relevance to the issue.

In common with Mozley, Hodge appealed to Jesus' sayings in the Fourth Gospel as "decisive proof of his divine mission."[153] But like Mozley, he did not address the question of whether the *reports* of Jesus' works have precisely the same evidential value for us today as the actual works themselves did for those who witnessed them. Both Mozley and Hodge appear to assume that they did. But the value that we assign to the reports of miracles rests upon a whole series of judgments that we make about the feasibility of the events in question and the trustworthiness of the reports of the events. All the orthodox theologians that we have considered readily conceded the importance of beliefs about God in assessing the question of feasibility and implicitly acknowledged the element of faith. It might be a rational faith, but it nevertheless remains faith. In assessing the value of reports, value judgments about the author, his competence, reliability, and proximity to the events in question are inescapable. For this reason Shedd's view of miracles as *tokens* may well come closer to John's view of miracles as *signs* (John 20:30) than the assumption that they are inescapable, verifiable proofs. For a sign is not a conclusive scientific demonstration, but a pointer or indication that calls for a response.

CONCLUSION

From Paley onward, orthodox theologians on both sides of the Atlantic repeatedly acknowledged the importance of approaching miracles within a framework of belief about God. Whether they realized it or not, the representatives of orthodoxy that we have been considering were making an important concession to Hume by admitting that without certain beliefs about God their attitude toward testimony to the miraculous would be very different. But it was not a concession that Hume could have savored with unmixed relish. For what it did was to extend the arena of debate that Hume himself found it convenient to ignore. The concession contained an implicit attack on the rationality of the secular view of the uniformity of nature that Hume himself had adopted as the vantage point for his attack on miracles, but that he himself had also questioned elsewhere. It is not without significance that Paley followed up his *View of the Evidences of Christianity* by writing his defense of *Natural Theology,* and that Hume composed his *Dialogues Concerning Natural Religion* as a sequel to his critique of miracles in his *Enquiry Concerning Human Understanding*. These works vividly illustrate the perception shared by many other thinkers that the view that one takes of miracles depends in the long run, not simply on isolated pieces of testimony, but upon the view that one takes of the testimony in relation to the view that one takes of the world in general.

It may be asked whether this point is anything new. The answer has to be in the negative. As we saw in the first chapter, this was a central issue for those who exercised their minds about miracles in the early centuries. It may even be said that the New Testament writers, together with those whom they describe in their accounts of miracles, did not come to the question with no framework of belief at all. No one appears to have based belief in God as such on miracles. Rather, the miracles were interpreted as signs that fitted into and modified an existing framework of belief. They were seen as saying something about what God was doing and about the person who wrought them. Although they modified the framework of belief, they did not establish that framework in the first place.

Whether such a framework of belief is to be established or demolished by an appeal to natural theology, with its arguments from causation, design, and purpose, as Paley and Hume thought, or by some other means is a subject beyond the scope of this investigation. What cannot be denied is the increasing clarity with which the importance of this framework of belief was recognized on all sides in the nineteenth century and the role that it continues to play in the discussions of the twentieth century.

IV

The Ongoing Debate

7

THE QUESTIONS
OF THE PHILOSOPHERS

At first sight contemporary literature on miracles looks like a jungle. Wherever we turn we are confronted by dense masses of argument. Here and there we catch a glimpse of a clearing and the promise of a path. Occasionally the path seems to lead somewhere, as in the case of C. S. Lewis's *Miracles*. But Lewis himself was cautious enough to qualify the title of his book by calling it *A Preliminary Study,* and various writers hint darkly that Lewis was neither a philosopher nor a theologian and that his arguments were technically flawed.[1] Most professional philosophers, on the other hand, seem content with discussing only aspects of the question in the abstract. To the layman, the professional philosophers seem so devoted to removing the logical specks from each other's eyes that it is not easy to see what their arguments add up to. The aim of the next three chapters is to assess the state of the debate today and to ask how this affects our view of miracles. At the risk of drawing invidious distinctions, we shall look first at the arguments of writers who are primarily philosophers and then at the arguments of those who are primarily apologists. In the final chapter we shall attempt to relate this to contemporary biblical scholarship. The philosophers that we shall look at include both believers and skeptics. What they have in common is an interest in the possibility of miracles occurring, in defining what a miracle is, and in recognizing a miracle, if and when it happens. As we shall see, these questions are interrelated. The apologist, on the other hand, is not only interested in these questions, but he is also interested in their bearing on faith. In particular, the apologist sets himself the question, "What role do miracles play in faith today?" When we have seen how the apologists answer this question, we shall be in a position to appreciate better the New Testament testimony to miracles and its significance for us today.

SKEPTICISM RESTATED

Philosophers, like other mortals, live in the shadow of the past. Nowhere is this more apparent than in their discussion of miracles. A case in point is that of Paul Tillich, who lays down three conditions for an event to qualify as a miracle:

> A genuine miracle is first of all an event which is astonishing, unusual, shaking, without contradicting the rational structure of reality. In the second place, it is an event which points to the mystery of being, expressing its relation to us in a definite way. In the third place, it is an occurrence which is received as a sign-event in an ecstatic experience.[2]

At first sight, Tillich might seem to be heading off a direct confrontation with science by capitulating to the demand that there can be no exceptions to the laws of nature. But the reasons that Tillich gives are not scientific but philosophical arguments, which could be traced back through nineteenth-century German Idealism to the sixteenth-century rationalism of Spinoza. Like Spinoza, Tillich believed that reality is a single rational whole. God is not to be thought of as a being who exists over and above the world, who occasionally interferes in the natural processes he has created. Tillich dismissed such a view as *supranaturalism,* and ridiculed the traditional view of miracles as nothing less than *demonic:*

> Miracles cannot be interpreted in terms of a supranatural interference in natural processes. If such an interpretation were true, the manifestation of the ground of being would destroy the structure of being; God would be split with himself, as religious dualism has asserted. It would be more adequate to call such a miracle "demonic," not because it is produced by "demons," but because it discloses a "structure of destruction."[3]

Tillich could assimilate laws of science into his scheme because they represented attempts to grasp the rational structure of being. Exceptions to such laws were felt by him to be a threat not so much to the coherence and competence of science as to the unitary, rational structure of his pantheistic view of the world. Not only does Tillich's view suggest an ultimate identity between the laws of science and the thoughts of God; it implies that God can have no other thoughts. On his view, miracles differ from ordinary events only in their capacity to awaken in us a sense of Being that manifests itself in all beings. In essence, Tillich's view was a restatement of the closed system of being, advocated by Spinoza, in which God is the immanent ground of all things. Inevitably, supernatural interventions were just as much a threat to Tillich as they were to Spinoza. But to thinkers who take a different view of the relationship of mind to matter, the possibility of God having thoughts different from the laws of nature is certainly not disruptive of their view of the divine being. It suggests, as we shall see, a possibility of how miracles might be envisaged.

Most philosophical discussions of miracles come to the question from an angle that is very different from Tillich's. It is not the shadow of Spinoza that lies over them but that of David Hume. Here again natural law figures at the center of the debate, but the background is not that of rationalism but of empiricism. We need not retrace our steps by rehearsing all the arguments already noted about Hume. It is, however, important to observe the direction that recent discussion has taken.

Hume defined a miracle as "a violation of the laws of nature." Although he acknowledged that the laws of nature were statistical in character, he thought of them as inviolable, since they were established by "a firm and unalterable experience." On this basis, miracles were by definition impossible. Hume's discussion oscillated between this tough-minded stance, which rejected miracles out of hand, and the somewhat less dogmatic view that argued that it was always more likely that testimony to miracles might be mistaken than that a miracle should have actually occurred. In either case, Hume left his readers with the impression that the events reported as miracles just could not have happened.

Hume's more recent followers have shown a greater degree of circumspection. As T. R. Miles points out, "If an event is sufficiently well attested, no one is entitled to argue that it could not have happened."[4] But to say this is (as Miles's own discussion shows) not to settle the question. On the one hand, Miles's observation raises the question of whether the event that was previously thought to be a miracle was really a miracle after all. On the other hand, the point also raises the question of what constitutes good attestation.

Antony Flew, who is second to none among modern philosophers in his admiration of David Hume, acknowledges "a rather wooden dogmatism of disbelief" in Hume.[5] Against his own high, skeptical principles, Hume tended to believe in common with other enlightened thinkers of his day that eighteenth-century science could say the last word about what was possible. Ignorance of abnormal psychology and psychosomatic medicine caused Hume to dismiss as unhistorical events that a twentieth-century empiricist like Flew could readily accept. But to say this is to enlarge the circle of the historically feasible at the expense of the supernaturally caused. In a similar vein Patrick Nowell-Smith throws down the following challenge to the advocate of supernatural explanations:

> Let him consider the meaning of the word "explanation" and let him ask whether this notion does not involve that of a law or hypothesis capable of predictive expansion. And then let him ask whether such an explanation would not be natural, in whatever terms it was couched, and how the notion of "the supernatural" could play any part in it.[6]

The same basic point has been stated in various ways, such as by observing that what was previously thought to be law L requires to be modified in the light of greater knowledge to become L_1, L_2, L_3 (and so on), in order to take account of apparent exceptions.[7] Similarly, Terence Penelhum argues that the skeptic is utterly rational when he responds to miraculous claims by saying "either that there is an existing formulation of natural law that will account for the event or that natural law can be so redescribed as to take account of it."[8] The point is not exactly new, and those who make it do not claim any novelty for it. In the nineteenth century J. S. Mill observed succinctly that "We cannot admit a proposition as a law of nature, and yet believe a fact in real contradiction of it. We must disbelieve the alleged fact, or believe that we were mistaken in admitting the supposed law."[9] In the thirteenth century Thomas Aquinas noted that the simple and credulous believed that the attraction of iron by a magnet involved the supernatural.[10] However, no effect produced by natural causes could count as a miracle. The difference between Aquinas and the modern successors of Hume consists in the fact that, whereas Thomas reserved the right to attribute supernatural causes to given events, the latter insist that all events are capable in principle of natural explanation.

THE POSSIBILITY OF MIRACLES REASSERTED

Among the philosophers who have challenged this view are R. F. Holland, Ninian Smart, Richard Swinburne, and Ian T. Ramsey. In a notable essay entitled "The Miraculous,"[11] Holland argues that the conception of miracles as violations of natural law is inadequate, because it is "unduly restrictive" and because it is "not restrictive enough."[12] Holland proceeds to identify two kinds of miracles: those which fall under the *contingency* or *coincidence concept* and those which fall under the *violation concept*. As an instance of the *contingency* or *coincidence* category Holland describes the case of a child riding a toy motor-car who strays onto a railway crossing. The car gets stuck and the child does not see the oncoming train or his mother's frantic efforts to warn him of the danger. The train stops and a terrible accident is averted— not because the driver saw the child, but because the driver was taken ill. He released pressure on the automatic control lever, and the train automatically came to a stop. In such a case no law of nature was violated. All the factors in the situation were capable of natural explanations. But the mother regarded the event as a miracle. All the factors in the situation were contingent in the sense that they did not have to occur. They just happened to have coincided. But the coincidence was not like that between the rise of the Ming dynasty and the arrival of the dynasty of Lancaster, which just happened to occur simultaneously, but which had no apparent interrelating connections. In the child's case the combination of factors resulted in an event that was seen by the mother as providential, gracious, and significant.

Depending upon their perspective, one person might interpret the event as fortuitous, another as a stroke of luck, and yet another person as an expression of the grace of God. In each case the reference is the same. But the meaning attached to it depends in part upon the frame of reference that is brought to the interpretation. From a detached standpoint, the event itself may not be sufficiently unambiguous to change the frame of reference. The person who believes in luck may see it as yet another instance of good luck in the world. The agnostic may see it as evidence that not all events in the world are bad. The religious person may see it as an event that counts toward confirming God's providential care.

To establish the *contingency concept* of the miraculous as a possible one, Holland deems it sufficient to point out that there are genuine contingencies in the world and that some of them are regarded as having religious significance.[13] We shall postpone until later a discussion of whether this is a useful category for interpreting biblical miracles. In the meantime it may be observed that, taken in isolation, no single instance of such a miracle might be sufficient to convert a person's thinking from agnosticism or superstition to belief in a personal, caring God. Beliefs, in any case, are not normally changed by a single, strong argument or a single, isolated experience. If, however, other contingent (not necessarily miraculous) experiences point in the same direction and are better interpreted by adopting a framework of theistic belief, a coincidence such as Holland has described could also better be interpreted religiously. For it would then cease to be an odd, isolated event, and would be assimilated into a broader, encompassing world view. When such a change of thought occurs, a paradigm shift has occurred. Instead of using luck, chance, or impersonal fate as the paradigm or key idea that makes the best sense of experience, the person concerned has now come to the belief that the world and life fall into a more meaningful pattern if they are seen in relation to a personal God. In such a case the contingent miracle is seen as having a significant part in the total pattern of events.

Turning to the *violation concept* of miracle, Holland lays down two truth conditions that must be fulfilled in order to acknowledge any event of this type as a miracle: "(1) that it is impossible, and (2) that it has happened."[14] The event must have occurred in order to be regarded as an event at all. It must be "impossible" in order to be distinguished from ordinary events or miracles that fall into the contingency category. In putting forward this paradoxical concept, Holland anticipates various objections. He is skeptical about vague appeals to the statistical character of modern science and indeterminacy in subatomic physics as a means of explaining the miraculous in natural terms. Such appeals rest upon a confusion of categories, and misunderstand the limited range of reference that such ideas have. Holland defends his notion of conceptual impossibility on the grounds that there is more than one kind of conceptual impossibility. To speak of a round square or a female father would be to perpetrate self-contradictory nonsense. But if an event is empirically certain and at the same time conceptually impossible, Holland insists that the conditions have been met for treating it as an instance of the violation concept of the miraculous.

Holland offers three examples of such a miracle, and none of them is entirely free from objections of one kind or another. Two of his examples are hypothetical: a horse kept alive without food, and levitation without physical support. The third is the story of the turning of water into wine in John 2. In the first two cases the conditions are so described as to rule out all possibility of physical explanation. But the objection may be made that Holland has specified truth conditions necessary for an event to qualify as an instance of the *violation concept,* but that no known actual event has occurred that meets Holland's stringent criteria. The skeptic or agnostic (or, for that matter, some New Testament scholars) might add that the miracle at Cana also fails on this score. They might agree with Holland that the story is told in such a way as to preclude natural explanation. There was no way of constructing and at the same time concealing elaborate apparatus that might produce the atomic and molecular transformations necessary in a winelike potion. As Holland remarks, those who are alleged to have drunk the wine were "practiced wine-bibbers, capable of detecting at once the difference between a true wine and a concocted variety in the 'British Wine, Ruby Type' category."[15] The account makes it clear that at one moment there was water and at a later moment there was wine. Even if we set aside the suggestion that the story might be a piece of myth or allegory, we have to acknowledge that there is a difference between saying that the episode was empirically certain for the author and saying that it is empirically certain for us today. For we have no means of verifying the event apart from asserting confidence in the general trustworthiness of the author. The believer may appeal to the authority of Scripture as the Word of God as the ground on which he bases his belief in John's veracity. But to adopt this line of defense is to make a statement of faith. The believer may have good grounds for asserting the validity of this procedure. In so doing he has shifted his position from the claim that the event is empirically certain, with all its implications concerning objective testability, to a confession of belief that the event is empirically certain. In this latter case there is no way of testing its certainty. The believer is confessing that he is prepared to take the author's word for it.

Holland appears to have salvaged the *violation concept* of miracle as a meaningful concept but at the price of disqualifying from consideration all alleged miracles in the more remote past. Apart from the resurrection of Jesus,[16] the most that we can assert on their behalf is that they were empirically certain for the authors who reported them and that we have grounds for believing their reports. But in the case of an extraordinary event said to have taken place nearly two thousand years ago for which we have testimony in one, two, three, or at most four authors (who may or may not have been independent witnesses), we do not have the same degree of empirical certainty that we have in an ordinary event in the more recent past witnessed by a number of people. The possibilities of confirming and verifying the former seem to fall well short of empirical certainty.

In his discussion "Miracles and David Hume," Ninian Smart also addresses the question of miracles and their violations of the laws of nature. He draws the distinction between large-scale laws, like the law of gravitation, which have a general applicability, and small-scale laws that cater for anomalies and that in turn require modification of the large-scale law. However, Smart points out that in the very nature of the case

> Miracles are not experimental, repeatable. They are particular, peculiar
> events occurring in idiosyncratic human situations. They are not small-
> scale laws. Consequently they do not destroy large-scale laws. Formally,
> they may seem to destroy the "Always" statements of the scientific laws;
> but they have not the genuine deadly power of the negative instance.[17]

The believer does not deny that miracles are caused, but holds that they are "the result of supernatural causation."[18] Such causation differs from causation on the natural level. Events like the freezing over of a pond may be explained by referring to the prevailing weather conditions and also to the law that water freezes at thirty-two degrees Fahrenheit, but Smart questions whether we can speak of "laws of supernature" that are open to our inspection in the same way as the laws of nature.[19] Moreover, scientific explanations have a predictive value. They not only describe particular states of affairs that have been observed in one particular laboratory. Their validity as scientific explanations means that they hold good wherever the same conditions are to be found. Smart shrinks from saying that miracles could likewise be expected, given the appropriate conditions.

Smart concludes by stating his conviction that "There is no reason in the nature of things why occasional random and inexplicable events should not occur."[20] He agrees with Hume in thinking that there is no absolute necessity why things should always continue to operate in the same way. "Thus we cannot rule out in advance the possibility that the miraculous, which is meant to be scientifically inexplicable, may occur."[21] Smart, therefore, sees miracles as nonrepeatable counterinstances to the laws of nature. Because of their nonrepeatable character, they are not sufficient to warrant modifications in the laws of nature as we know them:

> For what we mean by a genuine negative instance (the one which has
> the deadly power of destroying the law) is an experimentally repeatable
> exception. But the miracle does not fall into this category—otherwise
> it would itself be a new small-scale law, not a "violation" of regularity.[22]

There is, however, an important difference between a miracle and a mere random event. Whereas the occurrence of the latter is purely fortuitous, miracles are attributed by believers to an unobservable cause, namely God. They are interpreted as such in the context of what is believed about his character. They do not function as external guarantees of the truth of revelation, but belong to the pattern of divine self-disclosure.

In many ways Smart's position is an attractive one, since it appears to allow the possibility of miracles and at the same time avoid a head-on conflict with science. His view of large-scale and small-scale laws seems, to the layperson at least, to make sense. But his view of random events does not seem to be altogether free from objections. The phrase "random event" is ambiguous. It could refer to an unexpected occurrence that is historically unique. But the historically unique does not necessarily violate the laws of nature. Even though we are never in a position to analyze exhaustively all the factors in any given situation, our experience of the world suggests that there are no causeless events. To speak of "history" and "causes" raises the further complex question of the relationship of mental and spiritual causes to physical effects. But even here we seem to be in a different realm from that required by Smart's notion of a "random event." The latter seems to require by definition not only that it does not fit into any known laws or categories, but that it is incapable ever of being made so to fit.

The objector may well ask Professor Smart whether this latter notion of a "random event" that is *in principle* incapable of being subsumed under any kind of scientific explanation is meaningful and realistic. It may be that all that is meant here is that the random event that provides the nonrecurring counterinstance to the scientific law is really something that is so rare that no one has yet been able to offer an explanation. In such a case the event is not actually a violation of a known law but something that the scientist has not got around to understanding. Counterinstances to laws do not seem to be capable of being relegated to the category of pure randomness, utterly beyond the scope of scientific explanation. Rather, they suggest that their occurrence is to be explained in terms other than those that are currently available. In other words, the "random event" that at first looks like a violation may well violate one set of laws but turn out to be an instance of another set. If the "random event" in question is regarded as a miracle, it does not necessarily cease to be a miracle. It simply has to be reclassified under what Holland calls the *contingency concept*.

If, however, the term "random event" is intended to denote something that defies not only all available explanations but an occurrence that in principle is incapable of scientific explanation, the objector may well go on to ask whether there are any conceivable instances of such events apart from miracles. If religious miracles are the sole instances of events that fall into the latter category, it might appear that the category has been invented just for them, in which case the quasi-scientific underpinning of miracles by calling them nonrepeatable counterinstances of scientific laws looks somewhat suspect. The apologist might be tempted to come to Smart's aid by drawing attention to quantum physics and by alluding to Heisenberg's principle of indeterminacy, on the assumption that modern physics has completely set aside Newtonian mechanics.[23] But the relevance and precise significance of this point is far from clear. Modern nuclear physics has not completely replaced Newton's laws, which still remain valid within their appropriate limits and on the level of their relevance. The principle of uncertainty or indeterminacy relates to questions such as those concerning the position of an electron in relation to its velocity. The more accurately the former is measured, the greater is the uncertainty about predicting the latter. The uncertainty applies to the atomic and subatomic levels. But even here, as Ian G. Barbour observes, "if *a very large number* of atoms is involved, these statistical irregularities will tend to average out, and the over-all behavior of the total aggregate over a period of time will be found to conform accurately to that calculated from the probability-distribution."[24] Once we get above the nuclear level the random behavior is replaced by behavior that seems in principle capable of being described in terms of law.

Mary Hesse, who is professor of the philosophy of science at Cambridge, makes this observation:

> There is no doubt that abandonment of the deterministic world-view in physics has made it more difficult to regard the existing state of science as finally legislative of what is and what is not possible in nature. The very fact that what appeared for three centuries to be an absolutely true and universal theory has been shown to be false must cast doubt on all future claims of science to have reached such a universal theory. Science is continually growing and changing, sometimes quite radically. It is far less easy to see it to-day as a monolithic and cumulative progress towards the whole truth than was the case a hundred years ago. We are by no means sure, even in physics, that existing quantum theories will last many decades. Moreover, we have no guarantee that existing theories will prove adequate in sciences other than physics, and in the sciences of complex systems such as the human psyche and human social groups we have only the bare beginnings of any theories at all. Miracles which are religiously significant must be regarded as social phenomena of great complexity, and in the absence of any clear idea what "laws of nature" would look like in this domain, it is impossible to know what a "violation" would look like either.[25]

While this statement gives encouragement to those who wish to see miracles as events that may ultimately be explicable but still be religiously significant (which is Hesse's own position),[26] it lends no support for entertaining the possibility of random events that contradict all possible laws but are infrequent enough never to overthrow them.

In point of fact, if miracles could somehow be explained in terms of the random behavior of atoms and electrons, the apologist would find himself in the uncongenial position of (1) having explained miracles in terms of a purely naturalistic explanation; (2) having reduced miracles to the level of random events on a par with other random events; and (3) having unwittingly cut out God from the entire operation. For in this case the miracle would be attributable to the fortuitous behavior of the atoms. The apologist, on the other hand, wants to say that it is precisely because of the divine *ordering* of the atoms that the miracle came about.

In other words, we seem to be back where we started. The appeal to indeterminacy as an aid to making miracles more credible owes its attraction to the dubious assumption that atoms and electrons are somehow more amenable to God's control than entities on a larger scale. But at whatever level we posit the divine ordering we are brought back to the question of the relationship of the physical world to the transcendent.

For Mary Hesse, "The fundamental problem is not about miracles, but about transcendence."[27] The same could be said of C. S. Lewis who felt that nothing could be built on the principle of indeterminacy, if only because he could not suppress the feeling that "some new scientific development may not tomorrow abolish this whole idea of a lawless Subnature."[28] If we may for a moment anticipate the discussion of Lewis's attitude toward miracles that will come in the next chapter, Lewis's position may be contrasted with that of Smart in one further important respect. Smart argues that miracles are nonrepeatable with the qualifying admission that "pilgrimages to Lourdes might be held to belie this judgment."[29] Healers and the healed of other persuasions would also challenge his view. But C. S. Lewis's view extends the range and scope of repeatable miracles by seeing them in terms of the Old Creation and the New Creation. Miracles like healings and the stilling of the storm are seen by Lewis as instances of control over nature. Other miracles, like Jesus' walking on the water and the resurrection, are seen by Lewis not as unique events but as incursions into the present order by God's New Creation.[30] On Lewis's view these events are unique only in the sense of being historically unique. In and of themselves he believes that they are manifestations of a new order that broke into the world with Jesus Christ. Admittedly such a view is bound up with Lewis's faith perspective. Such supernature is not open to our scientific examination. What Lewis is doing here is to offer a theological, rather than a scientific, explanation of New Testament miracle stories. Moreover, he does this using the resurrection of Jesus as a paradigm for interpreting the other miracle stories. But before we explore Lewis and other Christian apologists, we need to conclude our examination of recent philosophical writing on the subject of miracles.

Richard Swinburne's incisive study *The Concept of Miracle*[31] is largely a response to the arguments of David Hume and the ramifications pursued by his successors. We have already had occasion to note some of Swinburne's rejoinders to the eighteenth-century philosopher. In dealing with the question of violations of the laws of nature Swinburne offers an elaboration of the position adopted by Holland and Smart, which he concludes by defining such violations in terms of nonrepeatable counterinstances of laws based on statistical evidence. To this he adds the following sober reminder:

> All claims about what are the laws of nature are corrigible. However much support any purported law has at the moment, one day it may prove to be no true law. So likewise will be all claims about what does or does not violate the laws of nature. When an event apparently violates such laws, the appearance may arise simply because no one has thought of the true law which could explain the event, or, while they have thought of it, it is so complex relative to the data as rightly to be dismissed before even being tested, or too complex to be adopted without further testing and the tests too difficult in practice to carry out. New scientific knowledge may later turn up which forces us to revise any such claims about what violates laws of nature. But then all claims to knowledge about the physical world are corrigible, and we must reach provisional conclusions about them on the evidence available to us. We have to some ex-

tent good evidence about what are the laws of nature, and some of them are so well established and account for so many data that any modifications to them which we could suggest to account for the odd counter-instance would be so clumsy and *ad hoc* as to upset the whole structure of science. In such cases the evidence is strong that if the purported counter-instance occurred it was a violation of the law of nature.[32]

Swinburne notes that the following events (if they occurred) would qualify as violations: levitation, resurrection from the dead of someone clinically dead for twenty-four hours, turning of water into wine without the assistance of chemical apparatus or catalysts, and a person recovering from polio in a minute. Readers of Holland and Smart will be familiar enough with this checklist. Reservations have already been voiced concerning some of the items here noted. From a logical standpoint, Swinburne seems to be technically correct in saying that science must reckon with anomalies. However, the objector may well ask whether the anomalies that Swinburne proposes to satisfy the requirements of the *violation concept* of miracle are the same kind of anomaly that he believes science must reckon with. The examples that he notes are either hypothetical or drawn from history. They are not recurrent or generally observable. They do not exhibit the same kind of recurrent randomness that is claimed in the field of subatomic physics. The kind of anomaly recognized by the scientist is an event for which there is no current explanation. Even though it may be impracticable to devise a method for testing a theory about them, such events remain within the category of the explicable-but-not-yet-explained. The *violation concept* of miracle has to operate with the category of the never-to-be-explained. Otherwise, it reverts to a form of the *contingency concept* by saying, in effect, that although we do not know, or may never know, an explanation for what happened, we nevertheless believe that there is one.

Swinburne notes Holland's *contingency concept,* and observes that "The notion of coincidence is perfectly comprehensible, and, given a religious system established on good grounds, the concept of religious significance seems perfectly comprehensible and applicable."[33] His discussion up to this point appears to be a recapitulation of the view found in Holland and Smart, only exploring more fully the notion of scientific law. It is when he turns to the question of historical evidence that he breaks new ground.

Swinburne argues that there are basically four types of factors operative in historical evidence: (1) our own apparent memories (the word "apparent" is inserted to allow for the possibility of mistakes detected in comparison with other evidence); (2) the testimony of others; (3) physical traces (e.g., footprints, fingerprints, ashes, bomb craters, artifacts, and other empirically discernible effects); and (4) our contemporary understanding of what is possible.[34] This fourth category is not an item of evidence, like the first three. It functions in relation to all three as a category in interpretation and as a check. But it is not absolute, for it may itself be modified by the evidence turned up by the other categories.

Hume's discussion of miracles was limited to the second and fourth types, the testimony of others and his understanding of what was possible. In dealing with the biblical miracles, the first type, our own apparent memories, is automatically excluded, except in relation to type four. For clearly, no one alive today is in a position to remember a biblical miracle. However, if someone recalls an event similar to something reported in the Bible, it would affect type four, our current understanding of what is possible, and thus in turn positively influence appreciation of an event recorded in Scripture. In detective work type three is clearly important. But this type is by no means limited to criminal investigation. The use of C_{14} dating to determine the age of artifacts belongs to this category. The use of documents, buildings, artifacts of various kinds, and anything physical belongs here. It is arguable that the existence of the church as an effect of the resurrection of Jesus belongs to this category.[35]

In assessing the value of evidence, Swinburne argues that "The most basic principle is to accept as many pieces of evidence as possible."[36] But in cases where evidence and current beliefs point in different directions various subsidiary principles come into play. The first of these is that (apart from empirical evidence about relative reliability) different kinds of evidence ought to be given different weight. Thus, one would trust one's own apparent memory (unless one had reason to distrust it) rather than someone else's, as the other person could conceivably be mistaken or lying. The second subsidiary principle is that different pieces of evidence ought to be given weights according to the empirical evidence that may be available about their reliability. If Jones and Smith disagree, we need to look into the general reliability of both. The third subsidiary principle is not to reject coincident evidence, unless the evidence of its falsity is extremely strong, and unless explanation can be given for its coincidence.

It is sometimes urged that historical claims cannot be repeatedly tested in the way that scientific claims can be tested, on the grounds that any given historical event occurred just once, whereas it is possible to go on repeating scientific experiments indefinitely. Swinburne rightly cautions against overestimating the significance of this point. For while the event in question cannot be repeated, there is no limit to examination of the evidence, the criteria, or fresh data by anyone who cares to look at them.[37] In one other important respect, historical investigation may be compared with scientific investigation. If there is enough evidence for maintaining that an event has occurred, it may be sufficient to counter the presumption that such events do not occur. However, Swinburne concedes Hume's general point "that we should accept the historical evidence, viz. a man's apparent memory, the testimony of others and traces, only if the falsity of the latter would be 'more miraculous', i.e. more improbable 'than the events which he relates.' "[38]

There is, however, an important consideration that drastically modifies the situation. In dealing with accounts of the past, the historian often has only one item of evidence on which to base a judgment whether an event occurred as reported. Should he accept it, because his source says so, or should he reject it, because he has only one account of it? The answer to this question is determined by the background beliefs that the historian brings to the issue and that determine the general probability of the event in question. If a purported action would seem to be both possible and in character, a comparatively slight degree of evidence is required in order to accept its trustworthiness. Swinburne concludes by suggesting that the same kind of consideration may be brought to the question of miracles. In this case, the inclining factor is our beliefs about God:

> If any of these arguments have any weight, we would need only slender historical evidence of certain miracles to have reasonable grounds to believe in their occurrence, just as we need only slender historical evidence to have reasonable grounds for belief in the occurrence of events whose occurrence is rendered probable by natural laws. We take natural laws to show the improbability of violations thereof because they are well-established parts of our overall view of how the world works. But if they are relevant for this reason, then so is any other part of our overall view of how the world works. And if from our study of its operation we conclude that we have evidence for the existence of a God of such a character as to be liable to intervene in the natural order under certain circumstances, the overall world-view gives not a high prior improbability, but a high prior probability to the occurrence of miracles under those circumstances.[39]

Two further points may be noted before we leave Swinburne's argument. The first is that the observations he makes about historical evidence are valid, whether we apply them to miracles that we believe belong to the *violation concept* or whether we apply them to events of the *contingency* kind. The second observation is that Swinburne is conscious that Archdeacon Paley made much the same point nearly two hundred years before him. As we noted already in the discussion of Paley, such a standpoint is not a case of simple evidentialism that behaves as if the data alone, apart from any other considerations, presented irrefragable evidence. But neither is it a simple fideism that makes acceptance of miracles a matter of blind faith. Both the decision to accept as historical the events we call miracles and the decision to reject them are decisions that cannot be separated from the world view that we bring to their consideration. They stand or fall, not as isolated events, but in conjunction with the world view in which we locate them.[40]

In his Inaugural Lecture to the Nolloth Chair of the Philosophy of the Christian Religion at Oxford in 1951, Ian T. Ramsey offered a somewhat different approach to the question of miracles and science. Ramsey entitled his lecture "Miracles: An Exercise in Logical Mapwork." He brought to his theme an expertise in linguistic philosophy that led him to explore different kinds of meaning in language in the aftermath of logical positivism. The logical positivists had claimed that religious language was factually meaningless, because it could not be verified in the same way that scientific statements could be verified by controlled experiment. They had condescendingly allowed that it could be emotive, expressing the individual emotional reactions to situations in life. But they had denied that it was cognitive in the sense of conveying factually significant statements.

Ramsey boldly chose the subject of miracles as the base from which to launch his analysis of language and meaning. He began by suggesting that the logical analysis of language was like constructing a map:

> To construct an ordinary map is to express schematically the geographical setting of towns and villages in terms of the symbols for hill and rivers, roads and railways. Working with this analogy we may say that logical mapwork is somewhat similarly concerned to exhibit the propositional settings in which concepts are set, to exhibit the linguistic context in which the particular concept sentences have their place.[41]

He went on to suggest that it is a mistake to think that all forms of discourse employ the same conventions, capable of being located on a single map. Just as the geographer employs different maps, using different projections and different conventions for different purposes, so we must recognize differences in the logic and conventions for different types of language.

The language of science employs a high degree of abstraction and generalization. To the extent that it strives toward comprehensiveness in dealing with uniformities and repeated patterns it is forced to abstract from the particular situation only those features that are relevant to the expression of general laws. The complexities of science force the scientist to abandon the language of everyday terms and employ the abstract conventions of mathematics, physics, and chemistry. In one sense science seeks to be comprehensive. Each new discovery is absorbed into the existing body of knowledge. But in another sense the language of science is never comprehensive. Ramsey argues that it is characterized by two permanent limitations. On the one hand, it is marked by a permanent incompleteness. No matter how far advanced science may be, there will always be new facts and new questions. On the other hand, the more science progresses, the more selective its language must be. For this reason Ramsey suggests that *"Both* to unite scientific languages at their different abstractive levels *as well as* to give *all* levels their factual reference, words will be wanted which lie outside all scientific languages, and which in uniting them also relate them to the *Fact* which all the abstractive selections of scientific fact presuppose."[42] Such words belong to metaphysics.

Whereas Smart and Swinburne wish to find a place for miracles among the nonrepetitive counterinstances recognized by the scientist, Ramsey argues that it is precisely on account of its general character that scientific language has no room for the word "miracle" within it. To treat miracles in scientific language "is either to ignore or to dissolve away all irregular features as the very condition of linguistic inclusion."[43] However, Ramsey believes that "the word 'God' does not work as a high-grade scientific word at all. It is *not* part of a 'hypothesis.' God-sentences do not belong to the logic of science."[44] But this is not to say that religious language has no empirical justification. It is rather to recognize that it has a different structure. It is more akin to the language of history.

Whereas science deals in abstractions and generalizations, history deals with the particular, the concrete, and the personal. "History is pre-eminently a technique for securing from a selected 'clue' an extended insight at a concrete personal level."[45] All historical language uses language from elsewhere. The historian does not devise his own language, but uses the language that is already available. Moreover, the language of history points to metaphysics. For in employing words like "person" and "I," the historian indicates his awareness of a reality that transcends the limits of purely objective description.[46] Neither the scientist nor the historian can dispense with metaphysical words, for such words coordinate the boundaries of the various disciplines and serve as indexes, uniting the several languages, each of which has its own particular logic.[47] For Ramsey metaphysical words are not vestiges of obsolete, esoteric branches of philosophy. They are required by science, history, and everyday life to give expression to the concrete unity of experience that transcends observable particulars:

> Metaphysical words are, then, more than a pious jingle of "regulative" words, because they are that part of a language system whose empirical necessity arises from the fact that experience is not exhaustively described in terms of any number of parts which are "objective" in any number of senses. The ultimate justification of metaphysical words lies in the fact that there is a non-inferential awareness more concrete than the observable facts which characterize it abstractly and objectively. Metaphysical words are, then, related in a curious way to the residue; and any *total* language map relates at once to the concrete non-inferential awareness and to the "data" which are abstractly discernible.[48]

With this in mind, Ramsey turns to the question of divine activity. He speaks of two *orders* of activity. In the *first order* the language of science is appropriate. It operates on the objective level. God is "generally" active in providence. In the *second order* God is said to be personally active. We are aware of him in a noninferential way, comparable with the way in which we are aware of ourselves. We are not aware of ourselves as an "I," which we infer from inspecting some aspect of our bodily action. Our knowledge of ourselves as an "I" is intuitive rather than inferential. From here Ramsey proceeds to argue that "The striking character of miracles is . . . to be related to their historical significance and extension and not at all to their scientific illegality, which is, indeed, a pseudo-category."[49] The question "Do miracles occur?" is not a scientific question. Even if it is reformulated as a historical question as to whether a miracle did occur on such and such an occasion, Ramsey contends that it cannot be answered on a purely scientific level. In fact, the question resolves itself into three other questions:

1. Have we examined, as far as in us lies, as much "evidence" as possible, i.e., original documents, traditional doctrine and so on?

2. Is theistic Kata-language the most adequate Kata-language available, and hence justified for methodological use by history? . . .

3. Was the person, or persons, in the particular miracle-claiming situation justified in claiming that "God's personal activity" was needed fully to describe this non-inferential awareness?[50]

With regard to the first of these questions, Ramsey suggests that an affirmative answer will be given, if the miracle gives "a stable historical insight" that gains "significance and relevance" as other events are adduced. With regard to the second question and the term *Kata-language,* Ramsey sees the language of theism as a kind of supplementary language, employing what he earlier called *second-order* statements. It serves as an index, pointing to dimensions of reality that cannot be subsumed under scientific language. To speak of miracles implies commending the language of theism as an essential supplement to the language of science. With regard to the third question, Ramsey sees the term "miracle" as "a metaphysical word to name and characterize those empirical situations when our non-inferential awareness cannot be adequately described in any language which does not extend to, and link together, the words 'personal (second-order) activity' and the word 'God'."[51]

In his much-acclaimed book, *Religious Language,* published some six years after his inaugural lecture, Ramsey reiterated his basic position. "A miracle is a non-conforming event, a *miraculum* whose non-conformity, whose oddness evokes, gives rise to, what we have called a characteristically theological situation. With a miracle, a situation 'comes alive,' the light dawns, the penny drops."[52] By this time he had supplemented his map-language with talk about models and qualifiers. A model is "a situation with which we are all familiar, and which can be used for reaching another situation with which we are not so familiar; one which, without the model, we should not recognize so easily."[53] A qualifier is "a directive which prescribes a special way of developing those 'model' situations."[54] To speak of "a breach of natural law" is to employ a *qualified model.* It is not a contradiction in terms, but a reminder that science is never capable of giving exhaustive descriptions. No sooner is a law broken, than it has to be mended by reformulation. Hence, miracles are not to be thought of in terms of breaches of the laws of science, but as configurations of occasions of personal, transcendent self-disclosure. In a sense, "miracle" and "free will" are "logical parallels":

Each claims a "personal" situation which needs *more than* scientific language to talk about it. "Free will" does not deny determinism any more than it *necessarily implies* indeterminism; rather it claims a characteristically "personal" situation which the language of causal connectedness never exhausts. So with a "miracle" situation: it neither denies nor asserts the applicability of the language of scientific law to the spatio-temporal features it contains, but it claims that such language never tells the full story. It thus claims about the *objective* features of a certain situation what free-will claims about the *subjective* features of other situations: it makes (we may say) a "free-will" claim about the Universe.[55]

In trying to assess Ian Ramsey's contribution to the debate on miracles, importance must be given to his attempt to distinguish different types of language and the logic of their meaning. Language is not a single, unified, verbal picture of reality, in which words have a one-to-one correspondence with whatever they refer to. We need to pay attention not only to the meaning of detached words but also to the explicit or implicit grammar. Indeed, it is impossible to discern meaning apart from grammar. Ramsey's approach gives recognition to the variety of maps and models that we employ both consciously and unconsciously to describe reality. Such maps owe their unity not to the fact that the symbols on them are mutually interchangeable, but to the fact that, where valid, they draw attention to and enable us to explore some feature of reality. It is the referent that gives the unity, not some presumed univocal or interchangeable character of the maps. The fuller the picture we need, the more we need to identify the object of our concern on different kinds of maps.

Important too is Ramsey's discussion of the transcendent, which in terms of one map may not appear to be transcendent at all, but in terms of another may disclose its transcendence. A note of caution must be entered at this point. Frequently we interweave different types of discourse. When the change is made from historical to scientific language, it is not as though we had spent the morning speaking English and then lapsed into Japanese for an hour or two. Even scientific language mixes the rarified abstractions of equations with everyday language, especially at those points where the equations are explained and applied. Conversely, in history appeal is made to science to determine and explain the boundaries of the feasible. As we have seen time and time again from David Hume onward, in making historical judgments people have at the back of their minds a picture (however rudimentary and incoherent) of what is scientifically possible. This is true of both the professional historian and the ordinary layperson trying to make up his or her mind.

Ramsey himself seems to have made up his mind about miracles by tacitly allowing science not to leave any gaps beyond its potential reach. On the level of scientific explanation there seems to be in principle no such thing as a real breach of a natural law. In other words, Ramsey's talk about "non-conforming events" draws attention not to their scientific irregularities, but to their function in "disclosure situations." Presumably the word "miracle" is used in this connection because the event is so unusual and unexpected that it evokes a sense of wonder at the personal transcendence manifested through the event in question. In other words, what Ramsey offers is an anticipation of Holland's *contingency concept* of miracle. But whereas Holland was prepared to say that some events appear to be classifiable as instances of the *violation concept* of miracle, Ramsey appears to have felt, rightly or wrongly, that this distinction was not worth pursuing.

FURTHER REFINEMENTS

The 1970's saw a steady stream of articles mulling over the issues raised by Smart, Holland, Swinburne, and Ramsey, sometimes making explicit reference to this quartet of philosophers, sometimes going over much the same ground in an independent fashion, and sometimes advancing arguments propounded by earlier philosophers and apologists.

The Princeton philosopher Malcolm L. Diamond argued that "it is logically possible for religious thinkers to affirm the supernaturalistic interpretation, but that the conceptual cost is too great."[56] He granted that scientific laws were corrigible, and was persuaded that utterly extraordinary cures had taken place at Lourdes. But he was reluctant to take the further step of ascribing a supernatural cause to such cures. He felt uncomfortable with the suggestion that such healings might be ascribed to a higher law:

> Even if it is the case that God's grace has a "law" of its own, it would take an infinite intelligence like God's to discern it. The "law" would remain inaccessible, in principle, to our limited intellects. We never, for example, learn why some supplicants are miraculously cured, while the prayers of others go unanswered.[57]

Diamond went on to endorse Guy Robinson's protests against the idea of exceptions to natural law, along the lines advocated by Holland, Smart, and Swinburne.[58] For to admit the possibility of genuine exceptions, natural or supernatural, would either stop the scientific enterprise or make it completely capricious. The cost of supernaturalism is the sacrifice of scientific autonomy. Diamond, therefore, concludes that the supernaturalistic interpretation of unusual events requires demythologizing, and God's revelatory activity understood within the fabric of scientific understanding, leaving room for an existentialist approach to faith.

At the other end of the scale, Tan Tai Wei endorses the efforts of Smart, Holland, and Swinburne to leave the door open for rare phenomena that are in principle inexplicable.[59] Miracles are not even to be thought of as "divine behavioral regularities," because God does not normally behave in that way. God may be said to move in mysterious ways, his wonders to perform. Such ways are not unintelligible to God, although they remain so for us. Miracles belong to those ways, and hence we must resist the attempt to make sense of them. George Landrum also argues against attempts to subsume miracles under natural laws. Since natural events cannot be against natural laws, Landrum suggests that miracles fall outside natural law.[60] On his view one need not presume that miracles are unrepeatable. The Bible itself reports repeated instances of exorcisms and healing. Nor need one suppose that miracles are the only entities to exist outside natural law. Angels and their actions (on the assumption that they are not to be demythologized, along with miracles, in the manner recommended by Diamond and Bultmann) could also be conceived as belonging to a universe that could be at least in part understood, but not explained by science alone.

Between Malcolm L. Diamond, on the one hand, and Tan Tai Wei and George Landrum, on the other hand, stand various philosophers who think that neither of these extremes is satisfactory and that more needs to be said in order to make the idea of miracles intelligible and reports of their occurrence convincing. Among the philosophers who have addressed the subject of miracles in the past decade we may note Michael J. Langford, George D. Chryssides, Robert Young, Douglas K. Erlandson, and Douglas Odegard.

Michael J. Langford appears to be advocating a form of the *contingency concept* of miracle, positing God as the divine mind that initiates the events that we call miracles.[61] He rejects the idea of direct divine interventions inserted in between ordinary events. Such a view suggests a "miracle of the gaps theory" that parallels the "God of the gaps theory."[62] Such a theory would be vulnerable in exactly the same ways as the "God of the gaps" view of God working in the world in those areas not yet explained by science. For as science proffers explanations, so the area of divine activity would shrink to its vanishing point. Langford suggests that we think of miracles in terms of "God working through minds in a way that is not totally dissimilar to our previous experience of minds."[63] He sees miracles as an outworking of the divine grace that works through human minds without violating them and that in turn produces tangible, physical results:

> Thus God (1) works as a mind, in and through human minds (2), in the natural order (3), in such a way as not to destroy freedom or order . . . . A miracle is an event which is the result of grace, which in turn has unleashed little-known or unsuspected human powers, triggered off by the interaction of human and divine minds.[64]

Such a view of miracles presupposes not only belief in the existence of God but a network of beliefs about God and the nature of mind. It recalls Kant's discussion of freedom and necessity and the extension of this by H. H. Farmer, which we shall examine later on.[65] Langford concedes that his view is more readily applicable to those miracles where psychosomatic influences may be conceivable, even though we remain far from knowing the scope of such influence. His view finds a kind of negative confirmation in the fact that miracles do not normally extend to the growth of lost limbs, which would seem to lie outside the sphere of psychosomatic factors. Langford does not pursue the question of how his views might apply to nature-miracles. His thesis is not offered as a complete solution, but as "a possible schema in terms of which the word 'miracle' can be seen to be intelligible to someone who believes in God, or who regards such belief as meaningful even though mistaken."[66]

Another thinker who is dissatisfied with the *violation concept* of miracle is George D. Chryssides. He argues that if the concept makes sense and even if such a violation could be identified, "it would be logically impossible to ascribe such an event to the activity of a rational agent."[67] His argument turns on what he calls the *Repeatability Requirement*. Causality is attributed to an agent on the basis of repeated conjunctions that can be seen to be related. Observation of past repeated conjunctions leads to the expectation of future ones. This brings Chryssides to observe:

> If I am correct in claiming that the assignment of agency implies predictability, then no event can be assigned to an agent unless it is in principle possible to subsume the putative effect brought about by his action under scientific law, for to be able to predict the circumstances in which the effect will recur *means* to be able to formulate a scientific law relating the alleged cause to the alleged effect.[68]

The upshot of the argument is that "there is an inherent self-contradiction in the notion of an agent performing a miracle."[69] This is not to say that very unusual events might not occur, but they would not be miracles in the sense of violations of the laws of nature.

It is doubtful whether the believer in miracles would feel quite as unsettled in his views as Chryssides thinks he or she ought to feel. Such a believer might respond to the argument by drawing attention to certain differences between causes in science and causes in history of which Chryssides shows himself only partially aware. He acknowledges that in cases of murder, the murderer does not have to go on proving his point. We know what kinds of actions are required in order to discharge guns. But Chryssides's discussion focuses on the predictability of physical conditions. In attributing the kind of causality that amounts to personal responsibility, the historian, the detective, the jury, and the judge take into account not only factors that are in principle repeatable and similar; they also, as it were, work backward, by trying to exclude the general to establish what remains of the particular. In such cases judgments about agency are made, not because a repeated conjunction can be demonstrated, but because a causal relationship is inferred, when all other possible factors are eliminated. If they cannot be satisfactorily eliminated, judgment about agency has to be suspended.

A feature of Chryssides's argument is the double assumption that miracles are by definition unrepeatable and that anything repeatable comes under the domain of *scientific* law. Both points are open to challenge. Clearly many of the healings, regarded by believers as miracles, were repeated. Even the resurrection of Jesus was not regarded by the apostle Paul as unique. To him it was the ground of the believer's own resurrection hope (Rom. 6:6; 1 Cor. 15:22f.; Col. 1:18; 3:1). It is not at all obvious that anything repeatable is adequately or necessarily describable in terms of scientific laws, or that all kinds of causation are reducible to the kinds of causes appropriate to science.

Chryssides's contribution to the discussion is perhaps best seen as a salutary warning not to lay too much stress on the ideas of violation, randomness, and unrepeatability. In attributing miracles to divine agency the believer is not focusing on their randomness. Negatively, the believer is confessing belief that other factors are either absent or insufficient to explain the event. Positively, the believer is asserting that the event is consistent with and expresses further the character of God, as perceived within his or her belief-system. Just as on a physical level causality may be attributed on the basis of accepted paradigms of causality, so miracles are interpreted in the light of accepted paradigms of divine agency. Moreover, within a belief-system the miracles themselves become part of the paradigm for interpreting the future hope. The miracle is not seen as a unique random occurrence, but as a manifestation of an order of reality that will supersede the present order with all its physicality. This is, of course, part of a confession of faith. But whatever else, it cannot be dismissed on the grounds of "inherent self-contradiction."[70]

The present writer finds himself closer to the positions of Robert Young[71] and Douglas K. Erlandson,[72] though not without making important qualifications. Both of them express reservations about the *violation concept* of miracle. Young suggests that miracles might best be viewed in terms of the doctrine of "the plurality of causes," which he finds supported by Walther Eichrodt's discussion of miracles in the Old Testament.[73] To be a candidate for the cause of a specified event, the purported cause must be among those and only those conditions that occur relevant to the event. Young contends that "when a miracle occurs, God is an active agent-factor in the set of factors (out of the perhaps several possible sets sufficient for the event's occurrence) which actually was causally operative. His presence (*ceteris paribus*) alters the outcome from what it (perhaps) would have been if, *contrary to fact,* he had not been present."[74] Thus, in terms of the logic of historical investigation of the resurrection of Jesus, "God's presence as an active agent-factor most adequately accounts for the facts established which stand in need of explanation (e.g. the empty tomb, the subsequent behaviour of the witnesses and so on) . . . . This approach would be generalisable for all miracles."[75] The point of his procedure is "to show that miracles are conceivable and then to ask whether we could justifiably claim to identify an actual instance."[76] Young sees miracles as part of revelation, rather than as proof of revelation.[77] In claiming that any event is a miracle, we are expressing a human judgment, subject to the limitations of all human judgments. But this is part of the price that we have to pay in making factual claims.

Before we turn to Erlandson in this account of the views of contemporary philosophers, we may pause to ask what is the difference between Young's position and Holland's *contingency concept.* Young dismisses the latter on two counts. First, to admit identifiable finite factors in producing an event of religious significance seems to rule out talk of God by the simple application of Occam's razor. Secondly, the concept seems too weak to sustain the notion of miracle exemplified in the biblical accounts.[78] In response to this, it may well be asked whether the same application of Occam's razor—

that entities are not to be multiplied beyond necessity—would not eliminate all reference to divine agency in the ordinary events of life to which the believer gives a religious significance. The answer to this depends on whether we can see and justify a sense of divine agency in and through such occurrences. Young proffers his account as an alternative to both contingency and violation. But it is very difficult to see how it can avoid being either one or the other. For if it is not contingency, then in some sense it involves violation; and if it is not violation, then it involves some form of contingency. Admittedly, the contingency in question posits causes beyond the range of present scientific explanation. Nevertheless, God's relation to the events that we call miracles does not involve direct intervention and the suspension of all causes. Rather, God's action is "a factor in the causally operative set of factors."[79]

Douglas K. Erlandson seems to be advocating a similar position when he argues that "the believer can hold that certain *particular* events are the result of interventions by divine agency and are thus not to be explained scientifically but nevertheless can grant the scientist autonomy to investigate all *types* of events."[80] He contends that the kind of violations posited by Swinburne and others do not tell us why their bizarreness and disruptive qualities should make us despair of ever offering a scientific explanation.[81] He meets the challenge of Robinson and Diamond, who think that the integrity of science would be undermined by the admission of such violations, by contending that "God's interventions do not involve evasion of the laws of nature; rather, human finitude prevents understanding the ways of God, and as a result certain events are seen as miracles."[82]

Erlandson sees God

> as a supersensible agent (i.e. an agent in whole or in part imperceptible to the human senses) who is part of the universe (i.e. the entire space-time sphere). His interventions bear a similarity to the interventions of human agents in being one part of the universe interacting with another part. But while they share certain characteristics (e.g. purposiveness) God's interventions are often more grandiose and mysterious.[83]

Erlandson goes on to argue that to emphasize inexplicability and mystery to the exclusion of all else is likely to lead astray. "Inexplicability or mystery *is* an element of the miraculous, but it must be of a certain sort—it must fit a pattern."[84] This leads him to what appears to be a restatement of the *contingency concept,* which allows him to entertain both scientific and theological explanations for such events as the Israelites' crossing of the Red Sea, Joshua's long day, and even the Virgin Birth. What makes the parting of the Red Sea for Moses a miracle and other partings not turns on the pattern of events of which the respective incidents form a part:

> The believer may admit that the crossing of the Red Sea on dry ground is not in itself a miracle. But in the case of the exodus he perceives it as part of a larger set of events which form a pattern indicating providen-

tial guidance by Jehovah of the children of Israel. Similarly, in the case of the Virgin Birth, the believer sees a pattern surrounding many aspects of the life of Jesus, of which this forms a part. On the other hand, the believer might not see any such pattern when a lone adventurer crosses the Red Sea or when a poor virgin in India gives birth to a child who will soon die of malnutrition.[85]

Hence, in response to the challenge of Robinson, Diamond, and indeed of anyone who thinks that belief in miracles demands the intellectual sacrifice of ways of looking at the world that have demonstrated their validity, Erlandson throws out an impressive counterchallenge. All events are, in principle, open to scientific investigation. This is not simply a matter of apologetics for the benefit of the skeptics and for calling Robinson's and Diamond's bluff. It is a duty for the believing scientist:

> Even were the scientist a believer in the miraculous he would not have the option of "opting out." This is because (a) confronting an anomaly never *in itself* gives him this option, but does so only if the anomaly is an event conforming to a very special pattern; and (b) since the scientist is concerned with devising theories to explain *types* of events, even if the believer claims that a *particular* anomalous event is a miracle, the scientist still has a duty to devise a theory for that type of event.[86]

In trying to assess Erlandson's position, believers of a more orthodox stamp may well be puzzled by his preference for speaking of God as *part of* the universe, as opposed to *outside,* that is, in a nonspatial sense. His intention seems to be to safeguard divine immanence, and to make intelligible God's ability to answer prayer requests (which are obviously spatiotemporal events), which seems to Erlandson to be rendered more difficult if God is thought to be a being *outside* the world. It is questionable whether Erlandson's preferred way of speaking really meets this need. To speak of God as *part of* the universe suggests a way of thinking about God as one finite (admittedly greater) being alongside other beings and as something that is somewhat less than the whole and indeed in some sense dependent on it. Whether this is really Erlandson's intention is another matter. The rest of his arguments suggests a more traditional theistic understanding of God. Clearly this is an issue of the most far-reaching consequences and is of the utmost significance to the subject of miracles, but it lies outside the scope of the present discussion.

In general, it must be said that there seems to be something fundamentally right in Erlandson's basic contention that all events are in principle open to scientific investigation. If Christian believers claim that certain events connected with their beliefs are historical, this claim entails the corollary that these events are open to examination by whatever means that are appropriate. It may be that we just do not have enough data to carry out an examination of any given event. To that extent, any truth-claims that we may make about the event will be based on faith. Or it may be that scientific knowledge is inadequate to advance an account. In that case, the scientist must acknowledge his limitations, just as he does in other cases that defy current explanation. But we are here talking about principles, and in this respect Erlandson's claim that miracles, like all other events, are *prima facie* open to scientific investigation cannot be faulted.

However, the question may be asked whether Erlandson is not backtracking on his apparent no-holds-barred attitude at the point where he seems to grant exemption to those anomalies that conform to a religious pattern for which he claims a *different explanation.*[87] At this point he appears to be re-introducing the *violation concept* by the back door. When Erlandson says that science may be able to explain some virgin births, but that a different explanation is required for the Virgin Birth of Jesus, he seems to be taking back with his right hand what he has previously given with his left. What Erlandson says about the need to interpret miracles in terms of significant patterns of events is an important insight. But it seems to the present writer that recognition must be given to different, but overlapping, levels of explanation. In the case of the crossing of the Red Sea, Moses is said to have stretched out his hand over the sea, "and the Lord drove the sea back by a strong east wind all night, and made the sea dry land, and the waters were divided" (Exod. 14:21). It was not a case of *either* a natural explanation *or* a super-natural, theological explanation, but of both. Both explanations were appropriate at the appropriate levels of understanding. The question that this raises is twofold. Should we think of miracles generally as having these two levels of explanation, and, if so, what justifies the theological explanation in those situations where natural factors can be identified or suggested?

We shall return to these questions in the final two chapters of this study. In the meantime I would offer a preliminary answer to these questions by drawing on various ideas that we have noted from time to time throughout this book. In the first place, miracles for the Christian believer are not bizarre, random events. They are acts of God that reveal something of the character of God. In some instances, God as a personal being orders nature in a way comparable with the way in which we as personal beings order nature. In everyday life we do not suspend the normal patterns of cause and effect. But as personal agents we are able to initiate some sequences of cause and effect and terminate others. In the case of a miracle like the dividing of the Red Sea, we appear to have an instance of what Holland and others have termed the *contingency concept* of miracle. In this case, there appears to be no suspension or violation of the laws of nature but an ordering of them by a personal being for a gracious purpose.

However, in other instances of events alleged to be miracles such causal factors are not readily identifiable. We may, with the skeptic, choose to say that the reported event was not an event at all and attribute the report to a mistake of some kind. Alternatively, we may allow the possibility that the event actually occurred in the belief that a rational explanation may be forth-coming one day. Such a view might be entertained by the skeptic or by a believer, who would thus see the event as an instance of the *contingency concept*. There is, however, a further option. This is to posit the event as an instance of an order different from the order we call nature, impinging on the natural order. Admittedly, on this view, such impingements are rare—in fact too rare to warrant the reformulation of scientific laws. In the past, various Christian thinkers have suggested that such events were not so much violations of the laws of nature as the coming into play of the laws of a higher divine order. More recently, Douglas Odegard has suggested that the idea of a miracle as a violation of the laws of nature necessarily carries with it the idea of divine intervention.[88] He writes, "We can explain a law violation as an instance of a kind of event which is impossible unless a god produces an instance."[89]

To take this view is to offer a general metaphysical hypothesis. It leaves open the question of what evidence might warrant the conclusion that any alleged miracle had actually occurred and was indeed a miracle of this kind. Moreover, as Odegard recognizes, this way of looking at miracles prevents us from arguing from the fact of the miracle to the existence of God. For, in order to say that the event is a miracle, we have also to say at the same time that it was caused by God. However, it is at least *prima facie* possible to give reasons for saying that the event is best explained as a divine act and for seeing how it relates to our broader view of God and reality.

Whether we take a skeptical view of miracle stories, or believe that they may all turn out to be instances of contingency, or whether we see some in terms of contingency and others in terms of the higher order of God's action impinging on our accustomed order, depends on two sets of factors. On the one hand, there is the evidence that (unless we have experienced a miracle at first hand) consists largely of reports. On the other hand, there is a metaphysical or theological view of reality that we take. In assessing a report we do so in terms of this larger world view. In practice, the relationship between reports (whether they be of miracles or of anything else) and our world view is reciprocal, constantly being modified in the light of new experience, more information, further reflection, deeper insight, and so on. Once so processed, a report or an item of new information becomes itself part of our world view, and thus in turn plays a part in evaluating further reports and items of information.

If this is so, the question of miracles is not the simple one of asking whether we have enough evidence to say that this or that event is a violation of the laws of nature. It requires us to ask what the miracle in question looks like in relation to our convictions about the nature of reality. But in saying this, we are already encroaching on the theme of the next two chapters.

8

THE ANSWERS
OF THE APOLOGISTS

Broadly speaking, Christian apologists find themselves pushed into two camps over the question of miracles. This is no less true today than it has been through the centuries, although the second camp seems to be increasingly more numerous. The first camp may be labeled the offensive camp. Its leaders see miracles as objective events that give irrefragable proof of divine intervention. Such events are ascertainable by anyone who cares to use the normal techniques employed by secular historians investigating secular history. Miracles are seen as providing objective grounds for believing, and do not require any special faith-commitment as a prerequisite to accepting them. The second camp may be labeled the defensive camp. To this camp belong those thinkers who believe in the possibility of miracles, but do not think that it is possible to offer hard historical evidence to show that every biblical miracle really happened in such a way as to compel belief. Here the emphasis is negative in the sense that the apologist is concerned to show that his acceptance of miracles is not incompatible with a rational view of the world and that he has good ground for seeing miracles in harmony with his broader view of God and of God's ultimate purposes.

In this chapter we shall look at three groups of apologists: American evangelicals, Roman Catholics, and some British writers. This is not to suggest that these groups represent three distinctive schools of thought. What they have in common is a concern for apologetics and the presentation of the historic Christian faith. American evangelicalism has traditionally placed greater emphasis on taking the initiative by launching an aggressive case for the Christian faith. Most of the writers we shall be looking at are the lineal descendants of Archibald Alexander and the classical Calvinistic argument that miracles provide evidence for belief. Those of the post-World War II generation clearly demonstrate a concern to update this position by responding directly to the questions of contemporary philosophy. Traditionally the Roman Catholic Church has also viewed miracles as divine attestation of its position and authority. However, we may discern a certain shift of emphasis in moving away from simplistic evidentialism to a theological appreciation of miracles in their character as signs. In British Protestant theology apologetics has never had the same status as a subject in its own right that it acquired in American evangelicalism or in Roman Catholicism. Scholars tend to be either biblical theologians, historians, or philosophers of religion. For this reason the work of thinkers like Ian Ramsey and Richard Swinburne usually comes under the heading of philosophy, and we have already discussed it in that context. On the other hand, British theology has maintained a long-standing concern for the truth of the Christian faith. A number of writers who were scholars of distinction in other fields have made important contributions to apologetics. In so doing, they have offered some new perspectives on the question of miracles.

AMERICAN EVANGELICAL APOLOGISTS

In looking at American evangelicalism, we shall focus on B. B. Warfield, Edward John Carnell, John Warwick Montgomery, and Norman Geisler as representatives of three generations of thinkers who span the twentieth century. In many ways Benjamin Breckinridge Warfield (1851–1921) was the doyen of American evangelical polemicists. Between 1887 and 1921 he occupied the chair of Didactic and Polemical Theology at Princeton Theological Seminary. Although he has been dead for over sixty years, his views still carry great weight in evangelical circles on a wide range of issues. In 1917-18 Warfield delivered the Thomas Smyth Lectures at Columbia Theological Seminary, South Carolina, which were published under the title *Counterfeit Miracles* (1918) and later retitled *Miracles: Yesterday and Today, True and False*.[1]

Warfield's book was marked by the solid erudition and commitment to Reformed evangelicalism that characterized his other writings. But the book largely falls outside the scope of the present study in view of the fact that Warfield was concerned with postbiblical miracles, or to be more precise, the denial of postbiblical miracles. In the opening pages Warfield reiterated the traditional Calvinistic view that miracles continued in the apostolic church "as part of the credentials of the Apostles as the authoritative agents of God in founding the church. Their function thus confined them to distinctively the Apostolic Church, and they necessarily passed away with it."[2] On the subject of Jesus' miracles Warfield contented himself with the somewhat poetic reflection, "The signs which accompanied His Ministry were but the trailing clouds of glory which He brought from heaven, which is His home. The number of miracles which He wrought may easily be underrated."[3] The miracles of the apostles were the "crowning sign" of their divine commission. It is not clear from this whether Warfield regarded such signs as indisputable proof demanding assent from the twentieth-century reader or as a testimony inviting faith. For like Conyers Middleton (on whom Warfield leaned heavily in his rejection of miracles in the postapostolic church), Warfield refrained from applying to the New Testament the same scrutiny that he applied to all other accounts of miracles.[4] Beginning with the second century and moving through the Middle Ages to Roman Catholic miracles, Irvingite gifts, and accounts of modern faith healing and mind-cures, and culminating in a discussion of why Mrs. Mary Baker Eddy found it necessary to visit a dentist, Warfield's work remains an incomparable inventory of objections to the miraculous.

A certain poignancy attaches to Warfield's work in view of the debilitating illness of his wife throughout their married life. Warfield's view of divine activity in the present age encompassed the providential ordering of all things in accordance with God's eternal decrees, regeneration, sanctification, and the illumination of the Scripture by the Holy Spirit. But it precluded supernatural healing of the kind recorded in the New Testament. Warfield shared the view, preserved in the article on "Miracle" in *The Westminster Dictionary of the Bible,* that God does not work miracles "except for great cause and for a religious purpose. They belong to the history of redemption, and there is no genuine miracle without an adequate occasion for it in God's redemptive revelation of himself."[5] They are not established by the number of witnesses, but by the character and qualifications of the witnesses. Moreover, miracles are not scattered throughout the length and breadth of Scripture. They are almost exclusively confined to four main periods of great significance in redemptive history: the redemption of Israel from Egypt and the settlement in Canaan, the life-and-death struggle with heathenism under Elijah and Elisha; the book of Daniel, which attests Yahweh's supremacy; and the introduction of Christianity, "when miracles attested the person of Christ and his doctrine."

It is curious that in the article Warfield wrote on "Jesus Christ" for *The New Schaff-Herzog Encyclopedia of Religious Knowledge*[6] miracles play a very small part. We again find Warfield claiming that their number is generally underestimated. He even ventures a thought that goes far beyond the biblical evidence: "For a time disease and death must have been almost banished from the land." However, "the purport of His miracles was that the kingdom of God was already present in its King."[7]

Somewhat earlier Warfield had discussed the apologetic role of miracles in a series of articles entitled "The Question of Miracle" that appeared in *The Bible Student* between March and June 1903.[8] Warfield began by attempting to define a miracle. He sought to outflank David Hume and his followers by insisting that a miracle was not "a violation, or suspension, or transgression of the laws or forces of nature." It was not "contranatural," but "extra-natural," or more specifically "super-natural."[9] Natural forces remain operative throughout. But Warfield refused to speak of their "cooperation." Although miracles take place within nature, "in no sense, in whole or in part" could they be considered "the product of nature."[10] Hence, Warfield offers the following defining characteristics:

> A miracle then is specifically an effect in the external world, produced by the immediate efficiency of God. Its *differentiae* are: (1) that it oc-

curs in the external world, and thus is objectively real and not a merely mental phenomenon; and (2) that its cause is a new super-natural force, intruded into the complex of nature, and not a natural force under whatever wise and powerful manipulation.[11]

In other words, Warfield appears to preclude from the outset all possibility of an instance of what in the last chapter we called the *contingency concept* of a miracle from qualifying as a genuine miracle. It may be noted in passing that Warfield does not at this stage attempt to examine any actual instances of miracles in order to form his definition. In fact, his definition, like his method in general, appears to be based on logical reflection on the implications of certain basic ideas, rather than close examination of particular cases.

At various points Warfield appears to be a hard evidentialist, arguing that miracles can be recognized as objective, supernaturally caused events by anyone who takes the trouble to look fairly at the evidence. He detects inconsistency and unbelief behind the view that entertains the possibility of a miracle occurring, yet wonders whether the evidence is strong enough to assert it as an objective historical fact. "If it occurs, it ought to be capable of being shown to have occurred."[12] But Warfield's own case seems to involve a certain amount of backtracking or lack of perception as to the real nature of his argument. For within a single paragraph he advances the following contradictory statements:

> How we can infer from any study of the ordinary course of things, however protracted, profound, or complete, that an extraordinary event never occurs; and how we can infer from the conviction that such an extraordinary event never occurs. that it is impossible; it is not easy to see. . . . The atheist, the materialist, the pantheist are within their rights in denying the possibility of miracle. But none other is. So soon we adopt the postulate of a personal God and a creation, so soon miracles cease to be "impossible" in any exact sense of the word. We may hold them to be improbable, to the verge of the unprovable: but their *possibility* is inherent in the very nature of God as personal and the author of the universal frame.[13]

The first sentence is logical enough, but it begs the question of whether "extraordinary events" are the same as miracles. However, Warfield's claim is contradicted by the second sentence, which admits that the atheist, the materialist, and the pantheist are within their rights to deny the possibility of miracles. The whole argument is further modified by the admission of belief in a personal Creator God as the condition for granting the feasibility of miracles. It would seem from this that Warfield was ready to concede that miracles could not be admitted as objective proof that would compel belief in someone who was not prepared to accept a theistic world view.

Somewhat naively Warfield proceeds to the conclusion that "The question of miracles, then, is after all just a question of evidence."[14] But it is precisely the presuppositions that we bring to the weighing of evidence that determines our evaluation of it. The subsequent argument is itself an illustration for this. For Warfield goes on to claim that the probability of "testimony being true rests in part on the known or presumable trustworthiness of the witnesses available in the case, anterior to their testimony to the particular fact now under consideration."[15] It is on this ground that Warfield proclaims the accounts of the raising of Lazarus (John 11) and the restoration of the sight of the man born blind (John 9) as historical events,[16] even though we have only the testimony of the Fourth Gospel to vouch for them. It is not because Warfield has overwhelming evidence outside the testimony of the Fourth Gospel for these unusual events. In fact he has no corroborating evidence at all. Nor can he appeal to the intrinsic feasibility of John's reports on the grounds that they tell of events comparable with similar events in his own experience. For Warfield was committed to the belief that miracles ceased with the apostolic age, and hence there could be no events in subsequent history comparable with the miracles reported in the Gospels and Acts. In short, Warfield accepted the accounts of the miracles in the Fourth Gospel because he believed the work to be trustworthy in its reporting. But this was, in fact, a faith-position bound up with theological considerations.

The role of theological considerations is further evidenced by the part that Warfield assigns to sin, not only in his interpretation of the meaning of miracles but in his assessment of their possibility:

> The entrance of sin into the world is . . . the sufficient occasion of the entrance also of miracle. Extraordinary exigencies (we speak as a man) are the sufficient explanation of extraordinary expedients. If, then, we conceive the extraordinary events of the Scriptural record as part and parcel of the redemptive work of God—and this is how they are uniformly represented in the Scriptural record itself—surely the presumption which is held to lie against them is transmitted into a presumption in their favor, as appropriate elements in a great remedial scheme, by means of which the broken scheme of nature is mended and restored.[17]

Warfield's determination to approach the New Testament miracles from the standpoint of prior belief-commitments is also evidenced by his insistence on the importance of taking the New Testament at face value,[18] and his desire to see miracles within the context of creation, the incarnation, and the resurrection of Christ. Such "extraordinary works of God recorded in Scripture" cannot "be subsumed under the category of natural law." Although it may be questioned whether such events fit into the category of what is normally called miracle, they fit Warfield's broad conception of miracles as events supernaturally wrought. Moreover, the role that Warfield assigns to creation, the incarnation, and the resurrection is pivotal in his apologetic for miracles:

> The admission of the truly miraculous character of these three will not only itself suffice to fill the category of "miracle," taken in its strictest sense, with an undeniable content, and so to vindicate the main proposition that miracles have happened; but will tend to drag into that category others in their train.[19]

There is a certain vagueness in Warfield's talk about tending "to drag into that category others in their train." Warfield's main contention seems to be that if God can create the world, become incarnate, and raise Jesus from the dead, he can also perform lesser, related wonders. But to say that God can perform greater wonders is not the same as saying that he must have performed lesser wonders. Nor can we simply assume that accounts of lesser wonders are guaranteed as objective historical events by our belief in the greater wonders. The believer may accept the lesser wonders as part of his faith, but if so, he must recognize that this is a faith-commitment. Belief in God the Creator does not necessarily entail the multiplication of the loaves and fishes and the turning of water into wine. Indeed, if one starts from the premise of God's normal working in sustaining creation, one would be inclined not to expect such sudden changes at all. Warfield contends that "From the resurrection of the dead we may advance to other miracles which have to do with spiritual entities, such as, for example, the cure of demoniacs which can scarcely be subsumed under the operation of natural forces."[20] This raises the hermeneutical question of how we should interpret the Gospel accounts of exorcism. Some readers may conclude that in linking resurrection from the dead with spiritual healing Warfield is mixing categories of activity, and wonder whether there is an intrinsic connection between the two. But to pursue these questions at this stage would obscure the main point to be noted, which is that Warfield's approach to the New Testament miracles is by no means the straightforward, objective evidentialism that it has been imagined to be and that he himself perhaps thought it to be.

In the year 1901 members of the Junior Class of Princeton Theological Seminary were required to answer the following question in their Examination in Didactic and Polemic Theology: "Show that Miracles are possible, capable of proof and have occurred."[21] Doubtless the class had been already well primed in the kind of teaching outlined above. One wonders how Warfield himself would have reacted to a student who pointed out that Warfield's own approach to miracles was not a matter of objective proof that created faith. Rather, they have a place as part of the fabric of a belief-system in which beliefs not only about the trustworthiness of the Gospels and the acceptance of their reports at face value, but also the prior commitment to beliefs about sin, creation, incarnation, and resurrection play a decisive part. This decisive part not only affects their interpretation (which actually tends to be pushed into the background in Warfield's writings) but also the question of their possibility and actuality. The point to be stressed is not that this is necessarily wrong, but that Warfield's position must be recognized for what it is. Warfield cannot simply be counted as an objective evidentialist belonging to the offensive camp of apologists who had established the objectivity of the biblical miracles quite apart from faith-commitments. Still less can his position be used as a vantage point from which to attack others as half-hearted or "neo-orthodox" in view of their recognition of belief-commitments. For belief-commitments of various kinds were built into the very fabric of Warfield's position.

In the generation after Warfield, E. J. Carnell adopted a similar stance in *An Introduction to Christian Apologetics* (1948). Like Warfield, Carnell rejected postbiblical miracles. He could even remark that "the doctrine that miracles no longer occur is one of those fundamental canons which separate Protestantism from Roman Catholicism."[22] He went on to reiterate the Reformed view that "Miracles are a seal and sign of special, covenantal revelation; but revelation has ceased. There cannot, therefore, be new miracles." Carnell's central concern was not, however, the inner-Christian debate about the extent of revelation and miracles, but the difficulties presented to believer and unbeliever alike by reading the biblical reports of miracles in the modern scientific age. He met this difficulty by insisting that "The Christian defines nature as what God does with His creation, and a natural law as but a mathematically exact description upon the part of man of how God has elected to order His creation."[23] Miracles differ from ordinary events not by being greater manifestations of God's power, but by being different manifestations of that power.

In the course of Carnell's argument the resurrection of Jesus occupies the supreme place as a test case of a miraculous event that no scientist can explain away in terms of physical laws. The significance of the point is that if this miracle can be accepted, the other miracles recorded in Scripture that are obviously lesser in kind can also be accepted. However, this point raises the question of whether there is a necessary relationship between the other miracles and the resurrection. It also raises the question of whether the other miracles are accepted on the basis of historical evidence or on warrant of divinely inspired Scripture. If it is on the former basis, the believer has to acknowledge that the evidence is comparatively slight. For whereas there is considerable evidence for the resurrection of Jesus throughout the New Testament, the historical evidence for many of the miracles is limited to the testimony of at most the four Gospels and sometimes to that of only one Gospel. If, however, miracles are accepted on the latter basis because they are reported in Scripture, which is divinely inspired, it has to be acknowledged that the miracles themselves have *ipso facto* ceased to be independent items of evidence that compel faith and have become themselves objects of faith.

Carnell's position appears at times to combine these two views. He goes on to claim that, far from ruining the predictive character of empirical science, "miracles are the very thing which save it." The core of his argument is stated in the following passage:

> Miracles are a sign and a seal of the veracity of special revelation, revelation which assures us exactly how God has elected to dispose of His universe. In this revelation we read that He Who made us, and Who can also destroy us, has graciously chosen to keep the universe regular according to the covenant which He made with Noah and his seed forever. If

the scientist rejects miracles to keep his mechanical order, he loses his right to that mechanical order, for, without miracles to guarantee revelation, he can claim no external reference point; and without an external reference point to serve as a fulcrum, the scientist is closed up to the shifting sand of history. In such a case, then, how can the scientist appeal to the changeless conviction "that the universe is mechanical," when from flux and change only flux and change can come? The scientist simply exchanges what he thinks is a "whim of deity" for what is actually a "whim of time and space." Why the latter guarantees perseverance of a mechanical world, when the former seemingly is impotent so to do, is not easy to see.[24]

Perhaps the "scientist" might retort that he does not expect any such guarantee of perseverance, and that he does not view the world as "mechanical." He might even concede that a biblically grounded view of God as Creator offers him a possibility of seeing meaning and purpose in nature and history that would otherwise be denied him. But such a view would be a presupposition, brought to the interpretation of the world and confirmed or invalidated by its capacity to interpret. In such a case miracles might be accepted as part of that general interpretation. They would function, not as independent evidence of divine control over nature which could be directly inspected, but as indicators within the belief-system of the significance of certain persons and events.

This appears to have been Carnell's view, and is supported by his claim that "The Christian teaches that a miracle is verified by systematic coherence."[25] But when Carnell goes on to say that a miracle requires "no more testimony to establish its veracity than is needed to establish other historical facts," the question seems to be once more confused. Although his ensuing argument makes some telling points against Hume on the subject of historical testimony, he certainly does not bring to the scrutiny of biblical miracles the same kind of historical and scientific scrutiny that B. B. Warfield brought to nonbiblical miracles before pronouncing them counterfeit. In fact, Carnell appears to exempt them from historical scrutiny altogether and offers instead a series of reflections on the historicity of Napoleon Bonaparte, recalling Whately's celebrated tract written over a century earlier. Clearly, American evangelical fascination with this argument did not end with Carnell, for variations on the theme of Napoleon's uniqueness have been repeated by John Warwick Montgomery and Norman L. Geisler in their several writings.

In discussing the question of interpretation, Carnell rightly acknowledges the importance of presuppositions when he observes that "a philosopher's major postulates are chosen for their ability to explain the greatest area of reality."[26] But in the very next breath Carnell seems to create enormous difficulties for himself when he says that "the Christian view of God and the world . . . is based on the Biblical miracles." For he himself has already invoked belief in God as Creator in order to think of natural laws in such a way as to allow for the possibility of miracles. He cannot then logically appeal to miracles as independent, logical historical evidence that provides the basis for his entire scheme of thought. Carnell seems to come perilously close to making the same point function as both the premise and the conclusion of his argument for a biblical-theistic view of the world. However, as we observed in the discussion of Richard Swinburne earlier, the weight that we give to any item of evidence does not depend solely upon the amount of literary testimony available. It depends upon the overall feasibility that we assign to any given item of testimony or evidence. We have to acknowledge in the case of the New Testament miracles that, historically speaking, we are limited to at most four sources for the account of miracles performed by Jesus. We have no direct access to the events in question. The Gospels themselves have been variously interpreted as historical documents. If we acknowledge the miracles as historical events, as the present writer does, it is not on the basis of overwhelming historical evidence as such, but as events consonant with biblically grounded beliefs about God. Within this scheme of belief, the miracles function as *signs* pointing to further perceptions about Jesus but not as irrefragable objective proofs.

Carnell, like other apologists before him, seems to draw no distinction between a sign and a proof. But quite apart from the semantic difference between signs and proofs, there is the question of whether we can really treat miracle stories as demonstrative proofs. In support of his position, Carnell cites such passages as Matthew 11:4-5 ("Go and tell John what you hear and see: the blind receive their sight and the lame walk, lepers are cleansed and the deaf hear, and the dead are raised up, and the poor have the good news preached to them") and John 5:36 ("these very works which I am doing bear witness that the Father has sent me"). When Carnell claims that "without miracles we cannot be assured that he who bears a revelation actually is from God,"[27] he appears to be restating the traditional apologetic view that miracles function as objective, historical credentials of divine attestation. However, this claim obscures the historical gap between direct personal witness of a miracle and secondhand reports of alleged miracles. Reports of events, especially at this distance in time, do not have the same evidential force as direct experience of events themselves. It is all too easy for apologetic zeal to merge the two and act as if the report were the same as the event.

This is a question that confronts both the unbeliever and the believer as they ask themselves what to make of the miracle stories. Those who were eyewitnesses to an alleged miracle were in a different position from us who read the account of it some nineteen centuries later. They were in a position to ask questions and check facts in a way that we cannot do. In the case of the account of the healing of the man blind from birth, the skeptics went to the length of verifying with the parents of the man the claim that this was in fact their son who had truly been born blind (John 9:19f.). But we are not in a position to put the same questions to them and ask such supplementary questions as would verify their veracity. In one sense, people living in the modern age are in a better position to examine miraculous claims, in that they have access to modern medical and scientific knowledge. But in another sense, they are in a worse position to examine such reports, because they do not have direct access to the cases. The data available to us are not the cases themselves but the hearsay witness of the narratives. Even if we take a high view of those narratives, as the present writer does, we cannot avoid recognizing the difference between accepting an unverifiable report on trust (which is the position of the believer today) and being confronted by an event beyond the scope of human capacities to contrive (which was the position, according to the narratives, of the people who witnessed Jesus' works). It was to the generation who had witnessed Jesus' works that Jesus said (according to John 15:24), "If I had not done among them the works which no one else did, they would not have sin; but now they have seen and hated both me and my Father." To that generation they were a demonstration of divine activity; to us they are a report of that demonstration which functions as a sign pointing to the identity of Jesus inviting the commitment of faith (cf. John 20:30f.).

The subject of miracles has continued to provoke keen debate among evangelical scholars in North America of the postwar generation. Evidence of this can be seen in the December 1978 issue of the *Journal of the American Scientific Affiliation* (vol. 30, no. 4), which was devoted to the question. The papers are characterized by a new level of expertise in evangelical scholarship and a desire to dialogue with, if not do battle with, secular scholars of rank. In his paper "Science, Theology and the Miraculous," John Warwick Montgomery argued that:

> The more willing we are to allow empirical evidence of the unique and non-analogous to stand, modifying our general conceptions of regularity accordingly, the better scientists and philosophers we become. And the more willing we are as Christians to employ the biblical and classic miracle apologetic, the more effectively we can give a reason to our dark age of secularism for the hope that is within us.[28]

The earlier part of Montgomery's paper was devoted to a reply to Hume, in the course of which he endorsed Mary Hesse's view that "abandonment of the deterministic world-view in physics has made it more difficult to regard the existing state of science as finally legislative of what is and what is not possible in nature."[29] He went on to endorse the definition of R. F. Holland, noted in the previous chapter, which viewed a miracle as an event that was (1) empirically certain (i.e., as having actually occurred); (2) conceptually impossible (i.e., inexplicable without appealing beyond our experience); and (3) religious (i.e., calling for a religious explanation).[30] After examining some of Antony Flew's arguments, Montgomery asserted that, in assessing something new, the general (i.e., our view of the way things are and what is possible) must always yield to the particular since

> (1) the historian's knowledge of the general is never complete, so he can never be sure he ought to rule out an event or interpretation simply

because it is new to him, and (2) he must always guard against obliterating the uniqueness of individual historical events by forcing them into a Procrustean bed of regular, general patterns. Only the primary-source evidence for an event can ultimately determine whether it occurred or not, and only that same evidence will establish the proper interpretation of the event.[31]

These considerations underlie Montgomery's argument for "the paramount miraculous event" of Christ's resurrection, which cannot be explained away and which leads Montgomery to affirm Christ's deity.[32] This empirical event, like the turning of water into wine and Gospel accounts of the healing of leprosy, cannot be accounted for by natural explanations. To attempt to do so would be to place a "blind faith" in natural causes. Montgomery compares the inexplicable anomalies presented by miracles with the inexplicable wave-particle paradox accepted by the modern physicist in his study of light. If scientists can live with this and other paradoxes forced on them by the weight of empirical evidence, we should allow the empirical evidence of the miraculous in history to shape our views, even though we cannot explain it.

The ensuing articles in *The Journal of the American Scientific Affiliation* constituted a series of rejoinders that raised serious questions about the viability of Montgomery's argument. In "The Problem of Miracle in the Apologetic from History," Stephen J. Wykstra disclaimed the intention of debunking the appeal to history altogether. Nevertheless, he detected serious flaws in the argument as Montgomery had presented it. Wykstra pointed out that the shift from Newtonian to Einsteinian physics (to which Montgomery in company with many others appealed) has very little philosophical relevance to the question of whether we have the right to rule out the possibility of miraculous events:

> The correct epistemological moral to draw from the Einsteinian revolution is thus not: "Aha, now we see that miracles are possible after all!"; rather it is: "If we can no longer claim to *know* what natural processes in themselves are capable of producing, how then can we know whether any startling anomaly is a 'miracle'?" The crucial question is thus underscored: If miracles do occur, by what criteria can we distinguish them, *qua miracles,* from those natural events that are startling only because our theories of nature (and the expectations these theories give us) are defective?[33]

If we look back to Montgomery's article to see what kind of response he might make to this, it is clear that Montgomery does not wish to entertain the idea that miracles could ultimately be instances of the *contingency concept,* discussed in the previous chapter. For, on the one hand, he expressly rejects this possibility,[34] and, on the other hand, it is precisely on the scientifically inexplicable that he builds his apologetic case. Moreover, it may be noted that while he endorses Max Black's charge that the concept of cause is "a peculiar, unsystematic, and erratic notion"[35] (in the interests of challenging a closed view of the universe), Montgomery appears to make tacit use of it later on (in judging deity to be the adequate and necessary cause for Jesus' resurrection and for other miracles).

Perhaps Montgomery himself sensed that there was something at least paradoxical in this phase of the argument, for he insists that the event of the resurrection is not self-explanatory. Indeed, "the most satisfactory interpretation of an event such as the Resurrection will be the construction placed upon it by the person who himself brings the event about, even if that construction involves the category of miracle."[36] However, to say this implies that the interpretation is judged adequate to the presumed cause.

Montgomery's use of the resurrection in apologetics raises several further questions. Wykstra detects a certain circularity in the argument:

> Originally, the apologist argued that we are justified in believing Jesus' teachings *because* his authority has received Divine attestation via miracles—events which clearly could only come from God. But now, the reason offered for believing that the crucial event *is* indeed a miracle is that Jesus teaches that it is, i.e. that "only God himself" could produce it. The circle is closed.[37]

Wykstra also detects a certain existential element in Montgomery's thought, despite its apparent claims to be an apologetic based on objective, empirical evidence.[38] This point is vividly illustrated in the following passage from Montgomery's article:

> The conquest of death for all men is the very predicate of deity that a race dead in trespasses and sins can most easily recognize, for it meets man's most basic existential need to transcend the meaninglessness of finite existence. Not to worship One who gives you the gift of eternal life is hopelessly to misread what the gift tells you about the Giver. No more worthy candidate for deity is in principle imaginable than the One who conquers death in mankind's behalf. And it should go without saying that the Giver of such a gift has to be regarded metaphysically positive ("God"), not negative (an archdemon) because of the positive character of His gift in relation to human need.[39]

Perhaps Montgomery thinks of this heartfelt need as part of the empirical evidence. But we need to reflect that the gift we have in present time is not a *resurrection body* of the same order as Christ's and thus would be of similar empirical evidential value, but rather a sense of spiritual satisfaction that is bound up with believing, but that Montgomery himself has pronounced to be "philosophically indistinguishable from heartburn."[40]

There seems to be something theologically and apologetically inexact about Montgomery's appeal to the resurrection of Jesus. On the one hand, he presents it as the clinching proof of Christ's divinity.[41] On the other hand, he fails to make clear what he perceives to be the connection between Christ's resurrection and the miracles recounted in the Gospels. By way of comment on these questions we should give our attention to the following points. New Testament apologetic never argues that Christ raised himself from the dead or that his personal divinity was the ground of his resurrection. The characteristic emphasis falls on the fact that God the Father,[42] or the Spirit of God,[43] raised him from the dead and so vindicated him as the Christ and Savior. Whereas Montgomery argues that "every major apologist in Christian history" from the early church to the mid-eighteenth century "confidently argued from the historical facticity of our Lord's miracles to the veracity of His claims and the consequent moral obligation to accept them,"[44] with the implication that we should do the same, Montgomery's argument is not, in fact, based on the historically demonstrable facticity of Jesus' miracles in general but on that of Jesus' resurrection in particular. It is not made clear whether Montgomery thinks that the miracles have independent, historical evidential value, or whether he thinks that they are feasible on the grounds that having accepted the greater miracle of the resurrection, it is conceptually easier to accept lesser miracles. We noted earlier that Montgomery accepts the stipulations laid down by R.F. Holland for an event to qualify as an instance of the violation concept of a miracle. It must be empirically certain, conceptually impossible, and religiously significant. In his discussion of miracles in "Science, Theology and the Miraculous," Montgomery focuses on the second, hints at the third, but appears to omit to establish the first altogether.[45] If this is true, his apologetic is not a straightforward return to classical apologetics as practiced before the advent of David Hume. Demonstrable, objective facticity has been tacitly narrowed down to the resurrection of Jesus. But even here, as Wykstra pointed out, the argument ceases to be purely objective at the crucial point where one must decide on the interpretation to be placed on the event. In the last analysis, the interpretation is based on a faith-decision, bound up with various assumptions.

Montgomery is surely right in stressing the importance of empirical evidence of a unique, nonanalogous kind, and in seeing the resurrection of Jesus as such evidence and the cornerstone of the apologist's appeal to history. But his zeal for objectivity leads him to overplay his hand. However, a number of other evangelical scholars are very alive to the possibility of doing just this. Commenting on the problem of dealing with apparent anomalies to the laws of science and identifying such alleged events as miracles, Wykstra writes,

> The only readily apparent way for the apologist from history to avoid the horns of this dilemma, then, is to adopt a policy of systematic inconsistency with respect to the probability-estimating procedures he employs. He must employ the normal procedures when appraising the possibilities envisioned by naturalistic alternatives to the resurrection hypothesis, and abstain from these procedures when gauging the probability of the resurrection. Such a policy might not be as indefensible as it at first blush appears to be. After all, if and when God does intervene in the normal course of events, one would not expect the normal probability-estimating procedures to be appropriate.[46]

In a joint article that wrestles with this problem, entitled "Science and the Concept of Miracle," David and Randall Basinger detect confusions in the kind of approach advocated by Swinburne that we discussed in the previous chapter. They argue that it is impossible for the Christian or any theist "to contend justifiably that any given occurrence is in fact miraculous, as it is always possible that relevant scientific laws will be developed sometime in the future ."[47] They argue that the traditional apologetic claim that miracles are permanently inexplicable events, requiring a divine explanation, is no longer viable, as such events cannot be identified for certain. They suggest, therefore, that

> The most viable alternative... is to define "miracle" as a religious concept (an act of God) which derives its uniqueness not from its explicability status, but from the fact that it is part of an unusual event sequence.[48]

They concede that the identification of the miraculous in this way introduces a large element of subjectivity that correspondingly weakens the objective apologetic status of the miraculous. Nevertheless, they contend that those who feel uncomfortable with this "weaker" view of miracles must develop an alternative "objective identification criterion that is built neither on the explicability status nor the timing or the sequencing of the event in question."[49]

In this connection, it is worth noting the observation of Werner Schaaffs, the German physicist whose book *Theology, Physics, and Miracles* (1974) was published in the United States under evangelical auspices.[50] Much of Schaaffs's book is concerned with explaining modern physics for the layperson. To that extent it could be said to be devoted to the explicability of miracles. After considering the examples of the burning bush, the crossing of the Red Sea, and the Star of Bethlehem, Schaaffs reaches the following conclusion:

> I repeat: the really miraculous element in the bibical miracles is the time of their occurrence; for, insofar as we possess the necessary scientific knowledge, we know that the occurrence of the event is a definite possibility, as long as we wait long enough. According to the biblical accounts, the time at which a miracle occurs is determined by things that cannot be conceived or influenced physically, i.e., the spiritual distress of a person or a community, the answering of a prayer ("Out of the depths I cry to thee, O Lord! Lord, hear my voice!"), and lastly and chiefly, God's sovereign intervention.[51]

In this and other statements, Schaaffs seems to be saying much the same as the Basingers.

The work of Norman L. Geisler represents a return to a more traditional, evidentialist apologetic approach. In his *Christian Apologetics* (1976) Geisler drew a distinction between *first class miracles* and *second class miracles*. The latter term covers those supernaturally guided events "whose natural *process* can be described scientifically (and perhaps even reduplicated by humanly controlled natural means) but whose end *product* in the total picture is best explained by invoking the supernatural."[52] The former term embraces exceptions to the natural process. Broadly speaking, the distinction corresponds to the one noted earlier between the *contingency* and *violation* concepts of miracle. Geisler was even willing to entertain the thought that first class miracles might be reducible to second class ones, on the ground that one day science might be able to understand how virgin births and resurrections occur. However, this would not destroy the miraculous or eliminate its evidential value, since explanation on this level would not undermine the teleological significance of the event in question.[53]

In his more recent work, *Miracles and Modern Thought* (1982), Geisler refocuses his definition by seeking to avoid the question of violation of natural laws and by attempting to define a miracle positively in terms that echo C. S. Lewis. He defines a miracle as "a *new effect* produced by the introduction of a supernatural cause":

> In brief, a miracle is a divine intervention into, or an interruption of the regular course of the world that produces a purposeful but unusual event that would not (or could not) have occurred otherwise. The natural world is the world of regular, observable, and predictable events. Hence, a miracle by definition cannot be predicted by natural means.[54]

Miracles and Modern Thought is written in the form of a college textbook in the Christian Free University Curriculum Series. In it Geisler ranges back and forth from Spinoza and Hume to contemporaries like Antony Flew and Malcolm L. Diamond. However, he does not intend there to provide a chronological account of ideas, but to answer a series of questions ranging from the possibility and credibility of miracles to their relation to nature and their actuality. The various skeptical writers cited are noted because they bring into sharp focus particular objections that demand an answer.

Geisler's work is characterized by clarity of exposition and forceful apologetic intent. It stands in the evidentialist tradition of Archibald Alexander and John Locke, whose names do not play any significant part in his argument, and Richard Whately, whose *Historical Doubts Relative to Napoleon Buonaparte* is referred to several times in admiration and approval. There is, however, a deep ambiguity that runs through the book. It concerns the precise value of miracles as evidence. At various points Geisler speaks of the "evidential value" of miracles.[55] In his concluding chapter, he repudiates the claims of other religions to miracles as "self-canceling," and asserts that "Only Christianity provides a unique set of claims and unique series of supernatural credentials. Therefore, we believe only Christianity is miraculously confirmed to be true."[56] To this extent, Geisler appears to belong to what at the beginning of this chapter we called the offensive camp of apologists, as distinct from the defensive camp. However, the precise nature of Geisler's argument indicates after all that he takes the miracle stories of the Gospels on trust as part of his belief-system and that it is only within that context that they have "evidential value." To say this is not to minimize Geisler's achievement or to question the validity of this conclusion. Rather, it is to give recognition to the part played by miracles in the thought of a leading conservative apologist, and to suggest that his position is not radically different from some scholars whom conservatives think of as neo-orthodox.

There are several reasons for drawing this conclusion. Not the least significant is Geisler's contention that

> Miracles cannot be identified without a logically prior commitment (on whatever grounds) to the existence of God. One cannot know acts of God to have occurred unless one postulates a God who can act. One can only discover God's "fingerprints" in the world if he posits a God whose "fingerprints" are known. But theists have just as much right simply to *believe* that the ultimate cause of these Godlike events is supernatural as naturalists do believe that ultimately there is a natural cause for all events, even though they do not know what it is. Indeed, rational theists are in an even better position, since they have provided rational grounds for their belief in the supernatural realm.[57]

Alongside this quotation may be placed Geisler's summary conclusion to his entire book:

> To summarize the results of our study, we may conclude that (1) miracles are identifiable in a theistic universe, (2) the Bible provides us with the identifying characteristics of a miracle, and (3) the resurrection of Christ possesses these characteristics. Therefore, a miracle can be identified as having occurred. Miracles are not only possible, but they are actual.[58]

What Geisler is acknowledging here is a prior commitment to a Christian, theistic belief-system as the prerequisite for identifying miracles. If this is so, then miracles can no longer serve as independent pieces of evidence for the truth of that belief-system. For miracles can be recognized and accepted only in relation to the system of belief. This point is further exemplified by Geisler's discussion of criteria for distinguishing reports of genuine miracles from pseudo-miracles. Again he appeals to the "context of theistic claims" that enable us to see that biblical miracles are not mere anomalies of nature, but have meaning and purpose.[59] In rejecting the claims of false miracle-workers and miracles from other religions, the decisive factor for Geisler is not empirical evidence, but the theological and moral values of the Christian belief-system.[60] In making this point, Geisler is clearly following in the footsteps of Calvin, the church fathers, and the biblical writers.[61] We are not questioning the value of this argument but noting the role of prior belief-commitments in the discernment of miracles.

It should be observed that Geisler is concerned to establish the rationality of this prior Christian belief-system. He does so positively and negatively. A great deal of the book is devoted to showing the non sequiturs in the arguments of those who would claim that miracles are impossible. At most such views represent a faith-commitment on the part of those who deny miracles. We need not reiterate this negative part of Geisler's discussion, as we have already examined at length arguments against miracles from Spinoza and Hume onward. Positively, however, Geisler seeks to establish the validity of a theistic framework within which to interpret miracles by invoking the cosmological argument for the existence of God. Geisler states the premises of the argument in the following way:

1. Something exists.
2. Nothing cannot cause something; only something can cause something.
3. The effect resembles its cause in some significant way(s).[62]

Reflection on these premises leads Geisler to infer the existence of a necessary and eternal first cause that must be different from the world, for the world is finite and (in the view of modern scientists) subject to entropy. Because the effect bears marks of intelligence, we must posit an intelligence as the cause. This argument is supplemented by a moral one which argues from personal moral values and imperatives to a personal ground for them.

Due allowance must be made for the fact that Geisler's work is not intended to be a monograph on the existence and attributes of God. Even so, there appear to be too many gaps in the argument to make it an adequate basis for a rational, evidential approach to miracles. It appears to take for granted that the universe is a single system that owes its origin to a single source, namely God. It does not show that there can only be one God. It does not show that the God that is the inferred conclusion of the argument is identical with the triune God of the Bible and of Christian faith and theology. It does not show that this God could not be identified with the God known in other religions who might conceivably act graciously in performing miracles outside the context of the Christian church. Moreover, Geisler's form of the cosmological argument does not obviously lead to acknowledgment of a God who might be expected to intervene in or interrupt the regular course of the world. It appears to be assumed that if such a God brought the world into being, it would not be beyond his power to interrupt and intervene.

What at most we are entitled to infer from this is that belief in miracles is not incompatible with theistic belief, provided that one has adequate grounds for believing that miracles are compatible with the character of God. But when Geisler enlarges on the character of God, it is not on the basis of his rational, natural theology, but upon his beliefs about God derived from the Bible. Perhaps the most we can say is that miracles cannot be ruled out by general considerations, but they can only be identified and known by biblical revelation.[63] This leads to Geisler's final question concerning the actuality of miracles, which he explains as follows:

> Granting the context of a theistic universe that would make miracles possible and identifiable, can an event be identified as a miracle? Or, if God exists, what (if any) event(s) from His perspective can be called miraculous?[64]

With his answer to this question we are brought back once more to the ambiguous character of Geisler's evidentialism. For in point of fact, he does not examine the historicity of any particular miracles reported by the Gospels as having been performed by Jesus. Instead, he offers a series of general considerations concerning the trustworthiness of the Gospels as early, accurate pieces of reporting, and an argument for the historicity of the resurrection of Jesus, which is described as "in many respects . . . the cornerstone miracle of Christianity."[65] Geisler puts forward a number of cogent arguments for regarding the resurrection of Jesus as a historical event. However, as pointed out earlier in discussing John Warwick Montgomery, it is an over-simplification to treat the resurrection as an automatic proof of the deity of Christ and to assume that, because there are grounds for asserting the resurrection of Jesus to be a historical event, the miracles attributed to Jesus in the Gospels have the same degree of evidential certainty.

Perhaps the precise nature of the question which exercises evangelicals needs to be underscored. The point at issue is not whether Jesus performed miracles, but whether miracles may be regarded as objective, historically testable evidence, which compels assent and which thus serves as independent "supernatural credentials" for Christianity. We must recognize that we do not have the same degree of attestation for, say, the turning of the water into wine at Cana (John 2) and the raising of Lazarus (John 11) as for the resurrection of Jesus. We are told of the raising of the widow's son at Nain only in Luke 7:11–17. The stilling of the storm is mentioned in the three Synoptic Gospels (Matt. 8:23–27; Mark 4:35–41; Luke 8:22–25), but not by John. For these and other miracles we do not have the same degree of scrutinizable testimony that we have for the resurrection. Moreover, although the Christian church would be impoverished without these stories, it is conceivable that it could exist without them, whereas it is inconceivable that Christianity would ever have come into existence without the resurrection of Jesus. We may agree that the Gospel records bear marks of authenticity and integrity. But to say, for example, that Luke gives accurate geographical information at points where his statements can be corroborated is somewhat different from saying that his reports concerning miracles are equally dependable. For it is beyond our capability to corroborate them. What we have in the case of the miracle stories is not the same kind of testable evidence, but testimonies to events that challenge belief and invite trust. In the last analysis, we cannot get away from an element of decision over whether to believe or disbelieve. For this reason it seems to me that miracles play an important part in the testimony to Jesus. They play an important part within the belief-system of Christianity. The miracle stories of the Gospels are part of the testimony of the biblical writings, and as such are part of the Christian revelation. They are compatible with Christian theism, but because they function within the scheme of Christian theism, they cannot serve as objective, independent, evidential grounds for that system.

It is possible that Geisler's work represents a turning point in evangelical thinking. Its best sections are those where the author defends the feasibility of entertaining the possibility of miracles against the attacks of the skeptics. But in its recognition of the importance of approaching the miracle stories within the context of a framework of belief and in its guarded, ambivalent attitude as to the exact evidential value of particular miracle stories, Geisler's work may represent the end of the line of the strict evidentialist approach to the Gospel miracles. It is a line that Roman Catholic and British Protestant writers on this subject have already passed.

ROMAN CATHOLIC APOLOGISTS

In the discussion of miracles in Chapter Six, we had occasion to compare nineteenth-century Roman Catholic attitudes with contemporary attitudes and to note a tempering of the hard evidentialist position.[66] This tempering may be seen in Avery Dulles's *History of Apologetics* (1971), which reviews both Protestant and Catholic apologetics from New Testament times to the present day, and in the attitudes of such writers as Leopold Sabourin and Johann Baptist Metz. Sabourin's *The Divine Miracles Discussed and Defended* (1977) is an important contribution to biblical studies. Although he is primarily concerned with New Testament interpretation, Sabourin felt it necessary to preface his work with a brief account of presuppositions that drew the conclusion that

> Although faith in the strict sense may not be necessary to recognise a miracle, basic dispositions certainly are, mainly a certain openness to realities higher than the purely natural, and the readiness to accept the evidence in whatever direction it may lead. This is one of the important presuppositions for initiating any study of truly miraculous phenomena.[67]

Writing on the subject of "Miracle" in *Sacramentum Mundi*, J. B. Metz is even more specific. He acknowledges that, theologically speaking, a miracle "cannot be a sign which compels assent. It does not make the thing signified a perspicuous manageable truth. It is a sign which is a summons."[68] Metz goes on to question whether science is the proper field in which to assess miracles. "The natural sciences work on the methodical presumption that reality is fundamentally calculable." This is legitimate within the realm of the calculable, where any alleged miracle is merely an embarrassment that inspires the scientist to seek a new set of explanations. For this reason Metz thinks it best not to define a miracle in terms of a breach or violation of the laws of nature. His conclusion is on the same lines as Sabourin's. A miracle is

> a (positive) sign of the fact that all reality is included in the historical dispensation of God. It can be seen by all those whose outlook on the world is dominated by interpersonal relationships in their basic search for the meaning and wholeness of life.[69]

In other words, our perception of a miracle (which includes our judgment of whether it might have happened or not) depends upon the frame of reference or world view we bring to it. A purely deterministic, scientific world view would reject miracles out of hand from the start. But a view that is willing to entertain the possibility of a divine ordering of the world may see in miracles a sign of that personal ordering.

Perhaps the most impressive contemporary general study of miracles from a Roman Catholic standpoint is Louis Monden's *Signs and Wonders: A Study of the Miraculous Element in Religion* (1966).[70] It is a work of massive learning, exhaustive research, and deep Catholic piety. In some ways it cuts across the philosophical lines of debate that we have been tracing with its philosophical discussion about the feasibility of miracles in the light of modern science. The name of David Hume merits mention in only two places. But in another sense the work is a contribution to the ongoing debate. It answers the question of whether miracles are possible by producing a documented account of the "major miracles in the Catholic church," notably the healings associated with Lourdes. On the basis of his acceptance of these cures as ongoing signs of divine activity of a piece with miracles performed in the church through the ages, Monden senses no need to defend miracles as unique violations of the order of nature that happened long ago. Rather, the task that he sets for himself is to analyze the nature and role of miracles in the Christian religion on the basis of their actuality.

Monden sees his position as fully consonant with the teaching of the First Vatican Council. At the same time he feels the need to appreciate miracles within a framework of faith. Within a purely naturalistic framework miracles would have no place. But,

> Once recognized as plausible within the framework of man's supernatural calling, miracles become immeasurably more probable in view of the concrete act which makes this calling a reality—the redemptive act of the divine Incarnation.[71]

Miracles are like the church and the sacraments, and stand in the line which is "the normal prolongation of the Incarnation."[72] In a manner reminiscent of Athanasius, Monden argues that

> Mankind, whose life the Word comes to share, is sinful and fallen from grace; in order to make men share in his divine life he has first to cure, purify, and ransom them. Thus the miraculous, as a perceptible sign of this divine message, must carry a redemptive significance.[73]

According to Monden, "A miracle is something that happens in the physical world; but its true significance springs from its spiritual meaning."[74]

The purpose of miracles is "less to show God's sovereign power than to signify his redemptive love."[75] They are *sign-acts*. All relationships between God and man are effected by means of symbols, for God is not known directly but indirectly through the medium of something else, whether it be the human words contained in Scripture, the bread and wine in the Lord's

Supper, or the cup of cold water given in the name of Christ. Miracles are "set apart from natural happenings not by the fact that they demonstrate a manifestation of power, but rather because their unusual nature makes them better fitted to be signs."[76] Miracles, like grace in general, do not destroy nature, but liberate, ennoble, and renew it. Echoing Ambrose of Milan, Monden claims that miracles are like Jesus' fulfillment of the law. Neither nature nor the law are set aside; they are rather fulfilled.[77]

This leads Monden to describe the characteristics of the Christian miracle, which he does from the standpoint of faith. Because miracles belong to revelation, they cannot simply be defined in terms of violations of the natural order. The character of any alleged miracle has to be taken into account in any assessment of its factuality. Negatively, any alleged miracle associated with immorality, charlatanism, trickery, magic, illusion, sensuality, or mere sensationalism must be ruled out. The apocryphal story of the child Jesus making birds of clay and giving them life is dismissed on the grounds of sheer irrelevance.[78] By their very nature miracles are not appeals to sensationalism; they are never performed merely to impress. It was for this reason that Jesus refused to perform signs. "A Miracle is Christian only if it helps us to believe rather than relieve us of the necessity of faith."[79] Moreover, there is a sense in which miracles are reminders of the fact that the world is not yet glorified:

> If it is to be a Christian miracle, moreover, it should not give the impression that this passing world is now already glorified, that paradise has already been regained. The miracle must rather give a glimpse of what is to come; it is a kind of smile by which God lightens the path of his Church as it follows the *Via Crucis* which is mortal life. The sudden growth of a new leg, strikingly sensational as this might be, would express but ill God's grace; it would be less suitable to our fallen status, it would be less a sign of salvation, than are the ordinary examples of healings at Lourdes. Oft-times these leave even traces of scars, and thus recall to us the marks upon his blessed body which our risen Saviour wished to preserve in order that they might recall to his disciples the strength of the bond that unites the state of glory to the redemptive work of the Holy Cross.[80]

These negative characteristics of true miracles are balanced by positive characteristics.[81] When performed by a saint, they testify to the human agent's character as being transformed by God's saving revelation. In addition, they testify to a divine mission, and they occur in the context of prayer and a divine message. In short, they point beyond themselves to the redemptive activity of God.

Monden thinks that it is a mistake to see miracles only as weapons in apologetic controversy. Their primary importance is not to impress unbelievers. Rather, their real significance is in the life of believers and the whole context of Christian living. "Merely natural knowledge can attain only to a God who remains yet afar off: by faith, we come into his presence, the source of all our joy: we confront the God who saves."[82] To the unbeliever miracles serve as external signs, summoning him to a knowledge possible only through faith. "The signified reality glimpsed in signs is not the supernatural element as such, but rather the supernatural as a naturally knowable fact."[83] Man is brought face to face with the message and tidings of supernatural salvation, but the sense of these tidings can be grasped only in faith.

In the ensuing discussion Monden seeks to show how this view harmonizes with the stance on miracles taken by the First Vatican Council. Miracles are like the Court of the Gentiles in the Temple at Jerusalem[84]—they are not the Holy One himself, nor are they the Holy of Holies of the divine presence. Nevertheless, they bring the outsider to the place where he can apprehend the divine presence at a distance. The holiness and presence of God will not grip him until he actually passes beyond wonders and enters the Holy Place of faith. Miracle thus plays a primary role in "setting up the prudential motives of faith."[85]

> The fact that God has employed miracles is a precise indication of his regard for the human spirit as being conjoined to human flesh: it constitutes a divine recognition of our total humanity. If Christ made the matter of the Jews' hunger after miracles a matter of reproach to them, it was because he saw in it a symptom of their unbelief. He, himself, wrought a continuous succession of miracles, and he appealed to them as guarantees of his divine mission. Both internal and external signs have each their own worth, and it is a complementary one.[86]

The particular persuasive force of miracles is bound up with what Monden calls their "regular irregularity."[87] In asserting this traditional Catholic view, Monden stands in marked contrast with Warfield, Carnell, and the Calvinistic view, which saw miracles as divine attestations that ceased with the apostolic age and the completion of the canon of Scripture. By contrast, Monden echoes the sentiment of the First Vatican Council that miracles are "one of those characteristic manifestations which make it possible for the Church to be 'a sign lifted up among the nations.' "[88] Just as Warfield had a vested interest in disproving all claims to miracles after the apostolic age, especially in the Roman Catholic Church, Monden has a vested interest in demonstrating the veracity of such claims within the Catholic Church and at the same time disputing miraculous claims outside the Catholic Church (which, if genuine, might seem to rob it of its uniqueness). A substantial part of Monden's work is devoted to these issues, but to pursue them would take us beyond the scope of our present investigation.

However, it is not Monden's intention to reduce miracles to apologetic shots to be fired across the ecclesiastical battle lines in the war between Catholicism and Protestantism. Monden sees miracles as sacramental signs, pointing back to the incarnation and forward to humankind's eschatological hope:

> Faith . . . sees in the miraculous an earnest of the glory which will fill *the new heaven and the new earth;* faith discerns therein the love of God

who shall be all in all; it finds in the miraculous the certification of *that hope which dwells within us.*[89] Like dogmas and sacraments, so too a miracle becomes a symbol of faith and a supernatural expression of God's Word. In distinction to the dogmatic statement, it is a *symbolic act,* a "word-event"—*parole-événement*—as Jean Guitton felicitously says. While the sacrament gives external forms to divine action, the *word-event* expresses the divine speech. It imparts not an infusion but a message of grace. In a legitimate sense, therefore, we may speak of a miracle, apprehended by faith, as a "dogmatic symbol,"[90] or a "sacrament." Being at once sign and reality, it anticipates what is promised and announces that our definitive salvation is at hand.[91]

In saying this, Monden is conscious of standing in the tradition of Augustine. It was a view adumbrated in the nineteenth century by the Anglican Archbishop of Dublin, R. C. Trench, and the Scottish Free Church theologian, A. B. Bruce. It is a view that has also been developed by twentieth-century British apologists.

BRITISH WRITERS

At the beginning of this chapter we spoke of two camps of apologists, the offensive and the defensive. The majority of British apologists stand firmly in the defensive camp. In 1924 the Cambridge philosopher of religion, F. R. Tennant, delivered three lectures in the University of London that were subsequently published under the title *Miracle and its Philosophical Presuppositions.* From his lucid and penetrating review of the subject from Spinoza onward, Tennant drew two main conclusions. On the one hand, modern science has "put an end to the dogma of the impossibility of miracles."[92] On the other hand, no one is in a position to claim that certain events are miraculous, "so long as our scientific knowledge of Nature is inexhaustive."[93] Wonders, therefore, "cannot be used to prove theistic or Christian revelation in the sense of affording rigorous demonstration of doctrine."[94] From this Tennant proceeded to the conclusion that miracles have no evidential value for us today:

> Christianity does not presuppose the Christian miracles; they presuppose Christianity, though they are by no means bound up with Christianity. . . . Testimony, we have seen, cannot reach to divine agency. . . . I will conclude then, as I began, by suggesting that the controversy about miracle has become of but historical interest save for its instructiveness as to what are and what are not to be taken for the essential presuppositions and necessary implications of Christian and theistic belief.[95]

The Oxford New Testament scholar B. H. Streeter was even less sanguine on the subject. Writing in 1912 in a volume entitled *Foundations: A Statement of Christian Belief in Terms of Modern Thought: By Seven Oxford Men,* Streeter attributed the desire for miracles to "the weakness of our faith" which demands "a sign that God *does* rule."[96] After reviewing the evidence for the empty tomb and the appearances of Christ, Streeter concluded that although this was a sign that satisfied the apostles, it can "be no convincing sign to us."[97] For him the resurrection appearances were objective visions, "directly caused by the Lord Himself veritably alive and in communion with them."[98] This was more satisfactory than basing everything on a view of miracle that the passage of time and the growth of knowledge made increasingly insecure.

Streeter's coauthor, William Temple, the future Archbishop of Canterbury, took a more positive view. Coming from a background of Oxford Idealism, Temple declared:

> We do not know what Matter is when we look at Matter alone; only when Spirit dwells in Matter and uses it as a tool do we learn the capacities of Matter. . . . So, too, we do not know what Humanity really is, of what achievements it is capable, until Divinity indwells it. If we are to form a right conception of God we must look at Christ. The wise question is not, "Is Christ Divine?" but, "What is God like?" And the answer to that is "Christ." So, too, we must not form a conception of Humanity and either ask if Christ is Human or insist on reducing Him to the limits of our conception; we must ask, "What is Humanity?" and look at Christ to find the answer. We only know what Matter is when Spirit dwells in it; we only know what Man is when God dwells in him.[99]

When applied to the question of miracles, this view led Temple to the following conjecture, which would provide a theoretical basis for entertaining not only miracles and the sinlessness of Christ but a way of thinking about God and the world in general:

> We find that if a man is thus united to God, Nature is his servant, not his master, and he may (so the story tells us) walk upon the water; the fetters of social influence cannot bind him, and he may be sinless, though tempted, in a sinful world. The incapacities which we thought inseparable from humanity are accidental after all, just as the stubbornness of lifeless matter is no necessary quality of matter. The machine-like character of the Universe, with its rigid laws and uniformities, is given to it by our unspiritual way of handling it; to a man in whom God dwells everything is plastic that he may mould it to God's purpose.[100]

This view, which is here stated in embryo and which was touched on again in Temple's *Christus Veritas*,[101] received its fullest treatment in Temple's Gifford Lectures of 1932-34, *Nature, Man and God*. Temple argued that it was naive to think that "God made the world and imposed laws upon it, which it invariably observes unless He intervenes to modify the operation of His own laws."[102] From this springs the equally wrong view that God's majesty requires us to think that God would have imposed such invariable laws on the world from the beginning. Temple's alternative was to see the "World-Process" as "the medium of God's personal action":

> If we adopt this view we shall have also to hold that no Law of Nature as discovered by physical science is ultimate. It is a general statement

of that course of conduct in Nature which is sustained by the purposive action of God so long and so far as it will serve His purpose. No doubt it is true that the same cause will always produce the same effect in the same circumstances. Our contention is that an element in every actual cause, and indeed the determinant element, is the active purpose of God fulfilling itself with that perfect constancy which calls for an infinite graduation of adjustments in the process. Where any adjustment is so considerable as to attract notice it is called a miracle; but it is not a specimen of a class, it is an illustration of the general character of the World-Process.[103]

This approach led Temple to think of miracles, not so much as objective proofs that functioned as validations of revelation, but as a form of revelation itself:

It is thus characteristic of God that He should usually act by what to us is uniformity (though the appearance even of this may conceal variations too delicate for our perception and too small to affect our confidence in action), just as it is characteristic of Him to vary His action when the occasion is sufficient. Yet there is inevitably a peculiarly revealing quality in the occasional variations, both because they show what occasions are in the divine judgement sufficient, and because they are the issue of a specially directed activity in face of the sufficient occasion, whereas the general uniformity obviously does not issue from such specially directed activity.[104]

What Temple is offering here is clearly not an argument for the historicity of any given miracle, but a metaphysical and theological view of the world, endeavoring to see the physical world in relation to a personal, theistic view of God. It is this personal, dynamic theism that provides a framework for entertaining the feasibility of miracles. This kind of approach characterized the best of British apologetic thinking on the subject of miracles.

In the prewar period the most significant contributions to the discussion came from the pens of D. S. Cairns, Principal of the United Free Church College, Aberdeen, and H. H. Farmer, professor of systematic theology at Westminster College, Cambridge, and subsequently Norris-Hulse Professor of Divinity in the University of Cambridge. In 1928 Cairns published *The Faith that Rebels: A Re-Examination of the Miracles of Jesus.*[105] In 1935 Farmer produced *The World and God: A Study of Prayer, Providence and Miracle in Christian Experience.*[106] Both books represented a moderate but positive outlook that was sensitive to modern thought. Neither Cairns nor Farmer believed that modern knowledge required the abandonment of miracles, but both urged that their place in Christian thinking should be reassessed.

Cairns argued that the traditional view of miracles as divine interventions in the generally orderly course of nature, as a form of supernatural attestation, did not really fit the New Testament picture of Jesus or the role the New Testament assigns to faith.[107] He felt equally uncomfortable with the traditional Protestant view that God should limit such supernatural working to given periods as well as with the liberal view that rejected physical miracles altogether. [108] Instead of treating miracles as objective evidence given to accredit revelation, Cairns proposed that miracles should be seen as "part of the substance of the revelation."[109] Cairns's central thesis is expressed in the following statement:

> It is quite impossible, given the Old Testament and Jewish presuppositions, to regard these signs of Jesus as something accidental and external to the rest of the record. . . ; and if Jesus were what the Gospels suppose Him to be, the ideally pure and representative Man, and as such the Founder of the new order, then it was essential that He should work just such "signs" (to speak broadly and generally) as they represent Him to have wrought. These signs, therefore, are integral parts of the revelation, and not adjuncts to it. They are revelations of the ideal purpose of God for mankind, and therefore of His character. They must therefore necessarily influence our idea of God. Inasmuch, also, as they imply the coming into the order of nature of powers that cannot be explained in terms of mere nature, they must inevitably affect our whole conception of the world. And finally, as they are works wrought through the Perfect Man, and are meant by Him to be imitated by imperfect men, they must affect our conceptions of the possibilities of man, and the possibilities and range of prayer.[110]

The bulk of Cairns's book was devoted to working out the implications of this view. Cairns's language has the unmistakable flavor of prewar, British pulpit rhetoric of the scholarly, free-church variety. On the face of it, he seems to be downplaying the divinity of Christ. At the same time, he is making two important points that need to be borne in mind in considering the New Testament writings. On the one hand, Cairns insists that theology and apologetics cannot be neatly separated, as if the factual aspect of miracles can be objectively established independently of theological considerations and as if form and content had no real bearing on each other. To concentrate on establishing the objective historicity of the miracles as supernatural wonders to the neglect of their theological significance is to miss the whole point. On the other hand, Cairns is drawing attention to an aspect of the Gospel miracles that has generally been neglected through preoccupation with apologetic questions, namely the roles of faith and the Holy Spirit. As he puts it:

> The Synoptics sometimes approach these signs from the human side, and speak of them as wrought through faith. But sometimes they go deeper, and speak of them as wrought by the Spirit. We are just to their whole conception only when we say that they were one and all wrought by the Spirit of God through the faith of man and, above all, through the faith of the Son of Man, "the leader and perfection of faith" (Heb. xii.20).[111]

The approach of H. H. Farmer was less exegetical and more philosophical. Nevertheless, it pointed in the same general direction. Farmer argued that

> Miracle being fundamentally a religious category and not a scientific or philosophic one, the proper place to begin is within the sphere of living religion itself. To define miracle *in limine,* for example, as an event involving suspension of natural laws is to begin in the wrong place.[112]

Like Cairns, Farmer argued that the idea of miracle should be assimilated to revelation. It should be seen in the context of a view of reality in which the ultimate is personal. One effect of this is to make clear "why it is impossible ever to establish by intellectual proof that quality of an event which makes it miraculous to the religious mind."[113] For revelation is "God speaking to the individual personally," and "it is impossible to take up a personal situation into a general proposition or syllogism without its concrete, historical, livingly personal quality vanishing in a cloud of abstractions."[114]

Farmer detected a common element of need and succor in the New Testament accounts of miracles. On this basis, he even felt able to formulate the principle: *"the more intensely personal and individual the succour of God is felt to be, the more appropriate and inevitable the word miracle becomes on the religious man's lips."*[115] At this point Farmer introduced an example of a mother praying for a child who was judged by the best medical evidence to be incurably sick. Farmer pronounces such a recovery to be a miracle only when three conditions are fulfilled.

> First, there is an awareness of serious crisis or need or threat of disaster in the personal life, and of helplessness to deal with it adequately and victoriously through the exercise of ordinary, unaided human powers. Second, there is a more or less conscious and explicit turning to God for assistance. Third, there is an awareness of an *ad hoc* response of God to the situation and to man's petitioning inadequacy in it, so that the crisis is met, the need satisfied, the danger averted in an event, or combination of events, which would not have taken place had man not so petitioned and God so acted.[116]

What is striking here is the similarity between Farmer's view and R. F. Holland's *contingency concept* of miracle, discussed in the previous chapter, but anticipated by Farmer exactly thirty years earlier. The most significant difference lies in the fact that in Holland's account the miracle occurs without prior intercessory prayer. In both cases the event is seen in retrospect as miraculous and in both cases natural factors are not excluded. The miracle lies in the coincidence of factors, which include both human need and divine succor.

In looking at miracles and the laws of nature, Farmer argued that

> The question . . . is not one of causation as against non-causation, or of order against disorder, but whether a certain type of causation and order, namely that involved in the idea of God initiating events in accordance with His wisdom in relation to individual situations, is so contradictory of that type of causation and order which science presupposes and investigates that we are forced to choose between them, and believe either in miracle or in science, but not in both.[117]

Basically, this was a religious question rather than a scientific question for Farmer. This view was not simply based on the contention that the observed regularities of science are "transcripts, made from a certain selected angle, of what hitherto has been found to happen in the phenomenal world, which thus provide a basis for judging future probabilities."[118] Farmer's view was bound up with a view of personal identity that he himself traced back to Immanuel Kant. The essence of the argument is contained in the following passage:

> If I pick up a stone and throw it, it seems self-evident to me at the moment of the act, that had I not done so the stone would have remained where it was; and it seems equally self-evident that a scientist could do much in examining from his angle what has taken place—the relation of the speed and weight of the stone to the path it describes, etc.—and in predicting what will take place if I again interfere and throw other stones, provided that the general environment, so far as it concerns the stones and their flight, remains constant. Man's whole life is built up on this awareness that he is related to a system which is permanent enough to be resolved into regularities, and plastic enough to leave at least some room for his own will to shape it to his own ends. How this should be possible is a puzzling enough question to the philosopher, and there have been those who have supposed that I only *appear* to initiate events by will, my volition being as much determined by all that has gone before as each succeeding position of the stone is when once it has started on its flight. The unsatisfactoriness of such a theory has often enough been demonstrated; our interest here is in what is not the least important thing in the demonstration, namely the simple fact that nobody has ever succeeded in living as though it were true. The power to initiate events relevantly to ends and occasions is bound up with the fundamental conditions of our existence, and nobody is in the least puzzled by the fact that the work of science goes on alongside the daily exercises of that power; indeed the experiments of science are one example of the exercise of it. If, then, what is familiar in man's relation to his world is declared, on theoretical grounds, to be impossible when it is transferred to God, it may be presumed that theory has somewhere got wide of the facts in a way that should be possible to lay bare.[119]

In taking up this position, Farmer preempts the contemporary philosophical attack on miracles that allows their possibility at the price of converting them into ordinary events that are in principle explicable. In one important point at least, Farmer anticipated Ian T. Ramsey's contention that the scientist and the historian operate with two different kinds of maps of reality. Farmer pointed out that

> Every situation is the result of the convergence of a number of different causal series, and science can in a measure disentangle those series in which it happens to be interested, and trace them out a certain distance; but it is in the end quite unable to say why those particular causal series should have coincided and converged together to produce just that situation, and not other ones to produce another situation entirely different.[120]

To that extent, Farmer could describe the universe as a "transcendent" that lies entirely outside the scope of the laboratory methods of science. Natural science may be compared with the attempt to trace various colored threads on the underside of an embroidery. Much can be detected about their different course and their relationship. But it is beyond the scope of the scientist, speaking as scientist, to say why those colors should have been brought together at all on that particular piece of cloth, so that when it is turned over, it displays an exquisite pattern.[121] Science explains how things behave; it does not answer the metaphysical questions as to why they behave as they do. For Farmer, science and theology offer complementary outlooks. He does not claim to be able to resolve all possible tensions between them, but at least he believes that he has shown a way of thinking about their possible relationship.

Of the British writers of the wartime and postwar generation who have discussed the question of miracles, Alan Richardson, J. S. Lawton, and C. S. Lewis are the most outstanding. Richardson's study *The Miracle Stories of the Gospels* (1941) was a major contribution to biblical studies, and we will take note of it in the next chapter. But Richardson also discussed the apologetic aspect of miracles in his *Christian Apologetics* (1947) and in his Bampton Lectures for 1962, *History: Sacred and Profane* (1964). Richardson was professor of Christian theology in the University of Nottingham before becoming Dean of York shortly before his death. His standpoint was comparable with that of Farmer, but it was more biblically and historically oriented. Richardson saw himself taking the same stance as Augustine, when the latter declared that "A Miracle is not contrary to nature, but to what is known of nature."[122] With Augustine he could see everything in the universe as miraculous, but at the same time could recognize that certain events awaken a sense of wonder, humility, and awareness of the presence of God.[123]

In a sense Richardson's standpoint was complementary to that of Farmer. Whereas Farmer stressed the transcendence of the personal self in initiating, ordering, and terminating physical events that are themselves subject to physical laws, Richardson argued that, "from the standpoint of God Himself, there can be no such thing as 'miracle' [in the sense of an event outside natural law or beyond the scope of all possible knowledge] . . . since if He is God, He must *ex hypothesi* know how all the laws of nature work."[124] In principle, therefore, the biblical miracles are all subsumable under laws that are known to God, if not to man.

Central to Richardson's thought was his contention that "To the New Testament writers the miracles of Jesus were, for those who had eyes to see, signs that enabled them to penetrate the mystery of His person."[125] Like Cairns, Richardson saw these signs as part of the revelation and not as external, objective proofs that guaranteed the revelation quite apart from experience and faith. Richardson believed that apologetics had taken a wrong turn in trying to secure objective guarantees for revelation. In revelation there is always a subjective element, just because it is a personal matter, not an objective matter. This is not to say that Richardson retreated into pure subjectivism. He believed that there were good grounds for adopting a Christian, supernatural interpretation. He argued that the alternative to the miracle-working Jesus of the Gospels was not the high-minded ethical Jesus of liberalism, but sheer historical skepticism. For the only Jesus that we can discover in the New Testament is one who is said to have worked miracles.

In his *Christian Apologetics* Richardson argued that Christians are not in a position to go to non-Christians with a piece of objective history that necessarily would compel their assent to the statement that the miracles really happened:

> They will be able to see "what happened" only when they see through the apostles' eyes, when they accept the categories of interpretation used, or, in other words, when they see Jesus as the Christ of the Church's faith. We cannot by argument cause them to see in this way; all that we can do is to show that the apostolic interpretation of Jesus gives a vital moment in the world's life, and that the alternative to this interpretation is a *lacuna* in history, an admission of ignorance about "what happened" at precisely that historical moment at which the Christian Church and its faith were born.[126]

In *History: Sacred and Profane* Richardson set his approach in the wider context of his view of historical writing in general. He repudiated the idea of purely objective history writing. For once the historian gets beyond certain generally acknowledged "facts," like dates, he has moved from the realm of chronicle to that of interpretation. The "facts" that the historian deals with are not directly observable, repeated events. The historian cannot request a rerun of the Battle of Waterloo or the events that led up to the Declaration of Independence. He cannot directly observe what went on in the minds of the participants. The most he can do is to construct his interpretation on the basis of the data available to him in the light of what C. L. Becker called the historian's "settled convictions as to the nature of man and the world." Such convictions may be revised from time to time in the light of new data, new experience, and further reflection upon them. Nevertheless, Richardson insists that absolute objectivity in history writing is a chimera. Insight is gained only by interpretation, which inevitably contains a subjective element. Admittedly the data, procedures, and conclusions are open to checking by anyone with sufficient skill, knowledge, and patience to undertake the task. But the process of historical interpretation can never be reduced to a purely objective process:

> The historians' final judgment of the evidence will, then, in the last resort, and after as rigorous a critical appraisal as he can make, be determined by the man he is. Nothing can abolish the personal element from the decision about what is and what is not a "fact" when once we have moved outside the realm of technical history, which, being more or less verifiable by anyone who has acquired the necessary expertise, is relatively detached and noncontroversial.[127]

It was because of this personal element in historical interpretation that Richardson argued that there could be such a thing as a Christian interpretation of history but not a Christian chemistry:

> There is a public and verifiable scientific interpretation of nature, but it does not answer our deep existential questions: there is no such public and verifiable interpretation of history, which nevertheless does convey insight into our existential predicaments, but not insights which can be verified by scientific means. Faith and historical interpretation are indissolubly joined together. That is why there can be a Christian interpretation of history but not a Christian chemistry. Failure to understand the relation of faith and history has led recent scholars to offer a "scientific" account of the origins of the Christian Church and its faith; so far from being "scientific," their subjective presuppositions are visible on every page and determine at every point "what could not have happened." The result is a general picture of Christian beginnings at variance with the evidence of the sources.[128]

For Richardson, the decision of whether or not to adopt the outlook of the New Testament writers with regard to Jesus and his miracles is bound up with the decision of whether or not to accept their testimony to the resurrection of Jesus as a historical event. In the case of the miracle stories we have only the word of the evangelists. There is no way of verifying or falsifying their word beyond all possible doubt. But the resurrection of Jesus is a different question. It is not one incident among many. It is an event that underlies the whole existence of the church, an event of such magnitude that, had it not occurred, it is highly questionable whether there would have been a Christian church at all.

For this reason Richardson takes issue with Günther Bornkamm who says that

> The event of Christ's resurrection from the dead, his life and his eternal reign, are things removed from historical scholarship. History cannot ascertain and establish conclusively the facts about them as it can with other events of the past. The last historical fact available to it is the Easter faith of the first disciples.[129]

Such observations have become a commonplace of New Testament scholarship. They imply that faith is something that can be ascertained by the historian, but its cause cannot be. But to Richardson,

> such an attitude involves the abandoning of historical method altogether, for the historian cannot admit that there are any "last facts" in history, for they would be causeless events. . . . The historian, if he is to be true to his calling, is bound to go on to consider various possible explanations of the alleged happening or, if he can, to find a new and better one.[130]

This does not mean that there are no occasions when the historian may suspend judgment. On the contrary, he must do so when the evidence is in-

conclusive or insufficient or when the question lies outside his competence.
But in the case of the resurrection of Jesus, Richardson insists that "Either
Christ's resurrection called the Church's faith into being or we must give
some more rationally coherent account of how that faith with all its tremen-
dous consequences arose."[131] In Richardson's mind, the belief that Jesus was
raised from the dead offers a much more satisfactory answer to the question
posed by the existence of the church and its testimony than the rival theories
of mistaken belief, fraud, and sheer agnosticism. But no decision can be made
apart from faith, whether it be of a Christian kind or faith in the settled
convictions of agnosticism or materialistic atheism:

> Historians are not provided by their critical studies with a technique that
> enables them to escape the decision of faith; and in this matter, as in
> others, every man is (in Becker's phrase but not quite in his sense) "his
> own historian."[132]

In line with the general direction of the British scholars whom we have
noted is the position of J. S. Lawton. Lawton's *Miracles and Revelation*
(1959) is a history of attitudes toward miracles in British thought from the
age of deism onward. He concludes his masterly and definitive survey with
a number of comments on the changing attitudes toward miracles. At one
time miracles were thought of as the bulwark of the faith. They then became
an embarrassment. In Lawton's view, a further change has now taken place:

> Miracle has actually moved from the circumference to the very centre
> of revelation. No longer are the signs of the supernatural thought of as
> mere credentials, but as part of the very substance of what is revealed.
> The Resurrection and the mighty works are seen as an essential part of
> the drama by which God personally discloses Himself, and by which He
> achieves victory over evil and the creation of a new humanity.[133]

Lawton observes that Cartesian philosophy had fostered the idea that man's
apprehension of the external world could be expressed in terms of knowledge,
doubt, and ignorance, and that scientific knowledge was the model for all
knowledge. Christian apologists, therefore, sought to express Christian truth
in the same terms. But our knowledge of the nature, scope, and limitations
of both science and history has grown and changed. The same is true of
theological knowledge. In a manner comparable with that of Richardson,
Lawton observes:

> It has come to be realized that the acts of God in history can only be
> apprehended for what they are by the exercise of a human decision which
> includes all the intuitive aspects of personality, in the same way as these
> are called for in the most vital concerns between man and man. But this
> does not mean that religious faith and sacred history are two separate
> domains, any more than our trust in a human friend can be dissociated
> from our knowledge of the things he has done for us. Against the liberal
> idea of the merely historic recognition of the origins of Christianity, and
> the catholic modernist plan for a faith divorced from a literal Incarna-

tion, English conservative theology has contended masterfully that the wholeness and uniqueness of the Christian revelation consists in its sacramental mediation through history. Consequently, its right apprehension involves an act of the whole man: his intellect, his spiritual discernment and his will to surrender to God's Word.[134]

Of all the books on miracles none has enjoyed greater popularity than C. S. Lewis's *Miracles: A Preliminary Study* (1947). At the time of publication it met a mixed reception from the reviewers, ranging from acclamations of excellence to complaints of Lewis's lack of understanding of scientific, historical, and theological method.[135] But for the general public Lewis had produced a work that was clear and cogent. As in his other apologetic writings, Lewis shunned footnotes and cross-references to scholarly literature and wrote in the kind of direct, self-assured conversational style that left the reader wondering why nobody else had put it that way before. As a matter of fact, there were plenty of people who had put forward similar ideas. Half of Lewis's book consisted of a defense of a metaphysical view of the world that had marked similarities with the views of such contemporaries of Lewis as William Temple, A. E. Taylor, and H. H. Farmer. What Lewis possessed was a unique gift for expressing metaphysical and theological argument in everyday language. To this was added a disarming candor and a fearless capacity for grasping nettles.

This latter gift grew as the years went by. Perhaps it was encouraged by the fact that he wrote as an amateur in the fields of theology and philosophy. Clearly this is not true in the strict monetary sense, for his books far outsold those of the professionals in these fields. But it is true in the sense that Lewis's professional education and expertise lay in the realm of English literature. He was an amateur in theology in the triple sense of being one who had no technical training in it, did not practice it as his main profession, but nevertheless had a deep love of it. Thus Lewis stood outside the guild of professional theologians and steadfastly refused to be inhibited by them. He said what he thought. In his epilogue to *Miracles* he urged his readers to turn straight to the New Testament rather than to books about it. When they turn to books by modern scholars, he cautioned, readers should remember that they go "as sheep among wolves," and that they will meet naturalistic assumptions and beggings of the question on every side.[136] Nevertheless, Lewis was not oblivious to the opinions of others. A Socratic Club debate with Elizabeth Anscombe, who in later years became professor of philosophy at Cambridge, led him to rewrite the third chapter of *Miracles*. In the first edition it was entitled "The Self-Contradiction of the Naturalist"; in the 1960 version it was called "The Cardinal Difficulty of the Naturalist."[137]

A somewhat earlier statement of Lewis's views was given in a sermon on "Miracles" that he delivered in 1942 and has been reprinted in the anthology *God in the Dock* (1970). The following account of Lewis's position draws on both the book and the earlier sermon. Comparison of the wording of the two works suggests that *Miracles* is an elaboration of the earlier piece. At some points the wording is scarcely altered. Both discussions were essentially defensive. Unlike a number of American apologists who have drawn on Lewis in an attempt to develop an objective evidential case for proving the truth of Christianity, Lewis's argument was really about the feasibility of miracles and their significance as revelations of God in Christ. In *God in the Dock* Lewis bluntly stated that "Whatever experiences we may have, we shall not regard them as miraculous if we already hold a philosophy which excludes the supernatural."[138] The determined agnostic, cast into the Lake of Fire at the end of the world, would continue forever to regard the experience as an illusion and find explanations in psychoanalysis or cerebral pathology. "If a man doubts whether he is dreaming or waking, no experiment can solve his doubt, since every experiment may itself be part of the dream. Experience proves this, or that, or nothing, according to the preconceptions we bring to it."[139] The question of preconceptions was one that was to take up thirteen of the seventeen chapters of *Miracles*, which Lewis aptly subtitled *A Preliminary Study*. These first thirteen chapters were in effect an essay in philosophical theology, exploring the defects of naturalism and commending the feasibility of a theistic view of God and the world. The last four chapters suggested ways of looking at the miracle stories of the Gospels that showed their feasibility as acts of God in Christ, when considered within the framework of Lewis's theistic world view.

To Lewis there were basically two ways of looking at the world and our experience—naturalism and supernaturalism.[140] The naturalist thinks that there is nothing but nature. Nature means everything that is. Moreover, it happens of its own accord. On this view naturalism is another way of describing atheistic materialism. But is also verges on determinism, the view that effects are determined by antecedent, physical causes. To Lewis, this was the Achilles' heel of naturalism. For if all our thinking is determined by physical factors over which we have no control, we have no way of forming valid judgments about anything. The deathblow to strict determinism is given in the following words, which Lewis quotes from J. B. S. Haldane:

> If my mental processes are determined wholly by the motions of atoms
> in my brain, I have no reason to suppose that my beliefs are true . . .
> and hence I have no reason for supposing my brain to be composed of
> atoms.[141]

In its first form in the first edition of *Miracles*, Lewis's argument against naturalism was admittedly simplistic. It virtually equated naturalism with determinism.[142] Having found determinism to be self-refuting, the way was clear for Lewis to draw a distinction between "Reason" and "Nature," and conclude that "rational thought is not part of the system of Nature."[143] Thus, the human mind was in a sense "supernatural." This in turn led Lewis to posit a "cosmic mind" that is not "the product of mindless Nature . . . but the basic, original, self-existent Fact which exists in its own right. But to admit *that* sort of cosmic mind is to admit a God outside Nature, a transcendent and supernatural God."[144]

In point of fact, Lewis retained these conclusions in the second version of his argument, but attempted a more circumspect attack on naturalism. A feature of this revised argument was the distinction between causes and grounds. In response to Miss Anscombe's charges of specious argument, Lewis recognized that physical causes were not the same as rational grounds. The naturalist might entertain various theories of causation and offer rational grounds for his beliefs. The physical explanation of brain behavior operates on one level; the question of rationality of thought operates on another level entirely. Lewis thus felt obliged to revise his argument and moderate its tone. Instead of speaking of the self-contradictions of naturalism, he spoke of the difficulties of naturalism. Nevertheless, there still remained the cardinal one of the existence of the mind, which Lewis argued to be "supernatural," in the sense that "It must break sufficiently free from that universal chain [of physical cause and effect] in order to be determined by what it knows."[145]

A second line of argument in favor of a theistic supernaturalism took the form of a reminder of the way people (including naturalists) appeal to moral values and obligations. The fact that such values and obligations transcend nature points to a source that Lewis identifies with God.[146] However, as Lewis recognized, neither of his arguments for the existence of God necessitated the existence of a miracle-working God.[147] With a deistic or pantheistic God miracles are out of the question. But with the transcendent, personal God of Christian faith we come to "a sort of Rubicon. One goes across; or not. But if one does, there is no manner of security against miracles. One may be in for *anything*."[148]

In saying this, Lewis makes a leap of faith from natural theology to revealed religion. From now on he is increasingly concerned to interpret the miracles of the Gospel stories in terms of belief in the Christian Creator-God. His primary concern is to explain how miracles are thinkable in terms of this framework of belief. In what he called "A Chapter of Red Herrings," Lewis had already pointed out the absurdity of assuming that people in the ancient world were more prone to believe in miracles because they understood less of nature. As he points out,

> A moment's thought shows this to be nonsense: and the story of the Virgin Birth is a particularly striking example. When St. Joseph discovered that his fiancee was going to have a baby, he not unnaturally decided to repudiate her. Why? Because he knew just as well as any modern gynaecologist that in the ordinary course of nature women do not have babies unless they have lain with men.[149]

In saying this, Lewis is laying the foundations for his developed view of miracles. For Lewis, a miracle is not a violation of the laws of nature but "an interference with Nature by supernatural power."[150] What we call laws of nature are formulations concerning their observed regularities. It is only against the background of these regularities that we can even speak of miracles. On the basis of our past experience of the regularities of nature, we are entitled to predict how nature will generally behave under similar circumstances. But the scientist is concerned only with general patterns. When man, as a personal being, does something to nature, he does not suspend the laws—he merely rearranges the patterns of physical behavior. Man thus could be said to interfere with the laws of nature. The same can also be said of God. When God has taken the initiative in interfering in this way, the regular patterns of nature once more take over:

> It is therefore inaccurate to define a miracle as something that breaks the laws of Nature. It doesn't. If I knock out my pipe I alter the position of a great many atoms: in the long run, and to an infinitesimal degree, of all the atoms there are. Nature digests or assimilates this event with perfect ease and harmonises it in a twinkling with all other events. It is one more bit of raw material for the laws to apply to, and they apply. I have simply thrown one event into the general cataract of events and it finds itself at home there and conforms to all other events. If God annihilates or creates or deflects a unit of matter He has created a new situation at that point. Immediately all Nature domiciles this new situation, makes it at home in her realm, adapts all other events to it. It finds itself conforming to all the laws. If God creates a miraculous spermatozoon in the body of a virgin, it does not proceed to break any laws. The laws at once take it over. Nature is ready. Pregnancy follows, according to all the normal laws, and nine months later a child is born.[151]

In short, "A miracle is emphatically not an event without cause or without results. Its cause is the activity of God: its results follow according to Natural law."[152] Clearly Lewis is using nontechnical layman's language. The word "cause" is an open-ended term, used in a broad sense to cover whatever causal relationships may be appropriate. The terms "nature"and "law" are likewise open-ended. At the same time, it may be noted that Lewis wisely refrained from getting embroiled in discussions of indeterminism and quantum physics. He was dubious about basing anything on the unpredictable behavior of subatomic particles. As a layman, he could not help thinking that physicists mean

> no more than that the movements of individual units are permanently incalculable *to us*, not that they are in themselves random and lawless. And even if they mean the latter, a layman can hardly feel any certainty that some new scientific development may not tomorrow abolish this whole idea of a lawless Subnature.[153]

In point of fact, Lewis operated with what is often called a closed system of the universe, in the sense that on the physical level everything worked in terms of whatever causes and effects are deemed appropriate by the relevant sciences. Lewis's supernaturalism consisted in the assertion that personality (both human and divine) introduces a new factor of a different order in the initiation and termination of the sequences of cause and effect.

At this point two further observations may be made. The first concerns the tone of Lewis's language. It is a reminder that, although Lewis appears increasingly to speak with absolute certainty about what God is or is not doing in performing miracles, Lewis's pronouncements are really no more than a hypothetical explanation from the standpoint of faith. His position certainly holds many attractions for an orthodox Christian. Nevertheless, like all views of the miraculous (including its denial), Lewis's view remains a conjecture, bound up with a particular view of reality, which is designed to give a possible account of the veracity of the miracle stories of the New Testament. The second observation concerns the similarity of Lewis's personal supernaturalism with the views advanced by H. H. Farmer a decade earlier, not to mention William Temple, A. E. Taylor, Alan Richardson, and the broad Augustinian tradition that lived on in Anglicanism. In particular, there is a striking resemblance with Farmer's view of God's transcendent personality ordering causes within nature for his own ends.

If Lewis's metaphysics were of a piece with those of his contemporaries, his theological interpretation of miracles was not without parallels. In common with many Anglicans of his generation, Lewis saw the incarnation as the grand, central miracle.[154] The centrality of the incarnation had been a major theme of Anglican theologians from Maurice and Westcott to Gore and Temple. However, in *God in the Dock* Lewis expresses his indebtedness to two writers in particular for helping him to see a rationale for the miracles of Jesus. Lewis first discovered this rationale in the nineteenth-century Scottish minister and novelist, George MacDonald. He later found it anticipated by Athanasius, the fourth-century champion of Nicene orthodox christology. In response to the question of why God did not choose to reveal himself in the "nobler parts of creation" but preferred instead to come as a man, Athanasius observed:

> Our Lord took a body like to ours and lived as a man in order that those who had refused to recognize Him in His superintendence and captaincy of the whole universe might come to recognize from the works He did here below in the body that what dwelled in this body was the Word of God.[155]

Lewis saw this as an expression of the pronouncement in John 5:19: "The Son can do nothing of his own accord, but only what he sees the Father doing." He went on to explain it in the following manner:

> There is an activity of God displayed throughout creation, a wholesale activity let us say which men refuse to recognize. The miracles done by God incarnate, living as a man in Palestine, perform the very same things as this wholesale activity, but at a different speed and on a smaller scale. One of their chief purposes is that men, having seen a thing done by personal power on the small scale, may recognize, when they see the same

thing done on the large scale, that the power behind it is also personal—is indeed the very same person who lived among us two thousand years ago. The miracles in fact are a retelling in small letters of the very same story which is written across the whole world in letters too large for some of us to see.[156]

Moreover, miracles have a double purpose:

> The miracle has only half its effect if it only convinces us that Christ is God: it will have its full effect if whenever we see a vineyard or drink a glass of wine we remember that here works He who sat at the wedding party in Cana. Every year God makes a little corn into much corn: the seed is sown and there is an increase, and men, according to the fashion of their age, say "It is Ceres, it is Adonis, it is the Corn-King," or else "It is the laws of nature." The close-up, the translation, of this annual wonder is the feeding of the five thousand. Bread is not made there out of nothing. Bread is not made of stones, as the Devil once suggested to Our Lord in vain. A little bread is made into much bread. The Son will do nothing but what He sees the Father do. There is, so to speak, a family *style*.[157]

In the same way, the miracles of healing are to be seen in the context of God as the Lord and giver of life. The one miracle of destruction, the cursing of the fig tree (Matt. 21:19; Mark 11:13–20), is likewise to be viewed as an act that is "also in harmony with God's wholesale activity. His bodily hand held out in symbolic wrath blasted a single fig tree; but no tree died that year in Palestine, or any year, or in any land, or even ever will, save because He has done something, or (more likely) ceased to do something, to it."[158]

The miracles that Lewis has described so far are seen as small-scale acts of God that are broadly comparable with God's large-scale actions in creation. There is, however, a second class of miracles that "foretell what God has not yet done, but will do, universally."[159] In *Miracles* Lewis termed these two classes of miracles "Miracles of the Old Creation" and "Miracles of the New Creation"[160]—language reminiscent of his Narnia chronicles, which were to be his next major undertaking:

> The miracles of Reversal all belong to the New Creation. It is a miracle of Reversal when the dead are raised. Old Nature knows nothing of this process: it involves playing backwards a film that we have always seen played forwards. The one or two instances of it in the Gospels are early flowers—what we call spring flowers, because they are prophetic, although they really bloom while it is still winter. And the miracles of Perfecting or of Glory, the Transfiguration, and Resurrection, and the Ascension, are even more emphatically of the New Creation. They are the true spring, or even the summer of the world's new year. The Captain, the forerunner is already in May or June, though His followers on the earth are still living in the frosts and east winds of Old Nature—for "spring comes slowly up this way."[161]

Whereas Lewis saw the miracles of the old creation in relation to the incarnation, he looked at those of the new creation in relation to the resurrection and ascension of Jesus.[162] The resurrection of Jesus introduces a new order. Jesus had a resurrection body that was neither a mere resuscitation of his former corpse nor a ghostlike apparition:

> The records represent Christ as passing after death (as no man had passed before) neither into a purely, that is, negatively, "spiritual" mode of existence nor into a "natural" life such as we know, but into a life which has its own, new Nature. It represents Him as withdrawing six weeks later, into some different mode of existence. It says—He says—that He goes "to prepare a place for us." This presumably means that He is about to create that whole new Nature which will provide the environment or conditions for His glorified humanity and, in Him, for ours.[163]

Lewis regarded the accounts of Jesus walking on the water (Matt. 14:22-33; Mark 6:45-52; John 6:16-21) as an anticipation of what the New Order would be like. The relationship of spirit and nature is so altered that nature is subject to spirit.[164] In a general sense magic is an attempt to get this kind of power over nature—but without paying the price. If unchecked, the result would be chaos. But in the case of Jesus, this power over nature is achieved only in obedience to the Father who is the true Lord of nature. The raising of Lazarus (John 11) is also an act of reversal, an anticipation of the New Order. Similarly, the transfiguration of Jesus (Matt. 17:1-9; Mark 9:2-10; Luke 9:28-36) is "an anticipatory glimpse of something to come."[165] In these miracles of the new creation there is a reversal of the entropy of the created world, as we know it, and the introduction of a new order.[166]

We have already taken note of Lewis's acknowledged debt to Athanasius. His debt to George MacDonald (1840-1905) came about chronologically earlier and was more pervasive. A chance reading of MacDonald's romantic novel *Phantastes* resulted in the conversion and baptism (to use his own language) of Lewis's imagination.[167] MacDonald's novels were nineteenth-century forerunners of the mythopoeic, allegorical fantasies that Lewis and Tolkien were to write in the twentieth century. But perhaps Lewis's discussions of miracles owed a particular debt to MacDonald. For certainly there is a marked affinity between Lewis's treatment of the miracles of the old and new creations and MacDonald's devotional thoughts on miracles. In 1871 MacDonald published *The Miracles of Our Lord*. In it he shunned all philosophical and critical questions, and offered instead a series of meditations on the Gospel stories.

In essence Lewis's doctrine of the miracles of the old creation is contained in MacDonald's opening exhortation:

> Let us then recognize the works of the Father as epitomized in the miracles of the Son. What in the hands of the Father are the mighty motions and progresses and conquests of life, in the hands of the Son are miracles.

I do not myself believe that He valued the working of these miracles as He valued the utterance of truth in words. But all that He did had one root, *obedience,* in which alone can any son be free. And what is the highest obedience? Simply a following of the Father, a doing of what the Father does. Every true father wills that his child should be as he is in his deepest love, in his highest hopes. All that Jesus does is of His Father. What we see in the Son is the Father. What His works mean concerning Him, they mean concerning the Father.[168]

Like Lewis after him, MacDonald saw Jesus' miracles of producing bread and wine as "condensed" mysteries, paralleling what the Father is doing more slowly and more grandly on a large scale.[169] On the other hand, MacDonald's treatment of the raising of Lazarus, the walking on the water, and the resurrection anticipate Lewis's doctrine of the miracles of the new creation. There is a reversal of the order of nature and the appearance of a new order. MacDonald suggests that in order to walk on water, a change was necessary before the body of the Son of Man could move, like the Spirit of old, upon the face of the waters. The change affected not the water but the human body, subject to the indwelling spirit.[170] With Jesus' resurrection a new order of being is introduced. Again this was anticipated by the transfiguration.[171]

In drawing attention to MacDonald's discussion of Jesus' miracles, I am not implying that Lewis simply appropriated the ideas of someone else. At the same time the anticipation of Lewis's ideas by MacDonald (not to mention Athanasius) in the area of theological interpretation and by William Temple, H. H. Farmer, and A. E. Taylor in the area of metaphysical explanation suggests that Lewis's work on miracles was not quite as original as it is often thought to be.[172] What Lewis possessed was a great gift for digesting and appropriating the ideas of others, so that, when he expressed them, they really were his own.

In at least one other important respect Lewis drew on the ideas of others. This concerns his use of myth. Indeed, it would seem that it took some considerable effort on the part of Hugo Dyson, Owen Barfield, and J. R. R. Tolkien to persuade Lewis in the early thirties that myths were not lies but expressions of intuitive insights.[173] As a result of a conversation with Tolkien in September 1931, Lewis became persuaded that, whereas in pagan myths God used the minds of poets and their images to express fragments of eternal truth, in Christianity God himself was the poet and the images that he used were real men and actual history. As a consequence, Lewis confessed that he had "just passed on from believing in God to definitely believing in Christ—in Christianity."[174]

Lewis's discussion of myth and miracles may well be compared with those of D. F. Strauss and Wilhelm Bousset. However, Lewis's position completely reverses their ideas. Strauss detected the presence of myth in the New Testament on the grounds that the stories attributed to Jesus actions that in the Old Testament were attributed to Yahweh. Bousset found proof of myth in the Gospel stories on grounds of alleged parallels in pagan sources. Both writers dismissed the New Testament stories on the grounds that they bore no analogy to a scientific understanding of the laws of nature. Lewis grasped this nettle by replying in effect that the Gospel stories were not yet more instances of fictitious nonevents; rather, we should think of them as the actualization in history of God's answer to the needs felt in man's deep religious experiences.

In the course of this study, we have observed from time to time the role played by analogy in the discussion of miracles. In the thought of Hume, Strauss, and Troeltsch, analogy is used to show the improbability of miracles. The term "analogy" hardly figures in C. S. Lewis's discussion of the subject, but nevertheless he makes implicit use of the concept. In his metaphysical defense of supernaturalism Lewis sees an implicit analogy between human personal action in interfering with the laws of nature and divine personal action in interfering with them. If man is capable of determining in his limited way what factors may come into play in nature, it is all the more feasible to think that the Creator of the universe may determine what factors may come into play in nature. But analogy also figures implicitly in Lewis's theological interpretation of miracles. The miracles of the old creation are to be interpreted by analogy with God's work in creation. The miracles of the new creation are to be seen as the analogical first fruits of the new order inaugurated by the resurrection of Jesus.

If, in developing these thoughts, Lewis was indebted to others who had thought them before him, nothing can detract from his creative power in putting them together in such a forceful and highly suggestive manner. At certain points Lewis's argument is open to question. Can we really think of the feeding of the five thousand and the miracle at Cana as simply the acceleration of natural processes? Does the thought of acceleration really help to make the event more credible? Moreover, it leaves unexplained how the bread came to be baked and the wine fermented. All this puts a large question mark against Lewis's idea of miracles of the old creation.

At a crucial juncture in his argument Lewis appears to make a curious about-face. At the outset of both his discussions of miracles Lewis strongly insists upon the importance of the right preconceptions as the prerequisite for accepting miracles. He labors hard to demonstrate the inadequacies of naturalism and to erect a metaphysical framework of personal supernaturalism as the necessary context for gauging the historical actuality of miracles and their theological significance. However, in the passages cited from *God in the Dock*, where Lewis refers to Athanasius and gives his rationale for miracles, he appears to stand his own argument on its head. The reason for miracles lies in man's refusal to recognize the "wholesale activity of God. . . . The miracles in fact are a retelling in small letters of the very same story which is written across the whole world in letters too large for some of us to see."[175] Apart from the fact that Lewis does not make clear whether he thinks incapacity to see God's activity is due to an intellectual or moral failure on man's part, he does not explain how *reports* of miracles will remedy this defect for man today. Moreover, our ability to apprehend miracles is said by Lewis to depend precisely on our ability to see them in the context of a personal supernaturalism that is based on general reflections on the "wholesale activity of God." It may well be that Lewis himself sensed that there was something fundamentally wrong with this argument, for in his later study of *Miracles* he appears to have removed the obvious self-contradiction and smoothed the whole thing out. In *Miracles* he reformulated the argument as follows:

> I contend that in all these miracles alike the incarnate God does suddenly and locally something that God has done or will do in general. Each miracle writes for us in small letters something that God has already written, or will write, in letters almost too large to be noticed, across the whole canvas of Nature. They focus at a particular point either God's actual, or His future operations on the universe. When they reproduce operations we have already seen on the large scale they are miracles of the Old Creation: when they focus those which are still to come they are miracles of the New. Not one of them is isolated or anomalous: each carries the signature of the God whom we know through conscience and from Nature. Their authenticity is attested by the *style*.[176]

Clearly a concept of analogy permeates Lewis's thinking. In *Miracles* he seeks to establish the framework for it by drawing on arguments from natural theology and concluding that we can make better sense of the world on the premises of a personal, supernatural theism than we can on the premises of naturalism. But there was also an intuitive side to Lewis's mind, which is clearly present in his Narnia stories and his view of myth. For through the medium of myth the mind grasps in an indirect and noninferential way something of the reality of God. This intuitive apprehension of God underlies Lewis's discussion of miracles. It appears, for example, in Lewis's assumed identification of the personal God of nature with the God of the Bible and of Christian faith.[177] When Lewis talks about the "authenticity" of the New Testament miracle stories being "attested by the *style*," he is not comparing their *style* with that of the personal being posited by his natural theology (who on his own admission could not be expected to perform miracles) but with the God of the Bible. Even so, to speak of God's *style* does not imply that Yahweh was in the habit of repeating miracles. Rather, Lewis's thought is best seen as the expression of an intuitive conviction that the miracle stories of the Gospels bear some kind of analogical correspondence with the acts of God the Creator. Whether Lewis was correct in his representation of all the miracle stories is another question. His work is at bottom a defense of the propriety of intuitively seeing the miracle stories as acts of the same God who the Bible tells us is the Creator. What he had done was not to demonstrate the actual historicity of any given miracle, but to suggest a conceivable frame of reference within which the miracle stories of the Gospels were conceivable as historical events. Lewis called his book on miracles *A Preliminary Study*. He did not go on to write a sequel. But in what he did, he left behind fruitful suggestions that deserve to be followed up.

9

CRITICAL CROSSCURRENTS

The question of miracles has claimed the attention of three groups of scholars: philosophers, apologists, and students of the New Testament. In this chapter we shall look at the third group. The approach will be deliberately selective; our aim will be to observe different types of approach, noting presuppositions and methods, rather than to attempt a comprehensive survey of the critical investigation of the New Testament miracle stories. At the same time, the definition of what constitutes a student of the New Testament has been intentionally broadened beyond the confines of the guild of professional New Testament teachers, in order to permit us to take note of scholars as diverse as Karl Barth and J. D. M. Derrett. In their different ways, both have made important contributions to the understanding of the New Testament miracle stories. Neo-orthodoxy is included here because of its concern for a theology grounded in biblical revelation and because of its influence on twentieth-century theology. We shall, therefore, consider the critical study of the Gospel miracles under four headings: (1) Neo-orthodoxy; (2) Bultmann, Form Criticism, and Demythologization; (3) Alan Richardson and Biblical Theology; and (4) Trends in Contemporary Critical Study. It will be readily apparent that there are numerous crosscurrents of thought, each reflecting varied assumptions, presuppositions, and methods of approach. There is no overall consensus. Yet an examination of critical crosscurrents will help to identify the issues and options before the modern critical mind.

NEO-ORTHODOXY

The term neo-orthodoxy is an emotive one. To conservative, right-wing Christians it suggests compromise and failure to recognize God's truth in the Bible for what it is. To the radicals on the left it denotes an anachronistic attempt to revive the orthodoxy of the early church and the Reformers in a way that pays only lip service to the realities of modern thought. Already the great leaders of neo-orthodoxy—Brunner, Barth, and Bultmann—have been dismissed as somewhat *passé*. They have fallen into the temporary oblivion that attends most prominent figures for the first ten years after their deaths. However, there are some signs of renewed interest in them, especially in Barth. If for no other reason than that of their considerable influence during their lifetimes, Brunner, Barth, and Bultmann deserve mention at this point. The fact that these three were at odds with each other scarcely requires elaboration. There can be no question about Bultmann being the most radical of the three. But it is certainly arguable that Bultmann's chief desire was to restore the dimension of the transcendence of God to twentieth-century Christianity and proclaim the central significance of the cross and resurrection of Christ. Both these concerns were characteristic of the neo-orthodoxy that played such a big part in Protestant theology from the 1920s to the 1960s. At the same time miracles could hardly be said to be central to neo-orthodox thought. In this section, however, we shall look at the thought of Brunner, Barth, and Bonhoeffer. Because Bultmann was primarily a New Testament scholar, we shall consider him in the next section.

In his massive and influential book *The Mediator* (1927), Emil Brunner (1889–1966) relegated the subject of miracles to a footnote in which he pointed out that miracles were an embarrassment to modern immanentism, but were central to the religion of the Bible. They were "signs" of Christ, and "as such they should be studied and pondered with as much earnestness as His words."[1] However, Brunner did not follow through on his own recommendation in the context of his study of the mediator. He took a step toward rectifying this in the second volume of his *Dogmatics,* where he briefly defended the propriety of belief in miracles and included an appendix on the question of miracles and demythologizing. Brunner's view was that the rejection of miracles is bound up with philosophical considerations that may be either explicit or implicit. But if we believe in the God of biblical revelation, we must recognize that the laws of nature are relative and that God is not tied to them. In order to restore his creation, God has to intervene as the Redeemer:

> Thus the God of the Bible, both of the Old and of the New Testament, is the living God, who intervenes in the course of history. He is the God who works miracles, in contrast to both the Absolute of speculative philosophy, and the deity of Mysticism, who, as original Truth, stands above or behind all that happens, but takes no part in the events themselves.[2]

In his discussion of the rejection of miracles in the name of demythologizing,[3] Brunner detected what he regarded as the unwarranted assumptions of a "closed universe" and the "uniform interrelatedness of nature." In a manner comparable with his British contemporaries, William Temple, H. H. Farmer, and C. S. Lewis, Brunner saw personal freedom as the key factor in grasping man's and God's transcendence over the laws of nature. Only when one recognizes this freedom can a really fruitful discussion of demythologizing begin. To Brunner, the old apologetic proof from miracles was unconvincing:

> We believe in the miracles of Jesus when we already believe in Him, but not before. And even then we do not give up the right to criticize this or that recorded miracle, this or that marvel as due rather to the "myth-forming imagination" than to the historical fact. But a modern theologian ought to be open to the possibility that the great miracle (of revelation) may produce most unusual results.[4]

Having opened the door to the possibility of miracles in this way, Brunner does not seem to have ventured through it himself. Biblical miracles play no significant part in his doctrines of revelation and reconciliation.

A similar practical lack of interest in the biblical miracles may be detected in Karl Barth (1886–1968). The index to his compendious *Church Dogmatics* contains scarcely more than two dozen references to miracles, and when we look at them, most turn out to be passing allusions. We have to go through nine massive part-volumes before we reach Barth's illuminating discussion of Jesus' miracles, which he gives in the context of his exposition of "The Royal Man" (§ 64) in IV,2. If we compare Barth and Brunner on the subject of miracles, their attitudes appear to correspond to their respective views on natural theology. Brunner's interest was largely apologetic, and centered on the formal question of the feasibility of miracles in the context of God's relations to the natural world. Barth ignored this question. Declaring that miracles were mysteries of the sovereign activity of God, Barth concentrated on the theological significance of the New Testament witness.

Barth's initial emphasis fell on the fact that we cannot know or speak of the hidden God who reveals himself in Jesus Christ "apart from the miracle of His grace."[5] Miracle is "simply the revelation of the divine glory otherwise hidden from us, on the strength of which we can believe and honour Him elsewhere as Creator and Lord."[6] Miracles are displays of the divine omnipotence, which is no different from God's omnipotence in other acts:

> The power in which God is Lord over all created powers is in itself one and the same power, whether God uses and manifests it for us in the usual or in an unusual way. It is certainly not the function of biblical miracles to present to men a special divine omnipotence, a higher one, exercised and used in a series of exceptions. On the contrary, their function is to remind men by signs, by visible illustrations of His Word, that God is omnipotent (as He calls us into His kingdom by His Word), and therefore that the omnipotence of God and God Himself are not to be identified with the created powers in themselves and as such, or with their sum or substance, as we are constantly inclined to think in view of the usual course of events.[7]

On the basis of this assertion of divine omnipotence as the necessary ground for grasping the feasibility of miracles, Barth thus saw miracles as revelatory signs, or acts of God illustrating and proclaiming the same message as the Word of God. They could no more be proved by objective means than the Word itself could be so proved. But within the scheme of revelation they have a positive function as a demonstration of Christ's person. Moreover, the demonstration is itself a revelation of that person:

> The Gospel records of the miracles and acts of Jesus are not just formal proofs of His Messiahship, of His divine mission, authority and power, but as such they are objective manifestations of His character as the Conqueror not only of sin but also of evil and death, as the Destroyer of the destroyer, as the Saviour in the most inclusive sense. He not only forgives the sins of men; He also removes the source of their suffering.[8]

But all miracles are mysteries. The form cannot be separated from the matter, or the matter from the form. There is no way in which we can trace the event directly back to God. Men see the earthly form through which God reveals himself, but they cannot penetrate the mystery. They can only respond in faith, obedience, and joy.[9]

It is against this background that Barth offers a brief, but suggestive, theological interpretation of the Gospel miracles.[10] He concedes that the healing miracles of Jesus bear formal similarities with those attributed to Apollonius of Tyana, Vespasian, Hadrian, or even to the disciples of the Pharisees (Matt. 12:27; Luke 11:19).[11] And he notes the widely held conviction that the New Testament descriptions of exorcism are really the ancient world's way of describing psychotherapy. But if Jesus' healings were really of this kind, "they would have become only relatively extraordinary actions."[12] The decisive difference for Barth consists in the fact that "the new thing" about these other healings "is only a revelation of the depth of the old—a depth which was always there and could even be discerned."[13] However, "according to the proclamation in the Word of Jesus the alien and miraculous and inconceivable thing that takes place in His actions in the world, and in defiance of all human being and perception and understanding, is nothing other than the kingdom of God."[14]

Barth discerns the following six "symptoms" that indicate a difference between Jesus' miraculous healings, other kinds of healing, and reports of healing:[15]

(1) According to the Gospel accounts, Jesus did not set himself up as a healer or seek publicity through his healings. In the majority of cases Jesus did not take the initiative. "He is almost like His own spectator" (cf. Mark 5:30; 6:56).

(2) Jesus did not use any therapeutic techniques. He made pronouncements, but these do not have the character of incantations. Occasionally he laid his hands on people (e.g., Mark 6:5; Luke 4:10). On three occasions he touched the blind and deaf with spittle (Mark 7:33; 8:23; John 9:6). But this did not amount to a technique. One cannot discern any art or craft that he practiced either as a doctor or a magician. As distinct from psychotherapy, there was no preparation or repeated consultations. He called those who were healed to prayer, or he prayed for them himself.

(3) Jesus never performed any miracles in his own interests or for the preservation or deliverance of his own person. He expressly rejected the temptation to do so (Matt. 4:2ff.; 26:53), and was mocked for saving others, while being unable to save himself (Matt. 27:42). He did not expect or receive rewards for his actions, and commanded his disciples to adopt the attitude, "Freely you have received, freely give" (Matt. 10:8). What is expected of those who are helped by him is simply that they should "give glory to God" (Luke 17:18)—and nothing more.

(4) The miracles of Jesus were not part of an organized attempt to ameliorate world conditions or initiate general welfare programs. Jesus' well-doing never became an institution. It did not lead to the founding of a Lourdes. The cures did not prevent the beneficiaries from succumbing to other ailments and eventually from dying. The five thousand were not repeatedly miraculously fed.

(5) The miracles of Jesus do not have an independent, autonomous value. They perform a twofold service to faith and the call to faith: they are "the cosmic actualisations of His kerygma, and are performed in this context to summon men to faith." Apart from this context, they are like the words of Jesus that fall by the wayside, on stony ground, or among thorns (Mark 4:4f.). For Bethsaida, Chorazin, and Capernaum, where miracles produced no repentance, they become signs of judgment and the occasion of denunciation (Matt. 11:20f.). It was because Jesus was not prepared to perform miracles in a vacuum that he refused the desire of the Pharisees for a sign (Mark 8:11f.; Matt. 16:4). This also explains why he commanded those who were healed not to speak of what had taken place. Barth believes that the meaning of Mark 6:5 is that Jesus could not will to work miracles in his own city, because they would be gaped at as the revelation of some superior world or power, or be marvelled at simply because of their effects. "The Jesus of the Gospels could not and would not work miracles merely as a means of propaganda among those who would not accept His preaching and be converted and believe." Other types of "miracles" claim attention for very different reasons.

(6) Not only the miracles described by John but also those in the Synoptic Gospels have "a symbolic quality." The restoration of sight, hearing, and the ability to walk, and the raising of the dead have a certain analogy to salvation. Whereas form critics had suggested that the story of the miraculous draught of fishes (Luke 5:4f.; John 21:1f.) had grown out of a saying about "fishers of men" (Mark 1:17), Barth saw the miracles as parabolic history, attesting in events what was also declared in the Word. For example, the feedings of the multitudes point in the direction of the Lord's Supper; the calming of the storm is a lesson in history for the church; and the exorcisms reveal Jesus as the victor over the cosmic powers of evil. The church fathers were well aware of this dimension of the miracle stories, but modern fear of allegorizing has led to a refusal to look in this direction at all. However, Barth suggests that a distinctive feature of biblical miracles is that they are

parables as well as history, and that a miracle "that is not a parable as well as history, is a miracle of a very different type."

Thus, although the Gospel miracles appear to bear formal similarities with healings and wonders elsewhere, Barth contends that these six "distinctive symptoms" are indications of essential differences. What is more, these differences show us that Jesus' miracles are bound up with the kingdom of God, which has drawn near in Jesus. The Fourth Evangelist goes out of his way to point out that John the Baptist "did no miracle"; his greatness consisted in bearing true witness to Jesus (John 10:41). It is through Jesus' acts that the divine glory is manifested (John 2:11). This glory is the new thing to which history, including the miracles of Elijah and Elisha, is pointing. In astonishment at an exorcism, the crowds remark that "It was never so seen in Israel" (Matt. 9:33), even though exorcisms had been performed by the disciples of the Pharisees (Matt. 12:27; Luke 11:19). "The new thing which was now seen was that 'the kingdom of God is now come unto you' (Mt. 12[28]). Whether it was recognized or not, this was the thing which was to be seen in the acts of Jesus."[16]

This leads Barth to offer a series of further reflections on miracles and the kingdom of God. He saw Jesus' actions as his "response to human misery" in its many forms.[17] Sometimes the need was relatively trivial and scarcely more than an embarrassment, like the shortage of wine at Cana (John 2:1f.) or the need to pay the temple tax (Matt. 17:27). The miraculously fed multitudes were scarcely on the point of starvation. But throughout Jesus had a deep concern for those with whom things were going badly (Mark 1:40; 2:17; 9:22f.; 10:47; cf. Matt 4:24; 8:17, 25; 15:30). The result of Jesus' actions is release from torment and embarrassment. Man "can breathe again. He can be a man again—a whole man in this elemental sense. His existence as a creature in the natural cosmos is normalised."[18]

In this connection Barth contends that the important thing about the needy in the miracle stories is not that they are sinners but that they are sufferers:

> Jesus does not first look at their past, then at their tragic present in the light of it. But from their present he creates for them a new future. He does not ask, therefore, concerning their sin. He does not hold it against them. He does not denounce them because of it. The help and blessing that He brings are quite irrespective of their sin. He acts almost (indeed exactly) in the same way as His Father in heaven, who causes His sun to shine on the good and the evil, and His rain to fall on the just and unjust (Mt. 5[45]).[19]

Even in those passages where sin is mentioned, Barth contends that the evil concerned was either not the result of personal sin, as in the case of the man born blind (John 9:2f.; cf. Luke 13:1), or that Jesus focused on the forgiveness of sin (Mark 2:5, 11) and future avoidance of it (John 5:14).

What is revealed in the miracles is God's deity and power and the fact that God puts himself on man's side. This is epitomized in Jesus' words to the woman who touched his garment: "Daughter, your faith has made you well; go in peace, and be healed of your disease" (Mark 5:34).

> His activity is first and foremost the Gospel in action. Only then is it the new Law which condemns the sins that he [man] has committed and warns him not to commit fresh sin, thus closing the door by which chaos has invaded his life and being. It is a matter of saving his life and being, and of doing this for the sake of God's glory. For the glory of God is threatened by man's destruction. Hence God cannot tolerate that man should perish.[20]

Barth supports this contention by a series of exegetical reflections. In his comments on the Fourth Gospel Barth places himself in that relatively small company of theologians who have noticed that the works of Jesus are depicted as the works of the Father in and through him:

> In John's Gospel there are frequent references to the "works" of Jesus, and primarily and concretely this term is used to denote His miracles. He, Jesus, has to do them (Jn. 10[37]), or "work" them (9[4]). But He does them in the name of the Father (10[25]). The Father has given Him these works to "finish" (5[36]). Strictly, it is the indwelling Father Himself who does them (14[10]). Strictly, then, they are the "works of God" (9[3]), given to Jesus to do, to work, to finish, in order to attest Him, and in His person the salvation and life granted by God to man (5[36]), that life which is the light of men (1[4]).[21]

The fact that Jesus performed many of his healings on the Sabbath points in the same direction. It was not that Jesus was concerned with the formal exercise of freedom in relation to Sabbath regulations. Rather, Jesus healed deliberately and gladly on the Sabbath, "because His own coming meant that the seventh and last day, the great day of Yahweh had dawned, and healing was the specific Word of God that He had come to accomplish on this day (in the name of God and in fulfillment of His own work)" (cf. Mark 3:4; 3:10f.; 14:1f.; John 5:9; 8:12; 9:14f.).[22] Barth sees the liberating, life-giving work of "the indwelling Father" brought into sharp focus in the stories of the raising of Jairus's daughter (Mark 5:38f.), of the widow of Nain's son (Luke 7:14), and of Lazarus (John 11).

Similarly, Barth refuses to see the stories of exorcism as either a piece of pedagogic accommodation on the part of Jesus to current Jewish beliefs or an expression of theological and cultural naiveté. They, too, point in the same direction as the other stories. The "whole action of Jesus is stated in the words: 'Who went about doing good, and healing all that were oppressed of the devil; for God was with him' " (Acts 10:38).[23] "The activity of Jesus, and revealed in it God Himself and His Kingdom, are a defiance of the power of destruction which enslaves man, of *phthora* in all its forms."[24]

Finally, Barth gives prolonged consideration to the role of faith in relation to miracles. Barth concludes that the faith which the Gospels talk about is not concerned with philosophical entertainment of the theoretical possibility of miracles. "The distinctive feature of the New Testament faith in miracles is that it was faith in Jesus and therefore in God as the faithful and merciful God of the covenant with Israel; and in this way and as such it was this confidence in His power."[25] But there is the further question of whether faith precedes miracles or follows them. Clearly, in a number of instances faith is the precondition of Jesus' response (Matt. 8:10; 9:18, 23, 28; 14:31; 17:20; Mark 2:4f.; 4:40; 5:36; 11:23; Luke 7:50; 17:6). However, the healing of the blind man in John produces faith (John 9:35). Other acts, particularly those described in John, either produce faith or are expected to produce faith (John 10:37f.; 12:37; 20:31; cf. 4:48; 6:30; Matt. 11:4ff., 20f.; Luke 24:19). But they can also provoke opposition, as in the case of Jesus' exorcisms (Mark 3:22–27; Matt. 12:24–29; Luke 11:15–22; John 7:20; 8:48; 10:20). John 11:47f. depicts the raising of Lazarus as the crowning event that led the council to resolve on Jesus' destruction. Barth, therefore, denies that the miracles were mechanically effective instruments to produce faith. Jesus steadfastly refused to produce miraculous credentials (Matt. 12:38–42; 16:1–4; Mark 8:11–12; Luke 11:16, 29–32; John 6:30ff.).

Barth explains Jesus' refusal to perform signs as follows:

> Those who did not ask for His mercy, and therefore for the Son of David, the Son of Man, for the faithfulness and omnipotence of the God of Israel, asked in vain for the acts of Jesus, and, even if they saw them, saw them in vain. They might well see an act of power, but they did not see the sign of the coming kingdom. They could not come to faith in this way.[26]

Jesus' acts were no more "an infallible means" to producing faith than were his spoken words. The purpose of the works and the words of Jesus was to direct attention beyond themselves to the person behind them. When faith is said to save a person in the New Testament, "faith is only secondarily described as a disposition or attitude or act of man. It is this, but the decisive thing is that it also reaches behind this whole sphere to a primary thing for which it proceeds as a human action when man is awakened and called to it."[27] Faith has its origin and goal in the action of God in Christ, and it is not true faith (in the New Testament sense of the term) apart from Christ. Thus, on Barth's view, it would be true to say that in some instances Jesus performed miracles in response to a faith that was kindled by him, while in other instances his miraculous work kindled the faith. In neither case can faith be separated from Jesus. Miracles are to be seen in the context of the grace of God. They attest "the epiphany of the Son of Man," and as such they are signs and anticipations of the restoration of glory and peace in the final revelation of the will and kingdom of God.

Of the leading continental neo-orthodox theologians, Barth is the one who gives the most positive account of miracles. In contrast, Barth's one-time student, Dietrich Bonhoeffer (1906–1945), sought to explore the idea of a new "religionless Christianity." Reflecting in prison on Bultmann's essay on "New Testament and Mythology," he wrote to Eberhard Bethge:

My view of it today would be, not that he went "too far," as most people thought, but that he didn't go far enough. It's not only the "mythological" concepts, such as miracle, ascension, and so on (which are not in principle separable from the concepts of God, faith, etc.), but "religious" concepts generally, which are problematic. You can't, as Bultmann supposes, separate God and miracle, but you must be able to interpret *both* in a "non-religious" sense. Bultmann's approach is fundamentally still a liberal one (i.e. abridging the gospel), whereas I'm trying to think theologically.[28]

To Bonhoeffer, Barth had started out on the right lines toward a "religionless Christianity," but he had stopped short at a "positivism of revelation," which was merely a restoration of the old.[29] In his musings on what a "religionless Christianity" might look like, Bonhoeffer believed that Christians should learn to live before God as if God were not there. They must recognize that the world has come of age, and belief in a God who intervenes in the world is just not realistic:

> So our coming of age leads us to a true recognition of our situation before God. God would have us know that we must live as men who manage our lives without him. The God who is with us is the God who forsakes us (Mark 15.34). The God who lets us live in the world without the working hypothesis of God is the God before whom we stand continually. Before God and with God we live without God. . . .

> Here is the decisive difference between Christianity and all religions. Man's religiosity makes him look in his distress to the power of God in the world: God is the *deus ex machina*. The Bible directs man to God's powerlessness and suffering; only the suffering-God can help. To that extent we may say that the development towards the world's coming of age outlined above, which has done away with a false conception of God, opens up a way of seeing the God of the Bible, who wins power and space in the world by his weakness. This will probably be the starting-point for our "secular interpretation."[30]

Bonhoeffer's ideas made a considerable impact on Christian thought, especially in the 1960s, when talk about the secularization of the gospel was at its height. It coincided with the high watermark of the influence of Bultmann and Tillich, and Bonhoeffer was perceived as the martyred prophet of a new form of Christianity. What was not so often seen was that his talk of the world come of age was an echo of Kant's view of enlightenment,[31] and that Bonhoeffer's restatement of Christianity, with its emphasis on heroically following in the footsteps of Christ with no expectations of God doing anything, bore a marked resemblance to the moral deism of Kant's religion within the limits of reason alone. In prison Bonhoeffer could hardly be expected to have documented his ideas with footnotes explaining his sources. At the same time, no competent German student of theology could have graduated without at least reading allusions in the standard German histories of philosophy to Kant's essay on enlightenment. The era that Kant had seen as dawning had now fully arrived for Bonhoeffer. The Christian church, therefore, must reshape its attitudes accordingly. Bonhoeffer's message was not simply that deism was correct. He saw God's withdrawal from the world as essential to the gospel of suffering and discipleship.

BULTMANN, FORM CRITICISM, AND DEMYTHOLOGIZATION

The leading prophet of the need to restate the gospel in terms of a modern world view was not Bonhoeffer, but Rudolf Bultmann (1884–1976). In his "Autobiographical Reflections" Bultmann acknowledged his theological kinship with Barth and the neo-orthodox movement of the 1920s in its protest against the liberalism that saw the Christian faith as a phenomenon of religious and cultural history:

> It seemed to me that, distinguished from such a view, the new theology correctly saw that Christian faith is the answer to the Word of the transcendent God which encounters man, and that theology has to deal with this Word and the man who has been encountered by it.[32]

However, Bultmann went on to say that this judgment never led him into a simple condemnation of "liberal" theology:

> On the contrary I have endeavoured throughout my entire work to carry further the tradition of historical-critical research as it was practiced in "liberal" theology and to make our recent theological knowledge the more fruitful as a result.

Bultmann's theology cannot be understood unless we appreciate it in the light of these declared intentions.

Bultmann's first major work, *The History of the Synoptic Tradition* (1919, E.T. 1963), together with Martin Dibelius's *From Tradition to Gospel* (1919, E.T. 1935), helped to establish form criticism as a tool and technique of New Testament scholarship, and in so doing laid the foundations for subsequent redaction criticism. Bultmann did not invent form criticism, nor did he see it as an alternative to the older literary source criticism. He saw himself building on the foundations already laid by Johannes Weiss, William Wrede, K. L. Schmidt, Julius Wellhausen, and Hermann Gunkel. Whereas the older critics had come to believe that Mark was the oldest of the four Gospels, and represented more or less a historical portrait of Jesus (which had been embellished by Matthew, Luke, and John for their own didactic and apologetic purposes), Bultmann maintained that Mark itself was made up of a series of disconnected individual units, which had themselves been shaped (and in many cases created) by the faith of the church. It was therefore necessary to analyze the forms in which the stories and sayings have been preserved in order to detect their "life situation" (or, to use Gunkel's immortal phrase, their *Sitz im Leben*) in the early church. To Bultmann, form criticism was not simply an exercise in descriptive classification. He saw it as an endeavor "to throw some light on the history of the tradition before it took literary form."[33]

Bultmann concluded from his elaborate analysis of the forms of the Gospel stories and teaching attributed to Jesus that Gospel material was shaped and largely created to meet the apologetic and polemical needs of the early church:

> The collection of the material of the tradition began in the primitive *Palestinian Church*. Apologetic and polemic led to the collection and production of apophthegmatic sections. The demands of edification and the vitality of the prophetic spirit in the church resulted in the handing on, the production and the collection of prophetic and apocalyptic sayings of the Lord. Further collections of dominical sayings grew out of the need for paraenesis and Church discipline. It is only natural that stories of Jesus should be told and handed down in the Church—biographical apophthegms, miracle stories and others. And just as surely as the miracle stories and such like were used in propaganda and apologetic as proofs of messiahship, so is it impossible to regard any one interest as the dominant factor; as it is generally not right to ask question [sic] about purpose and need only; for a spiritual possession objectifies itself also without any special aim.[34]

This process, which started in the Palestinian church, was taken over by the Hellenistic church and adapted to its own needs. Like Wilhelm Bousset (whose professorial chair at Giessen Bultmann briefly assumed before going on to Marburg), Bultmann believed that the idea of Lordship was adopted by the Hellenistic church from the saviors of pagan religion.[35] The Christ who is preached in the New Testament "is not the historic Jesus, but the Christ of the faith and the cult. . . . The kerygma of Christ is cultic legend and the *Gospels are expanded cult legends*."[36]

Bultmann saw the Gospel of Mark as the first product of a new literary genre that emerged in the Hellenistic church. In no sense can it be regarded as a biography depicting historical events as they happened:

> Mark was the creator of this sort of Gospel; the Christ myth gives his book, the book of secret epiphanies, not indeed a biographical unity, but a unity based upon the myth of the kerygma. . . . Matthew and Luke strengthened the mythical side of the gospel at points by many miracle stories and by their infancy narratives and Easter stories. But generally speaking they have not really developed the Mark type any further, but have simply made use of an historical tradition not accessible to Mark but available to them.[37]

Although Bultmann saw broad analogies in other forms of literature, including the stories of the miracle-worker Apollonius of Tyana,[38] he insisted that the Gospels were a unique form of literature.

The central section of *The History of the Synoptic Tradition* is devoted to a descriptive analysis of stories and legends. The latter consisted of "those parts of the tradition which are not miracle stories in the proper sense, but instead of being historical in character are religious and edifying."[39] Sometimes they include the miraculous, but they need not. For example, the "cult legends" of the Last Supper do not contain anything distinctively miraculous. The decisive difference for Bultmann lay in the fact that they were not unities in themselves, but gained their point only when set in their context. A number of miracle stories occur in apophthegms, or sayings of Jesus, set in a brief context (e.g., Mark 3:1-6; Luke 13:10-17; 14:1-6; 17:11-19).[40] Indeed, some miracles began merely as sayings that somehow got converted into events. But the healing of the paralytic (Mark 2:1-12) is "miracle story proper," drawing attention to the faith that overcomes material difficulties and directing attention to the miracle-worker who merits such trust. The story lacks any psychological interest in the sufferer. "The miracle working word, Jesus' command and its execution which demonstrates its effectiveness are typical characteristics, as is the impression made upon the onlookers."[41] Similarly, the exorcism in Mark 1:21-28 "is plainly meant to give a paradigmatic illustration of the ministry of Jesus."[42] The passage

> exhibits the typical characteristics of a miracle story, and especially of an exorcism: (1) the demon recognizes the exorcist and puts up a struggle; (2) a threat and a command by the exorcist; (3) the demon comes out, making a demonstration; (4) an impression is made on the spectators.[43]

By contrast Luke's handling of the incident (Luke 4:35) "shows that Luke no longer understands the motif, but instead emphasizes the healing itself as much as possible"(!)

It goes without saying that for Bultmann the extraordinary character of these stories, combined with a detection of the writer's intentions, make it self-evident that they have no basis in history. Bultmann's handling of the miracle stories is a long catalog consisting of brief comments on style, form, and the handling of the material. He agreed with Martin Dibelius that "it is of the very essence of the gospel to contain miracle stories."[44] Their purpose was to demonstrate not the character but the messianic authority or divine power of Jesus. The faith that is mentioned in the Gospels "is not a believing attitude to Jesus' preaching or to his Person in the modern sense of the word, but is a trust in the miracle worker which is his proper due."[45] This discrimination between different types of faith was to play an increasingly significant part in Bultmann's thought as the years went by.

Bultmann's handling of the miracle stories was not only an exercise in form criticism. It drew on the work of members of the History of Religions school, and indeed should be seen as a synthesis of the methods of the two schools of thought. Unlike D. F. Strauss who looked to the Old Testament as the quarry from which the early church dug its myths about Jesus, Bultmann turned to non-Christian literature and later rabbinic writings. At first sight Bultmann's listing of parallels in pagan and Jewish sources looks very impressive. But a number of these sources are those we have noted already in discussing Bousset, where we saw how tenuous was the connection with the Gospel accounts. In other instances, the parallels amount to no more than noting the length of sickness, the dangerous character of the disease, the ineffective treatment of the physicians, doubt and contemptuous treatment of the healer, and the effectiveness of the healer.[46] Such observations hardly invalidate an account of healing, whether in the New Testament or elsewhere. They are precisely the kind of observations that might be expected in any account of healing. Similarly, the observation of disturbances at exorcisms[47] might be expected to corroborate the accounts as authentic.

Bultmann's entire discussion is marked by erudition in his knowledge of sources and sheer lack of discrimination. This is evidenced by the wholesale character of his general allusions to fairy stories, from Ovid to the brothers Grimm. It suffices Bultmann to note that "The process of transferring some available miracle story to a hero (or healer or even a god) is frequently to be found in the history of literature and religion."[48] It is implied, rather than shown, that such stories were attributed to Jesus. Bultmann does not pause to discuss whether the pagan sources bear real, material similarities to the Gospel stories. He does not enter into questions of dating. He refrains from exploring whether the non-Christian source could conceivably have been known or used by the Gospel tradition, or whether the secular source could have drawn on the Christian one. It is sufficient to list the sources of alleged parallels in the interests of dismissing all such stories as unhistorical.

Twenty years after the first edition of *The History of the Synoptic Tradition*, Bultmann published *The Gospel of John* (1941). He applied to the miracles of the Fourth Gospel the ideas that he had already developed. The miracle at Cana was drawn from the Dionysus cult, adapted to become an epiphany of the Revealer.[49] Although John had his own signs-source, his use of it was unashamedly apologetic. The raising of Lazarus is seen in the context of the Revealer's secret victory over the world. Bultmann thought of revelation here in terms of a Christian Gnosticism. The account in John 11 is a "description of the primitive faith of those who need the external miracle in order to recognize Jesus as the Revealer."[50]

In the same year that he published his commentary on John, Bultmann produced his epoch-making essay "New Testament and Mythology," which initiated the demythologizing debate that was to preoccupy New Testament scholarship for the next quarter of a century.[51] In retrospect the work was not quite as innovative as it first seemed to be. Rather, it brought into sharp focus the implications of the work of the History of Religions school and the picture of Christianity that Bultmann himself had been working on during the previous twenty-five years. Once more Bultmann dissociated himself from previous liberalism only to restate liberal ideas in a more radical way. Whereas earlier liberals had held that some elements in the Gospel story, like the virgin birth, the magi, and the empty tomb, had been mythical, Bultmann argued that the entire thought-world of the New Testament was mythical. The alleged three-decker universe of heaven, earth, and hell; angels and demons; divine interventions; the heavenly redeemer; salvation, resurrection, and judgment—all were mythical concepts used by the first-century church to express their faith. These ideas were drawn from the mythological thought-worlds of Jewish apocalyptic and Hellenistic Gnosticism. But this mythological way of looking at the world is rendered obsolete by modern science, which does not admit divine interventions and explains what was hitherto regarded as supernatural in terms of chemistry, physics, and psychology. Nevertheless, there was a certain point to myth. Although it does not represent an objective picture of the world as it is, it is a vehicle for expressing man's awareness of an intangible reality. What needs to be done is to demythologize the message of the New Testament so that the true offense of Christianity may be seen and heard.

In his own interpretation of what the New Testament message was all about, Bultmann drew on the categories of Heidegger's existentialism. He saw Paul's teaching about the flesh as saying what Heidegger was saying when he spoke of inauthentic existence. The life of faith corresponded to Heidegger's concept of authentic existence, in which man was liberated from concern for self-contrived, tangible security, enabling him to be genuinely open to the future. There was, however, a point beyond which Bultmann himself would not demythologize, and for which Bultmann has been criticized by friends and foes alike. He retained the concepts of God, the cross, and resurrection (though he made it clear that he did not believe in penal satisfaction and the resuscitation of corpses). Bultmann's conclusion reiterates the position that he had maintained since the 1920s and which bears certain similarities to that of Barth and Brunner in the importance that Bultmann attaches to the word of God:

> The word of preaching confronts us as the word of God. It is not for us to question its credentials. It is we who are questioned, we who are asked whether we will believe the word or reject it. But in answering this question, in accepting the word of preaching as the word of God and the death and resurrection of Christ as the eschatological event, we are given an opportunity of understanding ourselves. Faith and unbelief are never blind, arbitrary decisions. They offer us the alternative between accepting or rejecting that which can illuminate our understanding of ourselves.
>
> The real Easter faith is faith in the word of preaching which brings illumination. If the event of Easter Day is in any sense an event additional to the event of the cross, it is nothing else than the rise of faith in the risen Lord, since it was this faith which led to the apostolic preaching. The resurrection itself is not an event of past history.[52]

Bultmann went on to add that faith cannot be buttressed by appeals to allegedly objective historical facts:

> It is precisely its immunity from proof which secures the Christian proc-
> lamation against the charge of being mythological. The transcendence
> of God is not as in myth reduced to immanence. Instead, we have the
> paradox of a transcendent God present and active in history: "The Word
> became flesh."[53]

Bultmann went on to elaborate his position in numerous writings, including his lectures at Yale and Vanderbilt, *Jesus Christ and Mythology,*
where he acknowledged that language about God is essentially analogical.[54]
However, he specifically addressed the subject of miracles in a paper entitled
"The Question of Wonder."[55] Here he declared that a wonder, in the sense
of "a violation of the conformity to law which governs all nature," is impossible for us today, "because we understand the processes of nature as
governed by law."[56] The idea of miracles must be abandoned not only because
it contradicts the universal validity of natural law posited by modern science,
but also because it is a purely intellectual notion and not a notion of faith.
Admittedly, the Bible presents certain events as miracles. But for Bultmann
this fact merely underlines the necessity of critical methods and recognition
of the fact that the biblical writers had not fully appreciated their own presuppositions and the nature of God's actions.

Nevertheless, there is a sense of wonder that Bultmann wishes to retain
and that does not involve rejecting the authority of Scripture. It is not,
however, the sense of a wonder as an observable event that leads to the conclusion that God exists. Rather, it is God's hidden action in revelation and
the forgiveness of sins. Indeed, "there is . . . only *one* wonder: the wonder
of the *revelation*, the revelation of the grace of God for the godless, the revelation of forgiveness."[57] This event is not to be understood as part of the world
process in which God is some kind of first cause. Indeed, it is contrary to
the world process—which is precisely what constitutes its miraculous character. It is a hidden event that cannot be objectified.

We shall have occasion to note responses to Bultmann as we go along,
but at this point it may be appropriate to make a passing observation about
Bultmann's underlying philosophy. A great deal of discussion has centered
on his existentialism. But existentialism is not the only, or even the most important factor. Certainly, Bultmann acknowledged his debt to Heidegger's
existentialism, whose categories he used in his analysis of the life of faith
as contrasted with life apart from faith. But Bultmann never completely
dissolved the gospel into existential self-awareness and openness. He retained
the concept of a personal, transcendent God who reveals himself in grace,
whereas Heidegger abandoned God in favor of Being. It would seem to be
nearer the mark to take Bultmann's self-evaluation seriously, and see him
as one who stood in the Protestant tradition of acknowledging the sovereign
grace of God in his Word but who tried to combine this with radical criticism
that made use of the history of religions. At the same time, his thought has
a neo-Kantian substructure that pushes God to a realm beyond the objective
world of time and space in which nature is governed by natural law.

Anton Fridrichsen's *The Problem of Miracle in Primitive Christianity* (1925)[58] appeared in its original French form four years after Bultmann's *History of the Synoptic Tradition*. However, in subsequent revisions of his work Bultmann made use of the Norwegian scholar's work, which had begun as a dissertation at Strasbourg. Fridrichsen subsequently enjoyed a distinguished career at Uppsala. His influence on New Testament studies continues to be felt through his own writings and the work of outstanding students like Krister Stendahl, Bertil Gärtner, Harald Riesenfeld, and Birger Gerhardsson. Fridrichsen studied in Germany, and in some respects came out of the same intellectual milieu as Bultmann, at least in their grounding in form criticism and the history of religions. He had a certain kinship with Bultmann, who dedicated the second volume of his *Glauben und Verstehen* (1952) to "Anton Fridrichsen, faithful friend in good and evil days." But there were also marked differences. Fridrichsen did not share Bultmann's philosophical background. He was prepared to acknowledge that

> Jesus undoubtedly healed those who were sick and those commonly called demoniacs. Those around him believed that they were witnesses to his wonders. But the difficulties begin when we ask "what happened" and "how did these things happen?" At bottom, this is a mystery. What we can ascertain is the impression produced by the "miracles" and the stylized redaction to which the tradition subjected them. This is all we can discover in historical study.[59]

Fridrichsen thus appears to adopt a somewhat more positive attitude toward miracles than Bultmann, allowing that behind all the stories lies the activity of Jesus, though this is ultimately a mystery. Yet he went on to argue that the earliest preaching concentrated on Jesus' redemptive work and paid only scant attention to miracles. Moreover, he rejected the idea that the Gospels were in any way based on historical "remembrance" of Jesus.[60] In common with other form critics he argued that "the tradition took shape chiefly under the influence of the religious needs and circumstances of the church."[61] But whereas Bultmann was concerned to compile a catalog of alleged parallels to the miracle stories in non-Christian literature, Fridrichsen concentrated on a phenomenological descriptive analysis of the New Testament itself. He showed that miracles were integral not only to the gospel tradition but also to the Christian mission (cf. Rom.15:19; 2 Cor. 12:12; Mark 16:17; Acts 5:15; 19:11ff.; 20:7ff.; 28:1ff.). Indeed, it was the close connection with miracle that "distinguished the primitive Christian mission from the Jewish mission and the propaganda of philosophic popularization."[62] However, Fridrichsen detected a certain downplaying of the significance of miracles and exorcisms already in the accounts of Jesus. When John the Baptist asked from prison whether Jesus really was the coming messiah, the reply that he was given pointed to the healings and preaching of the gospel in terms of fulfilled prophecy (Matt. 11:2, 6; cf. Isa. 29:18ff.; 35:5ff.; 61:1). This shows Jesus was no mere passing thaumaturge, but the one promised in prophecy.[63] Jesus is clearly presented in the Gospels as the one who has overcome Satan (Mark 3:22–27; Matt. 12:24–29; Luke 11:15–18). However, the warning to the disciples not to prize too highly their authority over demons, but to rejoice that their names are written in heaven, is seen by Fridrichsen as a warning to the church not to attach too great an importance to miracles.[64] Paul's emphasis on love in 1 Corinthians 13 represents a further devaluation of miraculous gifts, as do the various warnings in the Gospels about false prophets (Matt. 7:15–23; 24:24; Mark 13:22; cf. 2 Cor. 11:13–15; 2 Thess. 2:3–9; 1 John 4:1; 2 Pet. 2:1; Rev. 16–20). Fridrichsen saw all this as indicative of the declining role of miracles in the faith and life of the church. He concluded his survey on an ambiguous note:

> In the great church the source of miracles was on the point of drying up. Though it has never completely run dry in the church catholic, it does flow between the banks of faith and superstition. Enthusiasm as the essential characteristic of the church's life is dead for ever and support for miracle has fallen with it.
>
> Enthusiasm was destined gradually to disappear; psychologically such a development was inescapable. At the very outset complications loomed up and produced a critical attitude toward miracle. It is this state of mind and all it implies which we have tried to analyse in the preceding chapters.[65]

ALAN RICHARDSON AND BIBLICAL THEOLOGY

In the year that Bultmann launched his demythologizing program in Germany, Alan Richardson published in England *The Miracle-Stories of the Gospels* (1941). The work rapidly established itself as a classic statement of the biblical theology movement. In part it was a reply to the form-critical approach to miracles, and from time to time Richardson responded directly to the contentions of the form critics. He repudiated the claims of Bultmann and Martin Dibelius that the "tales" of miracles were borrowed from stories of gods, saviors, and miracle-workers in the ancient world, and were then adapted to attest the superiority of Jesus as a miracle-worker.[66] In so doing, he also rejected the form-critical distinction between such stories and what the form critics called paradigms, apophthegms, or pronouncement-stories, the point of the latter being to edify and instruct in the ways of salvation. Richardson observed that both Bultmann and Dibelius frequently found themselves in difficulties in their attempts to preserve a sharp distinction between the two. He also made it clear that Bultmann's attempt to discern a special form in the miracle stories was downright fatuous in view of the fact that it would be extremely difficult to report any case of healing, ancient or modern, without noting the malady, the actions of the healer, and the effect of the cure (which were allegedly distinctive features of the miracle stories).[67] However, Richardson's main point was not to respond piecemeal to the particular arguments of the form critics or to examine the catalog of alleged parallel miracles in the history of religions. The aim of his study was to develop a positive statement of how the miracle stories are presented in the New Testament, showing how they relate to the thought of the Bible. Whereas Bultmann presented the miracle stories as a carry-over into the beliefs of the early church of the obsolete, mythical beliefs of the ancient world generally, Richardson insisted that the stories could not be properly understood apart from the religious ideas of the Old Testament.

Richardson also questioned some of the basic assumptions of form criticism. He saw no need to draw a sharp distinction between the miracle stories and the paradigms, on the assumption that the former were designed simply to impress, whereas the latter were concerned with preaching and instruction. Both alike were the work of the same body of preachers and teachers. There was not the slightest evidence for the existence of a separate body of miracle-story tellers in the early church. In his list of ministries (1 Cor. 12:28), the apostle Paul did not say, "He gave some to be story-tellers." Central to Richardson's case was his contention that "the object of the miracle-stories, no less than of the paradigms, is to awaken saving faith in the person of Christ as the Word of God."[68]

In arguing this case, Richardson was not only challenging a basic assumption of the trend-setting form critics; he was also breaking with traditional apologetics in its assumption that the miracle stories somehow provided objective, historical evidence for the truth of Christian beliefs. Paradoxically, the skeptical form critics and the orthodox apologists shared a common premise—that the miracles were so extraordinary and their circumstances such, that the only possible conclusion that could be drawn was that these events had actually happened and that the one who worked them was divine. But neither the form critics nor the orthodox paid much attention to what the particular miracle stories were saying. The impression is frequently given that one miracle is as good as another, so long as it serves its apologetic purpose in validating the supernatural credentials of the miracle-worker. What Richardson did was to insist that the miracle stories were of a piece with the teaching of Jesus. They were not external, objective proofs of the truth of the Christian revelation; rather, they were themselves part of the Christian message. In saying this, Richardson was laying down an exegetical foundation for the apologetic position that he was to develop later and which we examined in the previous chapter. He was also siding with such writers as F. D. Maurice, B. F. Westcott, A. B. Bruce, and R. C. Trench in the nineteenth century, though of these names only Trench's figures in his discussion.

Richardson questioned the common view that the Fourth Evangelist adopted a different attitude toward the miracles of Jesus from that of the Synoptists. The latter are sometimes said to present the miracles as spontaneous works of compassion, where John saw them as evidences or signs that demonstrate who Jesus is. Richardson commented:

> As against this view, we would draw no such clear distinction between
> the Synoptists and St. John. In all the Gospels Jesus is unwilling to work
> miracles as mere displays, but the motive of compassion is not promi-

nent and certainly is not primary either in the Synoptists or in St. John; in the Synoptists no less than in St. John the miracles are evidence (not to the general public, but only to those who have eyes to see) as to Who Jesus is. This, we shall maintain, is their *raison d'être* in all four Gospels.[69]

Richardson went on to set out the role of miracles in the New Testament in relation to the kingdom of God. He saw a threefold connection: (1) Miracles were manifestations of the powers of the New Age demonstrated in Jesus; (2) they were signs of the kingdom; moreover (3), they should be seen as prophetic signs.

In connection with the thought of miracles as manifestations of the powers of the New Age, Richardson drew attention to the expectation that the Holy Spirit would be poured out in the "last days" (cf. Acts 2:17f.; Joel 2:28f.; Isa. 44:3; Ezek. 1:19; Zech. 12:10). He noted the role of the Holy Spirit and references to the kingdom in the exorcisms of Jesus (Mark 3:22-30; Matt. 12:25-37; Luke 11:17-23) and in Jesus' use of prophecy, "The Spirit of the Lord is upon me . . ." (Luke 4:18f.; cf. Isa. 61:1f.). He also noted Paul's attribution of gifts of healing to the Spirit (1 Cor. 12:7-11; cf. Rom. 15:18f.; Heb. 6:5) and the mission of the disciples in connection with the preaching of the kingdom, healing, and exorcism (Mark 6:7-13; Matt. 9:35-10:23; Luke 9:1-6; 10:1-20). From this, Richardson concluded that "The early church's belief in miracle through the power of the Holy Spirit was an expression of her eschatological faith."[70] Similarly, Jesus' reply to John the Baptist's question whether he was the coming one, in terms of his fulfillment of prophecy (Matt. 11:4f.; Luke 7:22; cf. Isa. 61:1; 35:5f.), leaves no doubt about the intention "to assert that the Messianic Age of the Isaianic prediction had already arrived. The significance of the miracles of Jesus lies in the fact that they are the miracles of the New Age."[71] On the other hand, "Inability to perceive the true significance of His miracles was regarded by Jesus as equivalent to the rejection of His Gospel" (cf. Matt. 11:20f.; 13:58; Mark 6:5; Luke 10:13).[72]

In speaking of the miracles of Jesus as signs of the kingdom, Richardson has in mind such pronouncements as Matthew 12:28: "But if it is by the Spirit of God that I cast out demons, then the kingdom of God has come upon you" (cf. Luke 11:20). There is an implied opposition between the kingdom of God and the kingdom of Satan, which come into open conflict in the exorcisms (cf. Mark 3:34; Matt. 12:25; Luke 11:17). Moreover, Richardson is consciously adopting biblical terminology when he speaks of miracles as signs.[73] The Fourth Gospel repeatedly makes use of the word *sēmeion*, sign, in connection with miracles (John 2:11, 18, 23; 3:2; 4:54; 6:2, 14, 26, 30; 7:31; 9:16; 10:41; 11:47; 12:18, 37; 20:30). But the concept of miracles as signs is by no means confined to John. Acts 2:22 represents Peter at Pentecost as saying: "Men of Israel, hear these words: Jesus of Nazareth, a man attested to you by God with mighty works and wonders and signs which God did through him in your midst . . ." (cf. Acts 10:38). Apart from the quotation from Joel in Acts 2:19, the work "wonders" (*terata*) is never used without the "signs" (*sēmeia*), and even in that passage it is identified with "signs" shortly afterward.

Commenting on Jesus' refusal to perform signs on demand (Matt. 12:38–42; 16:1–4; Mark 8:11–13; Luke 11:16, 29–32; cf. John 2:18–22; 6:30), Richardson observes:

> The attitude of Jesus would seem to have been, on the one hand, the refusal to work wonders to compel belief or to satisfy curiosity, and on the other hand, the insistence that His miracles were truly signs *to those who had eyes to see*. "Having eyes see ye not?" (Mark viii.18). "Blessed are the eyes which see" (Luke x.23). In both these sayings it is surely correct to understand a deep spiritual meaning in the use of the word "see."[74]

In the miracles there is a veiling of the power of God. Indeed, there is a sense in which they are comparable with the parables of Jesus:

> The truth would seem to be that the early Church regarded the miracles as it regarded the parables, namely, as revelations or signs to those to whom it was given to know the mystery of the Kingdom of God (Mark iv.11f.). To the "outsider" the miracles were mere portents, the acts of one wonder-worker amongst many; to the believer they were unique— not so much in outward form or action, as in their inner spiritual significance as *Gesta Christi*.[75]

Richardson went on to develop an impressive argument for understanding the actions of Jesus as prophetic signs. Such signs had been a long-standing part of the Jewish prophetic tradition. They were not intended to prove the message of the prophet, or provide some kind of independent, objective attestation. Rather, they illustrated and embodied in a visible way what the message said orally. Like the verbal message of the prophet, the meaning of the prophetic act required discernment and invited a response. Thus Isaiah went naked as a sign of the foretold desolation (Isa. 20:2f.). Micah rolled in the dust (Mic. 1:10). Jeremiah wore a yoke as a sign that the people should submit to Nebuchadnezzar (Jer. 27:2ff.). Ezekiel predicted the reunion of Judah and Ephraim by joining two sticks (Ezek. 37:15ff.). In New Testament times John the Baptist had dressed in the traditional likeness of Elijah, the expected forerunner of the Day of the Lord (Mark 1:6; cf. 2 Kings 1:8). The Judaean-Christian prophet Agabus bound his own hands and feet with Paul's girdle as a sign of Paul's captivity (Acts 21:10f.). Moreover, John's baptism was a symbolic act of cleansing for the penitent.

Jesus himself stood in this tradition and used symbolic acts to illustrate his teaching. His action of taking a child into his arms (Mark 9:36; cf. 10:13–16) embodied and exemplified the Father's love. He instructed his disciples to shake the dust off their feet as a testimony to the unbelieving cities (Mark 6:11). He dramatized the nonpolitical character of his messiahship by riding into the Holy City in the manner of the prophecy of Zechariah 9:9. His symbolic cleansing of the temple fulfilled the prophecy of Malachi 3:1-3. The Last Supper may also be viewed as a prophetic sign, as may John's account of Jesus washing his disciples' feet (John 13:4ff.).

It is Richardson's contention that the miracle stories are not to be viewed as something independent or accidental to the teaching activity of Jesus. Nor should they be regarded as a series of isolated acts, included in the Gospel narratives as knockdown proofs of Jesus' divinity. Rather, they should be seen as prophetic signs accompanying and embodying his message. Insofar as they do this, they are disclosures of his person. It may be further observed that the connection between miracles as the signs of a prophet is made explicitly in John 6:14: "When the people saw the sign which he had done, they said, 'This is indeed the prophet who is to come into the world!' " The inference is drawn here that the feeding of the five thousand is no ordinary prophetic sign. It is the sign of the eschatological prophet.

Jesus' actions in touching the sick were not, as form critics suppose, instances of the manipulative magical techniques of the thaumaturge. They belong to the sign-language of Jesus. However, in other instances he is said to heal, exorcise, or control nature with a word, without any accompanying bodily action (Matt. 8:16; Mark 1:25; 3:5; 4:39; 5:8; 9:25; 10:52). Richardson observes:

> To anyone familiar with the Old Testament it is immediately obvious that the power of Jesus's word demonstrates His participation in the creative power of God, Who both made and rules the world by the word of His mouth (cf. Gen. i.3, 6, 9, etc.; Ps. xxxiii.6, 9; cxlvii.18, etc.). The significance that Jesus shares with God the characteristic mode of His activity cannot be overstressed. We are moving, not in the atmosphere of Hellenistic magic, but in the wholly opposed thought-world of the Bible.[76]

In the light of these considerations, Richardson proceeds to examine in detail the miracles reported in the Gospels. Far from being a curious tale devoid of religious and moral value, the cursing of the fig tree is seen as a symbolic act of judgment against the background of Old Testament language concerning judgment (Mark 11:12-14, 20-25; cf. Luke 13:6-9; Jer. 8:13; Joel 1:7; Ezek. 17:24; Hos. 9:10, 16f.).[77] The healing miracles are, "as it were, symbolic demonstrations of God's forgiveness in action."[78] They have nothing to do with faith cures in the modern sense. "The modern mind which professes to find belief in the healing work of Jesus easier on account of the successes of modern psycho-therapy is still a long way removed from the New Testament faith in Christ the Saviour."[79] With regard to the exorcisms, Richardson observes that they raised the christological question

> not only because they demonstrate the supernatural power of Christ over the forces of evil (cf. Mark iii. 22-30, Matt. xii. 22ff., Luke xi. 14ff.), but also because the possession by the daemons of superhuman insight enables them to penetrate the mystery, inscrutable to flesh and blood (cf. Matt. xvi. 17), of Who Jesus is. It is a characteristic of the Marcan

tradition that the daemons bear unwilling witness to that very Lordship which the Church proclaims.[80]

The miracle stories clearly have a didactic value for Richardson, though he never suggests that they were invented for that purpose. The two Gentile miracles, the healings of the centurion's servant (Matt. 8:5–13; Luke 7:1–10) and the Syrophoenician woman's daughter (Mark 7:24–30; Matt. 15:21–28), embody God's concern for the Gentiles. The latter story illustrates Paul's conception of the divine economy: "The power of God unto salvation . . . to the Jew first, but also to the Greek" (Rom 1:16; cf. 10:12).[81]

Whole generations of Christian apologists had treated miracles and the fulfillment of prophecy as objective proofs of the divinity of Christ, running, as it were, on parallel but separate tracks. In dealing with the accounts of the healing of the blind and deaf, Richardson pointed out that the significance of these stories lies precisely in the fulfillment of prophecy. In particular, the healing of the deaf-mute, the blind man of Bethsaida, and Blind Bartimaeus (Mark 7:31–37; 8:22–26; 10:46–52) are signs of the arrival of the Day of the Lord (cf. Isa. 29:18; 32:3f.; 42:7; 61:1; Ezek. 24:27).[82]

To use language that has become current since Richardson wrote his study, it may be said that there is a *grammar* of biblical prophetic language, and that the reports of such healings must be read in terms of this grammar. The same may be said of the accounts of Jesus stilling the storm (Matt. 8:23–27; Mark 4:35–41; Luke 8:22–25) and walking on the water (Matt. 14:22–33; Mark 6:45–52; John 6:16–21). Yahweh is the one who makes the storm be still and brings those who sail to their desired haven (Ps. 107:23–30). He is the one who stills the raging of the sea (Ps. 89:9; cf. 29:3; 46:3; 93:3f.; Nahum 1:4), and even tramples the sea (Job 9:8; Hab. 3:15). What is said of Yahweh in these passages is implied of Jesus in the stilling of the storm and his walking on the water. Once more, the grammar of Old Testament theology provides the means for interpreting the miracles. The twin themes of creation and redemption in the Old Testament are refocused in the healing and nature miracles of the New Testament. But Richardson finds a further motif in the stilling of the storm that suggests that Mark drew no sharp distinction between the healing and nature miracles. According to Mark 4:39, Jesus not only "rebuked" the storm, but commanded it to "Be muzzled!" The same two words were used in the exorcism of the unclean spirit in Mark 1:25. To Richardson this indicates the vanquishing of demonic power in both the exorcism and the stilling of the storm. With Hoskyns and Davey he observes that Mark may have seen in the juxtaposition of the exorcism of the Legion of demons (Mark 5:1–20) and the stilling of the storm (Mark 4:35–41) a fulfillment of Psalm 65:7: "Who stilleth the roaring of the seas, the roaring of their waves, and the madness of the peoples."[83]

In Mark 4:41 the awestruck disciples ask, "Who then is this, that even wind and sea obey him?" In Mark 6:50 Jesus greets the terrified disciples using the "I am" formula of the divine name (cf. Exod. 3:14).[84] Richardson observes that "Dibelius is as far as possible from the truth when he speaks of an 'epiphany motive' or says that the Walking on the Water is 'an example of the secularization of the Christian narrative by non-Christian motives.' "[85] When read in terms of the grammar of Old Testament theology, Old Testament statements about Yahweh find specific fulfillment in the actions of Jesus.

The feeding of the five thousand (Matt. 14:13–21; Mark 6:32–44; Luke 9:10–17; John 6:1–15) and the four thousand (Matt. 15:32–39; Mark 8:1–10) are to be understood as acts or signs of the Messiah. They would have been looked for in the expected prophet who would be like Moses (Deut. 18:15ff.; John 6:14). He is greater than both Moses and Elijah (Exod. 16; Num. 11; 2 Kings 4:42–44), for he gives the bread of life. Again the feedings are seen as symbolic acts, bearing parallels with the Last Supper (Mark 6:41; 8:6; cf. 14:22; 1 Cor. 11:23f.). The feeding of the four thousand is not a "doublet" of the first account that was carelessly repeated. Rather, the two accounts symbolize the offering of salvation "to the Jew first, but also to the Greek" (Rom. 1:16), for the second account is set in the Hellenistic region of the Decapolis.[86]

In comparing the outlook of the four evangelists on the subject of miracles,[87] Richardson saw Mark as a theological meditation on the significance of the person and actions of Jesus, based on the stories that he had received. He questioned the common assumption that Matthew sought to heighten the miraculous effect in Mark, since the details that Matthew adds do not really increase the miraculous nature of Jesus' actions. He did, however, see a conscious emphasis on messianic fulfillment (Matt. 8:17; cf. Isa. 53:4f.; Matt. 15:29–31; 21:14) and haggadic features in Matthew's stories. Both Luke and Matthew reproduce most of Mark's miracle stories without substantially altering their meaning, though sometimes they abbreviate them. However, the symbolic use of the stories is less elaborate in Luke. Although Luke does not introduce a new perspective, he has some distinctive material in his account of the draught of fishes, the widow of Nain's son, the woman healed on the Sabbath, the dropsical man healed on the Sabbath, and the ten lepers (Luke 5:1–11; 7:11–17; 13:10–17; 14:1–6; 17:11–19).

Although John introduces no new motives, he stresses the signlike quality of the miracles. Richardson suggests that the fact that John records seven miracles is bound up with the symbolic character of the number seven. Furthermore, each miracle has a symbolic significance. Through all of them runs the theme of the revelation of Christ's glory, though the full truth is known only to those who respond in faith. Otherwise, the signs serve to condemn those who reject them. The changing of water into wine at Cana (2:1–11) is a sign that Judaism must be purified and transformed in order to find its fulfillment in Christ, who as the Son of God brings new life to the world. The healing of the nobleman's son (4:16–54) brings out the nature of true faith, which goes beyond mere curiosity to trust Jesus as the Lord and giver of life. The healing of the impotent man (5:2–9) has affinities with Mark's account of the healing of the paralytic. It deals with the questions of sin and sickness and the Sabbath, and identifies Jesus' work with that of the Father (5:17, 25–29). The feeding of the five thousand (6:4–13) leads to the discourse on the true identity of the bread of life. Jesus' walking on the water (6:15–21) leads to the later theme of Jesus going to prepare a place for the disciples (14:3) and his promise not to leave them desolate (14:18; cf. 16:5–7, 16–22). The healing of the man born blind (9:1–7) elaborates similar synoptic themes and touches on the connection between sin and sickness, which in this case does not exist. However, John elaborates the themes that are only implicit in Mark, that Christ is the light of the world, by which people are led from darkness and error to faith and sight. The raising of Lazarus (11:1–46) illustrates the truth that Christ is the resurrection and the life of all the faithful.

These considerations bring Richardson to the point that we noted when we considered his work in the previous chapter in connection with apologetics. In considering the historical and religious value of the miracle stories, Richardson utterly rejects the suggestion that the miracles of the gospel were "the figments of a legend-loving Christian community." They had in fact a direct connection not only with his ministry but with his crucifixion. "Jesus was not crucified because he taught an ethic of love. . . . It was because Jesus by His signs had demonstrated that He was the resurrection and the life, the fulfillment of Judaism and the hope of the world, that He was put to death."[88] For us today, no less than those of Jesus' day, there is a need to penetrate the incognito of Jesus. For even the miracles are not direct revelations of God that present God immediately to human eyes. The miracles, like Jesus himself, demand interpretation. On scientific grounds it is possible to conclude that something happened. But it is only when we discern in faith the significance of the miracles that we can appreciate them as signs of the kingdom and revelations of the Son of God, so that in believing we may have life in his name (John 20:31).[89]

TRENDS IN CONTEMPORARY CRITICAL STUDY

The years after the Second World War have witnessed an unabated torrent of theological literature, a high proportion of which is concerned with New Testament interpretation. A striking feature of some of it is a curious absence of reference to the miracles of Jesus in works discussing trends in New Testament studies and even christology.[90] Clearly, embarrassment with the whole subject of miracles must be in some measure responsible for this act of conscious or unconscious suppression. But even so conservative a scholar as Donald Guthrie could apparently find no room for a discussion of the theological significance of miracles in his massive, thousand-page *New Testament Theology* (1981).[91]

Other scholars have, however, found an important place for miracles in their studies. Like Alan Richardson, Herman Ridderbos saw the miracles of Jesus as veiled signs of the kingdom of God.[92] In his encyclopedic study,

The Miracles of Jesus (1965), H. van der Loos examined the individual stories against the background of the history of interpretation. His conclusions were also comparable with Richardson's.[93] Jesus manifested himself in both word and deed, and the latter includes miracles. Both word and miracle are functions of the kingdom of God. Miracles occur over and above ordinary events, and against the known order of things. They have a "concealed" character that lays them open to various conflicting explanations. What the believer calls a "miracle" may be ascribed by an unbeliever to "unknown causes." Attempts to explain miracles are the understandable product of the naturalistic and rational desire to reduce the unacceptable manner in which salvation happens in miracles to something that is acceptable. For van der Loos, miracles are "intrahistorical" events that serve as functions of the kingdom of God revealing salvation in particular concrete ways. But they are also "suprahistorical," in that they are acts of God, and as such are signs of his eschatological action. Hence, they have a kerygmatic significance. In miracles creation and future meet together. Like Richardson, van der Loos stresses the role of faith in the discernment of miracles. This is not the faith that periodically entertains the hope that one day all miracles will be explained. It is, rather, the faith that recognizes that ultimately one is faced with the alternative, whether to believe that Jesus performed feats over and above nature, or not to believe.

Van der Loos conceded that at various points the theology of the community and legendary threads of thought may have influenced the form in which the stories were told. But like all human study the results of investigations in these areas always must remain disputable. What is beyond dispute is the order of a new reality in the deeds of Jesus, proclaiming his freedom, power, and love as the Son and Lord sent by the Father.

Whereas Bultmann saw demons as part of the mythical thought-world of the first century, Ragnar Leivestad saw Christ's conquest of the forces of evil as the major theme of the New Testament.[94] James Kallas took this idea even further in his study *The Significance of the Synoptic Miracles* (1961). Kallas welcomed Alan Richardson's achievement in presenting the miracles as organically related to the other parts of Jesus' activity, but he detected a "mortal weakness" in what he believes to be Richardson's stress on theological interpretation at the expense of history.[95] Moreover, Kallas's conception of the kingdom and Jesus' role in it is intended to provide a theological correction to Richardson. Kallas argued that Jesus understood the kingdom in terms of the Book of Daniel, and that this involved a new order, preceded by a cosmic conflict with Satan and the demons. With Richardson he maintained that the miracles have "precisely the same message as the words of Jesus."[96] But this message was not simply one of timeless spiritual truths:

> The Kingdom meant the defeat of Satan, and the recreation, the restoration, of the world that Satan had stolen and subjugated. Thus the command to preach the kingdom was never separated from the command to cast out demons and to heal the sick, from the command to begin

the shattering of Satan's stranglegrip of the fallen creation (Matt. 8:16f.; 9:35; 10:7f.; Mark 6:7, 12f.; Luke 4:17ff.; 8:16f.; 10:1, 9; 13:31f.).[97]

Kallas agreed with Rudolf Otto in saying that the exorcism of demons was the center of Jesus' message, but repudiated Otto's attempt to attribute the maladies described in the New Testament to purely psychological and neurological factors.[98] What God had made good has become sick, demon-possessed, and dominated by Satan. Jesus' message of the kingdom cannot be spiritualized away:

> When we do that, internalize the message and interpret it in existential terms seeing the forces of evil as inner impulses and not as malignant forces acting from the outside, when we try to update and modernize the message of Jesus, relegating this conflict motif to the scrapheap of outmoded thought, then we have lost that which was central and formative in the gospel record.[99]

The nature miracles, Kallas insists, are also to be interpreted in terms of Christ's conflict with demonic forces. Jesus rebuked the wind as he would any other demon, and stilled the sea as he stilled those who were possessed by evil spirits (Mark 4:37–41).[100] Other nature miracles illustrate the rebirth of the creation. The miracle stories, therefore, are not merely accidental to the teaching of Jesus. Insight into their significance calls for a reappraisal of the prevailing fashions in theology that reduce the kingdom of God to spiritual truths, existential experiences of outmoded eschatological concepts.

R. H. Fuller has rightly pointed out that Kallas sometimes overplays his hand, particularly in his dismissal of the symbolic and spiritual significance of miracle stories.[101] He does not appreciate the symbolism of the feeding of the five thousand as an anticipation of the messianic banquet or see how this might be related to his own interpretation of the kingdom. Further, he does not appear to appreciate how Mark deliberately places the cure of the blind man at Bethsaida before the opening of the eyes of the disciples to Jesus' messiahship at Caesarea Philippi (Mark 8:22–30) and that of Blind Bartimaeus after the revelation of Jesus' servant-messiahship (Mark 10:46–52). The symbolic significance of blindness is clinched by Mark 8:18. Fuller sees a fundamental weakness in Kallas's failure to distinguish between various levels in the synoptic tradition—namely Jesus himself, the oral tradition, the primary sources Mark and Q, and the later evangelists Matthew and Luke. In other words, he neglects source and form criticism as the key to exegesis. Clearly the questions that Fuller raises are important ones. Nevertheless, Kallas has drawn attention to an important aspect of both the kingdom of God and the miracle stories in the Synoptic Gospels. Seminal ideas need to be appreciated for what they are rather than be rejected out of hand for not being the same as the mature fruit.

It could hardly be said that the demonic occupies the center stage of scholarly interest, although the researches of Otto Böcher in Germany have explored the pervasive influence of demon possession in the New Testament era.[102] Böcher argues that Jesus' activity as an exorcist is inseparable from his eschatological self-understanding, and that the early church overcame demons through the crucified and risen Lord. Moreover, this triumph was closely connected with baptism. Almost simultaneous with the publication of Böcher's *Christus Exorcista* in 1972 came the report in Britain of the Bishop of Exeter's Commission on Exorcism.[103] In some quarters it was greeted as a deplorable revival of medieval theology. But the need of such a commission is itself testimony to the widely felt influence of the occult and the demonic, and of the need to do something about it.

In his brief examination of exorcism in the New Testament, which opened the report, J. H. Crehan drew attention to the place of exorcism in the world of Palestinian Jewry and the Dispersion.[104] Crehan argued that it was to be expected that the messiah would possess the powers of an exorcist. He further claimed that Matthew, in particular, clearly distinguished between different categories of illness (Matt. 4:24; 12:22; 17:15, 18), and that the attribution to Satan of certain conditions was not simply a case of accommodation to the language of the day about illness. The account of the healing of the lunatic boy in Matthew 17 indicates that the boy had the symptoms of epilepsy, but this does not preclude demon possession as the cause.

Similar views have been put forward by John Richards, John Wilkinson, and others, who argue that a diagnosis of epilepsy in the story of Mark 9:14–27, Luke 9:37–43, and Matt. 17:14–18 does not automatically exclude demon possession as the cause.[105] Epilepsy covers an ill-defined group of disorders characterized by fits or seizures. The case in question may have been an instance of idiopathic epilepsy for which modern medicine knows no cure and for which the cause may have been a spiritual malady. John Richards offers the following comment:

> Had the lad in the Gospel story suffered from symptomatic epilepsy our Lord could only have cured him by an act of healing rather than exorcism, just as he healed the man with an impediment in his speech (Mark 7:32–7) and a blind man (Mark 8:22–5) by the laying-on of hands, but a dumb and a blind *demoniac* by exorcism (Matthew 12:2ff.).[106]

Studies like the report on *Exorcism*, John Richards's *But Deliver Us from Evil* (1974), and the series of articles by evangelical scholars in *The Churchman* on the subject of possession[107] have pastoral concerns as their primary orientation. At the same time they illustrate the role of analogy in interpretation that we have noted throughout this study. Bultmann, like all his skeptical predecessors, used his understanding of the world as his frame of reference for interpreting the ancient world. Because he saw no analogies between his world and the world of the New Testament, he dismissed the latter as mythical. The writers that we have just been considering argue, in effect, that there are analogies between the two worlds and that they mutually illuminate each other. On the periphery of modern medicine and psychotherapy stands the world of the demonic. Its existence and structures throw light on the Gospels. At the same time the Gospels bear witness to one who has conquered the demonic and in whose name demons are expelled today.

The main focus of attention for New Testament scholars of the postwar generation has been form criticism and redaction criticism, and many of the most important discussions of the miracle stories have approached them from the standpoint of the form of the stories and the way that the different evangelists handle them. R. H. Fuller's *Interpreting the Miracles* (1963) did this on a more popular, nontechnical level. While criticizing fundamentalists for taking the New Testament at its face vaue and believing that all the miracles occurred literally as described, Fuller nevertheless agrees with them in saying that both the nature and healing miracles "proclaim to us a God of miracles, a God who acts, who intervenes and interferes in specific events."[108] Miracles cannot be treated as objective proofs or humanitarian examples. "The gospel miracles are not tales of what happened in far-off Palestine two thousand years ago, but proclamations of the works of Christ today."[109]

A study that has attracted considerable interest and endorsement is H. J. Held's "Matthew as Interpreter of the Miracle Stories."[110] Held argues that Matthew's Gospel is a retelling of Mark that abbreviates Mark's account in order to emphasize the themes of christology, faith, and discipleship. Matthew's manner of narration is formal. He omits secondary people and actions, and makes conversation the center of the stories, frequently using catchword connections to express actual relationships in a self-contained pericope. The principle that shapes his miracle stories is that faith and miracle belong together. He brings out more strongly than Mark and Luke the actual circumstances of the faith that saves. These conclusions lead Held to reject the positions of Bultmann and Dibelius. In Matthew's hands, the stories approximate more to paradigms or pronouncement stories, designed to illustrate aspects of christology, faith, and discipleship. Following Schniewind and Schlatter, Held sees the collection of miracle stories in chapters 8 and 9 as having a christological function. He observes that Mark has two groups of miracle stories (Mark 1:21–45; 4:35–5:43) and Luke three (Luke 4:31–5:26; 7:1–17; 8:22–56). Matthew, however, puts them together in a single cycle:

> The similarly-worded verses in Matt. 4.23 and Matt. 9.35 show by their contents (summary account of the activity of Jesus in word and deed) and their position (in the one case before the Sermon on the Mount and in the other immediately after the chapters containing the miracles), that Matthew's purpose in the chapters enclosed by these verses is to portray the double office of Christ: his teaching and his healing activity. His collection of the miraculous deeds of Jesus thus has a Christological function. The evangelist presents Jesus at the beginning of his Gospel not only as the Messiah of the word (in the Sermon on the Mount) but also as the Messiah of deed (by his miraculous deeds).[111]

Held goes on to note four christological themes in Matthew's presentation of the miracle stories: (1) Jesus fulfills prophecy (Matt. 8:17; cf. Isa. 53:4;

Matt. 11:5; cf. Isa. 53:5f.; 61:1) and also the requirements of the law (Matt. 8:4; cf. Lev. 14:2); (2) he is the Servant of the Lord who takes the cause of the helpless, and proves himself with might to be the one who shows mercy, just as Yahweh does; (3) he is the helper and Lord of his community; and (4) he gives his disciples a share in his authority.

In his discussion of the details of Matthew's presentation of the miracle stories, Held seeks to show that Matthew both transmits and interprets the miracle stories. His approach coincides with that of his mentor, Günther Bornkamm, in his handling of "The Stilling of the Storm in Matthew."[112] Bornkamm sees in the story

> a description of the dangers against which Jesus warns anyone who over-thoughtlessly presses to become a disciple: here is, in fact, the Son of Man who has not where to lay his head. At the same time, however, the story shows him as the one who subdues the demonic powers and brings the *basileia* of God and who therefore can also demand and is able to reward the sacrifice of abandoning earthly ties such as stand in the way of the second follower. In this sense the story becomes a kerygmatic paradigm of the danger and glory of discipleship.[113]

Contemporary New Testament scholarship has paid increasing attention to the form of presentation of the miracle stories. Heinrich Greeven's examination of Matthew's account of the healing of the paralytic leads him to conclude that Matthew had a somewhat different intention from Mark and Luke in his presentation of the story.[114] Both of the latter placed greater emphasis on Jesus' missionary activity, but Matthew is more concerned to instruct the community of believers who already believe.

Interest in the tendencies and motifs of the narratives is shared by evangelical, Catholic, and Jewish scholars alike. In the *Festschrift* for George E. Ladd, Ralph P. Martin compared the accounts in Matthew and Luke of the healing of the "centurion's" son/servant.[115] Martin ascribed the difference in the two stories to a difference of motive. "The intention of the evangelists is one of selective emphasis, each writer inserting and highlighting the details which will give point and purpose to his overruling theological *Tendenz*."[116] He saw Luke's account as secondary. His details about the elders and friends were given, not primarily to pick up the theme of the Gentiles' indebtedness to Israel, but to give independent attestation to the Roman's worthiness and humility in the context of Luke's overall concern to endorse the legitimacy of preaching to the Gentiles. Luke wants to demonstrate how the church of his generation came genetically out of "true Israel," of which the Gentile soldier (like Cornelius in Acts 10:34f.) is an illustrious example. This is reflected in the way Luke phrases the Lord's word in Luke 7:9. Matthew's phrasing of the same reply (8:12) emphasizes the failure of Israel to respond to the Messiah's call and claim. In accentuating faith in Jesus' naked word and adding the universalistic observations of Matthew 8:11–12, Matthew was, in effect, championing the Pauline gospel against Jewish and Jewish-Christian particularism. At the same time Matthew was justifying the rejection of Israel that was still insisting on signs (cf. Matt. 12:39; 16:4; Luke 11:29; 1 Cor. 1:22), and in rejecting Jesus had cut itself off from God's purposes. Martin sees two themes developing *pari passu* in Matthew: (1) Gentile interest and inclusion within God's covenant (Matt. 2:1–12; 4:15; 12:18, 21; 13:38; 21:43; 22:9, 10; 28:18–20), and (2) Jewish rejection and exclusion from the kingdom (Matt. 3:9, 10; 8:11, 12; 21:43; 22:7, 8; 27:25). He therefore saw the story as further corroboration of the thesis that Matthew's church was composed of liberalized Jewish Christians who saw that "God's people of the new covenant is the church embracing all nations," because in God's design the gospel produces a church that is "not Jewish-Christian, but universal."[117]

A redaction-critical approach to the saying about the sign of John (Matt. 12:39; 16:4; Luke 11:29), which is commonly traced to the so-called Q source of sayings, presumed to underlie the material common to Matthew and Luke, has been undertaken by Richard A. Edwards.[118] Edwards posits a Q community that rewrote the refusal of a sign in Mark, so as to express its understanding of Jesus' resurrection. In turn, Edwards argues, Luke and Matthew redacted the traditions that they received. Clearly this type of approach to redaction involves considerable skepticism about the historical value of the Gospels in their present form and an equal degree of optimism about what may be speculated about Q and the Q community.

The discernment of motifs also plays a prominent part in Robert Meye's discussion, "Psalm 107 as 'Horizon' for Interpreting the Miracle Stories of Mark 4:35–8:26," which (like Martin's study noted above) appears in the *Festschrift* for George E. Ladd.[119] Meye sees the section as a unity, which begins by posing the question, "Who then is this, that even wind and sea obey him?" (Mark 4:41), but does not give the answer until the completion of the long succession of miracle stories (Mark 8:27–30). Meye's proposal cuts across Bultmann's form-critical skepticism. It rejects the thesis of Theodore Weeden that Mark was engaged in a sharp polemic against a group that glorified in the miraculous, failing to perceive that Jesus' way was the way of humility and suffering.[120] For Meye seeks to show that the miracles have a positive message that is bound up with the way of humility and suffering. Like Alan Richardson, Meye attempts to understand the miracles in the context of the Old Testament, but he thinks that Richardson is wrong in downgrading the element of compassion, for God's gracious compassion and steadfast love in deliverance are fundamental themes of the Old Testament in general and Psalm 107 and the miracles in Mark in particular.

Psalm 107 celebrates the mighty acts of God, experienced by his people, calling on them to praise his redemptive deliverance (vv. 1–2) and concluding with the call, "Whoever is wise, let him give heed to these things; let men consider the steadfast love of the Lord" (v. 43). In between, the psalmist celebrates "four typical experiences of deliverance in which God intervened upon hearing the cry of the people."[121] The parallel between these four types of experience and those exhibited in the miracles recorded in Mark is too great to be accidental. It may be set out in the following tabular way:

1. Deliverance from hunger and thirst in the wilderness
   (Ps. 107:4–9; cf. Mark 6:30–44; 8:1–10, 14–21).

2. Deliverance from darkness and distressing bondage
   (Ps. 107:10–16; cf. Mark 5:1–20; 6:13; 7:24–30).

3. Deliverance from sickness
   (Ps. 107:17–22; cf. Mark 5:21–6:5, 13, 53–56; 7:31–37; 8:22–26).

4. Deliverance from peril at sea
   (Ps. 107:23–32; cf. Mark 4:35–41; 6:45–52).

Meye proceeds to draw attention to further details that Mark and Psalm 107 have in common. In verse 11 God is called "the Most High"; the same title is used in the synoptic tradition only in Mark 5:7. Moreover, the context of both passages is concerned with deliverance from bondage. In the Psalm the sick can take no food (vv. 17–22; cf. Mark 5:43). The theme of God's compassionate, steadfast love is recurrent in the Psalm (vv. 1, 15, 21, 31, 43); it is emphasized particularly by Mark in comparison with Matthew and Luke (Mark 4:38; 5:19; 6:34; 8:2). The call to understanding with which the Psalm concludes (v. 43) is echoed in Mark 8:17, 21. The proclamation of God's redemptive deeds (Ps. 107:1–3, 22, 32) also finds an echo in the proclamation of Jesus' deeds, despite Jesus' command to silence lest the nature of his messiahship be misunderstood (Mark 5:19f., 27, 43; 7:37). The summons of the redeemed from all quarters (Ps. 107:2) has its parallels in Mark 1:37, 45; 3:7f.; and 7:24, 26.

Whereas the Psalm speaks of Yahweh's deliverance directly without reference to human agents, the miracle stories of Mark link Yahweh's deliverance with Jesus, the Son of God, "the incarnate manifestation of the Father."[122] This thought is brought out elsewhere (e.g., Mark 8:38; 9:7; 12:19). The fact that miracles may be performed by false Christs and false prophets (Mark 13:22) in no way detracts from those performed by the true Christ. The works of the true Son of God are works of the Father, whereas the works of others are not.

Meye's line of approach raises many questions. Did Jesus himself view his actions as a fulfillment of the Psalm? Or was it the work of the evangelist's religious imagination, steeped in Old Testament tradition? The Psalm itself is not explicitly quoted in the pericope. May we not see similar themes in other Psalms and other Old Testament passages? The present writer would offer the following tentative comments. The points of similarity between Psalm 107 and Mark's account of Jesus' miracles are too striking to be dismissed as coincidental. The Psalm does indeed seem to provide a horizon or, as I would prefer to say, a frame of reference for interpreting the activity of Jesus. The word "horizon" suggests an all-encompassing boundary, by reference to which one may determine one's position. There are elements in the pericope, like Mark 7:1–23 with its focus on "What Defiles a Man," which, as Meye points out, do "not readily fit into a collection of miracle stories."[123] But this story would fit the frame of reference concerned with cleansing, a theme that also runs through Mark, as will be shown in the concluding chapter of this book. It therefore seems right to see the Psalm as an important factor in interpreting Mark, alongside others.

Meye's argument could, in fact, be extended to include earlier material. If the Psalm provides a key for understanding the deliverance from evil spirits and sickness in chapters 5, 7, and 8, could it not also provide a similar key for chapters 1, 2, and 3? Psalm 107:17 says that "Some were sick through their sinful ways." In response to their cry, the Lord "sent forth his word and healed them, and delivered them from destruction." In Mark 2:5 Jesus says to the paralytic, "My son, your sins are forgiven." This immediately provokes the comment that this is blasphemy: "Who can forgive sins but God alone?" Mark intends his readers to see that there are only two constructions that can be placed on Jesus' utterance. Either he is uttering blasphemy, or he is uttering the word of God. (Perhaps as a subsidiary theme, the words "My son" are intended to be a further indication that Jesus is acting *in loco parentis*, i.e., in the place of the heavenly Father.) Moreover, this section of the Psalm concludes with the call, "Let them thank the LORD for his steadfast love, for his wonderful works to the sons of men! And let them offer sacrifices of thanksgiving, and tell of his deeds in songs of joy!" (vv. 21f.). The account in Mark concludes with an observation that may well seem to echo this: "And he rose, and immediately took up the pallet and went out before them all; so that they were all amazed and glorified God, saying, 'We never saw anything like this!' " (v. 12).

The theme of deliverance from bondage, distress, and destruction is a major theme of the Old Testament. Psalm 107 puts it in sharp focus, making it clear that it is the Lord who is the deliverer. This theme, already introduced in Mark 1 and 2, comes to a climax in Mark 3, where Jesus is accused of casting out demons by Beelzebul. In reply Jesus points to the self-contradiction in thinking that Satan would deliver from himself what is in his possession. It is not Jesus who commits blasphemy, but the accusers who attribute to Satan the activity of the Spirit of God (Mark 3:29f.). Such blasphemers will never be delivered.

If we ask how it came to be that the Psalm influenced Mark in the composition of his Gospel or perhaps Jesus himself in construing his activity in terms of the Psalm, the essential clue may lie in the use of the Psalms in the Jewish lectionary. Michael D. Goulder believes that the Psalms were used in an annual cycle from Nisan. He thinks that Psalm 107 may have been the Psalm for Tishri IV, and that it did indeed influence Mark in his account of the stilling of the storm.[124] Goulder himself sees lectionary function as a much more promising key to understanding the Gospels and their composition than the prevailing fashions in form criticism. However, as a major contributor to *The Myth of God Incarnate*, he would doubtless disclaim any attempt to see the supernatural acts attributed to Jesus in Mark 1–8 as historical.[125] Nevertheless, the question may well be asked how far Jesus himself was influenced by the lectionary in view of his practice of synagogue attendance.

Precise attention to the Jewish world of the first century characterizes the impressive investigations of J. Duncan M. Derrett. Coming from a Jewish background and possessing an unrivaled knowledge of law in the Jewish and ancient world, Derrett, who is Professor of Oriental Laws in the University of London, has thrown new light on incidents in the Gospels. In his discussion "Water into Wine"[126] he offers a more convincing alternative explanation for the miracle at Cana than the alleged desire to demonstrate the superiority of Christ over pagan wine deities, which, in any case, would not have carried much weight with the Jews who first transmitted the story. Derrett suggests that the story be read in the context of Jewish wedding conventions, with the obligation to provide a gift, part of which would be devoted to the wedding feast. The appearance of the disciples at the wedding caused an additional strain on the resources of and potential embarrassment to the bridegroom. Jesus' provision of the wine meets his obligations as a guest and shows solidarity with the groom in not putting him to shame.

The story of the coin in the fish's mouth is not strictly a miracle story.[127] Again the background is Jewish law. Jesus could have claimed exemption from the temple tax on the grounds that he and the disciples were employed in God's service. But the collectors were not rabbis, capable of determining this. To save them from embarrassment and also to avoid drawing on funds that were otherwise committed to God's service, Jesus directed Peter to an item of lost property that, in Jewish law, the finder could keep. For in such a case, the establishment of ownership was out of the question. The fish involved would probably have been the scaleless cat-fish, *Clarias lazera*, an omnivorous predator that the Jew was prohibited from eating, and that no Jewish fisherman would have attempted to catch.

Derrett has also examined the stories of the Syrophoenician woman, the centurion's boy,[128] and the Gerasene demoniac.[129] Whereas form critics are inclined to dismiss the last story as an attempt to heighten the divine claims made by the evangelists on behalf of Jesus, Derrett offers an alternative approach. Although the present form of the story indicates use in Christian liturgy and preaching, Derrett traces its origins to reminiscence. Again Derrett draws on his wealth of knowledge of both Scripture and the ancient world. He sees numerous Old Testament passages (including Exod. 14–15; Pss. 8:7; 68:7; 107:10–16; Isa. 65:1–7; 66:17–20; Zech. 13:2; Nahum 1:4, 11–15) as formative in the story. Although Jesus would have been liable for damage to property under other circumstances, the bestiality implicit in the account (Mark 5:12) required that all affected animals be put to death (Lev. 20:15f.). Pigs, which were a favorite sacrificial animal in Greece and Rome, were destined for sacrifice, the majority of them (Derrett claims) for sacrifice to demons or idols. In terms of Jewish thought, Jesus was not only not liable for damage to the property of others; he had performed a righteous act. Derrett concludes that the episode teaches that, so far as demon-possession was concerned, Jesus was an acknowledged expert, who saw the subjective condition of *possession* as intrinsically hostile to his mission wherever it occurred, whether amongst nominally observant Jews or lapsed Jews (as this one probably was), or gentiles. The mind not prepared to welcome the Holy Spirit, and to take it as a final and exclusive guide, is territory into which the ambassadors of the kingdom must penetrate, land which they must claim for their sovereign.[130]

The kind of approach represented by Meye, Goulder, and Derrett in their different ways recognizes the importance of tendencies and context in the narratives, but departs from a good deal of form criticism with its pre-occupation with pure form. Nevertheless, form criticism continues to influence the study of the miracle stories among both Protestant and Catholic scholars. At this point we can do no more than mention names of authors and their works in the expectation of exploring the relevance of form-critical methods in a sequel to the present study.[131] The same must be said of the relevance of structural analysis,[132] numerous other studies of a more general nature that discuss the miracles of Jesus,[133] and various studies dealing especially with the signs recorded in John.[134] In this sequel, I plan to examine the individual miracle stories in the light of contemporary scholarship and explore their bearing on the Christian faith. In the meantime it is important to notice several currents of thought that would erode the traditional Christian understanding of Jesus.

The first, and perhaps most important, of these currents of thought is the thesis that Jesus belonged to the category of "divine man" *(theios anēr)* in the Hellenistic world. In other words, he was just another charismatic miracle-worker of much the same kind as Apollonius of Tyana. The idea is not exactly new. It was canvassed by the deists and investigated by F. C. Baur. In the 1930s it was elaborated by Ludwig Bieler,[135] and more recently it has been utilized by such scholars as H. D. Betz and Helmut Koester, who see in the Gospels traces of "divine man" christology.[136] Miracle stories and the title "Son of God" are seen as an attempt to invest Jesus with the characteristics of a "divine man." The "divine man" of early Christianity is thought to be the product of the "divine man" of the Hellenistic world assimilated to Old Testament Jewish heroes. In Hellenistic Judaism Moses was deemed to be a Jewish version of the divine man, and this in turn provided a model and impetus for presenting Jesus as the latest and greatest in the succession of "divine men." Some scholars, like Theodore J. Weeden, Sr., have suggested a somewhat more subtle hypothesis, and have seen in the Gospels an attempt to critique the triumphalist christology based on the idea. In particular, Weeden conjectured that this type of christology was associated with the disciples, and that Mark wrote his Gospel, committed to a suffering servant christology, in order to combat triumphalism.[137]

In the past decade the *theios anēr* idea has been subjected to critical scrutiny by David L. Tiede[138] and Carl H. Holladay.[139] W. L. Lane has examined its relevance to Mark's christology.[140] Weeden himself has subsequently conceded that the category "may prove unsatisfactory for describing the Christology and discipleship of Mark's opponents."[141] Both Tiede and Holladay show that *theios anēr* is an imprecise idea. Contrary to assumptions, it was not associated in the sources where it occurs with miracle working. Indeed, Holladay contends that,

> Apart from the expression *theios anēr* itself, in those passages where "language of deification" was employed, there was no visible tendency to authenticate such claims by appeals to miracles or miracle traditions. . . .

> Our fundamental criticism of the use of the expression *theios anēr* in Christological discussions arises from its intrinsic ambiguity. Long before this study, several scholars had already begun to express doubts about the legitimacy and impropriety of using *theios anēr* as a *terminus technicus* or as a concrete, well defined category, but this study has tended to reinforce those doubts. The obvious again needs pointing out: the single word *theios* was capable of *at least* four distinct meanings, with room for intermediate shades, and this fluidity has been amply attested with the Hellenistic-Jewish authors, specifically Josephus and Philo. Thus, because *theios anēr* is automatically capable of *at least* four meanings, including "divine man," "inspired man," "a man, in some sense, related to God," and "extraordinary man," it is less possible to speak without further ado of *a theios anēr* Christology, as if *theios anēr* had only one meaning, especially as if the two notions of divinity and miracle-working were essential ingredients.[142]

It scarcely needs to be added that the term itself is never used in the New Testament. But it is worthwhile to note with Holladay the difficulties of assuming that the Hellenistic milieu of the early church somehow provided a catalyst for producing christological changes that would otherwise have been impossible in a purely Jewish setting. Holladay contends that Hellenization seems, in some instances, to have made it more difficult for Jews to conceive of a divine man. Philo, who used the term *theios anēr*, toned down Moses' activity as a miracle-worker. The more Hellenistic the milieu for the sermons in Acts, the more the portrayal of Jesus as a miracle-worker diminishes. It is present in the Jewish context of the sermons in Acts 2:22 and 10:38, but is absent from the account of Paul's preaching in Athens in Acts 17.[143] This point is in itself further confirmation that the New Testament writers did not look at miracles and fulfilled prophecy as two independent, all-purpose, objective proofs. What distinguished Jesus precisely from others who performed signs and wonders was the fact that his works fulfilled Old Testament prophecy and were in character with the God of the Old Testament. In other words, it is not the Hellenistic world that provides the milieu for New Testament christology but the Judaism that had its roots in the Old Testament. The signs of Jesus were signs that could be properly understood only within such a framework of belief and experience.[144]

From time to time attempts have been made to relate the exorcisms and activity of Jesus to the world of magic. In *Some Notes on the Demonology in the New Testament* (1950), S. Eitrem argued that "the effective background" for Jesus' healings and exorcisms was "contemporary magic."[145] More recently John M. Hull has written a study entitled *Hellenistic Magic and the Synoptic Tradition* (1974).[146] Hull argues that Mark, and more especially Luke, saw Jesus as a Master-Magician, whereas Matthew saw the danger in doing this, and tried to expunge all allusions to magic from his Gospel. The first part of his study consists of a descriptive analysis of magic in the Hellenistic world, drawn mainly from Egyptian papyri dating from the third and fourth centuries A.D., and supplemented by tablets, ostraca, inscriptions, and allusions in ancient writers.[147] It is clear that magicians figured in the world of the early church, but in the writings of Luke, the author whom Hull sees to be most influenced by magic, magicians and exorcists are presented as enemies of Christ and the Spirit (Acts 8:19–24; 13:4–12), and the conversion of the Ephesians resulted in the mass burning of magical books (Acts 19:18f.).[148]

The word of command "Ephphatha" (meaning "Be opened"; Mark 7:34) was not a meaningless incantation like *abracadabra*. It is better understood as a speech-act, comparable with the creative word of the Father, which brings things into being through the divine act of utterance. Jesus' use of spittle (Mark 7:33; 8:23; John 9:6) may be compared with similar uses elsewhere.[149] It does not appear to have been used in an act of conjuration. The context may be that of folk medicine, where spittle had an apotropaic force. F. Fenner has argued that spittle, once it has left the mouth, replaces the "soul of the breath" and becomes "condensed breath."[150] If this is so, Jesus' actions in Mark may be a symbolic way of indicating that the Spirit which filled him was at work in healing the dumb and the blind. In both instances the act was accompanied by the symbolic touch of Jesus' hands and his spoken word. In the Fourth Gospel, Jesus' actions are clearly represented as an act of anointing, using the dust of the ground and his own spittle accompanied by the spoken word.[151]

Whereas Hull sought to make a case for claiming that the Gospel narratives were influenced by magical motifs, he stopped short at speculating whether Jesus thought of himself as a magician. In *Jesus the Magician* (1978) Morton Smith sought to show that involvement in magic is the key that explains the life of Jesus and the Jews' rejection of him. From his study of Christian and Jewish sources, against the background of magic in the ancient world, Smith discerns three pictures of Jesus: (1) the "official portrait" of Jesus Christ, the Son of God, given by the Gospels; (2) "Jesus the magician" as pictured in the hostile sources; and (3) the primitive Christian picture of "Jesus the god" that lies behind the Gospel portrait. "All three are expressions of propaganda and each is inherently incredible, since they all explain the phenomena of Jesus' life in terms of a mythological world of deities and demons that do not exist."[152] These explanations must therefore be discarded, as must obvious inventions like walking on water and multiplying food. But Jesus may well have quieted lunatics, persuaded himself and his disciples that they would appear in glory, and had such confidence in his own powers that he attributed the cessation of a storm to his own word of command. But over and above this, Smith contends that many features of Jesus' behavior are best explained by the hypothesis that Jesus knew and used magic. He concedes that he cannot draw a sharp line between religion and magic, or attempt to define magic in the abstract.[153] Nevertheless, he sees numerous parallels between the Gospels and magical practices, and attributes the absence of positive identification in Christian sources to sustained efforts at censorship.

Both Celsus and Jewish sources claim that Jesus learned magic in Egypt. Smith is inclined to see Matthew's account of the flight of the holy family to Egypt (Matt. 2:13–23) as an implausible cover-up, designed to counter such allegations.[154] He finds implications of magic in the descriptions of Christianity given by secular historians.[155] Further, he sees magical associations in various artifacts and spells dating from the second century A.D. onward,[156] which he takes to be confirmations of his contention that Christianity was bound up with magic from the beginning. Indications of magic are detected in the Gospels themselves:

> The gospels' story of the descent of the spirit is matched by the outsiders' charge, "he has a demon." Here we have contrary evaluations of substantially the same supposed "fact." The gospels' myth of the descent of the spirit has several points in common with magical texts for much the same purpose—the heavens opened, the bird as a messenger or spirit, the result, that he is made "the Son." Such a group of agreements makes it seem that the gospel story came from a person whose imagination was shaped by knowledge of magical texts or ceremonies. Whether or not this person was Jesus is uncertain.[157]

Smith sees parallels with magic in the title "son of God."[158] But, "the clearest evidence of Jesus' knowledge and use of magic is the eucharist, a magical rite of a familiar sort."[159] Smith finds independent confirmation in Celsus's account of Jesus for accepting the main outline of the life and passion of Jesus that is given in the Gospels. What gives coherence to the picture of Jesus is that it fits that of a magician.

There is a sense in which those who place a different construction on the Gospels may feel indebted to Morton Smith's work. This arises from the way in which he forces his readers to recognize the strong element of the demonic in the events associated with Jesus. Each generation is inclined to patronize the naiveté of its predecessors. Albert Schweitzer taught his generation to smile at the simplistic picture of the moral teacher painted by the nineteenth-century liberals. But the eschatological and existential Jesus of twentieth-century scholarship is sealed in a kind of invisible, airtight container that prevents him from having any real contact with the demon-possessed world of the first century. In our technological Western world we fail to appreciate the fine but real line between religion and magic. Thus, we are apt to miss the confrontation presented in the Gospels, and in so doing we may miss the full force of the temptations of Jesus (with their inducements to dabble in magic and the demonic) and the accusations running through the Gospels that Jesus was in league with Satan.

In a curious way Morton Smith resembles Albert Schweitzer. The latter made an impressive case for interpreting Jesus in terms of thoroughgoing eschatology, but declined to believe that eschatology. Smith sees the pervasive influence of magic, but gives no credence to it. Magic belongs to the scrap heap of obsolete ideas, and functions in the book as the principal means of discrediting Jesus, the Gospels, and Christianity. In this single-minded *tour de force*, Smith tends to obscure the fact that the sources on which he builds his case for Jesus' indebtedness to magic belong to different ages, which are all considerably later than the Gospels. Just as the Gnosticism that Bultmann believed to have provided the New Testament with many of its key concepts is now widely recognized to be itself indebted to Christianity for these ideas, so the same may be said of the magical texts to which Smith appeals. Clearly magic existed for centuries before Christianity, but it also drew on Christianity. Evidence of this process is apparent in the Acts of the Apostles, where the professed convert, Simon Magus, sought to acquire the power of the Holy Spirit for his own practice of magic (Acts 8:19–24). Before they can be used as evidence of Christian borrowing from magic, it needs to be shown that the magical texts of the Christian era were not themselves products of the syncretism that assimilates Christian terms and ideas to magical practices.

In a sense, Morton Smith's argument is an elaborate statement of the charge that, according to the Gospels, was brought against Jesus from the start, namely that his actions were evil, that he was demon-possessed and even in league with Satan (Mark 2:7; 3:20–30; Matt. 9:34; 10:25; Luke 11:19f.; John 7:20; 8:48–59; 10:19–39).[160] Perhaps the greatest service that Smith's book can perform is to state very forcibly the question, "By what power did Jesus act?"

An answer to this question that is very different from Smith's has come from the Jewish scholar Geza Vermes, in his book *Jesus the Jew* (1973). Vermes observes that "The representation of Jesus in the Gospels as a man whose supernatural abilities derived, not from secret powers, but from immediate contact with God, proves him to be a genuine charismatic, the true heir of an age-old prophetic religious line."[161] In particular, Vermes sees affinities between Jesus and Honi the Circle-Drawer and Hanina ben Dosa.[162] The former was so called because he once drew a circle, stood inside it, and successfully interceded for rain. The latter was a Galilean charismatic of the first century A.D., who is said to have survived a poisonous snake-bite, healed at a distance, interceded for rain, and delivered people from physical peril, especially that caused by evil spirits. Hanina lived in total poverty like Jesus, but, unlike him, was married. Vermes sees in Jesus, Hanina, and the Hasidim generally a lack of interest in legal and ritual affairs and a corresponding moral concern. The charismatics' informal familiarity with God and confidence in the efficacy of their words brought them into conflict with the Pharisees and staunch upholders of institutional religion. Vermes disclaims, however, that the discovery of resemblances between Jesus as representative of charismatic Judaism implies that Jesus was simply one of them and nothing more.[163] Clearly, Vermes's interpretation of Jesus completely cuts across the magical interpretation of Morton Smith. However, if comparison with first-century Jewish charismatics serves to illuminate the background and tradition out of which Jesus came, it also serves to emphasize the differences between Jesus and his contemporaries.[164]

V

Postscript:
A Question of Perspective

10

CHRISTIAN APOLOGETICS AND MIRACLES

The aim of this postscript is not to attempt the impossible by offering a simple summary of nineteen centuries of involved and often bitter argument. It is rather to offer some personal reflections on the state and shape of the question of Jesus' miracles. We shall look at it from two perspectives: in the present chapter we shall examine the place of miracles in Christian apologetics, and in the final chapter I shall make some suggestions concerning the place of the Gospel miracles in New Testament interpretation.

PERSPECTIVES AND EVIDENCE

Early on in the present century Reinhold Seeberg made the observation that "Miracle was once the foundations of all apologetics, then it became an apologetic crutch, and today it is not infrequently regarded as a cross for apologetics to bear."[1] Broadly speaking Seeberg was right, but it would be an oversimplification to divide church history into three successive stages characterized by increasing lukewarmness on the subject of miracles. It would be equally naive for modern man to think that miracles were somehow much easier to accept in the ancient world than they are today. If miracles were as commonplace in antiquity as we popularly assume, they would hardly have counted as miracles at all and would have been indistinguishable from the normal course of events. As a matter of fact, miracles in the Old Testament are very few and far between. In those that are mentioned, stress is frequently laid on Yahweh's control of nature (as in the plagues on Egypt and the crossing of the Red Sea) rather than on violations of nature.[2] If there was a difference between ancient and modern attitudes toward miracles, it did not turn on actual testimony to the miraculous. Despite the vast difference between modern man's understanding of nature and science and that of his ancient counterpart, the miraculous was still miraculous for ancient man. It differed radically from his expectations based on the normal course of nature. The basic difference between the believer and the skeptic was then, as it is now, a difference between frames of reference and frameworks of belief.

The shifts of attitude of which Seeberg speaks have less to do with the actual testimony of the miracle stories (which remains what it has been since the Gospels were written) than with the frame of reference within which we interpret the stories. We recognize things and people only when we relate them to what we know (or think we know) already. The same applies to the discernment of truth, meaning, and significance. All perception and knowledge involve interpretation. What we call facts are items of information that we have processed within our schemes of reference. In our knowledge of the past, whether it be what happened last week, last year, or two thousand years ago, we do not have direct access to the events themselves. History writing is not an action-replay of the actual events. Rather, it is a construct in verbal form, placed by the historian on a heterogeneous body of data in the light of the frames of reference within which he is operating.[3] There is always a reciprocal relationship between data and frames of reference. What Seeberg was attempting to describe was bound up with shifting attitudes toward God, the supernatural, and nature in general, which in turn affected attitudes toward miracles in particular.

From time to time in this study attention has been drawn to the role that analogy plays in discussion about miracles. It is perhaps the most decisive factor for both the skeptic and the believer. For it is only by considering the analogies between miracle stories and our frames of reference (or the lack of them) that judgments about their truth are made. Long before Ernst Troeltsch had formulated his views on analogy as a methodological principle in history, Hume and Spinoza had employed the basic idea in their critiques of miracles. The same could be said of skeptics through the ages. At bottom the skeptical rejection of miracles turns on the claim that miracles bear no analogy to the common uniformities of experience on which future expectations are based. In practice, this means that, having once settled his convictions about the possible, the skeptic demands a great deal of evidence and argument in order to change them. He more readily attributes unverifiable reports of miracles to lack of knowledge on the part of the reporter, credulity, the inflamed religious imagination, or sheer deceit, than allow them to shake his convictions.

Modern skeptics are perhaps less inclined to dismiss the historicity of all alleged miracles than were their counterparts in previous centuries. More is known today about psychosomatic factors in illness and healing. Modern medicine recognizes the phenomenon of remission. But in such cases the skeptic simply changes his categories. He grants the possible facticity of the report, but at the price of denying its miraculous character. If no explanation is at hand, the event is relegated to the twilight domain of anomalies awaiting elucidation by the onward march of science. These conclusions are bound up with two convictions. One is that reports of miracles are so improbable that it is a near certainty that they cannot be taken at anything like face value. The other is that miracles are violations of the laws of nature; therefore, if natural and other factors can be identified, they cease to be miracles. If such factors cannot be identified, the facticity of the event is denied. The result is a heads-I-win-tails-you-lose argument.

In some respects, the thought processes of the believer are similar to those of the skeptic. He too has his settled convictions about reality that determine his views about possibility and truth. Indeed, it is only on the basis of his experience of the uniformities of nature that he is able to make claims about God's control of events and the possibility of miracles. For unless there is a background of normal uniformities, one cannot identify at all anything different. The very idea of a miracle presupposes both a uniformity of events and the occurrence of something so unexpected and unusual that it defies explanation in terms of nature taking its normal course. By the very nature of the case, miracles are not the kind of recurrent events on which one could build scientific theories and projections. In fact, it is part of the believer's case that miracles would not occur at all, but for the intervention of God.

Sometimes Christian apologists have spoken as if they could first establish the objective facticity of miracles and then proceed to demonstrate their connections with God. Miracles are then seen as some kind of objective authentication of the apologist's belief-system. This procedure is a dubious one, fraught with difficulties; and it is certainly questionable whether anyone in the Bible thought of miracles in this way. Usually the apologist is selective in the miracles that he chooses to use. He tends to prefer cases of healing to those of miraculous feeding or control of the elements, as the former are *prima facie* deemed more credible in the light of psychosomatic knowledge. But in making this move, the apologist lays himself open to the retort that there is nothing supernatural about such a case. It could simply be another mystery of nature's marvels.

In the case of the miracles reported in the Gospels we have to acknowledge that they are *reports*. They are not events to which we have direct access. An interval of nearly two thousand years separates us from them. We may, of course, peruse the reports and ask questions about their transmission and veracity. But the existence of five thousand manuscript copies of the Greek New Testament does not in itself guarantee the truth of the reports any more than five thousand copies of a newspaper would guarantee the truth of a front-page story. In the case of the Gospels we have no direct access to the people involved. We cannot cross-check their stories with outside sources, or examine the previous and subsequent case histories of those who were healed. At most we have only four accounts that were clearly not always independent, and even then they do not always give the same stories. If the believer says that he believes the reports because they are contained in the divinely inspired Scriptures, or even because he believes in the general trustworthiness of the authors of Scripture, he is believing the miracle stories because of Scripture rather than Scripture because it is accredited by miracles.

From this standpoint the attempt to base Christian faith on the miracle stories of the Gospels might appear a forlorn undertaking. But I would agree with Alan Richardson's observation that the alternative to the miracle-working Jesus of the Gospels is not the ethical teacher of liberal theology but sheer historical skepticism. There is no way by which we can detach the miracle stories from the Gospels and get back to a non-miracle-working Jesus. I would also agree with the argument propounded by Richard Swinburne concerning the importance of inclining factors in assessing items of historical evidence.

If we believe that an alleged occurrence is compatible with our overall view of how things are, the way they work, and with what we believe about such-and-such a person, we need only a comparatively slight amount of evidence in order to give credence to it. Indeed, a great deal of history is of this character, and it is on this type of reasoning that the outcome of many court cases depends. For some events, like the outbreak of the Second World War, there is obviously an abundance of evidence. But the more specific the question, the more the historian has to renounce multiple attestation and rely on his interpretation of single documents. The issue then becomes one of how well the interpretation fits the wider body of overall accepted ideas.

The same is true in the case of the Gospel stories about Jesus. It is not a case of balancing conflicting testimonies against each other. It is rather a matter of asking how the testimony to miracles fits our overall view of reality. Here again analogy plays a decisive part. It has long been apparent that the older, hard evidentialism that tried to treat miracles as solid, objective, incontrovertible evidence of divine authenticity was in fact somewhat simplistic. We do not have to look far in the writings of the evidentialists before we find them making all kinds of theological presuppositions about the nature of God and his purposes for the world in order to explain the feasibility of the miracle stories. This is true of the doyen of British evidentialists, Archdeacon Paley, and also of such Americans as Archibald Alexander, B. B. Warfield, and their successors. But equally the skeptic approaches the same miracle stories with presuppositions that affect his reading of them. Whether we take a skeptical or a believing attitude to the miracle stories, we have to recognize a reciprocal relationship between our view of the stories themselves and our wider view of reality. It has now become commonplace in philosophy to observe that all facts are theory-laden. Nowhere is this more apparent than in our attitudes toward the miracle stories of the Gospels.

A number of writers take the view that one must settle one's overall wider view of reality first and then deal with the miracle stories accordingly. Clearly this is what David Hume was doing in the eighteenth century, and it is what other skeptics, including Bultmann, have done in our own day. A major difficulty with this attitude arises from the fact that, once adopted, nothing is allowed to count against it. Nothing new can be admitted. The evaluation of historical testimony to the contrary is settled in advance. On the other hand, Christian apologists like C. S. Lewis and Norman L. Geisler

stress prior commitment to a theistic world view as the prerequisite for identifying, and thus for believing in, miracles. The impression may well be given
that here, too, the question is settled in advance, and no empirical evidence
could count against the apologist's prior belief-commitments.

To my mind, the procedure is much less cut and dried than the apologists
of both faith and skepticism appear to admit. They are apt to give the impression that people go through a phase in life during which they work out
their world views. Once this has been achieved, all that remains is to clear
up details. No doubt people do go through such phases. But only those whose
thoughts remain petrified do not modify and amplify their world views as
they grow in experience and insight. Perhaps it is the occupational hazard
of the apologist to become so engrossed in defending his position that he
might not notice things that could cause him to change his mind.

It is both an oversimplification and a questionable move to claim that
we cannot recognize miracles without a logically prior commitment to the
existence of God, especially if such a commitment is based on natural
theology. It may be that some people find convincing the arguments of natural
theology as a prior step to faith. So far as I can see, however, natural theology
is more often used in order to provide some kind of reinforcement for resolving questions that have arisen once an initial commitment has been made.
Similarly, Hume's arguments against miracles and his arguments against the
existence of God were developed as a defense of the skepticism he had already
adopted.

In Chapter Eight we noted some of the difficulties in moving from a
natural theology based on general arguments to a Christian theology based
on the Bible. We need not repeat them here, except to draw attention to the
leap of faith required to get from one to the other, especially when the God
of natural theology is expected to provide an adequate basis for believing
in the miracle-working God of the Bible. However, the kind of critique of
naturalism that C. S. Lewis undertook is probably best seen as an attempt
to highlight the inadequacies of naturalistic materialism as a comprehensive
world view, in order to prepare the ground for presenting the cogency of
the Christian view of God, based on the Bible.

For many of those who have come to believe in miracles, the question
is not a three-step process, one that begins by establishing the existence and
character of God on general grounds, then seeks to identify the God of the
Bible with such a being, and finally fits Jesus and the miracles into this
framework. It is more a matter of finding the miracle-working God of the
Bible as the One who answers our deepest human needs in Jesus Christ. In
such a case, the question of the existence of God is not logically prior to
that of Jesus who works miracles. It is a matter of a growing apprehension
of God in Christ through the Holy Spirit. The way of the Gospels is the way
of following a path by which the Son makes known the Father and the Father
illuminates the Son. The point of departure is not necessarily a committed

conviction about the existence of God. It may be some deep human need that finds an answer in some incident, a saying, or a story and in turn becomes a means of focusing our thoughts about God, Christ, and the miracles.

As I read the Gospels, the miracle stories were not intended by the evangelists to provide objective, extrinsic proofs of the divinity of Jesus and the authenticity of his teaching. They were told to enable those who heard them to focus on the Father through the Son and the Son in relation to the Father. The process of understanding them is not like that of erecting a two-story building in which the second story (christology) is built on top of the first story (doctrine of God). It is more like a focusing process in which the Father and the Son are progressively brought into focus as the story unfolds. Both the Father and the Son may be initially out of focus. To begin with, the reader may have only the most inchoate ideas about God. He or she may be willing to acknowledge his existence only hypothetically and tentatively. The miracle stories, like the accounts of Jesus' teaching and other actions, contribute not only to our understanding of Jesus but also to our understanding of God.

When viewed in this light, the miracles of Jesus are as much a manifestation of the incarnation of God as are the teaching and other actions of Jesus. To some this might seem to be an apologetic retreat. To me this is not a loss but a positive gain. From time to time we have observed how the evidentialist position of many apologists turned out, on closer inspection, to be so qualified as to be a form of presuppositionalism. The result is more like an exposition of the truth conditions that would have to obtain in order to regard the reports of miracles as factual. As such the exercise is valuable, but it is not quite the same as what the evidentialists appear to think it to be. Moreover, the evidentialist approach of former days appears to have assumed that signs and proofs were the same. But a sign is not the same as a proof. It is never completely free from ambiguity. It is a pointer, an indication. As such, it falls short of conclusive demonstration. The miracles recorded in the Gospels serve as indicators, summoning a response of insight, faith, and obedience.

Furthermore, there is a difference between seeing a sign for oneself and reading a report of it. Jesus' contemporaries were confronted by the signs he wrought, according to the witness of the New Testament (John 15:24; 20:30; Acts 2:22; 10:38). We today are not so confronted; rather, we are confronted by reports of those signs. We are not in a position to verify like the onlookers whether the man said to be born blind in John 9 was really born blind and healed by Jesus. This story, like the other miracle stories, comes to us as a report of a sign, and not as some kind of irrefutable, objective demonstration. It invites us to make a response to Jesus and revise our views of God and reality as a precondition to further insight.

There is another point that apologists over the ages do not seem to have fully appreciated. From the early Fathers onward, miracles and fulfilled prophecy have been appealed to as two parallel, but separate, objective proofs of Christian truth-claims. But in the New Testament itself miracles and prophecy were not two independent and unrelated tracks of arguments. Moreover, the miracles of Jesus were not simply to be differentiated from those of others by being bigger, better, and more authentic. As we noted in the previous chapters in connection with the so-called "divine man" christologies, the appeal to the miracles of Jesus belongs specifically to the context of the proclamation of Jesus among the Jewish people. Within that context, the miracles of Jesus were not all-purpose signs, comparable with, but greater than, those of other miracle-workers. They were signs that fulfilled messianic prophecy and works that accomplished the work of the Father. The latter may be said to be the characteristic emphasis of the Fourth Gospel (cf. John 4:34; 5:17, 19-29, 36; 6:27-40; 9:3f.; 10:25, 32f., 37f.; 14:10-12; 15:24; 17:4; 20:30f.). The theme that the miracles of Jesus were the fulfillment of messianic prophecy is central to the message of the Synoptic Gospels. I shall argue later on that this is what Mark sees as the point of John the Baptist's prophecy as recorded in Mark 1:8. Luke's account of Jesus reading in the synagogue at Nazareth from the book of Isaiah the prophecy concerning the Spirit of the Lord anointing the Messiah to perform his works, sets the context of the teaching, healing, and all the other works of Jesus (Luke 4:18f.; cf. Isa. 61:1f.). Matthew's story of Jesus' reply to John the Baptist's question whether he was the coming One makes a similar point. Jesus' answer did not simply appeal to the stupendous nature of his works, but to the character of those works as fulfillment of prophecy (Matt. 11:5; cf. Isa. 35:5f.; 61:1; Luke 7:17f.). The actions of Jesus focus on prophecy, and prophecy focuses on the actions of Jesus. Both focus not only on the identity of Jesus but also on the identity of the Father.

MIRACLES AND THE RESURRECTION

In the present study I have deliberately left to one side the virgin birth and the resurrection of Jesus. The reason for this is that our concern has been with the miracles that were said to be wrought by Jesus rather than those that were, so to speak, wrought upon him. In the final chapter I will comment on the conception stories in Matthew and Luke. In the meantime, one or two observations may be made concerning the place of the resurrection in the New Testament. First, we may repeat the observation made in Chapter Eight in connection with John Warwick Montgomery's view of the resurrection of Jesus. The New Testament writers do not argue, as some of the church fathers did, that Jesus rose from the dead because he was divine, and because what is divine cannot die. Characteristically they speak of Jesus being raised from the dead or being raised by the Father (cf. Acts 2:24; 4:10; 10:40; 1 Cor. 15:4, 12ff., 20, 23, 38; Gal. 1:1; etc.), or even by the Spirit of holiness (Rom. 1:4).[4] The point that we are making is made in the interests of trying to discern the thrust of New Testament apologetics. The resurrection of Jesus is the ultimate vindication by God the Father of Jesus, whom he had attested by signs, wonders, and the Holy Spirit during his lifetime (cf. Acts 2:22, 36; 10:38, 42f.).

This last point is heavily underlined by the circumstances of Jesus' death, which in turn throws into sharp relief the alternative constructions that may be placed on Jesus' person. In terms of the Law, the only construction that could be placed upon Jesus' death on the cross was that he was under the curse of God (Gal. 3:13; cf. Deut. 21:23). The clinching factor in Jesus' condemnation was, according to Matthew 26:65 and Mark 14:64 (cf. John 10:36), his claim to be the messianic Son of God, which to the high priest was an act of blasphemy. In the Gospel narratives, charges of blasphemy dated from the very outset of Jesus' ministry (Matt. 9:3; cf. Mark 2:7). Almost as early was the charge that Jesus was in league with Satan or was demon possessed (Matt. 12:22-30; cf. 9:34; Mark 3:22-27; Luke 11:14-23; John 7:20; 8:48, 52; 10:20). King Herod may well have believed that Jesus was practicing necromancy (Mark 6:14; cf. Matt. 14:1; Luke 9:7ff.; cf. Mark 8:28) by conjuring the spirit of John the Baptist. Blasphemy in the name of the Lord was a capital offense (Lev. 24:16). The use of the divine name in magic and unlawful cursing were likewise worthy of death (Exod. 20:7; Deut. 5:11). So, too, was dabbling in magic, the occult, and alien divinities (Deut. 13:1-18). This probably explains the oath "Jesus be cursed" (1 Cor. 12:3), which may well be an expression of the attitudes of official Judaism to Jesus that had surfaced in Corinth.

These observations may seem to have taken us some way from the questions of the role of the resurrection in Christian apologetics. The point of them, however, is to show what was at stake in the stance of contemporary, official Judaism and in early Christian apologetics. To the official Judaism of Jesus' day, Jesus was a blasphemer who dealt in the occult and who was thus rightly put to death, especially if his activities might prompt an unfortunate clash with the Roman authorities. Perhaps the Christian church has never fully appreciated the importance of Deuteronomy 13 for the official Jewish understanding of Jesus. It provides the all-important clue to the attitude of the Jewish leaders. The decision to get rid of Jesus was not prompted simply by envy and malice. In their eyes Jesus was a messianic pretender and false prophet who sought to justify his deviant teaching and practices by signs and wonders.[5] To the Jewish leaders, signs and wonders were proof of *guilt* providing clear-cut evidence (if only they could get competent witnesses to testify) that would justify the purging of evil from the midst of the people of God. In the apostolic preaching, the resurrection of Jesus was God's vindication and exaltation of the One in whom God (and not Satan) had been active all along.

Christian apologists have rightly appealed to the resurrection of Jesus as a historical event, and as such a cornerstone of Christian faith.[6] It figures in the New Testament not as one miracle alongside the others but as the seal on all that Jesus was and is. It is supported by testimony, but it is also the *raison d'être* of the church. Without it, the Christian faith would be in vain and the Christian representation of God would be a misrepresentation (1 Cor. 15:14-15). It is the fact that presupposes the entire New Testament and the existence of the church. In relation to the other miracles, the New Testament writers do not think of the resurrection as the supreme test of credibility for all miracles. They do not argue, as some modern apologists appear to argue, that if God could pull that off, then he could easily pull off all the rest. Their thought is, rather, that God's raising of Jesus shows conclusively that all the other activities of Jesus were also the work of God. The resurrection of Jesus is related to the miracles of Jesus in the sense of identifying and confirming the truth that "God was with him" (Acts 10:38).

For this reason I would express reservations concerning Pannenberg's christology "from below" and the precise part that the resurrection plays in his thought.[7] Pannenberg rightly sees the resurrection of Jesus as a historical event, accessible to the historian in a manner comparable to the way in which other events in history are accessible. He sees it as an event that, nevertheless, bursts the analogies of everyday experience and that therefore opens up new perspectives.[8] With this I find myself in full agreement. At the same time, Pannenberg's christology "from below" appears to demand the suspension of all judgment concerning God's activity in Jesus until after the resurrection. At that point a christology "from above," developed from God's perspective, is allowed to take over.

A major difficulty about such a two-phase approach to christology arises from the fact that nothing can be apprehended and described from a standpoint of absolute neutrality. The original disciples of Jesus were as much "below" after the resurrection as they were before it. They were obliged to use the conceptual tools of their everyday language to testify to the risen Christ in much the same way that they did to describe his actions before the resurrection. Words belong to language, and language has its grammars. Nothing can be described or discussed apart from them. Moreover, perception is never simply a matter of taking a look and seeing. We do not describe things, events, and people merely on the level of surface phenomena. The acts of recognition and description involve making judgments about what lies behind appearances. In a sense, these acts involve making judgments as it were "from behind" as well as "from below" and "from above." Thus, when people in the Gospels identified Jesus with "the Son of David," "Elijah," "one of the prophets," "the Christ," or "Beelzebul," they were reaching beyond what they saw in order to identify it in terms of a category and a framework of interpretation.

Such activity did not begin with the resurrection. It is part of the normal process of recognition. There are times, of course, when the wrong categories and frameworks are applied. There are other times when people are uncertain as to the appropriate category and framework. They may go backward and forward between conflicting ones. They may need more information and more thought to arrive at a more appropriate judgment. But in no case is it a matter remaining with surface descriptions.

What the resurrection does in the apologetics of the New Testament is not to introduce the transcendent element of the divine presence for the first time. Nor does it imply that God's presence in Jesus was previously obscure or utterly ambiguous. Rather, it confirms the identity of God's personal presence in Jesus, and thus vindicates him and the faith of those who followed him. In short, it could be said that the christology "from above," associated with the resurrection, served to confirm and clinch the earlier christology "from above," which the followers of Jesus had apprehended with increasing sureness as they saw and heard Jesus, and as they walked with him. The same may be said of the experience of the Spirit at Pentecost. The church's experience of the Spirit was a confirmation that the Spirit they knew was the same Spirit that filled Jesus and was the power behind Jesus' acts (cf. Acts 2:22 and 10:38 with 1:8; 2:33; 11:16; Luke 4:18; John 20:20).

VIOLATIONS AND CONTINGENCY

We shall return to the role of the Spirit in our discussion of the place of miracles in New Testament interpretation. But before we leave the question of Christian apologetics and miracles, I must comment on the question of whether miracles should be viewed as violations of the laws of nature. Some writers have seen the essence of miracle to consist in the fact that a miracle is a clear-cut violation of the laws of nature, and yet empirically certain. David Hume, on the other hand, regarded the idea of a violation of the laws of nature as tantamount to a self-refutation. Some thinkers have drawn a distinction between the violation concept of miracle and the coincidence or contingency concept. In the latter case there is no obvious violation of nature, but rather an ordering of events that indicates gracious, purposive activity of a higher order. From time to time, apologists have suggested that miracles were somehow instances of natural processes that were speeded up. Among those who have made this suggestion was C. S. Lewis, who assigned such miracles to the "old creation," and other miracles to the "new creation."

For myself, I do not think that the idea of miracles as the acceleration of natural processes really works. In any case, we are still left with a miracle. We have not explained what happened. Moreover, we have to recognize that it is one thing to say that fish are daily multiplied in the sea and wheat grown in abundance in the fields. It is another thing to say how dead fish could multiply on land and loaves multiply without benefit of planting the seed, growing period, harvesting, and baking. In short, such explanations do not really help. Where miracles of this sort are believed, they must be believed as mysteries or not at all.

It seems to me that the distinction between miracles of the "old creation" and miracles of the "new creation" is not as helpful as it might appear to be at first sight, if it is invoked as an explanation of the nature miracles. If anything, the so-called nature miracles of Jesus would seem to belong to the "new creation" rather than to the "old." Clearly, many of Jesus' activities, even on the most orthodox of interpretations, had a contingent aspect. He ate, he walked, he slept, he talked, he touched people. Such activities belong to the realm of cause and effect. What the miracles do, however, is to focus attention on the redemptive Creator who is present in his creation. (Much the same could be said of Jesus' teaching, which, in speaking to our human condition, draws us to the One who created man and redeems him.)

In trying to define miracles it is safest to begin with Augustine's open-ended definition of a miracle as "whatever appears that is difficult or unusual above the hope and power of them who wonder." In a similar vein, C. S. Lewis offered a useful, rule-of-thumb definition of a miracle as "an interference with Nature by supernatural power." If we start with a definition of miracles on these lines, we avoid putting ourselves in the invidious position of identifying divine activity only with those instances where nature appears to be set aside and no explanation at all is possible. There is a double danger with such a view. It banishes God from the normal, and it suffers from the same weakness as the old God-of-the-gaps apologetics. If God is to be found only in the gaps of our natural knowledge, he progressively dies the death of a thousand explanations, as science gradually fills those gaps.

I think that C. S. Lewis's instincts were sound in deterring him from seeking a basis for the miraculous in what the layperson might imagine to be the random universe of quantum physics. The universe is not open because ultimately it is chaotic at the center. It is open in the sense that it is a contingent universe that has a place for personal activity both within its structures and at its source. Lewis was not alone in seeing that vague, uninformed appeals to modern physics were really a cul-de-sac for the Christian apologist. More recently T. F. Torrance has observed that

> we are to think of the miraculous acts of Jesus within the limits, conditions, and objectivities of our world, not as involving in any way the suspension of the space-time structures which we call "natural law," far less implying the abrogation of the God-given order in nature they express, but rather as the re-creating and deepening of that order in the face of all that threatens to break it down through sin, disease, violence, death, or evil of any kind.[9]

My own view is that those thinkers, like H. H. Farmer, were right in seeing an analogy between our personal action in the world and God. Like all analogies, however, it has its limitations. We do not exist in the way that God exists. Nevertheless, our personal action, which does not suspend laws of nature, but rather orders them, may be an important clue as to how we may think of divine activity in the world. As personal beings, we do not stand outside the sequence of cause and effect. Personal action consists rather in initiating some sequences and terminating others. We stand within the process and at the same time enjoy a measure of transcendence.

If there is a sense in which man is made as the image of God, as Christians believe, it may be that this can serve as a model for thinking of divine activity. However, there is a fundamental difference between the acts of a creature within the world and the acts of the Creator in creating. The same Creator may act within the world and he may act upon the world. In both cases there is a resultant order. Thus in the last resort, all miracles may turn out to be expressions of contingency, though the contingency may include that of the "new creation," as well as that of the "old." The kind of miracles that Christians believe in are not pure random manifestations. They are manifestations of a divine ordering of the nature with which we are familiar, and of the eschatological order of Christian hope. In neither case could they have come about if nature had been left to itself. For this reason miracles cannot be the object of scientific investigation, for science can only deal with nature as it is left to itself.

To speak in this way is, of course, to make a confession of faith. It is to suggest what truth-conditions would have to obtain in order to speak meaningfully of miracles. It is to suggest, as it were, a grammar of belief, in terms of which miracles have a meaningful place. Beyond this the philosopher and the apologist cannot go; they can only debate whether such perspectives are reasonable. Beyond that each individual must make up his or her own mind.

11

THE PLACE OF THE GOSPEL MIRACLES IN NEW TESTAMENT INTERPRETATION

In what follows I shall not attempt to examine in detail the individual miracle stories. Nor shall I be concerned with the important question of sources and how the Gospels in their present form relate to them. These questions require a separate book. My present aim is the more modest one of making some suggestions toward identifying the place of the miracles in the Gospels, as they now stand, and asking what these stories might be saying to us. Curiously enough, this kind of exercise appears to be somewhat neglected, but I think that it is necessary for two reasons.

In the area of philosophy and apologetics the questions of the possibility and the significance of miracles have all too often been debated in the abstract without paying too much attention to what the Gospels may actually be saying about the activities of Jesus. It is therefore important to philosophy and apologetics, not to mention systematic theology, to ask what is the place of miracles in the Gospels and what significance the Gospels themselves attach to them.

It is also important to ask these questions for the sake of understanding the New Testament. In all walks of life, modern pressure to specialize encourages a piecemeal approach, from which theology is by no means exempt. Not only is there a danger of Christian philosophers and apologists constructing their systems with only minimal regard to the sources and historical origins of their faith, it is also possible for biblical scholars to ignore the philosophical dimensions of their work. Moreover, there is considerable pressure on scholars to adopt a piecemeal approach to their investigations.

On the one hand, conservatives and radicals are both prone to the temptation to treat the sayings and incidents of the Gospels piecemeal without asking what each evangelist might be trying to say with his Gospel. On this basis, they all too often construct their christologies first and then ask what they should make of the miracle stories. On the other hand, the fascination of constructing a *Sitz im Leben* for items of Gospel material in the life of the first-century church seems to have contributed to a general neglect of what the Gospels might be saying as a whole. It leads scholars to seek an origin for sayings and incidents anywhere but in the life of Jesus himself.

The present chapter is in a sense a postscript to what has gone before. It is written as an exploratory inquiry into the way the Gospels present the miracle stories and relate them to their proclamation of the gospel of Christ. Perhaps inevitably this involves some change of style and approach, as questions of biblical exegesis become the center of concern. Moreover, this shift of focus involves a shift from the critical examination of technical writings of others to a personal and preliminary mapping out of the subject under discussion. Inevitably this will open up new fields of inquiry. But if we do not ask ourselves what the Gospels are saying in terms of their own thought world, discussion of the biblical miracles in the realms of philosophy and apologetics could easily degenerate into an exercise in futility.

PERSPECTIVES IN CHRISTOLOGY

In order to appreciate the place of miracles in the christology of the evangelists as well as in Christian belief, some ground clearing may be necessary. First of all, it seems to me that we do not help ourselves if we assume, without more ado, that the term "Son of God" provides a self-explanatory rationale for the miracles. This assumption appears to be made by two groups of people for opposite reasons. On the one hand are those traditionalists who attempt to base their belief in the incarnation primarily on Jesus' express declaration that he was the Son of God. The confession by Peter (Matt. 16:16), the testimony of the centurion (Mark 15:39), and Jesus' own admission to the chief priest (Mark 14:61f.) are seen to be clinching proof of his claims to personal deity. The underlying logic here is the belief that to be the son of someone involves being of the same substance as the parent. Since God is divine, Jesus must be divine. Therefore, he must be capable of performing by himself divine acts, that is, miracles, as corroborative proof of his divinity. The other group that treats the term as a divine title are the liberal and radical opponents of the traditionalists. They see in the use of the title an attempt on the part of the evangelists and the early church to divinize Jesus. Bound up with this is the assumption that Jesus could not have been in any sense divine to start with, since he was a man. Members of this group then feel free to throw around charges of myth-making and to ridicule the idea of a divine Son of God concealed within a human son of man.

Although these arguments continue to be propounded on both sides with energy, dexterity, and scholarship, it seems to me that neither side has quite got the point of the initial meaning of the title, or done full justice to the complexity of the New Testament picture.[1] This is not to say that the term "Son of God" did not take on new depths of meaning for the church, in view of their experience of Jesus and in particular of the resurrection and the coming of the Holy Spirit after Pentecost. But the evidence of the Gospels, as they reflect the historical situation in which Jesus spoke and acted, suggests that "Son of God" had a range of connotations that were not necessarily divine. It is an oversimplification to say that the title "Son of God" expresses Jesus' divinity and "Son of Man" his humanity.

Luke, for example, took the remark of the centurion at the cross to be a Jewish idiom, and translated it for his readers to express his conviction that Jesus was truly righteous or innocent (Greek *dikaios*; Luke 23:47). Either we must conclude that Luke was deliberately toning down Mark's high christology, or that he recognized the title as an idiom that meant something different from our modern interpretations.

Furthermore, earlier in his Gospel Luke describes Adam as "the son of God" (Luke 3:38). No one would dream of asserting the divinity of Adam on those grounds. It is interesting to note that Luke places this description of Adam as "the son of God" between his accounts of Jesus' baptism and temptation—where Jesus is also identified as the Son of God. At the climax of the story of Jesus' baptism, a voice from heaven declares, "Thou art my beloved Son; with thee I am well pleased" (Luke 3:22). Satan's temptation of Jesus turns on the premise, "If you are the Son of God . . ." (Luke 4:3, 9). These passages raise, rather than settle, the question of how Luke understood the term "Son of God."

The title "Son of God" did, in fact, have an established usage that did not carry with it the connotation of personal deity. It denoted God's representative, the righteous servant, to whom God had given authority to rule and govern, and who stands in a filial relationship to God.[2] In this sense Luke may have described Adam as the Son of God in view of his being created in the image of God with authority and responsibility for the care of God's creation.[3] There is a case for arguing that "Son of God" and "Son of Man" ultimately converge in their meaning. In the background of the idea of "The Son of Man" there may well lie the ideas of descent from Adam and the role of his chosen descendants in fulfilling the mandate that was originally given to Adam. In biblical Hebrew *ʾāḏām* is both the name of Adam and the ordinary word for "man." There is much to suggest that "Son of Man" describes Yahweh's faithful and righteous servant who fulfills his elect calling despite all opposition and who is given authority to reign.[4] Matthew traces his genealogy of Jesus back to Abraham (Matt. 1:1, 2), with whom God made his covenant and from whom the nation of Israel ultimately descended. In tracing Jesus back to Adam, Luke may well have envisaged the renewal of humankind through Jesus and Jesus' role in the kingdom.

It would take us too far afield to trace the complex discussions of recent years concerning the titles of Jesus. But we may draw attention to the fact that in an Old Testament passage that plays a significant part in the New Testament, the king of Israel was designated as God's son (Ps. 2:7). The passage may also be compared with Nathan's prophecy to David, made in respect of his son: "I will be his father, and he shall be my son" (2 Sam. 7:14). Nathan's prophecy was quoted in a collection of messianic testimonies from Qumran (1Q flor. 10f.; cf. 4Q 243). Psalm 2:7 is cited in Acts 13:33; Hebrews 1:5; 5:5; and 2 Peter 1:17. Psalm 2:7 also provides the source of the identification of Jesus with God's Son by the voice from heaven after his baptism and the descent of the Spirit (Mark 1:11; Matt. 3:17; Luke 3:22; cf. John 1:34). The identification of Jesus with God's beloved, in whom he delights, further identifies Jesus with God's servant upon whom he has put his Spirit (Isa. 42:1).

The two allusions to the Old Testament made by the voice from heaven do not in themselves make Jesus a divine being. They identify him with the messianic king and servant of the Lord of Old Testament prophetic expectation. Peter's confession of Jesus as the Christ (Christ being simply the Greek form of the Hebrew word for Messiah, or anointed one) is entirely in line with this identification of Jesus (Matt. 16:16; Mark 8:29; Luke 9:20; cf. John 6:69). When viewed in the light of Jewish idioms, the addition in Matthew of the words "the Son of the living God" may not be, as is often supposed, a heightened two-step christology, in which Peter confessed Jesus as the Messiah, and then took a step further by professing his belief that Jesus was also the Second Person of the Trinity. In the context of Matthew 16:16, there is evidently a Jewish parallelism in which "Christ" and "Son of God" are complementary terms expressing Peter's realization that Jesus was the messianic king of prophetic expectation. Possession of this insight, Jesus adds, is a gift of the Father himself.

For the same reasons, it must be doubted whether the high priest was questioning Jesus on whether he claimed to be the Second Person of the Trinity, when he demanded of Jesus whether he was "the Christ, the Son of the Blessed" (Mark 14:61; cf. Matt. 26:63; Luke 22:67). What is significant is that Jesus not only replies in the affirmative, but his reply, according to the evangelists, immediately identifies the Son of God with the *Son of Man* who will be seen to be vindicated at the right hand of power (Matt. 26:64; Mark 14:62; Luke 22:69). The language of this reply is the language applied in Daniel 7:13 to the "one like a son of man" to whom is given dominion. It is also the language of Psalm 110:1, which also belongs to the thought-world of kingship. The juxtaposition of "Son of God" and "Son of Man" at this crucial point further confirms the suggestion that the meaning of the two terms ultimately converges. This is further confirmed by the mockery of the chief priests and their minions at the cross. They identified Jesus' answer that he was the Son of God as a claim to be the "King of Israel" (Matt. 27:42). In the Fourth Gospel, with its explicit high christology, it may be noted that "Son of God" and "Christ" are juxtaposed (John 20:31; cf. 1:20, 25, 49; 4:25, 29; 7:26f., 41f.; 9:22; 11:27; 12:34; 17:3). John's Gospel lays heavy emphasis on the kingship of Jesus as the Christ (cf. John 6:15; 18:36f.; 19:14–21).

All this may seem to have taken us several steps away from the subject of miracles and several steps backward from the traditional approach to the divinity of Christ. However, we are making these points in order to try to identify more precisely how the evangelists approached Jesus' person in relation to the pronouncements and acts that they record. Two observations may be made at this point. The first is to underscore the point that, while historically the expression "Son of God" did not necessarily denote personal divinity, this does not mean that it was incapable of being filled with a new content. If its initial application to Jesus suggests the connotation of messianic kingship, this does not rule out the personal presence of God in Jesus that afforded the grounds for the redefinition of divine sonship in later Christian theology. On the other hand, the evangelists were not tritheists. Therefore, my second observation is to say that tritheism is not a satisfactory model for understanding the Gospels, which were composed within the horizons of Jewish monotheism. The evangelists do not depict the Father, the Son, and the Holy Spirit as three separate deities, who could each be said to be God because each was made of the same divine substance and as a divine individual performed divine acts. The Christian church has always repudiated tritheism. But in saying this we are brought back to the question of how the evangelists depict Jesus.

A generation ago, the Scottish theologian D. M. Baillie wrote a book which he entitled *God Was in Christ* (1948). The title, which was drawn from Paul's declaration that "God was in Christ reconciling the world to himself" (2 Cor. 5:19), was indicative of the thrust of Baillie's proposals for a new understanding of the incarnation. Baillie was impressed by the need to recognize that Jesus was a real, actual human being. He was not just some kind of manifestation of impersonal humanity. He was a real, actual man. This much is clear from the New Testament, and it is part and parcel of the orthodox Chalcedonian faith. This conviction is reinforced by the entire quest of the historical Jesus. But the nineteenth-century liberal quest discovered a Jesus who was really a reflection of the nineteenth-century liberal scholar. The Dialectical Theology of Barth, Brunner, and Bultmann redressed the balance and recovered something of the divine transcendence in Jesus, but at the expense of losing the historical Jesus. Barth and Brunner did not appear to be interested in him at all, and Bultmann's skeptical form criticism taught that the historical Jesus was forever buried from our view beneath the tangled mass of early Christian piety.

In response to all this, Baillie confessed (as I would) that he could not get rid of the conviction that the early church was not uninterested in what Jesus said and did. He thought it absurd to think that the church would go to extreme lengths to invent sayings and actions of Jesus, and show no concern at all for Jesus himself. Baillie turned to the more moderate form criticism of C. H. Dodd who, on the basis of his examination of diverse strata of Gospel passages, reached the conclusion that "all of them in their different ways exhibit Jesus as a historical personality distinguished from other religious personalities of His time by His friendly attitude to the outcasts of society."[5] This in turn provided Baillie with a way of linking revelation with the historical Jesus.

For Baillie, revelation was not some esoteric, mystical, or existential Word, unrelated to the life of Jesus. Jesus' life itself, including his words and acts, was a revelation of the Father reconciling the world to himself through Jesus. As a model for thinking about the incarnation, Baillie suggested the Christian's experience of the paradox of grace, in which he knows that he owes everything to God, but at the same time he remains truly a human, responsible individual.[6] In the course of his argument Baillie revived the idea of Cairns, Gore, Westcott, and others, that we should not think of the miracles of Jesus as works of his personal deity. Rather, they should be seen as the works of the Father operating through his humanity. To support his point, Baillie drew attention to those passages in the Gospels where Jesus looked to the Father as the source of his healing power, and bade those who were healed to give glory to God rather than himself (Mark 5:19; 7:34; Luke 17:18).[7] The Fourth Gospel gives the following answer to Philip's request to be shown the Father: "Do you not believe that I am in the Father and the Father in me? The words that I say to you I do not speak on my own authority; but the Father who dwells in me does his works" (John 14:10). Similar thoughts are found in John 5:19, 30; 7:16, 18, 28f.; 12:49.

Although he does not say so in so many words, it would appear that, on Baillie's reading of this passage, the "I" refers to the human Jesus and "the Father" refers to God. In other words, the passage is not an explication of inner-Trinitarian relationships. Rather, it is a declaration of the incarnation of the Father in Jesus. With such deft application of the surgeon's scalpel, Baillie cut away the problems of how many wills, minds, and persons there were in Jesus. He obviated the need to posit, for example, a human will, the will of the divine Son within Jesus, and the will of the Father in both. By appealing to the paradox of grace, in which the believer is conscious of his own will and responsibility and at the same time is conscious of God's will and grace, Baillie presented a model that would not resolve the tension of divine presence in human life. Nevertheless, the model made the tension feasible. Baillie anticipated the question of whether we could all be Christs by saying that grace is always a matter of divine initiative, and by pointing out that the New Testament itself links the believer's sonship with that of Christ.[8] Although Baillie went on to talk about the doctrine of the Trinity, the reader is left wondering what has really become of it. Although he saw it as essential, Baillie's trinitarianism was a symbolic way of describing the church's experience of the God who was incarnate in Jesus and who is known to us today. Put bluntly, we are left with an incarnation of the Father. It is a form of unitarianism, evoking the ghost of Schleiermacher, but speaking with a Scottish accent.[9]

Baillie's position is not without its strong points. The attention that he paid to the role of the Father in the ministry of Jesus redressed a balance that was apt to be lost by traditionalists bent on attributing everything to the personal divinity of Jesus. But the price that Baillie paid for this was his implicit unitarianism and his conspicuous neglect of what the Gospels had to say about the Spirit, the Word, and the Wisdom of God. More recent scholarship has attempted to balance this, but at the risk of lurching in the opposite direction. The past decade has seen the emergence of a Spirit christology that has attempted to give due recognition to the role of the Spirit in the life and ministry of Jesus. But the impression is readily given that at heart Spirit christology wants to teach the incarnation of the Spirit. The Second Person of the Trinity is now replaced by the Third. Thus, J. D. G. Dunn writes, "Certainly it is quite clear that if we can indeed properly speak of the 'divinity' of the *historical* Jesus, we can only do so in terms of his experience of God: *his 'divinity' means his relationship with the Father as son and the Spirit of God in him.*"[10]

In making this point, Dunn cites the support of the late G. W. H. Lampe's study, "The Holy Spirit and the Person of Christ."[11] Lampe himself advocated an "inspirational" (though not Adoptionist) christology, as opposed to the "incarnational" christology of orthodoxy. In his 1976 Bampton Lectures, *God as Spirit*, Lampe went on to develop this view. However, he made it evident that he did not think of the Spirit as the Third Person of the Trinity. Rather, for Lampe the Holy Spirit is a way of denoting the immanent creativity of God. With this Lampe also reverted to a form of unitarianism. Whether Dunn, with his evangelical and charismatic connections, would go quite so far is not quite clear, although at times he appears to come very close to Lampe's view.[12] What is clear is his contention that *"The eschatological kingdom was present for Jesus only because the eschatological Spirit was present in and through him."*[13] He sees Jesus' exorcisms as a manifestation of the kingdom of God through the Spirit working through Jesus, and he sees the miracles of Jesus as the work of a charismatic personality, comparable with the activities of the "psychic 5%" of humanity capable of drawing on "sources of energy" of which the ordinary man is only rarely aware and who may transmit power from a richer source of energy outside himself.[14]

The researches of Lampe, Dunn, and others pose the question of whether contemporary scholarship is pushing us in the direction of a charismatic unitarianism. My personal response would be that we have much to learn from Spirit christology. But like D. M. Baillie's work a generation ago, in some ways it goes too far and in others it does not go far enough. Although it may sound anachronistic to the New Testament specialists, I think that the Gospels are far more Trinitarian in their picture of Jesus than the experts give them credit for. Obviously, in a postscript to a survey of the history of ideas, I cannot set out my proposals in the same kind of detail that one would expect in a study of the christology of the Gospels. However, the following outline may serve as a basis for further investigation. It also indicates how the miracle stories may relate to the christology of the Gospels.

THE GOSPEL ACCORDING TO MARK

As a starting point, it might be useful to recall the christology presented at two crucial points in the Acts of the Apostles. The first passage is taken from the account of Peter's preaching at Pentecost, the second from his preaching to Cornelius. In both instances the preaching was connected with the gift of the Spirit and the opening of the church (first to the Jews at large and then to the Gentiles at large):

> Men of Israel, hear these words: Jesus of Nazareth, a man attested to you by God with mighty works and wonders and signs which God did through him in your midst, as you yourselves know. . . . (Acts 2:22)

> You know the word which he sent to Israel, preaching good news of peace by Jesus Christ (he is Lord of all), the word which was proclaimed throughout all Judea, beginning from Galilee after the baptism which John preached: how God anointed Jesus of Nazareth with the Holy Spirit and with power; how he went about doing good and healing all that were oppressed by the devil, for God was with him. (Acts 10:36–38)

At first sight the christology presented here seems unpromising from the more traditionalist standpoint, for it seems to say much less than what orthodoxy wants to say. Christ is now Lord of all, but in its accounts of Jesus' ministry the christology stresses the humanity of Jesus and attributes his mighty works to God or the Holy Spirit. On the other hand, this could well be the most primitive christology of all in the postresurrection Jewish church. In my view, it coincides with the christology of the first three Gospels. Indeed, if there is any link between Mark and Peter, as Papias claimed, and if these passages truly represent the standpoint of Peter, it could well be that the christological perspective presented by Mark is a fuller representation of Peter's view of Jesus.[15]

In my opinion a neglected key to the understanding of the structure of Mark's Gospel and to his christology is the prophecy of John the Baptist: "I have baptized you with water; but he will baptize you with the Holy Spirit" (Mark 1:8). The same prophecy is in fact recorded by Matthew 3:11 and Luke 3:16, both of which add the words "and with fire." The Fourth Gospel contains a similar statement in the form of John's testimony: "I myself did not know him; but he who sent me to baptize with water said to me, 'He on whom you see the Spirit descend and remain, this is he who baptizes with the Holy Spirit' " (John 1:33). However, for present purposes we shall concentrate on Mark.

Broadly speaking, there are three main lines of interpretation of this prophecy concerning baptism with the Holy Spirit. In traditional Catholic theology, the baptism of the Spirit is linked with the rite of water baptism. In Reformed theology, it is linked with conversion, regeneration, and justification by faith. In Pentecostal and charismatic theology, baptism with the Holy Spirit is linked with postconversion deepening experiences of grace and gifts for ministry. Put bluntly, all three interpretations bypass the actual ministry of Jesus and see the prophecy taking effect only with the coming of the Spirit at Pentecost. Although they see the Spirit as the Spirit sent by Jesus, they appear to treat the actual ministry of Jesus as irrelevant to the baptism of the Spirit, except as some kind of prelude. Perhaps a reason for this is a tendency to read the prophecy of John the Baptist as if it were the same as the prophecy in Acts 1:5 and 11:16. But these prophecies were the utterances of Jesus himself either in his earthly days or as the risen Christ. My suggestion, therefore, is that we need to understand the prophecy of Mark 1:8 as a prophecy that relates to the activity of Jesus in his earthly ministry. In short, his entire ministry was an expression of the baptism of the Holy Spirit. This, of course, does not preclude his ministry of the baptism of the Holy Spirit after Pentecost. Rather, it lays the foundation for it,[16] and sets the scene for the entire Gospel. Mark is not so much a biography of Jesus as an interpretation of him in terms of this theme.

To support this interpretation, I would draw attention to a number of factors. First of all is the "you" in the Baptist's prophecy that evidently refers to the hearers, drawn from "all the country of Judea, and all the people of Jerusalem" (Mark 1:5). Second is the word "baptize" itself, drawn from the Greek *baptizō*, which the Christian church did not translate, but chose to transliterate. Clearly, it was connected with washing, cleansing, plunging, and immersing into. What John did with water, Jesus would do with the Spirit. Third is Mark's account of what Jesus did. But before we look at that, it is worth pausing to observe the role of the Spirit in eschatological expectation.

In connection with the Day of the Lord and the renewal of Israel, Isaiah 4:3f. links the themes of cleansing, burning, judgment, and the Spirit:

> And he who is left in Zion and remains in Jerusalem will be called holy,
> everyone who has been recorded for life in Jerusalem, when the Lord
> shall have washed away the filth of the daughters of Zion and cleansed
> the bloodstains of Jerusalem from its midst in a spirit of judgment and
> by a spirit of burning.

The coming of the Spirit in the end-time, as the means of cleansing, renewal, and the establishment of righteousness, is widely attested in the Old Testament (e.g., Isa. 32:15; 44:3; Ezek. 18:31; 36:25ff.; 37:14; 39:29; Joel 2:28-32; cf. Acts 2:17-21).[17] Some of these passages speak of the outpouring of the Spirit upon the nation, as God's servant. Other passages link the Spirit with wisdom, knowledge, and understanding (e.g., Isa. 11:2; 40:13f.), while still others speak of the Spirit and the Lord's anointed or the Lord's servant (Isa. 11:2; 42:1; 48:16; 59:19-21; 61:1).[18]

In addition to these references to the Spirit, we may note the prophecy of Malachi concerning the return of the Lord to his temple, the day of his coming, his refining "like a refiner's fire and like fullers' soap," and his purification of the sons of Levi "till they present right offerings to the Lord," so that the offering of Judah and Jerusalem may be pleasing to the Lord (Mal. 3:1–5). The evangelists took Malachi's prophecy of the messenger who would prepare the way of the Lord as being fulfilled in the ministry of John the Baptist (Mal. 3:1; Matt. 11:10; Mark 1:2; Luke 1:17, 76; 7:27). He was the Elijah who would come before the great and terrible Day of the Lord (Mal. 4:5; Matt. 17:11; Mark 9:12; Luke 1:17). Implicit in this understanding is the identification of Jesus as the one in whom the Lord would return to his temple and refine God's people.

Relevant too is the expectation of the Qumran community, illustrated by the following extract from the Community Rule that links the thought of cleansing, instruction, and the Spirit of truth:

> God will then purify every deed of Man with his truth; He will refine for Himself the human frame by rooting out all spirit of falsehood from the bounds of his flesh. He will cleanse him of all wicked deeds with the spirit of holiness; like purifying waters He will shed upon him the spirit of truth (to cleanse him) of all abomination and falsehood. And he shall be plunged into the spirit of purification that he may instruct the upright in the knowledge of the Most High and teach the wisdom of the sons of heaven to the perfect of way. For God has chosen them for an everlasting Covenant and all the glory of Adam shall be theirs. There shall be no more lies and all the works of falsehood shall be put to shame.[19]

The Qumran community view of the two opposing Spirits is echoed in the Gospels in the contrast between Beelzebul and the Holy Spirit. It is brought into sharp focus by the question: By what Spirit is Jesus teaching and performing all his works? The Qumran community looked to the Teacher of Righteousness. The evangelists saw in Jesus the one in whom messianic prophecy was fulfilled and the one in whom expectation of the Spirit was met. These were not two separate lines of prophecy; they coincided in Jesus. For the messiah was the messiah precisely because he was anointed by the Spirit. This thought is illustrated elsewhere in intertestamental literature by such passages as Psalms of Solomon 17:37; Ethiopic Enoch 49:3; and Testament of Levi 18:6ff.

With this in mind, we may perhaps see a little more clearly what Mark is saying in his Gospel. Immediately following John the Baptist's prophecy of the One who "will baptize you with the Holy Spirit," Mark gives an account of Jesus' baptism at the hands of John, the descent of the Spirit, and the voice from heaven (Mark 1:9–11). It may be noted that the New Testament writers never suggest that Jesus himself was baptized by the Spirit— the Spirit descended *after* his baptism. As we observed earlier, the voice from heaven identifies Jesus with the servant on whom God has put his Spirit (Isa. 42:1) and the messianic son-king now installed in office.[20] Significantly, it is the Spirit that drives Jesus into the wilderness, where he is tempted by Satan (Mark 1:12–13). There are at least two themes in the temptation of Jesus.

One is the theme of the testing of God's Son, comparable with the way that Israel as God's Son was tested in the wilderness.[21] The other theme surfaces more explicitly in Mark 3:22-30 and is elaborated in Matthew 4:1-11 and Luke 4:1-13. This was the temptation to achieve his vocation by resorting to magic and Satanism, with the tempting prospect of short-cuts and avoidance of the demands of righteousness. As the messianic Son of God, he was not exempt from such temptations; they were all the more acute.

Then follows Mark's account of the beginning of Jesus' ministry (1:14-15). After the arrest of John the Baptist, Jesus announces that "The time is fulfilled, and the kingdom of God is at hand; repent and believe the gospel." What comes next is all related to the kingdom or reign of God. First we are told of the response of the disciples to Jesus' call (1:16-20). This is followed by an account of the first public act of Jesus' ministry, which occurs on the Sabbath in the synagogue at Capernaum (1:21-28) and concerns a man with "an unclean spirit." The spirit recognizes Jesus as "the Holy One of God." I believe that Mark intends his reader to see a juxtaposition of two spirits: the unclean spirit in the man and the Holy Spirit who has descended upon Jesus and who now leads him. It is by the Holy Spirit that the unclean spirit is driven out and the man is made clean. In other words, Mark may well be intending us to see this episode as the first instance of Jesus baptizing with the Holy Spirit.

The rest of Mark 1 is taken up with the account of further exorcisms and healings and people's responses: Peter's mother-in-law, the sick and the possessed at sundown, and a leper. All these are implicitly or explicitly instances of cleansing (which is an important aspect of baptism) and of the life-giving power of the Spirit. With his account of the healing of the paralytic (2:1-12), Mark introduces a further aspect of cleansing, the forgiveness of sins. In so doing he also introduces the possible alternative construction that could be placed on Jesus' actions, the possibility that he was committing blasphemy by putting himself in the place of God (v. 7).

This episode, which is told in some detail, leads to a series of further episodes and sayings culminating with the parable of the sower and other parables (4:1-33). In a sense this caps the climax, or perhaps better the anticlimax, of Jesus' ministry so far. What these episodes have in common is the fact that they illustrate response and reaction to Jesus. When the people see the paralytic take up his pallet and walk, "they were all amazed and glorified God, saying, 'We never saw anything like this!' " (2:12). It is, as it were, as if the Day of the Lord has dawned, and as if the prophecy of Isaiah 35:6 has found fulfillment (a point noted elsewhere in Matt. 11:5; Luke 7:22). Levi is less effusive but gives a response in action rather than words (2:13-14). In answer to the call, "Follow me," he follows Jesus. As chapter 2 proceeds we are shown the mounting conflict with the Pharisees, which is occasioned by Jesus' mingling with tax collectors and sinners. This leads to the pronouncements about the bridegroom, new cloth, and new wine

(2:18–22). It is aggravated by the disciples plucking corn on the Sabbath. These stories culminate with the pronouncement that the Son of Man is lord even of the Sabbath (3:28).

The account of the healing of the man with a withered hand, again in a synagogue on the Sabbath, intensifies the conflict (3:1–6). It issues in the ironical collaboration of the former enemies, the Herodians and the Pharisees uniting to "destroy him" on the grounds that he had "restored" the man's hand. The reason for this (as I shall argue more fully when I discuss Matthew's account) is that both groups see Jesus as a false prophet who performs signs and wonders to justify his teaching and who must be purged from the midst of the people in accordance with the Law (Deut. 13:5). Jesus counters this threat by withdrawing, but great crowds follow, including those from Gentile regions. He heals and casts out unclean spirits who declare him to be the Son of God, but Jesus again commands them not to make him known (Mark 3:11; cf. 1:25, 34). After this the twelve are called to be with him and are given authority to cast out demons (3:13–19).

At this point Mark presents what I would call the anticlimax of his Gospel. It is the negative counterpart to the positive confession at Caesarea Philippi of Jesus as the Christ, which Peter makes later on (8:27–30). It concerns the charge (one might even say "confession") that Jesus "is possessed by Beelzebul, and by the prince of demons he casts out demons" (3:22). The conflict has been building up from the first. It is possible that enemies of John the Baptist who had witnessed or received secondhand reports of what they might have considered the bizarre episode of Jesus' baptism and subsequent departure into the wilderness, had entertained such ideas for some time. After all, the wilderness where Jesus was driven by the Spirit was also the abode of evil spirits (cf. Tob. 8:3; and the discussion of Matt. 12:43–45 below). Such ideas might have been given substance by Jesus' "blasphemy" in connection with the sin of the paralytic and his attitude toward the Sabbath. The charge was doubtless the result of the Pharisees and Herodians taking council how to destroy him (3:6). Jesus' outrageous and "blasphemous" behavior could well be attributed to Satanic influence, for which the Law prescribed punishment by death.

Jesus' response to the charge is to draw attention to the self-contradiction implied in the thoughts of Satan casting out Satan, of a kingdom divided against itself, and the impossibility of the goods of the strong man's house being plundered without first binding the strong man (3:23–27). This leads once more to the question of blasphemy, but this time it is Jesus who makes the pronouncement. Some blasphemies will be forgiven, "but whoever blasphemes against the Holy Spirit never has forgiveness, but is guilty of an eternal sin" (3:29). This pronouncement has been the subject of a great deal of discussion. However, the context indicates that the blasphemy in question is to attribute to Satan what in fact is the work of the Holy Spirit.[22] This interpretation is reinforced by Mark's comment: "for they said, 'He has an unclean spirit' " (3:30).

The incident throws light not only on the structure of Mark's Gospel but upon his understanding of Jesus, the kingdom, and the Spirit. Jesus' reference to the self-contradiction of a divided kingdom suggests a kingdom of Satan over against the kingdom of God. The former includes all who are bound in any way by Satan, both the possessed and Jesus' enemies. The allusion to the "house" suggests that what was once the house of Abraham has now become the house of Satan. Over against the house and kingdom of Satan, Jesus' works make manifest the kingdom of God. Mark's concluding comment in verse 30 indicates that Jesus' accusers could not be more wrong. What they attributed to an unclean spirit was in fact the work of the Holy Spirit.

The suggestion that Mark has an ongoing interest in audience reaction is further evidenced by the account of Jesus' mother and brothers standing "outside" and calling to him, and Jesus' response, "Here are my mother and brothers! Whoever does the will of God is my brother, and sister, and mother" (3:34f.). This passage reinforces the picture of Jesus, over against the interpretation of his enemies, as one who does the will of God. But it also draws attention to a category of people who are neither open followers of Jesus nor overt opponents. They are those who stand "outside" and in whom the word of God has not yet produced lasting fruit. It is at this point that Mark gives the parable of the sower (4:1–20), which he presents as Jesus' comment on the varied response to the word that he has sown and the factors, including Satanic interference, that prevent or promote its growth.

The account we have given of Jesus' ministry so far could well be called a Spirit christology. It has seen all of Jesus' activities as the activity of the Spirit of God in and through him. Thus, the healing miracles of Jesus, together with his exorcisms and pronouncement of forgiveness of sins, are presented by Mark in the overall context of the activity of the Spirit of God. It is this activity of the Spirit in and through Jesus which constitutes the presence of the kingdom, or the reign of God. To this extent it could be said that Mark has an explicit Spirit christology. But to say this is to speak from only one perspective. Alongside the explicit Spirit christology, Mark presents an implicit Word christology. Jesus preaches "the gospel of God" (1:14). He commands the disciples to follow him (1:17). The unclean spirit is rebuked and exorcised by Jesus' word of command (1:25). The people are amazed at the "new teaching" and "authority" of Jesus (1:27), though they themselves remain in the position of those who, like the seeds sown in rocky ground, receive the word with joy but have no root. It is by the word spoken by Jesus that the leper is made clean (1:41). He declares to the paralytic the word of forgiveness of sins, which only God may speak (2:5, 7). Jesus' numerous pronouncements in Mark 2 present God's pronouncements. The man with the withered hand is likewise healed by the word of Jesus (3:5). Jesus gives the authority to preach and to cast out demons to his disciples (3:14f.). Lest there be any doubt as to what Jesus is doing, the interpretation of the parable of the sower declares that the sower sows the word (4:14).

The parable, like the other parables that Jesus told, is a mystery of the kingdom of God (4:11; cf. 4:30), the point of which is to speak "the word to them, as they were able to hear it" (4:33). In short, alongside the explicit Spirit christology Mark presents an implicit Word christology. Jesus is the one who utters the word of God. He speaks as only God himself is entitled to speak. His speech-acts, like the speech-acts of God in the Old Testament, accomplish what is uttered. Together they determine the precise nature of Jesus' messiahship and sonship.

It is at this point that Mark introduces the nature miracles alongside further accounts of exorcism and healing. At this stage in our study we cannot go through all the stories of all four Gospels in an attempt to show how they illustrate the points that have been argued. I find myself in agreement with those exegetes, like Alan Richardson,[23] who see in Jesus' actions and words the embodiment of the actions and words of the Father and Creator. In a sense the stories that follow the Beelzebul controversy and the parable of the sower reiterate the picture that Mark has already presented. But apart from the interlude reporting the fate of John the Baptist, there is a respite in Mark 5 and 6 from religious opposition to Jesus. The center of the conflict here is with man's enemies, the unclean spirits, disease, death, man's physical needs, and the elements.

In these episodes, as R. P. Meye has shown in his discussion of Psalm 107 as a horizon for the interpretation of the miracle stories here, Jesus embodies and actualizes God's response to his people's needs.[24] The expression *in loco parentis* may be said to take on a new meaning. Normally it refers to an adult acting in the place of a parent; here, however, the Son acts in the place of the Father. He does what God does—or rather, the works that only God can do are wrought by Jesus. In a sense, the emphasis here comes close to the Johannine emphasis on Jesus as the Son who does the works of the Father. With his exorcism and healing works, Jesus is the healer of Israel (cf. Isa. 55:18ff.). With the nature miracles we are brought a step beyond the baptism of Israel by the Spirit through Jesus. We are shown the Creator and Redeemer. We are shown the man through whom God will truly reign on earth. In this sense, the miracles that find their culmination in Mark 8 anticipate the transfiguration, where Jesus is revealed as greater than Moses and Elijah and is confirmed as God's beloved Son (Mark 9:7; cf. 1:1, 11; Matt. 17:5; Luke 9:35; John 12:28ff.). If we were to examine the language of the Servant Song of Isaiah 42:1ff., from which the term "beloved" is taken, together with the Son theme of Psalm 2, which is also echoed here, we would see that it is concerned with the universal redemptive reign of Yahweh through his servant.

But at the very center of Mark's stories of provision, rescue, and reign stands the story of the imprisonment and beheading of John the Baptist (6:14-29). It is a reminder that God does not always come to the immediate relief of his servants. It is a reminder to the disciples, and perhaps even to

Jesus himself, of a fact he knew all along, that the ways of God do not exempt his servants from pain, suffering, and desolation.

With the debate in Mark 7 on what defiles a man, the question of cleanness and cleansing takes on a new turn. The traditions of the scribes and Pharisees make void the word of God (7:13). Ritual cleansings, which include the washing (Greek *baptismous*) of cups, pots, and vessels (v. 4), fail to deal with what really defiles a person. For it is the evil thoughts from within, out of the heart, that defile (vv. 21–23). This chapter presents a further aspect of Jesus, as the One who has come to cleanse the people of God. Perhaps verses 21–23 are incidentally an oblique description of Jesus' opponents.

The numerous other acts of Jesus culminate in the climactic episode of Peter's confession of Jesus as the Christ (8:29). The title Christ is a transliteration of the Greek word *christos*. Like the Hebrew word Messiah *(mašiah)* which it translates, Christ means the anointed one. It is to be understood as the messiah of Old Testament expectation. Specifically, Jesus is the One who was anointed by the Spirit at his baptism and who thus fills the role of the Spirit-anointed messiah. Mark's account of the actions and teaching of Jesus up to this point is intended to show how Jesus filled the role of the messianic Son of God and Son of Man (Mark 1:1, 11, 24; 2:10, 28; 3:11; 5:7; cf. 9:7).

From the beginning the title of Christ involved cost, conflict, and suffering. From the very first act of exorcism, the first instance of baptism with the Holy Spirit, messiahship meant conflict. Before Jesus could be anointed by the Spirit, he himself had to be baptized in water. The confession of Jesus as the Christ immediately prompts the reminder that the Son of Man—God's faithful representative to whom God gives the dominion of his kingdom—must suffer and be put to death by the very people who might be expected to be God's true representatives (8:31, 34–38). The passion predictions in Mark 8:31 and 9:12 state what might have been expected in view of the treatment meted out to John the Baptist, the Beelzebul charge, and the request for a sign, which was evidently a trap (8:11). Peter's suggestion of an easier way out renews the temptations that confronted Jesus as the Christ from the very first. The voice from heaven had acknowledged him as the Son, and this was immediately followed by Satanic temptation. In both instances Jesus repudiates Satan and goes the way of the Spirit-anointed Christ (8:33; cf. 1:1–13; 9:7, 12–13, 30–32).

The incidents and teachings of Mark 9 and 10 illustrate the way of God's kingdom, the way of the cleansed Israel. As events move rapidly to their climax, the theme of baptism is reintroduced in two significant ways. It occurs first in Jesus' response to the request of James and John to sit at his right and left hand in glory. Jesus asks whether they are able to drink the cup that he drinks and be baptized with the baptism with which he is baptized, and goes on to promise them that they will indeed do so (10:38f.). If baptism means something like being immersed in the Spirit with the consequences of being cleansed and purged as a result of going through the refining fires, we may construe Jesus' reply as follows. The implications of his own baptism by John and anointing by the Spirit mean that he must fulfill his calling to the bitter end. To be the messianic Son of Man means a vocation "not to be served but to serve, and to give his life as a ransom for many" (10:45). Likewise, the followers of the Son of Man must fulfill the implications of the baptism of the Spirit. The theme of the cup that Jesus must drink is reintroduced at the Last Supper (14:23-25) and in the Garden of Gethsemane (14:36). The need to watch and pray lest the disciples enter into temptation is linked with the saying, "The spirit is indeed willing, but the flesh is weak" (14:38). It may make better sense of the passage, and also bring it into line with the role of the Spirit in Jesus' temptation and Mark's understanding of the Spirit generally, if we read this as an allusion to the willingness of the Holy Spirit.[25]

The other incident in which the theme of baptism is introduced is the cleansing of the temple (11:15-19). In a sense this incident represents the climax of the Gospel, for in coming to Jerusalem and specifically in coming to the temple, Jesus was fulfilling the prophecy of Malachi 3. John the Baptist had fulfilled the prophecy of the coming Elijah. Now the Lord was indeed suddenly coming to his temple. Like a refiner's fire he was seeking to purify the sons of Levi, so that the offering of Judah and Jerusalem would be pleasing to the Lord (cf. Mal. 3:1-4). Once more the question of Jesus' authority is raised (11:27-33). Appropriately, it is put by the religious leaders. In response, Jesus asks them whether the baptism of John was from heaven (i.e., from God) or from men. This question belongs to a whole series of dilemmas that surface in the final days of Jesus' ministry. They include the question of paying taxes to Caesar (12:13-17), married relationships in the resurrection (12:18-27), the great commandment (12:28-35), and the identity of the Son of David (12:35-37). The way one responds to these questions determines one's attitude toward the kingdom in general. The question of John's baptism was indeed such a dilemma. The answer given determines how one fits into the various parables of Jesus, including that of the vineyard, which Jesus proceeds to tell (12:1-11), and which prompts proceedings for his arrest (v. 12). The question of John's baptism was not designed simply to throw the questioners into confusion; it raises the further question of Jesus' relationship to John, Jesus' messiahship, and the relationship of John's water baptism to Jesus' baptism with the Holy Spirit. An affirmative answer implies acknowledgment not only that John was wrongfully beheaded, but that he was indeed the forerunner of the Christ and that he had prophetically spoken the word of God in proclaiming that Jesus was the one who would baptize with the Holy Spirit.

With this we are brought full circle in Mark's account of the ministry of Jesus. There is a reciprocal relationship between Mark's understanding of the Spirit and his understanding of the Christ. It is an intriguing question whether the chief priests, scribes, and elders who now decline to give answer, preferring to confess ignorance about the origin of John's baptism than to say what they think before the people, are the same as the scribes who came from Jerusalem with the charge that Jesus was possessed by Beelzebul. At any rate, Jesus also declines to tell them "by what authority I do these things" (11:33).

We clearly cannot comment here on all the many fascinating aspects of Mark's presentation of Jesus in his final week of ministry as the Christ. However, it is important to note that in the eschatological discourse Jesus endorses the standpoint of Deuteronomy 13. Signs and wonders, in and of themselves, are not conclusive evidence of the true prophet or the Christ (Mark 13:22; cf. Matt. 24:24; Luke 17:23). Indeed, it is a sign of the false Christ and false prophet that he will try to deceive the elect by such means. To that extent it may be said that Jesus and his adversaries shared the same premises. For both, truth according to the Word of God inspired by the Spirit of God is the decisive test. Significantly, this point is made in the discussion in the temple of the identity of the Christ as both David's son and Lord. How is it that David "inspired by the Holy Spirit" calls him Lord, if he is his son (12:35-37; cf. Matt. 22:41-46; Luke 20:41-44; Ps. 110:1)? The decisive factor is not whether Jesus performs impressive signs and wonders, but whether he is the one who fulfills through the Spirit of God the Word of God that was uttered by the Spirit of God (cf. also Mark 12:10, 24, 28-34).

Much has been written about the so-called *messianic secret* in Mark,[26] which is bound up with the command to the spirits to be silent and the command to the healed not to make him known. It seems to me that we could equally well say with J. D. G. Dunn that Mark is as much concerned with the question of messianic *misunderstanding* as he is with a messianic secret.[27] Certainly we can say that according to Mark, Jesus will not allow the unclean spirits to testify to him. Regardless of whether they are formally correct in their recognition of Jesus, Jesus commands them to be silent. Indeed, if Jesus had countenanced their testimony, he could have been justifiably incriminated for being in league with the demons. Jesus will have nothing to do with Satan and his minions, though ironically he was accused of doing his works by their power. If Jesus had been arrested on account of their testimony, his ministry would have terminated prematurely. Moreover, so long as the unclean spirits remain in possession of those who they afflict, Jesus' mission is not accomplished.

In a sense the messianic secret was as much a *Holy Spirit secret* as a messianic secret. On the one hand, recognition of who Jesus is and what his work accomplishes is bound up with recognition of the activity of the Spirit of God in him. On the other hand, the titles Messiah and Christ mean the Anointed One. If we ask, "By what or by whom is the Christ anointed?" the answer is that he is anointed by the Holy Spirit of God. In other words, the title Christ carries with it the implication of being anointed by the Holy Spirit. We are apt to assume that when the title Christ is used, it refers exclusively to Jesus. If the above account is in any way correct, the title contains an implicit reference to the anointing of Jesus by the Holy Spirit (cf. Acts 10:38). This applies particularly to Peter's confession of Jesus as the Christ (Mark 8:29). It helps to explain the comparative lack of explicit references to the Holy Spirit in the evangelists' accounts of Jesus' ministry. If the above interpretation of Mark is correct, there is an undercurrent of allusions to the Holy Spirit throughout Jesus' ministry, not least in the title Christ, which was seen by the high priest as the ultimate blasphemy (Mark 14:61-64).

The point of the messianic secret is its challenge to spontaneous recognition of Jesus as the Spirit-anointed Christ. As such it is diametrically opposed to the construction placed on Jesus by his enemies, which saw him as a false prophet or messianic pretender who performed signs and wonders to accredit himself, but who was really possessed by Satan. To that extent, the messianic secret might equally well be called a *Word of God secret*. For as the Anointed One, Jesus spoke the Word of God with authority. His utterances pose the question of whether his words are the Word of God or whether they are blasphemy. They also raise the question of his authority. As Matthew and Luke bring out with even greater clarity, the words of Jesus are inseparable from his actions. Jesus stands or falls by the construction that is to be placed on them both together.

By outlining Jesus' ministry in Mark, I have attempted to provide a context for the miracle stories as they are presented in the Gospel. There are very many questions I have left untouched. I have said nothing about the particular form given to the stories in relation to the question of the church for which Mark wrote. Nevertheless, I believe that New Testament scholarship must take as its starting point the Gospel of Mark as it stands, before it tries to construct theories of Mark's sources and their possible edificatory role in the life of the early community. If it does not do this, it runs the risk of failing to see the forest for the trees. On the above construction the actions of Jesus cannot be separated from his teaching. Nor can we attribute this or that saying or act to one member of the Trinity, while consigning other sayings or acts to another member. On this view the Holy Spirit did not suddenly swing into action at Pentecost, taking over from where Jesus left off. After Pentecost the Spirit is the Spirit of Christ; before Pentecost Christ is the Christ of the Spirit of the Lord.

THE GOSPEL ACCORDING TO MATTHEW

If we ask how the picture of Jesus and his miracles in the other Gospels compares with that of Mark, there are obvious differences as well as similarities. All four evangelists record the cleansing of the temple (Matt. 21:12-13; Mark 11:15-17; Luke 19:45-46; John 2:13-17). In the Synoptics it comes at the climax of Jesus' ministry. It is seen as Jesus' attempt to restore the temple to a house of prayer. The Synoptics proceed to the question of authority and record Jesus' question about the baptism of John (Matt. 21:23-27; Mark 11:27-33; Luke 20:1-8). Thus all three give substance to the suggestion that this was the climactic act of baptism or cleansing by the Spirit through Jesus who had divine authority to do this. John, however, places the cleansing of the temple at the beginning of his Gospel for thematic purposes, to provide a context for all that follows.

Both Matthew and Luke give birth and infancy narratives. Perhaps it would be more accurate to say that they both also include conception narratives in which they attribute Jesus' birth to the Holy Spirit (Matt. 1:18, 20; Luke 1:35, cf. also 80). Luke also mentions the Holy Spirit in connection with the ministry prophesied for John the Baptist (1:15, 17) and the gift of prophetic utterance (1:41, 67; 2:25). Luke clearly sees in these manifestations of the Spirit anticipations of the eschatological outpouring of the Spirit that he describes at Pentecost (Acts 2:17-21; cf. Joel 2:27-32). Both Matthew and Luke correct the impression that the Spirit only came upon Jesus after his baptism. In other words, they oppose any adoptionist ideas that might be gleaned by reading Mark alone. At the same time, they make it clear that the descent of the Spirit after Jesus' baptism was the special anointing by the Spirit of God that inaugurated and empowered Jesus' ministry.

We have already observed how all four evangelists record the prophecy of John the Baptist concerning Jesus' baptism with the Holy Spirit (Matt. 3:11; Mark 1:8; Luke 3:16; John 1:33). All four mention the descent of the Spirit (Matt. 3:16; Mark 1:10; Luke 3:22; John 1:32f.). The Synoptists all mention the Spirit leading Jesus into the wilderness to be tempted (Matt. 4:1; Mark 1:12; Luke 4:1). Luke presses the point still further. He mentions how "Jesus returned in the power of the Spirit into Galilee" (4:14), and describes the incident in the synagogue at Nazareth, where Jesus read from Isaiah 61:1f.:

> The Spirit of the Lord is upon me, because he has anointed me to preach good news to the poor. He has sent me to proclaim release to the captives and recovering of sight to the blind, to set at liberty those who are oppressed, to proclaim the acceptable year of the Lord. (Luke 4:18-19)

In other words, Luke makes it even more explicit than Mark that Jesus' messiahship is to be thought of in terms of the anointing by the Spirit; that the healing miracles and exorcisms, no less than Jesus' preaching and teaching, are to be attributed to this anointing by the Spirit, and that all this is a fulfillment of messianic prophecy.

Matthew does not record this prophecy, but as he cites another messianic prophecy from Isaiah that was partly cited by the voice from heaven at Jesus' baptism, Matthew interprets Jesus' healings as fulfillment of Isaiah 42:1-4:

> Behold, my servant whom I have chosen, my beloved with whom my soul is well pleased. I will put my Spirit upon him, and he shall proclaim justice to the Gentiles. He will not wrangle or cry aloud, nor will any

one hear his voice in the streets; he will not break a bruised reed or quench
a smoldering wick, till he brings justice to victory; and in his name will
the Gentiles hope. (Matt. 12:18–21)

In citing this passage Matthew is laying the foundation for the disciple-making
mission to all nations, "baptizing them in the name of the Father and of
the Son and of the Holy Spirit" (Matt. 28:19). Jesus' ministry of the Spirit
is to be carried on by his disciples. Formerly he was physically present; to
the close of the age he will be invisibly present.

The citation from Isaiah follows shortly after the healing of the man
with the withered hand. As in Mark, the incident provides the occasion of
the Pharisees' decision to take counsel to destroy him (12:14; cf. Luke 6:11).
It leads directly to the charge of casting out demons by Beelzebul (12:24),
which is the answer that the Pharisees give to the people's question of whether
Jesus might be the expected Son of David. Matthew makes the connection
between Jesus' works, the kingdom, and the Spirit even more explicit than
Mark. In addition to the self-contradictions in the imputation noted by Mark,
Matthew records the following question and observation:

> And if I cast out demons by Beelzebul, by whom do your sons cast them
> out? Therefore they shall be your judges. But if it is by the Spirit of God
> that I cast out demons, then the kingdom of God has come upon you.
> (12:27f.; cf. also 9:34; 10:25)

This answer suggests that, while the sons of the Pharisees were endowed with
the Spirit in a limited way to perform this ministry, Jesus as the Christ is
anointed by the same Spirit to perform his messianic ministry. This leads
to the saying on blasphemy, where again Matthew's version is even more
explicit than Mark's. The pronouncement that "whoever speaks against the
Holy Spirit will not be forgiven, either in this age or in the age to come"
(v. 32), puts it beyond all doubt that the attribution to Beelzebul of the
manifest work of the Spirit of God by Jesus' enemies at the present time
is the true blasphemy. This is followed by a series of warnings against idle
words (12:33–37).

Before Matthew records the episode concerning Jesus' mother and
brothers standing outside (12:46–50) and the parable of the sower and the
other parables of the kingdom (13:1–52), which thus preserves the general
configuration of events in Mark, he inserts Jesus' response to the scribes'
and Pharisees' request for a sign (12:38–42) and the pronouncement about
the unclean spirit (12:43–45). Jesus' refusal to perform a sign has sometimes
been taken to imply that he performed no miracles at all, and the miracles
in the Gospels were the invention of zealous Christians who felt an urgent
need to remedy this lack. However, this is not the only way of looking at
this episode.

Jesus did not perform signs merely for the sake of impressing people,
or providing them with such conclusive evidence that they could be sure that
they were not making a mistake in believing in him. His works were works

of compassion, restoration, and redemption. They were such that could be identified by those who studied and loved the Scriptures with the works of the One on whom God would put his Spirit. The very people that demanded a sign were those who had attributed the actions of Jesus to Beelzebul, and in so doing had failed to see that Jesus was the One prophesied by Isaiah. This in itself was an indication that the questioners were not concerned with the truth of God, as set out in the Scriptures. This point is further underscored by the allusion to "an evil and adulterous generation" that seeks a sign. Adultery was an image of apostasy (cf. Isa. 57:3 and the Book of Hosea). But the saying may also reflect the fact that the questioners evidently condoned, or at least did not speak out against, the treatment meted out to John the Baptist for his condemnation of the adulterous relationship of Herod Antipas and Herodias (cf. Matt. 11:2ff.; 14:1-12; 19:1-19). Some of them had evidently sought John's baptism, but had been warned by John to "bear fruit that fits repentance" (3:7-10). John had then gone on to say that while he baptized them with water, the coming One would baptize with the Holy Spirit and with fire, and would separate the wheat from the chaff, burning the latter with unquenchable fire (3:11-13).

Those who sought the sign had evidently not taken either John's warning or his prophecy to heart. To be more interested in signs than the righteousness of the Law was indicative of the attitude of the generation. Moreover, if Jesus had performed a sign, he would have walked straight into a trap. For a sign could readily have been construed as none other than the work of Beelzebul. Matthew's temptation stories tell of Satanic enticements to perform just such signs (4:1-11). The temptations were temptations to use the power of the Spirit for selfish ends, and to gain a following by means of impressive, but nonredemptive signs. However, the student of the Law knew full well that signs were at best inconclusive and at worst incriminating evidence of magic and the occult. They required that the person who wrought the sign should be put to death (Deut. 13), so that the evil would be purged out of the midst of the people. The word used in Matthew for a sign (Greek *sēmeion*) is the same word that is used in the Greek version of Deuteronomy 13 in connection with the prophet or dreamer who performs signs in order to persuade people of his teaching and to lead them astray. The same word is used in Matthew 24:24 and Mark 13:22 of the signs performed by false Christs and false prophets to lead astray the elect. In these passages the underlying thought is that of Deuteronomy 13, but here "the elect" are the church rather than the nation of Israel.

If Jesus had performed a sign, it could well have been construed as support for his interpretation of the Law, which differed radically from the accepted traditions (cf. the Sermon on the Mount, Matt. 5-7) and his attitude toward the Sabbath. Whereas Jesus could not readily be purged out of the midst of the people for his teaching, an impromptu sign might provide clinching evidence that Jesus really was in league with Beelzebul and could legally be executed in accordance with the decision that had already been taken (Matt.

12:14). They would have evidence of a deed done before competent witnesses, namely themselves, as distinct from hearsay, rumor, and the unreliable witness of members of the lower strata of society and women, whose testimony had no legal standing.

Perhaps the scribes and Pharisees hoped for a nature miracle that could more readily be construed as a piece of magic. This suggestion is supported by at least two considerations. On the one hand, their charge of demon-possession had just been torn to shreds. It could not stand up any more. On the other hand, they may have heard rumors about Jesus' nature miracles. In Mark's brief account, the request by the Pharisees for a sign from heaven is represented as a deliberate test (8:11) that immediately follows the feeding of the four thousand. If viewed within a magical frame of reference, something like that could readily be interpreted as a magical act, designed to lead the people astray. The scribes and Pharisees would have fulfilled the Law by taking the first steps toward removing the wonder-working false prophet from the midst of the people of God.

Jesus' response to the request for a sign is to say that no sign will be given except that of the prophet Jonah (Matt. 12:39; cf. 16:4; Luke 11:29). In one sense Jesus' miracles can be seen as prophetic signs, illustrating and embodying his message. This was the sense of the earlier allusion to Isaiah 42:1-4 (12:18-21) and Jesus' response to John the Baptist, who had asked from prison whether Jesus was the One who was to come (11:1-6; cf. Isa. 35:5-6; 61:1). In contrast to the Pharisees who had asked for a sign but were given a verbal reply, John appears to have asked for a verbal reply (though no doubt expecting some new action) but was directed to Jesus' past actions as signs. But these were signs for those who believed the Law and the Prophets and sought to understand Jesus from that perspective. To the evil and adulterous generation no sign would be given except the sign of the prophet Jonah.

The use of the name Jonah may well have had connotations for the rabbinic mind that are not readily apparent to modern English and American readers. The name Jonah means "dove." It recalls "the Spirit of God descending like a dove, and alighting on him" (Matt. 3:16). This connotation would pick up the earlier issue at the heart of the Beelzebul charge, of whether the actions of Jesus are to be attributed to Satan or to the Spirit of God. In late Jewish thought the dove was a symbol of the Spirit of God, of wisdom, and of the people of God (cf. Hos. 7:11; 11:11; Ps. 74:19). Part of the message of the Book of Jonah is that Jonah represents the people of God. But the point on which Jesus focuses attention is the *sign* of Jonah. Unlike other prophetic signs that were performed *by* the prophet, the sign of Jonah was one that was done *to* him. Similarly, the sign that will be granted to the evil and adulterous generation is not one performed by Jesus but upon him.

Moreover, the student of the Law and the Prophets would know that the swallowing of Jonah by the great fish came about as a consequence of a judgment on Jonah. Those who threw him overboard did so as an act of sacrifice, in order to remove evil from their midst, and so avert a worse disaster than the storm that was tossing the ship (Jonah 1:14ff.). Likewise, the death of Jesus, as a consequence of the charges of blasphemy and Satanism, would be a judgment on Jesus that would remove the evil from the midst of Israel and avert national shipwreck. But the rescue of Jonah reverses the judgment and reinstates the prophet. The restoration and vindication of Jesus will likewise be a reversal of the verdict and actions of those who seek to put him to death. It will also be a vindication of the wisdom of God and of those like the Ninevites who responded to the proclamation of the Word of God (Matt. 12:42).

The saying about the unclean spirit (Matt. 12:43-45; cf. Luke 11:24-26) also takes up the charge that had been leveled against Jesus. An outward response had been made to the preaching and baptism of John the Baptist. The Pharisees were among those who had come to John, though they had been rebuked by him (Matt. 3:7-10; cf. 7:30). They had not really got rid of the evil spirit. They had presented themselves for water baptism. Whatever outward reformation they may have shown, they had certainly not been baptized with the Holy Spirit. Their subsequent actions will show the last state to be worse than the first.

A deeper underlying motif may also be discerned in this saying. It contains an allusion to the Day of Atonement ritual, described in Leviticus 16 and the Mishnah tractate Yoma, and to the necessity of driving what is unclean out of the camp, that "they may not defile the camp, in the midst of which I dwell" (Num. 5:3b). The Day of Atonement was a day of purgation. Having made atonement for the sins of the people, the high priest laid his hands on a goat. Having confessed the sins of the people over it, he drove it into the wilderness. The goat stood for Azazel who, we are told in the Book of Enoch, is the leader of rebel angels and the seducer of man. While we may be unaware of the precise allusions in Jesus' statement about the unclean spirit when viewed in the context that we are suggesting, it is clear that the saying is a charge turning the Beelzebul accusation against those who conceived it. The sins and the spirit that inspired them have not been disposed of by the Day of Atonement rites. Far from purging evil from the midst of the people of God, the religious leaders are themselves more than ever in the grip of evil spirits.

These comments are intended to serve as an indication of Matthew's overall perspective which, if anything, brings out even more clearly than Mark the decisive role of the Spirit in Jesus' messiahship and the two conflicting interpretations that were placed on him. What was said earlier about a Word christology alongside the Spirit christology in Mark could be said even more emphatically of Matthew. In response to the very first temptation (which comes immediately after the descent of the Spirit) Jesus declares, "It is written, Man shall not live by bread alone, but by every word that proceeds from the mouth of God" (Matt. 4:4; cf. Deut. 8:3). As the temptations, and indeed the rest of the Gospel, proceed, Jesus is portrayed not only as One who lives by every word that proceeds out of the mouth of God. The word of God proceeds out of his own mouth. In delivering the Sermon on the Mount, "he taught them as one who had authority, and not as their scribes" (Matt. 7:29). His healings, like his other actions, fulfill the word of God (e.g., Matt. 3:15; 8:17; cf. Isa. 53:4). But in his exorcisms, healing, restoration to life, forgiving, and rebuking of the storm he also speaks the word of God (see, e.g., Matt. 8 and 9).

For more detailed investigation of Matthew's handling of the miracle stories, I would draw particular attention to Birger Gerhardsson's study, *The Mighty Acts of Jesus According to Matthew* (1979).[28] Gerhardsson sees Matthew presenting the activity of Jesus in two phases. During the first, God is with him and he is active in strength. He is the healer of Israel (e.g., Matt. 8:16f.; cf. Isa. 53:4; Matt. 9:33 and the fulfillment of prophecy already noted). His ministry is directed not toward the disciples, but toward the crowds, the sick, the outsiders. Bound up with this is a concern to make Jesus understood by his readers. Jesus' power and the faith of men is the theme of Jesus' nontherapeutic miracles. This leads to new insight. Whereas the therapeutic miracles were continually recurring, the nontherapeutic miracles were occasional events, the meaning of which is for the benefit of the disciples (Matt. 8:23–27; 14:13–33; 15:29–39; 17:24–27; 21:18–22). The disciples themselves are given authority to participate in the work of Jesus (Matt. 12:1, 8). The second phase that Gerhardsson sees in Matthew is the period of weakness, which is the period of the passion.

We may observe that for the Synoptic evangelists, but especially for Matthew, the miracles are like the parables (Matt. 13:10–17; cf. Mark 4:11; Luke 8:9f.). In both cases, discernment of meaning requires faith, a right attitude, and grace. "Blessed is he who takes no offense at me" (Matt. 11:6). "Blessed are you, Simon Bar-Jona! For flesh and blood has not revealed this to you, but my Father who is in heaven" (16:17; cf. 11:27). The Sermon on the Mount recognizes the possibility of prophesying, casting out demons, and doing many mighty works in Jesus' name, only to be cast out as an evildoer not known by Jesus (7:21–23). The pronouncement is consistent with the attitude toward signs in chapters 12 and 24, discussed above. It underscores the importance of right relationships over outward acts.

Moreover, the distinction between two successive phases in Jesus' life and ministry of strength followed by weakness cannot be regarded as an absolute one. For the One who stills the storm has just said that, unlike the foxes and birds, the Son of Man has nowhere to lay his head (8:20–27). His sheer fatigue causes him to sleep in the boat, though he does not have a place of his own. He who cast the demons into the swine also obliged the Gadarenes by leaving their neighborhood (8:34). He is the one who, according to the infancy narratives, received royal gifts, but was deemed illegitimate by Joseph, who was obliged to flee the country with his family on account of Herod's search and destroy mission (2:14).

In other words, a paradox between strength and weakness may be discerned throughout Matthew's story. In his own person he fulfills the Emmanuel prophecy of the sign that God is with his people (1:23; cf. Isa. 7:14). It is a sign that he fulfills through his humble birth. As Son of God he has dominion and authority (11:27; 14:30, 33; 16:16; 22:42-44; 28:19). But the way of the Son of God is that of righteous obedience in the face of temptation (3:15; 4:3-10). The paradox between strength and weakness finds climactic, ironical expression in the mockery of the chief priests, scribes, and elders: "He saved others; he cannot save himself. He is the King of Israel; let him come down now from the cross, and we will believe in him. He trusts in God; let God deliver him now, if he desires him; for he said, 'I am the Son of God' " (27:42-43). Both Mark and Luke have abbreviated versions of this (Mark 15:32; Luke 23:35). But it is Matthew who brings out the paradox the most strongly and records the final ironical demand of a conclusive sign from his triumphant adversaries. The situation has a striking parallel in the Wisdom of Solomon 2:18: "For if the righteous man is God's son, he will uphold him and deliver him out of the hand of his adversaries."

In Matthew's account of the trial and crucifixion of Jesus there is a juxtaposition of the titles "Son of God" and "King of Israel" (27:40, 42; cf. 11, 29, 37). It may well contain a *double entendre*, for the title "King of Israel" was one that belonged especially to Yahweh (Isa. 44:6; cf. 42:21). The kingship of Yahweh was a theme of the so-called enthronement psalms (Pss. 47:8; 93:1; 96:10; 97:1; 99:1). In messianic theology the universal reign of Yahweh was combined with the hoped-for reign of the messiah. Thus, a note of scorn is clearly audible when the adversaries of Jesus called him "The King of the Jews." In recording Jesus' dying words the evangelist himself appears to set a certain distance between God and Jesus in the cry "My God, my God, why hast thou forsaken me?" (27:46; cf. Mark 15:34). To some this sounded like a cry to Elijah, which from the perspective of magic, necromancy, or occultism would seem to be a last, desperate effort to invoke supernatural (though not divine) power. From the perspective of Psalm 22, however, it was the opening words of a psalm in which the psalmist knows the desolation of the righteous, but finds strength and ultimate vindication in the Lord. The final verses of the psalm find a fulfillment in the final verses of Matthew's Gospel. The universal dominion that is Yahweh's is given to the risen Lord (28:18; cf. Ps. 22:28ff.).

In describing Jesus' death Matthew uses the words *aphēken to pneuma*—literally, "he let go the spirit" (Matt. 27:50; cf. John 19:30). English translations usually take this to mean that he yielded up his human spirit. Certainly, the human spirit is a well-established meaning for *pneuma* (cf. Gen. 35:18). But *pneuma* is also the recognized term for the Spirit of God. The two senses occur together in Psalm 51:10ff., 17. In view of all that Matthew has said about the Spirit in Jesus' conception and anointing as the ground of his sonship and ministry, it may be asked whether Matthew's wording here is not intended as a *double entendre*, and that his death meant the departure of the Spirit of God.

THE GOSPEL ACCORDING TO LUKE

On the question of Luke's approach, Paul J. Achtemeier has made an important contribution in "The Lukan Perspective on the Miracles of Jesus: A Preliminary Sketch."[29] He observes that Luke has omitted six of Mark's stories and added some ten of his own.[30] Achtemeier discerns in Luke a concerted attempt to remove vagueness and ambiguity in Mark's wording. Luke directs attention away from the recipient and toward Jesus (cf. 18:35-43 with Mark 10:46-52). Analysis of the form of Luke's stories shows a predilection for adding a reaction from the crowd, usually to praise God for what they had seen. Luke arranges his material so as to bring out the importance of miracles in Jesus' mission and their relationship with discipleship. He attempts to balance Jesus' miracle working with his teaching. Following the reading of Isaiah 61:1f. in the synagogue at Nazareth (4:18ff.), Luke stresses both the prophetic and the healing work of Jesus. We may note that this leads to a conflict that focuses on the refusal of the people to accept Jesus on these terms, and how this typifies the response to God's action in the past. It results in an attempt on Jesus' life (4:29). As yet there is no open charge of blasphemy or demon possession. The event occurs in Nazareth before the exorcism in Capernaum. But there is clear resentment of Jesus' presumption.

Achtemeier sees a further balance of teaching and miracle working in Luke 4:31-37; 5:12-16 and in the way in which Luke arranges teaching and healing in chapters 6 and 7. Even where his source contains only one element, Luke seeks to supply the other. He eliminates detail in order to focus on Jesus. In his handling of John the Baptist's question, Luke emphasizes Jesus' current miracles (7:18-23; cf. Matt. 11:2-6). This episode is preceded by two stories (7:1-17), both of which concern raisings to life and give point to the declaration that "the dead are raised," among the healing and preaching activities of Jesus (7:22; cf. Isa. 29:18-19; 35:5-6; 61:1). Here, too, we may add, Jesus' works are not simply impressive feats. They are the works of God or works of the Spirit that fulfill prophecy.

Luke draws attention to the human response to Jesus' acts. It is frequently a combination of amazement, fear, and glorification (5:25f.; 7:16; 8:35, 37, 43; 9:43; 13:13; 17:15; 18:43), though the fear is generally confined to the onlookers. If faith is a ground of healing, praise to God is the proper outcome (17:18f.). Mighty works, whether performed by Jesus or the disciples, show that the kingdom of God is present and demand a positive response (10:9, 13-20; 11:14-23; 17:20f.). The kingdom of God is not something future; it is already in the midst of the questioners.

Like Matthew and Mark, Luke brings out the conflict with Satan and the question of whether it is by the Spirit of God or Beelzebul that Jesus does his works. But Luke does so in his own way. The subjection of the demons to the seventy whom Jesus sent out to every place where he was about to come, is evidence of the fall of Satan from heaven (10:17-20). But the seventy are not to rejoice in power for its own sake, but because they belong to God who is the source of their power. In his account of Jesus' baptism, anointing, temptation, return, and reading of Isaiah 61, Luke has already stressed the role of the Spirit. The return of the seventy is an occasion for Jesus' rejoicing in the Holy Spirit (10:21). Luke places the saying on blasphemy against the Holy Spirit in the context of a series of sayings and thus detaches it from the Beelzebul controversy (12:10). However, he gives the controversy central place (11:14–26), and makes it clear that it is by the Holy Spirit that Jesus works and the disciples are also to work.

Luke brings this out in various ways. He understands the saying about the Father's delight to give gifts to those who ask to be specifically a delight of the heavenly Father to "give the Holy Spirit to those who ask him" (11:13; cf. Matt. 7:11). Whereas Matthew places his saying in the Sermon on the Mount, Luke place his saying immediately before the Beelzebul controversy. When Luke gives his version of the saying about blasphemy against the Holy Spirit, he goes on to link it with the promise that the Holy Spirit will teach the disciples what to say in their hour of trial (12:12; cf. Matt. 10:20). Luke thus appears to have in mind the thought that the Spirit of God that was upon Jesus will be given to the disciples. This is in accordance with his understanding of the baptism of the Spirit as the promised gift of the Spirit to the disciples (Acts 1:5; 11:16). They will be immersed in the Spirit, as they are sent by the Lord in fulfillment of his mission.[31]

Although this is Luke's primary focus when he speaks of the baptism with the Spirit, the elements that we noted in Mark are not eliminated in Luke. Moreover, the ascription of Jesus' works to the Spirit and their centrality to the kingdom of God in the narration of the Beelzebul controversy is asserted in the pronouncement, "But if it is by the finger of God that I cast out demons, then the kingdom of God has come upon you" (11:20). Luke clearly has more in mind than exorcism in the strict sense. For the context makes it clear that the reason for the dumbness of the man whom Jesus has just cured is a dumb spirit (11:14). The healing of a woman who had "a spirit of infirmity" for eighteen years is described as a release from the bondage of Satan (13:10, 16; cf. 11:21f.). In his account of the healing of Simon Peter's mother-in-law, Luke describes how Jesus "rebuked the fever," which leaves her (4:39). He thus uses the language of exorcism for physical ailments. In describing his mission, Jesus closely links the casting out of demons, the performance of cures, and prophecy (13:31–35). What is described in Luke 11:20 may, therefore, be understood as a part of Jesus' ministry, which is descriptive of the whole (cf. 4:18f.). The expression "finger of God," like the more common "hand of God," was an established way of speaking about God in action and appears to be synonymous with "Spirit of God."[32] Thus, for example, the heavens could be ascribed to the work of God's fingers (Ps. 8:3) and God's breath or spirit (Ps. 33:6). The connection between the laying on of hands and the gift of the Spirit may well be related to this matrix of ideas. It may well also be that Luke's phraseology has preserved the original idiomatic form of wording, whereas Matthew has translated it.

Two conclusions may be noted from a comparison of Matthew with Luke. On the one hand, although Luke is generally thought of as the theologian of the Holy Spirit in the New Testament, Matthew's emphasis on the Spirit is no less great than Luke's.[33] Indeed, with his concern to balance teaching with healing and exorcisms, and to show how the disciples were also given the Spirit, Luke gives a wider context to the point that is so clear in Mark—that Jesus' ministry fulfills John the Baptist's prophecy that Jesus will baptize with the Holy Spirit. On the other hand, Luke clearly presents Jesus as the One on whom the Spirit of the Lord has come, to fulfill the redemptive ministry prophesied by Isaiah, which includes both healing and preaching.

THE GOSPEL ACCORDING TO JOHN

I have argued that Matthew, Mark, and Luke have an explicit Spirit christology and an implicit Word christology. Their understanding of Christ cannot be appreciated apart from the unique activity of the Spirit. At the same time, they make it clear that the words of Jesus are the speech-acts of God himself. The two activities are inseparable, but it is the activity of the Spirit that is the initial focus of attention providing the context for his utterance of the Word. With John's Gospel, it is the other way around. John begins with the express declaration that "In the beginning was the Word, and the Word was with God, and the Word was God. . . . And the Word became flesh and dwelt among us, full of grace and truth; we have beheld his glory, glory as of the only Son from the Father" (1:1, 14). In John the word "Son" refers to the eternal Word of God who became incarnate. As such he is divine, preexistent, and the appointed executor of the Father (3:16–21, 31–36; 6:33, 50, 58, 62; 7:28; 8:14–20; 10:36; 16:28; 17:1–5, 17, 21–24). John begins with an explicit Word christology. His Gospel culminates, however, with a Spirit christology. For the risen Jesus breathes on the disciples and says to them, "Receive the Holy Spirit" (20:22).

Underlying this action are two implications. The immediate one is the fact that the word "Spirit" in both Hebrew (*rûaḥ*) and Greek (*pneuma*) means "wind" and "breath." The action was thus in the tradition of prophetic signs, carrying with it the further implication that the life-force that makes possible the incarnation of the Word of God was none other than the life-force of God himself being bestowed upon the disciples. They would thus have a new relationship with God as they fulfilled the mission of Jesus (cf. John 7:38f.; cf. 14:11f.). As John's Gospel unfolds, the Spirit aspect of christology is developed. John records the Baptist's testimony, "I myself did not know him; but he who sent me to baptize with water said to me, 'He on whom you see the Spirit descend and remain, this is he who baptizes with the Holy Spirit.' And I have seen and have borne witness that this is the Son of God"

(1:33f.). It is not without significance that the Pharisees saw baptism as an activity of the Christ, Elijah, or the eschatological prophet (1:25). But John points out that his baptism was merely baptism with water. The Fourth Gospel goes on to say that Jesus' disciples also baptized with water (4:1–2; cf. 3:22). Still later the evangelist notes the observation of many who came to Jesus, who said that "John did no sign, but everything that John said about this man was true" (10:41).

It may well be that Jesus' declarations concerning being born from above and of the Spirit in John 3:3–6 contain an allusion to himself, as the Son of Man who has "descended from heaven" (3:13). Nicodemus says to Jesus, "Rabbi, we know that you are a teacher come from God; for no one can do these signs that you do, unless God is with him" (3:2). Yet Nicodemus was "a man of the Pharisees . . . a ruler of the Jews" (3:1). Perhaps we are intended to see here a minority, dissentient voice among the Pharisees, one that refused to go along with the majority who denounced Jesus as demon-possessed as a means of discrediting his teaching. For Nicodemus the teaching was authenticated by the signs. These evidently included the signs that Jesus did at the Passover in Jerusalem (2:23). The demand for a sign to justify Jesus' cleansing of the temple (2:18) corresponds to the question in the Synoptics concerning his authority. Jesus' response concerning the destruction of the temple of his body (2:19–22) corresponds to the sign of Jonah in Matthew and Luke. Nicodemus' failure to comprehend the working of the Spirit, despite the fact that he is a teacher of Israel (3:10), may well include an allusion to the role of the Spirit in the prophecies of Isaiah concerning the Lord's anointed. At the same time, the passage (esp. vv. 5–8) emphasizes the necessity of rebirth by the Spirit for everyone who would enter the kingdom of God.

John 7:39 stresses that the Spirit was not yet given to believers because Jesus was not yet glorified. But John 1:32 and 20:22 make it clear that Jesus himself was filled with the Spirit. The Paraclete sayings of John 14:16, 17, 25 and 16:7–15 constitute a bridge between Jesus' possession of the Spirit and Jesus' bestowal of the Spirit.

Whereas the Synoptic Gospels give prominence to the Beelzebul charge, John records the equally damning charge that Jesus is a Samaritan and has a demon (8:48; cf. 7:20; 10:20). Here, too, it is linked with attempts to kill Jesus on the grounds that he is leading people astray (7:12, 20, 25; 8:59; 10:33). It may be that Jesus' teaching was seen as a form of Samaritan deviation from the pure Jewish faith, and that such deviations were associated in the Jewish mind with demons. There is evidence of esteem of magical powers in Samaria.[34] The response of the woman at Jacob's well in Samaria suggests that she thought that Jesus was making magical claims to draw water without implements (4:11). Significantly, the question of drinking is linked with drinking of the Spirit (cf. 7:37; an image that occurs elsewhere in 1 Cor. 10:4; 12:13). The reply that Jesus gives links the Spirit of God with truth (John 4:24). God who is Spirit must be worshiped in the Spirit and in truth. This leads immediately to the woman's confession, identifying the Anointed

One with the revelation of truth: "The woman said to him, 'I know that Messiah is coming (he who is called Christ); when he comes, he will show us all things.' Jesus said to her, 'I who speak to you am he' " (4:25-26). The frequent references in John to the Christ remind the reader that he is the Anointed One, and at the same time raise the question, "With what is he anointed?" The answer has already been given in John 1:33f. (cf. 1:41).

Caiaphas justified Jesus' death by calling it the ultimate act of expediency, one that will avert the national disaster that would come about through the people being led astray by following Jesus' signs (11:47-53). Thus, in John's Gospel the motivation for getting rid of Jesus is essentially the same as that in the Synoptic Gospels. The rebuttal of the charge of demon-possession also affords significant comparisons. Attention is drawn to the patent absurdity of the idea of a demon opening the eyes of the blind (10:21). The question is raised, "When the Christ appears, will he do more signs than this man has done?" (7:31). But whereas in Matthew and Luke, Jesus refers his works to the Spirit of God, in John they are related to the eternal Word of God that is incarnate in Jesus (7:16ff.; 8:51-58). The Spirit motif is implicit rather than explicit in John. In the Synoptics attribution of the works of Jesus to Satan are seen as blasphemy against the Holy Spirit. In John false accusation of Jesus is attributed to the devil (8:44). It is not Abraham who is the father of those who accuse Jesus in the interests of removing him from the midst of the people, but the devil who (in allusion to Gen. 3) was a murderer from the beginning and who is the father of lies.

The charge of blasphemy figures in John 10:33, 36, where it is linked with Jesus' identity as Son of God. Here, as in the Synoptics, the title is understood dynamically. It is immediately related to the one who does the works of the Father, in whom is the Father and who is in the Father. "If I am not doing the works of my Father, then do not believe me; but if I do them, even though you do not believe me, believe the works, that you may know and understand that the Father is in me and I am in the Father" (10:37f.; cf. 5:20-27, 35ff.; 7:27f.; 8:28; 9:3f.; 14:10f.; 15:24; 17:2ff., 21). Whereas Matthew and Luke develop the thought that the works of Jesus are the works of the Spirit-anointed Christ, and as such fulfill prophecy, in John the works of Jesus are identifiable as the works of the Father. As such they reveal the divine glory, in accordance with the Scriptures, and they also bring glory to God (5:41-47; cf. 1:14; 2:11; 5:41, 44; 7:18; 8:50, 54; 9:24; 11:4, 40; 12:41, 43; 17:5, 22, 24). It is a characteristic of human beings, especially the false accusers of Jesus, that they seek their own glory. It is the characteristic of Jesus' works that they reveal the glory of God and bring glory to God.

In John the works of Jesus are signs that demand a response. As Eduard Lohse and Eduard Schweizer have pointed out, John is here adopting an Old Testament concept. Each sign is not to be considered by itself; it "has significance only as a pointer to something different."[35] The signs in John are not like the signs demanded by the Pharisees in the Synoptic Gospels or by the Jews in John 6:30 (cf. 2:23; 4:48). They are not provided simply to validate the message as external, objective proof. Rather, they are more like the prophetic signs of the Old Testament the prophet performed to illustrate and embody his message. The prophetic signs of the Old Testament were largely nonsupernatural, in that they did not generally involve violations of the laws of nature. In riding into Jerusalem on an ass (12:25; cf. Zech. 9:9) and in washing the disciples' feet (13:12–17), Jesus was performing similar signs. Indeed, the feeding of the five thousand leads to the observation that Jesus was "the prophet who is to come into the world" (John 6:14). But insofar as Jesus was more than a prophet, in fact, the Word of God made flesh, his signs also had a supernatural dimension.

John makes no reference to exorcisms. Instead, he describes seven signs: the turning of water into wine (2:1–11); the healing of the nobleman's son (4:46–54); the healing of the lame man by the pool (5:1–18); the feeding of the five thousand (6:1–14); the walking on the water (6:16–21); the healing of the blind man (9:1–41); and the raising of Lazarus (11:1–44). The choice of seven may reflect the idea of the perfect number, completeness, or the days of creation or the restoration of creation. It has been suggested that these signs respectively show Jesus' lordship over quality, space, time, quantity, nature, misfortune, and death.[36] The main narrative in John reaches the climactic conclusion with these verses:

> Now Jesus did many other signs in the presence of the disciples, which are not written in this book; but these are written that you may believe that Jesus is the Christ, the Son of God, and that believing you may have life in his name. (20:30–31)

It is not for nothing that scholars like R. E. Brown interpret the Fourth Gospel as "The Book of Signs."[37] However, if we speak in this way, it is important to remember that the signs illustrate and embody the teaching of Jesus. The signs are interwoven in a series of discourses and discussions that they illustrate. They are thus prophetic signs in the tradition of Old Testament prophecy. They do not lead away to another God, like the signs of the false prophet who is to be condemned and destroyed. Rather, they illustrate and embody the work of the Father, and as such reveal God's glory.

Despite the emphasis on the signs of Jesus in John 20:30–31, signs have an ambivalent value. The preceding verse caps the account of Thomas's unbelieving attitude toward the resurrection with the question, "Have you believed because you have seen me? Blessed are those who have not seen and yet believe" (20:29). Lohse observes that

> Jesus' miracles exert no incontrovertible power before which all must bow, but rather, like his preaching, consistently provoke a double reaction (7.40f.; 9.16; 10.19; 11.45f.). On the one hand stands faith, which understands the signs of Jesus as a revelation (2.11; 4.46–54). But on the other hand, the signs of Jesus release the embittered hatred of the Jews, which brings him to the cross.[38]

Throughout the Gospel, the signs of Jesus (like the teaching of Jesus) provoke both belief (2:11, 23; 4:50, 53; 5:9; 6:14, 21; 9:11, 17, 33, 38; 11:27,
45; 12:11) and unbelief (5:18; 6:66; 9:16, 24, 29, 40f.; 11:53). The desire for
signs and wonders, which does not get beyond being impressed with the
remarkable, could be compared with what the Synoptic parable of the sower
likens to seed fallen on the path or among thorns (2:24f.; 3:2; 4:48; 6:2;
12:18). For the reader of the Gospel, the purpose in recording the signs of
Jesus is not to provide conclusive proof but to provide grounds for *believing*
in the Christ, the Son of God, so that the *believer* may have life in his name.

MIRACLES AND THE TRINITY

If we were to stand back and ask ourselves how we should think of the Spirit
and Word of God in relation to Jesus, it may be helpful to recall an observation made by Karl Rahner in his small but important book *The Trinity*:

> Throughout the Old Testament there runs the basic theme that God is
> the absolute mystery, whom nobody can see without dying, and that it
> is nevertheless this God *himself* who conversed with the Fathers through
> his actions in history. This revealing self-manifestation is, in the Old Testa-
> ment, mediated mostly (not to mention Yahweh's Angel, etc.) by the
> "Word," which, while causing God to be present in power, also represents
> him; and by the "Spirit," who helps men to understand and to announce
> the Word. When these two are not active, Yahweh has retreated from
> his people. When he bestows upon the "holy remnant" his renewed and
> forever victorious mercy, he sends *the* prophet with his Word in the
> fullness of the Spirit. (The Torah and Wisdom doctrine of sapiential
> literature is only a more individualistic version of the same conception.
> It pays less attention to historical development.) God is present in the
> unity of Word and Spirit.[39]

Somewhat earlier and somewhat more tersely Rahner urges that "A
revelation of the Father without the Logos and his incarnation would be like
speaking without words."[40] But equally well, it could be said that a revelation of the Father without his Spirit would be like speaking without breath.
For without breath it is impossible to speak a word. From time to time in
this Postscript we have drawn attention to the fact that both the Hebrew
and the Greek words for Spirit mean wind or breath. In a sense, wind and
breath coincide, for from the physical standpoint they both consist of air.
But it is moving air. Thus, both wind and breath also symbolize energy and
life. Both senses are present in the New Testament. The Spirit came as a
rushing wind at Pentecost (Acts 2:2). Referring to the Spirit, Jesus observed
that the wind blows where it wills (John 3:8). But Spirit, in the sense of the
divine breath, is clearly intended in the action of the risen Jesus, when he
breathed on the disciples and said, "Receive the Holy Spirit" (John 20:22).

If we look further back into the Old Testament we find that in Genesis
1 creation is attributed to the Word of God. To adapt the language that we

have used of christologies, it could be said that Genesis 1 teaches an explicit Word doctrine of creation in its references to God speaking and at the same time an implicit Spirit doctrine of creation in its allusions to the Spirit.[41] Psalm 33:6 brings the two ideas expressly together in the parallelism: "By the word of the Lord the heavens were made, and all their host by the breath of his mouth." From one standpoint creation is the work of God's Word; from another, it is the work of his breath. Breath is the vital power of life;[42] it is also the means by which words are articulated. A similar idea is expressed in the New Testament in the observation that all Scripture is God-breathed (theopneustos; 2 Tim. 3:16). In other words, the Word of God in Scripture is articulated by the breath of God. In order to speak, we need breath. The Word of God, which is the expression of the mind of God, is articulated by the breath or Spirit of God. We cannot have the Word without the Spirit, or the Spirit without the Word.

Our study of miracles is pointing us in the same direction. From one standpoint, the miracles of Jesus are the work of the Spirit or divine breath in and through him. From another, they are wrought by the Word of God that he uttered and that, according to John, was made flesh in him. From yet another standpoint, both these activities were the work of the Father. For the Spirit is the Spirit of the Father and the Word is the Word of the Father.

A great deal of Christian thought has been inclined to relate the miracles of Jesus to the exclusive personal action of Jesus and has sought to treat them in isolation from the activity of the Father and the Spirit. Yet this left the question of what to do with the references to the Spirit and to the Father in the Gospel miracle stories. In the light of our study, it would seem that to begin with the incarnation in this way is to begin at the wrong end. We need to see the miracles and indeed the incarnation in the context of the Trinity. We need to remember, too, that when the classical confessions of the Christian faith speak of the three divine Persons, they are not teaching tritheism. The word Person did not carry with it the idea of an autonomous individual with a mind, will, and feelings of his own. Nor did it denote a merely temporary manifestation or fashion of speaking. It denoted what Calvin called "a 'subsistence' in God's essence."[43] The three Persons of the Trinity are three ways in which God is God. The question of miracles is really a question of the Trinity. To see it in broader perspective, we need to look more carefully at what the Old and New Testaments and intertestamental literature have to say about the Spirit of God, the Word and Wisdom of God, and indeed about the Fatherhood of God.[44] Perhaps this may open up the way for a renewed Augustinian approach to the Trinity in terms of God's eternal, personal oneness in threeness. But these must remain questions for other studies.

ENDNOTES

1. MIRACLES AND APOLOGETICS FROM THE EARLY CHURCH TO THE REFORMATION

1. Cf. G. W. H. Lampe, "Miracles and Early Christian Apologetic," in C. F. D. Moule, ed., *Miracles: Cambridge Studies in their Philosophy and History* (London: Mowbrays, 1965), 203–18; M. F. Wiles, "Miracles in the Early Church," ibid., 219–34; J. Speigl, "Die Rolle der Wunder in Vorkonstantinischen Christentum," *Zeitschrift für Katholische Theologie* 92 (1970): 287–312; and especially R. M. Grant, *Miracle and Natural Law in Graeco-Roman and Early Christian Thought* (Amsterdam: North Holland Publishing Co., 1952).

2. *Against Celsus* 1.46; quoted from H. Chadwick, *Origen: Contra Celsum* (Cambridge: Cambridge Univ. Press, 1953), 42.

3. *Dialogue with Trypho* 69; quoted from R. P. C. Hanson, tr. and ed., *Selections from Justin Martyr's Dialogue with Trypho, A Jew* (London: Lutterworth Press, 1963), 43.

4. *On the Incarnation* 18; quoted from E. R. Hardy and C. C. Richardson, eds., *Christology of the Later Fathers,* Library of Christian Classics, vol. 3 (Philadelphia: Westminster Press; London: SCM Press, 1954), 72.

5. *An Address on Religious Instruction* (also known as *Catechetical Oration)* 34; quoted from Hardy and Richardson, op. cit., 313f.; cf. *Against Eunomius* 5.5.

6. Cf. Justin, *Dialogue with Trypho* 39; *First Apology* 48; Eusebius, *Ecclesiastical History* 2.3.2; Theophilus, *To Autolychus* 1.13; Arnobius, *Against the Heathen* 1.42–51.

7. Cf. the apocryphal *Acts* of John, Paul, and Peter, noted by Lampe, op. cit., 205ff.

8. Cf. Cicero's criticism of the Stoics in *On the Nature of the Gods* 3.92. See further R. Walzer, *Galen on Jews and Christians* (London: Oxford Univ. Press, 1949), 28ff. On science and nature in the ancient world see R. G. Collingwood, *The Idea of Nature* (Oxford: Clarendon Press, 1945), and C. Singer, *A Short History of Scientific Ideas to 1900* (Oxford: Clarendon Press, 1959).

9. Pliny, *Natural History* 2.5.26.

10. Cf. H. Weinel, *Die Wirkungen des Geistes und der Geister im nachapostolischen Zeitalter bis auf Irenäus* (Tübingen: J. C. B. Mohr, 1899), 116.

11. Jerome D. Frank, *Persuasion and Healing: A Comparative Study in Psychotherapy*, rev. ed. (New York: Schocken Books, 1974), 58–66; Ari Kiev, ed., *Magic, Faith and Healing: Studies in Primitive Psychiatry Today* (New York: The Free Press, 1964).

12. Justin, *Dialogue with Trypho* 7; Irenaeus, *Against the Heresies* 1.13.3f., 23; 2.31f.; Tertullian, *Apology* 22; Tatian, *Address to the Greeks* 12–18; Athenagoras, *A Plea for the Christians* 26–27; cf. Origen, *Against Celsus* 7.3.

13. Origen, *Against Celsus* 1.6, 28, 67f.; 2.32, 51; 5.45; 6.41; 8.80.

14. *Against Celsus* 1.67 (H. Chadwick, op. cit., 62). On this whole question see Eugene V. Gallagher, *Divine Man or Magician: Celsus and Origen on Jesus,* Society for Biblical Literature Dissertation Series 64 (Chico: Scholars Press, 1982).

15. *Against Celsus* 1.68 (Chadwick, 63).

16. *Commentary on John* 2.28; quoted from A. Menzies, ed., *The Ante-Nicene Fathers,* vol. 10 (reprint, Grand Rapids: Wm. B. Eerdmans, 1950), 342.

17. Tertullian pointed out that false prophets could perform signs (Matt. 24:24) and Lactantius noted that the pagan magician Apollonius was reported to have performed wonderful deeds. Tertullian confessed that he had to "deny that evidence simply of this sort was sufficient as a testimony to Him. He himself afterwards deprived it of its authority, because He declared that many would come and 'show great signs and wonders,' so as to turn aside the very elect. . . . wherefore Christ should not be believed in simply on account of His miracles . . ." (*Against Marcion* 3.3; quoted from A. Roberts and J. Donaldson, eds., *The Ante-Nicene Fathers,* vol. 3 [Grand Rapids: Wm. B. Eerdmans, 1951], 322). For both Tertullian and Lactantius (*The Divine Institutions* 5.3), Jesus' fulfillment of prophecy offered a surer proof (cf. also Justin, *First Apology* 31–35, and the works noted above in n. 6). For a survey of early church apologetics see Avery Dulles, *A History of Apologetics,* Theological Resources Series (Philadelphia: Westminster Press; London: Hutchinson, 1971), 22–71.

18. *Against Celsus* 1.2 (Chadwick, 8); cf. the arguments of Lessing and Hume discussed below in chs. 4 and 5.

19. *Against Celsus* 1.46.

20. *Ibid.,* 2.8; 7.8.

21. In C. F. D. Moule, ed., op. cit., 225 (see note 1).

22. In J. Hick, ed., *The Myth of God Incarnate* (Philadelphia: Westminster Press; London: SCM Press, 1977), 1–10, 148–66. Similarly, R. M. Grant believes that "the church fathers in general were too much under the spell of Greek rationalism to be able to avoid rationalising their own myths. They had to treat the miracles of faith as if they were events subject to sense-perception. Perhaps their treatment was in part due to pressure from the non-philosophical *simpliciores.* In any case, by such 'misplaced concretion' they lost the values they were trying to defend. These miracle stories were actually symbols, stories conveying pictures of the freedom and the power of God, who was at work in human history and would ultimately vindicate those who trusted and obeyed him" (*Miracle and Natural Law in Graeco-Roman and Early Christian Thought,* 268f.). Grant concludes his magisterial review of thought on the subject by urging the futility of trying to prove miracles and at the same time admitting that the attempt "to prove that miracles cannot take place is almost equally difficult." Grant's underlying philosophy appears to be akin to that of Paul Tillich (see ch. 7 below) and that of Richard Kroner, whose view he endorses when Kroner writes, "Miracles can be verified or rejected by means of scientific thought as little as the laws of nature can be comprehended with the power of religious imagination; they occur and are meaningful in a sphere quite different from that of science and thought" (Grant, op. cit., 268; cf. R. Kroner, *The Religious Function of the Imagination* [New Haven: Yale Univ. Press, 1941], 42f.). Both the interpretation of miracles and the underlying philosophy here bear a marked resemblance to the views of D. F. Strauss in the nineteenth century (see ch. 5 below).

23. F. MacNutt, *Healing* (Notre Dame: Ave Maria Press, 1974), and *The Power to Heal* (Notre Dame: Ave Maria Press, 1977).

24. B. B. Warfield, *Miracles: Yesterday and Today, True and False* (1918; reprint, Grand Rapids: Wm. B. Eerdmans, 1954), 6.

25. *On the Profit of Believing* 34; quoted from P. Schaff, ed., *A Select Library of the Nicene and Post-Nicene Fathers,* 1st ser., vol. 3 (reprinted, Grand Rapids: Wm. B. Eerdmans, 1956), 362.

26. *Of True Religion* 47; quoted from J. H. S. Burleigh, ed., *Augustine: Earlier Writings,* The Library of Christian Classics, vol. 6 (Philadelphia: Westminster Press; London: SCM Press, 1953), 248.

27. Acts 2:4; 10:45f.

28. Acts 5:15.

29. Cf. Ambrose, *Letter* 22; Augustine, *Confessions* 9.7.16; *The City of God* 22.8; *Sermon* 286.5.

30. *The Retractations,* tr. Sister Mary Inez Bogan, *The Fathers of the Church,* vol. 60 (Washington, D.C.: The Catholic Univ. of America Press, 1968), 55; cf. *The City of God* 21 and 22.

31. R. M. Grant sees especially a Stoic influence (op. cit., 218).

32. *Reply to Faustus the Manichaean* 26.3; quoted from P. Schaff, ed., op. cit., 4:321f. Elsewhere Augustine urges that miracles should be seen in the larger context of the miracle of creation: "Now any marvellous thing that is wrought in this universe is assuredly less than this whole universe, that is heaven and earth and all things that in them are, which God assuredly

created. But the means by which he created it are as hidden and incomprehensible to man as he himself is who created it. . . . Man is greater even than any miracle performed by any man's agency" *(The City of God* 10.12, tr. David S. Wiesen, Loeb Classical Library, vol. 3, books 8–11 [Cambridge, Mass.: Harvard Univ. Press; London: Heinemann, 1958], 308).

33. *The Trinity* 3.9.16; quoted from Augustine, *The Trinity,* tr. S. McKenna, *The Fathers of the Church,* vol. 55 (Washington, D.C.: The Catholic Univ. of America Press, 1963), 112. R. M. Grant traces this idea of the seeds through Philo to Stoicism (op. cit., 219).

34. Cf. E. and M.-L. Keller, *Miracles in Dispute: A Continuing Debate* (London: SCM Press, 1969), 25.

35. *Literal Commentary on Genesis* 6.13.24.

36. *Expositions on the Book of Psalms,* Ps. 91 (90), 14; quoted from P. Schaff, ed., op. cit., 8:450.

37. "The concept of space which we use in the Nicene Creed is one that is relatively closed, so to speak, on our side where it has to do with physical existence, but is one which is infinitely open to God's side" (Torrance, *Space, Time and Incarnation* [London: Oxford Univ. Press, 1969], 18).

38. *Literal Commentary on Genesis* 6.13.24.

39. *Tractates on the Gospel of John* 17, quoted from P. Schaff, *A Select Library of the Nicene and Post-Nicene Fathers,* 1st ser., vol. 7 (reprint, Grand Rapids: Wm. B. Eerdmans, 1956), 111.

40. *Against Apollinaris,* 28.

41. *Dissertations on Subjects Connected with the Incarnation* (London: John Murray, 1907), 165f. Gore's italics, citing John 11:41; Matt. 12:28; Luke 5:17; cf. B. F. Westcott, *The Epistle to the Hebrews* (London and New York: Macmillan, 1892²), 66.

42. See the edition of T. C. O'Brien, St. Thomas Aquinas, *Summa Theologiae* 14, *Divine Government* (1a2ae. 103–109) (London: Blackfriars in conjunction with Eyre and Spottiswoode; New York: McGraw-Hill, 1975).

43. *Summa Theologiae* I, Q. 105, art. 6 (O'Brien, 81). For a recent discussion of medieval miracles see Benedicta Ward, *Miracles and the Medieval Mind: Theory, Record and Event, 1000–1215* (London: Scholar Press; Philadelphia: Univ. of Pennsylvania Press, 1982). Sister Benedicta maintains that the presuppositions behind medieval thinking on miracles are to be found chiefly in Augustine.

44. *Summa Theologiae* I, Q. 105, art. 7; cf. above, n. 25.

45. Ibid. (O'Brien, 85).

46. Ibid., I, Q. 105, art. 8 (O'Brien, 87).

47. *Summa Contra Gentiles* 3.102.3; quoted from Saint Thomas Aquinas, *On the Truth of the Catholic Faith: Summa Contra Gentiles,* Book Three: Providence, Part II, tr. Vernon J. Bourke (Garden City, N.Y.: Doubleday, Image Books, 1956), 81.

48. Ibid. 3.102.4.

49. Ibid. 3.102.6 (Bourke, 85).

50. Ibid. 3.103.8 (Bourke, 88).

51. Ibid. 3.104–105.

52. Ibid. 3.106.

53. *Martin Luther's Doctrine of Christ,* Yale Publications in Religion 14 (New Haven: Yale Univ. Press, 1970), 41f.

54. *Sermons on the Gospel of John: Chapters 14–16,* vol. 24 in *Luther's Works,* ed. J. Pelikan and D. E. Poellot (St. Louis: Concordia Publishing House, 1961), 73.

55. See above, n. 40. Like Gregory of Nyssa, Luther attributes the miracles of Jesus to his divine nature. Commenting on Jesus' claim to be able to take his life again (John 10:18), Luther asserts: "Therefore He cannot be only man but must also be God. The fact that He is to be destroyed and die is proof of His humanity. But that He will rise again, that He raises Himself from death, bears witness to His divinity and to His divine power to quicken the dead; for this is not the work of a human being. In this way Christ reveals His true divinity and humanity to the Jews. And we, too, believe that there are two natures, the divine and the human, in the one Person of Christ" (ibid., *Chapters 1–14,* vol. 22 in *Luther's Works* [1957], 247).

56. *Luther's Works,* 24:64.

57. Ibid., 66. For later Lutheran thought on the relation of Christ's humanity and divinity in his miracles see Martin Chemnitz, *The Two Natures of Christ* (1578), tr. J. A. O. Preus (St. Louis: Concordia Publishing House, 1971), 219–20, 295–96, 475–85.

58. Cf. ibid., 14:114, n. 9.

59. Ibid., 24:67.

60. Ibid., 79f.

61. In a meditation on John 6:1-15 Luther observed: "In this section of the Gospel Christ teaches us again to believe that we should not be anxious for the belly and food, and spurs us on with a miraculous work, as if he should be saying here with the deed what he said in words in Matthew 6: 'Seek first the kingdom of God and his righteousness, then all such will be well with you' " (*Luthers Werke*, Weimarer Ausgabe, XVII/2, 223, author's translation).

62. Ibid., 64f.

63. "So in the mass also, the foremost promise of all, he adds as a memorial sign of such a great promise his own body and his own blood in the bread and the wine, when he says: 'Do this in remembrance of me' [Luke 22:19; 1 Cor. 11:24-25]. And so in baptism, to the words of promise he adds the sign of immersion in water. We may learn from this that in every promise of God two things are presented to us, the word and the sign, so that we are to understand the word to be the testament, but the sign to be the sacrament" (*The Babylonian Captivity of the Church*, *Luther's Works*, 36, *Word and Sacrament*, 2, ed. A. R. Wentz, General Editor H. T. Lehmann [Philadelphia: Muhlenberg Press, 1959], 44).

64. *Luther's Works*, 24:79.

65. Ibid., 192.

66. *Institutes of the Christian Religion*, 2 vols., ed. J. T. McNeill, tr. F. L. Battles, The Library of Christian Classics, vol. 20 (Philadelphia: Westminster Press; London: SCM Press, 1960), 17f.

67. Ibid., 16f. (this section added in the 1539 edition).

68. Ibid., 17.

69. Ibid.; cf. Augustine, *Tractates on the Gospel According to John* 13.17.

70. *Institutes* 1.8.6 (McNeill, 86).

71. Ibid. 1.8.5-7.

72. Ibid. 4.19.6 (McNeill, 2:1454); cf. 4.19.18.

73. Ibid. 1.13.13 (McNeill, 1:136).

74. Ibid. 4.14.18 (McNeill, 2:1294).

75. Ibid. 4.19.18 (McNeill, 2:1466).

2. THE SEVENTEENTH-CENTURY CRUCIBLE

1. Pyrrho (ca. 360–ca. 270 B.C.) is regarded as the first great "skeptic" or "inquirer" (which was the original meaning of the Greek word *skeptikos*). With the rediscovery in the sixteenth century of the writings of the Pyrrhonist Sextus Empiricus, the codifier of Greek skepticism who lived in the last half of the second century and the first quarter of the third century A.D., the arguments of the Greek skeptics entered the theological and philosophical debates of Western Europe. For detailed investigation of points noted below see the seminal work of Richard H. Popkin, *The History of Scepticism from Erasmus to Descartes* (Assen: Van Gorcum and Co., 1960; rev. ed., New York: Harper Torchbooks, 1968).

2. *Discourse on Method* (1637), pts. 2, 4; *Meditations* (1641), 1-3; cf. Popkin's discussion, op. cit., 175-217, which sees Descartes as a "conqueror of scepticism" and yet a "sceptique malgré lui."

In response to a correspondent who drew attention to a parallel in Augustine's *On the Trinity* 10.10, 12 to the *cogito ergo sum*, Descartes replied that Augustine used the idea to show the image of the Trinity in man, whereas he used it "to establish that this conscious *I* is an immaterial substance with no corporeal element" (Letter dated Leyden, November 1640, in E. Anscombe and P. Geach, eds., *Descartes: Philosophical Writings* [London: Nelson, 1954], 263). In a letter thought to be addressed to the Marquis of Newcastle, dating from March or April 1648, he described it as "a proof of our soul's capacity for receiving from God an intuitive kind of knowledge" (ibid., 301). The argument is also found in Augustine, *On Free Will* 2.3.7; *On True Religion* 73; *Against the Academicians* 3.11.25-26; *Soliloquies* 2.1.1; *On the Blessed Life* 2.2.7; *On the Trinity* 10.10.16; 15.12.21. It is more than possible that he encountered it in his student days at La Flèche, and in later life he may have forgotten its source.

3. According to Christoph Matthäus Pfaff, *Dissertationes Anti-Baelius* (Tübingen, 1719), I:3-4 (cf. Popkin, op. cit., 217).

4. David Hume, *An Enquiry Concerning Human Understanding*, sec. XII, pt. 2, 126, cited

from Hume's *Enquiries*, ed. L. A. Selby-Bigge, 3rd ed. rev. P. H. Nidditch (Oxford: Clarendon Press, 1975), 158f.

Section XII of the *Enquiry Concerning Human Understanding* is entitled "Of the Academical or Sceptical Philosophy." Pt. I contains this comment: "There is a species of scepticism, *antecedent* to all study of philosophy, which is much inculcated by Des Cartes and others, as a sovereign preservative against error and precipitate judgement. It recommends an universal doubt, not only of all our former opinions and principles, but also of our very faculties; of whose veracity, say they, we must assure ourselves, by a chain of reasoning, deduced from some original principle, which cannot possibly be fallacious or deceitful. But neither is there any such original principle, which has a prerogative above others, that are self-evident and convincing: or if there were, could we advance a step beyond it, but by the use of those very faculties, of which we are supposed to be already diffident. The Cartesian doubt, therefore, were it ever possible to be attained by any human creature (as it plainly is not) would be entirely incurable; and no reasoning could ever bring us to a state of assurance and conviction upon any subject" (ibid., #116, 149f.).

5. Quoted from H. F. Stewart, *Pascal's Pensées with an English Translation and Brief Notes and an Introduction* (New York: Pantheon Books, 1950), #383, 205.

6. John Donne, *LXXX Sermons*, 1640, #XXII, dated March 25, 1627 (cf. R. Hooykaas, *The Principle of Uniformity in Geology, Biology and Theology: Natural Law and Divine Miracle* [Leiden: E. J. Brill, 1963], 225).

7. Cf. above, p. 8, with Hooykaas, ibid., who notes that Nicholas Oresme, Pierre D'Ailly, and Calvin also tried to narrow the gulf between miracles and natural events.

8. Cf. R. M. Burns, *The Great Debate on Miracles: From Joseph Granvill to David Hume* (Lewisburg: Bucknell Univ. Press, 1981), 38. On British thought on science and religion in this period see also R. S. Westfall, *Science and Religion in Seventeenth-Century England* (New Haven: Yale Univ. Press, 1958), and Henry G. van Leeuwen, *The Problem of Certainty in English Thought, 1630-1690*, International Archives of the History of Ideas 3 (The Hague: Martinus Nijhoff, 1963).

9. John Wilkins, *Of the Principles and Duties of Natural Religion* (1693), reprinted with a new introduction by Henry G. van Leeuwen (New York and London: Johnson Reprint Corporation, 1969), 23 (author's italics).

10. Ibid., 30f. (author's italics).

11. Ibid., 37f., 97f.; cf. Pascal, op. cit., 117ff.; Van Leeuwen, op. cit., 68.

12. *Tractatus Theologico-Politicus* (1670), ch. 6; quoted from *The Chief Works of Benedict de Spinoza*, tr. R. H. M. Elwes, vol. I (reprint, New York: Dover Publications, 1955), 81.

13. Ibid.

14. Cf. *Ethics*, pt. I (R. H. M. Elwes, tr., op. cit., 2:45-81); A. G. Wernham, ed., *The Political Works of Benedict de Spinoza* (Oxford: The Clarendon Press, 1965), 15.

15. F. Copleston, *A History of Philosophy,* vol. 4 (London: Burns & Oates, 1958), 208f.

16. *The Canons of the Synod of Dort*, I, 6-9 (text in P. Schaff, ed., *The Creeds of Christendom,* vol. 3 [reprint, Grand Rapids: Baker Book House, 1977], 582f.).

17. *Tractatus Theologico-Politicus*, ch. 6 (Elwes, op. cit., 1:83).

18. Ibid., 86.

19. Ibid., 87.

20. Ibid., 87ff.

21. Ibid., 88. Spinoza's view of the golden calf is, to say the least, paradoxical. In the light of the history of religions, the calf itself could be seen as the symbolic representation of an immanent deity that would be much nearer to Spinoza's own concept of *deus sive natura* than the transcendent Yahweh of the Old Testament. For recent critical interpretations see J. P. Hyatt, *Exodus,* New Century Bible Commentary (reprint, Grand Rapids: Wm. B. Eerdmans; London: Marshall, Morgan & Scott, 1971), 300-306; B. S. Childs, *Exodus: A Commentary,* Old Testament Library (London: SCM; Philadelphia: Westminster, 1974), 553-81.

22. *Tractatus Theologico-Politicus*, ch. 6 (Elwes, op. cit., 1:91).

23. Ibid., 92. Spinoza found biblical support for the fixity of nature in Ps. 148:6; Jer. 31:35; Eccles. 1:10ff.; 3:11 (ibid., 96).

24. Ibid., 93.

25. Ibid., 94.

26. Alluding to Eccles. 1:10: "there is nothing new under the sun."

27. Ibid., 97.

28. Cited from Hobbes's Introduction in the edition of Nelle Fuller in *Great Books of the Western World*, vol. 23 (Chicago: Encyclopaedia Britannica, Inc., 1952), 47. For Hobbes's background see Samuel I. Mintz, *The Hunting of Leviathan: Seventeenth-Century Reactions to the Materialism and Moral Philosophy of Thomas Hobbes* (Cambridge: Cambridge Univ. Press, 1962).

29. Chapter 46; Fuller, 267.

30. Following these two disasters Parliament passed a bill for the suppression of atheism, and a committee was formed to investigate Hobbes. The charges were eventually dropped, probably due to the intervention of his patron, Charles II. However, Hobbes was forbidden to publish his opinions.

31. Fuller, op. cit., 188.

32. Ibid., 189. Hobbes argued from Matt. 13:58 and Mark 6:5 that Jesus performed miracles only for the elect, as it was the elect alone who had faith. Taken at its face value, this theological point would have met the approval of the Calvinistic Puritans who governed England at the time when *Leviathan* was published. As a piece of irony, however, implying that only the self-styled elect believers could believe in miracles, the point anticipated David Hume by nearly a century.

33. Ibid., 190.

34. Ibid., 190f.

35. Ibid., 191.

36. Cited from *Pascal: Pensées,* tr. A. J. Krailsheimer (Harmondsworth: Penguin Books, 1966), 309.

37. By 1659 Pascal himself had arranged some of the thoughts in order and had given them titles. The task of editing and arranging the fragments has occupied scholars from the time of Pascal's death until the present day. Recent work by Louis Lafuma and Jean Mesnard has resulted in a more definitive French text. Their work has been used by Krailsheimer in his translation (n. 36). Krailsheimer's text is cited below on the question of miracles. It has the advantage of grouping together Pascal's thought on both the New Testament miracles and those associated with Port-Royal. However, Pascal's numerous references to Pyrrhonism and the Pyrrhonists are obscured by Krailsheimer's use of "scepticism" and "sceptics" as interpretative translations. For students and scholars his work would have been enhanced by the inclusion of a comparative table listing the numbers of the various *Pensées* in different editions.

38. Krailsheimer, #131, p. 162.

39. Ibid., #418 (The Wager), pp. 149–53; cf. #110, p. 58; #131, pp. 62–66.

40. Ibid., 357; cf. #84, p. 52; ##140–46, pp. 72–74; ##167–88, pp. 83–85.

41. Ibid., #189, pp. 85f.

42. Ibid., #379, p. 138; c. #378, pp. 137f.

43. Ibid., #832, p. 284.

44. Ibid., #844, p. 290.

45. Ibid., #846, p. 291. The section quoted alludes to Mark 2:2–12; Luke 10:20; 16:31; John 3:2.

46. Ibid., #835, p. 286.

47. Cf. B. Robert Kreiser, *Miracles, Convulsions, and Ecclesiastical Politics in Early Eighteenth-Century Paris* (Princeton, N.J.: Princeton Univ. Press, 1978), 70–72. In Krailsheimer's translation, which follows Lafuma's text, the *Pensées* dealing with the Port-Royal miracles and the implied divine vindication of their cause come at the climax of the entire work (##859–912, pp. 295–306).

48. Ibid., #878, p. 299.

49. Cf. W. Notestein, *A History of Witchcraft in England from 1558 to 1718* (1911; reprint, New York: Russell and Russell, 1965); G. L. Kittredge, *Witchcraft in Old and New England* (1929; reprint, New York: Russell and Russell, 1956); and C. Hole, *Witchcraft in England* (Totowa, N.J.: Rowman and Littlefield, 1977).

50. *Sadducismus-Triumphatus* (reprint, Gainesville, Fla.: Scholars Facsimiles and Reprints, 1966).

51. Ibid., 76.

52. Ibid., 87.

53. Ibid., 101.

54. R. M. Burns, *The Great Debate on Miracles*, 49.

55. *Sadducismus, Triumphatus*, 125.

56. Cited by Burns, op. cit., 55, from Boyle Manuscripts, Royal Society, London, vol. 7, fol. 120–22.

57. *An Essay Concerning Human Understanding,* ed. and abr. A. S. Pringle-Pattison (Oxford: Clarendon Press, 1924, 1967), 2.1.2 (p. 42).

58. Ibid., 4.17.23 (p. 354).

59. Ibid., 4.18.2 (p. 355).

60. See John Locke, *The Reasonableness of Christianity with a Discourse of Miracles* and part of *A Third Letter Concerning Toleration,* ed. and intro. I. T. Ramsey (London: A. & C. Black, 1958).

61. Op. cit., 4.19.4 (p. 360).

62. Ibid., 4.18.5 (pp. 356f.).

63. Ibid., 4.18.3 (pp. 355f.).

64. Ibid., 4.16.14 (p. 343); 4.18.7 (p. 357).

65. Ibid., 4.19.15 (p.363).

66. Cf. I. T. Ramsey, op. cit., 13f., 37, 76f.

67. Ibid., 79.

68. Ibid., 80. For use of the argument by the seventeenth-century Latitudinarian Edward Stillingfleet, and later by the deists and their opponents, see J. C. A. Gaskin, *Hume's Philosophy of Religion* (London: Macmillan, 1978), 106ff., 179.

69. Ramsey, 82.

70. Ibid., 81f.

71. Ibid., 83.

72. Ibid., 84.

73. *A Third Letter Concerning Toleration*, ch. 10 (ibid., 90–99).

3. THE AGE OF DEISM

1. *Instruction Chrétienne*, vol. 2 (Geneva, 1564), "Epistre," dated December 12, 1563. Etymologically the term derives from the Latin *deus* (God). It may be compared with *theism*, which derives from the Greek *theos* (God). Whereas theism denotes belief in a God who is both transcendent and immanent, deism precludes immanent divine activity in the world.

For the varied uses of the term, an account of deism, and bibliography see E. C. Mossner, "Deism," in P. Edwards, ed., *The Encyclopedia of Philosophy,* vol. 2 (New York: Macmillan; London: Collier Macmillan, 1967), 326–36.

2. Thomas Halyburton's *Natural Religion Insufficient, and Revealed Necessary to Man's Happiness in his Present State* (1714) contains a detailed exposition of Lord Herbert's position and that of his disciple, Charles Blount (see *The Works* of Thomas Halyburton, with an Essay on his Life and Writings by Robert Burns [Glasgow: Blackie and Son, 1837], 253–501).

3. For the Greek text and a modern English translation see the critical edition of F. C. Conybeare, Philostratus, *The Life of Apolloneus of Tyana,* Loeb Classical Library, vols. 1–2 (Cambridge, Mass.: Harvard Univ. Press; London: William Heinemann, 1912; rev. ed. 1950).

Comparison of Jesus with "divine men" in the Hellenistic world has received scholarly attention in more recent times. See G. Petzke, *Die Traditionen über Apollonius von Tyana und das Neue Testament,* Studia ad Corpus Hellenisticum Novi Testamenti 1 (Leiden: E. J. Brill, 1970); D. L. Tiede, *The Charismatic Figure as Miracle Worker,* SBL Dissertation Series 1 (Missoula, Mont.: Univ. of Montana, 1972); C. H. Holladay, *Theios Aner in Hellenistic Judaism: A Critique of the Use of this Category in New Testament Christology,* SBL Dissertation Series 40 (Missoula, Mont.: Scholars Press, 1977).

4. The quotation was one of several printed on the title page. It was taken from a sermon preached before the Society for the Propagation of the Gospel in Foreign Parts on February 17, 1715 (*Works*, 3:346, 348). Sherlock went on to argue that the gospel has "a claim to be received independent of those miracles which were wrought for its confirmation" (350).

5. Op. cit., 135 (cited from the facsimile reprint of the first edition, New York and London: Garland Publishing, Inc., 1978).

6. *A View of the Principal Deistical Writers* (London, 1754), 1:444.

7. *The Great Debate on Miracles: From Joseph Glanvill to David Hume* (Lewisburg: Bucknell Univ. Press; London and Toronto: Associated Univ. Presses, 1981), 70; cf. John Toland, *Christianity Not Mysterious*, 152f.; Charles Blount, *The Oracles of Reason* (London, 1693), 12; Thomas Morgan, *The Moral Philosopher* (London, 1737), 1:98f. The following discussion of the deists

and their influence is indebted to the research of R. M. Burns, whose work in this field represents the most important contribution to date.

8. Burns, 72.

9. Burns (ibid., 277) claims that Thomas Chubb provided one of the most balanced and sophisticated treatments in his *Enquiry Concerning the Books of the New Testament in Four Tracts* (London, 1734), *The Author's Farewell*, secs. 6, 8, 9, 10, in *Posthumous Works,* vol. 2 (London, 1748), and *Discourses on Miracles* (London, 1741). Less judicious was Peter Annet's *The Resurrection of Jesus Considered in Answer to the Tryal of the Witnesses* (London, 1744) and *Examination of the Character of St. Paul* (London, 1742). More intemperate was Woolston's *Six Discourses* (London, 1727–28).

Their views may be compared with David Hume, *Enquiries Concerning Human Understanding and Concerning the Principles of Morals*, ed. L. A. Selby-Bigge, 3rd ed. with text and notes rev. P. H. Nidditch (Oxford: Clarendon Press, 1975), #92, pp. 116f.

10. *The Moral Philosopher,* 2:31; cf. Hume, #93, pp. 117f.

11. *Christianity Not Mysterious*, 154; cf. Hume, ##95–100, pp. 121–30; Chubb, *Posthumous Works*, 2:198–200.

12. Hume, #95, p. 122.

13. Burns, 72.

14. In his First *Discourse on the Miracles of our Saviour*, 2nd ed. (London, 1727), 51.

15. *Posthumous Works,* 2:227, cf. 35f.; cf. Thomas Morgan, *Letter To Eusebius* (London, 1739), 8f. and *The Moral Philosopher*, 1:98.

16. First *Discourse*, 4.

17. Ibid., 15.

18. Ibid., 34; Third *Discourse,* 5–8; Fourth *Discourse,* 29; cf. Chubb, *Posthumous Works*, 2:182–93.

19. Woolston, Third *Discourse,* 50; cf. 43.

20. Cf. the views of Locke discussed in the previous chapter and the position of Samuel Chandler, *A Vindication of the Christian Religion* (1725), 81, 83 (noted by Burns, op. cit., 81f.). Chandler dismissed the stories of Apollonius moving vessels of wine and water to entertain guests, understanding the language of the birds, and conversing with the ghost of Achilles. Chandler concluded that "the very telling of such stories is enough to confute them." Similarly, he dismisses many of "the pretended miracles of the Church of Rome" for not being "agreeable to the notions we have of the perfections of divine wisdom."

21. This point is forcibly argued by R. M. Burns, op. cit., 83f., 247–51. Burns contends that R. S. Westfall is incorrect in attributing opposition to miracles to the growing influence of a mechanical world view (Westfall, *Science and Religion in Seventeenth-Century England* [New Haven: Yale Univ. Press, 1958], 96). Burns finds no direct evidence of this in the writings of the major deists, and only indirect evidence of this in the writings of such opponents of the deists as Samuel Clarke, John Leng, and John Conybeare.

22. *Christianity Not Mysterious*, 150.

23. Ibid., 156.

24. *The Religion of Nature Delineated,* 2nd ed. (1722), 109.

25. *Supernaturals Examined*, 44.

26. Ibid., 56–58.

27. Ibid., 63; cf. 64.

28. Ibid., 66f.

29. Burns, op. cit., 90, n. 84, which cites Hume's *Treatise of Human Nature*, ed. L. A. Selby-Bigge (Oxford: Clarendon Press, 1888), 461, as evidence of Hume's knowledge of Wollaston's work.

30. Cf. Burns, 96, who gives a valuable discussion of attitudes toward miracles among the orthodox divines (96–130).

31. William Fleetwood (1656–1733) was a Fellow of King's College, Cambridge, and successively Bishop of St. Asaph (1708) and of Ely (1714). His *Essay* contained material that he had collected for the Boyle Lectureship, but ill health prevented him from giving the lectures. Fleetwood's *Essay* provoked John Locke to reply with his *Discourse of Miracles*.

32. Cited from *The Works* of Samuel Clarke, vol. 2 (London, 1738; reprint, New York and London: Garland Publishing Co., 1978), 607.

33. Ibid., 701.

34. Ibid.

35. Ibid.

36. Ibid., 702.

37. Cf. Brampton Gurdon, *The Pretended Difficulties in Nature or Reveal'd Religion no Excuse for Infidelity,* Boyle Lectures 1721-22 (London, 1723); Thomas Stackhouse, *A Fair State of the Controversy between Mr. Woolston and his Adversaries* (London, 1729); John Chapman, *Eusebius* (Cambridge, 1739 [a reply to Morgan's *Moral Philosopher,* which in turn provoked Morgan's *Letter to Eusebius*]); Abraham Le Moine, *A Treatise on Miracles* (London, 1747); Hugh Farmer, *Dissertation on Miracles* (London, 1771), and *An Examination of the Late Mr. Le Moine's Treatise on Miracles* (London, 1772 [a reply to charges that he had plagiarized Le Moine]). These writers became progressively adamant in their insistence on the evidential, coercive force of miracles. All except Le Moine and Farmer could have provided Hume with ample evidence of this position.

38. *Dissertation on Miracles,* Preface, p. i.

39. Sixth *Discourse,* 27.

40. Ibid., 38.

41. *The Works of Bishop Sherlock, with Some Account of his Life, Summary of Each Discourse, Notes, & c.* by the Rev. T. S. Hughes, vol. 5 (London: A. J. Valpy, 1830), 216. The illustration figured more than once in the debates of the time. Locke told the story of a Dutch ambassador who assured the King of Siam that in cold weather water could become so hard that an elephant could stand on it. To this the king replied: "Hitherto I have believed the strange things you have told me, because I look upon you as a sober fair man; but now I am sure you lie" *(An Essay Concerning Human Understanding,* 4.15.5., ed. A. S. Pringle-Pattison [Oxford: Clarendon Press, 1924], 336). Cf. Joseph Butler, *The Analogy of Religion, Natural and Revealed, to the Constitution and Course of Nature* (1736), Introduction, #3 *(The Works of Joseph Butler,* ed. W. E. Gladstone, vol. 1 [Oxford: Clarendon Press, 1896], 5). David Hume also discussed the significance of this analogy in his *Enquiry Concerning Human Understanding* (1748), X, #89 (Hume's *Enquiries,* ed. L. A. Selby-Bigge, 2nd ed. [Oxford: Clarendon Press, 1902], 113f.). It was noted too by J. S. Mill, *A System of Logic,* 8th ed. (reprint, London: Longmann, 1925), 111.

42. In 1739 Annet published *Judging for Ourselves: Or Free Thinking, The Great Duty of Religion.* He attacked Sherlock in *The Resurrection of Jesus Consider'd: In answer to the Tryal of the Witnesses. By a Moral Philosopher,* which went through three editions in 1744; *The Resurrection Reconsider'd* (1744), *The Sequel of the Resurrection Consider'd* (1745); and *The Resurrection Defenders Stript of all Defence* (1745). Annet replied to the criticisms of Gilbert West in *Supernaturals Examined* (1747). West replied with his *Observations on the History and Evidences of the Resurrection of Jesus Christ* (1747) for which the University of Oxford conferred on him the degree of D.C.L. Sherlock himself replied to Annet in *The Sequel of the Trial of the Witnesses of the Resurrection: Being An Answer to the Exceptions of a Late Pamphlet, Intitled, 'The Resurrection of Jesus Considered by a Moral Philosopher.'* Revised by the Author of the Trial of the Witnesses (1749; *Works,* 5:227-325). Sherlock's writings on the resurrection complemented his earlier work on *The Use and Intent of Prophecy* (1725; rev. ed. 1749).

Other orthodox works relating to the controversy were Samuel Chandler's study *The Witnesses of the Resurrection of Jesus Christ* (1730), which followed his previous *Discourse on the Nature and use of Miracles* (1725) and *Vindication of the Christian Religion* (1725); Richard Smallbroke's two-volume work *Vindication of our Saviour's Miracles* (1729), and Thomas Stackhouse's *Fair State of the Controversy between Mr. Woolston and his Adversaries* (1730).

43. Cf. J. S. Lawton, *Miracles and Revelation* (London: Lutterworth Press, 1959), 51, 63f.; L. Stephen, *History of English Thought in the Eighteenth-Century,* vol. 1, 3rd ed. (1902; reprint, London: Rupert Hart Davis, 1962), 183f., 209f.

44. Benjamin Hoadly, *Letter to Mr. Fleetwood* (London, 1702), reprinted in *Several Tracts Collected in One Volume* (London, 1715); John Leng, *The Natural Obligations to Believe the Principles of Religion and Divine Revelation,* Boyle Lectures 1717-18, 7th ed. (London, 1727); John Conybeare, *The Nature, Possibility and Certainty of Miracles* (London, 1721), and *A Defence of Revealed Religion against the Exceptions of a Late Writer in his Book entitled "Christianity as Old as the Creation"* (London, 1732); James Foster, *The Usefulness, Truth and Excellency of the Christian Revelation Defended: Against the Objections Contained in a Late Book Entitled "Christianity as Old as the Creation"* (London, 1731); Arthur Ashley Sykes, *A Brief Discourse Concerning the Credibility of Miracles and Revelation* (London, 1742). On these writers see R. M. Burns, op. cit., 107-11.

45. *Five Types of Ethical Theory* (New York: Harcourt Brace, 1930), 5.

46. *The Works of Joseph Butler, D.C.L.,* ed. the Right Hon. W. E. Gladstone, vol. 1, *The Analogy of Religion* (Oxford: Clarendon Press, 1896), 5. A similar position had already been argued by Bishop Berkeley and others (cf. G. R. Cragg, *Reason and Authority in the Eighteenth Century* [Cambridge: Cambridge Univ. Press, 1964], 110, 115).

47. "The Empirical sciences are systems of theories. The logic of scientific knowledge can therefore be described as a theory of theories" (Karl Popper, *The Logic of Scientific Discovery* [London: Hutchinson, 6th impression rev., 1972], 59). "Thus not only the more abstract explanatory theories transcend experience, but even the most ordinary singular statements. For even ordinary singular statements are always *interpretations of 'the facts' in the light of theories"* (423; Popper's italics).

48. In Gladstone, op. cit., 1:177.

49. Ibid., 188.

50. *Institutes of the Christian Religion,* 1.3.1, 2; 1.5.1–4.

51. In Gladstone, op. cit., 1:189.

52. Ibid., 190.

53. Ibid., 192.

54. Ibid., 213.

55. Ibid., 218f.

56. Ibid., 219.

57. Ibid., 219. The bishop's thoughts about electricity should be seen against his historical background. For it was only from the 1730s onward that experiments were being performed to determine the nature of static electricity.

58. Ibid., 220.

59. Ibid., 248; cf. 247, 376f.

60. Ibid., 302.

61. Ibid., 304f.

62. Ibid., 306.

63. Ibid., 307.

64. Ibid., 309.

65. Ibid., 317.

66. Ibid., 216f.; cf. L. Stephen, op. cit., 1:339; J. S. Mill, *A System of Logic,* 8th ed. (reprint, London: Longmans, Green and Co., 1925), 407–18; and Anders Jeffner, *Butler and Hume on Religion* (Stockholm: Diakonistyrelsens Bokforlag, 1966), 122. However, R. M. Burns contends that this is a complete misunderstanding of Butler's point (op. cit., 128). He argues that Butler is trying to show that the question of predictability of an event has nothing to do with our difficulties in believing it. We have no difficulty in believing ordinary events that are unpredictable. Moreover, the predictability of divine actions cannot be judged by the predictability of ordinary human actions or natural events.

67. In Gladstone, op. cit., 1:302f.

68. In the accounts of the apostolic preaching in Acts the resurrection of Jesus is crucial (Acts 2:32; 3:26; 4:10, 33; 5:31; 10:40; 13:30; 17:31; 22:10; 25:19; 26:15). However, it should be noted that in the two key sermons of Peter at Jerusalem and Caesarea, where the church was opened to the Jews and Gentiles respectively and the Holy Spirit came upon those who were admitted, the works of Jesus are seen as attestation by God (Acts 2:22) and the Holy Spirit (Acts 10:38).

69. The relevant literature is immense. A recent very thorough investigation of the course of events that also contains an extensive bibliography is that of B. Robert Kreiser, *Miracles, Convulsions, and Ecclesiastical Politics in Early Eighteenth-Century Paris* (Princeton, N.J.: Princeton Univ. Press, 1978).

70. *Enthusiasm: A Chapter in the History of Religion: With Special Reference to the XVII and XVIII Centuries* (Oxford: Clarendon Press, 1950), 372–88.

71. *Signs and Wonders: A Study of the Miraculous Element in Religion* (New York: Desclée, 1966), 309-21.

72. Ibid., 321.

73. *Miracles: Yesterday and Today, True and False* (1918; Grand Rapids: Wm. B. Eerdmans, 1954), 31.

74. Cf. ibid., 36.

75. From *My Own Life,,* dated April 18, 1776, text in E. C. Mossner, *The Life of David Hume,* 2nd ed. (Oxford: Clarendon Press, 1980), 612; see also 223, 286–94.

76. *Free Answer to Dr. Middleton's Free Inquiry* . . . (1749).

77. *A Vindication of the Miraculous Power which Subsisted in the First Three Centuries of the Christian Church* (1750). J. Chapman's *Miraculous Powers of the Primitive Church* (1752) appeared too late for inclusion. But the *Free Enquiry* discussed Chapman's *Discovery of the Miraculous Powers of the Primitive Church* (1747) as well as other writers including Daniel Waterland.

78. *A Free Inquiry into the Miraculous Powers which are Supposed to have Subsisted in the Christian Church, from the Earliest Ages through Several Successive Centuries, To which is Added a Letter from Rome, Shewing an Exact Conformity between Popery and Paganism: or the Religion of the Present Romans, Derived from that of their Heathen Ancestors* (London: Sherwood and Co., 1825), 3f.

79. Ibid., 19f.

80. Ibid., 20.

81. Ibid., 20f.

82. Ibid., 22. Origen had observed that demons were driven out of many sufferers "without any curious magical art or sorcerer's device, but with prayer and very simple adjurations and formulas such as the simplest person could use. For generally speaking it is uneducated people who do this kind of work. The power in the word of Christ shows the worthlessness and weakness of the daemons; for it is not necessary to have a wise man who is competent in the rational proofs of the faith in order that they should be defeated and yield to expulsion from the soul and body of a man" (*Against Celsus* 7.4; cf. 1.6; cited from H. Chadwick, ed., *Origen: Contra Celsum* [Cambridge: Cambridge Univ. Press, 1953], 398).

83. Mark 9:38–41 = Luke 9:49f.; 1 Cor. 12:10, 28f.; Gal. 3:5; Heb. 2:4 (?). Mention may also be made of the unnamed seventy disciples whose mission included healing and exorcism (Luke 10:1–20). Alongside this, Philip is said to have performed signs, exorcisms, and healings in the course of his preaching ministry (Acts 8:4–8). Acts presents a number of parallels between Peter and Paul. Both at an early point in their ministry healed lame men (Acts 3:2ff.; 14:8ff.); both exorcised demons (Acts 5:16; 16:18); both had triumphant encounters with sorcerers (Acts 8:18ff.; 13:6ff.); both raised the dead (Acts 9:36ff.; 20:9ff.); and both had miraculous escapes from prison (Acts 12:7ff.; 16:25ff.). Further, the healing effect of Peter's shadow may be compared with that of the cloths from Paul's body (Acts 5:15; 19:11f.). On this see F. F. Bruce, *Commentary on the Book of Acts,* The New London Commentary (London: Marshall, Morgan and Scott, 1954), 387ff.

84. Middleton, op. cit., 25f.

85. The pieces of material were evidently sweat-rags and aprons that Paul had tied around his head and waist while engaged in leather-working. The incident recalls the story of those who were healed by touching the fringe of Jesus' cloak (Mark 5:27ff.; 6:56) and the healing effect of Peter's shadow (Acts 5:15).

86. Cf. n. 82.

87. Warfield, op. cit., 31.

88. Middleton, op. cit., 26.

89. Justin saw the position of the human nose on the face as a symbol of the cross of Christ *(First Apology* 55; Middleton, op. cit., 28). On his view of the origin of the Septuagint translation of the Old Testament into Greek see Justin, *Hortatory Address to the Greeks* 13 (Middleton, 38).

90. *Against Heresies* 3.25.2 (Middleton, op. cit., 50); 5.33.3 (Middleton, 47).

91. Op. cit., 71.

92. Ibid., 75; cf. Irenaeus, *Against Heresies* 2.32.4 ("Yet, moreover, as I have said, the dead have been raised up, and remained among us for many years"). Eusebius also mentions the testimony of Papias "that the resurrection of a dead body took place in this day" (*Ecclesiastical History* 3.39.9). Middleton dismisses this as another of the "fabulous stories delivered by that weak man."

93. Middleton, op. cit., 77.

94. Ibid., 80.

95. Ibid., 81.

96. Ibid., 83.

97. Ibid., 85. Mention of Jewish exorcists is made by several church fathers (Justin, *Dialogue with Trypho* 85; Irenaeus, *Against Heresies* 2.6.2; Origen, *Against Celsus* 1.24f.; 5.45; cf. 2.51). Josephus tells of the exorcism performed by Eleazar in the presence of Vespasian and his troops, employing a ring with a drug or root under its seal, the name of Solomon, and allegedly draw-

ing the demon through the nostrils of the sufferer (*Antiquities of the Jews* 8.2.5). As proof of the exorcism the spirit overturned a cup or basin of water. Josephus claimed to have seen the event himself.

98. Middleton, op. cit., 88.

99. Ibid., 97–117.

100. Ibid., 117ff.

101. Ibid., 124.

102. Ibid., 176, citing J. Chapman, *Miscellaneous Tracts,* 175f.

103. Middleton, op. cit., 177.

104. Ibid., 191–94.

105. Ibid., 194–200.

106. Ibid., 200–15.

107. Ibid., 216–34.

108. Ibid., 218.

109. Ibid., 219f.

110. Ibid., 220.

111. Ibid., 225ff.; cf. David Hume, *An Enquiry Concerning Human Understanding*, in Hume's *Enquiries*, ed. L. A. Selby-Bigge, 2nd ed. (1902; reprint, Oxford: Clarendon Press, 1961), 124f., 344ff.; E. C. Mossner, *The Life of David Hume,* 95, 288, 419.

112. Middleton, op. cit., 227.

113. Ibid., 114.

114. Warfield, op. cit., 6.

115. *Journal*, January 28, 1749. In his entry for August 12, 1771, Wesley commented on Shinstra's *Letter Against Fanaticism:* "In truth, I cannot but fear Mr. Shinstra is in the same class with Dr. Conyers Middleton, and aims every blow, though he seems to look another way, at the fanatics who wrote the Bible." Between Jan. 4 and 24, 1749, Wesley wrote an extended letter to Middleton in which he examined Middleton's arguments in detail (*The Letters of the Rev. John Wesley, A.M.*, ed. John Telford [London: Epworth Press, 1931]), 2:312–88.

116. Stephen, op. cit., 1:227.

117. E. C. Mossner in *The Encyclopedia of Philosophy,* ed. P. Edwards, vol. 3 (New York: Macmillan, 1967), 328f.

118. Cited from the reprint of chapters 15 and 16 under the title *History of Christianity: Comprising All that Relates to the Progress of the Christian Religion in "The History of the Decline and Fall of the Roman Empire," and A Vindication of Some Passages in the 15th and 16th Chapters* (New York: Peter Eckler, 1923), 107.

119. Cf. n. 113. Gibbon was a great admirer of Hume, who repaid the former's compliments with a letter expressing great admiration for Gibbon's *Decline and Fall* when it appeared in 1776 (cf. E. C. Mossner, *The Life of David Hume,* 229f., 589f.).

120. Gibbon, op. cit., 148f.; citing Irenaeus, *Against Heresies* 1 Preface, and Middleton, *Free Inquiry,* 96.

121. Gibbon, op. cit., 151; cf. Hume, op. cit., 110–16.

122. Gibbon, op. cit., 131.

123. Ibid., 154.

124. Cf. Sir Isaac Newton, *Theological Manuscripts*, selected and edited by H. McLachlan (Liverpool: Univ. of Liverpool Press, 1950).

125. "I. Absolute, true, and mathematical time, of itself, and from its own nature, flows equably without relation to anything external, and by another name is called duration: relative, apparent, and common time, is some sensible and external (whether accurate or unequable) measure of duration by the means of motion, which is commonly used instead of true time; such as an hour, a day, a month, a year.

"II. Absolute space, in its own nature, without relation to anything external, remains always similar and immovable. Relative space is some movable dimension or measure of the absolute spaces; which our senses determine by its position to bodies; and which is commonly taken for immovable space; such as the dimension of a subterraneous, an aerial, or celestial space, determined by its position in respect of the earth. Absolute and relative space are the same in figure and magnitude; but they do not remain always numerically the same. For if the earth, for instance, moves, a space of our air, which relatively and in respect of the earth remains always the same, will at one time be one part of the absolute space into which the air passes; at another time it will be another part of the same, and so, absolutely understood, it will be continually changed" (*Mathematical Principles of Natural Philosophy* [1687], Definitions, cited from Sir Isaac Newton, *Mathematical Principles of Natural Philosophy* and *Optics;* and Christiaan Huygens, *Treatise on Light,* Great Books of the Western World [Chicago: Encyclopaedia Britannica, 1952], 8f.).

126. Cf. "General Scholium" (ibid., 369–72) for Newton's views about space, time, motion, and God. God "is omnipresent not *virtually* only, but also *substantially*; for virtue cannot subsist with substance. In him are all things contained and moved" (p. 370). Newton supposed that those irregularities in the heavens which could not be explained by his mathematical formulae were due to the direct intervention of God (Newton, *Optics* [1704], III:1, Q. 31; ibid., 541f.). Many years later the French astronomer Pierre Simon Laplace (1749-1827) solved the mathematical problem posed by the irregularities and is reputed to have remarked to Napoleon that he no longer needed the hypothesis of God (A. Richardson, *The Bible in the Age of Science* [London: SCM Press, 1961], 28).

127. "Is not the sensory of animals that place to which the sensitive substance is present, and into which the sensible species of things are carried through the nerves to the brain, that they may be perceived by their immediate presence to that substance? And these things being rightly dispatched, does it not appear from phenomena that there is a Being incorporeal, living, intelligent, omnipresent, who in infinite space (as it were in his sensory) sees the things themselves intimately, and throughly perceives them, and comprehends them wholly by their immediate presence to himself?" (*Optics* [1704], III:1, Q. 28; ibid., 529).

128. "And the instinct of brutes and insects can be the effect of nothing else than the wisdom and skill of a powerful, ever-living agent, who being in all places, is more able by His will to move the bodies within His boundless uniform sensorium, and thereby to form and reform the parts of the Universe, than we are by our will to move the parts of our own bodies. And yet we ought not to consider the world as the body of God, or the several parts thereof as the parts of God. He is a uniform Being, void of organs, members or parts, and they are his creatures subordinate to him, and subservient to His will; and He is no more the soul of them than the soul of man is the soul of the species of things carried through the organs of sense into the place of its sensation, where it perceives them by means of its immediate presence, without the intervention of any third thing" (ibid., Q. 31; pp. 542f.).

129. Cf. H. McLachlan, op. cit., 17f. The passage in brackets was crossed out. McLachlan regards it as consonant with Newton's view of the operations of the deity, but thinks that Newton had second thoughts and preferred the following clause.

130. Reprinted in H. G. Alexander, ed., *The Leibniz-Clarke Correspondence, Together with Extracts from Newton's Principia and Opticks* (New York: Philosophical Library Inc., 1956). Leibniz (1646-1716) was a universal scholar with international contacts. His later years were clouded by a dispute with the Newtonians over whether he or Newton had first discovered the infinitesimal calculus.

131. In Alexander, op. cit., 11f.; cf. Leibniz's letter to the Abbé Conti of April 9, 1716: "I call a *miracle* any event which can only occur through the power of the Creator, its reason not lying in the nature of created things; and when nevertheless one would attribute to it the qualities or powers of created things, then I call this quality a *scholastic occult quality*; that is one that it is impossible to render clear, such as a primitive heaviness; for the occult qualities which are chimerical are those whose cause we do not know but do not exclude" (187f.).

132. Ibid.,14.

133. Cf. N. L. Torrey, *Voltaire and the English Deists* (New Haven: Yale Univ. Press, 1930; reprint, Archon Books, 1967).

134. In addition to the translation into French and German of individual works, deistic ideas were disseminated through works like G. W. Alberti, *Briefe betreffend den allerneusten Zustand der Religion und der Wissenschaften in Gross-Britannien* (1752-54); J. A. Trinius, *Freydenker-Lexikon* (1759); U. G. Thorschmid, *Freydenker-Bibliothek* (1765-67). G. V. Lechler, *Geschichte des englischen Deismus* (1841; reprint, Hildesheim: Georg Olms, 1965), documented the impact of deism in Germany.

135. Reprint, New York: Kraus Reprint Co., 1970. Allen declared that it was not his design to examine particularly the history of miracles, but claimed that ancient miracles cannot prove revelations. He argued that men ought not to deem miraculous that which they cannot understand. Miracles cannot be instructive to mankind, and prayer cannot be attended with miraculous consequences. After dealing with miracles in ch. 7, he went on to attack prophecy and special revelations in ch. 8.

136. The work was published in facsimile with an introduction by Cyrus Adler (Washington: Government Printing Office, 1904). For the critical edition see *Jefferson's Extracts from the Gospels: "The Philosophy of Jesus" and "The Life and Morals of Jesus,"* ed. Dickinson W. Adams, ass't. ed. Ruth W. Lester, intro. Eugene R. Sheridan, *The Papers of Thomas Jefferson, Second Series* (Princeton: Princeton Univ. Press, 1983).

137. C. Adler, ed., op. cit. 18.

138. Disappointment caused by public neglect of his philosophical writings led Hume to turn to history, and it was as a man of letters and as historian (albeit an infidel) that Hume was acclaimed in the eighteenth century. Hume held Bishop Butler in high regard, and modeled his figure of Cleanthes on him in the *Dialogues* (E. C. Mossner, "The Enigma of Hume," *Mind* 45 [1936]: 334–49).

4. DAVID HUME

1. David Hume, *Enquiries Concerning Human Understanding and Concerning the Principles of Morals*, ed. L. A. Selby-Bigge, 3rd ed. with text and notes rev. P. H. Nidditch (Oxford: Clarendon Press, 1975), viii. Quotations are taken from this edition, giving section and page numbers. It may be noted, however, that Hume first called his work *Philosophical Essays Concerning Human Understanding*.

2. See "My Own Life," in E. C. Mossner, *The Life of David Hume,* 2nd ed. (Oxford: Clarendon Press, 1980), 615.

3. A. E. Taylor on "David Hume and the Miraculous," in *Philosophical Studies* (London: Macmillan, 1934), 365.

4. *Enquiry Concerning Human Understanding*, #86, p. 109. Hume is citing Tillotson's *Discourse Against Transubstantiation* (1684) (cf. *Works*, 2:448).

5. *Enquiry*, #86, p. 110.

6. Ibid., 109.

7. In a letter dated June 7, 1762, addressed to his critic, the Rev. George Campbell, with whom he enjoyed an amicable exchange, Hume claimed to have first propounded his argument against miracles in discussion with a Jesuit in the cloisters of the Collège de la Flèche. This was in response to the Jesuit's account of a miracle that had occurred there. According to Hume, the Jesuit observed that "it was impossible for that argument to have any solidity, because it operated equally against the Gospel as the Catholic miracles:—which observation I thought proper to admit as a sufficient answer." Hume went on to say to Campbell, "I believe that you will allow, that the freedom at least of this reasoning makes it somewhat extraordinary to have been the product of a convent of Jesuits, though perhaps you may think the sophistry of it savours plainly of the place of its birth" (J. Y. T. Greig, *Letters of David Hume,* vol. 1 [Oxford: Clarendon Press, 1932], 361).

The date of the origin of the essay is a matter of some debate. Hume had spent some time at La Flèche in his youth, and revisited La Flèche between 1735 and 1737. This was evidently the period referred to in the letter. Some scholars think that the essay was composed between 1734 and 1737, in view of a letter Hume addressed to Henry Home on December 2, 1737, where he expressed his resolve not to publish his "reasonings concerning miracles" and his hope to gain an introduction to Bishop Butler (R. Klibansky and E. C. Mossner, eds., *New Letters of David Hume* [Oxford: The University Press, 1954], 2f.).

This has prompted the suggestion that Hume originally intended to include his argument in his *Treatise of Human Nature*. But it is not clear that the essay existed in its present form at that date. Various considerations, including the detached, urbane style of writing that characterizes the essay and Hume's later writings, may indicate that it was composed some time in the 1740s. However, it seems clear that Hume's opposition to the apologetic use of miracles had its genesis in France at a time when the Saint-Medard miracles were provoking a considerable stir, which coincided with the great deistic debate in England on the miracles and the resurrection of Jesus. For discussion of the origin of Hume's essay see R. M. Burns, *The Great Debate on Miracles*, 131–41.

8. A. Flew, *Hume's Philosophy of Belief: A Study of his First Inquiry* (New York: The Humanities Press, 1961), 176.

9. *Enquiry,* #87, p. 110; cf. John Locke, *An Essay Concerning Human Understanding* 2, 1, 2; 4, 12, 9; and the full title of Hume's *Treatise of Human Nature: Being An Attempt to introduce the experimental Method of Reasoning into Moral Subjects.*

10. *Enquiry*, #87, pp. 110f.

11. Ibid., #88, p. 111.

12. Ibid., #60, pp. 76f.; cf. *A Treatise of Human Nature*, ed. L. A. Selby-Bigge (1888; Oxford: Clarendon Press, 1967), 1.3.14, pp. 155–72.

13. *Enquiry*, #59, p. 75; cf. Locke's comments on the role of intuition in certainty (*An Essay Concerning Human Understanding*, 4.2.1ff.).

14. Cf. W. Pannenberg, *Basic Questions in Theology*, vol. 1 (London: SCM Press, 1970), 43ff.; C. Brown, ed., *History, Criticism and Faith: Four Exploratory Studies* (Downers Grove, Ill.: Inter-Varsity Press, 1976), 171–77; and the discussion of Ernst Troeltsch in ch. 5, below. Hume used the word "analogy" in #99 (p. 128) and spoke of the rules of analogy in the footnote to #89 (p. 114), dealing with the Indian prince and ice, which he inserted in the second edition of the essay.

15. *Enquiry*, #88, p. 112.

16. Ibid., #89, p. 113.

17. Ibid., #88, p. 112.

18. Ibid., #90, p. 114.

19. Cf. ch. 3, n. 41.

20. *Enquiry*, #89, pp. 113f.

21. Ibid., #90, n. 1, p. 115.

22. Ibid., #90, p. 115.

23. Cited from *A Discourse Concerning the Unchangeable Obligations of Natural Religion, and the Truth and Certainty of the Christian Revelation,* the Boyle Lectures for 1705, in *The Works of Samuel Clarke, D.D.,* ed. John Clarke, vol. 2 (1838; reprint, New York and London: Garland Publishing, Inc., 1978), 701. Clarke was an eminent eighteenth-century divine who had been influenced by Newton. His Boyle Lectures defended rational theology against Locke's empiricism. Though a critic of the deists, he was suspected by some of deistic tendencies. As noted in ch. 2, the question of the other forms of supernatural agency was one that occupied Joseph Glanvill and others.

24. J. Boswell, *Papers*, 12:227 (cf. E. C. Mossner, op. cit., 51, 597).

25. *Enquiry*, #91, p. 116.

26. Ibid., #92, pp. 116f.

27. Ibid., #93, pp. 118f.

28. Ibid., #94, p. 119.

29. Ibid., #95, pp. 121f.

30. Ibid., #96, p. 122; cf. Tacitus, *Histories,* 4.81; and Suetonius, *Life of Vespasian,* 8 (7).2. See further A. Flew, op. cit., 183f.

31. *Enquiry*, #96, p. 123.

32. Ibid., #96, pp. 123f.; cf. Cardinal de Retz, *Mémoires*, 4:550. See further A. Flew, op. cit., 184.

33. *Enquiry*, #96, pp. 124f.; cf. 344–46. Conyers Middleton had also discussed the miracles (cf. above, ch. 3). Hume noted the work by the former freethinker and member of parliament Carré de Montgéron, *La Verité des Miracles opérés à l'intercession de M. de Pâris et autres appelans, demontrée contre M. l'Archevêque de Sens,* vols. 1–3 (1737–48), and the anonymous *Recueil des Miracles opérés au Tombeau de M. de Pâris,* vols. 1–2 (1733). See further A. Flew, op. cit., 184f., and the discussion above in ch. 3.

34. *Enquiry*, #99, p. 128.

35. Ibid.

36. Ibid., #100, pp. 129f.

37. Ibid., 130.

38. Ibid., #101, p. 131.

39. Cf. Sir Leslie Stephen, op. cit., 1:330–43; the articles by Stephen and others on the writers mentioned in the *Dictionary of National Biography*, which was edited by Stephen; J. S. Lawton, op. cit., 55ff., 68ff.; R. M. Burns, op. cit., 176–246.

40. E. C. Mossner, op. cit., 292.

41. *Journal*, March 5, 1769 (edition cited, 3:360).

42. Cf. above, ch. 3, n. 66.

43. Op. cit., 32.

44. Flew, *Hume's Philosophy of Belief* (see n. 8 above).

45. Taylor, op. cit., 332.

46. *The Encyclopedia of Philosophy*, ed. P. Edwards, vol. 5 (New York: Macmillan and Free Press; London: Collier Macmillan, 1967), 351.

47. Ibid.

48. Taylor, op. cit., 339.

49. Ibid., 349.

50. Taylor thinks that Hume is deliberately criticizing Newtonian science (op. cit., 332f., 345, 349). On the basis of Hume's epistemology, science goes beyond the limits of pure experience no less than dogmatic theology. But Flew protests that Hume elsewhere showed great respect for Newtonian science (op. cit., 211f.). A case can be made out for his Newtonianism in view of his stress on experimental method (cf. N. Capaldi, *David Hume: The Newtonian Philosopher* [Boston: Twayne, 1975]). But in that case it could be said that he was using some Newtonian methods to exhibit the irrationality of Newtonianism.

51. Flew, op. cit., 204; *The Encyclopedia of Philosophy*, 5:351.

52. Flew, op. cit., 204.

53. Ibid., 208.

54. Reprinted in D. Z. Phillips, ed., *Religion and Understanding* (Oxford: Blackwell, 1967), 155–70.

55. Ibid., 167.

56. "We cannot admit a proposition as a law of nature, and yet believe a fact in real contradiction to it. We must disbelieve the alleged fact, or believe that we were mistaken in admitting the supposed law" (J. S. Mill, *A System of Logic*, 8th ed. [reprint, London: Longmans, Green, 1925], 3.25.2, p. 409). "The Definition of a miracle as a suspension or a contravention of the order of nature is self-contradictory; because all we know of the order of nature is derived from our observation of the course of events of which the so-called miracle is a part" (T. H. Huxley, *Collected Essays*, vol. 6 [London: Macmillan, 1894], 157).

See further the discussions of the question by P. Nowell-Smith, "Miracles," in A. Flew and A. MacIntyre, eds., *New Essays in Philosophical Theology* (London: SCM Press, 1955), 243–53; A. Flew, *Hume's Philosophy of Belief*, 202ff., and *The Encyclopedia of Philosophy*, 5:349ff.; Terence Penelhum, *Religion and Rationality* (New York: Random House, 1971), 267–80; Ninian Smart, *Philosophers and Religious Truth*, 2nd ed. (London: SCM Press, 1969), 25–49; Richard Swinburne, *The Concept of Miracle* (London: Macmillan, St. Martin's Press, 1970), 18ff., 26ff.; David Basinger, "Miracles and Apologetics: A Response," *Christian Scholars Review* 9 (1979–80): 348–53.

57. Cf. above, ch. 1, n. 25.

58. Cf. above, ch. 3, n. 59.

59. Basinger, op. cit., 353.

60. "Hume on Miracles, History, and Apologetics," *Christian Scholars Review* 8 (1978–79): 324.

61. Swinburne, op. cit., 35.

62. Cf. Alan Richardson, *History: Sacred and Profane,* Bampton Lectures for 1962 (London: SCM Press, 1964), 195–200; Wolfhart Pannenberg, *Jesus—God and Man* (London: SCM Press; Philadelphia: Westminster Press, 1968), 88–105; see esp. p. 98.

63. Cf. Taylor, op. cit., 333.

64. Swinburne, op. cit., 17.

65. Op. cit., 60f.

66. Matt. 24:24; 1 Cor. 11:14; 2 Thess. 2:9ff.; cf. Deut. 13.

67. Cf. Matt. 5:43ff.; Acts 14:16f.; 17:24–31; Rom. 1:19f.; 13:1ff.; 1 Pet. 3:13ff.; Rev. 22:2.

68. Rom. 1:18–32; Acts 17:22–31. For the idea of general revelation see G. Bornkamm, "The Revelation of God's Wrath (Romans 1–3)," in *Early Christian Experience* (London: SCM Press, 1969), 47–70.

69. Acts 14:15; cf. Acts 14:11 with Acts 28:6.

70. *Hume's Philosophy of Belief,* 179; cf. C. S. Peirce, *Values in a Universe of Chance,* ed. P. P. Wiener (New York: Doubleday Anchor, 1958), 292f.

71. See above, ch. 3, n. 47.

72. Cf. Thomas S. Kuhn, *The Structure of Scientific Revolutions,* 2nd ed. (Chicago: Univ. of Chicago Press, 1970).

5. CONTINENTAL SKEPTICISM

1. "Beantwortung der Frage: Was ist Aufklärung?", *Berlinische Monatschrift*, vol. 4, no. 12 (1784):481–94, *Gesammelte Schriften*, 8:35–42 (author's translation). There is an English translation of the work by Lewis White Beck in Kant's *Foundations of the Metaphysics of Morals and What is Enlightenment?* (Indianapolis-New York: Bobbs-Merrill, 1959).

2. *Critique of Pure Reason*, tr. Norman Kemp Smith (1929; London: Macmillan, 1973). Kant set out the categories in four groups of three: Quantity (Unity, Plurality, Totality), Quality (Reality, Negation, Limitation), Relation (Of Inherence and Subsistence, Of Causality and Dependence, Of Community—reciprocity between agent and patient), and Modality (Possibility-Impossibility, Existence-Non-existence, Necessity-Contingency) (113).

3. Ibid., 86f.; cf. *Prolegomena to Any Future Metaphysics*, ed. Lewis White Beck (Indianapolis-New York: Bobbs-Merrill, 1950), 89.

4. *Prolegomena*, 87; cf. *Critique of Pure Reason*, 393–421.

5. *Critique of Pure Reason*, 495–514.

6. *Critique of Practical Reason,* tr. Lewis White Beck (Indianapolis-New York: Bobbs-Merrill, 1956), 114–39.

7. Ibid., 127; cf. *Critique of Pure Reason*, 218–33 for the doctrine that "All alterations take place in conformity with the law of the connection of cause and effect."

8. Ibid., 30.

9. *Religion within the Limits of Reason Alone*, tr. with an introduction and notes by Theodore M. Greene and Hoyt H. Hudson (1934; New York: Harper, 1960), 3.

10. Ibid., 5f.

11. Ibid., 145. This was the title of a section in Book IV that carried the general title, "Concerning Service and Pseudo-Service under the Sovereignty of the Good Principle, or, Concerning Religion and Clericalism." Unlike the first three books, Kant did not submit Book IV for official approval.

12. Ibid., 56.

13. Ibid., 57.

14. Ibid., 54f. Kant was aware of the critical work of K. F. Bahrdt and H. S. Reimarus, which will be discussed below. He rejected both because of their dubious moral implications (76).

15. Ibid., 78.

16. Ibid., 79; cf. John 4:48. Kant's claim that the commands of duty are "primordially engraved upon the heart of man through reason" recalls Calvin's contention that "a sense of divinity is by nature engraven on human hearts" (*Institutes*, 1.4.4).

17. Ibid., 80.

18. Ibid., 81.

19. Ibid., 82.

20. Ibid., xxxii–xxxvii.

21. An English translation of *Fragments from Reimarus* was made by the one-time Anglican vicar Charles Voysey (London: Williams and Norgate, 1879; reprint, Lexington, Ky.: American Theological Library Association, 1962). More recent versions are that of G. W. Buchanan, *The Goal of Jesus and His Disciples* (Leiden: E. J. Brill, 1970), and *Reimarus: Fragments*, ed. C. H. Talbert, tr. R. S. Fraser (Philadelphia: Fortress Press, 1970; London: SCM Press, 1971). Quotations below are from Talbert's edition, giving section and page numbers. Gerhard Alexander has edited a critical edition of the complete work, *Apologie oder Schutzschrift für die vernünftigen Verehrer Gottes*, 2 vols. (Frankfurt: Insel Verlag, 1972).

22. Schweitzer, *The Quest of the Historical Jesus: A Critical Study of its Progress from Reimarus to Wrede*, E.T. 2nd ed. (1911; reprint, London: Black, 1956), 23.

23. Matt. 27:46 (cf. C. H. Talbert, op. cit., #8, p. 150).

24. Schweitzer, op. cit., 26.

25. *Hermann Samuel Reimarus and his Apology* (cf. Talbert, op. cit., 44–57).

26. Cf. Talbert, op. cit., 11–18; G. W. Buchanan, op. cit., 5ff.; N. L. Torrey, *Voltaire and the English Deists* (Yale, 1930; reprint, Archon Books, 1967).

27. Talbert, op. cit., #46, p. 230.

28. Ibid., #48, p. 233; cf. also #52, p. 239.

29. Ibid., #49, p. 234.

30. Ibid., #48, pp. 232f.

31. Ibid., #57, p. 253.

32. Ibid.

33. Ibid., #5, p. 143.

34. Schweitzer, op. cit., 23.

35. Cf. *Lessing's Theological Writings,* ed. H. Chadwick (London: Black, 1956). Perhaps the best account of Lessing's theology is G. Pons, *Gotthold Ephraïm Lessing et le Christianisme,* Germanica 5 (Paris: Didier, 1964).

36. Origen, *Against Celsus* 1.2 (cf. above, ch. 1, n. 18).

37. H. Chadwick, op. cit., 52.

38. Ibid., 53.

39. Ibid. See also n. 42 below.

40. This was the theme of the famous parable of three rings in *Nathan the Wise,* Act III, Scene 7, adapted from Boccaccio's *Decameron.* Three brothers quarrel over which of them has a magical ring capable of making its owner loved by God and man. Each of the brothers, who represent Christianity, Judaism, and Islam, have been left a ring by their father, but only one is genuine. A wise judge counsels the brothers each to behave as if he has the true ring. Their behavior will reveal the truth. The idea that the great religions of the world will one day transcend themselves in a universal religion of morality and love was further developed in *The Education of the Human Race* (1780; H. Chadwick, op. cit., 82–98). It anticipated Kant's similar approach in *Religion within the Limits of Reason Alone.*

41. Cf. Alexander Altmann, *Moses Mendelssohn: A Biographical Study* (London: Routledge and Kegan Paul, 1973), 253–56, 553–69.

42. Ibid., 538, citing *Moses Mendelssohns Gesammelte Schriften,* ed. G. B. Mendelssohn, vol. 3 (1843–45), 315.

43. *Briefe über die Bibel im Volkston. Eine Wochenschrift von einem Prediger auf dem Lande* (Halle, 1782 onward). These were succeeded by *Ausführung des Plans und Zwecks Jesu. In Briefen an Wahrheit suchende Leser* (Berlin, 1784–92). For summary appraisal see Albert Schweitzer, op. cit., 38–44; and Ernst and Marie-Luise Keller, *Miracles in Dispute: A Continuing Debate* (London: SCM Press, 1969), 67–79.

44. *Ausführung,* Letter 66 (cf. Keller, op. cit., 73).

45. Hase, *Das Leben Jesu. Lehrbuch Zunächst für akademische Vorlesungen* (1829), 2nd ed. (Leipzig, 1853), from which quotations here are given. The 5th ed. (1865) was replaced by the *Geschichte Jesu. Nach akademischen Vorlesungen* (1876).

46. Ibid., #58, p. 110.

47. Ibid., #97, p. 172.

48. Cf. above, ch. 1, nn. 34–36.

49. Hase, op. cit., #147, pp. 267f.

50. Schweitzer, op. cit., 60.

51. Ibid., 61.

52. E.T. *The Christian Faith* (Edinburgh: T. & T. Clark, 1928), #94, p. 384. Perhaps the best overall introduction is M. Redeker, *Schleiermacher: Life and Thought* (Philadelphia: Fortress Press, 1973). For other works see T. N. Tice, *Schleiermacher Bibliography, With Brief Introductions, Annotations and Index,* Princeton Pamphlets 12 (Princeton, N.J.: Princeton Theological Seminary, 1966).

53. *The Christian Faith,* #103, p. 441.

54. Ibid., 448.

55. Ibid., citing Matt. 16:16; John 1:14, 16; 4:42; 6:68f.; 7:25f.

56. Ibid.

57. Ibid., 449.

58. Ibid.

59. Based on lectures delivered in 1832 and published in 1864. The first English version was edited by J. C. Verheyden (Philadelphia: Fortress Press; London: SCM Press, 1975).

60. Ibid., 190–229.

61. Ibid., 228.

62. Ibid., 227.

63. Ibid., 229.

64. Tr. and ed. Leander E. Keck (Philadelphia: Fortress Press; London: SCM Press, 1977).

65. Ibid., 86.

66. Ibid., 160.

67. Ibid., 162.

68. The work was originally translated by George Eliot and published in three volumes in 1846. A second English edition was published in one volume in 1892 with revised pagination. This text has been reprinted in the edition of Peter C. Hodgson (Philadelphia: Fortress Press, 1972; London: SCM Press, 1973). Quotations are from this edition. Keck and Hodgson provide significant background material in their respective editions of Strauss. A recent important study is Horton Harris, *David Friedrich Strauss and His Theology,* Monograph Supplements to the Scottish Journal of Theology (Cambridge: Cambridge Univ. Press, 1973).

69. Hodgson, op. cit., #8, p. 52; cf. ##6-7, pp. 46-52.

70. Ibid.

71. Ibid., #15, p. 86.

72. Ibid., #14, p. 78.

73. Ibid., 79.

74. Ibid.; cf. Schleiermacher, *The Christian Faith,* ##46f.

75. Hodgson, op. cit., #91, p. 413.

76. Ibid., #92, pp. 422f.; #93, p. 435; #101, p. 496.

77. Ibid., #94, pp. 437-41.

78. Ibid., #95, p. 445.

79. Ibid., #96, pp. 452ff.

80. Ibid., #96, p. 457.

81. Ibid., #97, p. 460.

82. Ibid., #100, p. 476; cf. R. Bultmann, *The History of the Synoptic Tradition* (Oxford: Basil Blackwell, 1963), 12ff., 209ff. Strauss offered a similar explanation for the cursing of the fig tree (#104, 527-34).

83. Hodgson, op. cit., #100, p. 495. Among the sources that Strauss cited in support of this position was F. C. Baur, "Apollonius von Tyana und Christus, oder das Verhältnis des Pythagoreismus zum Christentum. Ein Beitrag zur Religionsgeschichte der ersten Jahrhunderte nach Christus," *Tübinger Zeitschrift für Theologie* 4 (1832):3-235. Strauss had been a pupil of Baur.

84. Hodgson, op. cit., #101, p. 504. Strauss cites Iamblichus, *Vita Pythagorae* 136; Porphyry, 29; and Lucian, *Philopseudes* 13. It may be noted that these authors all belonged to the Christian era: Iamblichus (ca. 250-ca. 325); Porphyry (ca. 232-ca. 305); Lucian (b. ca. 120).

85. Hodgson, op. cit., #102, pp. 507-19.

86. Ibid., #103, pp. 519-27.

87. Cf. Hodgson's Introduction, xxxvi.

88. Ibid., #98, p. 470; #101, p. 496.

89. Ibid., #149, p. 773.

90. Ibid., #150, p. 777.

91. Ibid.

92. Ibid., #151, p. 781.

93. See further H. Harris, op. cit., 259-73; C. Hartlich and W. Sachs, *Der Ursprung des Mythosbegriffes in der modernen Bibelwissenschaft* (Tübingen: J. C. B. Mohr, 1952); Roger A. Johnson, *The Origins of Demythologizing: Philosophy and Historiography in the Theology of Rudolf Bultmann* (Leiden: Brill, 1974).

94. Cf. Bultmann's "Autobiographical Reflections" in C. W. Kegley, ed., *The Theology of Rudolf Bultmann* (London: SCM Press, 1966), xix-xxv.

95. Hick, ed., *The Myth of God Incarnate* (Philadelphia: Westminster Press; London: SCM Press, 1977), 8ff., 117ff., 161ff., 167-85. For responses to the book see M. D. Goulder, ed., *Incarnation and Myth: The Debate Continued* (London: SCM Press; Grand Rapids: Wm. B. Eerdmans, 1979).

96. Strauss himself coined the term to designate those who, like himself, adopted a modified Hegelianism (*Streitschriften zur Verteidigung meiner Schriften über das Leben Jesu,* Nr. 3, 1837).

97. *The Essence of Christianity,* reprinted with an introductory essay by Karl Barth and foreword by H. Richard Niebuhr (New York: Harper, 1957), xxxv. For a recent study of Feuerbach see Marx W. Wartofsky, *Feuerbach* (Cambridge: Cambridge Univ. Press, 1977, 1982).

98. Ibid., 206.

99. Ibid., 207.

100. Ibid., 128f.

101. Ibid., 129.

102. Ibid., 130.

103. Ibid., 133.
104. Ibid., 133f.
105. Cf. E. and M.-L. Keller, op. cit., 94–108, 145–56.
106. Ernst Bloch, *Das Prinzip der Hoffnung,* Gesamtausgabe 5 (Frankfurt am Main: Suhrkamp Verlag, 1959), 1392–1550.
107. Authorized translation (London: Williams and Norgate, 1879), 1:213.
108. Ibid., 2:437f.; cf. H. Harris, op. cit., 200–12.
109. On the history of New Testament criticism see Albert Schweitzer, *The Quest of the Historical Jesus: A Critical Study of its Progress from Reimarus to Wrede* (1906, E.T. 1910), reprinted with an introduction by James M. Robinson (New York: Macmillan, 1968); W. G. Kümmel, *The New Testament: The History of the Investigation of its Problems* (Nashville and New York: Abingdon Press, 1972); S. Neill, *The Interpretation of the New Testament, 1861–1961,* The Firth Lectures 1962 (London: Oxford Univ. Press, 1964); A. I. C. Heron, *A Century of Protestant Thought* (Philadelphia: Westminster Press, 1980).
110. Augustine, *De Consensu Evangelistarum* 1.2–3.
111. Karl Lachmann, "De Ordine narrationum in evangeliis synopticis," *Theologische Studien und Kritiken* 8 (1835):570–90, reprinted in his *Novum Testamentum Graece et Latine,* vol. 2 (1850). The most important sections are translated by N. H. Palmer in "Lachmann's Argument," *New Testament Studies* 13 (1966–67):368–78.
The priority of Matthew continues to have powerful advocates, as can be seen from such recent publications as W. R. Farmer, *The Synoptic Problem: A Critical Analysis* (Macon: Mercer Univ. Press, 1976); Hans-Herbert Stoldt, *History and Criticism of the Marcan Hypothesis* (Macon: Mercer Univ. Press; Edinburgh: T. & T. Clark, 1980); Bernard Orchard, *The Griesbach Solution to the Synoptic Question,* vol. 1, *Matthew, Luke and Mark* (Manchester: Koinonia Press, 1975); Bernard Orchard and Thomas R. W. Longstaff, eds., *J. J. Griesbach: Synoptic and Text-Critical Studies, 1776-1976,* Society for New Testament Studies Monograph Series 34 (Cambridge: Cambridge Univ. Press, 1978). However, the theory has been rigorously criticized by C. M. Tuckett, *The Revival of the Griesbach Hypothesis: An Analysis and Appraisal,* Society for New Testament Studies Monograph Series 44 (Cambridge: Cambridge Univ. Press, 1983).
112. F. C. Baur, *Vorlesungen über neutestamentliche Theologie,* ed. Ferdinand Friedrich Baur (Leipzig: Fues's Verlag, 1864), 46. For recent reappraisals of Baur see Peter C. Hodgson, *The Formation of Historical Theology: A Study of Ferdinand Christian Baur* (New York: Harper and Row, 1966); and Horton Harris, *The Tübingen School* (Oxford: Clarendon Press, 1975).
113. *The Christian Doctrine of Justification and Reconciliation* (Edinburgh: T. & T. Clark, 1902), 451. For a contemporary appraisal of Ritschl see Philip Hefner, *Faith and the Vitalities of History: A Theological Study Based on the Work of Albrecht Ritschl* (New York: Harper and Row, 1966).
114. *What is Christianity? Sixteen Lectures Delivered in the University of Berlin during the Winter-Term, 1899–1900* (London: Williams and Norgate; New York: G. P. Putnam's Sons, 1901), 28f. Harnack held that the miracle stories of the Gospels could be explained by allotting them to the following five categories: "(1) Stories which had their origin in an exaggerated view of natural events of an impressive character; (2) stories which had their origin in sayings or parables, or in the projection of inner experiences on to the external world; (3) stories such as arose in the interests of the fulfilment of Old Testament sayings; (4) stories of surprising cures effected by Jesus' spiritual force; (5) stories of which we cannot fathom the secret" (28). He left it to the reader to decide which story fit which category.
For recent reassessments of Harnack see G. Wayne Glick, *The Reality of Christianity: A Study of Adolf von Harnack as Historian and Theologian* (New York: Harper and Row, 1967); Wilhelm Pauck, *Harnack and Troeltsch: Two Historical Theologians* (New York: Oxford Univ. Press, 1968).
115. *What is Christianity?,* 51.
116. Ibid., 59.
117. Ibid., 144.
118. Ibid., 37.
119. *Christianity at the Cross-Roads* (1909), reprint with a Foreword by A. R. Vidler (London: George Allen & Unwin, 1963), 49.
120. Schweitzer, op. cit., 399.
121. Author's translation from Ernst Troeltsch, *Gesammelte Schriften,* vol. 2, 2nd ed. (1922; reprint, Darmstadt: Scientia Verlag Aalen, 1962), 732. Troeltsch examined the subject of "Historiography" in the *Encyclopedia of Religion and Ethics,* ed. James Hastings (Edinburgh:

T. & T. Clark; New York: Charles Scribner's Sons, 1913), 6:716–23; reprint in John Macquarrie, ed., *Contemporary Religious Thinkers: From Idealist Metaphysicians to Existential Theologians* (London: SCM Press, 1968), 76–97.

122. See "What Does 'Essence of Christianity' Mean?" (1903, 1913) in Ernst Troeltsch, *Writings on Theology and Religion,* tr. and ed. Robert Morgan and Michael Pye (Atlanta: John Knox Press; London: Gerald Duckworth & Co., 1977), 124–79.

123. Ernst Troeltsch, *The Absoluteness of Christianity and the History of Religions* (1901, 3rd ed. 1929; Atlanta: John Knox Press, 1971; London: SCM Press, 1972), 131. Cf. also Benjamin A. Reist, *Towards a Theology of Involvement: A Study of Ernst Troeltsch* (London: SCM Press, 1966); and John Powell Clayton, ed., *Ernst Troeltsch and the Future of Theology* (Cambridge: Cambridge Univ. Press, 1976).

124. *The Absoluteness of Christianity,* 112.

125. Wilhelm Bousset, *Kyrios Christos: A History of the Belief in Christ from the Beginnings of Christianity to Irenaeus* (1913), English translation with an Introductory Word from the 5th German edition by Rudolf Bultmann (Nashville and New York: Abingdon Press, 1970), 98. In his earlier study *Jesus,* Bousset maintained that Jesus' "healing activity lies entirely within the bounds of what is psychologically conceivable, and this feature of the life of Jesus has absolutely nothing unique about it. The history of religion offers countless analogies to it down to the most recent times. . . . There are in fact but very few stories which record an absolutely miraculous and impossible event, or one for which no analogy can be found. These few must then be cast aside as the mere outgrowths of legend" (New York: G. P. Putnam's Sons; London: Williams and Norgate, 1906), 48, 54.

126. *Kyrios Christos,* 98.

127. Ibid., 103.

128. Ibid., 100.

129. Ibid., 101, where Bousset gave references to Otto Weinreich, *Antike Heilungswunder: Untersuchungen zum Wunderglauben der Griechen und Römer* (Giessen, 1909); Paul Fiebig *Jüdische Wundergeschichten des neutestamentlichen Zeitalters unter besonderer Berücksichtigung ihres Verhältnisses zum Neuen Testament* (Tübingen, 1911); and Johannes Weiss in *Die Religion in Geschichte und Gegenwart,* 1st ed., 3:2188.

130. *The Lover of Lies, Or the Doubter (Philopseudes sive Incredulus),* 11. The translation given here is that of A. M. Harmon, *Lucian,* Loeb Classical Library, vol. 3 (Cambridge, Mass.: Harvard Univ. Press; London: William Heinemann Ltd., 1921), 337. It is possible that Lucian was actually satirizing Christian miracle stories, and that Jesus is here characterized as a Babylonian. Lucian satirized numerous outlooks that were not materialistic. The call to Midas to "Cheer up" (*tharrei*) may echo Jesus' *tharsei* (Matt. 9:2). The form *tharrei* was used increasingly from the later Attic writers. It also had associations with the Eleusinian mysteries.

131. Pliny, *Natural History* 7.37.124, tr. H. Rackham, Loeb Classical Library, vol. 2 (Cambridge, Mass.: Harvard Univ. Press; London: William Heinemann Ltd., 1942), 589.

132. Celsus, *De Medicina* 2.6.16, tr. W. G. Spencer, Loeb Classical Library, vol. 1 (Cambridge, Mass.: Harvard Univ. Press; London: William Heinemann Ltd., 1935), 115. The observation occurs in a passage commenting on the faulty and premature diagnosis of death. In Apuleius, *Florida* 19, the story is treated as an absolute miracle. However, this work is dated much later (ca. 160–70).

133. Bousset, op. cit., 101; cf. Baba Mezia 59b; Jerusalem Talmud Berachoth 9, 1; Matt. 8:23–27; Mark 4:34–41; Luke 8:22–25.

134. *The Lover of Lies, Or the Doubter,* 13 (edition cited, p. 339). The Hyperboreans were a legendary race of Apollo worshipers, living in the far North and revered by the Greeks. If Lucian was satirically identifying the Christians with them, the reference to the peasant brogues might be an allusion to Jesus' background. Similarly, the reference to flying through the air might allude to the acension. The calling of "mouldy corpses" to life and the implication of magic might also reflect on incidents in the Gospels.

135. Bousset, op. cit., 101.

136. Ibid., 103. Bousset notes that the water-into-wine stories associated with Dionysos are related by Pliny, *Natural History* 31.13; Diodorus Siculus, 3.66; Pausanias, 6.26.1–2; Athenaios, 1.61. He also notes that the early Christian festival of the Epiphany coincided with the beginning of the festival of Dionysos on the night of January 5–6. In early Christian liturgy January 6 was recognized as the anniversary of the wedding at Cana. The possible connection between the story in John 2:1–11 and Dionysos has been much discussed. Some see in the story an attempt on the part of the evangelist to claim superiority for Christ over Dionysos, while others

see the story as symbolic of salvation through Christ. For a review of interpretations see H. Van der Loos, *The Miracles of Jesus,* Supplements to Novum Testamentum 9 (Leiden: E. J. Brill, 1965), 590–618. Van der Loos concludes that the story does not depict a bacchantic feast or express any struggle between Jesus and Dionysos. The changes that Jesus performed were in secret, and were intended to confirm and deepen the faith of the believer. J. D. M. Derrett argues that the story should be seen against the background of Jewish wedding customs ("Water into Wine," in *Law in the New Testament* [London: Darton, Longman and Todd, 1970], 228–46). The bridegroom or his parents had invited Jesus without reckoning what it might cost them. Jesus recognized moral obligations without swerving from his self-imposed poverty.

137. See above, n. 129; and cf. Richard Reitzenstein, *Hellenistic Mystery Religions: Their Basic Ideas and Significance* (1910; 3rd ed. 1927), Pittsburgh Theological Monograph Series 15 (Pittsburgh: The Pickwick Press, 1978); R. Reitzenstein, *Hellenistische Wundererzählungen* (1906; reprint, Stuttgart: B. C. Teubner, 1974).

138. Bousset, op. cit., 7.

139. *Philosophical Fragments, Or A Fragment of Philosophy* (1844), tr. D. F. Swenson, rev. Howard V. Hong with intro. Niels Thulstrup (Princeton, N.J. : Princeton Univ. Press, 1962), 130.

140. *Training in Christianity* (1850), tr. Walter Lowrie (1941; Princeton, N.J.: Princeton Univ. Press, 1972), 135.

141. Ibid., 28f.; cf. *Philosophical Fragments,* 61–88; and *Concluding Unscientific Postscript* (1846), tr. D. F. Swenson and W. Lowrie (Princeton, N.J.: Princeton Univ. Press, 1941), 169–224. The *Postscript* contains a lengthy discussion of the significance of Lessing's views on history (59–113).

142. Ibid., 127.

143. Ibid.

144. Ibid., 124f.

6. ORTHODOXY EMBATTLED

1. *Lectures on the Present Position of Catholics in England: Addressed to the Brothers of the Oratory in the Summer of 1851* (London: Burns, Oates and Co., n.d.), 306.

2. The essay on "The Miracles of Scripture" was written in 1825-26 for the *Encyclopaedia Metropolitana* as a sequel to a memoir of Apollonius of Tyana. "The Miracles of Early Ecclesiastical History" was written in 1842-43. They were subsequently combined in a single volume (1870). References below are to the new impression (London: Longmans, Green and Co., 1911).

3. Ibid., 4. Newman did not include answers to prayer under miracles on the grounds that such answers did not violate God's "usual system" (67).

4. Ibid., 11.

5. Ibid., 17f.

6. Ibid., 13–48.

7. Ibid., 16. Newman does not specify where this argument may be found. He appears to be thinking of the *ad hominem* claim that "it is impossible for us to know the attributes or actions of such a Being, otherwise from the experience which we have of his productions, in the usual course of nature" (David Hume, *An Enquiry Concerning Human Understanding,* #99). The observation was made in connection with the appeal to miracles as a basis for any new system of religion. However, Hume did not believe that any idea of God could be formed from the observation of nature (cf. esp. his *Dialogues Concerning Natural Religion,* 1779).

8. Ibid., 31. Newman acknowledged that some of the biblical stories (e.g., Eve's temptation by the serpent, Balaam's ass, Jonah and the whale, the devils sent into the herd of swine) "are by themselves more or less improbable, being unequal in dignity to the rest" (30). But they were "supported by the system in which they are found." Moreover, in some of them a further purpose may be discernible, such as to demonstrate the reality of demon possession, as in the case of the Gadarene swine. Such features are, however, lacking in many of the apocryphal, pagan, and rabbinic miracles (28–48).

9. Ibid., 42f.

10. Ibid., 45.

11. Ibid., 48.

12. Ibid., 116.

13. Ibid., 118. The final section of Newman's essay consisted of a detailed discussion of the evidence for nine miracles in the early church: the thundering legion, the change of water into oil by St. Narcissus, the change of the course of the Lycus by St. Gregory, the appearance of the cross to Constantine, the discovery of the Holy Cross by St. Helena, the sudden death of Arius, the fiery eruption on Julian's attempt to rebuild the temple, the recovery of the blind man by the relics of the martyrs, and speech without tongues by the African confessors.

14. John Henry Newman, *An Essay on the Development of Christian Doctrine, The Edition of 1845,* edited with Introduction by J. M. Cameron (Harmondsworth: Penguin Books, 1974). Newman's revised edition of 1878 does not affect the argument at this point. For further discussion see Owen Chadwick, *From Bousset to Newman: The Idea of Doctrinal Development* (Cambridge: Cambridge Univ. Press, 1957), and P. Toon, *The Development of Doctrine in the Church* (Grand Rapids: Wm. B. Eerdmans, 1979).

15. E. A. Abbott, *Philomythus: An Antidote to Credulity; A Discussion of Cardinal Newman's Essay on Ecclesiastical Miracles,* 2nd ed. (London and New York, 1891).

16. The dogma of the Immaculate Conception had been defined by Pius IX in the Bull *Ineffabilis Deus* (1854). No doubt Bernadette Soubirous had heard references to the Immaculate Conception in church. Though the words attributed to the vision were grammatical, they were not strictly coherent.

17. Cf. E. W. Kemp, *Canonization and Authority in the Western Church* (London: Oxford Univ. Press, 1948).

18. L. Sabourin, *The Divine Miracles Discussed and Defended* (Rome: Officium Libri Catholici—Catholic Book Agency, 1977), 172. In his review of eleven officially recognized miraculous cures at Lourdes, Sabourin draws heavily on D. J. West, *Eleven Lourdes Miracles* (London: Duckworth, 1957). West complains of the lack of thoroughness in the investigation of cases, which he believes does not preclude wrong diagnosis and natural remission of the illnesses. Sabourin also reviews other cases not connected with Lourdes, as does B. B. Warfield in *Miracles: Yesterday and Today, True and False* (1918; Grand Rapids: Wm. B. Eerdmans, 1954), 71-124.

19. *Constitutio Dogmatica de Fide Catholica,* ch. 3; cf. Canons 3 and 4 (*The Church Teaches: Documents of the Church in English Translation* [St. Louis: B. Herder Book Co., 1960 ed.], #64; cf. ##71, 72; Latin in *Enchiridion Symbolorum definitionum et Declarationum de Rebus Fidei et Morum,* ed. H. Denzinger, rev. A. Schönmetzer, 32nd ed. [Barcelona, Freiburg, Rome: Herder, 1963], ##3009, 3033,3034).

20. *The Church Teaches,* #88 (Denzinger-Schönmetzer, #3539).

21. Cited from the anonymous translation of *The History of the Origins of Christianity: Book I. The Life of Jesus* (London: Mathieson & Company, n.d.), xi-xii.

22. Ibid., liii.

23. Ibid., xiii.

24. In chapter 16, which was devoted to miracles, Renan explained that Jesus was an exorcist and thaumaturgist in spite of himself (ibid., 147-55). "Jesus had no more idea than the majority of his countrymen of a rational medical science; he shared the general belief that healing was to be effected by religious practices, and such a belief was perfectly consistent" (150). He fell into the pattern of holy men, sanctioned by supernatural powers, established by Elijah and Elisha in the Old Testament and Apollonius of Tyana in the ancient world. Renan regarded Jesus' reluctance to perform miracles and have them publicly proclaimed as evidence of his disinclination to act as a thaumaturgist. Renan concluded that "The miracles of Jesus were a violence done to him by his age, a concession forced from him by a passing necessity. The exorcist and the thaumaturgist have alike passed away; but the religious reformer will live eternally" (155). Evidently Renan felt that he could not explain away all Jesus' reported acts, and thus hinted at natural explanations, though he himself refrained from offering any.

Among the replies to Renan was M.-J. Lagrange's *Christ and Renan: A Commentary on Ernest Renan's "The Life of Jesus,"* tr. Maisie Ward (London: Sheed and Ward, 1928). On Renan's career see H. W. Wardman, *Ernest Renan: A Critical Biography* (London: Univ. of London, The Athlone Press, 1964).

25. On Modernism in general see B. M. G. Reardon, ed., *Roman Catholic Modernism* (London: Adam and Charles Black, 1970); Alec R. Vidler, *A Variety of Catholic Modernists* (Cambridge: Cambridge Univ. Press, 1970); John Ratté, *Three Modernists: Alfred Loisy, George Tyrrell, William L. Sullivan* (London: Sheed and Ward, 1968); John J. Heaney, *The Modernist Crisis* (London: Geoffrey Chapman, 1969); Émile Poulat, *Histoire, Dogme et Critique dans la Crise Moderniste* (Paris: Casterman, 1962).

On the question of Modernism and miracles see Louis Monden, *Signs and Wonders: A Study of the Miraculous Element in Religion* (New York: Desclée, 1966), 51ff.; and the definitive study by François Rodé, *Le Miracle dans la Controverse Moderniste,* Théologie Historique 3 (Paris: Beauchesne et ses Fils, 1965).

26. See Maurice Blondel, *The Letter on Apologetics and History and Dogma,* tr. Alexander Dru and Illtyd Trethowan (London: Harvill Press, 1964).

27. Ibid., 134f.

28. Ibid., 135.

29. Cited from *History and Dogma* (1904), ibid., 226.

30. The work was translated into English in 1903 and has been reprinted with an introduction by Bernard B. Scott in the Lives of Jesus Series (Philadelphia: Fortress Press, 1976).

31. Ibid., 166.

32. Ibid.

33. Cf. Loisy's complementary study of *The Origins of the New Testament* (1936), tr. L. P. Jacks (London: George Allen and Unwin Ltd., 1950), 79f., 124f., 204, 213f.

Loisy gave an account of his life and thought in *My Duel with the Vatican: The Autobiography of a Catholic Modernist,* authorized translation by R. W. Boynton with a new introduction by E. H. Smith (New York: Greenwood Press, 1968). For a major study see Albert Houtin and Félix Sartiaux, *Alfred Loisy: Sa Vie, Son Oeuvre,* Manuscript edited and published with a bibliography of Loisy's works and a bio-bibliographical index of his contemporaries by Émile Poulat (Paris: Éditions du Centre National de la Recherche Scientifique, 1960).

34. Blondel, op. cit., 240f.

35. Ibid., 275f.

36. "Essai sur la Notion du Miracle," *Annales de Philosophie Chrétienne* (1906), 242; cf. F. Rode, op. cit., 192.

37. Second meeting of *Société Française de Philosophie,* December 28, 1911, 135; cf. F. Rodé, op. cit., 232.

38. *Dogmatic Constitution on the Church, Lumen Gentium,* ch. 1, 5 (tr. in A. Flannery, ed., *Vatican Council II: The Conciliar and Postconciliar Documents* [Grand Rapids: Wm. B. Eerdmans, 1975], 352f.).

39. *Catholicism* (Minneapolis: Winston Press, Study Edition, 1981), 328.

40. The edition cited below is *Paley's View of the Evidences of Christianity, Comprising the Text of Paley, Verbatim; with Examination Questions, Arranged at the Foot of Each Page of the Text, and a Full Analysis Prefixed to Each Chapter by the Rev. George Fisk,* 4th ed. (Cambridge: J. Hall & Son, 1864). Paley's various writings were standard textbooks at Cambridge well into the nineteenth century. The *Evidences* survived as a textbook until 1920. Among the countless students who studied Paley's *Natural Theology* was Charles Darwin. See further M. L. Clarke, *Paley: Evidences for the Man* (London: S.P.C.K., 1974), 126–34.

41. *Paley's View of the Evidences of Christianity,* 1.

42. Ibid., 3.

43. Ibid., 2–5.

44. Ibid., 7f.; cf. M. L. Clarke, op. cit., 102ff.

45. *Paley's View,* 6.

46. Ibid., 167.

47. Ibid., 155.

48. *Aids to Reflection* (1825), cited from the edition revised by Thomas Fenby, *Aids to Reflection in the Formation of a Manly Character on the Several Grounds of Prudence, Morality and Religion* (Liverpool: Edward Howell, 1874), 363.

49. In 1798 Coleridge went to Germany to study Kantian philosophy. He followed Kant in rejecting the traditional proof of the existence of God, but his own view of reality stressed the role of intuition in the apprehension of being. He spoke like an Idealist when he talked about the antithesis of thought and being and overcoming through the synthesis of faith. At times he could speak like a pantheist, but on other occasions his thought appears to be thoroughly theistic. While in Germany he became familiar with the work of Reimarus and Lessing. This left its mark on Coleridge's posthumous *Confessions of an Inquiring Spirit* (1840, reprint ed. H. St. J. Hart (London: Adam and Charles Black, 1956]). For appraisals of Coleridge's religious thought see B. M. G. Reardon, *From Coleridge to Gore: A Century of Religious Thought in Britain* (London: Longman, 1971); Norman Fruman, *Coleridge, the Damaged Archangel* (London: George Allen and Unwin, 1972); James D. Boulger, *Coleridge as Religious Thinker* (New Haven: Yale Univ. Press, 1961); J. Robert Barth, *Coleridge and Christian Doctrine* (Cambridge,

Mass.: Harvard Univ. Press, 1969); Thomas McFarland, *Coleridge and the Pantheistic Tradition* (Oxford: Clarendon Press, 1969); Charles Richard Sanders, *Coleridge and the Broad Church Movement* (1942; reprint, New York: Octagon Books, 1972); Basil Willey, *Nineteenth Century Studies: Coleridge to Matthew Arnold* (London: Chatto and Windus, 1949). A somewhat incomplete collection of *The Complete Works of Samuel Taylor Coleridge* in seven volumes was edited by W. G. T. Shedd (New York: Harper and Brothers, 1853-84).

50. Cited from the periodical *The Friend*, which Coleridge published at irregular intervals between 1809 and 1810 and which he revised in volume form (ed. Shedd, 2:468).

51. Notebook 38 (1829), cited by P. Barth, op. cit., 41.

52. *The Friend* (ed. Shedd, 2:394).

53. Notebook 48 (1830), cited by P. Barth, op. cit., 41.

54. J. S. Mill, *Dissertations and Discussions,* vol. 1 (1867), 330, 394; cf. Reardon, op. cit., 60.

55. J. S. Mill, *A System of Logic, Rationative and Inductive, Being A Connected View of the Principles of Evidence and the Methods of Scientific Investigation* (London: Longmans, Green and Co., New Impression, 1925), 410.

56. Reprint, New York: AMS Press, 1970, 224f.

57. Ibid., 228.

58. For a recent account of the book and the controversy that it provoked see Ieuan Ellis, *Seven Against Christ: A Study of "Essays and Reviews,"* Studies in the History of Christian Thought (Leiden: E. J. Brill, 1980).

59. Cited from the 7th ed. (London: Longman, Green, Longman and Roberts, 1861), 109.

60. Ibid., 133.

61. Ibid., 143.

62. Ibid., 144.

63. *Literature and Dogma: An Essay Towards a Better Apprehension of the Bible* (London: Smith, Elder and Co., 1886), xii.

64. Ibid., 96.

65. *God and the Bible* (Boston: James R. Osgood and Co., 1876), 72.

66. Ibid., 81f.

67. Cassels was a retired Bombay merchant who was interested in scholarship and whose work survived into the twentieth century. Two volumes of *Supernatural Religion: An Inquiry into the Reality of Divine Revelation* appeared in 1874. The third volume was published in 1877. Quotations are from the 2nd revised edition, 1874. The work ranged widely over early Christianity and drew on German scholarship. Cassel's treatment of the early Fathers drew a reply from J. B. Lightfoot in a series of articles in the *Contemporary Review* (1874-75), which were subsequently published in *Essays on the Work Entitled Supernatural Religion* (London and New York: Macmillan, 1889).

68. J. S. Mill, *System of Logic*, 408; cf. Cassels, op. cit., 1:80.

69. Mill, *System of Logic*, 408f.; cf. Cassels, op. cit., 1:81.

70. Cassels, op. cit., 1:92.

71. Arnold, *God and the Bible,* 74.

72. Ibid., 83.

73. Cited from the Everyman's Library edition of Sir John Robert Seeley, *Ecce Homo,* with an introduction by Sir Oliver Lodge (1908; London: J. M. Dent; New York: E. P. Dutton, 1932), 7. On the general background to Seeley see David L. Pals, *The Victorian "Lives" of Jesus* (San Antonio: Trinity Univ. Press, 1982).

74. *Ecce Homo*, 7f.

75. Ibid., 38f.

76. Ibid., 72; cf. 42.

77. Quotations are from the edition edited by A. R. Vidler, 2 vols. (London: SCM Press, 1958). Important studies of Maurice include A. M. Ramsey, *F. D. Maurice and the Conflicts of Modern Theology* (London: SCM Press, 1951); W. M. Davies, *An Introduction to F. D. Maurice's Theology* (London: S.P.C.K., 1964); and A. R. Vidler, *F. D. Maurice and Company: Nineteenth Century Studies* (London: SCM Press, 1966).

78. Cited from a letter to the Rev. Isaac Taylor, dated April 10, 1860, in Frederick Maurice, ed., *The Life of Frederick Denison Maurice, Chiefly Told in His Own Letters,* 4th ed., vol. 2 (London: Macmillan, 1885), 358.

79. *Theological Essays* (1853; reprint with an introduction by E. F. Carpenter [London: James Clarke, 1957], 276f.).

80. *The Kingdom of Christ*, 2:170; cf. *The Life of Frederick Denison Maurice*, 2:453ff., and

A. R. Vidler, op. cit., 158ff.

81. *The Kingdom of Christ,* 2:172.

82. Ibid., 2:171.

83. Edwin Hodder, *The Life and Work of the Seventh Earl of Shaftesbury, K.G.* (London: Cassell and Company, 1887), 272. It should be noted that this comment was not prompted by Maurice's attitude toward miracles, but by his theological stance generally and its application to social questions. To many people Maurice was a dangerous and somewhat unorthodox thinker. He was dismissed from his chair of theology at King's College, London, for his attack in his *Theological Essays* on the endlessness of future punishment. He was a leader of Christian Socialism. His appointment in 1866 to the Knightbridge Chair of Moral Philosophy at Cambridge was an indication of the growing acceptability of his views.

84. Ibid., 591. Hodder observes that scarcely a day passed when Shaftesbury was not protesting against attacks on the orthodox faith. He was a leader of the protest against *Essays and Reviews.*.

85. Letter dated January 10, 1866, in Arthur Westcott, *Life and Letters of Brooke Foss Westcott,* vol. 1 (London: Macmillan, 1903), 289.

86. For an appraisal of Westcott's achievements see Henry Chadwick, *The Vindication of Christianity in Westcott's Thought,* The Bishop Westcott Memorial Lecture 1960 (Cambridge: Cambridge Univ. Press, 1961).

87. *What is Revelation?* (Cambridge: Macmillan, 1859; reprint, New York: AMS Press, 1975), 57.

88. Ibid., 62.

89. Ibid., 75.

90. *Characteristics of the Gospel Miracles* (Cambridge: Macmillan, 1859), 15ff.; cf. Augustine, *Tractates on the Gospel of John* 9.1; *Sermon* 126.4; *Expositions on the Book of the Psalms* 90.6. See also the discussion of Augustine in Chapter One of this book.

91. Ibid., 17.

92. Ibid., 27.

93. Ibid., 29.

94. Ibid., 11f.

95. Ibid., 21.

96. Ibid., 37.

97. Ibid., 49ff.

98. Ibid., 43f. Westcott drew attention to the pain, grief, and human cost to Jesus in doing the Father's will. The miracles were not sheer prodigies.

99. See ch. 1, n. 41. Westcott exercised an influence on Gore from the time when Gore was his pupil at Harrow.

100. Westcott, op. cit., 63.

101. Ibid., 89.

102. Ibid., 97.

103. Chadwick, op. cit., 7, 9.

104. *F. D. Maurice and Company,* 226.

105. *Notes on the Miracles of Our Lord,* 15th ed. (London: Kegan Paul, Trench, Trübner and Co., 1895), 91.

106. Ibid., 94.

107. Ibid., 98.

108. Ibid., 29; cf. Rev. 13:2; Gregory the Great, *Moralia in Job* 20.7; Augustine, *The City of God* 10.16; *Against Faustus* 13.5.

109. Trench, op. cit., 99. Trench notes "the admirable words of Calvin . . . on the Holy Scripture as ultimately *autopistos,* its own proof" (*Institutes* 1.7.4f.).

110. Trench, op. cit., 75.

111. Ibid., 76.

112. Ibid., 75f.

113. Ibid., 16f.

114. Ibid., 102; cf. 27, 29, 75.

115. *Eight Lectures on Miracles,* 7th ed. (London: Rivingtons, 1886), 25.

116. Ibid., 23.

117. Ibid., 46.

118. Ibid., 54.

119. Ibid., 58.
120. Ibid., 74.
121. Ibid., 79.
122. Ibid., 81; cf. John Hick, "Theology and Verification," *Theology Today* 17 (1960), reprinted in J. Hick, ed., *The Existence of God* (New York: Macmillan; London: Collier-Macmillan, 1964), 253-74; and "Eschatological Verification Reconsidered," *Religious Studies* 13 (1977): 189-202.
123. Mozley, op. cit., 110; cf. Blaise Pascal, *Oeuvres,* ed. P. Faugère, vol. 2 (Paris: Hachette, 1895), 151.
124. Mozley, op. cit., 129f.
125. Ibid., 159f.
126. Ibid., 161-87.
127. R. W. Church, *Occasional Papers,* vol. 2 (London: Macmillan, 1897), 82f. (reprinted from *The Times,* June 5, 1866).
128. C. A. Row, *Christian Evidences Viewed in Relation to Modern Thought,* Bampton Lectures 1877, 5th ed. (London: Norgate, 1888), xiv; cf. 54-72.
129. Ibid., 63.
130. H. D. McDonald, *Theories of Revelation: An Historical Study, 1860-1960* (London: Allen and Unwin, 1963), 58. McDonald sees a tendency to minimize miracles in such writers as J. R. Illingworth, *Personality Human and Divine* (1894), 203f.; and H. Drummond, *The New Evangelism* (1899), 107ff. In addition to McDonald's work, see also B. M. G. Reardon, *From Coleridge to Gore: A Century of Religious Thought in Britain* (London: Longman, 1971), for a review of thought in this period. A. B. Bruce (see following note) also reviews trends of thought. In America, Horace Bushnell's *Nature and the Supernatural* (1858) saw God working through nature in a way analogous to the human will transcending nature in operating in and through its laws. Bushnell saw miracles as part of the divine law of nature.
131. A. B. Bruce, *The Miraculous Element in the Gospels: A Course of Lectures on the "Ely Foundation," Delivered in Union Theological Seminary* (New York: A. C. Armstrong; London: Hodder and Stoughton, 1886), 43.
132. Ibid., 46.
133. Ibid., 258.
134. Ibid., 309.
135. *The Plan of a Theological Seminary Adopted by the General Assembly . . . A.D. 1811* (Philadelphia, 1811), 13; cited from Jack B. Rogers and Donald K. McKim, *The Authority and Interpretation of the Bible: A Historical Approach* (San Francisco: Harper and Row, 1979), 269.
136. *Evidences of the Authenticity, Inspiration, and Canonical Authority of the Holy Scriptures,* 2nd ed. (Philadelphia: Presbyterian Board of Publication, 1836), 76f.
137. Ibid., 88.
138. Ibid., 89.
139. Ibid., 67f.
140. *Nature and the Supernatural* (New York: Charles Scribner & Co., 1871), 38.
141. Ibid., 363f.
142. Ibid., 364.
143. Ibid., 365; cf. Calvin, *Institutes* 1.9.1-3; Westminster Confession 1.5.
144. A. A. Hodge, *The Life of Charles Hodge D.D., LL.D.* (New York: Charles Scribner's Sons, 1880), 521.
145. *Systematic Theology,* vol. 1 (1871; reprint, Grand Rapids: Wm. B. Eerdmans, 1952), 617-36.
146. *Dogmatic Theology,* vol. 1 (1888; reprint, Grand Rapids: Zondervan, n.d.), 533-46.
147. Westminster Confession (1647), 5.3; cf. Hodge, *Systematic Theology* 1:617f.; Shedd, op. cit., 1:533.
148. Shedd, op. cit., 1:536.
149. Ibid., 546.
150. Ibid., 632.
151. Ibid., 635.
152. Ibid., 636.
153. Ibid., citing John 5:20, 36; 7:17; 10:25, 38; cf. Mozley's appeal to John 15:24 and 5:36 (op. cit., 1.25; cf. above, nn. 146f.).

7. THE QUESTIONS OF THE PHILOSOPHERS

1. Cf. E. and M.-L. Keller, *Miracles in Dispute: A Continuing Debate* (London: SCM Press, 1969), 192–97; T. R. Miles, *Religion and the Scientific Outlook* (London: George Allen and Unwin, 1959), 190f.

2. *Systematic Theology,* vol. 1 (London: Nisbet, 1953), 130.

3. Ibid., 1:129.

4. Miles, op. cit., 189.

5. *The Encyclopedia of Philosophy,* ed. P. Edwards, 5:351.

6. In *New Essays in Philosophical Theology*, ed. A. Flew and A. MacIntyre (London: SCM Press, 1955), 253; cf. A. Flew, *God and Philosophy* (London: Hutchinson, 1966), 150.

7. Cf. Richard Swinburne, *The Concept of Miracle* (London: Macmillan, 1970), 26–32.

8. *Religion and Rationality: An Introduction to the Philosophy of Religion* (New York: Random House, 1971), 277.

9. *A System of Logic*, 8th ed. (reprint, London: Longmans, Green, 1925), 3.25.2, p. 409.

10. *Summa Contra Gentiles* 3.102.3.

11. R. F. Holland, "The Miraculous," *American Philosophical Quarterly* 2 (1965):43–51; reprinted in D. Z. Phillips, ed., *Religion and Understanding* (Oxford: Blackwell, 1967), 155–70. References are to the latter.

12. Ibid., 155.

13. Ibid., 157.

14. Ibid., 163.

15. Ibid., 168.

16. From the standpoint of evidence, the resurrection of Jesus stands apart from miracles attributed to Jesus in the Gospels. The latter are attested by individual reports. The resurrection of Jesus, however, is attested not only by individual reports; it is the presupposition of the existence of the Christian church. The present writer's position is set out in his article on "The Resurrection in Contemporary Theology" in C. Brown, ed., *The New International Dictionary of New Testament Theology*, vol. III (Exeter: Paternoster Press; Grand Rapids: Zondervan, 1978), 281–309).

17. Smart, *Philosophers and Religious Truth,* 2nd ed. (London: SCM Press, 1964), 37.

18. Ibid., 38.

19. Ibid.

20. Ibid., 48.

21. Ibid.

22. Ibid.

23. For discussions of indeterminacy see Ian G. Barbour, *Issues in Science and Religion* (Englewood Cliffs: Prentice-Hall; London: SCM Press, 1966), 298–309, 395–99; E. L. Mascall, *Christian Theology and Natural Science: Some Questions in their Relations,* The Bampton Lectures, 1956 (London: Longmans, Green and Co., 1956), 167–207; W. Heisenberg, *Physics and Philosophy: The Revolution in Modern Science* (New York: Harper and Brothers, 1958); John Dillenberger, *Protestant Thought and Natural Science: A Historical Interpretation* (Garden City, N.Y.: Doubleday, 1960), 270–79, 284f.; Werner Schaaffs, *Theology, Physics, and Miracles* (Washington: Canon Press, 1974).

24. Barbour, op. cit., 278.

25. In C. F. D. Moule, ed., *Miracles: Cambridge Studies in their Philosophy and History* (London: A. R. Mowbray; New York: Morehouse-Barlow, 1965), 38f.

26. Ibid., 41.

27. Ibid., 42.

28. C. S. Lewis, *Miracles: A Preliminary Study* (London: Geoffrey Bles, 1947), cited from the Fontana Books edition, 3rd ed. rev. (1960), 18.

29. Smart, op. cit., 39.

30. Lewis, op. cit., 136–67.

31. London: Macmillan, St. Martin's Press, 1970.

32. Ibid., 31f. In *The Concept of Miracle* and also in his more recent discussion, "Arguments from History and Miracles" in *The Existence of God* (Oxford: Clarendon Press, 1979), 225–43, Swinburne considers whether laws of nature are universal or statistical in character. Universal laws take the form of the generalization "All A's are B," whereas statistical laws take the form: "99.99% of A's are B." In the case of universal laws Swinburne now prefers to speak of "violations," whereas in the case of statistical laws he speaks of "quasi violations." In such a case

the occurrence of a miracle would not be sufficient to warrant the replacing of law L by L[1], because it would add to the complexity of the law and because there is every reason to suppose that any predictions on the basis of the modified law would be false.

33. *The Concept of Miracle*, 10.

34. Ibid., 33-37.

35. Cf. Alan Richardson, *History: Sacred and Profane,* The Bampton Lectures for 1962 (London: SCM Press, 1964), 199f.; Wolfhart Pannenberg, *Jesus—God and Man* (London: SCM Press, 1968), 98.

36. *The Concept of Miracle,* 37.

37. Ibid., 42.

38. Ibid., 51.

39. Ibid., 68f.

40. In *The Existence of God* Swinburne concludes that as a class miracles provide a weak confirmation of theism (pp. 242f.). This is a general conclusion based on the nature of the evidence in the light of probability. However, this conclusion may be upgraded or downgraded in the light of more detailed consideration of particular evidence. Moreover, theism is not based primarily on miracles. The case for Christian theism depends upon a complex of considerations.

41. Reprinted in *The Miracles and the Resurrection: Some Recent Studies,* by I. T. Ramsey, G. H. Boobyer, F. N. Davey, M. C. Perry, and Henry J. Cadbury, Theological Collections 3 (London: S.P.C.K., 1964), 2.

42. Ibid., 7.

43. Ibid., 8.

44. Ibid., 9.

45. Ibid., 13.

46. At this point Ramsey engages in a debate with Gilbert Ryle, arguing that "I"-language points to personal identity that transcends objective "me"-language.

47. Ramsey, op. cit., 15.

48. Ibid., 21.

49. Ibid., 26.

50. Ibid., 28.

51. Ibid., 27.

52. *Religious Language: An Empirical Placing of Theological Phrases* (London: SCM Press, 1957), 144; cf. op. cit., 21.

53. *Religious Language,* 61. Ramsey went on to develop his views in various works, including *Models and Mystery* (London: Oxford Univ. Press, 1964); *Models for Divine Activity* (London: SCM Press, 1973); and *Christian Empiricism,* ed. Jerry H. Gill (London: Sheldon Press, 1974). For a brief appraisal see H. P. Owen, "The Philosophical Theology of I. T. Ramsey," *Theology* 74 (1971):67-74.

54. *Religious Language,* 62.

55. Ibid., 147.

56. "Miracles," *Religious Studies* 9 (1973):309. The article adopts substantially the same standpoint as Diamond's discussion of the subject in his *Contemporary Philosophy and Religious Thought: An Introduction to the Philosophy of Religion* (New York: McGraw-Hill, 1974), 57-74.

57. *Contemporary Philosophy,* 57.

58. Ibid., 317; cf. Guy Robinson, "Miracles," *Ratio* 9 (1967):155-66.

59. "Professor Langford's Meaning of 'Miracle'," *Religious Studies* 8 (1972):251-55; cf. also Tan Tai Wei, "Recent Discussions on Miracles," *Sophia* 11 (1972); and "Mr. Young on Miracles," *Religious Studies* 10 (1974):333-37.

60. "What a Miracle Really Is," *Religious Studies* 12 (1976):49-57.

61. "The Problem of the Meaning of 'Miracle,' " *Religious Studies* 7 (1971):43-52.

62. Ibid., 47; cf. C. A. Coulson, *Science and Christian Belief* (London: Oxford Univ. Press, 1955), 64.

63. *Religious Studies* 7, 48f.

64. Ibid., 50.

65. Immanuel Kant, "Possibility of Causality through Freedom, in Harmony with the Universal Law of Natural Necessity," in *Critique of Pure Reason,* tr. Norman Kemp Smith, rev. (London: Macmillan, 1933), 467-79; cf. H. H. Farmer, *The World and God: A Study of Prayer, Providence and Miracle in Christian Experience* (London: Nisbet, 1935), 159.

66. *Religious Studies* 7, 52.

67. Chryssides, "Miracles and Agents," *Religious Studies* 11 (1975):321.

68. Ibid., 322.

69. Ibid., 327.

70. The above comments may be compared with those of Herbert Burhenn in "Attributing Miracles to Agents—Reply to George D. Chryssides," *Religious Studies* 13 (1977):485-89. Burhenn detects a number of odd and even question-begging features in Chryssides's discussion. He suggests that it is better to explore the teleological character of miracles than to focus on the question of causation in the oversimple way deemed necessary by Chryssides.

71. "Miracles and Epistemology," *Religious Studies* 8 (1972):115-26; and "Miracles and Credibility," *Religious Studies* 16 (1980):465-68.

72. "A New Look at Miracles," *Religious Studies* 13 (1977):417-28.

73. *Religious Studies* 8, 120; cf. W. Eichrodt, *Theology of the Old Testament,* vol. 2 (London: SCM Press, 1961), 162-67.

74. Ibid., 123.

75. Ibid., 125.

76. *Religious Studies* 16, 467.

77. Ibid.

78. *Religious Studies* 8, 116.

79. *Religious Studies* 16, 465.

80. *Religious Studies* 13, 417.

81. Ibid., 419; cf. R. Swinburne, op. cit., 27-32; and Margaret A. Boden, "Miracles and Scientific Explanation," *Ratio* 11 (1969):140.

82. *Religious Studies* 13, 421.

83. Ibid.

84. Ibid., 423.

85. Ibid., 426. For attempts to explain the Virgin Birth in terms of the mutation of sex chromosomes in the instant of conception see E. L. Mascall, *Theology and the Gospel of Christ: An Essay in Reorientation* (London: S.P.C.K., 1977), 132ff., 195ff.; Cletus Wessels, *The Mother of God, Her Physical Maternity: A Reappraisal* (River Forest, Ill.: Aquinas Library, 1964).

86. *Religious Studies* 13, 427.

87. Ibid.

88. "Miracles and Good Evidence," *Religious Studies* 18 (1982):37-46.

89. Ibid., 46.

8. THE ANSWERS OF THE APOLOGISTS

1. Originally published by Scribner's. References below are to the reprint published by Wm. B. Eerdmans Publishing Co., Grand Rapids, 1954.

2. Ibid., 6.

3. Ibid., 3.

4. Warfield discussed "The Supernatural Birth of Jesus" in *Christology and Criticism* (New York: Oxford Univ. Press, 1929), 447-58. The same volume lists several articles on the resurrection of Jesus (459). But neither this volume nor *The Lord of Glory* (1907; New York: American Tract Society; reprint, Grand Rapids: Zondervan, n.d.), which is a study of the title of Jesus, contains a detailed study of biblical miracles.

5. *The Westminster Dictionary of the Bible,* ed. John D. Davis, rev. and rewritten by Henry Snyder Gehman (Philadelphia: Westminster Press, 1944), 399. Warfield was a contributor to the original work, which first appeared in 1898.

6. New York and London: Funk and Wagnalls Co., 1910, 6:150-60; reprinted in *Christology and Criticism*, 149-77.

7. Ibid., 173.

8. Reprinted in B. B. Warfield, *Selected Shorter Writings,* ed. John E. Meeter, vol. 2 (Phillipsburg: Presbyterian and Reformed, 1973), 167-204.

9. Ibid., 168.

10. Ibid., 169.

11. Ibid., 170; cf. 197.

12. Ibid., 171.

13. Ibid., 175.

14. Ibid.

15. Ibid., 189.

16. Ibid., 180.

17. Ibid., 193. At this point Warfield noted a similarity between his own position and that of Abraham Kuyper who interpreted miracles within the context of God's renewal of the whole cosmos (*Encyclopedia of Sacred Theology*, reprinted with the new title *Principles of Sacred Theology*, with an introduction by B. B. Warfield [Grand Rapids: Wm. B. Eerdmans, 1954], 414; cf. 420–28). This position may also be compared with that of C. S. Lewis noted below.

18. Ibid., 200.

19. Ibid.

20. Ibid., 202.

21. The question is taken from a copy of the examination questions that came into my possession. The subject of miracles regularly featured in the examinations of this period.

22. *An Introduction to Christian Apologetics: A Philosophic Defense of the Trinitarian-Theistic Faith* (Grand Rapids: Wm. B. Eerdmans, 1948), 272; cf. 269. In reviewing C. S. Lewis's *Miracles*, which had been published the previous year, Carnell acknowledged Lewis's work as a real contribution to apologetics, though it gave "evidence of theological uncertainty at points" and did not struggle with the relation between miracles and the canon (*United Evangelical Action* 6 [1948]:24). Clearly Carnell was disappointed in the fact that Lewis saw no evident connection between miracles and the establishment of the canon of Scripture.

23. *Introduction*, 251.

24. Ibid., 258.

25. Ibid., 261.

26. Ibid., 273.

27. Ibid., 269. The kind of miracles Carnell had in mind here were what he called "absolute miracles," which defied all natural explanation and which he clearly distinguished from instances of "the convergence of the *ordinary* operations of God's general providence in nature in such a way that, by the confluence of laws, a special blessing is borne home" (274).

28. "Science, Theology and the Miraculous," *Journal of the American Scientific Affiliation* 30 (Dec. 1978):152f. Montgomery's paper, which was originally delivered at the Lee College Symposium on the Theological Implications of Science in 1977, has been reprinted in Montgomery's *Faith Founded on Fact: Essays in Evangelical Apologetics* (Nashville and New York: Thomas Nelson, 1978), 43–78. References given here are to the journal article.

29. Hesse, op. cit., 147; cf. C. F. D. Moule, ed., *Miracles,* 38 (cited above on p. 179).

30. Holland, op. cit., 147 (cf. above, pp. 175).

31. Montgomery, op. cit., 148.

32. Ibid., 149f.

33. *Journal of the American Scientific Affiliation*, 156.

34. Ibid., 150ff.

35. Ibid., 146; cf. Max Black, *Models and Metaphors* (Ithaca, N.Y.: Cornell Univ. Press, 1962), 169.

36. *Journal of the American Scientific Affiliation*, 150; cf. 157.

37. Ibid., 157.

38. Ibid., 157ff.

39. Ibid., 150.

40. Ibid., 146.

41. "In sum, the Resurrection does point unequivocally to the truth of Jesus' claim to Godhead. . . . And it should be noted with care that once the facticity of Christ's Resurrection has been granted, all explanations for it reduce to two: Christ's own (He rose because He was God) and any and every interpretation of the event in contradiction to this explanation" (ibid., 150). Apart from noting the tautological character of the latter sentence, it may be questioned what claims Montgomery has in mind. Are they claims made on behalf of Christ (in which case they are value judgments made by others), or are they claims attributable to Christ himself (in which case it is not clear which precise claims Montgomery has in mind)?

42. Cf. Acts 2:24, 32f.; 4:10ff.; 5:31f.; 10:40–43; 13:34, 39; 17:31; Rom. 10:9; 1 Cor. 15:4; 2 Cor. 4:14; Phil. 2:9; 1 Thess. 1:10.

Even those passages which use an intransitive form of the verb do not necessarily imply that the ground of the resurrection of Jesus was his personal divinity (e.g., Mark 9:31; 10:34; 14:28; 16:6). They leave open the question of the cause of the resurrection. John 10:17f. implies a delegated authority. John 2:19 should be understood as the word of the Father uttered by Jesus (cf. John 14:10; 17:8).

No New Testament passage argues the resurrection from the intrinsic immortal divinity of the Son. In fact, the title "Son of God" was not self-evidently a title of divinity, but a designation of righteous relation to God that belonged to Davidic kingship and messiahship (cf. Ps. 2:7; Luke 3:38; Matt. 3:17; Acts 13:33; Heb. 1:5; 5:5; 2 Pet. 1:17). This interpretation best fits Peter's confession of Jesus as the Christ, the Son of the living God (Matt. 16:16), and the high priest's question (Mark 14:61). The centurion's confession at the foot of the cross was a confession of Jesus' righteousness (Mark 15:39; cf. Luke 23:47).

43. Rom. 1:4; cf. 6:4, 9; 8:34; 1 Tim. 3:16.

44. *Journal of the American Scientific Affiliation*, 145.

45. Ibid., 151.

46. Ibid., 161.

47. Ibid., 166.

48. Ibid., 168.

49. Ibid.

50. Published by the Canon Press in Washington, D.C., with a foreword by John W. Klotz and a comment from the publisher by Harold O. J. Brown.

51. Ibid., 56; cf. 67ff.

52. *Christian Apologetics* (Grand Rapids: Baker Book House, 1976), 227.

53. Ibid., 278.

54. *Miracles and Modern Thought* (Grand Rapids: Zondervan; Dallas: Probe Ministries International, 1982), 13.

55. Ibid., 75; cf. 115, 154.

56. Ibid., 152.

57. Ibid., 75.

58. Ibid., 154.

59. Ibid., 123.

60. Ibid., 121.

61. Cf. ch. 1, nn. 15, 16, 17, 66, 68, 69.

62. Geisler, op. cit., 69.

63. Ibid., 116–23.

64. Ibid., 136.

65. Ibid., 147.

66. See above, pp. 137ff.

67. *The Divine Miracles Discussed and Defended* (Rome: Officium Libri Catholici, 1977), 17. On this subject Sabourin expresses his debt to J. de Tonquedec, *Introduction à l'Étude du Merveilleux et du Miracle* (Paris, 1916), and the same author's "Miracle" in the *Dictionnaire Apologetique de la Foi Catholique* (Paris, 1926; E.T. *Miracles* [West Baden College, 1955]).

68. *Sacramentum Mundi: An Encyclopedia of Theology*, ed. Karl Rahner et al., vol. 4 (New York: Herder and Herder; London: Burns and Oates, 1969), 45.

69. Ibid., 46.

70. The work originally appeared in Flemish with the title *Het Wonder*, from which Monden made an enlarged French version *Le Miracle, Signe de Salut* (Bruges: Desclée de Brouwer, 1960) on which the English translation is based (New York: Desclée, 1966), with a foreword by Avery Dulles.

71. Ibid., 25.

72. Ibid., 29.

73. Ibid.; cf. Athanasius, *On the Incarnation* 8, 9, 14, 16, 20, 21, 38, 43, 44, 49, 54.

74. Monden, op. cit., 31.

75. Ibid., 37.

76. Ibid., 43.

77. Ibid., 57; cf. Ambrose, *Commentary on Luke* 5.

78. Monden, op. cit., 60; cf. *The Infancy Story of Thomas*, 2 (in E. Hennecke, *New Testament Apocrypha*, ed. W. Schneemelcher, vol. 1 [London: Lutterworth Press, 1963], 392f.).

79. Monden, op. cit., 62. Monden utterly rejects the attitude that looks at "the most abnormal as being the most *convincing* miracle," which is illustrated in the sally recounted by Anatole France: "Being at Lourdes during August, I visited the grotto where countless crutches are hung as emblems of cures which have been effected. My companion pointed out these trophies

to me, and whispered: 'Just one wooden leg would say more than all these' " (60; cf. Anatole France, *Le Jardin d'Épicure* [Paris, 1897], 203f.).

80. Monden, op. cit., 62f.

81. Ibid., 70ff.

82. Ibid., 80.

83. Ibid., 84f.

84. Ibid., 86. The illustration is taken from G. Söhngen, "Wunderzeichen und Glaube," in *Die Einheit der Theologie* (Munich, 1952), 270.

85. Monden, op. cit., 89.

86. Ibid., 93.

87. Ibid., 94. In using this expression Monden is thinking of the recurrence of miracles through the ages. This recurrence is not sufficient for them to be regarded simply as natural events, although Monden later concedes that "No *science* true to its nature can ever declare a phenomenon unexplainable" (343). In his ensuing discussion Monden stresses the religious significance of miracles as signs.

With regard to biblical miracles, Monden approaches them in the light of contemporary miracles, justifying their historicity by analogy with more recent, accepted miracles. "Once we admit, in fact, that true miracles can happen, we can no longer doubt the genuine character of the miracles narrated in the Gospel, for they bear the stamp of authenticity down to their smallest details. Their sober simplicity and characteristic starkness, the dignified, grave and self-forgetful manner of Jesus in achieving them, their perfect accordance with the personality of the Lord, his teaching and the work of salvation, their harmony with the sacramental symbolism and the language of the parables—all these authenticating signs. . . , which place the miracles of Christ at the opposite extreme from prodigies typical of apocryphal accounts or modern charlatans, reveal their full apologetic meaning in the light of the contemporary miracle" (351).

88. Ibid., 94; citing the *Dogmatic Constitution on the Faith*, ch. 3, which echoes the phraseology of Isa. 11:12 (Denzinger-Schönmetzer, #3014; *The Church Teaches*, #68).

89. 1 Cor. 15:28; 1 Pet. 3:15.

90. Cf. J. Guitton, *Le Problème de Jésus*, vol. 2, *Divinité et Résurrection* (Paris, 1953), 245; G. Söhngen, *Symbol und Wirklichkeit im Kultmysterium*, 2nd ed. (Bonn, 1940), 82-94.

91. Monden, op. cit., 100.

92. Tennant, *Miracle and its Philosophical Presuppositions* (Cambridge: Cambridge Univ. Press, 1925), 23.

93. Ibid., 67.

94. Ibid.

95. Ibid., 94f.; cf. F. R. Tennant, *Philosophical Theology*, vol. 2, *The World, The Soul and God* (Cambridge: Cambridge Univ. Press, 1930), 215ff.

96. *Foundations* (London: Macmillan, 1912), 129.

97. Ibid., 140.

98. Ibid., 136.

99. Ibid., 259.

100. Ibid.

101. *Christus Veritas: An Essay* (London: Macmillan, 1924), 100.

102. *Nature, Man and God: Being the Gifford Lectures Delivered in the University of Glasgow in the Academical Years 1932-33 and 1933-1934* (London: Macmillan, 1934), 267.

103. Ibid. Temple's use of the word "process" should not be confused with the Process Thought of A. N. Whitehead and subsequent Process Theology. Temple viewed his thought as Dialectical Realism, characterized by transcendent, personal theism. Temple was critical of Whitehead's attempt to make God and the world correlative. He believed that the world was open to the determination of the transcendent God. In his view, "Whitehead surreptitiously introduces thoughts which properly belong to Personality, though ostensibly he stops short at the category of organism. Because he stops there, he has to present God and the world as completely correlated to each other. . . . *But Personality is always transcendent in relation to Process*" (260f., Temple's italics; cf. pp. 246-74 for Temple's views on transcendence and Whitehead's shortcomings). On Temple's thought generally and his philosophical background see Owen C. Thomas, *William Temple's Philosophy of Religion* (London: S.P.C.K.; Greenwich, Conn.: Seabury Press, 1961).

104. *Nature, Man and God*, 302f.

105. Cairns, *The Faith that Rebels,* 3rd ed. (London: SCM Press, 1929).

106. Farmer, *The World and God,* 2nd ed. (London: Nisbet, 1936).

107. Cairns, op. cit., 29f.

108. Ibid., 31f.

109. Ibid., 6.

110. Ibid., 92f.

111. Ibid., 93.

112. Farmer, op. cit., 108. Farmer reiterated his position in the brief tract *Are Miracles Possible?* (London: National Society, S.P.C.K., 1960).

113. *The World and God,* 114.

114. Ibid. The point may be compared with Calvin's view (*Institutes* 1.7.4–5) and the observation of Ludwig Wittgenstein: " 'You can't hear God speak to someone else, you can hear him only if you are being addressed.'—That is a grammatical remark" (*Zettel,* #717, ed. G. E. M. Anscombe and G. H. von Wright [Oxford: Basil Blackwell, 1967], 124e).

115. *The World and God,* 118 (Farmer's italics).

116. Ibid., 122f.

117. Ibid., 145f.

118. Ibid., 149.

119. Ibid., 146f.; cf. 159, 161, and Kant, *Critique of Pure Reason,* section on "Possibility of Causality through Freedom" (see above, ch. 5, n. 66).

120. *The World and God,* 153; cf. above, ch. 7, n. 65.

121. Ibid., 153f.; cf. K. Beth, *Das Wunder* (1908), 23.

122. Richardson, *Christian Apologetics* (London: SCM Press, 1947), 154; cf. Augustine, *The City of God* 21.8. Richardson also notes the passage from *Against Faustus the Manichaean* 26.3, and *The City of God* 10.12, discussed above in ch. 1.

123. Richardson, op. cit., 155f.

124. Ibid., 155.

125. Ibid., 172. For vindication and elaboration of this position Richardson referred his readers to *The Miracle Stories of the Gospel* (London: SCM Press, 1971).

126. *Christian Apologetics,* 171f.

127. *History: Sacred and Profane,* Bampton Lectures for 1962 (London: SCM Press, 1964), 203. For a discussion of Richardson's position generally see J. Navone, *History and Faith in the Thought of Alan Richardson* (London: SCM Press, 1966).

128. History, 208.

129. G. Bornkamm, *Jesus of Nazareth* (1960; London: Hodder and Stoughton; New York: Harper and Brothers, rev. ed. 1963), 180.

130. *History,* 196f.

131. Ibid., 209.

132. Ibid., 212.

133. Lawton, *Miracles and Revelation* (London: Lutterworth Press, 1959), 254f.

134. Ibid., 255f.

135. See the reviews noted and summarized by Joe R. Christopher and Joan K. Ostling in *C. S. Lewis: An Annotated Check List of Writings about Him and His Works* (Kent, Ohio: Kent State Univ. Press, 1973), 268–72.

136. *Miracles: A Preliminary Study* (1947), cited from the rev. ed. (London: Collins, Fontana Books, 1960), 168; cf. "Modern Theology and Biblical Criticism," in *Christian Reflections*, ed. Walter Hooper (London: Geoffrey Bles, 1967), 152–66.

Lewis's *Miracles* coincided with the publication of *The Rise of Christianity*, by the freethinking Bishop of Birmingham, E. W. Barnes (London: Longmans, Green and Co., 1947). The bishop, who rejected miracles in the name of science, is thought to have been the model for the episcopal ghost in *The Great Divorce* (R. L. Green and W. Hooper, *C. S. Lewis: A Biography* [New York and London: Harcourt, Brace, Jovanovich, 1974], 227). His position was the kind that Lewis was attacking in *Miracles.*

137. The debate was held at the meeting of the Socratic Club. Miss Anscombe's paper is reprinted from the *Socratic Digest* in *The Collected Philosophical Papers of G. E. M. Anscombe,* vol. 2, *Metaphysics and the Philosophy of Mind* (Minneapolis: Univ. of Minneapolis Press, 1981), 224–32. A resumé of the discussion and a note by Lewis are appended. See further Richard Webster in *Seven: An Anglo-American Literary Review* 2 (1981):21-23.

138. *God in the Dock: Essays on Theology and Ethics,* ed. Walter Hooper (Grand Rapids: Wm. B. Eerdmans, 1970), 25.

139. Ibid., 25f.

140. *Miracles,* 9–15.
141. Ibid., 19; citing J. B. S. Haldane, *Possible Worlds,* 209.
142. Ibid., 28, 30.
143. Ibid., 31.
144. Ibid., 34f.
145. Ibid., 27.
146. Ibid., 38–48.
147. Ibid., 50.
148. Ibid., 98.
149. Ibid., 50.
150. Ibid., 9.
151. Ibid., 63.
152. Ibid., 64.
153. Ibid., 17.
154. Ibid., 112ff.; cf. Lewis B. Smedes, *The Incarnation: Trends in Modern Anglican Thought* (Kampen: J. H. Kok, 1953).
155. *God in the Dock,* 28f.; cf. Athanasius, *On the Incarnation,* #43.
156. *God in the Dock,* 29; cf. *Miracles,* 139.
157. *God in the Dock,* 29f.; cf. *Miracles,* 140.
158. *God in the Dock,* 30; cf. *Miracles,* 144f.
159. *God in the Dock,* 32.
160. These themes form the subjects of chapters 15 and 16 respectively.
161. *Miracles,* 146.
162. Ibid., 146ff.
163. Ibid., 153.
164. Ibid., 154.
165. Ibid., 156.
166. Ibid., 158.
167. See C. S. Lewis's introduction to the reprint of George MacDonald's *Phantastes and Lilith* (Grand Rapids: Wm. B. Eerdmans, 1964), 11.
168. George MacDonald, *The Miracles of Our Lord* (1871; reprint, ed. Rolland Hein [Wheaton, Ill.: Harold Shaw Publishers, 1980]), 14.
169. Ibid., 13; cf. 20ff., 143ff.; and C. S. Lewis, ed., *George MacDonald: An Anthology* (New York: Macmillan, 1947), 31, 46, 54.
170. MacDonald, op. cit., 142.
171. Ibid., 153–66.
172. Green and Hooper note that "Besides an immense amount of reading in philosophers and educationalists from Plato to the present, Lewis spent many hours in the Bodleian poring over the mammoth *Encyclopaedia of Religion and Ethics*" (op. cit., 218). Certainly, various affinities may be noted between Lewis's natural theology and A. E. Taylor's article on "Theism," vol. 12 (Edinburgh: T. & T. Clark, 1921), 261–87, and between J. A. MacCullough's discussion of "Miracles" (8:676–90).

Taylor's critique of Hume was noted above in ch. 4. Taylor, who was a devout Anglican, was the doyen of prewar British philosophical theologians. He defended the existence of God on lines similar to Lewis's in his popular study *Does God Exist?* (London: Macmillan, 1945). There are a number of striking resemblances with Taylor's Gifford Lectures for 1926-28, *The Faith of a Moralist* (London: Macmillan, 1937). Taylor speaks of nature and supernature. He argues that "the very notion of miracle should be possible only to a conscious or unconscious rationalist" (2:189). He concluded: "Except as interpreted in the light of antecedent belief in God, no marvel, however stupendous, however well authenticated, and however marked its results on the life of mankind, would be more than a rare and curious fact" (2:195f.).

Lewis's remarks about the skeptic in the Lake of Fire (*God in the Dock,* 25) sound like an echo of Taylor's conclusion: "If a man does not see God in the *cursus ordinarius* of nature and human life, 'neither will he believe, though one rose from the dead.' Or at least we should perhaps say, he may in fact be converted by the rising of one from the dead, but he will owe the fact of that conversion to the weakness of his logic; his conversion will prove that, whatever his good points, he is no *esprit juste*" (2:196). In Lewis's hands, Taylor's thought seems to have undergone a metamorphosis, in which it has sloughed Taylor's dry, pedantic humor, and assumed the terse, colorful imagery that so endeared Lewis to his vast following.

173. Cf. Humphrey Carpenter, *The Inklings: C. S. Lewis, J. R. R. Tolkien, Charles Williams*

and their Friends (Boston: Houghton Mifflin, 1979), 42–45; and Lewis's letter to Arthur Greeves dated October 18, 1931, in Walter Hooper, ed., *They Stand Together: The Letters of C. S. Lewis to Arthur Greeves (1914–1963)* (New York: Macmillan, 1979), 426–28.

174. Cited from Lewis's letter to Arthur Greeves dated October 1, 1931, in W. Hooper, op. cit., 425.

175. *God in the Dock,* 29; cf. above, n. 156.

176. *Miracles,* 138f.

177. Cf. Lewis's concession that he did not maintain "that God's creation of Nature can be proved as rigorously as God's existence, but it seems to me overwhelmingly probable, so probable that no one who approached the question with an open mind would very seriously entertain any other hypothesis" (*Miracles,* 37). Lewis went on to assert the superiority of the Genesis stories (though told in the manner of a popular poet or folk tale) over nonbiblical creation legends, contending that in the biblical accounts, "The idea of *creation* in the rigorous sense of the word is there fully grasped." From this point onward Lewis operated increasingly on the assumption of the truth of the biblical accounts of God as the Creator.

9. CRITICAL CROSSCURRENTS

1. *The Mediator: A Study of the Central Doctrine of the Christian Faith* (E.T., London: Lutterworth Press, 1934), 424n.

2. *Dogmatics,* vol. 2, *The Christian Doctrine of Creation and Redemption* (E.T., London: Lutterworth Press, 1952), 161.

3. Ibid., 186–92.

4. Ibid., 192; cf. *Revelation and Reason* (E.T., London: SCM Press, 1947), 304f.

5. *Church Dogmatics*, II,1, *The Doctrine of God* (Edinburgh: T. & T. Clark, 1957), 199.

6. Ibid., 509.

7. Ibid., 539.

8. *Church Dogmatics*, III,3, *The Doctrine of Creation* (1960), 311.

9. *Church Dogmatics,* III,4 (1961), 320f.; cf. IV,1, *The Doctrine of Reconciliation* (1956), 207, 646; IV,2 (1958), 147f., 232, 340.

10. *Church Dogmatics*, IV,2, 212–47.

11. Ibid., 212.

12. Ibid., 213.

13. Ibid., 216.

14. Ibid., 215.

15. Ibid., 216–18.

16. Ibid., 219.

17. Ibid., 221.

18. Ibid., 222.

19. Ibid., 223.

20. Ibid., 226.

21. Ibid.

22. Ibid.

23. Ibid., 228.

24. Ibid., 232.

25. Ibid., 236.

26. Ibid., 239.

27. Ibid., 240.

28. Letter to Eberhard Bethge from Tegel prison, May 5, 1944 in Dietrich Bonhoeffer, *Letters and Papers from Prison*, The Enlarged Edition, ed. Eberhard Bethge (London: SCM Press, 1971), 285.

29. Letter to Bethge from Tegel, April 30, 1944 (ibid., 280).

30. Letter to Bethge from Tegel, July 16, 1944 (ibid., 361).

31. Cf. ch. 5, n. 1.

32. Charles W. Kegley, ed., *The Theology of Rudolf Bultmann* (London: SCM Press, 1966), xxiv.

33. *The History of the Synoptic Tradition,* tr. John Marsh, 2nd ed. (Oxford: Basil Blackwell; New York: Harper & Row, 1968), 4.

34. Ibid., 368.
35. Ibid., 369.
36. Ibid., 370f.
37. Ibid., 371.
38. Ibid., 211, 221.
39. Ibid., 244.
40. Ibid., 209.
41. Ibid., 213.
42. Ibid., 209.
43. Ibid., 210.
44. Ibid., 218f. In *From Tradition to Gospel* (New York: Charles Scribner's Sons, 1935), 70-103, Dibelius treated the miracle stories as "Tales" that freely used extraneous material for propaganda purposes.
45. Ibid., 219.
46. Ibid., 221.
47. Ibid., 225, 231f.
48. Ibid., 228.
49. *The Gospel of John: A Commentary* (Oxford: Basil Blackwell; Philadelphia: Westminster Press, 1971), 120f.; cf. *The History of the Synoptic Tradition*, 238. Cf. Morton Smith, "On the Wine God in Palestine," *Salo W. Baron Jubilee Volume* (1975), English section, 815ff., with J. D. M. Derrett, "Water into Wine" (n. 126, below).
50. *Gospel of John*, 405.
51. Hans-Werner Bartsch, ed., *Kerygma and Myth: A Theological Debate*, vols. 1 and 2 combined with enlarged bibliography (E.T., London: S.P.C.K., 1972), 1-44. The volume includes a selection of responses from the first two volumes of *Kerygma und Mythos* and Karl Barth's tongue-in-cheek "Rudolph Bultmann—An Attempt to Understand Him." For a succinct appraisal of the question of myth see F. F. Bruce, "Myth and History" in Colin Brown, ed., *History, Criticism and Faith: Four Exploratory Studies* (London and Downers Grove: Inter-Varsity Press, 1976), 79-100. More extensive discussions of myth, religious language, and hermeneutics include Wolfhart Pannenberg, "The Later Dimensions of Myth in Biblical and Christian Tradition" in *Basic Questions in Theology*, vol. 3 (London: SCM Press, 1973), 1-79; Roger A. Johnson, *The Origins of Demythologizing: Philosophy and Historiography in the Theology of Rudolf Bultmann,* Studies in the History of Religions (Supplements to Numen) 28 (Leiden: E. J. Brill, 1974); G. B. Caird, *The Language and Imagery of the Bible* (Philadelphia: Westminster Press, 1980); A. C. Thiselton, *The Two Horizons: New Testament Hermeneutics and Philosophical Description with Special Reference to Heidegger, Bultmann, Gadamer and Wittgenstein* (Exeter: Paternoster Press; Grand Rapids: Wm. B. Eerdmans, 1980). The present writer has attempted an appraisal of Bultmann's thought in "Bultmann Revisited," *The Churchman* 88 (1974):167-87. For a comprehensive account see Walter Schmithals, *An Introduction to the Theology of Rudolph Bultmann* (London: SCM Press, 1968).
52. In Bartsch, op. cit., 41f.; cf. *Jesus and the Word* (1926; E.T., New York: Charles Scribner's Sons, [1934] 1958), 217ff.
53. Bartsch, 44.
54. *Jesus Christ and Mythology* (New York: Charles Scribner's Sons, 1958; London: SCM Press, 1960), 68f.
55. In *Faith and Understanding* (E.T., London: SCM Press, 1969), 247-61.
56. Ibid., 247.
57. Ibid., 254.
58. English translation with a foreword by Krister Stendahl and an introduction by Roy A. Harrisville (Minneapolis: Augsburg Publishing House, 1972).
59. Ibid., 26f.
60. Ibid., 50.
61. Ibid., 51.
62. Ibid., 56.
63. Ibid., 99.
64. Ibid., 135f.
65. Ibid., 158.
66. *The Miracle-Stories of the Gospels* (London: SCM Press, 1941), 24f.; cf. M. Dibelius, op. cit., 70ff.
67. Ibid., 28.

68. Ibid., 26.
69. Ibid., 31; cf. p. 33, where Richardson notes that allusions to compassion occur in Mark only three times apart from the oblique allusion in Mark 9:22. They occur twice in connection with the feeding miracles (6:34; 8:2) and once in the healing of a leper (1:41). Luke omits all Mark's references to compassion, but refers to it in connection with the widow of Nain's son (Luke 7:13) and in the parables of the Good Samaritan (10:33) and the Prodigal Son (15:20). Matthew is the evangelist who stresses compassion the most (Matt. 9:36; 14:14; 15:32; 20:34), though he omits mention of it in Matthew 8:3, which is his parallel to Mark 1:41. John does not mention compassion at all.
70. Ibid., 40.
71. Ibid., 43.
72. Ibid.
73. Ibid.
74. Ibid., 48.
75. Ibid., 48f.; cf. pp. 11ff., where Richardson draws attention to the themes of the hiddenness of the kingdom and of divine wisdom.
76. Ibid., 53f.
77. Ibid., 55ff.
78. Ibid., 62.
79. Ibid., 63.
80. Ibid., 72; cf. Mark 1:24, 34; 3:11; 5:7; James 2:19.
81. Ibid., 79.
82. Ibid., 82f.
83. Ibid., 92; cf. Sir Edwyn Hoskyns and Noel Davey, *The Riddle of the New Testament,* rev. ed. (London: Faber and Faber, 1936), 154. Hoskyns and Davey stressed the prophetic fulfillment motif.
84. *Miracle Stories,* 92. The words that the RSV translates as "It is I" are in the Greek *ego eimi,* "I am," which recalls the divine name in Exodus 3:14 and the "I am" sayings in John. John 6:20 also gives these words in Jesus' reply followed by a command not to be afraid.
85. Ibid., 93; cf. Dibelius, op. cit., 277.
86. *Miracle Stories,* 97f.
87. Ibid., 100-22.
88. Ibid., 135.
89. Ibid., 137f.
90. Cf. Gerhard F. Hasel, *New Testament Theology: Basic Directions in the Current Debate* (Grand Rapids: Wm. B. Eerdmans, 1978); Patrick Henry, *New Directions in New Testament Study* (Philadelphia: Westminster Press, 1979); Harvey K. McArthur, ed., *In Search of the Historical Jesus* (New York: Charles Scribner's Sons, 1969; London: S.P.C.K., 1970); Leander E. Keck, *A Future for the Historical Jesus: The Place of Jesus in Preaching and Theology* (New York and Nashville: Abingdon Press, 1971; London: SCM Press, 1972).
91. *New Testament Theology* (Leicester and Downers Grove: Inter-Varsity Press, 1981). In his account of christological events Guthrie moves from the virgin birth straight to the resurrection and ascension.
92. *The Coming of the Kingdom* (Philadelphia: Presbyterian and Reformed, 1962), 11-121; cf. G. E. Ladd, *Jesus and the Kingdom: The Eschatology of Biblical Realism* (London: S.P.C.K., 1966), 207.
93. *The Miracles of Jesus,* Supplements to Novum Testamentum 9 (Leiden: E. J. Brill, 1968), 699-706.
94. *Christ the Conqueror: Ideas of Conflict and Victory in the New Testament* (London: S.P.C.K., 1954).
95. *The Significance of the Synoptic Miracles* (London: S.P.C.K., 1961), 3ff. However, Kallas seems to miss the point that the miracle stories are both parabolic and historical, and he fails to appreciate Richardson's position on the force of historical argument.
96. Ibid., 77.
97. Ibid., 81.
98. Ibid., 86; cf. Rudolf Otto, *The Kingdom of God and the Son of Man: A Study in the History of Religion* (London: Lutterworth Press, 1938), 106, 346f.
99. *Significance of the Synoptic Miracles,* 88.
100. Ibid., 89.
101. R. H. Fuller, *Interpreting the Miracles* (London: SCM Press, 1963), 124f.

102. Otto Böcher, *Dämonenfurcht und Dämonenabwehr, Ein Beitrag zur Vorgeschichte der Christlichen Taufe,* Beiträge zur Wissenschaft vom Alten und Neuen Testament 90 (Stuttgart: Verlag W. Kohlhammer, 1970); *Christus Exorcista: Dämonismus und Taufe im Neuen Testament,* BWANT 96 (Stuttgart: Verlag W. Kohlhammer, 1972). More recently the question of exorcism in Luke has been examined by W. Kirschläger in *Jesus exorzistisches Wirken aus der Sicht des Lukas,* Österreichische Bibel-Studien 3 (Österreichisches Katholisches Bibelwerk, 1981).

103. *Exorcism: The Report of a Commission Convened by the Bishop of Exeter,* ed. Dom Robert Petitpierre, O.S.B. (London: S.P.C.K., 1972). Other members of the commission were T. Corbishley, J. H. Crehan, P. Ferguson-Davie, M. H. B. Joyce, E. L. Mascall, and W. D. Omand.

104. Ibid., 11f.; cf. Acts 10:38; 13:10; 19:13. The Genesis Apocryphon 20, which was read at Qumran, represents Abraham as an exorcist who laid hands on Pharaoh and expelled an evil spirit. Jewish views of exorcism are contained in the Testaments of the Twelve Patriarchs, which was also read at Qumran. The exorcism of seven demons from Mary Magdalene (Luke 8:2; cf. Matt. 12:45) may be compared with the doctrine of the seven spirits in the Testament of Reuben 2:1; 3:2.

105. Cf. John Richards, *But Deliver Us from Evil: An Introduction to the Demonic Dimension in Pastoral Care* (London: Darton, Longman and Todd, 1974), 98-105; John Wilkinson, "The Case of the Epileptic Boy," *Expository Times* 79 (1967-68), 39-42; see also Jean Lhermitte, *Diabolical Possession—True and False* (London: Burns and Oates, 1963); W. M. Alexander, *Demonic Possession in the New Testament: Its Historical, Medical and Theological Aspects* (1902; reprint, Grand Rapids: Baker Book House, 1980). By contrast, S. V. McCasland seeks to explain possession in terms of mental illness and sees the story of the boy as simply an ancient way of describing epilepsy (*By the Finger of God: Demon Possession and Exorcism in Early Christianity in the Light of Modern Views of Mental Illness* [New York: Macmillan, 1951]).

106. Richards, op. cit., 103.

107. *The Churchman* 94 (1980) was devoted to the topics of possession and exorcism. It included: Graham Dow, "The Case for the Existence of Demons" (199-208), Peter H. Lawrence and Graham H. Twelftree, "Demon-Possession and Exorcism in the New Testament" (210-25); Myrtle S. Langley, "Spirit-Possession, Exorcism and Social Context: An Anthropological Perspective with Theological Implications" (226-45); and M. G. Barker, "Possession and the Occult—A Psychiatrist's View" (246-53). Barker, who is highly critical of modern tendencies to ascribe mental illness to possession and in so doing to disclaim responsibility for actions, has a joint article with D. Whitwell on "Possession in Psychiatric Patients in Britain" in the *British Journal of Medical Psychology* 53 (1980).

108. Fuller, op. cit., 122.

109. Ibid., 114.

110. Text in Günther Bornkamm, Gerhard Barth, and Heinz-Joachim Held, *Tradition and Interpretation in Matthew* (London: SCM Press, 1963), 165-299.

111. Ibid., 246; cf. J. Schniewind, *Das Evangelium nach Matthäus,* Das Neue Testament Deutsch 2 (Göttingen: Vandenhoeck und Ruprecht, 1936), 37, 106; Adolf Schlatter, *Der Evangelist Matthäus* (reprint, Stuttgart: Calwer Verlag, 1963), 120.

112. Bornkamm et al., op. cit., 52-57.

113. Ibid., 57. Bornkamm notes that the word "rebuke" is the regular expression for rebuking the demonic powers (Matt. 17:18; Mark 9:25; Luke 9:42; Mark 1:25; Luke 4:35). In common with Schniewind, Hoskyns, and Davey, he observes that Yahweh's subduing of the flood and rescuing from the raging waves of the sea is already in the Old Testament an illustration of the experience of the community (cf. Pss. 29:3; 65:8; 89:10; 93:4; 107:25ff.; 124:4f.). The *basileia* of God is his kingdom or, more precisely, his kingly rule.

114. H. Greeven, "Die Heilung des Gelahmten nach Matthäus," *Wort und Dienst, Jahrbuch der Theologischen Schule Bethel,* Neue Folge 4 (1955), 65-78.

115. "The Pericope of the Healing of the 'Centurion's' Servant/Son (Matt. 8:5-13 par. Luke 7:1-10): Some Exegetical Notes," in Robert A. Guelich, ed., *Unity and Diversity in New Testament Theology: Essays in Honor of George E. Ladd* (Grand Rapids: Wm. B. Eerdmans, 1978), 14-22.

116. Ibid., 17.

117. Ibid., 18, citing N. A. Dahl, "Die Passionsgeschichte bei Matthäus," *New Testament Studies* 2 (1955-56): 17-32, esp. 23.

118. *The Sign of Jonah in the Theology of the Evangelists and Q,* Studies in Biblical Theology, 2nd ser. 18 (London: SCM Press, 1971).

119. Text in Guelich, op. cit., 1-13.

120. Ibid., 2; cf. Theodore J. Weeden, Sr., *Mark—Traditions in Conflict* (Philadelphia: Fortress Press, 1971).

121. In Guelich, 6f.

122. Ibid., 11.

123. Ibid., 3.

124. M. D. Goulder, *The Evangelists' Calendar: A Lectionary Explanation of the Development of Scripture,* The Speaker's Lectures in Biblical Studies (London: S.P.C.K., 1978), 263.

125. In *The Myth of God Incarnate,* ed. John Hick (London: SCM Press, 1977), Goulder wrote two papers. In the first he presented Jesus as "the Man of universal destiny." In the second he argued for a Samaritan origin for the Christian myths about Jesus. However, the latter argument seems to be undermined by his own attempts to see the Jewish lectionary as the formative influence in the shaping of the Gospels. Goulder also edited *Incarnation and Myth: The Debate Continued* (London: SCM Press, 1979).

126. *Biblische Zeitschrift* 7 (1963), 80-97; reprinted in *Law in the New Testament* (London: Darton, Longman and Todd, 1970), 228-46.

127. "Peter's Penny," *Novum Testamentum* 6 (1963): 1-15; reprinted ibid., 247-65.

128. J. D. M. Derrett, *Studies in the New Testament,* vol. 1 (Leiden: E. J. Brill, 1977), 143-69.

129. "Legend and Event: The Gerasene Demoniac: An Inquest into History and Liturgical Projection," in E. A. Livingstone, ed., *Studia Biblica 1978,* vol. 2, *Papers on the Gospels, Sixth International Congress on Biblical Studies, Oxford 3-7, April 1978,* Journal for the Study of the New Testament, Supplement Series 2 (Sheffield, 1980), 63-73.

130. Ibid., 70.

131. For example, the Roman Catholic scholar Rudolf Pesch examines the miracle stories from the standpoint of form, motive, and tradition history in *Jesu Ureigene Taten? Ein Beitrag zur Wunderfrage,* Quaestiones Disputatae 52 (Freiburg, Basel, Vienna: Herder, 1970); and *Der Besessene von Gerasa: Entstehung und Überlieferung einer Wundergeschichte,* Stuttgarter Bibelstudien 56 (Stuttgart: KBW Verlag, 1972). Pesch stresses the connection with the kingdom of God and the theological context. Similarly, Franz Mussner insists that the question of miracles is inseparable from the totality of salvation history and must be seen in the light of theological and form-critical perspectives in *The Miracles of Jesus: An Introduction* (Notre Dame: Univ. of Notre Dame, 1968). Another Roman Catholic scholar who draws attention to literary genre is John Paul Heil, *Jesus Walking on the Sea: Meaning and Gospel Functions of Matt 14:22-33, Mark 6:45-52 and John 6:15b-21,* Analecta Biblica 87 (Rome: Biblical Institute Press, 1981).

The overall role of miracles in the Gospels has been studied from the standpoint of tradition history by both Protestant and Catholic scholars. Among the major studies are Karl Kertelge, *Die Wunder Jesu im Markusevangelium. Eine redaktionsgeschichtliche Untersuchung* (Munich: Kösel-Verlag, 1970); Gerd Theissen, *Urchristliche Wundergeschichten. Ein Beitrag zur formgeschichtlichen Erforschung der synoptischen Evangelien* (Gütersloh: Gütersloher Verlagshaus Gerd Mohn, 1974; E.T. *The Miracle Stories of the Early Christian Tradition* [Edinburgh: T. & T. Clark; Philadelphia: Fortress, 1982]); Dietrich-Alex Koch, *Die Bedeutung der Wundererzählungen für die Christologie des Markusevangeliums* (Berlin: Walter de Gruyter, 1975); Ludger Schenke, *Die Wundererzählungen des Markusevangeliums,* Stuttgarter Biblische Beitrage (Stuttgart: Verlag Katholisches Bibelwerk, n.d. but ca. 1975).

These studies are characterized by interest in the form, motives, and role of the miracle stories. Theissen detects a social, a history of religions, and an existential function in the early Christian miracle stories. Kertelge argues that there is no single, uniform attitude toward miracles in Mark. The command to silence suggests an ambivalent attitude that makes them almost redundant, though Mark employs them in the interest of his christology. Kertelge detects a Hellenistic divine man (*theios anēr*) concept in the pre-Markan material behind the Gospel. Mark's achievement lies in the way in which he makes use of miracle material without succumbing to the temptation to entertain or become preoccupied by miracle stories. Both Koch and Schenke detect a tension in Mark's handling of the stories which is bound up with the messianic secret. Various motifs may be discerned, but Mark is anxious to stress the cross over against those who would glorify in acts of divine power.

Howard Clark Kee urges the importance of sociological factors in interpreting miracle stories in *Christian Origins in Sociological Perspective: Methods and Resources* (Philadelphia: Westminster Press, 1980) and *Miracle in the Early Christian World: A Study in Sociological Method* (New Haven: Yale Univ. Press, 1983). Unfortunately the latter book appeared too late to be taken into consideration in the present study. While the sociological approach has a positive contribution to make, overconcentration on the sociological function of the New Testament writings is open to the same methodological pitfalls as form criticism, that is, making passages answer questions that seem socially and devotionally appropriate to the church in later ages at the expense of neglecting the religious and social context of the event narrated. Great care needs to be exercised in avoiding anachronisms and the imposition of Greco-Roman ideas onto the Jewish thought-world. The impression is given that some advocates of the sociological approach have discounted in advance the possibility of the miracle stories having any discoverable basis in history and that all that remains for them to investigate is the sociological function of the stories as pious myths. To that extent the approach is an extension of that of Strauss, the History of Religions school, and Bultmann's form criticism.

Other studies include K. Tagawa, *Miracles et Évangile. La Pensée personelle de l'évangeliste Marc* (Paris: Presses Universitaires de France, 1966); A. Suhl, *Die Wunder Jesu. Ereignis und Überlieferung* (Gütersloh: Gütersloher Verlagshaus, 1968); Robert M. Fowler, *Loaves and Fishes: The Function of the Feeding Stories in the Gospel of Mark,* Society of Biblical Literature Dissertation Series 54 (Chico, Calif.: Scholars Press, 1981).

132. Volume 11 of *Semeia* (1978), ed. Robert W. Funk, was devoted to articles on *Early Christian Miracle Stories.* Henrikus Boers and Paul J. Achtemeier subjected Gerd Theissen's work (see previous note) to blistering criticism in their respective reviews ("Sisyphus and His Rock, Concerning Gerd Theissen," *Urchristliche Wundergeschichten,* 1–48; and "An Imperfect Union: Reflections on Gerd Theissen," *Urchristliche Wundergeschichten,* 49–68). Hans Dieter Betz wrote "The Early Christian Miracle Story: Some Observations on the Form Critical Problem," 69–81. Antoinette Clark Wire discussed "The Structure of the Gospel Miracle Stories and their Tellers," 83–113. Paul J. Achtemeier reflected on " 'And he followed him': Miracles and Discipleship in Mark 10:46-52," 115–45.

Other studies include Robert W. Funk, "The Form of the New Testament Healing Miracle Story," *Semeia* 12 (1978):57-95; Paul J. Achtemeier, "Toward the Isolation of pre-Markan Miracle Catenae," *Journal of Biblical Literature* 89 (1970):265-91; "The Origin and Function of the pre-Markan Miracle Catenae," ibid., 91 (1972):198-221; "Miracles and the historical Jesus," *Catholic Bible Quarterly* 37 (1975):471-91; and "The Lucan Perspective on the Miracles of Jesus: A Preliminary Sketch," *Journal of Biblical Literature* 94 (1975):547-62, reprinted in Charles H. Talbert, ed., *Perspectives on Luke-Acts,* Special Studies Series 5 (Danville: Association of Baptist Professors of Religion; Edinburgh: T. & T. Clark, 1978), 153-67.

It should be noted that the articles mentioned here vary in perspective and the emphasis that they place on structure. Estimates of structuralism vary. Its advocates see in it an important critical tool, while others see only the most meager and trite results, which bear little proportion to the effort required to master the techniques of the discipline.

133. These include Otto Betz and Werner Grimm, *Wesen und Wirklichkeit der Wunder Jesu,* Arbeiten zum Neuen Testament und Judentum 2 (Frankfurt am Main: Peter Lang, 1977); Xavier Léon-Dufour, ed., *Les Miracles de Jésus, Selon le Nouveau Testament* (Paris: Éditions du Seuil, 1977); Leopold Sabourin, *The Divine Miracles Discussed and Defended* (Rome: Officium Libri Catholici, 1977); Bruce Kaye and John Rogerson, *Miracles and Mysteries in the Bible* (Philadelphia: Westminster Press, 1978); Leonhard Goppelt, *Theology of the New Testament,* vol. 1 (Grand Rapids: Wm. B. Eerdmans, 1981), 154-57; A. E. Harvey, *Jesus and the Constraints of History,* Bampton Lectures 1980 (Philadelphia: Westminster Press, 1982), 98–119; Ben F. Meyer, *The Aims of Jesus* (London: SCM Press, 1979); A. Suhl, ed., *Der Wunderbegriff im Neuen Testament* (Darmstadt: Wissenschaftliche Buchgesellschaft, 1980); B. Wenisch, *Geschichten oder Geschichte? Theologie des Wunders* (Salzburg: Verlag St. Peter, 1981).

In earlier chapters reference has been made to C. F. D. Moule, ed., *Miracles: Cambridge Studies in their Philosophy and History* (London: A. R. Mowbray; New York: Morehouse-Barlow Co., 1965). In addition to discussions of the New Testament and early church, various articles discuss the Old Testament, Herodotus, Plutarch, the Wisdom of Solomon, and Josephus.

134. Apart from the numerous commentaries on John that discuss the miracles, mention may be made of several studies that discuss the role of signs in the Fourth Gospel. A trend in the study of the Fourth Gospel is to posit a signs-source that the evangelist incorporated and adapted. These studies include the following: Wilhelm Wilkens, *Zeichen und Werke. Ein Beitrag zur Theologie des 4. Evangeliums in Erzählungs- und Redestoff,* Abhandlungen zur Theologie des Alten und Neuen Testaments 55 (Zurich: Zwingli Verlag, 1969); Robert Tomson Fortna, *The Gospel of Signs: A Reconstruction of the Narrative Source Underlying the Fourth Gospel,* Society for New Testament Studies Monograph Series 11 (Cambridge: Cambridge Univ. Press, 1970);

W. Nicol, *The Sēmeia in the Fourth Gospel: Tradition and Redaction,* Supplements to Novum Testamentum 32 (Leiden: E. J. Brill, 1972).

135. Ludwig Bieler, *THEIOS ANĒR. Das Bild des "Göttlichen Menschen" in Spatantike und Frühchristentum* (Vienna: Oskar Höfels, 1935, 1936; reprint in one volume, Darmstadt: Wissenschaftliche Buchgesellschaft, 1976).

136. Hans Dieter Betz, "Jesus as Divine Man," in F. Thomas Trotter, ed., *Jesus and the Historian: Written in Honor of Ernest Cadman Colwell* (Philadelphia: Westminster Press, 1968), 114-33; and *Lukian von Samosata und das Neue Testament, Religionsgeschichtliche und paränetische Parallelen,* Texte und Untersuchungen 76 (Berlin: Akademie Verlag, 1961); Helmut Koester in James M. Robinson and Helmut Koester, eds., *Trajectories through Early Christianity* (Philadelphia: Fortress Press, 1971), 187ff., 216ff. For other writers who have used the idea see Carl H. Holladay (n. 139 below), 1-45.

137. Theodore J. Weeden, *Mark—Traditions in Conflict* (Philadelphia: Fortress Press, 1971; reprint with new preface, 1979).

138. David Lenz Tiede, *The Charismatic Figure as Miracle Worker,* Society of Biblical Literature Dissertation Series 1 (Missoula: S.B.L., 1972).

139. Carl H. Holladay, *Theios Anēr in Hellenistic-Judaism: A Critique of the Use of this Category in New Testament Christology,* Society of Biblical Literature Dissertation Series 40 (Missoula: Scholars Press, 1977).

140. W. L. Lane, *"Theios Aner* Christology and the Gospel of Mark," in Richard N. Longenecker and Merrill C. Tenney, eds., *New Dimensions in New Testament Study* (Grand Rapids: Zondervan), 144-61.

141. Weeden, op. cit., vii.

142. Holladay, op. cit., 237; cf. Josephus, *Antiquities* 3.180; Philo, *De Vita Mosis* 1.158; 2.188; *Quaestiones in Exodum* 2.29.40; *De Virtutibus* 177; et al.

Reservations about the utility of the divine man concept have recently been expressed by Eugene V. Gallagher in *Divine Man or Magician? Celsus and Origen on Jesus,* Society for Biblical Literature Dissertation Series 64 (Chico: Scholars Press, 1982).

143. Holladay, 239.

144. These considerations have bearing in reestimating the relevance of the alleged parallel with Apollonius of Tyana, the Neopythagorean sage and wandering ascetic who lived in the first century A.D. and who was reputed to possess exorcistic and miraculous powers. His exploits are recorded in a biographical romance by Philostratus that is regarded by classical scholars as highly untrustworthy. An anti-Christian writer, Hierocles of Nicomedia, paralleled Apollonius with Christ, provoking a reply from Eusebius who saw Apollonius not as an enemy of Christianity but as one who prepared the way for it in the pagan world. The texts of both Apollonius and Eusebius have been edited by F. C. Conybeare, *Philostratus: The Life of Apollonius of Tyana. The Epistles of Apollonius and the Treatise of Eusebius,* Loeb Classical Library, 2 vols. (Cambridge, Mass.: Harvard Univ. Press; London: William Heinemann Ltd., 1912 and reprints).

Apollonius has been investigated by G. Petzke in *Die Traditionen über Apollonius von Tyana und das Neue Testament,* Studia ad Corpus Hellenisticum Novi Testamenti 1 (Leiden: E. J. Brill, 1970); and "Historizität und Bedeutsamkeit von Wunderberichten. Möglichkeiten und Grenzen des religionsgeschichtliche Vergleiches," in Hans Dieter Betz and Luise Schottroff, *Neues Testament und christliche Existenz. Festschrift für Herbert Braun* (Tübingen: J. C. B. Mohr, 1973), 367-85.

The most striking parallel occurs in the comparison between Luke 7:11-17 and the *Life of Apollonius* 4.45, which tells how Apollonius encountered the funeral procession in Rome of a bride who had died in the hour of her marriage, and restored her. Philostratus leaves the question open whether Apollonius "detected some spark of life in her . . . or whether life was really extinct."

It is clear that the *Life of Apollonius* is much later than the Gospels. It was commissioned by the Empress Julia Domna, the wife of Septimius Severus, who instigated persecution of the church. Julia Domna, who collected a coterie of men of learning, provided Philostratus with sources. The circumstances and contents of the book have prompted the suggestion that Apollonius and his cult were deliberately fostered as a rival alternative to Christianity (cf. John Ferguson, *The Religions of the Roman Empire* [London: Thames and Hudson, 1960], 181-83). This view seems more likely than the explanation that it was written to conciliate Christians, for the work seems to contain nothing that would achieve that end. It seems more in line with the views of Alexander Severus who, instead of setting up images of the gods in his private shrine, erected statues of Alexander the Great, Orpheus, Apollonius of Tyana, Abraham, and Christ. The effect was to relativize Christian belief in Christ.

145. S. Eitrem, *Some Notes on the Demonology in the New Testament, Symbolae Osloenses Fasc. Supplet.* 12 (Oslo: A. W. Brøgger, 1950), 9.

146. *Hellenistic Magic and the Synoptic Tradition,* Studies in Biblical Theology, 2nd ser. 28 (London: SCM Press; Naperville, Ill.: Alec R. Allenson Inc., 1974).

147. Ibid., 5-19. A primary source is Karl Preisendanz, *Papyri Graecae Magicae: Die griechische Zauberpapyri,* vols. 1-3 (Leipzig and Berlin, 1928, 1931, and 1942; reprint, Stuttgart: Teubner, 1973). Early important references to magic include the *Apology* of Apuleius, Iamblichus, *De Mysteriis,* the Elder Pliny, *Naturalis Historia,* and the writings of Lucian of Samosata.

148. In response to Hull, Paul J. Achtemeier has shown that many of the alleged magical features said to penetrate Luke can be found in the other Gospels, and that Luke actually tones down and eliminates features that might be construed as magical ("The Lucan Perspective on the Miracles of Jesus: A Preliminary Sketch," in *Perspectives on Luke-Acts,* 161-64; cf. above, n. 132). While magical elements may be found in the accounts of the attitudes and actions of people, Luke does more to combat magic than to foster it.

149. Cf. H. van der Loos, op. cit., 306-11; W. Crooke, "Saliva," *Encyclopaedia of Religion and Ethics,* 11:100-104. Tacitus (*Historiae* 4.81) and Suetonius (*Vespasianus* 7) tell of the emperor Vespasian restoring the sight of a blind man at Alexandria by use of his spittle (cf. also Dio Cassius 65.8). The use of charms in healing was prohibited by the Mishnah (Sanhedrin 10.1), as was the use of spittle (Tosephta 12.10 [433]).

150. F. Fenner, *Die Krankheit im Neuen Testament. Eine Religions - und Medizingeschichtliche Untersuchung,* Untersuchungen zum Neuen Testament 18 (Leipzig: J. C. Hinrichs'sche Buchhandlung, 1930), 91f.

151. In addition to the sources noted above in n. 149, C. K. Barrett draws attention to the saying that one must not put fasting spittle on the eyes of the Sabbath (Y. Shabbath 14,14d, 17f.; *The Gospel according to St. John* [S.P.C.K., 1955], 296). Barrett sees here an application of the general principle that anointing on the Sabbath was allowed only with fluids commonly used for anointing on other days (cf. Shabbath 14.4). Irenaeus saw in the passage an allusion to Gen 2:7 (*Adversus Haereses* 5.15.2; cf. Chrysostom on John 9:3; and Job 4:19; 10:9; 33:6; 38:14 LXX; where clay rather than dust is the material out of which man is formed). The underlying thought is that he who made man out of earth cures him likewise (cf. E. C. Hoskyns, *The Fourth Gospel,* ed. F. N. Davey, 2nd ed. [London: Faber and Faber, 1947], 354).

152. Morton Smith, *Jesus the Magician* (San Francisco: Harper and Row, 1978), 149.

153. Ibid., 69.

154. Ibid., 46-50, 58; cf. Origen, *Against Celsus* 1.28.38; and the rabbinic sources referred to on pp. 178f., especially Shabbath 104b. Smith suggests that Paul's claim to bear "the marks of Jesus" (Gal. 6:17) were "most likely, the same marks that Jesus had carried," i.e., tattoo marks containing spells (48; cf. Preisendanz, op. cit., VII, 222-32; VIII, 65ff.).

155. Smith, 50-53; cf. Tacitus, *Annals* 15.3-8; Suetonius, *Life of Nero* 16.2; Younger Pliny, *Letters* 10.96.

156. Smith discusses a number of art works linking Christianity with magic (ibid., 61ff.). These include a magical gem with a crucifixion figure dated ca. A.D. 200, a later graffito depicting a crucifixion scene in which the crucified man has the head of a donkey, and a fourth-century gold glass plate depicting the raising of Lazarus in which Christ is evidently a magician bearing a wand.

The name of Jesus occurs in a number of spells (ibid., 63; cf. Preisendanz, op. cit., III, 420; IV, 1233, 3020; XII, 192).

157. Smith, 151.

158. Ibid. Smith observes that the invocation of the spirit in the Mithras liturgy ends with the magician's claim to be the Son. Smith sees the recognition of Jesus as the Son of God by the exorcised demons as further indication of magical practices. He strives to show that the title "Son of God" was not messianic but magical, occurring chiefly in connection with miracles and exorcism (39, 176f.). However, the argument has to be strained to the point of denying any messianic identification with the pronouncement of the voice from heaven at Jesus' baptism and likewise any connection with Ps. 2 and Isa. 42:1. Smith sees in several magical texts invocations of a supernatural spirit that result in the magician becoming a son (100ff.; cf. Preisendanz, IV, 154-221, 475-830).

159. Smith, 152; cf. 122ff., 146.

160. Ibid., 32ff. On the question of Jewish attitudes toward magic see R. Campbell Thompson, *Semitic Magic: Its Origin and Development* (1908; reprint, New York: Ktav Publishing House, 1971).

161. Geza Vermes, *Jesus the Jew: A Historian's Reading of the Gospels* (London: Collins, 1973), 69.

162. Ibid., 69-78, 241 (where Vermes gives details of his sources).

163. Ibid., 223.

164. Vermes's views may be compared with those of Martin Hengel who rejects the view that Jesus was some kind of rabbi and sees similarities between Jesus and the charismatic leaders of the Maccabean-Zealot tradition (*The Charismatic Leader and His Followers* [Edinburgh: T. & T. Clark; New York: Crossroad, 1981]).

Some seventy years ago Paul Fiebig and Adolf Schlatter were engaged in a debate over Jewish attitudes toward the miraculous. Fiebig considered much of the Gospel material as a legendary product of contemporary ideas. Schlatter strenuously denied any connection between Jewish miracle stories and the New Testament. He refused to antedate any rabbinic miracle stories, and urged that a distinction be drawn between Palestinian and Babylonian stories. He claimed that the example of Honi was more a case of answered prayer. See Paul Fiebig, *Rabbinische Wundergeschichten des Neutestamentlichen Zeitalters,* Kleine Texte für Vorlesgungen und Übungen 78 (Bonn: A. Marcus and E. Weber's Verlag, 1911); *Jüdische Wundergeschichten des Neutestamentlichen Zeitalters unter besonderer Berücksichtigung ihres Verhältnisses zum Neuen Testament bearbeitet* (Tübingen: J. C. B. Mohr, 1911); and *Antike Wundertexte,* rev. G. Delling, Kleine Texte für Vorlesungen und Übungen 79 (Berlin: Walter de Gruyter, 1960); Adolf Schlatter, *Das Wunder in der Synagoge,* Beiträge zur Förderung christlicher Theologie (Gütersloh: Bertelsmann, 1912).

The rabbinic writings contain numerous miracle stories, some of a trivial and fanciful kind. But the rabbis regarded miracles as of secondary importance. Following Deut. 13, the rabbis rejected miracles as a test of truth. Stress was laid on the daily wonders of divine providence. Such miracles as occur were foreordained and provided for in the act of creation. See further K. Kohler, "Miracle," *The Jewish Encyclopedia,* vol. 8 (New York: Funk and Wagnalls, 1904), 606f.; J. Licht, L. I. Rabinowitz, E. Schweid, and M. J. Graetz, "Miracle," *Encyclopaedia Judaica,* vol. 11 (Jerusalem: Ketev; New York: Macmillan, 1971),73-81; C. G. Montefiore and H. Loewe, *A Rabbinic Anthology,* with a Prolegomenon by Raphael Loewe (New York: Schocken Books, 1974, 1978), 334-41; Harold Remus, "Does Terminology Distinguish Early Christian from Pagan Miracles?" *Journal of Biblical Literature* 101 (1982): 531-51.

On the question of magic see further David E. Aune, "Magic in Early Christianity," in W. Haase, ed., *Aufstieg und Niedergang der römischen Welt. Geschichte und Kultur Roms im Spiegel der neueren Forschung* (Berlin: de Gruyter, 1980), XXIII/2, 1507-57. The ancient Jewish polemical account of Jesus, the *Toledoth Jeshu,* did not deny the actuality of Jesus' miracles but attributed them to his theft and magical use of the divine name (12:39-18:19; cf. Günter Schlichting, *Ein jüdisches Leben Jesu. Die verschollene Toledot-Jeschu-Fassung Tam u-mu'ād,* Wissenschaftliche Untersuchungen zum Neuen Testament 24 [Tübingen: J. C. B. Mohr, 1982], 97-123).

10. CHRISTIAN APOLOGETICS AND MIRACLES

1. Reinhold Seeberg, "Wunder," *Realenzyklopädie für Protestantische Theologie und Kirche,* ed. A. Hauck, vol. 21 (Leipzig: J. C. Hinrich'sche Buchhandlung, 1908), 562 (author's translation).

The present study has concentrated on the question of miracles in the English-speaking world. For further discussion of German thought see Urban Forell, *Wunderbegriffe und logische Analyse. Logisch-philosophische Analyse von Begriffen und Begriffsbildungen aus der deutschen protestantischen Theologie des 20. Jahrhunderts,* Forschungen zur systematischen und ökumenischen Theologie 17 (Göttingen: Vandenhoeck & Ruprecht, 1967); Bernhard Bron, *Das Wunder. Das theologische Wunderverständnis im Horizont der neuzeitlichen Natur- und Geschichtsbegriffs,* 2nd ed. (Göttingen: Vandenhoeck & Ruprecht, 1979).

2. Cf. Walther Eichrodt, *Theology of the Old Testament,* vol. 2 (London: SCM Press, 1967), 162–67.

3. For further discussion see Colin Brown, "History and the Believer," in Colin Brown, ed., *History, Criticism and Faith: Four Exploratory Studies* (Leicester and Downers Grove: Inter-Varsity Press, 1976), 147–224.

4. Perhaps the nearest that the New Testament comes to saying that Jesus raised himself is John 2:19. Even so, it may be observed that the utterance is of the Word of the Father that became flesh. Moreover, verse 22 reverts to the passive language of Jesus being raised from the dead. Similarly, the "power" referred to in John 10:18 is given by the Father. See further ch. 8, n. 42.

5. The continuing importance for Judaism of Deut. 13 is reflected in the Mishnah tractate *Sanh.* 10.4, which prescribes the death penalty for those who beguile the men of a city and lead them astray. The terms are given under which the penalty is to be inflicted. This, like similar statements in the Talmud, may reflect on attempts by Christians to proselytize among the Jewish people. *Sanh.* 7 deals with the death penalty in connection with acts forbidden by the Law, including blasphemy, idolatry, sorcery, and profanation of the Sabbath. The passage is replete with allusions to the Torah, including Lev. 18–24, Deut. 13, and Exod. 22:18; Deut. 18:10–11.

6. I have attempted to assess various viewpoints in "The Resurrection in Contemporary Theology," in Colin Brown, ed., *The New International Dictionary of New Testament Theology,* vol. 3 (Grand Rapids: Zondervan; Exeter: Paternoster Press, 1978), 281–305. My own views of the role of the resurrection of Jesus in New Testament apologetics may be compared with those of Markus Barth in Markus Barth and Verne H. Fletcher, *Acquittal by Resurrection* (New York: Holt, Rinehart and Winston, 1964). However, they were reached by a somewhat different path.

7. Wolfhart Pannenberg, *Jesus—God and Man* (Philadelphia: Westminster Press; London: SCM Press, 1968), 34ff., 65–114.

8. Wolfhart Pannenberg, *Basic Questions in Theology,* vol. 1 (Philadelphia: Fortress Press; London: SCM Press, 1970), 39–50.

9. T. F. Torrance, *Divine and Contingent Order* (Oxford: Oxford Univ. Press, 1981), 24.

11. THE PLACE OF MIRACLES IN NEW TESTAMENT INTERPRETATION

1. My understanding of the titles of Jesus in the New Testament is much indebted to C. F. D. Moule, *The Origin of Christology* (Cambridge: Cambridge Univ. Press, 1977), to which the reader is referred for further discussion, though Professor Moule is clearly not responsible for the views I argue here. For a somewhat different approach see F. F. Bruce, "The Background to the Son of Man Sayings," in H. H. Rowdon, ed., *Christ the Lord: Studies Presented to Donald Guthrie* (Leicester: Inter-Varsity Press, 1982), 50–70. Moule has further amplified his position in "Neglected Factors in the Problem of the 'Son of Man,'" *Essays in New Testament Interpretation* (Cambridge: Cambridge Univ. Press, 1982), 75–90.

2. Perhaps it was in this sense that the nation of Israel could be designated as God's Son (Exod. 4:22–23; Hos. 11:1). It may also be that this idea underlies the application of the term to angelic beings (Dan. 3:25; Job 38:7; Ps. 82:6).

For reviews of various applications of the title "Son of God" in Hellenistic culture, intertestamental Judaism, and the Qumran literature see, e.g., Martin Hengel, *The Son of God: The Origin of Christology and the History of Hellenistic Religion* (Philadelphia: Fortress Press; London: SCM Press, 1976); and J. D. G. Dunn, *Christology in the Making: A New Testament Inquiry into the Origins of the Doctrine of the Incarnation* (Philadelphia: Westminster Press; London: SCM Press, 1980), 14ff. Dunn observes that "it was obviously a widespread belief or convention that the king was a son of God either as descended from God or as representing God to his people. So too, both inside and outside Judaism, human beings could be called 'sons of God' either as somehow sharing the divine mind or as being specially favoured by God or pleasing to God" (16).

3. On the interpretation of the term "image of God" see D. J. A. Clines, "The Image of God in Man," *Tyndale Bulletin* 19 (1968): 53–103.

4. Cf. Moule, op. cit., 12–22, 24. On the Adamic background of "Son of Man" see Morna

D. Hooker, *The Son of Man in Mark* (London: S.P.C.K., 1967). Cf. also J. D. M. Derrett, "Judaica in St. Mark," *Studies in the New Testament,* vol. 1 (Leiden: E. J. Brill, 1977), 85-100. In his discussion of Jesus' usage of the title "Son of Man," Moule draws attention to the almost invariable presence of the word *the.* In his view "Son of Man" is not so much a title as "a symbol of a vocation to be utterly loyal, even to death, in the confidence of ultimate vindication in the heavenly court" (14). In other words, "the Son of Man" is not simply a rather awkward circumlocution for "I." It is as if Jesus were saying that it was his vocation to fulfill the role of the Son of Man as delineated in the Book of Daniel.

Despite the objections of more recent writers like Maurice Casey, *Son of Man: The Interpretation and Influence of Daniel 7* (London: S.P.C.K., 1979), and various rival proposals, I think that Moule's case is sustained for seeing Daniel 7 as a locus for Jesus' own interpretation. At the same time I think that New Testament scholarship has too readily ignored the Book of Ezekiel as a source. Both books are set in the context of the Exile. The son of man in Ezekiel is also called to be God's faithful, righteous representative in a time of trial and upheaval (Ezek. 2:3; 3:4-11). The son of man is called to consume the word of God and utter it to God's people, whether they hear or refuse to hear (3:1-11). Moreover, the son of man is filled and led by the Spirit in his vocation (2:2; 3:12, 14, 24; etc.). Moreover, "the punishment of the house of Israel" is laid upon him (4:4). So far as I can see, biblical scholarship has paid too little attention to Ezekiel as a role model for Jesus. In my view, we do not have to choose between Daniel and Ezekiel. Both contributed converging themes in defining the vocational role model that Jesus assumed. For a review of literature and interpretations of the "Son" titles of Jesus see O. Michel and I. H. Marshall, "Son," in C. Brown, ed., *The New International Dictionary of New Testament Theology,* vol. 3 (Grand Rapids: Zondervan; Exeter: Paternoster Press, 1978), 607-66.

5. D. M. Baillie, *God Was in Christ: An Essay on Incarnation and Atonement* (1948; London: Faber and Faber, quoted from the reprint of the second edition, 1973), 58; cf. C. H. Dodd, *History and the Gospel* (London: Nisbet, 1938), 90-101, discussing Mark 2:14; 2:15-17; Luke 19:2-10; 7:36-48; John 7:53-8:11; Luke 15:4-7 = Matt. 18:12f.; Luke 18:10-14; Matt. 11:16-19 = Luke 7:31-35; Matt. 21:32.

6. Baillie, 106-32.

7. Ibid., 125; cf. 13f., 224ff.

8. Ibid., 128-32; cf. John 17:21ff.; 20:17; Rom. 8:29; 1 Cor. 3:23; Gal. 2:20; Col. 1:18; Heb. 2:11.

9. In the course of his study Baillie drew on a massive array of nineteenth- and twentieth-century scholars. Schleiermacher merited only a single mention, despite the remarkable similarity between his basic approach to christology and Baillie's. What makes the point all the more striking is the fact that Baillie was one of the translators of Schleiermacher's *The Christian Faith* (1928). Perhaps it was that Schleiermacher's fortunes were at their lowest ebb when Baillie was writing, and Baillie may not have wanted to identify himself with him.

10. James D. G. Dunn, *Jesus and the Spirit: A Study of the Religious and Charismatic Experience of Jesus and the First Christians as Reflected in the New Testament* (Philadelphia: Westminster Press; London: SCM Press, 1975), 92 (Dunn's italics).

11. In S. W. Sykes and J. P. Clayton, eds., *Christ, Faith and History: Cambridge Studies in Christology* (Cambridge: Cambridge Univ. Press, 1972), 111-30.

12. *"Jesus seems to have understood the relation between himself and the Spirit in terms primarily of inspiration and empowering,* that is, as the power of God himself filling him and coming to manifestation through him" (*Christology in the Making,* 138, Dunn's italics; cf. also 136, 139). For Dunn's more recent views see his article "Rediscovery of the Spirit," *Expository Times* 94 (1982-83): 9-18.

13. *Jesus and the Spirit,* 48.

14. Ibid., 72. Dunn observes that "it is possible that the origin of the nature miracle reports is best explained in charismatic terms." He goes on to note Rudolf Otto's observation of "the power of the charismatic to satisfy the hunger of the recipients by a small gift which he has blessed" (cf. Otto, *The Kingdom of God and the Son of Man,* 347). The walking on the water may be explained by levitation or the psychical phenomenon of spiritual *operatio in distans* (73; cf. Otto, 350, 368-74).

15. Cf. Eusebius, *Ecclesiastical History* 3.39. For discussion of Mark's possible links with Peter see Ralph P. Martin, *Mark: Evangelist and Theologian* (Grand Rapids: Zondervan; Exeter: Paternoster Press, 1972), 52-60.

16. Among those who have drawn attention to the role of the Spirit in the ministry of Jesus

and its connection with the kingdom of God is J. E. Yates, *The Spirit and the Kingdom* (London: S.P.C.K., 1963; cf. also J. E. Yates, "The Form of Mark 1.8B," *New Testament Studies* 4 [1957-58]:334–38). Regrettably, Yates's work has not received the attention it deserves. Among those who take note of it is E. M. B. Green, but Green dismisses it prematurely on the grounds that Jesus "did not baptise with the Holy Spirit until after his death and resurrection" (*I Believe in the Holy Spirit* [London: Hodder and Stoughton; Grand Rapids: Wm. B. Eerdmans, 1975], 40). Green's appeal to John 7:39 ("the Spirit had not yet been given, because Jesus was not yet glorified") misses the point of John's observation, which has to do with the believer's future inner experience of the Spirit, as distinct from the manifestation of the Spirit in Jesus that was already evident (cf. John 3:6ff.). When Jesus breathed on the disciples and said, "Receive the Holy Spirit" (John 20:22), he was bestowing on them the Spirit that had already been manifest in his earthly ministry and resurrection life. Green contends that "It is the concerted teaching of the whole New Testament that the Christian experience of the Holy Spirit is possible only after the death and resurrection of Jesus." But this is at best a tautology that begs the question and ignores the evidence of the Spirit's activity in the ministry of Jesus.

In *Jesus and the Spirit,* J. D. G. Dunn ignores Yates's book altogether. However, in his earlier study *Baptism in the Holy Spirit,* Studies in Biblical Theology, 2nd ser. 15 (London: SCM Press, 1970), 20, Dunn noted the work only to reject it for reasons similar to Green's. Dunn did, however, note that C. H. Dodd, in a private communication, supported the basic thrust of Yates's argument.

The present writer's interpretation follows a somewhat different path from that of Yates. Whereas Yates stresses the sifting and judging of Israel through Jesus' ministry of the Spirit, I would stress the cleansing, purging, renewing, and healing work of the Spirit, which necessarily carries with it the sifting and judging of Israel.

An earlier important study is C. K. Barrett, *The Holy Spirit and the Gospel Tradition* (London: S.P.C.K., 1947).

17. Cf. I. H. Marshall, *The Gospel of Luke: A Commentary on the Greek Text,* The New International Greek Testament Commentary (Exeter: Paternoster Press; Grand Rapids: Wm. B. Eerdmans, 1978), 147f. Marshall draws attention to the contrast of water with Spirit (Isa. 44:3; Ezek. 35:25–27; 1QS 4:21) and of Spirit with fire (Joel 2:28–30; 1QS 4:13, 21). Judgment is associated with fire (Isa. 29:6; 31:9; Ezek. 38:22; Amos 7:14; Zeph. 1:18; 3:8; 2:11–13) and with wind, which is denoted by the same word in Hebrew and Greek as spirit (Isa. 40:24; 41:16; Jer. 4:11f.; Isa. 29:6; 30:27f.; Ezek. 1:4; 4 Ezra 13:10, 27).

The messiah is said to be endowed with Spirit (Isa. 11:2; Ps. Sol. 17:42; Ethiopic Enoch 49:3) and to bestow the Spirit (Test. Levi 18:6–11; Test. Judah 24:2, though some think that the latter are Christian interpolations).

18. Cf. J. D. G. Dunn, *Christology in the Making,* 129–36.

19. 1QS 4:20–23; cited from G. Vermes, *The Dead Sea Scrolls in English* (Harmondsworth: Penguin Books, 1962), 77f.

20. Psalm 2 is generally recognized as a royal psalm used at the enthronement of the king or at the yearly celebration of his accession (cf. A. A. Anderson, *The Book of Psalms,* vol. 1 [London: Oliphants, 1972], 63f.).

21. Cf. B. Gerhardsson, *The Testing of God's Son (Matt. 4:1–11 & Par.).* Coniectanea Biblica, New Testament Series 2:1 (Lund: Gleerup, 1966); W. Schneider and C. Brown, "Tempt," in C. Brown, ed., *The New International Dictionary of New Testament Theology,* vol. 3 (1978), 804–808.

22. Cf. H. Währisch and C. Brown, "Revile, Blaspheme, Slander," in C. Brown, ibid., 343ff. Important material that is pertinent to the general background of the Christian clash with Judaism is contained in Elisabeth Schüssler Fiorenza, ed., *Aspects of Religious Propaganda in Judaism and Early Christianity* (Notre Dame: Univ. of Notre Dame, 1976).

23. Cf. above, pp. 255–63.

24. Cf. above, pp. 268–70.

25. Cf. E. Schweizer, *The Good News According to Mark* (Richmond: John Knox Press, 1970), 314.

26. For details see C. Brown, "The Messianic Secret," op. cit., 506–11; C. M. Tuckett, ed., *The Messianic Secret* (Philadelphia: Fortress, 1983).

27. J. D. G. Dunn, "The Messianic Secret in Mark," *Tyndale Bulletin* 21 (1970): 92–117, esp. p. 100.

28. B. Gerhardsson, *The Mighty Acts of Jesus According to Matthew,* Scriptora Minora Regiae Societatis Humanorum Litterarum Lundensis 1978-1979:5 (Lund: Gleerup, 1979).

29. Reprinted in C. H. Talbert, ed., *Perspective on Luke–Acts* (Danville: Association of Baptist Professors of Religion; Edinburgh: T. & T. Clark, 1978), 153–67.

30. Luke omits the stories in Mark 6:45–52; 7:24–30; 7:31–37; 8:1–10; 8:22–26; 11:12–14, 20. He adds eight of his own (5:1–11; 7:1–10; 7:11–17; 11:14; 17:11–19; 22:50–51). Though reminiscent of Mark 3:1–6, Achtemeier considers Luke 13:10–17 and 14:1–6 as independent stories.

31. For a review of current thought on the subject see M. Max B. Turner, "Jesus and the Spirit in Lucan Perspective," *Tyndale Bulletin* 32 (1981): 3–42. Turner strenuously seeks to resist the implications of Spirit christology and the suggestion that Jesus' relation to the Spirit was archetypal for the church.

32. Cf. I. H. Marshall, op. cit., 475f. For "finger of God" see Exod. 8:19; Deut. 9:10 par. Exod. 31:18; Ps. 8:3. For "hand of God" see Exod. 7:4f.; 9:3, 15. For miracles in relation to the kingdom see John Bright, *The Kingdom of God* (New York and Nashville: Abingdon Press, 1963), 217f.

33. Cf. C. S. Rodd, "Spirit or Finger," *Expository Times* 72 (1960-61): 157f.

34. "The story of Simon Magus in Acts viii 14-24 indicates that possession of a spirit and magical powers were greatly esteemed in Samaria, an attitude that is echoed in later traditions about Simon and Dositheus" (R. E. Brown, *The Gospel According to John (i-xii)*, Anchor Bible [Garden City: Doubleday, 1966], 358).

35. E. Lohse, "Miracles in the Fourth Gospel," in Morna Hooker and Colin Hickling, eds., *What About the New Testament? Essays in Honour of Christopher Evans* (London: SCM Press, 1975), 72, citing E. Schweizer, *Ego Eimi,* 2nd ed. (Göttingen: Vandenhoeck & Ruprecht, 1965), 138.

36. M. C. Tenney, *John: The Gospel of Belief* (Grand Rapids: Wm. B. Eerdmans, 1948), 312.

37. Ibid., 39ff.

38. Lohse, op. cit., 73.

39. K. Rahner, *The Trinity* (New York: Seabury Press, 1974).

40. Ibid., 29.

41. Cf. Donald D. Evans, *The Logic of Self-Involvement: A Philosophical Study of Every-day Language with Special Reference to the Christian Language about God as Creator* (London: SCM Press, 1963), 168ff. In this connection Evans draws attention to Pss. 33:6; 104:29–30; Job 33:4; 34:14f.; Eccles. 12:7; Zech. 12:1; Rom. 5:5; Gal. 5:22.

42. Cf., e.g., Job 34:14f.; Ps. 104:29; Isa. 42:1, 5; Ezek. 37:6, 8-10, 14. For a brief review see Hans Walter Wolff, *Anthropology of the Old Testament* (Philadelphia: Fortress Press; London: SCM Press, 1974), 32-35. An older, but still important, analysis is C. A. Briggs, "The Use of RUḤ in the Old Testament," *Journal of Biblical Literature* 19 (1900), 132-45.

43. *Institutes* 1.13.6; cf. Augustine, *On the Trinity* 5.9; 7.4; Anselm, *Monologion* 38; Aquinas, *Summa Theologiae* I, Q. 29, art. 4; I, Q. 30, art. 1. See further Karl Barth, *Church Dogmatics,* I,1, 2nd ed. (Edinburgh: T. & T. Clark, 1949) 348-68; E. J. Fortman, *The Triune God: A Historical Study of the Doctrine of the Trinity* (Philadelphia: Westminster Press; London: Hutchinson, 1972). B. de Margerie, *The Christian Trinity in History* (Still River, Mass.: St. Bede's Publications, 1982).

44. Recent important studies of the Spirit include Hendrikus Berkhof, *The Doctrine of the Holy Spirit* (Richmond: John Knox Press, 1964); Lloyd Neve, *The Spirit of God in the Old Testament* (Tokyo: Seibunsha, 1972); George T. Montague, *The Holy Spirit: Growth of a Biblical Tradition* (New York: Paulist Press, 1976); C. F. D. Moule, *The Holy Spirit* (Grand Rapids: Wm. B. Eerdmans, 1978); Eduard Schweizer, *The Holy Spirit* (Philadelphia: Fortress Press, 1980); Daniel Lys, *Rûach: Le Souffle dans l'Ancien Testament. Enquête anthropologique à travers l'histoire théologique d'Israel* (Paris: Presses Universitaires de France, 1962); Max-Alain Chevalier, *Souffle de Dieu. Le Saint-Esprit dans le Nouveau Testament* (Paris: Éditions Beauchesne, 1978); Y. M.-J. Congar, *I Believe in the Holy Spirit,* 3 vols. (New York: Seabury; London: Chapman, 1983).

Approaches to christology from the standpoint of wisdom include M. Jack Suggs, *Wisdom, Christology and Law in Matthew's Gospel* (Cambridge, Mass.: Harvard Univ. Press, 1970); and R. G. Hamerton-Kelly, *Pre-Existence, Wisdom and the Son of Man: A Study of the Idea of Pre-Existence in the New Testament,* Society for New Testament Studies Monograph Series 21 (Cambridge: Cambridge Univ. Press, 1973). See also the brief study by G. N. Stanton, "Matthew 11:28-30: Comfortable Words?", *Expository Times* 94 (1982-83): 3-8. Hamerton-Kelly has also written a recent study entitled *God the Father: Theology and Patriarchy in the Teaching of Jesus* (Philadelphia: Fortress Press, 1979). See also R. L. Wilken, ed., *Aspects of Wisdom in Judaism and Early Christianity* (Notre Dame: Univ. of Notre Dame, 1975).

INDEXES

The letter "n" indicates a reference to the Endnotes.

SUBJECTS

NAMES